VISUAL BASIC® 2012
PROGRAMMER'S REFERENCE

Visual Basic® 2012

PROGRAMMER'S REFERENCE

Rod Stephens

WILEY

John Wiley & Sons, Inc.

Visual Basic® 2012 Programmer's Reference

Published by
John Wiley & Sons, Inc.
10475 Crosspoint Boulevard
Indianapolis, IN 46256
www.wiley.com

Copyright © 2012 by John Wiley & Sons, Inc., Indianapolis, Indiana

Published simultaneously in Canada

ISBN: 978-1-118-31407-4
ISBN: 978-1-118-33208-5 (ebk)
ISBN: 978-1-118-33535-2 (ebk)
ISBN: 978-1-118-43938-8 (ebk)

Manufactured in the United States of America

10 9 8 7 6 5 4 3 2 1

For general information on our other products and services please contact our Customer Care Department within the United States at (877) 762-2974, outside the United States at (317) 572-3993 or fax (317) 572-4002.

Wiley publishes in a variety of print and electronic formats and by print-on-demand. Some material included with standard print versions of this book may not be included in e-books or in print-on-demand. If this book refers to media such as a CD or DVD that is not included in the version you purchased, you may download this material at http://booksupport.wiley.com. For more information about Wiley products, visit www.wiley.com.

Library of Congress Control Number: 2012940034

ABOUT THE AUTHOR

 **ROD STEPHENS** started out as a mathematician, but while studying at MIT, he discovered how much fun programming is and has been programming professionally ever since. During his career, he has worked on an eclectic assortment of applications in such fields as telephone switching, billing, repair dispatching, tax processing, wastewater treatment, concert ticket sales, cartography, and training for professional football players.

Rod is a Microsoft Visual Basic Most Valuable Professional (MVP) and has taught introductory programming at ITT Technical Institute. He has written more than two dozen books that have been translated into languages from all over the world, and more than 250 magazine articles covering Visual Basic, C#, Visual Basic for Applications, Delphi, and Java.

Rod's popular *VB Helper* website (www.vb-helper.com) receives several million hits per month and contains thousands of pages of tips, tricks, and example programs for Visual Basic programmers, as well as example code for this book. His *C# Helper* website (www.csharphelper.com) contains similar material for C# programmers.

You can contact Rod at RodStephens@csharphelper.com or RodStephens@vb-helper.com.

ABOUT THE TECHNICAL EDITOR

BRIAN HOCHGURTEL has been doing .NET development for over ten years, and actually started his .NET experience with Rod Stephens when they wrote the Wiley book *Visual Basic .NET and XML* together in 2002. Currently Brian works as a SharePoint Developer and Administrator for a large defense contractor in Colorado.

CREDITS

Executive Editor
Robert Elliott

Senior Project Editor
Adaobi Obi Tulton

Technical Editor
Brian Hochgurtel

Production Editor
Daniel Scribner

Copy Editor
Kim Cofer

Editorial Manager
Mary Beth Wakefield

Freelancer Editorial Manager
Rosemarie Graham

Associate Director of Marketing
David Mayhew

Marketing Manager
Ashley Zurcher

Business Manager
Amy Knies

Production Manager
Tim Tate

Vice President and Executive Group Publisher
Richard Swadley

Vice President and Executive Publisher
Neil Edde

Associate Publisher
Jim Minatel

Project Coordinator, Cover
Katie Crocker

Proofreader
Nicole Hirschman

Indexer
Ron Strauss

Cover Designer
Ryan Sneed

Cover Image
© Erik Isakson / Tetra Images / JupiterImages

ACKNOWLEDGMENTS

THANKS TO BOB ELLIOTT, Adaobi Obi Tulton, Sydney Jones, Rayna Erlick, Kim Cofer, Daniel Scribner, and all of the others who worked so hard to make this book possible.

Thanks also to Brian Hochgurtel for giving me another perspective and the benefit of his valuable experience.

CONTENTS

INTRODUCTION

IT HAS BEEN SAID THAT SIR ISAAC NEWTON was the last person to know everything. He was an accomplished physicist (his three laws of motion were the basis of classical mechanics, which defined astrophysics for three centuries), mathematician (he was one of the inventors of calculus and developed Newton's Method for finding roots of equations), astronomer, natural philosopher, and alchemist (okay, maybe the last one was a mistake). He invented the reflecting telescope, a theory of color, and a law of cooling, and he studied the speed of sound.

Just as important, he was born before relativity, quantum mechanics, gene sequencing, thermodynamics, parallel computation, and a swarm of other extremely difficult branches of science.

If you ever used Visual Basic 3, you too could have known everything. Visual Basic 3 was a reasonably small but powerful language. Visual Basic 4 added classes to the language and made Visual Basic much more complicated. Versions 4, 5, and 6 added more support for database programming and other topics such as custom controls, but Visual Basic was still a fairly understandable language, and if you took the time you could become an expert in just about all of it.

Visual Basic .NET changed the language in much more fundamental ways and made it much harder to understand every last detail of Visual Basic. The .NET Framework added powerful new tools to Visual Basic, but those tools came at the cost of increased complexity. Associated technologies have been added to the language at an ever-increasing rate, so today it is impossible for anyone to be an expert on every topic that deals with Visual Basic.

To cover every nook and cranny in Visual Basic you would need an in-depth understanding of database technologies, custom controls, custom property editors, XML, cryptography, serialization, two- and three-dimensional graphics, multi-threading, reflection, the code document object model (DOM), diagnostics, globalization, web services, inter-process communication, work flow, Office, ASP, Windows Forms, WPF, and much more.

This book doesn't even attempt to cover all of these topics. Instead, it provides a broad, solid understanding of essential Visual Basic topics. It explains the powerful development environment that makes Visual Basic such a productive language. It describes the Visual Basic language itself and explains how to use it to perform a host of important development tasks.

It also explains the forms, windows, controls, and other objects that Visual Basic provides for building applications in a modern windowing environment.

This book may not cover every possible topic related to Visual Basic, but it does cover the majority of the technologies that developers need to build sophisticated applications.

SHOULD YOU USE VISUAL BASIC 2012?

Software engineers talk about five generations of languages (so far). A *first-generation language* (*1GL*) is *machine language*: 0s and 1s. For example, the binary command 00110010 00001110 00010010 00000000 might mean to combine the register CL with the value at address 12H by using the exclusive-or (XOR) operation. Pretty incomprehensible, right? You actually had to program some early computers by painstakingly toggling switches to enter 0s and 1s!

A *second-generation language* (*2GL*) is an *assembly language* that provides terse mnemonics for machine instructions. It provides few additional tools beyond an easier way to write machine code. In assembly language, the previous XOR command might look like "XOR CL, [12H]." It's a lot better than assembly language but it's still pretty hard to read. *Third-generation languages* (*3GLs*) are higher-level languages such as Pascal and FORTRAN. They provide much more sophisticated language elements such as subroutines, loops, and data structures. In Visual Basic, the previous example might look something like `total = total Xor value`.

> **WHERE DID THE REGISTER GO?**
>
> Higher-level languages generally don't directly use registers or memory addresses. Instead they work with variables with names such as `total` and `value`. The language's compiler automatically figures out when a value should be placed in a register or other location.

Fourth-generation languages (*4GLs*) are *natural languages*, such as SQL. They let developers use a language that is sort of similar to a human language to execute programming tasks. For example, the SQL statement "SELECT * FROM Customers WHERE Balance > 50" tells the database to return information about customers who owe more than $50.

Fifth-generation languages (*5GLs*) provide powerful, highly graphical development environments to allow developers to use the underlying language in more sophisticated ways. The emphasis is more on the development environment than on the language itself.

The Visual Studio development environment is an extremely powerful fifth-generation tool. It provides graphical editors to make building forms and editing properties easy and intuitive; IntelliSense to help developers remember what to type next; auto-completion so developers can use meaningful variable names without needing to waste time typing them completely by hand; tools that show call hierarchies indicating which routines call which others; and breakpoints, watches, and other advanced debugging tools that make building applications easier.

Visual Studio is so powerful that the answer to the question of whether you should use it is practically obvious: If you want to write powerful applications that run in a Windows operating system, you should use Visual Studio.

Visual Basic is not the only language that uses Visual Studio. The C# language does, too, so now the question is, should you use Visual Basic or C#?

LOTS OF LANGUAGES

Visual Studio also supports a few other languages including Visual C++, Visual J#, and Visual F#, and in theory it could support others in the future. Visual Studio was originally built for Visual Basic and C# so it provides the most support for these.

A Visual Basic programmer's joke asks, "What's the difference between Visual Basic .NET and C#? About three months!" The implication is that Visual Basic .NET syntax is easier to understand and building applications with it is faster. Similarly, C# programmers have their jokes about Visual Basic .NET, implying that C# is more powerful.

In fact, Visual Basic .NET is *not* a whole lot easier to use than C#, and C# is *not* significantly more powerful. The basic form of the two languages is very similar. Aside from a few stylistic differences (Visual Basic is line-oriented; C# uses lots of braces and semicolons), the languages are comparable. Both use the Visual Studio development environment, both provide access to the .NET Framework of support classes and tools, and both provide similar syntax for performing basic programming tasks.

The main difference between these languages is one of style. If you have experience with previous versions of Visual Basic, you will probably find Visual Basic 2012 easier to get used to. If you have experience with C++ or Java, you will probably find C# (or Visual C++ or Visual J#) easy to learn.

Visual Basic does have some ties with other Microsoft products that increase its value. For example, *Active Server Pages (ASP)* and ASP.NET use Visual Basic to create interactive web pages. Microsoft Office applications (Word, Excel, PowerPoint, and so forth) and many third-party tools use *Visual Basic for Applications (VBA)* as a macro programming language. If you know Visual Basic, you have a big head start in using these other languages. ASP and VBA are based on pre-.NET versions of Visual Basic, so you won't instantly know how to use them, but you'll have an advantage if you need to learn ASP or VBA.

If you are new to programming, either Visual Basic 2012 or C# is a good choice. I think Visual Basic 2012 is a little easier to learn, but I may be slightly biased because I've been using Visual Basic since long before C# was invented. You won't be making a big mistake either way, and you can easily switch later, if necessary.

WHO SHOULD READ THIS BOOK

This book is intended for programmers of all levels. It describes the Visual Basic 2012 language from scratch, so you don't need experience with previous versions of the language. The book also covers many intermediate and advanced topics. It covers topics in enough depth that even experienced developers will discover new tips, tricks, and language details. After you have mastered the language, you may still find useful tidbits throughout the book, and the reference appendices will help you look up easily forgotten details.

The chapters move quickly through the more introductory material. If you have never programmed before and are intimidated by computers, you might want to read a more introductory book first. If you are a beginner who's not afraid of the computer, you should have few problems learning Visual Basic 2012 from this book.

If you have programmed in any other language, fundamentals such as variable declarations, data types, and arrays should be familiar to you, so you should have no problem with this book. The index and reference appendices should be particularly useful in helping you translate from the languages you already know into the corresponding Visual Basic syntax.

HOW THIS BOOK IS ORGANIZED

The chapters in this book are divided into four parts plus appendices. The chapters in each part are described here. If you are an experienced programmer, you can use these descriptions to decide which chapters to skim and which to read in detail.

Part I: IDE

The chapters in this part of the book describe the Visual Studio *integrated development environment (IDE)* from a Visual Basic developer's point of view. The IDE is mostly the same for C# and other developers but there are a few differences such as which keyboard shortcuts perform which tasks.

Chapter 1, "Introduction to the IDE," explains how to get started using the Visual Studio integrated development environment. It tells how to configure the IDE for different kinds of development. It defines and describes Visual Basic projects and solutions, and shows how to create, run, and save a new project.

Chapter 2, "Menus, Toolbars, and Windows," describes the most useful and important commands available in the IDE's menus and toolbars. The IDE's menus and toolbars include hundreds of commands, so this chapter covers only those that are the most useful.

Chapter 3, "Windows Forms Designer," describes the designer you can use to build Windows Forms. It explains how to create, size, move, and copy controls. It tells how to set control properties and add code to respond to control events.

Chapter 4, "WPF Designer," explains how to use the Windows Presentation Foundation (WPF) form designer. This chapter is similar to Chapter 3 except that it covers WPF forms instead of Windows Forms.

Chapter 5, "Visual Basic Code Editor," describes one of the most important windows used by developers: the code editor. It explains how to write code, set breakpoints, use code snippets, and get the most out of IntelliSense.

Chapter 6, "Debugging," explains debugging tools provided by Visual Studio. It describes the debugging windows and explains techniques such as setting complex breakpoints to locate bugs.

Part II: Getting Started

The chapters in this part of the book explain the bulk of the Visual Basic language and the objects that support it. They explain the forms, windows, controls, and other objects that a program uses to build a user interface, and they tell how you can put code behind those objects to implement the program's functionality.

Chapter 7, "Selecting Windows Forms Controls," provides an overview of the Windows Forms controls that you can put on a form. It groups the controls by category to help you find the controls you can use for a particular purpose.

Chapter 8, "Using Windows Forms Controls," gives more detail about how you can use Windows Forms controls. It explains how you can create controls at design time or run time, how to set complex property values, and how to use useful properties that are common to many different kinds of controls. It explains how to add event handlers to process control events and how to validate user-entered data.

Chapter 9, "Windows Forms," describes the forms you use in a Windows Forms application. Technically, forms are just another kind of control, but their unique position in the application's architecture means they have some special properties, and this chapter describes them.

Chapter 10, "Selecting WPF Controls," provides an overview of WPF controls. It groups the controls by category to help you find the controls you can use for a particular purpose. This chapter is similar to Chapter 7 except it covers WPF controls instead of Windows Forms controls.

Chapter 11, "Using WPF Controls," gives more detail about how you can use WPF controls. This chapter is similar to Chapter 8 except it deals with WPF controls instead of Windows Forms controls.

Chapter 12, "WPF Windows," describes the windows that WPF applications use in place of Windows forms. This chapter is similar to Chapter 9 except it deals with WPF windows instead of Windows forms.

Chapter 13, "Program and Module Structure," describes the most important files that make up a Visual Basic project. It describes some of the hidden files that projects contain and explains some of the structure that you can give to code within a module, such as code regions and conditionally compiled code.

Chapter 14, "Data Types, Variables, and Constants," explains the standard data types provided by Visual Basic. It shows how to declare and initialize variables and constants, and explains variable scope. It discusses technical topics, such as value and reference types, passing parameters by value or reference, and creating parameter variables on the fly. It also explains how to create and initialize arrays, enumerated types, and structures.

Chapter 15, "Operators," describes the operators a program uses to perform calculations. These include mathematical operators (+, *, \), string operators (&), and Boolean operators (And, Or). The chapter explains operator precedence and potentially confusing type conversion issues that arise when an expression combines more than one type of operator (for example, arithmetic and Boolean).

Chapter 16, "Subroutines and Functions," explains how you can use subroutines and functions to break a program into manageable pieces. It describes routine overloading and scope. It also describes lambda functions and relaxed delegates.

Chapter 17, "Program Control Statements," describes the statements that a Visual Basic program uses to control code execution. These include decision statements, such as If, Then, and Else, and looping statements, such as For and Next.

Chapter 18, "Error Handling," explains error handling and debugging techniques. It describes the Try Catch structured error handler and discusses typical actions a program might take when it catches an error. It also describes important techniques for preventing errors and making errors more obvious when they do occur.

Chapter 19, "Database Controls and Objects," explains how to use the standard Visual Basic database controls. These include database components that manage connections to a database, DataSet components that hold data within an application, and data adapter controls that move data between databases and DataSets.

Chapter 20, "LINQ," describes language integrated query (LINQ) features. It explains how you can write SQL-like queries to select data from or into objects, XML, or database objects. It also explains PLINQ, a parallel version of LINQ that can provide improved performance on multi-core systems.

Chapter 21, "Metro-Style Applications," explains how to build Metro-style applications that run on Windows 8. It explains special considerations that you should take into account when writing Metro applications such as loading files asynchronously.

Part III: Object-Oriented Programming

This part explains fundamental concepts in object-oriented programming (OOP) with Visual Basic. It also describes some of the more important classes and objects that you can use when building an application.

Chapter 22, "OOP Concepts," explains the fundamental ideas behind object-oriented programming (OOP). It describes the three main features of OOP: encapsulation, polymorphism, and inheritance. It explains the benefits of these features, and tells how you can take advantage of them in Visual Basic.

Chapter 23, "Classes and Structures," explains how to declare and use classes and structures. It explains what classes and structures are, and it describes their differences. It shows the basic declaration syntax and tells how to create instances of classes and structures. It also explains some of the trickier class issues such as private class scope, declaring events, and shared variables and methods.

Chapter 24, "Namespaces," explains namespaces. It discusses how Visual Studio uses namespaces to categorize code and to prevent name collisions. It describes a project's root namespace, tells how Visual Basic uses namespaces to resolve names (such as function and class names), and demonstrates how you can add namespaces to an application yourself.

Chapter 25, "Collection Classes," explains classes included in the .NET Framework that you can use to hold groups of objects. It describes the various collection, dictionary, queue, and stack classes; tells how to make strongly typed versions of those classes; and gives some guidance on deciding which class to use under different circumstances.

Chapter 26, "Generics," explains how you can build classes that can work with arbitrary data types. For example, you can build a generic binary tree, and then later use it to build classes to represent binary trees of customer orders, employees, or work items.

Part IV: Interacting with the Environment

The chapters in this part of the book explain how an application can interact with its environment. They show how the program can save and load data in external sources (such as the system registry, resource files, and text files); work with the computer's printer, screen, keyboard, and mouse; and interact with the user through standard dialog box controls.

Chapter 27, "Printing," explains different ways that a program can send output to the printer. It shows how you can use the PrintDocument object to generate printout data. You can then use the PrintDocument to print the data immediately, use a PrintDialog control to let the user select the printer and set its characteristics, or use a PrintPreviewDialog control to let the user preview the results before printing.

Chapter 28, "Configuration and Resources," describes some of the ways that a Visual Basic program can store configuration and resource values for use at run time. Some of the most useful of these include environment variables, the registry, configuration files, and resource files.

Chapter 29, "Streams," explains the classes that a Visual Basic application can use to work with stream data. Streams allow you to manipulate different kinds of data, such as files or chunks of memory, in a uniform way.

Chapter 30, "Filesystem Objects," describes classes that let a Visual Basic application interact with the filesystem. These include classes such as Directory, DirectoryInfo, File, and FileInfo that make it easy to create, examine, move, search, rename, and delete directories and files.

Part V: Appendices

The book's appendices provide a categorized reference of the Visual Basic 2012 language. You can use them to quickly review the syntax of a particular command or to refresh your memory of what a particular class can do. The chapters earlier in the book give more context, explaining how to perform specific tasks and why one approach might be better than another.

Appendix A, "Useful Control Properties, Methods, and Events," describes properties, methods, and events that are useful with many different kinds of controls.

Appendix B, "Variable Declarations and Data Types," summarizes the syntax for declaring variables. It also gives the sizes and ranges of allowed values for the fundamental data types.

Appendix C, "Operators," summarizes the standard operators such as +, <<, OrElse, and Like. It also gives the syntax for operator overloading.

Appendix D, "Subroutine and Function Declarations," summarizes the syntax for subroutine, function, and property procedure declarations. It also summarizes the syntax for using lambda functions and lambda statements (subroutines).

Appendix E, "Control Statements," summarizes statements that control program flow, such as If Then, Select Case, and looping statements.

Appendix F, "Error Handling," summarizes Try Catch error handling blocks.

Appendix G, "Windows Forms Controls and Components," summarizes standard Windows Forms controls and components provided by Visual Basic 2012.

Appendix H, "WPF Controls," summarizes the most useful WPF controls.

Appendix I, "Visual Basic Power Packs," lists some additional tools that you can download to make Visual Basic development easier.

Appendix J, "Form Objects," describes forms. Forms are just another type of control but they play such a key role in Visual Basic applications that they deserve special attention in their own appendix.

Appendix K, "Classes and Structures," summarizes the syntax for declaring classes and structures, and defining their constructors and events.

Appendix L, "LINQ," summarizes LINQ and PLINQ syntax.

Appendix M, "Generics," summarizes the syntax for declaring generic classes.

Appendix N, "Graphics," summarizes the objects used to generate graphics in Visual Basic 2012. The earlier chapters in the book cover graphics only in passing while explaining how to print. This appendix provides more detail and a summary of the most useful graphics classes.

Appendix O, "Useful Exception Classes," lists some of the more useful exception classes defined by Visual Basic. You may want to throw these exceptions in your own code.

Appendix P, "Date and Time Format Specifiers," summarizes standard and custom specifiers that you can use to format dates and times. For example, they let you display a time using a 12-hour or 24-hour clock.

Appendix Q, "Other Format Specifiers," summarizes formatting for numbers and enumerated types.

Appendix R, "The Application Class," summarizes the Application class that provides properties and methods for controlling the current application.

Appendix S, "The My Namespace," describes the My namespace, which provides shortcuts to useful features scattered around other parts of the .NET Framework. It provides shortcuts for working with the application, computer hardware, application forms, resources, and the current user.

Appendix T, "Streams," summarizes the Visual Basic stream classes such as Stream, FileStream, MemoryStream, TextReader, and CryptoStream.

Appendix U, "Filesystem Classes," summarizes methods that an application can use to learn about and manipulate the filesystem. It explains classic Visual Basic methods such as FreeFile, WriteLine, and ChDir, as well as newer .NET Framework classes such as FileSystem, Directory, and File.

Appendix V, "Visual Studio Versions," describes the Visual Studio version that I used when writing this book and explains which versions you can use to reproduce the examples described here.

HOW TO USE THIS BOOK

If you are an experienced Visual Basic .NET programmer, you may want to skim the language basics covered in the first parts of the book. You may find a few new features that have appeared in Visual Basic 2012, so you probably shouldn't skip these chapters entirely, but most of the basic language features are the same as in previous versions.

Intermediate programmers and those with less experience with Visual Basic .NET should take these chapters a bit more slowly. The chapters in Part III, "Object-Oriented Programming," cover particularly tricky topics. Learning all the variations on inheritance and interfaces can be rather confusing so don't skip those chapters unless you have previous experience with object-oriented programming.

Beginners should spend more time on these first chapters because they set the stage for the material that follows. It will be a lot easier for you to follow a discussion of file management or regular expressions if you are not confused by the error-handling code that the examples take for granted.

Programming is a skill best learned by doing. You can pick up the book and read through it quickly if you like (well, as quickly as you can given how long it is), but the information is more likely to stick if you open the development environment and experiment with some programs of your own.

Learning by doing may encourage you to skip sections of the book. For example, Chapter 1 covers the IDE in detail. After you've read for a while, you may want to skip some sections and start experimenting with the environment on your own. I encourage you to do so. Lessons learned by doing last longer than those learned by reading. Later, when you have some experience with the development environment, you can go back and examine Chapter 1 in more detail to see if you missed anything during your experimentation.

The final part of the book is a Visual Basic 2012 reference. These appendices present more concise, categorized information about the language. You can use these appendices to recall the details of specific operations. For example, you can read Chapter 27 to learn what generic classes are for and how to create them. Later you can use Appendix M to refresh your memory of the syntax for declaring a generic class.

NECESSARY EQUIPMENT

To read this book and understand the examples, you will need no special equipment. To use Visual Basic 2012 and to run the examples found on the book's web page, you need any computer that can reasonably run Visual Basic 2012. That means a reasonably modern, fast computer with a lot of memory. See the Visual Basic 2012 documentation for Microsoft's exact requirements and recommendations. (I use a dual-core 1.83 GHz Intel Core 2CPU system with 2 GB of memory and 164 GB of hard disk space running Windows 7 Ultimate. It's a nice system and works well but I wouldn't say it's overkill.)

To build Visual Basic 2012 programs, you will also need a copy of Visual Basic 2012. You can download the free Express Edition of Visual Basic (and purchase other editions) at `www.microsoft.com/visualstudio/products`.

Don't bother trying to run the examples shown here if you have a pre-.NET version of Visual Basic such as Visual Basic 6. The changes between Visual Basic 6 and Visual Basic .NET are huge, and many Visual Basic .NET concepts don't translate well into Visual Basic 6. With some experience in C#, it would be much easier to translate the example programs into that language.

Much of the Visual Basic 2012 release is compatible with Visual Basic 2010 and earlier versions of Visual Basic .NET, however, so you can make many of the examples work with earlier versions of Visual Basic .NET. You will not be able to load the example programs downloaded from the book's website, however, because Visual Basic programs are not generally backward compatible with earlier versions. You will need to open the source code files in an editor such as WordPad and copy and paste the significant portions of the code into your version of Visual Basic.

CONVENTIONS

To help you get the most from the text and keep track of what's happening, a number of conventions have been used throughout the book.

For styles in the text:

➤   Important words are *highlighted* when they are introduced.

➤   Keyboard strokes are shown like this: Ctrl+A.

➤   Filenames, URLs, and code within the text are shown like this: `persistence.properties`. Code is presented in the following way:

```
We use a monofont type for most code examples.
```

SOURCE CODE

As you work through the examples in this book, you may choose either to type in all the code manually or to use the source code files that accompany the book. All the source code used in this book is available for download at `www.wrox.com`. Specifically for this book, the code download is on the Download Code tab at:

`www.wrox.com/remtitle.cgi?isbn=1118314077`

You can also search for the book at www.wrox.com by ISBN (the ISBN for this book is 978-1-118-31407-4) to find the code. And a complete list of code downloads for all current Wrox books is available at www.wrox.com/dynamic/books/download.aspx.

At the beginning of each chapter, we've provided a list of the major code files for the chapter. Throughout each chapter, you'll also find references to the names of code files as needed in the text.

Most of the code on www.wrox.com is compressed in a .ZIP, .RAR archive, or similar archive format appropriate to the platform. Once you download the code, just decompress it with an appropriate compression tool.

FIND IT FAST

Because many books have similar titles, you may find it easiest to locate the book by its ISBN: 978-1-118-31407-4.

Once you download the code, just decompress it with your favorite compression tool. Note that the programs won't run or even load in Visual Studio properly if you don't decompress them. If Visual Studio can't open an example program, make sure you have decompressed it.

Alternatively, you can go to the main Wrox code download page at www.wrox.com/dynamic/books/download.aspx to see the code available for this book and all other Wrox books.

You can also download the book's source code from its web page on my VB Helper website www.vb-helper.com/vb_prog_ref.htm. That page allows you to download all of the book's code in one big chunk or by individual chapter.

ERRATA

We make every effort to ensure that there are no errors in the text or in the code. However, no one is perfect, and mistakes do occur. If you find an error in one of my books, like a spelling mistake or faulty piece of code, I would be very grateful for your feedback. By sending in errata you may save another reader hours of frustration and at the same time you will be helping me provide higher quality information.

To find the errata page for this book, go to www.wrox.com and locate the title using the Search box or one of the title lists. Then, on the book details page, click the Book Errata link. On this page you can view all errata that have been submitted for this book and posted by Wrox editors. A complete book list including links to each book's errata is also available at www.wrox.com/misc-pages/booklist.shtml.

If you don't spot "your" error on the Book Errata page, go to www.wrox.com/contact/techsup-port.shtml and complete the form there to send us the error you have found. We'll check the information and, if appropriate, post a message to the book's errata page and fix the problem in subsequent editions of the book.

P2P.WROX.COM

For author and peer discussion, join the P2P forums at p2p.wrox.com. The forums are a web-based system for you to post messages relating to Wrox books and related technologies and interact with other readers and technology users. The forums offer a subscription feature to e-mail you topics of interest of your choosing when new posts are made to the forums. Wrox authors, editors, other industry experts, and your fellow readers are present on these forums.

At p2p.wrox.com you will find a number of different forums that will help you not only as you read this book but also as you develop your own applications. To join the forums, just follow these steps:

1. Go to p2p.wrox.com and click the Register link.
2. Read the terms of use and click Agree.
3. Complete the required information to join as well as any optional information you wish to provide and click Submit.
4. You will receive an e-mail with information describing how to verify your account and complete the joining process.

> **JOIN THE FUN**
>
> You can read messages in the forums without joining P2P, but in order to post your own messages, you must join.

Once you join, you can post new messages and respond to messages other users post. You can read messages at any time on the web. If you would like to have new messages from a particular forum e-mailed to you, click the Subscribe to this Forum icon by the forum name in the forum listing.

For more information about how to use the Wrox P2P, be sure to read the P2P FAQs for answers to questions about how the forum software works as well as many common questions specific to P2P and Wrox books. To read the FAQs, click the FAQ link on any P2P page.

Using the P2P forums allows other readers to benefit from your questions and any answers they generate. I monitor my book's forums and respond whenever I can help.

If you have other comments, suggestions, or questions that you don't want to post to the forums, feel free to e-mail me at RodStephens@vb-helper.com. I can't promise to solve every problem but I'll try to help you out if I can.

IMPORTANT URLS

Here's a summary of important URLs:

- ➤ `www.vb-helper.com` — My VB Helper website. Contains thousands of tips, tricks, and examples for Visual Basic developers.

- ➤ `www.vb-helper.com/vb_prog_reg.htm` — This book's web page on my VB Helper website. Includes basic information, code downloads, errata, and more.

- ➤ `p2p.wrox.com` — Wrox P2P forums.

- ➤ `www.wrox.com` — The Wrox website. Contains code downloads, errata, and other information. Search for the book by title or ISBN.

- ➤ `RodStephens@vb-helper.com` — My e-mail address. I hope to hear from you!

PART I
IDE

Introduction to the IDE

INTRODUCING THE IDE

The chapters in the first part of this book describe the Visual Studio integrated development environment (IDE). They explain the most important windows, menus, and toolbars that make up the environment, and show how to customize them to suit your needs. They explain some of the tools that provide help while you are writing Visual Basic applications and how to use the IDE to debug programs.

Even if you are an experienced Visual Basic programmer, you should at least skim this material. The IDE is *extremely* complex and provides hundreds (if not thousands) of commands, menus, toolbars, windows, context menus, and other tools for editing, running, and debugging Visual Basic projects.

Even after you've read these chapters, you should periodically spend some time wandering through the IDE to see what you've missed. Every month or so, spend a few minutes exploring little-used menus and right-clicking things to see what their context menus contain. As you become a more proficient Visual Basic programmer, you will find uses for tools that you may have dismissed or not understood before.

This chapter explains how to get started using the IDE. It tells how to configure the IDE for different kinds of development. It explains Visual Basic projects and solutions, and shows how to create, run, and save new projects. This chapter is mostly an introduction to the chapters that follow. The other chapters in this part of the book provide much more detail about particular tasks, such as using the IDE's menus, customizing menus and toolbars, and using the Windows Forms Designer to build forms.

DIFFERENT IDE APPEARANCES

Before you start reading about the IDE and viewing screen shots, it's important to understand that the Visual Studio IDE is *extremely* customizable. You can move, hide, or modify the menus, toolbars, and windows; create your own toolbars; dock, undock, or rearrange the toolbars and windows; and change the behavior of the built-in text editors (change their indentation, colors for different kinds of text, and so forth).

> **NOTE** *These chapters describe the basic Visual Studio development environment as it is initially installed. After you've moved things around to suit your needs, your IDE may look nothing like the pictures in this book. If a figure doesn't look exactly like what you see on your computer, don't worry too much about it.*

To avoid confusion, you should probably not customize the IDE's basic menus and toolbars too much. Removing the help commands from the Help menu and adding them to the Edit menu will only cause confusion later. Moving or removing commands will also make it more difficult to follow the examples in this and other books, and will make it more difficult to follow instructions given by others who might be able to help you when you have problems.

Instead of making drastic changes to the default menus and toolbars, hide the menus and toolbars that you don't want and create new customized toolbars to suit your needs. Then you can find the original standard toolbars if you decide you need them later.

The screens shown in this book may not look exactly like the ones on your system for several other reasons as well. Visual Studio looks different on different operating systems. The figures in this book were taken on a computer running Windows 8 so they display the Windows 8 look and feel. Additionally, some commands may not behave exactly the same way on different operating systems.

Visual Studio will also look different depending on which version you have installed. The free Visual Basic 2012 Express Edition product has fewer tools than other editions such as the high-end Team Suite. The figures in this book were captured while using Team Suite, so if you have another version, you may not see all of the tools shown here. Menu items, toolbars, and other details may also be slightly different for different versions. Usually you can find moved items with a little digging through the menus and customizations.

FOR MORE INFORMATION

You can learn about Visual Studio's free Express editions at http://www
.microsoft.com/express. Learn about Visual Basic in general at the Visual
Basic homepage: http://msdn.microsoft.com/vbasic.

Finally, you may be using different configuration settings from the ones used while writing this book. You can configure Visual Studio to use settings customized for developing projects using Visual Basic, C#, web tools, and other technologies. This book assumes your installation is configured for Visual Basic development, and the screen shots may look different if you have selected a different configuration. The following section says more about different IDE configurations and tells how you can select a particular configuration.

IDE CONFIGURATIONS

When you install it, Visual Studio asks you what kinds of development settings you want to use. The most obvious choice for a Visual Basic developer is Visual Basic Development Settings. This choice customizes Visual Studio to work more easily with Visual Basic, and is a good selection if you will focus on Visual Basic development.

Another reasonable choice is General Development Settings. This option makes Visual Studio behave more like Visual Studio 2003. It's a good choice if you're used to Visual Studio 2003, or if you expect to use other Visual Studio languages, such as C#, somewhat regularly because these settings are fairly effective for C# development and Visual Basic development.

This book assumes that you have configured Visual Studio for Visual Basic development. If you have chosen a different configuration, some of the figures in this book may look different from what you see on your screen. Some of the menu items available may be slightly different, or may appear in a different order. Usually, the items are available somewhere, but you may have to search a bit to find them.

If you later decide that you want to switch configurations, open the Tools menu and select Import and Export Settings to display the Import and Export Settings Wizard. Select the Reset All Settings option button and click Next. On the second page, tell the wizard whether to save your current settings and click Next. On the wizard's final page (shown in Figure 1-1), select the type of configuration you want and click Finish. When the wizard is done, click Close.

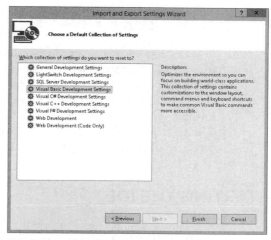

FIGURE 1-1: Use the Tools menu's Import and Export Settings command to change the Visual Studio configuration.

PROJECTS AND SOLUTIONS

Visual Studio groups files into projects and solutions. A *project* is a group of files that produces some specific output. This output may take many forms such as a compiled executable program, a dynamic-link library (DLL) of classes for use by other projects, or a control library for use on other Windows forms.

A *solution* is a group of one or more projects that should be managed together. For example, suppose that you are building a server application that provides access to your customer order database. You are also building a client program that each of your sales representatives will use to query the server application. Because these two projects are closely related, it might make sense to manage them in a single solution. When you open the solution, you get instant access to all the files in both projects.

Both projects and solutions can include associated files that are useful for building the application but that do not become part of a final compiled product. For example, a project might include the application's proposal and architecture documents. These are not included in the compiled code, but it can be useful to associate them with the project so they are easy to find, open, and edit while you are working on the project.

When you open the project, Visual Studio lists those documents along with the program files. If you double-click one of these documents, Visual Studio opens the file using an appropriate application. For example, if you double-click a file with a .doc, .docm, or .docx extension, Visual Studio normally opens it with Microsoft Word.

To associate one of these files with a project or solution, right-click the project file at the top of the Solution Explorer (more on the Solution Explorer shortly). In the context menu that appears, select the Add command's New Item entry, and use the resulting dialog box to select the file you want to add.

CUT OUT CLUTTER

You can add any file to a project or solution, but it's not a good idea to cram dozens of unrelated files into the same project. Although you may sometimes want to refer to an unrelated file while working on a project, the extra clutter brings additional chances for confusion. It will be less confusing to shrink the Visual Basic IDE to an icon and open the file using an external editor such as Word or WordPad. If you won't use a file very often with the project, don't add it.

STARTING THE IDE

When you launch Visual Studio, it initially displays the Start Page shown in Figure 1-2 by default. The Start Page's Recent Projects section lists projects that you have worked on recently and provides links that let you open an existing project or website, or create a new project or website. The Get Started tab contains links to help topics that may be useful to beginners.

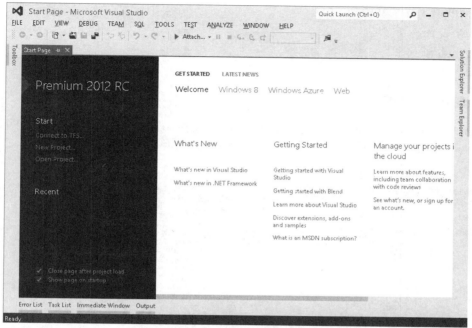

FIGURE 1-2: By default, Visual Studio initially displays the Start Page.

Click the Guidance and Resources tab to see general development topics such as a development overview, information about managing source code, and information about unit testing.

Click the Latest News tab to see an RSS feed listing current articles and stories about Visual Studio development. To change the feed, simply enter a new URL in the tab's text box.

Use the links on the left of the Start Page to open or create new projects. Click New Project to start a new project. Click Open Project to browse for a project to open. Click one of the Recent Project links to quickly open a project that you have recently edited.

Instead of displaying the Start Page, Visual Studio can take one of several other actions when it starts. To change the startup action, open the Tools menu and select Options. Then select the Show All Settings check box at the bottom of the dialog box so you can see all of the options and open the Environment folder's Startup item. In the At Startup drop-down box, you can select one of the following options:

➤ Open Home Page

➤ Load Last Loaded Solution

➤ Show Open Project Dialog Box

➤ Show New Project Dialog Box

➤   Show Empty Environment

➤   Show Start Page

Pick one and click OK.

CREATING A PROJECT

After you open Visual Studio, you can use the Start Page's New Project link or the File menu's New Project command to open the New Project dialog box shown in Figure 1-3.

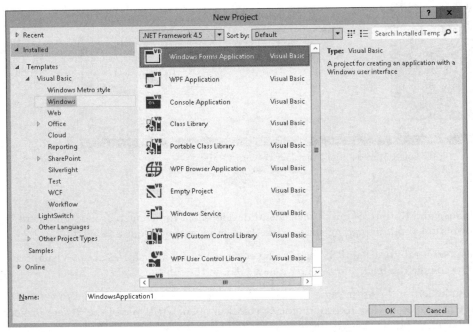

FIGURE 1-3: The New Project dialog box lets you start a new project.

Use the Templates tree view on the left to select the project category that you want. Then select a specific project type on the right. In Figure 1-3, the Windows Forms Application project type is selected. Enter a name for the new project in the text box at the bottom.

After you fill in the new project's information, click OK to create the project.

> **NOTE** *Visual Studio initially creates the project in a temporary directory. If you close the project without saving it, it is discarded.*

Figure 1-4 shows the IDE immediately after starting a new Windows Forms Application project. Remember that the IDE is extremely configurable, so it may not look much like Figure 1-4 after you have rearranged things to your liking (and I've arranged things to my liking here).

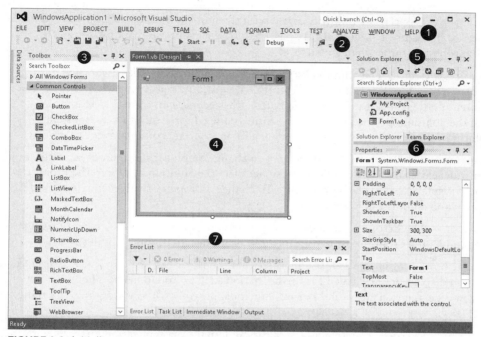

FIGURE 1-4: Initially a new project looks more or less like this.

The key pieces of the IDE are labeled with numbers in Figure 1-4. The following list briefly describes each of these pieces:

1. *Menus* — The menus contain standard Visual Studio commands. These generally manipulate the current solution and the modules it contains, although you can customize the menus as needed. Visual Studio changes the menus and their contents depending on the object you currently have selected. In Figure 1-4, a Form Designer (marked with the number 4) is open so the IDE is displaying the menus for editing forms.

2. *Toolbars* — Toolbars contain tools that you can use to perform frequently needed actions. The same commands may be available in menus, but they are easier and faster to use in toolbars. The IDE defines several standard toolbars such as Formatting, Debug, and Image Editor. You can also build your own custom toolbars to hold your favorite tools. Visual Studio changes the toolbars displayed to match the object you currently have selected.

3. *Toolbox* — The Toolbox contains tools appropriate for the item that you currently have selected and for the project type that you are working on. In Figure 1-4, a Form Designer

is selected in a Windows Forms application so the Toolbox contains tools appropriate for a Form Designer. These include Windows Forms controls and components, plus tools in the other Toolbox tabs.

4. *Form Designer* — A Form Designer lets you modify the graphical design of a form. Select a control tool from the Toolbox, and click and drag to place an instance of the control on the form. Use the Properties window (marked with the number 6) to change the new control's properties. In Figure 1-4, no control is selected, so the Properties window shows the form's properties rather than a control's.

5. *Solution Explorer* — The Solution Explorer lets you manage the files associated with the current solution. For example, in Figure 1-4, you could select Form1.vb in the Project Explorer and then click the View Code button (the second icon from the right at the top of the Solution Explorer) to open the form's code editor. You can also right-click an object in the Solution Explorer to get a list of appropriate commands for that object.

6. *Properties* — The Properties window lets you change an object's properties at design time. When you select an object in a Form Designer or in the Solution Explorer, the Properties window displays that object's properties. To change a property's value, simply click the property and enter the new value.

7. *Error List* — The Error List window shows errors and warnings in the current project. For example, if a program uses a variable that is not declared, this list will say so.

If you look at the bottom of Figure 1-4, you'll notice that the Error List window has a series of tabs. The Task List tab displays items flagged for further action such as To Do items. The Immediate window lets you type and execute Visual Basic commands, possibly while a program is running, but paused.

The Output tab shows output printed by the application. Usually an application interacts with the user through its forms and dialog boxes, but it can display information here, usually to help you debug the code.

WHAT WINDOWS?

If you don't see the Error List, Task List, and other windows, they are probably hidden. You can display many of them by selecting the appropriate item in the View menu. Commands to display some of the more exotic windows are located in other menus, such as the View menu's Other Windows submenu and the Debug menu's Windows submenu.

As soon as you create a new project, it is ready to run. If you open the Debug menu and select Start Debugging, the program will run. It displays only an empty form containing no controls, but the form automatically handles a multitude of mundane windowing tasks for you.

READY TO RUN

If you're using the Visual Basic environment settings, you can simply press F5 to start the program.

Before you write a single line of code, the form lets you resize, minimize, restore, maximize, and close the form. The form draws its title bar, borders, and system menu, and repaints itself as needed when it is covered and restored. The operating system also automatically handles many tasks such as displaying the form in the Windows taskbar and Task Manager. Some operating systems, such as Windows 7 and Vista, automatically generate thumbnail previews for the Flip and Flip 3D tools that you display by pressing Alt+Tab or Windows+Tab, respectively. Visual Basic and the operating system do a ton of work for you before you even touch the project!

The form contains no controls, can't open files, doesn't process data, in fact doesn't really do anything unique, but a lot of the setup is done for you. It handles the windowing chores for you so you can focus on your particular problem.

SAVING A PROJECT

Later chapters explain in depth how to add controls to a form and how to write code to interact with the form. For now, suppose you have built a project complete with controls and code.

If you try to close Visual Studio or start a new project, the dialog box shown in Figure 1-5 appears. Click Save to make the Save Project dialog box shown in Figure 1-6 appear. Click Discard to throw away the existing project. Click Cancel to continue editing the current project.

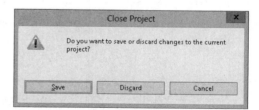

FIGURE 1-5: Before closing Visual Studio or starting a new project, you must decide what to do with the previous project.

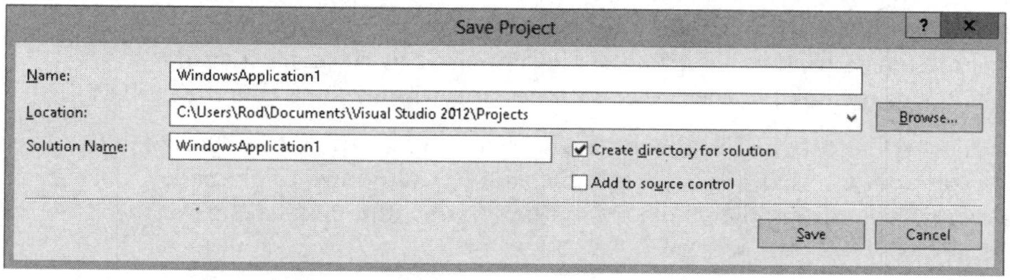

FIGURE 1-6: Use this dialog box to save a new project.

As you work with the new project, Visual Studio saves its form definitions and code in a temporary location. Each time you run the program, Visual Studio updates the files so it doesn't lose everything if it crashes. The files are still temporary, however.

When you are ready to make the new project permanent, open the File menu and select Save All to display the Save Project dialog box shown in Figure 1-6.

The Name field shows the name that you originally gave the project when you created it. Verify that the name is okay or change it.

Next, enter the location where you want the project saved. The default location is similar to the rather non-intuitive value shown in Figure 1-6. (This image was taken while I was logged in as the user named Developer. When you save a project, the "Developer" part of the location would be replaced with your username.)

Be sure to pick a good location before you click Save. The next time you build a project, the default will be the location you specify now so you won't need to be quite as careful in the future, assuming you want to build a lot of projects in the same directory.

If you check the Create Directory for Solution box, Visual Studio enables the Solution Name text box and adds an extra directory above the project directory to hold the solution. This is most useful when you want to include more than one project in a single solution. For example, you might want several projects in the same solution to sit in a common solution directory.

If you have Team Foundation Server installed, you can check the Add to Source Control box to place the new project's code under source control.

After you have entered the project name and location, and optionally specified a separate solution directory, click Save.

"SAVE AS" SURVIVAL SKILLS

The File menu's Save As commands let you save particular pieces of the solution in new files. For example, if you have a project named OfficeArrangerMain selected in Project Explorer, the File menu contains a command named Save OfficeArrangerMain As. This command lets you save the project file with a new name. Unfortunately it doesn't make a new copy of the whole project; it just makes a copy of the project file. That file contains information about the project on a high level such as references used by the project, files imported by the project, and the names of the forms included in the project. It does not contain the forms themselves.

Many beginners try to use the File menu's Save As commands to make copies of a project or a solution, but that doesn't work. Instead, use Windows Explorer to find the directory containing the whole project or solution and make a copy of the entire directory.

Similarly, if you want to back up a project or send someone a copy of a project, you need to use the entire solution directory, not just one or two of the many files that Visual Studio creates.

SUMMARY

This chapter explained how to get started using the Visual Studio integrated development environment. It showed how to configure the IDE for different kinds of development and explained that different configurations might make your version of Visual Studio look different from the screen shots shown in this book. It explained what Visual Basic projects and solutions are, and showed how to create, run, and save a new project.

The next few chapters describe parts of the IDE in greater detail. Chapter 2, "Menus, Toolbars, and Windows," describes the commands available in the IDE and the menus, toolbars, and secondary windows that hold them.

Menus, Toolbars, and Windows

WHAT'S IN THIS CHAPTER

➤ Finding IDE menus and tools

➤ Setting Option Explicit, Option Strict, and Option Infer

➤ Adding external tools to open a browser or send e-mail

➤ Rearranging IDE windows

➤ Displaying control properties and events

WROX.COM CODE DOWNLOADS FOR THIS CHAPTER

There are no code downloads for this chapter.

IDE TOOLS

The Visual Studio IDE is incredibly powerful and provides hundreds of tools for building and modifying projects. The price you pay for all of these powerful tools is extra complexity. Because so many tools are available, it can take some digging to find the tool you want, even if you know exactly what you need.

This chapter describes the menus, toolbars, and windows that contain the tools provided by the IDE. It explains some of the most useful tools provided by the IDE and tells where to find them, provided you haven't moved them while customizing the IDE.

This chapter also tells how you can customize the menus and toolbars to give you easy access to the commands that you use most frequently and how to hide those that you don't need.

MENUS

The IDE's menus contain standard Visual Studio commands. These are generally commands that manipulate the project and the modules it contains. Some of the concepts are similar to those used by any Windows application (File ⇨ New, File ⇨ Save, Edit ⇨ Copy), but many of the details are specific to Visual Studio programming, so the following sections describe them in a bit more detail.

The menus are customizable, so you can add, remove, and rearrange the menus and the items they contain. This can be quite confusing, however, if you later need to find a command that you have removed from its normal place in the menus. Some developers place extra commands in standard menus, particularly the Tools menu, but it is generally risky to remove standard menu items. Usually it is safest to leave the standard menus alone and make custom menus and toolbars to hold customizations.

Many of the menus' most useful commands are also available in other ways. Many provide keyboard shortcuts that make using them quick and easy. For example, Ctrl+N opens the New Project dialog box just as if you had selected the File ⇨ New Project menu command. If you find yourself using the same command very frequently, look in the menu and learn its keyboard shortcut to save time later.

Many menu commands are also available in standard toolbars. For example, the Debug toolbar contains many of the same commands that are in the Debug menu. If you use a set of menu commands frequently, you may want to display the corresponding toolbar to make using the commands easier.

Visual Studio also provides many commands through context menus. For example, if you right-click a project in the Solution Explorer, the context menu includes an Add Reference command that displays the Add Reference dialog box just as if you had invoked Project ⇨ Add Reference. Often it is easier to find a command by right-clicking an object related to whatever you want to do than it is to wander through the menus.

The following sections describe the general layout of the standard menus and briefly explain their most important commands. You might want to open the menus in Visual Studio as you read these sections, so you can follow along and see what other commands might be available.

> **MOVING MENUS**
>
> Visual Studio displays different menus and different commands in menus depending on what editor is active. For example, when you have a form open in the Windows Forms Designer, Visual Studio displays a Format menu that you can use to arrange controls on the form. When you have a code editor open, the Format menu is hidden because it doesn't apply to code.

File

The File menu contains commands that deal with creating, opening, saving, and closing projects and project files. The following list describes the most important commands contained in the File menu and its submenus:

➤ **New Project** — This command displays a dialog box that lets you create new Windows applications, class libraries, console applications, control libraries, and more. Select the type of project you want to start, enter a project name, and click OK.

➤ **New Web Site** — This command lets you start a new website project. It displays a dialog box where you can select the type of website to create from among choices such as ASP.NET Web Site, ASP.NET Empty Web Site, and WCF Service.

➤ **Open Project** — This command lets you open an existing project.

➤ **Open Web Site** — This command lets you open an existing website project.

➤ **Open File** — This command displays a dialog box that lets you select a file to open. The IDE uses integrated editors to let you edit the new file. For example, a simple bitmap editor lets you set a bitmap's size, change its number of colors, and draw on it. When you close the file, Visual Studio asks if you want to save it. Note that this doesn't automatically add the file to your current project. You can save the file and use the Project ➪ Add Existing Item command if you want to do that.

➤ **Add** — This submenu lets you add new items to the current solution. This submenu's most useful commands for Visual Basic developers are New Project and Existing Project, which add a new or existing Visual Basic project to the current solution.

➤ **Close** — This command closes the current editor. For example, if you were editing a form in the Windows Forms Designer, this command closes the designer.

➤ **Close Project** — This command closes the entire project and all of the files it contains. If you have a solution open, this command is labeled Close Solution and it closes the entire solution.

➤ **Save Form1.vb** — This command saves the currently open file, in this example, `Form1.vb`.

➤ **Save Form1.vb As** — This command lets you save the currently open file with a new name.

➤ **Save All** — This command saves all modified files. When you start a new project, the files are initially stored in a temporary location. This command allows you to pick a directory where the project should be saved permanently.

➤ **Export Template** — This command displays the Export Template Wizard, which enables you to create project or item templates that you can use later when making a new project.

➤ **Page Setup and Print** — The Page Setup and Print commands let you configure printer settings and print the current document. These commands are enabled only when it makes sense to print the current file. For example, they let you print if you have a code editor open because the code is text but they are disabled while you are using a Windows Forms Designer.

➤ **Recent Files and Recent Projects and Solutions** — The Recent Files and Recent Projects and Solutions submenus let you quickly reopen files, projects, and solutions that you have used recently.

Edit

The Edit menu contains commands that deal with manipulating text and other objects. These include standard commands such as the Undo, Redo, Cut, Copy, Paste, and Delete commands that you've seen in other Windows applications.

The following list describes other important commands contained in the Edit menu:

➤ **Find Symbol** — This command lets you search the application for a program symbol rather than a simple string. You can search for such items as namespaces, types, interfaces, properties, methods, constants, and variables.

➤ **Quick Find** — This command displays a Find dialog box where you can search the project for specific text. A drop-down menu lets you indicate whether the search should include the current document, the currently selected text, all open documents, the current project, or the current solution. Options let you determine such things as whether the text must match case or whole words.

➤ **Quick Replace** — This command displays the same dialog box as the Quick Find command except with some extra controls. It includes a text box where you can specify replacement text, and buttons that let you replace the currently found text or all occurrences of the text.

REGRETFUL REPLACEMENT

Be careful when using Quick Replace. Often it gets carried away and replaces substrings of larger strings so they don't make sense anymore. For example, suppose you want to replace the variable name "hand" with "handed." If you let Quick Replace run, it will change Handles clauses into "handedles" clauses, which will confuse Visual Basic. To reduce the chances of this type of error, keep the scope of the replacement as small as possible and check the result for weird side effects.

➤ **Go To** — This command lets you jump to a particular line number in the current file.

➤ **Insert File As Text** — This command lets you select a file and insert its text into the current location. This can be useful if the file contains a code snippet.

➤ **Advanced** — The Advanced submenu contains commands for performing more complex document formatting such as converting text to upper- or lowercase, controlling word wrap, and commenting and uncommenting code.

➤ **Bookmarks** — The Bookmarks submenu lets you add, remove, and clear bookmarks, and move to the next or previous bookmark. You can use bookmarks to move quickly to specific pieces of code that you have previously marked.

➤ **Outlining** — The Outlining submenu lets you expand or collapse sections of code, and turn outlining on and off. Collapsing code that you are not currently editing can make the rest of the code easier to read.

➤ **IntelliSense** — The IntelliSense submenu gives access to IntelliSense features. For example, its List Members command makes IntelliSense display the current object's properties, methods, and events.

➤ **Next Method and Previous Method** — The Next Method and Previous Method commands move to the next or previous method or class in the current document.

View

The View menu contains commands that let you hide or display different windows and toolbars in the Visual Studio IDE. The following list describes the View menu's most useful commands:

➤ **Code** — This command opens the selected file in a code editor window. For example, to edit a form's code, you can click the form in the Solution Explorer and then select View ➪ Code.

➤ **Designer** — This command opens the selected file in a graphical editor if one is defined for that type of file. For example, if the file is a form, this command opens the form in a graphical form editor. If the file is a class or a code module, the View menu hides this command because Visual Studio doesn't have a graphical editor for those file types.

➤ **Standard windows** — The next several commands in this menu list some explorers, Object Browser, Error List, Properties window, and Toolbox. These commands restore a previously hidden window.

➤ **Other Windows** — The Other Windows submenu lists other standard menus that are not listed in the View menu itself. These include the Bookmark window, Class View, Command window, Document Outline, Output, Task List, and many others. Like the standard windows commands, these commands are useful for recovering lost or hidden windows.

➤ **Tab Order** — If the currently visible document is a Windows Form that contains controls, the Tab Order command displays the tab order on top of each control. You can click the controls in the order you want them to have to set their tab orders quickly and easily. (If you are working with a WPF form, you must set the controls' TabIndex properties to set their tab order.)

➤ **Toolbars** — The Toolbars submenu lets you hide or display the currently defined toolbars. This submenu lists the standard toolbars in addition to any custom toolbars you have created.

➤ **Full Screen** — This command hides all toolbars and windows except for any editor windows that you currently have open. This gives you the most space possible for working with the files you have open. The command adds a small box to the title bar containing a Full Screen button that you can click to end full-screen mode.

➤ **Property Pages** — This command displays the current item's property pages. For example, if you select a project in the Solution Explorer, this command displays the application's property pages similar to those shown in Figure 2-1.

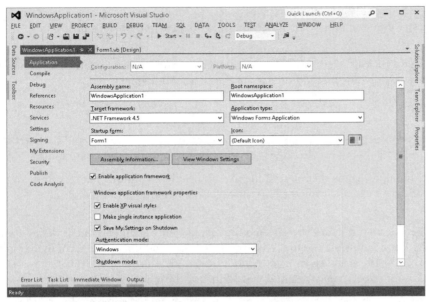

FIGURE 2-1: The View menu's Property Pages command displays an object's property pages.

Project

The Project menu contains commands that let you add and remove items to and from the project. Which commands are available depends on the currently selected item.

The following list describes the most important commands on the Project menu:

➤ **New items** — The first several commands let you add new items to the project. These commands are fairly self-explanatory. For example, the Add Class command adds a new class module to the project. Later chapters explain how to use each of these file types.

➤ **Add New Item** — This command displays a dialog box that lets you select from a wide assortment of items such as About Boxes, text files, bitmap files, and class modules.

EASY ICONS

You can build an icon, cursor, or other graphical file right inside Visual Studio. Use the Add New Item command to add the new file. Visual Studio's built-in editors let you draw these files, give them transparent backgrounds, and even set a cursor's hotspot. (The hotspot is the pixel that determines where the cursor is pointing. For example, an arrow cursor's hotspot is the tip of the arrow.) Note that integrated editors for some of these file types may be unavailable if you have the Express Edition, although lots of editors for these file types are available for download on the Internet.

➤ **Add Existing Item** — This command lets you browse for a file and add it to the project. This may be a Visual Basic file (such as a module, form, or class), or some other related file (such as a related document or image file).

➤ **Exclude From Project** — This command removes the currently selected item from the project. Note that this does not delete the file; it just removes it from the project.

➤ **Show All Files** — This command makes Solution Explorer list files that are normally hidden. These include resource files used by forms and hidden partial classes such as designer-generated form code. Normally, you don't need to work with these files, so they are hidden. Select this command to show them. Select the command again to hide them again.

➤ **Add Reference** — This command displays the Reference Manager shown in Figure 2-2. On the left select the category of the external object, class, or library that you want to find. For a .NET component, select the Assemblies category's Framework item. This is what you'll want most of the time. For a component object model (COM) component such as an ActiveX library or control built using Visual Basic 6, select the COM category. Click the Browse button to manually locate the file that you want to reference.

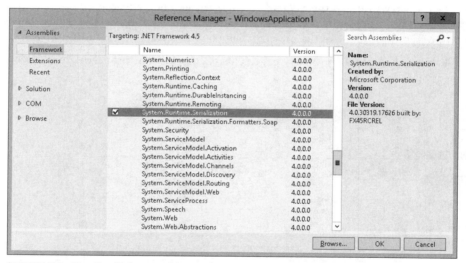

FIGURE 2-2: Use the Reference Manager to add references to libraries.

Scroll through the list of references until you find the one you want and click the Add button to select it. A checkmark to the left of an item shows that the item is selected. When you have made your selections, click OK to add the references to the project. After you have added a reference to the project, your code can refer to the reference's public objects. For example, if the file MyMathLibrary.dll defines a class named MathTools and that class defines a public function Fibonacci, a project with a reference to this DLL could use the following code:

```
Dim math_tools As New MyMathLibrary.MathTools
MessageBox.Show("Fib(5) = " & math_tools.Fibonacci(5))
```

➤ **Add Service Reference** — This command displays the dialog box shown in Figure 2-3. You can use this dialog box to find web services and add references to them so your project can invoke them across the Internet. Figure 2-3 shows a service reference for the TempConvert example service. For more information, go to `http://www.w3schools.com/webservices/tempconvert.asmx`.

➤ **WindowsApplication1 Properties** — This command displays the application's property pages shown in Figure 2-1.

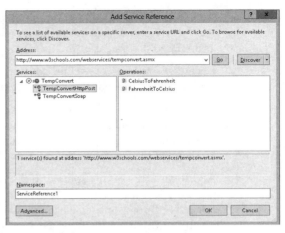

FIGURE 2-3: Use the Add Service Reference dialog box to add references to web services.

Use the tabs on the left of the application's property pages to view and modify different categories of application settings. You can leave many of the property values at their defaults, and many can be set in ways other than by using the property pages. For example, by default, the Assembly Name and Root Namespace values shown in Figure 2-1 are set to the name of the project when you first create it. For most projects, that's fine.

Figure 2-4 shows the Compile property page. This page holds four properties that deserve special mention.

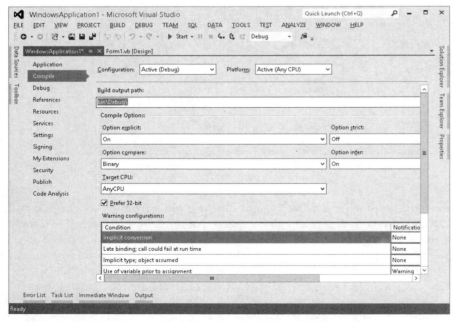

FIGURE 2-4: The Compile tab contains important properties for controlling code generation.

First, *Option Explicit* determines whether Visual Basic requires you to declare all variables before using them. Leaving this option turned off can sometimes lead to subtle bugs. For example, suppose you mistype a variable's name. If Option Explicit is Off, Visual Basic assumes that you are trying to create a new variable with a new name. The two variables are not the same, and that can lead to confusion. If you set Option Explicit to On, the compiler complains that the misspelled variable is not declared and the problem is easy to fix.

The second compiler option is *Option Strict*. When this option is turned off, Visual Studio allows your code to implicitly convert from one data type to another, even if the types are not always compatible. For example, your program might be able to assign the value in a string variable to an integer variable. That will work if the string happens to contain text such as "10" that is a number but fails if the string contains something else such as "ten."

If Option Strict is On, the IDE warns you at compile time that the two data types are incompatible, so you can easily resolve the problem while you are writing the code. You can still use conversion functions such as CInt, Int, and Integer.Parse to convert a string into an Integer, but you must take explicit action to do so. This makes you think about the code and reduces the chances that the conversion is just an accident. This also helps you use the correct data types and avoid unnecessary conversions that may make your program slower.

The third compiler directive, *Option Compare*, can take the values Binary or Text. If you set Option Compare to Binary, Visual Basic compares strings using their binary representations. If you set Option Compare to Text, Visual Basic compares strings using a case-insensitive method that depends on your computer's localization settings. Option Compare Binary is faster, but may not always produce the result you want.

The final compiler directive, *Option Infer*, determines whether you can omit the data type when declaring a variable and let Visual Basic deduce its data type from the context. For example, when it sees the statement Dim x = 1.2, Visual Basic assumes that x must be the Double data type.

The problem with inferred data types is that it is not obvious from the code what data type Visual Basic should use. In the statement Dim x = 1.2, you need to know Visual Basic's inference rules to know whether variable x is a Single, Double, or Decimal.

You can use an Option statement to set the values for each of these options at the top of a code module. For example, the following code turns Option Explicit on and Option Infer off for a module:

```
Option Explicit On
Option Infer Off
```

Instead of using Option statements in a file, you can use the property page shown in Figure 2-4 to set these options for all of the files in the application.

OPTION RECOMMENDATIONS

To avoid confusion and long debugging sessions, I recommend that you use the Compile property page to set Option Explicit on, Option Strict on, and Option Infer off to make Visual Basic as restrictive as possible. Then if you must loosen these restrictions in a particular file, you can add an Option statement at the top of the file. For example, you may need to set Option Infer on for a module that uses LINQ. See Chapter 20, "LINQ," for more information about LINQ.

Build

The Build menu contains commands that let you compile projects within a solution. The following list describes the most useful commands contained in the Build menu:

➤ **Build WindowsApplication1** — This command compiles the currently selected project, in this case the project WindowsApplication1. Visual Studio examines the project's files to see if any have changed since the last time it compiled the project. If any of the files have changed, Visual Studio saves and recompiles them.

➤ **Rebuild WindowsApplication1** — This command recompiles the currently selected project from scratch. It recompiles every file even if it has not been modified since the last time it was compiled.

➤ **Clean WindowsApplication1** — This command removes temporary and intermediate files that were created while building the application, leaving only the source files and the final result .exe and .dll files.

➤ **Publish WindowsApplication1** — This command displays the Publish Wizard, which walks you through the process of making your application available for distribution in a local file, file share, FTP site, or website.

If your solution contains more than one application, the Build menu also contains the solution-related commands Build Solution, Rebuild Solution, and Clean Solution. These are similar to their application counterparts except they apply to every application in the solution.

Debug

The Debug menu contains commands that help you debug a program. These commands help you run the program in the debugger, move through the code, set and clear breakpoints, and generally follow the code's execution to see what it's doing and hopefully what it's doing wrong.

For more information about the Debug menu and debugging Visual Basic code, see Chapter 6, "Debugging."

Data

The Data menu contains commands that deal with data and data sources. Some of the commands in this menu are visible and enabled only if you are designing a form and that form contains the proper data objects.

The following list describes the most useful Data menu commands:

➤ **Show Data Sources** — This command displays the Data Sources window, where you can work with the program's data sources. For example, you can drag and drop tables and fields from this window onto a form to create controls bound to the data source.

➤ **Preview Data** — This command displays a dialog box that lets you load data into a DataSet and view it at design time.

➤ **Add New Data Source** — This command displays the Data Source Configuration Wizard, which walks you through the process of adding a data source to the project.

Format

The Format menu contains commands that arrange controls on a form. The commands are grouped into submenus containing related commands. The following list describes the Format menu's submenus:

➤ **Align** — This submenu contains commands that align the controls you have selected in various ways. It contains the commands Lefts, Centers, Rights, Tops, Middles, Bottoms, and "to Grid." For example, the Lefts command aligns the controls so their left edges line up nicely. The "to Grid" command snaps the controls to the nearest grid position.

➤ **Make Same Size** — This submenu contains commands that make the dimensions of the controls you have selected the same. It contains the commands Width, Height, Both, and Size to Grid. The Size to Grid command adjusts the selected controls' widths so that they are a multiple of the alignment grid size. (This command is disabled unless the Windows Forms Designer's LayoutMode is set to SnapToGrid. To set this, open the Tools menu, select Options, go to the Windows Forms Designer tab, open the General subtab, and set the LayoutMode property.)

➤ **Horizontal Spacing** — This submenu contains commands that change the horizontal spacing between the controls you have selected. It contains the commands Make Equal, Increase, Decrease, and Remove.

➤ **Vertical Spacing** — This submenu contains the same commands as the Horizontal Spacing submenu except it adjusts the controls' vertical spacing.

➤ **Center in Form** — This submenu contains the commands Horizontally and Vertically that center the selected controls on the form either horizontally or vertically.

➤ **Order** — This submenu contains the commands Bring to Front and Send to Back, which move the selected controls to the top or bottom of the stacking order.

➤ **Lock Controls** — This command locks all of the controls on the form so that you cannot accidentally move or resize them by clicking and dragging, although you can still move and resize the controls by changing their Location and Size properties in the Properties window. Invoking this command again unlocks the controls.

Tools

The Tools menu contains miscellaneous tools that do not fit particularly well in the other menus. It also contains a few duplicates of commands in other menus to make them easier to find, and commands that modify the IDE itself.

The following list describes the Tools menu's most useful commands. Note that some of these commands appear only when a particular type of editor is open. Note also that some may not be available in Visual Studio Express Edition.

➤ **Attach to Process** — This command displays a dialog box to let you attach the debugger to a running process. This is useful for debugging programs that you cannot run directly in the Visual Studio IDE such as Windows services, which run automatically when the computer starts.

➤ **Connect to Database** — This command displays the Connection Properties dialog box, where you can define a database connection. The connection is added to the Server Explorer window. You can later use the connection to define data adapters and other objects that use a database connection.

➤ **Connect to Server** — This command displays a dialog box that lets you connect to a database server.

➤ **Code Snippets Manager** — This command displays the Code Snippets Manager, which you can use to add and remove code snippets.

➤ **Choose Toolbox Items** — This command displays a dialog box that lets you select the tools displayed in the Toolbox. For instance, some controls are not included in the Toolbox by default. You can use this command to add them if you will use them frequently.

➤ **Add-in Manager** — This command displays the Add-in Manager, which lists the add-in projects registered on the computer. You can use the Add-in Manager to enable or disable these add-ins.

➤ **Extension Manager** — This command displays an Extension Manager dialog box that lets you find Visual Studio extensions online and install them.

➤ **External Tools** — This command displays a dialog box that lets you add and remove commands from the Tools menu. For example, you could add a command to launch WordPad, MS Paint, WinZip, and other handy utilities from the Tools menu.

> **NOTE** *If you set an external tool's Command to the location of your favorite browser and its Arguments to a web address, you can easily open that address by selecting your tool from the Tools menu. You can even set the Arguments to a mailto address as in* `mailto:RodStephens@vb-helper.com` *to quickly send e-mail from the Tools menu.*

➤ **Import/Export Settings** — This command displays a dialog box that you can use to save, restore, or reset your Visual Studio IDE settings. Use this dialog box to configure your development environment for general development, project management, SQL Server development, Visual Basic, C#, C++, or web development.

➤ **Customize** — This command allows you to customize the Visual Studio IDE.

➤ **Options** — This command allows you to specify options for the Visual Studio IDE. See the following text for more details.

The Tools menu's Options command displays the dialog box shown in Figure 2-5. This dialog box contains a huge number of pages of options that configure the Visual Studio IDE.

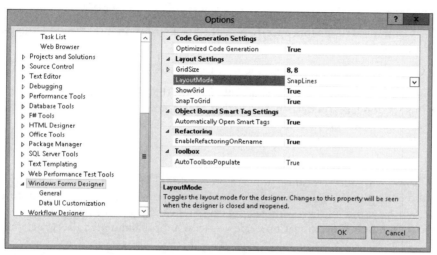

FIGURE 2-5: The Options dialog box lets you specify IDE options.

The following list describes the Options dialog box's most important categories:

➤ **Environment** — Contains general IDE settings such as whether the IDE uses tabs or multiple windows to display documents, the number of items shown in the most recently used file lists, and how often the IDE saves AutoRecover information. The Fonts and Colors subsection lets you determine the colors used by the editors for different types of text. For example, comments are shown in green by default, but you can change this color.

➤ **Projects and Solutions** — Contains the default settings for Option Explicit, Option Strict, and Option Compare.

➤ **Source Control** — Contains entries that deal with the source code control system (for example, Visual Studio Team Foundation Server or Visual SourceSafe). These systems provide file locking and differencing tools that let multiple developers work on the same project without interfering with each other.

➤ **Text Editor** — Contains entries that specify the text editor's features. For example, you can use these pages to determine whether long lines are automatically wrapped, whether line numbers are displayed, and whether the editor provides smart indentation. The Basic ➪ VB Specific subsection lets you specify options such as whether the editor uses outlining, displays procedure separators, or suggests corrections for errors.

➤ **Debugging** — Contains debugging settings such as whether the debugger displays messages as modules are loaded and unloaded, and whether it should allow Edit-and-Continue.

➤ **Database Tools** — Contains database parameters such as default lengths for fields of various types and how long to let long queries run before canceling them.

➤ **HTML Designer** — Contains options for configuring HTML Designer. These options determine such settings as the spacing of the display grid and whether the designer starts in source or design view.

➤ **Office Tools** — Contains settings that specify how the keyboard should work when you use Excel or Word files within Visual Studio.

➤ **Test Tools** — Contains settings that determine how testing tools behave.

➤ **Windows Forms Designer** — Contains settings that control the Windows Forms Designer. For example, this section lets you determine whether the designer uses a snap-to grid or snap lines and how far apart grid points are.

Test

The Test menu, which is not available in Visual Studio Express Edition, contains commands that control the Visual Studio testing tools. These tools let you perform such actions as coverage testing (to see if every line of code is executed), regression testing (to see if changes to the code broke anything), and load testing (to see how the application performs with a lot of simulated users running at the same time).

The following list briefly describes the Test menu's most useful commands:

➤ **New Test** — This command displays a dialog box that lets you create various kinds of tests for the application.

➤ **Load Metadata File** — This command lets you load a test metadata file. These XML files describe test lists, each of which can contain tests. This command lets you load test lists into different projects.

➤ **Create New Test List** — This command lets you make a new test list. Test lists let you group related tests so that you can execute them together. For example, you might have test lists for user interface testing, print tests, database tests, and so forth.

➤ **Run** — This command starts executing the currently active test project without the debugger.

➤ **Debug** — This command starts executing the currently active test project with the debugger.

➤ **Windows** — This command displays test-related windows including Test View, Test List Editor, Test Results, Code Coverage Results, and Test Runs.

Window

The Window menu contains commands that control Visual Studio's windows. Which commands are enabled depends on the type of window that has the focus. For example, if focus is on a code editor, the Split command is enabled and the Float, Dock, and Dock as Tabbed Document commands are disabled, but when the Solution Explorer window has the focus, the opposite is true.

The following list briefly describes the most useful of these commands:

➤ **Split** — This command splits a code window into two panes that can display different parts of the code at the same time. This command changes to Remove Split when you use it.

➤ **Float, Dock, Dock as Tabbed Document** — Secondary windows such as the Toolbox, Solution Explorer, and Properties windows can be displayed as dockable, floating, or tabbed documents. A dockable window can be attached to the edges of the IDE or docked with other secondary windows. A floating window stays in its own independent window even if you drag it to a position where it would normally dock. A tabbed document window is displayed in the main editing area in the center of the IDE with the forms, classes, and other project files.

➤ **Auto Hide** — This command puts a secondary window in Auto Hide mode. The window disappears, and its title is displayed at the IDE's nearest edge. When you click the title or hover over it, the window reappears so that you can use it. If you click another window, this window hides itself again automatically.

➤ **Hide** — This command removes the window.

➤ **Auto Hide All** — This command makes all secondary windows enter Auto Hide mode.

➤ **New Horizontal Tab Group** — This command splits the main document window horizontally so that you can view two different documents at the same time.

➤ **New Vertical Tab Group** — This command splits the main document window vertically so that you can view two different documents at the same time.

➤ **Close All Documents** — This command closes all documents.

➤ **Reset Window Layout** — This command resets the window layout to a default configuration.

➤ **Form1.vb** — The bottom part of the Window menu lists open documents such as form, code, and bitmap editors. The menu displays a checkmark next to the currently active document. You can select one of these entries to view the corresponding document.

➤ **Windows** — If you have too many open documents to display in the Window menu, select this command to see a list of the windows in a dialog box. This dialog box lets you switch to another document, close one or more documents, or save documents. By pressing Ctrl+Click or Shift+Click you can select more than one document and quickly close them.

Help

The Help menu displays the usual assortment of help commands. You should be familiar with most of these from previous experience. The following list summarizes some of the more interesting non-standard commands:

➤ **Set Help Preference** — This command lets you indicate whether you prefer to use local or online help.

➤ **MSDN Forums** — This command opens an MSDN community forums web page where you can post questions and search for answers.

➤ **Report a Bug** — This command opens Microsoft Connect where you can report bugs, make suggestions, and look for hot fixes for known problems.

➤ **Samples** — This command opens a Microsoft web page containing links to Visual Studio documentation and samples.

➤ **Customer Feedback Options** — This command displays a dialog box that lets you indicate whether you want to participate in Microsoft's anonymous Customer Experience Improvement Program. If you join, Microsoft collects anonymous information about your system configuration and how you use its software.

➤ **Check for Updates** — This command checks online for Visual Studio updates.

➤ **Technical Support** — This command opens a help page describing various support options. The page includes phone numbers and links to more information.

TOOLBARS

The Visual Studio toolbars are easy to rearrange. Simply grab the four gray dots on a toolbar's left or upper edge and drag the toolbar to its new position. Use the Tools menu's Customize command to show or hide toolbars. Select a toolbar and click the Modify Selection drop-down to make a toolbar dock to the IDE's top, left, right, or bottom edges.

You can use the IDE's menu commands to determine which toolbars are visible, to determine what they contain, and to make custom toolbars of your own.

Many menu commands are also available in standard toolbars. For example, the Debug toolbar contains many of the same commands that are in the Debug menu. If you use a set of menu commands frequently, you may want to display the corresponding toolbar to make using the commands easier. Alternatively, you can make your own custom toolbar and fill it with your favorite commands.

SECONDARY WINDOWS

You can rearrange secondary windows such as the Toolbox and Solution Explorer even more easily than you can rearrange toolbars. Click and drag the window's title bar to move it. As the window moves, the IDE displays drop icons and blue drop areas to help you dock the window, as shown in Figure 2-6. This figure probably looks somewhat confusing, but it's fairly easy to use.

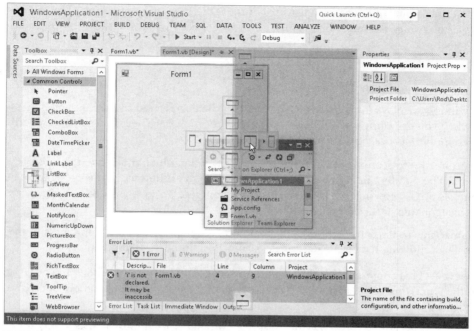

FIGURE 2-6: Use the IDE's docking icons to help you dock windows.

When you drag the window over another window, the IDE displays docking icons for the other window. In Figure 2-6, these are the icons in the center that look like little windows. In Figure 2-6 the cursor is hovering over one of these icons.

The four icons on the sides dock the window to the corresponding edge of the other window. The center icon places the dropped window in a tab within the other window.

When you drag the mouse over one of the docking icons, the IDE displays a pale blue rectangle to give you an idea of where the window will land if you drop it. In Figure 2-6, the mouse is over the main document window's right docking icon, so the blue rectangle shows the dropped window taking up the right half of the main document window.

If you drop a window somewhere other than on a docking icon, the window becomes free-floating.

When you drop a window on the main document area, it becomes a tabbed document within that area, and you cannot later pull it out. To free the window, select it and use the Window menu's Dock or Float command.

> **NOTE** *Sometimes the IDE is so cluttered with windows that it's hard to figure out exactly where the window will be dropped. It's usually fairly easy to just move the mouse around a bit and watch the pale blue rectangle to see what's happening.*

This section described some of the general features of the IDE's secondary windows. The following sections describe two of the most important of those secondary windows: the Toolbox and the Properties window.

Toolbox

The *Toolbox* window displays tools that you can use with the currently active document. The tools are available when you are editing a Windows Form, WPF Form, UserControl, web page, or other item that can contain objects such as controls and components.

The tools are grouped into sections called *tabs*, although they don't look much like the tabs on most documents. The Toolbox in Figure 2-6 displays tools for the Windows Forms Designer. The Common Controls tab is showing its tools as icons. The Containers and Menus & Toolbars tabs are listing their tools by name. Other tabs are hidden.

You can customize the Toolbox by right-clicking a tab and selecting one of the commands in the context menu. The following list briefly describes the most useful of these commands:

➤ **List View** — This command toggles the current tab to display tools as either a list of names (as in the Containers tab in Figure 2-6) or a series of icons (as in the Common Controls tab in Figure 2-6).

➤ **Show All** — This command shows or hides less commonly used tabs such as Data, WPF Interoperability, Visual Basic Power Packs, and many others.

➤ **Choose Items** — This command displays a dialog box where you can select the items that should appear in a tab.

➤ **Sort Items Alphabetically** — This command sorts the items within a Toolbox tab alphabetically.

➤ **Reset Toolbox** — This command restores the Toolbox to a default configuration. This removes any items you may have added by using the Choose Items command.

➤ **Add Tab** — This command creates a new tab where you can place your favorite tools. You can drag tools from one tab to another. Hold down the Ctrl key while dragging to add a copy of the tool to the new tab without removing it from the old tab.

➤ **Delete Tab** — This command deletes a tab.

➤ **Rename Tab** — This command lets you rename a tab.

➤ **Move Up, Move Down** — This command moves the clicked tab up or down in the Toolbox. You can also click and drag the tabs to new positions.

If you right-click a tool in the Toolbox, the context menu contains most of these commands plus Cut, Copy, Paste, Delete, and Rename Item.

Properties Window

When you are designing a form, the *Properties window* allows you to view and modify the properties of the form and of the controls that it contains. Figure 2-7 shows the Properties window displaying properties for a Button control named btnCalculate. You can see in the figure that the control's Text property is "Calculate" so that's what the button displays to the user.

Figure 2-7 shows some important features of the Properties window that deserve special mention. At the top of the window is a drop-down list that holds the names of all of the controls on the form. To select a control, you can either click it on the Windows Forms Designer or select it from this list.

The buttons in the row below the drop-down determine what items are displayed in the window and how they are arranged. If you click the left-most button, the window lists properties grouped by category. For example, the Appearance category contains properties that affect the control's appearance such as BackColor, Font, and Image. If you click the second icon that holds the letters A and Z, the window lists the control's properties alphabetically.

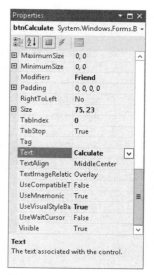

FIGURE 2-7: The Properties window lets you view and modify control properties.

> **NOTE** *Arranging properties alphabetically makes finding properties easier for many developers.*

The third icon makes the window display the control's properties, and the fourth icon (which displays a lightning bolt) makes the window display the control's events instead. (Yes, it's a little odd that the Properties window displays either properties or events, but there is no Events window.)

For more information on using the Properties window to edit properties and create event handlers in the Windows Forms Designer, see Chapter 3, "Windows Forms Designer."

SUMMARY

The Visual Studio integrated development environment provides a huge number of tools for manipulating projects. Menus and toolbars contain hundreds if not thousands of commands for creating, loading, saving, and editing different kinds of projects and files.

This chapter described the most useful and important commands available in the IDE's menus and toolbars. The kinds of menus, toolbars, and commands that are available depend on the type of window that currently has focus, in addition to the project's current state. For example, the Format menu contains commands that arrange controls on a form so most of its commands are enabled only when you are using a Windows Forms Designer and you have controls selected.

This chapter also described important IDE windows such as the Error List, Solution Explorer, and Properties window. One of the most important of those windows is the Toolbox, which is used mostly to add controls and components to forms in the Windows Form Designer. Chapter 3, "Windows Forms Designer," explains how to use the Windows Forms Designer to build the forms that make up most Windows applications.

3

Windows Forms Designer

WROX.COM CODE DOWNLOADS FOR THIS CHAPTER

There are no code downloads for this chapter.

INTRODUCING WINDOWS FORMS DESIGNER

The *Windows Forms Designer* allows you to design forms for typical applications that run on the Windows desktop. It lets you add, size, and move controls on a form. Together with the Properties window, it also lets you change a control's properties to determine its appearance and behavior.

This chapter provides an introduction to the Windows Forms Designer. It explains how to add controls to a form, move and size controls, set control properties, and add code to respond to control events. It also describes tips and tricks that make working with controls easier.

SETTING DESIGNER OPTIONS

When you first install Visual Studio, the Windows Forms Designer is configured to be quite usable. You can open a form immediately and use the Toolbox to place controls on it. You can use the mouse to move and resize controls. You can use the Format menu to arrange and size controls. Overall the **Windows Forms Designer provides a first-class** intuitive *WYSIWYG* ("what you see is what you **get") experience.**

Behind the scenes, however, **there are a few configuration options that control the designer's** behavior and that you should **know about to get the most out of the designer.**

To view the designer's options, **open the Tools menu, select Options, open the Windows Forms** Designer branch, and select **the General page to display the dialog box shown in Figure 3-1.**

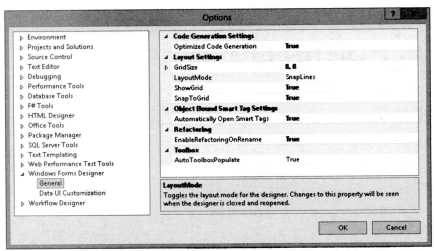

FIGURE 3-1: This dialog box lets you control the **Windows Forms Designer's behavior.**

The following list describes **the most important of these settings:**

➤ **Optimized Code Generation — Determines whether Visual Studio generates optimized** code. This setting is **here instead of some more code-oriented part of the Options dialog box** because some controls **may be incompatible with code optimization.**

➤ **Grid Size — Determines the horizontal and vertical dimensions of the sizing grid for use** when LayoutMode is **SnapToGrid.**

➤ **LayoutMode — Determines whether Visual Studio uses** *snap-to-grid* or *snap lines*. **If this** is SnapToGrid, objects **automatically snap to the nearest grid point when you drag or resize** them. When this is **SnapLines, resized controls automatically snap to lines that align** with the edges or **centers of other controls, or with the form's margins. Both of these** options make it **easy to build controls that are consistently sized and that align along their** edges. The two options have **a very different feel, however, so you might want to experiment** with both to see **which one you like best.**

➤ **Automatically Open Smart Tags — Determines whether Visual Studio displays smart tags** by default.

➤ **EnableRefactoringOnRename** — Determines whether Visual Studio performs refactoring when you rename a control. (*Refactoring* is the process of restructuring the code, hopefully to make it better.) If this setting is True and you change a control's name, Visual Studio updates any code that uses that control so it uses the new name. If this setting is False and you rename a control, any code that refers to the control still uses its old name, so the code will no longer work.

➤ **AutoToolboxPopulate** — Determines whether Visual Studio adds components built by the solution to the Toolbox window.

USEFUL OPTIONS

Which LayoutMode you should use is a matter of preference. I know many developers who use each style. The EnableRefactoringOnRename option can save you a lot of trouble when you rename controls, so it's almost always worth leaving the setting as True.

ADDING CONTROLS

The Windows Forms Designer allows you to add controls to a form in several ways.

First, if you double-click a control on the Toolbox, Visual Studio places an instance of the control on the form in a default location and at a default size. You can then use the mouse to move and resize the control.

NOTE *When you use this method, the new control is placed inside the currently selected container on the form. If the currently selected control is a GroupBox, the new control is placed inside the GroupBox. If the currently selected control is a TextBox that is inside a Panel, the new control is placed inside the Panel.*

Second, if you click a control in the Toolbox, the mouse cursor changes while the mouse is over the form. The new cursor looks like a plus sign with a small image of the control's Toolbox icon next to it. If you click the form, Visual Studio adds a control at that location with a default size. Instead of just clicking, you can click and drag to specify the new control's location and size. After you place the new control, the mouse returns to a pointer cursor so you can click existing controls to select them.

> **NOTE** *If you hold down the Control key when you click or drag on the form, the designer adds the new control to the form and keeps the control's Toolbox tool selected so you can add another instance of the control. For example, suppose you need to create a series of TextBoxes to hold a user's name, street, city, state, and ZIP code. Select the TextBox tool in the Toolbox. Then you can quickly use Ctrl+Click five times to create the TextBoxes. Press the Esc key to stop adding TextBoxes and then drag them into their correct positions.*

SELECTING CONTROLS

When you first create a control, the designer selects it. The designer indicates that the control is selected by surrounding it with white boxes. In Figure 3-2, the Button2 control is selected.

To select a control on the designer later, when you haven't just added it, simply click it.

You can click and drag to select a group of controls. As you drag the mouse, the designer displays a rectangle so you can tell which controls will be selected. When you release the mouse button, all of the controls that overlap the rectangle at least partly are selected.

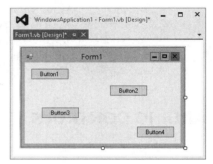

FIGURE 3-2: The designer surrounds a selected control with white boxes.

When you select a group of controls, the designer surrounds most of them with black boxes. It surrounds a special "master" control with white boxes. In Figure 3-3, four buttons are selected. Button1 is the "master" control so it is surrounded by white boxes.

The designer uses the "master" control to adjust the others if you use the Format menu's commands. For example, if you use the Format ⇨ Make Same Size ⇨ Height command, the designer gives the "black box" controls the same height as the "master" control. Similarly the Format ⇨ Align ⇨ Tops command moves the "black box" controls so their tops are aligned with the top of the "master" control.

To change the "master" control, simply click the control that you want to use as the "master."

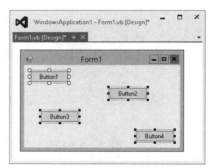

FIGURE 3-3: The selection's "master" control is surrounded by white boxes.

After you have selected some controls, you can Shift+Click or Ctrl+Click to add and remove single controls from the selection. You can Shift+Click-and-drag or Ctrl+Click-and-drag to add and remove groups of controls from the selection.

TRICKY CLICKS

Under some circumstances, the designer will not remove its selection even if you click the form off of the selected controls. To deselect all of the controls, either click a control that is not selected or press the Esc key.

COPYING CONTROLS

A particularly useful technique for building a series of similar controls is to build one and then use copy and paste to make others.

For example, to build the name, street, city, state, and ZIP code TextBoxes described in the previous section, you could start by adding the name TextBox to the form. Next, set all of the properties that you want the control copies to share. For example, you may want to adjust the TextBox's width, set its MaxLength property to 20, and set its Anchor property to Top, Left, Right so it resizes horizontally when its container resizes. Now select the control on the designer and press Ctrl+C to copy it. Then press Ctrl+V repeatedly to make copies for the other controls. Drag the controls into position and you have quickly built all of the controls with their shared properties already set.

CONTAINER CONFUSION

When you paste a copied control, the new control is placed inside whatever container is currently selected on the form. This can be confusing if you quickly copy and paste a container. For example, suppose you want to make three GroupBoxes. You build one and size it the way you want it. Then you press Ctrl+C, Ctrl+V, Ctrl+V. The first GroupBox is copied and the first copy is pasted inside the original GroupBox. Then the second copy is placed inside the first copy. The result is somewhat confusing and you'll probably need to drag the copies out onto the form before you can place them where you want.

You can also use copy and paste to copy a group of controls. For example, suppose you want to make name, street, city, state, and ZIP code TextBoxes but you also want Label controls to the left of the TextBoxes. First create the name Label and TextBox, set their properties, and position them so their baselines are lined up and the Label is to the left of the TextBox as desired. Click and drag to select both controls and then press Ctrl+C to copy them both. Now when you press Ctrl+V, the designer makes a copy of the Label and the TextBox. The copies have aligned baselines and the Label is to the left of the TextBox as in the originals. The new controls are even both selected so you can use the mouse to grab them both and drag them into position.

MOVING AND SIZING CONTROLS

Moving a control in the Windows Forms Designer is easy. Simply click the control and drag it to its new position.

To move a group of controls, select the controls that you want. Then click one of the controls and drag to move the whole group.

Note that you can drag controls in and out of container controls such as the FlowLayoutPanel, GroupBox, and Panel. When you drag a control into a new container, the mouse cursor acquires a little fuzzy rectangle on the lower right. If you are dragging a control and you see this appear, you know that dropping the control at the current position will move it into a new container. The new container indicator appears if you are dragging a control from the form into a container, from a container onto the form, or from one container to another.

Resizing a control is almost as easy as moving one. Click a control to select it. Then click and drag one of the white boxes surrounding the control to change its size.

To resize a group of controls, select the group. Then click and drag one of the boxes surrounding one of the controls. When you drag the mouse, the control beside the box you picked is resized as if it were the only control selected. The other selected controls resize in the same manner. For example, if you widen the clicked control by eight pixels, all of the other controls widen by eight pixels, too.

ARRANGING CONTROLS

The Format menu contains several submenus that hold tools that make arranging controls easier. For example, the Format menu's Align submenu contains commands that let you align controls vertically and horizontally along their edges or centers.

For a description of this menu's commands, see the section "Format" in Chapter 2, "Menus, Toolbars, and Windows." (Or just experiment with these commands — they aren't too complicated.)

For more information about how the selection's "white box master" control determines how other controls are adjusted, see the section "Selecting Controls" earlier in this chapter.

SETTING PROPERTIES

When you select a control, the Properties window allows you to view and edit the control's properties. For most properties, you can simply click the property and type a new value for the control. Some properties are more complex than others and provide drop-down lists or special dialog boxes to set the property's value. Most of the editors provided for setting property values are fairly self-explanatory, so they are not described in detail here.

> **NOTE** *You can press Ctrl+Z and Ctrl+Y to undo and redo changes in the Windows Form Designer, respectively, so you should feel free to experiment. You can change property values and add or remove controls and restore the form if you don't like the changes.*

In addition to using the Properties window to set a single control's properties one at a time, you can quickly set property values for groups of controls in a couple of ways. The following sections describe some of the most useful of these techniques.

Setting Group Properties

If you select a group of controls, you can sometimes use the Properties window to give all of the controls the same property value all at once. For example, suppose you select a group of TextBoxes. Then you can use the Properties window to simultaneously give them the same values for their Anchor, Text, MultiLine, Font, and other properties.

Sometimes, this even works when you select different kinds of controls at the same time. For example, if you select some TextBoxes and some Labels, you can set all of the controls' Text properties at the same time. You cannot set the TextBoxes' MultiLine properties, however, because the Labels do not have a MultiLine property.

> **BLANKING TEXT**
>
> One handy use for this technique is to set the Text property to a blank string for a group of TextBox controls. Unfortunately, if the selected TextBoxes have different Text values, the Properties window displays a blank value for the Text property. If you then try to make the property blank, the Properties window doesn't think you've changed the value, so it doesn't blank the controls' Text properties.
>
> To work around this restriction, first set the Text property to any non-blank value ("x" will do) to give all of the controls the same value. Then delete the Text value to blank all of the controls.

Using Smart Tags

Many controls display a *smart tag* when you select them on the designer. The smart tag looks like a little box containing a right-pointing triangle. When you click the smart tag, a small dialog box appears to let you perform common tasks for the control quickly and easily.

Figure 3-4 shows a PictureBox with the smart tag expanded. Because the smart tag's dialog box is visible, the smart tag indicator shows a left-pointing triangle. If you click this, the dialog box disappears.

The PictureBox control's smart tag dialog box lets you choose an image for the control, set the control's SizeMode, or dock the control in its container. These actions set the control's Image, SizeMode, and Dock properties.

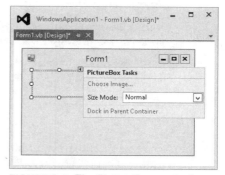

FIGURE 3-4: The PictureBox control's smart tag lets you set common control properties.

Many controls, particularly the more complicated kinds, provide smart tags to let you perform common actions without using the Properties window.

ADDING CODE TO CONTROLS

After you have added controls to a form and set their properties, the next step is to add code to the form that responds to control events and that manipulates the controls.

You use the code editor to write code that responds to control events. The code editor is described in Chapter 5, "Visual Basic Code Editor," but you can open the code editor from the Windows Forms Designer.

An *event handler* is a code routine that catches an event raised by a control and takes some action. Almost all program action is started from an event handler. Even actions started automatically by a timer or when a form first appears begin when an event handler catches a timer's events.

If you double-click a control on the Windows Forms Designer, Visual Studio creates an empty event handler to handle the control's default event and it opens the event handler in the code editor. For example, the following code shows the event handler the IDE built for a Button control named Button1. The default event for a Button is Click, so this code is a Click event handler.

```
Private Sub Button1_Click(sender As Object, e As EventArgs) Handles Button1.Click

End Sub
```

RELAX, DON'T WORRY

Relaxed delegates let you remove the parameters from the event handler's declaration if you don't need them. For example, if you use separate event handlers for each button, you probably don't need the parameters to figure out what's happening. If the user clicks the button named btnExit, the btnExit_Click event handler executes and the program can exit.

In this case, you can remove the parameters to simplify the code. The following code shows the simplified btnExit_Click event handler (without any code in it):

```
Private Sub btnExit_Click() Handles btnExit.Click

End Sub
```

Another way to build an event handler and open the code editor is to select the control on the Windows Forms Designer. Then click the Events icon (the lightning bolt) near the top of the Properties window to make the window show a list of events for the control as shown in

Figure 3-5. Double-click an event in the window to create an event handler for it and to open it in the code editor.

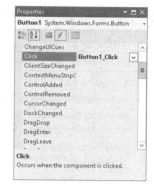

If you select more than one control in the Windows Forms Designer and then double-click an event, Visual Studio makes an event handler that catches the event for all of the selected controls. To create the following event handler, I selected three Buttons and double-clicked the Click event:

```
Private Sub Button2_Click(sender As Object, e As EventArgs) _
    Handles Button3.Click, Button2.Click, Button1.Click

End Sub
```

Note that I added the line continuation in the first line of the preceding code so it would fit in the book. Visual Studio makes it all one long line.

FIGURE 3-5: Click the Events icon to make the Properties window display a control's events.

The event handler's name is Button2_Click instead of Button1_Click or some other name because Button2 was the "white box master" control for the selected controls. See the section "Selecting Controls" earlier in this chapter for more information about a selection's "master" control.

TOO MANY HANDLERS

If you select a group of controls and then double-click them, Visual Studio makes a separate event handler for each control. If you want the same event handler to catch events from all of the controls, click the event handler button on the Properties window and then double-click the event name there instead.

SUMMARY

The Windows Forms Designer allows you to build forms for use in Windows applications. It lets you add controls to a form, and resize and move the controls. Together with the Properties window, it lets you view and modify control properties, and create event handlers to interact with the controls.

This chapter introduced the Windows Forms Designer and explained how you can take advantage of its features. Future chapters provide much more of the detail necessary for building forms. Chapter 7, "Selecting Windows Forms Controls," and Chapter 8, "Using Windows Forms Controls," provide more information about the kinds of controls you can use with the Windows Forms Designer. Chapter 9, "Windows Forms," says a lot more about how Windows Forms work and what you can do with them.

There are other ways to build applications that have user interfaces that run on the computer, however. Windows Presentation Foundation (WPF) lets you build applications that have a very different look and feel. Certain kinds of WPF applications can also run in the Windows 8 Metro interface, something that Windows Forms applications cannot do.

Chapter 4, "WPF Designer," describes the designer that you use to build Windows Presentation Foundation applications. In some ways it is similar to the Windows Forms Designer. For example, you use the Toolbox to place controls on the form, and you use the Properties window to view and edit control properties much as you do when using the Windows Forms Designer. In other ways the two designers are quite different, however, so you'll need the information in Chapter 4 if you want to build WPF applications.

WPF Designer

WROX.COM CODE DOWNLOADS FOR THIS CHAPTER

There are no code downloads for this chapter.

INTRODUCING WPF DESIGNER

Windows Forms controls allow you to build powerful desktop applications. *WPF* (*Windows Presentation Foundation*) is a new set of controls that you can also use to build desktop applications. While WPF and Windows Forms controls provide many similar features, the WPF controls are more closely tied to high performance graphics libraries so they can provide many sophisticated graphical features that are missing from Windows Forms controls. For example, WPF controls can draw themselves at any scale without losing resolution, can display gradient backgrounds, and can contain other controls in a more flexible and consistent way than Windows Forms controls can. For a specific example of this last feature, a Windows Forms Button control can hold only text. A WPF Button control can hold other controls such as a Grid that contains several Images and TextBlocks to make a much richer experience.

In addition to giving WPF new features, Microsoft is positioning it, or more precisely the Silverlight subset of WPF, for use in building applications on its future platforms. You can build applications in Silverlight for the Windows 8 operating system, the Windows Phone operating system, or web applications. Windows Forms programs still have an important role on desktop systems but Microsoft seems determined to make WPF and Silverlight be the development tools of the future. You can still build Windows Forms applications and run them on the Windows 8 desktop, but you need to use WPF to build programs that can run within the Windows 8 Metro interface.

The *WPF* (*Windows Presentation Foundation*) Designer allows you to build WPF windows (including those used by Metro-style applications) interactively much as the Windows Forms Designer lets you build Windows Forms. It provides a WYSIWYG (what you see is what you get) surface where you can add controls to a window. If you select one or more controls on the designer's surface, the Properties window displays the objects' properties and lets you edit many of them.

In addition to the WYSIWYG design surface, the designer provides a XAML (Extensible Application Markup Language) code editor. Here you can view and edit the XAML code that defines the user interface. This lets you edit properties and arrange controls in ways that are impossible using the WYSIWYG designer.

> **NOTE** *XAML is pronounced "zammel."*

This chapter provides an introduction to the WPF Designer. It explains how to add controls to a window, move and size controls, set control properties, and add code to respond to control events.

FOR MORE INFORMATION

Windows Presentation Foundation is quite large and complex, requiring you to learn about a whole new set of controls, objects, properties, animations, and other items. It even uses a whole new system for properties and events that isn't used by Windows Forms.

The chapters in this book cover WPF in enough detail to get you started and let you build an effective application, but there's much more to WPF. For more details, see my book *WPF Programmer's Reference: Windows Presentation Foundation with C# 2010 and .NET 4.0* (Stephens, Wrox, 2009). Some of the code examples use C# but most of the code uses XAML code, which is described by the book, so they're applicable to Visual Basic as well. You can learn more and download the book's example code in C# and Visual Basic versions on the book's web page at `http://www .vb-helper.com/wpf.htm`.

EDITOR WEAKNESSES

Visual Studio's Windows Forms Designer has been around for a long time, and over the years it has become extremely powerful. In contrast, the WPF Designer is relatively new and lacks many of the features included in its more mature cousin.

Although the WPF Designer is a WYSIWYG tool, it has a lot of weak spots. A small sampling of these weaknesses includes:

➤ The Properties window does not provide editors for many types of objects, and many of the editors it does provide are incomplete. For example, the Properties window provides no tools for editing a control's Clip property, which determines the geometry used to clip the control's contents.

➤ The Properties window provides tooltips describing properties but only when the mouse is hovering over the property's name, not while you are editing the property. Some of the tips are also fairly incomplete, saying things like Integer Canvas.ZIndex.

➤ The designer surface has no snap-to-grid mode.

➤ The XAML code editor's IntelliSense is incomplete and doesn't provide help in many places where it would be useful (although it's much better than nothing).

The WYSIWYG designer has enough weaknesses that it is often easier to build parts of a user interface by using the XAML code editor. For example, the designer provides no methods for making resources, styles, and templates, three items that are essential for building a maintainable interface. Fortunately, these things are not too difficult to build in the XAML code editor.

In all fairness, the WPF Designer has improved greatly since its first version and includes several enhancements added since the previous version, including better enumerated property support and primitive brush editors. It also crashes much less often and gets confused about how to draw its controls much less frequently. Hopefully it will catch up with the Windows Forms Designer someday.

All of these issues aside, the WPF Designer is a powerful tool. It lets you quickly build the basic structures of a WPF window and layout controls. You may need to rearrange controls somewhat and build additional elements such as resources and styles in the XAML editor, but the WYSIWYG surface can get you started.

Though the XAML editor also has shortcomings, it does provide the tools you need to fine-tune the user interface initially built by the designer surface. Together the two pieces of the WPF Designer give you everything you need to build aesthetically pleasing and compelling WPF user interfaces.

BUILDING WITH BLEND

Microsoft's Expression Blend product provides some of the features that are missing from the WPF Designer. For example, it provides better tools for creating styles and templates, better brush editors, and the ability to record property animations.

It still has its drawbacks (one being the fact that there is no free version) but it complements Visual Studio's WPF Designer nicely. Learn more about Expression Blend or download a trial copy at `http://www.microsoft.com/expression/products/blend_overview.aspx`.

RECOGNIZING DESIGNER WINDOWS

Figure 4-1 shows the Visual Studio IDE displaying the WPF Designer. You can rearrange the IDE's windows, but normally the Toolbox is on the left and the Properties window is on the right, below

Solution Explorer. The WPF Designer is shown in the middle with its WYSIWYG design surface on top and its XAML code editor on the bottom.

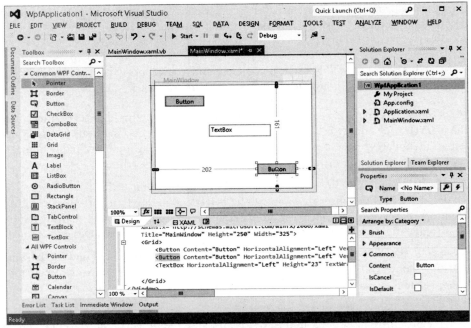

FIGURE 4-1: The WPF Designer includes a **WYSIWYG design surface** and a **XAML code editor**.

You can click the up and down arrow label between the WYSIWYG designer and the XAML editor to make the two switch panes. This is useful if you make one pane large and the other small. Then you can quickly switch back and forth, moving the one you want into the bigger pane as you move from using the WYSIWYG designer to the XAML editor.

If there is an error in the XAML code, the designer may display a message at its top indicating that errors exist. You can click that label to open the Error list to see the types of errors. You can then fix them in the XAML editor and refresh the designer.

ADDING CONTROLS

The WPF Designer allows you to add controls to a form in several ways that are similar to those provided by the Windows Forms Designer. If you are familiar with that topic you might want to skip this section.

First, if you double-click a control on the Toolbox, Visual Studio places an instance of the control on the window in a default location and at a default size. You can then use the mouse to move and resize the control.

CONTAINER CONFUSION

When you use this method, the new control is placed inside the currently selected container on the window. If the currently selected control is a StackPanel, the new control is placed inside the StackPanel. If the currently selected control is a TextBox that is inside a Grid, the new control is placed inside the Grid.

Second, if you click a control in the Toolbox, the mouse cursor changes to a crosshair while the mouse is over the window. If you click the window, Visual Studio adds a control at that location with a default size. Instead of just clicking, you can click and drag to specify the new control's location and size.

If you hold down the Ctrl key when you select a tool from the Toolbox, that tool remains selected even after you create a control on the window so you can add another instance of the control. For example, suppose you need to create a series of TextBoxes to hold a user's name, street, city, state, and ZIP code. Hold the Ctrl key and click the TextBox tool in the Toolbox. Then you can quickly click five times to create the TextBoxes. Click another tool or the arrow tool in the Toolbox to stop adding TextBoxes.

SELECTING CONTROLS

When you first create a control, the designer selects it. The designer indicates that the control is selected by surrounding it with light gray boxes. In Figure 4-1, the button on the lower right is selected.

To select a control on the designer later, simply click it. You can also click and drag to select a group of controls. As you drag the mouse, the designer displays a rectangle so you can tell which controls will be selected. When you release the mouse button, all of the controls that overlap the rectangle at least partly are selected.

When you select a group of controls, the designer surrounds them with light gray boxes and a light blue border.

After you have selected some controls, you can Shift+Click to add new controls to the selection or Ctrl+Click to toggle a control's membership in the selection. You can also Shift+Click-and-drag or Ctrl+Click-and-drag to add or toggle groups of controls from the selection.

NOTE *You can quickly deselect all controls by pressing the Esc key.*

MOVING AND SIZING CONTROLS

Moving controls in the WPF Designer is easy. Simply click and drag the control to its new position.

To move a group of controls, select the controls that you want to move. Then click one of the controls and drag to move the whole group.

Note that you can drag controls in and out of container controls such as the Grid or StackPanel. When you drag a control over a new container, the designer draws a box around the container and displays a tooltip that says "Press Alt to place inside *container*" where *container* is the name of the container. If the container doesn't have a name, the tooltip shows the container's control type in braces as in [Grid]. As the tooltip indicates, if you press Alt and then drop the control, it goes into the new container. If you drop the control without pressing Alt, the control lands above or below the container.

As you drag a control, the designer displays snap lines to show how the control lines up with other controls. It displays lines when the control's edges align with another control's edges. For some controls, it displays lines when the control's text baseline aligns with the text baselines of other controls.

Figure 4-2 shows the designer dragging the lower button. Four red dashed snap lines show that this control's edges line up with the left and right edges of the upper button, the left edge of the Rectangle control at the bottom, and the upper edge of the Ellipse control to the right.

Resizing a control is almost as easy as moving one. Click a control to select it. Then click and drag one of the light gray boxes surrounding the control to change its size.

If you hover the mouse near but not over a gray box at one of the control's corners, the cursor changes to a curved arrow. You can then click and drag to rotate the control.

If you hover the mouse near but not over a gray box on one of the control's edges, the cursor changes to two arrow heads separated by a slash. Then you can click and drag to skew the control. For example, if you drag the top of a TextBlock to the right, the result looks italicized.

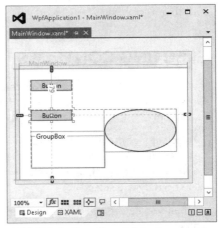

FIGURE 4-2: Snap lines show how moving controls align with other controls.

WPF controls provide a fairly complex set of properties to determine how they are anchored to their containers. Fortunately, the WPF Designer provides aids to make understanding control anchoring easier.

When you select a control, the designer displays symbols next to the container's edges showing how the control is anchored. A thin solid line ending in two closed chain links on the container's edge means the control's edge remains the same distance from the container's edge even when the container resizes. In Figure 4-2, the selected button's bottom and right edges are connected to its container's bottom and right edges. When the window resizes, the button moves to stay the same distance from those edges.

If you look closely at Figure 4-2, you can also see small numbers on the lines connecting the button's bottom and right edges to those of its container. In this example the numbers indicate that the button will remain 164 pixels from the container's right edge and 109 pixels from the container's bottom edge.

Broken chain links near the container's edge mean that edge is free to float if the container resizes. In Figure 4-2, the button's left and top edges are not anchored to the container's edges so the button will move and keep its original size if the container resizes.

If a control's opposite sides are both attached to the container, the control will grow and shrink as the container resizes so it can keep both edges the same distance from those of the container.

> **ATTACHMENT ANXIETY**
>
> The designer will not allow you to remove the attachment from all of a control's edges (so they all display broken chain links). If you remove one anchor, the designer changes the opposite side's anchor symbol to joined links if it isn't that way already.

You can easily change a control's edge anchors by simply clicking the symbol. If you click joined links, the designer breaks the links and vice versa.

SETTING PROPERTIES

When you select a control, the Properties window allows you to view and edit the control's properties. For Boolean properties, the Properties window displays a box that you can check or uncheck to indicate whether the property's value should be True or False.

For many other properties, you can simply click the property and type a new value for the control in a text box.

Still other properties provide custom editors to make it easier to set their values. For example, the Fill property is a brush that determines how the background of a control is filled. The Properties window provides a brush editor that lets you define the brush fairly easily.

SETTING GROUP PROPERTIES

If you select a group of controls, you can sometimes use the Properties window to give all of the controls the same property value all at once. For example, suppose you select a group of TextBoxes. Then you can use the Properties window to give them the same values for their Width, Height, Margin, MaxLength, and many other properties.

Sometimes, this even works if you select different kinds of controls at the same time. For example, if you select some TextBoxes and some Labels, you can set all of the controls' Width, Height, and

Margin properties at the same time. You cannot set the controls' MaxLength properties because the Labels do not have a MaxLength property.

ADDING CODE TO CONTROLS

After you have added the appropriate controls to a form and set their properties, the next step is to add code to the form that responds to control events and manipulates the controls.

You can add some kinds of code declaratively in the XAML editor. For example, you can make a trigger respond to a change in a control's property or to a control's event.

You can also write Visual Basic source code to respond to control events just as you would in a Windows Forms application. If you double-click a control on the WPF Designer, Visual Studio creates an empty event handler to catch the control's default event, and it opens the event handler in the code editor.

For example, the following code shows the event handler the IDE built for a Button control. The default event for a Button is Click, so this code is a Click event handler.

```
Private Sub Button_Click(sender As Object, e As RoutedEventArgs)

End Sub
```

SIT BACK AND RELAX

As is the case with Windows Forms, you can use relaxed delegates to remove unneeded parameters from event handlers. For example, the following code shows the previous event handler with the unnecessary parameters removed:

```
Private Sub Button_Click()

End Sub
```

Another way to build an event handler and open the code editor is to select the control on the WPF Designer. Then click the Events icon (the lightning bolt) near the top of the Properties window to make the window show a list of events for the control. Double-click an event in the window to open a new event handler for it in the code editor.

ATTACHMENT VARIATIONS

How the event is attached to the control depends on whether the control has a name. If the control's Name property is set to some value, Visual Studio uses a Handles clause in the Visual Basic code to indicate the control that uses the event. If the control does not have a name, Visual Studio defines the connection between the control and the event handler in the XAML code.

You can also create a new event handler for named controls within the code editor. The upper-left part of the code editor displays a drop-down listing the window's controls. If you select a control from the list, you can then pick an event for that control from a second drop-down in the code editor's upper right. If you select an event, the code editor makes a corresponding empty event handler.

SUMMARY

The WPF Designer allows you to build windows for use in WPF applications. It lets you add controls to the window, and to resize, move, and align the controls. Together with the Properties window, it lets you view and modify control properties, and create event handlers to interact with the controls.

This chapter introduced the WPF Designer and explained how you can take advantage of its features. Other chapters provide much more of the detail that is necessary for building windows. Chapter 10, "Selecting WPF Controls," and Chapter 11, "Using WPF Controls," provide more information about the kinds of controls you can use with the WPF Designer. Chapter 12, "WPF Windows," says more about WPF windows and pages.

The Windows Forms Designer and the WPF Designer let you add controls to forms and windows, respectively, but almost no program consists solely of controls. Most programs also include code behind the scenes to take action when different events occur, such as the user pressing a button. Chapter 5, "Visual Basic Code Editor," describes the code editor that you can use to edit the code that sits behind Windows Forms and WPF control events. Later chapters explain the Visual Basic language that you use within the code editor.

5

Visual Basic Code Editor

WHAT'S IN THIS CHAPTER

- ➤ Understanding margin icons
- ➤ Understanding IntelliSense
- ➤ Using code snippets
- ➤ Generating types from usage

WROX.COM CODE DOWNLOADS FOR THIS CHAPTER

The wrox.com code downloads for this chapter are found at `http://www.wrox.com/remtitle.cgi?isbn=9781118314074` on the Download Code tab. The code for this chapter is divided into the following major examples:

- ➤ Fibonacci
- ➤ FillArray

EDITING CODE

The Visual Studio IDE includes editors for many different kinds of documents, including several different kinds of code. For example, it has HyperText Markup Language (HTML), eXtensible Markup Language (XML), eXtensible Application Markup Language (XAML), and Visual Basic editors. These editors share some common features, such as displaying comments and keywords in different colors.

As a Visual Basic developer, you will use the Visual Basic code editor frequently, so you should spend a few minutes learning about its specialized features. The most obvious feature of the code editor is that it lets you type code into a module, but the code editor is far more than a simple text editor such as Notepad. It provides many features to make writing correct Visual Basic code easier.

This chapter describes some of the most important of these features. Many of these tools are invaluable for understanding and navigating through the code so, even if you have worked with Visual Studio before, you should take some time to read through this chapter and experiment with the tools it describes.

FANTASTIC FEATURES

The Visual Basic code editor provides many features that are not provided by other Visual Studio editors. For example, the HTML, XML, and XAML editors do not provide breakpoints or features that let you step through executing code.

Figure 5-1 shows the code editor displaying some Visual Basic code at run time. To make referring to the code lines easier, this figure displays line numbers. To display line numbers, invoke the Tools menu's Options command, navigate to the Text Editor ⇨ Basic ⇨ General page, and check the Line Numbers box.

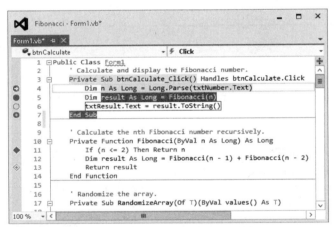

FIGURE 5-1: The Visual Basic code editor provides many features, including line numbers and icons that indicate break-points and bookmarks.

MARGIN ICONS

The gray margin to the left of the line numbers contains icons giving information about the corresponding lines of code. The following table describes the icons on lines 4 through 13.

LINE	ICON	INDICATES
4	Arrow	Execution is paused at this line
5	Red circle	A breakpoint
6	Hollow red circle	A disabled breakpoint

LINE	ICON	INDICATES
7	Red circle with plus sign	A breakpoint with a condition or hit count test
11	Red diamond	A breakpoint that executes an action when reached
12	Gray ribbon	A bookmark
13	Hollow diamond and plus sign	A disabled breakpoint with a hit test or condition that performs an action

---

BREAK TIME

A breakpoint is a line of code that you have flagged to stop execution so you can test and debug the program. When you run the program in the IDE, the program stops at the breakpoint and lets you see what routines called what other routines, examine variable values, change variables, and so forth to figure out what's happening. For more information on breakpoints and debugging, see Chapter 6, "Debugging."

These icons can combine to indicate more than one condition. For example, line 13 shows a blue and white rectangle to indicate a bookmark, a hollow red diamond to indicate a disabled breakpoint that performs an action, and a plus sign to indicate that the breakpoint has a condition or hit count test.

Note that the editor marks some of these lines in other ways than just an icon. It highlights the currently executing line with a yellow background. It marks lines that hold enabled breakpoints with white text on a red background. It surrounds lines with disabled breakpoints with red boxes.

To add or remove a simple breakpoint, click in the gray margin.

To make a more complex breakpoint, click in the margin to create a simple breakpoint. Then right-click the breakpoint icon and select one of the context menu's commands. The following list describes these commands:

➤ **Delete Breakpoint** — Removes the breakpoint.

➤ **Disable Breakpoint** — Disables the breakpoint. When the breakpoint is disabled, this command changes to Enable Breakpoint.

➤ **Location** — Lets you change the breakpoint's line number. Usually it is easier to click in the margin to remove the old breakpoint and then create a new one.

➤ **Condition** — Lets you place a condition on the breakpoint. For example, you can make the breakpoint stop execution only when the variable num_employees has a value greater than 100.

➤ **Hit Count** — Lets you set a hit count condition on the breakpoint. For example, you can make the breakpoint stop execution when it has been reached a certain number of times.

➤ **Filter** — Lets you restrict the breakpoint so it is set only in certain processes or threads.

➤ **When Hit** — Lets you specify the action that the breakpoint performs when it triggers. For example, it might display a message in the Output window.

➤ **Edit Labels** — Lets you add labels to a breakpoint. Later you can select this option to view, change, or remove the breakpoint's labels.

➤ **Export** — Lets you export information about the breakpoint into an XML file.

To add or remove a bookmark, place the cursor on a line and then click the Toggle Bookmark tool. You can find this tool, which looks like the blue and white bookmark icon, in the Text Editor toolbar, at the top of the Bookmarks window (View ⇨ Other Windows ⇨ Bookmark ⇨ Window), and in the Edit menu's Bookmarks submenu. Other bookmark tools let you move to the next or previous bookmark, the next or previous bookmark in the current folder, or the next or previous bookmark in the current document. Still others let you disable all bookmarks and delete a bookmark.

OUTLINING

By default, the code editor displays an outline view of code. If you look at the first line in Figure 5-1, you'll see a box with a minus sign in it just to the right of the line number. That box represents the outlining for the Form1 class. If you click this box, the editor collapses the class's definition and displays it as a box containing a plus sign. If you then click the new box, the editor expands the class's definition again.

Near the bottom of Figure 5-1, you can see that the RandomizeArray subroutine has been collapsed. The ellipsis and rectangle around the routine name provide an extra indication that this code is hidden.

The editor automatically creates outlining entries for namespaces, classes and their methods, and modules and their methods. You can also use the Region statement to group a section of code for outlining. For example, you can place several related subroutines in a region so you can collapse and expand the routines as a group.

Figure 5-2 shows more examples of outlining. Line 33 begins a region named Randomization Methods that contains two collapsed subroutines. Notice that the corresponding End Region statement includes a comment that I added giving the region's name. This is not required but it makes the code easier to understand when you are looking at the end of a region.

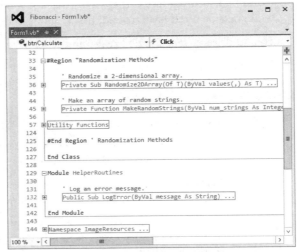

FIGURE 5-2: The code editor outlines namespaces, classes and their methods, modules and their methods, and regions.

Line 57 contains a collapsed region named Utility Functions. Notice that this region is nested inside the Randomization Methods region.

Line 129 starts a module named HelperRoutines that contains one collapsed subroutine.

Finally, line 144 holds the collapsed ImageResources namespace.

Notice that the line numbers skip values for any collapsed lines. For example, the Randomize2DArray subroutine is collapsed on line 36. This subroutine contains 7 lines (including the Sub statement), so the next visible line is labeled 43.

COLLAPSED CODE COMMENTS

Notice that comments before a subroutine are not collapsed with the subroutine. You can make reading collapsed code easier by placing a short descriptive comment before each routine.

TOOLTIPS

If you hover the mouse over a variable at design time, the editor displays a tooltip describing the variable. For example, if you hover over an integer variable named num_actions, the tooltip displays "Dim num_actions As Integer."

If you hover over a subroutine or function call (not the routine's definition, but a call to it), the tooltip displays information about that routine. For example, if you hover over a call to the Fibonacci function, the tooltip reads, "Private Function Fibonacci (n As Long) as Long."

At run time, if you hover over a variable, the tooltip displays the variable's value. If the variable is complex (such as an array or structure), the tooltip displays the variable's name and a plus sign. If you click or hover over the plus sign, the tooltip expands to show the variable's members.

In Figure 5-3, the mouse hovered over variable values. The editor displayed a plus sign and the text "values {Length=100}." When the mouse hovered over the plus sign, the editor displayed the values shown in the figure. Moving the mouse over the up and down arrows at the top and bottom of the list makes the values scroll.

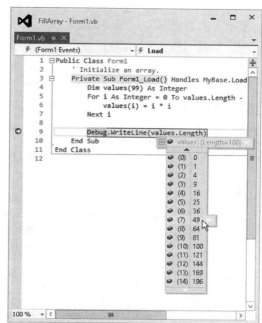

FIGURE 5-3: You can hover the mouse over a variable at run time to see its value.

If a variable has properties that are references to other objects, you can hover over their plus signs to expand those objects. You can continue following the plus signs to drill into the variable's object hierarchy as deeply as you like.

INTELLISENSE

If you start typing a line of code, the editor tries to anticipate what you will type. For example, if you type "Me." the editor knows that you are about to use one of the current object's properties or methods.

IntelliSense displays a list of the properties and methods that you might be trying to select. As you type more of the property or method name, IntelliSense scrolls to show the choices that match what you have typed so far.

In Figure 5-4, the code includes the text "Me.set," so IntelliSense is displaying the current object's methods that begin with the string "set."

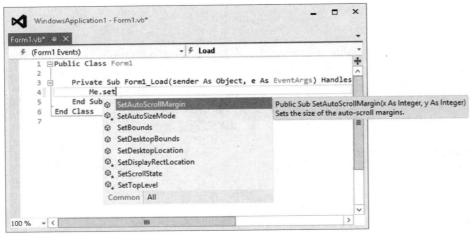

FIGURE 5-4: IntelliSense displays a list of properties and methods that you might be trying to type.

While the IntelliSense window is visible, you can use the up and down arrows to scroll through the list. While IntelliSense is displaying the item that you want to use, you can press the Tab key to accept that item and make IntelliSense type it for you. Press the Escape key to close the IntelliSense window and type the rest manually.

After you finish typing a method and its opening parenthesis, IntelliSense displays information about the method's parameters. Figure 5-5 shows parameter information for a form object's SetBounds method. This method takes four parameters: x, y, width, and height.

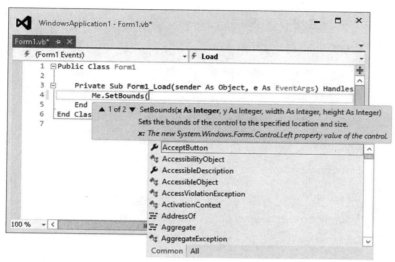

FIGURE 5-5: IntelliSense displays information about a method's parameters.

IntelliSense shows a brief description of the current parameter x. As you enter parameter values, IntelliSense moves on to describe the other parameters.

IntelliSense also indicates whether overloaded versions of the method exist. In Figure 5-5, the IntelliSense tooltip starts with "1 of 2" to indicate that it is describing the first of two available versions. You can use the up and down arrows to move through the list of overloaded versions.

CODE COLORING AND HIGHLIGHTING

The code editor displays different types of code items in different colors (although they all appear black or gray in this book). You can change the colors used for different items by selecting the Tools menu's Options command and opening the Environment ⇨ Fonts and Colors option page.

COLOR CONFUSION

To avoid confusion, you should probably leave the editor's colors alone unless you have a good reason to change them.

The following table describes some of the default colors that the code editor uses to highlight different code elements.

ITEM	HIGHLIGHTING
Comment	Green text
Compiler error	Underlined with a wavy blue underline
Keyword	Blue text
Other error	Underlined with a wavy purple underline
Preprocessor keyword	Blue text
Read-only region	Light gray background
User-defined types	Navy text
Warning	Underlined with a wavy green underline

A few other items that may sometimes be worth changing have white backgrounds and black text by default. These include identifiers (variable names, types, object properties and methods, namespace names, and so forth), and numbers.

When the code editor finds an error in your code, it highlights the error with a wavy underline. If you hover over the underline, the editor displays a tooltip describing the error. If Visual Studio can guess what you are trying to do, it adds a small flat rectangle to the end of the wavy error line to indicate that it may have useful suggestions.

The assignment statement `i = "12"` shown in Figure 5-6 has an error because it tried to assign a string value to an integer variable and that violates the Option Strict On setting. The editor displays the wavy error underline and a suggestion indicator because it thinks it knows a way to fix this error. The Error List window at the bottom also shows a description of the error.

If you hover over the suggestion indicator, the editor displays an error correction icon. If you click the icon, Visual Studio displays a dialog box describing the error and listing some actions that you may want to take. Figure 5-7 shows the suggestion dialog box for the error in Figure 5-6. If you click the text over the revised sample code, or if you double-click the sample code, the editor makes the change.

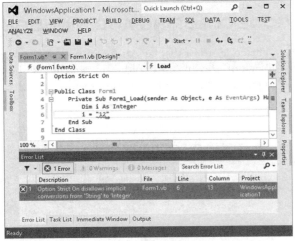

FIGURE 5-6: If the code editor thinks it can figure out what's wrong, it displays a suggestion indicator.

CODE SNIPPETS

A code snippet is a piece of code that you might find useful in many applications. It is stored in a snippet library so that you can quickly insert it into a new application.

Visual Studio comes with hundreds of snippets for performing standard tasks. Before you start working on a complicated piece of code, you should glance at the snippets that are already available to you. In fact, it would be worth your time to use the Code Snippet Manager available from the Tools menu to take a good look at the available snippets right now before you start a new project. There's little point in reinventing methods for calculating statistical values if someone has already done it and given you the code.

To insert a snippet, right-click where you want to insert the code and select Insert Snippet to make the editor display a list of snippet categories. Double-click a category to find the kinds of snippets that you want. If you select a snippet, a tooltip pops up to describe it. Figure 5-8 shows the editor preparing to insert the snippet named "Inserts a test method" from the Test snippet category.

Double-click the snippet to insert it into your code.

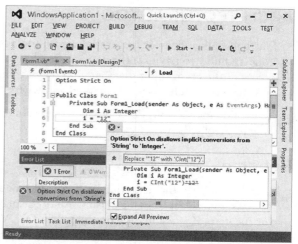

FIGURE 5-7: The error suggestion dialog box proposes likely solutions to an error.

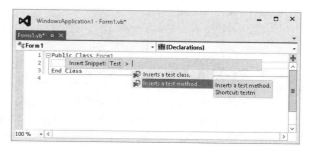

FIGURE 5-8: When you select a code snippet, a pop-up describes it.

The snippet may include values that you should replace in your code. These replacement values are highlighted with a light green background, and the first value is initially selected. If you hover the mouse over one of these values, a tooltip appears to describe the value. You can use the Tab key to jump between replacement values.

Figure 5-9 shows the code inserted by a snippet that creates a new property. The text newPropertyValue is highlighted and selected. Other selected text includes String and NewProperty. The mouse is hovering over newPropertyValue, so the tooltip explains that value's purpose.

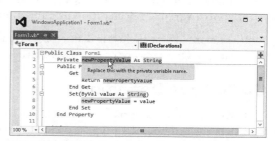

FIGURE 5-9: Values that you should replace in a snippet are highlighted.

ARCHITECTURAL TOOLS

The code editor provides several powerful tools that can help you understand the structure of your code and how to navigate through its pieces. They can give you a better understanding of how the pieces of the program fit together, and they can help you track down important code snippets, such as where a variable or type is defined and where one piece of code is called by others.

The following sections describe the most useful of these kinds of architectural tools and explain how to invoke them.

Rename

If you right-click the definition or occurrence of a symbol, such as a variable, subroutine, function, or class, and select Rename, Visual Studio displays a dialog box where you can enter a new name for the item. If you enter a name and click OK, Visual Studio updates all references to that symbol. If the symbol is a variable, it changes all references to the variable so they use the new name.

This is much safer than using a simple textual find-and-replace, which can wreak havoc with strings that contain your target string. For example, if you textually replace the variable name `factor` with `issue`, your Factorial function becomes Issueial. In contrast, if you right-click the `factor` variable, select Rename, and set the new name to `issue`, Visual Studio only updates references to the variable.

> **CORRUPTED COMMENTS**
>
> Unfortunately, Rename still leaves any comments that discuss the factor variable unchanged. You'll have to search the comments to fix them.

Go To Definition

If you right-click a symbol or type, such as a variable, function, or class, and select Go To Definition, the code editor jumps to the location where the symbol is defined. For example, it would jump to a variable's declaration or a function's definition.

If the symbol you clicked is defined by Visual Basic or a library rather than your code, Visual Studio opens the Object Browser and displays the symbol's definition there.

Go To Type Definition

If you right-click a variable and click Go To Type Definition, the code editor jumps to the location where the symbol's data type is defined. For example, if you right-click a variable of type Employee, the editor would jump to the definition of the Employee class.

If you click a variable that has one of the predefined data types such as Integer, Double, or String, the editor displays the Object Browser entry for that type.

Highlight References

Whenever the cursor sits on a symbol, the code editor highlights all references to that symbol by giving them a light gray background. It's a subtle effect, so you may not even notice it unless you're looking for it.

Reference highlighting makes it easier to see where a symbol such as a variable or subroutine is used, although it only really works locally. If a subroutine is called from many pieces of code that are far apart, you'll see only the ones that are currently visible in the code editor's window.

When you have a reference highlighted, you can use Ctrl+Shift+Up Arrow and Ctrl+Shift+Down Arrow to move to the next or previous reference.

To learn more about references to a symbol that are farther away, use the Find All References command described next.

Find All References

If you right-click a symbol such as a subroutine or variable and select Find All References, Visual Studio displays a list of everywhere in the program that uses that symbol.

For example, if you right-click a call to a function named Fibonacci, the list includes all calls to that function plus the function's definition.

You can double-click any of the listed references to make the code editor quickly jump to that reference.

Generate From Usage

The code editor can provide methods for automatically generating pieces of code in the form of suggested error corrections. For example, suppose you have not defined a Person class but you type the following code:

```
Dim new_student As New Person()
```

The code editor correctly flags this as an error because the Person class doesn't exist. It underlines the word Person with a blue squiggly line and displays a short red rectangle near it. If you hover over the rectangle, you'll see an error icon. If you then click the icon, Visual Studio displays a list of suggested corrections that include:

➤ Change Person to Version

➤ Generate 'Class Person'

➤ Generate New Type

The first choice assumes you have made a simple spelling error.

The second choice creates a new empty class named Person. You can fill in its properties and methods later.

The third choice displays the dialog box shown in Figure 5-10 so you can make Person another data type that might make sense such as an Enum or Structure. The dialog box lets you set the type's access to Default, Friend, or Public, and specify the file where Visual Studio should create the new type.

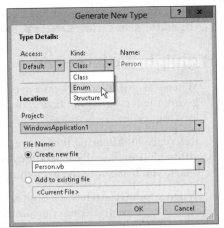

Now suppose you create an empty Person class and then type the following code:

```
new_student.FirstName = "Zaphod"
```

The code editor also flags this statement as an error. If you click the error icon this time, the suggested solution says:

Generate property stub for 'FirstName' in 'WindowsApplication1.Person'

FIGURE 5-10: The Generate New Type dialog box lets you create a new Class, Enum, or Structure.

If you click this text, Visual Studio adds the following simple property to the Person class:

```
Property FirstName As String
```

The code editor can also generate a constructor for the class if you enter the following code:

```
Dim another_person As New Person("Trillian")
```

This code is flagged as an error because no constructor is defined that takes a parameter. The error suggestions can make a constructor for you, although you'll need to edit it to give it code that handles the parameter.

This also causes a new error because the class now has a constructor that takes a single parameter, but not one that takes no parameters, so the earlier statement `Dim new_student As New Person()` is flagged as an error.

By now you can probably guess what's coming: If you click the error icon, the suggestions can make a constructor for this case, too.

Similarly, you can use the error suggestions to generate stubs for subroutines and functions. Simply use the new items as if they already exist, use the error suggestions to build stubs, and then fill in the appropriate code.

THE CODE EDITOR AT RUN TIME

The code editor behaves slightly differently at run time and design time. Many of its design-time features still work. Breakpoints, bookmarks, IntelliSense, and snippets still work.

At run time, the editor adds new tools for controlling the program's execution. Right-click a value and select Add Watch or QuickWatch to examine and monitor the value. Use the Step Into, Step Over, and Step Out commands on the Debug menu or toolbar to make the program walk through the code. Hover the mouse over a variable to see a tooltip giving the variable's value (see the section "Tooltips" earlier in this chapter for more information).

ESSENTIAL SHORTCUTS

Some very handy runtime shortcuts are F5 (Start Debugging), F8 (Step Into), Shift+F8 (Step Over), and Ctrl+F9 (Set Next Statement). Some particularly handy code editing shortcuts are F9 (Toggle Breakpoint) and Shift+Space (Open IntelliSense). You might want to write down these and any others that you use frequently.

(Note that some shortcuts are different if you don't have Visual Studio set up for Visual Basic development. If the IDE is customized for C# or general development, Step Over is F10 and Step Into is F11.)

Right-click and select Show Next Statement to move the cursor to the next statement that the program will execute. Select Run To Cursor to make the program continue running until it reaches the cursor's current line.

Right-click and select Set Next Statement to make the program skip to a new location. You can also drag the yellow arrow indicating the next statement to a new location in the left margin.

REPOSITION RESTRICTIONS

There are some restrictions on where you can move the execution position. For example, you cannot jump out of one routine and into another.

By using all of these runtime features, you can walk through the code while it executes and learn exactly what it is doing at each step. You can see the values of variables, follow paths of execution through If-Then statements, step in and out of routines, and run until particular conditions are met.

For more information on the Debug menu and its submenus, see the section "Debug" in Chapter 2, "Menus, Toolbars, and Windows." For more information on debugging techniques, see Chapter 6, "Debugging."

You can discover other runtime features by exploring the editor at run time. Right-click different parts of the editor to see which commands are available in that mode.

SUMMARY

The Visual Basic code editor is one of the most important IDE windows for Visual Basic developers. You can use the Windows Forms Designer alone to place controls on a form but the form can't do much without code behind those controls.

The Visual Basic code editor lets you type code into a module, but it also does much more. It provides tooltips that let you view variable values; outlining that lets you expand and collapse code, so you can focus on your current task; IntelliSense that helps you remember what methods are available and what their parameters are; code coloring and highlighting that immediately flags errors; and code snippets that let you reuse complex pieces of code that perform useful tasks. Architectural tools let you quickly find symbol and type definitions, jump to specific pieces of code, and easily see where a symbol is being used in the currently visible code. The code editor can even automatically generate stubs for classes, constructors, properties, and methods.

Many of these tools help you understand how the code works as you write it. Chapter 6, "Debugging," explains IDE tools that help you understand the code when it runs. Those tools let you walk through the code as it executes to see exactly what it is doing and what it is doing wrong.

Debugging

WROX.COM CODE DOWNLOADS FOR THIS CHAPTER

There are no code downloads for this chapter.

DEBUGGING AND TESTING

The Visual Basic code editor described in Chapter 5, "Visual Basic Code Editor," provides tools that make writing Visual Basic applications relatively easy. Features such as error indicators, tooltips, and IntelliSense help you write code that obeys the rules of Visual Basic syntax.

No code editor or any other tool can guarantee that the code you write actually does what you want it to do. *Debugging* is the process of modifying the code to make it run and produce correct results.

> **NOTE** *Testing tools such as those included in some versions of Visual Studio and third-party tools such as NUnit (`http://www.nunit.org`) can do a lot to ensure that your code runs correctly, but they work only if the code you write does the right things. If you need a billing system but write an inventory application, no tool will save you.*

Depending on the application's complexity, debugging can be extremely difficult. Although Visual Studio cannot do your debugging for you, it does include features that make debugging easier. It allows you to stop execution while the program is running so you can examine and modify variables, explore data structures, and step through the code to follow its execution path.

This chapter explains Visual Basic's most important debugging tools. It describes the tools available in the Debug menu and the other IDE windows that are most useful for debugging.

THE DEBUG MENU

The Debug menu contains commands that help you debug a program. These commands help you run the program in the debugger, move through the code, set and clear breakpoints, and generally follow the code's execution to see what it's doing and hopefully what it's doing wrong.

GIVE ME A BREAK

A breakpoint is a line of code that is marked to temporarily stop execution so you can test the code and figure out what's happening. The section "The Breakpoints Window" later in this chapter says a lot more about how to use breakpoints, but breakpoints are mentioned a lot between now and then so it's useful to have some idea of what they are now.

Effectively using these debugging tools can make finding problems in the code much easier, so you should spend some time learning how to use them. They can mean the difference between finding a tricky error in minutes, hours, or days.

The commands visible in the Debug window change depending on several conditions, such as the type of file you have open, whether the program is running, the line of code that contains the cursor, and whether that line contains a breakpoint. The following list briefly describes the most important menu items available while execution is stopped at a line of code that contains a breakpoint:

> ➤ **Windows** — This submenu's commands display other debugging-related windows. This submenu is described in more detail in the following section, "The Debug ➪ Windows Submenu."

> ➤ **Continue** — This command resumes program execution. The program runs until it finishes, it reaches another breakpoint, it encounters an error, or you stop it.

> ➤ **Break All** — This command stops execution of all programs running within the debugger. This may include more than one program if you are debugging more than one application at the same time. This can be useful, for example, if two programs work closely together.

➤ **Stop Debugging** — This command halts the program's execution and ends its debugging session. The program stops immediately, so it does not get a chance to execute any cleanup code that it may contain.

➤ **Step Into** — This command makes the debugger execute the current line of code. If that code invokes a function, subroutine, or some other procedure, the point of execution moves into that procedure. It is not always obvious whether a line of code invokes a procedure. For example, a line of code that sets an object's property may be simply setting a value or it may be invoking a property procedure.

➤ **Step Over** — This command makes the debugger execute the current line of code. If that code invokes a function, subroutine, or some other procedure, the debugger calls that routine but does not step into it, so you don't need to step through its code. However, if a breakpoint is set inside that routine, execution will stop at the breakpoint.

➤ **Step Out** — This command makes the debugger run until it leaves the routine it is currently executing. Execution pauses when the program reaches the line of code that called this routine.

➤ **QuickWatch** — This command displays a dialog box that gives information about the selected code object.

➤ **Exceptions** — This command displays the dialog box shown in Figure 6-1. When you select a Thrown check box, the debugger stops whenever the selected type of error occurs. If you select a User-unhandled check box, the debugger stops when the selected type of error occurs and the program does not catch it with error-handling code.

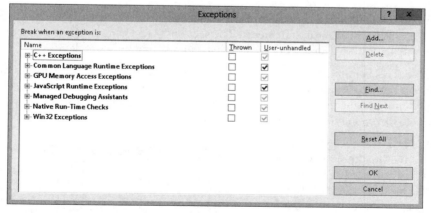

FIGURE 6-1: The Exceptions dialog box lets you determine how Visual Basic handles uncaught exceptions.

For example, suppose that your code calls a subroutine that causes a divide-by-zero exception. Use the dialog box to select Common Language Runtime Exceptions ➪ System ➪ System .DivideByZeroException (use the Find button to find it quickly). When you select the Thrown check box, the debugger stops in the subroutine when the divide-by-zero exception occurs, even if the code is protected by an error handler. When you select the User-unhandled check box, the debugger stops only if no error handler is active when the error occurs.

➤ **Toggle Breakpoint** — This command toggles whether the current code line contains a breakpoint. When execution reaches a line with an active breakpoint, execution pauses so you can examine the code and program variables. You can also toggle a line's breakpoint by clicking the margin to the left of the line in the code editor or by placing the cursor in the line of code and pressing F9.

➤ **New Breakpoint** — This submenu contains the Break At Function command. This command displays a dialog box that lets you specify a function where the program should break.

➤ **Delete All Breakpoints** — This command removes all breakpoints from the entire solution.

➤ **Disable All Breakpoints** — This command disables all breakpoints but leaves them in the solution so you can re-enable them later if you want.

➤ **Enable All Breakpoints** — This command enables all disabled breakpoints.

THE DEBUG ⇨ WINDOWS SUBMENU

The Debug menu's Windows submenu contains commands that display debugging-related windows. The following list briefly describes the most useful of these commands. The sections that follow this one provide more detail about the Breakpoints, Command, and Immediate windows.

➤ **Immediate** — This command displays the Immediate window, where you can type and execute ad hoc Visual Basic statements. The section "The Command and Immediate Windows" later in this chapter describes this window in a bit more detail.

➤ **Locals** — This command displays the Locals window, which displays the values of variables defined in the local context. To change a value, click it and enter the new value. Click the plus and minus signs to the left of a value to expand or collapse it. Note that a value may be an object, so you may be able to expand it further.

➤ **Breakpoints** — This command displays the Breakpoints window shown in Figure 6-2. This dialog box shows the solution's breakpoints, their locations, and their conditions. Select or clear the check boxes on the left to enable or disable breakpoints. Right-click a breakpoint to delete it or to edit its location, condition, hit count, action, and other properties.

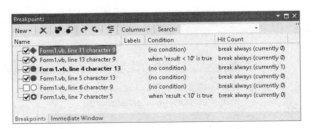

FIGURE 6-2: The Breakpoints window helps you manage breakpoints.

Use the dialog box's toolbar to create a new function breakpoint, delete a breakpoint, delete all breakpoints, enable or disable all breakpoints, go to a breakpoint's source code, and change the columns displayed by the dialog box. See the section "The Breakpoints Window" later in this chapter for more detail.

➤ **Output** — This command displays the Output window, which displays output produced by Debug and Trace statements.

➤ **Autos** — This command displays the Autos window, which displays the values of local and global variables used in the current line of code and in the previous line.

➤ **Call Stack** — This command displays the Call Stack window, which lists the routines that have called other routines to reach the program's current point of execution. Double-click a line to jump to the corresponding code in the program's call stack. This technique lets you move up the call stack to examine the code that called the routines that are running.

➤ **Threads** — This command displays the Threads window. A *thread* is a separate execution path that is running within a program. A *multi-threaded application* can have several threads running to perform more than one task at the same time. The Threads window lets you control the threads' priority and suspended status.

➤ **Parallel Tasks** — This command lists all of the application's running tasks. This is useful for debugging parallel applications.

➤ **Parallel Stacks** — This command shows the call stacks for tasks running in parallel.

➤ **Watch** — The Watch submenu contains the commands Watch 1, Watch 2, Watch 3, and Watch 4. These commands display four different watch windows that let you easily keep track of variable values. You can use each window to keep track of different sets of related variables. When you create a watch using the Debug menu's QuickWatch command described earlier, the new watch is placed in the Watch 1 window. You can click and drag watches from one watch window to another to make a copy of the watch in the second window.

You can also click the Name column in the empty line at the bottom of a watch window and enter an expression to watch.

> **WONDERFUL WATCHES**
>
> A useful IDE trick is to drag Watch windows 2, 3, and 4 onto Watch 1 so that they all become tabs on the same window. Then you can easily use the tabs to group and examine four sets of watches.

➤ **Modules** — This command displays the Modules window, which displays information about the DLL and EXE files used by the program. It shows each module's filename and path. It indicates whether the module is optimized, whether it is your code (rather than an installed library), and whether debugging symbols are loaded. The window shows each module's load order (lower-numbered modules are loaded first), version, and timestamp. Click a column to sort the modules by that column.

➤ **Processes** — This window lists processes that are attached to the Visual Studio session. This includes any programs launched by Visual Studio and processes that you attached to using the Debug menu's Attach to Process command.

Usually, when these debug windows are visible at run time, they occupy separate tabs in the same area at the bottom of the IDE. That lets you switch between them quickly and easily without them taking up too much space.

THE BREAKPOINTS WINDOW

A *breakpoint* is a line of code that you have flagged to stop execution. When the program reaches that line, execution stops and Visual Studio displays the code in a code editor window. This lets you examine or set variables, see which routine called the one containing the code, and otherwise try to figure out what the code is doing.

The Breakpoints window lists all the breakpoints you have defined for the program. This is useful for a couple of reasons. First, if you define a lot of breakpoints, it can be hard to find them all later. Although other commands let you disable, enable, or remove all of the breakpoints at once, at times you may need to find a particular breakpoint.

A common debugging strategy is to comment out broken code, add new code, and set a breakpoint near the modification so that you can see how the new code works. When you have finished testing the code, you probably want to remove either the old code or the new code, so you don't want to blindly remove all of the program's breakpoints.

The Breakpoints window lists all of the breakpoints and, if you double-click a breakpoint in the list, you can easily jump to the code that holds it.

Right-click a breakpoint and select Condition to display the dialog box shown in Figure 6-3. By default, a breakpoint stops execution whenever it is reached. You can use this dialog box to add an additional condition that determines whether the breakpoint activates when it is reached. In this example, the breakpoint stops execution only if the expression (n < 10) AndAlso (result > 1000) is True when the code reaches the breakpoint.

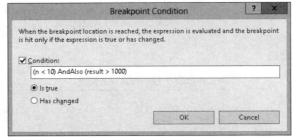

FIGURE 6-3: The Breakpoint Condition dialog box lets you specify a condition that determines whether Visual Studio stops at the breakpoint.

> **NOTE** *Note that specifying a breakpoint condition can slow execution considerably because Visual Basic must evaluate the condition frequently.*

Right-click a breakpoint and select Hit Count to display the Breakpoint Hit Count dialog box shown in Figure 6-4. Each time the code reaches a breakpoint, it increments the breakpoint's hit count. You can use this dialog box to make the breakpoint's activation depend on the hit count's value.

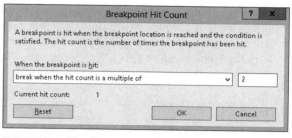

From the drop-down list you can select one of the following options:

FIGURE 6-4: The Breakpoint Hit Count dialog box lets you make a breakpoint's activation depend on the number of times the code has reached it.

➤ Break Always

➤ Break When the Hit Count Is Equal To

➤ Break When the Hit Count Is a Multiple Of

➤ Break When the Hit Count Is Greater Than or Equal To

If you select any but the first option, you can enter a value in the text box and the program will pause execution when the breakpoint has been reached the appropriate number of times. For example, if you select the option Break When the Hit Count Is a Multiple Of and enter 2 into the text box, execution will pause every second time it reaches the breakpoint.

Right-click a breakpoint and select When Hit to display the When Breakpoint Is Hit dialog box. This dialog box lets you specify the actions that Visual Basic takes when the breakpoint is activated. Select the Print a Message check box to make the program display a message in the Output window. Select the Continue Execution check box to make the program continue running without stopping after it displays its message.

THE COMMAND AND IMMEDIATE WINDOWS

The Command and Immediate windows enable you to execute commands while the program is stopped in the debugger. One of the more useful commands in each of these windows is the Debug .Print statement. For example, in the Command window, the command Debug.Print x displays the value of the variable x. In the Immediate window, the statement must follow normal Visual Basic syntax so the command is Debug.Print(x).

You can use a question mark as an abbreviation for Debug.Print. The following text shows how the command might appear in the Command window. Here the > symbol is the command prompt provided by the window and 123 is the result: the value of variable x. In the Immediate window, the statement would not include the > character.

```
>? x
123
```

The command >immed tells the Command window to open the Immediate window. Conversely, the command >cmd (you need to type the > in the Immediate window) tells the Immediate window to open the Command window.

Although there is some overlap between these two windows, they serve two mostly different purposes. The Command window can issue commands to the Visual Studio IDE. Typically, these are commands that do or could appear in menus and toolbars. For example, the following command uses the Debug menu's QuickWatch command to open a QuickWatch window for the variable first_name:

```
>Debug.QuickWatch first_name
```

One particularly useful command is Tools.Alias. This command lists command aliases defined by the IDE. For example, >Tools.Alias ? indicates that ? is the alias for Debug.Print and >Tools.Alias ?? indicates that ?? is the alias for Debug.QuickWatch.

The Command window includes some IntelliSense support. If you type the name of a menu, for example, Debug or Tools, IntelliSense will display the commands available within that menu.

The Command window issues commands to the IDE. In contrast, the Immediate window executes Visual Basic statements. For example, suppose that you have written a subroutine named CheckPrinter. Then the following statement in the Immediate window executes that subroutine:

```
CheckPrinter
```

You can execute subroutines in the Immediate window to quickly and easily test routines without writing user interface code to handle all possible situations. You can call a subroutine or function, passing it different parameters to see what happens. If you set breakpoints within the routine, the debugger will pause there.

You can also set the values of global variables and then call routines that use them. The following Immediate window commands set the value of the PrinterName variable and then call the CheckPrinter subroutine:

```
PrinterName = "LP_REMOTE"
CheckPrinter
```

You can execute much more complex statements in the Command and Immediate windows. For example, suppose that your program uses the following statement to open a file for reading:

```
Dim fs As FileStream = File.OpenRead(
  "C:\Program Files\Customer Orders\Summary" &
  DateTime.Now().ToString("yymmdd") & ".dat")
```

Suppose that the program is failing because some other part of the program is deleting the file. You can type the following code (all on one line) into the Immediate window to see if the file exists. As you step through different pieces of the code, you can use this statement repeatedly to learn when the file is deleted.

```
?System.IO.File.Exists("C:\Program Files\Customer Orders\Summary" &
  DateTime.Now().ToString("yymmdd") & ".dat")
```

The Immediate window evaluates the complicated string expression to produce a filename. It then uses the System.IO.File.Exists command to determine whether the file exists and displays True or False accordingly.

SUMMARY

Although Visual Basic cannot debug your applications for you, it provides all of the tools you need to get the job done. By using the tools in the Debug menu and the IDE's debugging-related windows, you can get a good idea about what your program is doing and what it is doing wrong.

This chapter and the others in the first part of this book described the basic pieces of the Visual Studio development environment. They described the windows, menus, and toolbars that you use to build and debug Visual Basic applications.

The next part of the book provides more detail about the steps you follow to build an application before you debug it. Chapter 7, "Selecting Windows Forms Controls," describes the most common controls that you can use to build Windows Forms applications. It explains the purposes of those controls to help you decide which controls to use in different situations.

PART II
Getting Started

7

Selecting Windows Forms Controls

WHAT'S IN THIS CHAPTER

➤ Control summaries

➤ Using controls to restrict selection

➤ Containing and arranging controls

➤ Selection controls

➤ Display and feedback controls

WROX.COM CODE DOWNLOADS FOR THIS CHAPTER

There are no code downloads for this chapter.

CONTROLS

A *control* is a programming entity that has a graphical component. A control sits on a form and interacts with the user, providing information and possibly allowing the user to manipulate it. Text boxes, labels, buttons, scroll bars, drop-down lists, menu items, toolstrips, and just about everything else that you can see and interact with in a Windows application is a control.

Controls are an extremely important part of any interactive application. They give information to the user (Label, ToolTip, TreeView, PictureBox) and organize the information so that it's easier to understand (GroupBox, Panel, TabControl). They enable the user to enter data (TextBox, RichTextBox, ComboBox, MonthCalendar), select options (RadioButton, CheckBox, ListBox), tell the application to take action (Button, MenuStrip, ContextMenuStrip), and interact with objects outside of the application (OpenFileDialog, SaveFileDialog, PrintDocument, PrintPreviewDialog). Some controls also provide support for other controls (ImageList, ToolTip, ContextMenuStrip, ErrorProvider).

This chapter provides a very brief description of the standard Windows Forms controls together with some tips that can help you decide which control to use for different purposes. Appendix G, "Windows Forms Controls and Components," covers the controls in much greater detail, describing each control's most useful properties, methods, and events.

CONTROLS OVERVIEW

Figure 7-1 shows the Visual Basic Toolbox displaying the standard Windows Forms controls. Because you can add and remove controls on the Toolbox, you may see a slightly different selection of tools on your computer.

The following table briefly describes the controls shown in Figure 7-1 in the order in which they appear in the figure (starting at the top, or row 1, and reading from left to right).

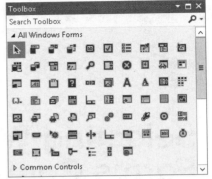

FIGURE 7-1: Visual Basic provides a large number of standard controls for Windows Forms.

CONTROL	PURPOSE
Row 1	
Pointer	This is the pointer tool, not a control. Click this tool to deselect any selected controls on a form. Then you can select new controls.
BackgroundWorker	Executes a task asynchronously and notifies the main program of its progress and when it is finished.
BindingNavigator	Provides a user interface for navigating through a data source. For example, it provides buttons that let the user move back and forth through the data, add records, delete records, and so forth.
BindingSource	Encapsulates a form's data source and provides methods for navigating through the data.
Button	A simple push button. When the user clicks it, the program can perform some action.
CheckBox	A box that the user can check and clear.
CheckedListBox	A list of items with check boxes that the user can check and clear.

CONTROL	PURPOSE
ColorDialog	Lets the user pick a standard or custom color.
ComboBox	A text box with an attached list or drop-down list that the user can use to enter or select a textual value.
ContextMenuStrip	A menu that appears when the user right-clicks a control. You set a control's ContextMenuStrip property to this control, and the rest is automatic.
Row 2	
DataGridView	A powerful grid control that lets you display large amounts of complex data with hierarchical or web-like relationships relatively easily.
DataSet	An in-memory store of data with properties similar to those of a relational database. It holds objects representing tables containing rows and columns, and can represent many database concepts such as indexes and foreign key relationships.
DateTimePicker	Lets the user select a date and time in one of several styles.
DirectoryEntry	Represents a node in an Active Directory hierarchy.
DirectorySearcher	Performs searches of an Active Directory hierarchy.
DomainUpDown	Lets the user scroll through a list of choices by clicking up-arrow and down-arrow buttons.
ErrorProvider	Displays an error indicator next to a control that is associated with an error.
EventLog	Provides access to Windows event logs.
FileSystemWatcher	Notifies the application of changes to a directory or file.
FlowLayoutPanel	Displays the controls it contains in rows or columns.
Row 3	
FolderBrowserDialog	Lets the user select a folder.
FontDialog	Lets the user specify a font's characteristics (name, size, boldness, and so forth).
GroupBox	Groups related controls for clarity. It also defines a default RadioButton group for any RadioButtons that it contains.
HelpProvider	Displays help for controls that have help if the user sets focus on the control and presses F1.
HScrollBar	A horizontal scroll bar.

continues

(continued)

CONTROL	PURPOSE
ImageList	Contains a series of images that other controls can use. For example, the images that a TabControl displays on its tabs are stored in an associated ImageList control. Your code can also pull images from an ImageList for its own use.
Label	Displays read-only text that the user cannot modify or select by clicking and dragging.
LinkLabel	Displays a label, parts of which may be hyperlinks. When the user clicks a hyperlink, the program can take some action.
ListBox	Displays a list of items that the user can select. Depending on the control's properties, the user can select one or several items at the same time.
ListView	Displays a list of items in one of four possible views: LargeIcon, SmallIcon, List, and Details.
Row 4	
MaskedTextBox	A text box that requires the input to match a specific format (such as a phone number or ZIP code format).
MenuStrip	Represents the form's main menus, submenus, and menu items.
MessageQueue	Provides communication between different applications.
MonthCalendar	Displays a calendar that allows the user to select a range of dates.
NotifyIcon	Displays an icon in the system tray or status area.
NumericUpDown	Lets the user change a number by clicking up- and down-arrow buttons, or by pressing up-arrow and down-arrow keys.
OpenFileDialog	Lets the user select a file for opening.
PageSetupDialog	Lets the user specify properties for printed pages. For example, it lets the user specify the printer's paper tray, page size, margins, and orientation (portrait or landscape).
Panel	A control container. The control can automatically provide scroll bars and defines a RadioButton group for any RadioButtons that it contains.
PerformanceCounter	Provides access to Windows performance counters.

CONTROL	PURPOSE
Row 5	
PictureBox	Displays a picture.
PrintDialog	Displays a standard print dialog box. The user can select the printer, pages to print, and printer settings.
PrintDocument	Represents output to be sent to the printer. A program can use this object to print and display print previews.
PrintPreviewControl	Displays a print preview within one of the application's forms.
PrintPreviewDialog	Displays a print preview in a standard dialog box.
Process	Allows the program to interact with processes, including starting and stopping them.
ProgressBar	Displays a series of colored bars to show the progress of a long operation.
PropertyGrid	Displays information about an object in a format similar to the one used by the Properties window at design time.
RadioButton	Represents one of an exclusive set of options. When the user selects a RadioButton, Visual Basic deselects all other RadioButton controls in the same group. Groups are defined by GroupBox and Panel controls and the Form class.
RichTextBox	A text box that supports Rich Text extensions. The control can display different pieces of text with different font names, sizes, bolding, and so forth. It also provides paragraph-level formatting for justification, bullets, hanging indentation, and more.
Row 6	
SaveFileDialog	Lets the user select the name of a file where the program will save data.
SerialPort	Represents a serial port and provides methods for controlling, reading from, and writing to it.
ServiceController	Represents a Windows service and lets you manipulate services.
SplitContainer	Lets the user drag a divider vertically or horizontally to split available space between two areas within the control.
Splitter	Provides a divider that the user can drag to split available space between two controls. The Dock properties and stacking orders of the controls and the Splitter determine how the controls are arranged and resized. The SplitContainer control automatically provides a Splitter between two containers, so it is usually easier and less confusing to use.

continues

(continued)

CONTROL	PURPOSE
StatusStrip	Provides an area (usually at the bottom of the form) where the application can display status messages, small pictures, and other indicators of the application's state.
TabControl	Displays a series of tabs attached to pages that contain their own controls. The user clicks a tab to display the associated page.
TableLayoutPanel	Displays the controls it contains in a grid.
TextBox	Displays some text that the user can edit.
Timer	Triggers an event periodically. The program can take action when the event occurs.
Row 7	
ToolStrip	Displays a series of buttons, drop-downs, and other tools that let the user control the application.
ToolStripContainer	A container that allows a ToolStrip control to dock to some or all of its edges. You might dock a ToolStripContainer to a form to allow the user to dock a ToolStrip to each of the form's edges.
ToolTip	Displays a tooltip if the user hovers the mouse over an associated control.
TrackBar	Allows the user to drag a pointer along a bar to select a numeric value.
TreeView	Displays hierarchical data in a graphical, tree-like form.
VScrollBar	A vertical scroll bar.
WebBrowser	A web browser in a control. You can place this control on a form and use its methods to navigate to a web page. The control displays the results exactly as if the user were using a standalone browser. One handy use for this control is displaying web-based help.

CHOOSING CONTROLS

Keeping all of the intricacies of each of these controls in mind at once is a daunting task. With so many powerful tools to choose from, it's not always easy to pick the one that's best for a particular situation.

To simplify error-handling code, you should generally pick the most restrictive control that can accomplish a given task, because more restrictive controls give the user fewer options for entering invalid data.

For example, suppose that the user must pick from the choices Small, Medium, and Large. The application could let the user type a value in a TextBox control, but then the user could type Huge or Weasel. The program would need to verify that the user typed one of the valid choices and display an error message if the text was invalid. The program might also need to use precious screen real estate to list the choices to help the user remember what to type.

A better idea would be to use a group of three RadioButton controls or a ComboBox with DropDownStyle set to DropDownList. Then the user can easily see the choices available and can only select a valid choice. If the program initializes the controls with a default value rather than leaves them initially undefined, it knows that there is always a valid choice selected.

COMMON SENSE DEFENSE

Restrictive controls also make the application more secure. By presenting users with a list of choices rather than letting them type in whatever they like, the program can protect itself from attack. For example, two of the most common attacks on websites are buffer overflow attacks, in which the attacker enters far more text than intended in a text box, and SQL injection attacks, in which the attacker enters carefully designed gibberish into a text box to confuse a database. Requiring the user to select options rather than typing neutralizes both of these attacks.

The following sections summarize different categories of controls and provide some tips about when to use each.

Containing and Arranging Controls

These controls contain, group, and help arrange other controls. These controls include FlowLayoutPanel, TableLayoutPanel, GroupBox, Panel, TabControl, and SplitContainer.

The FlowLayoutPanel arranges the controls it contains in rows or columns. For example, when its FlowDirection property is LeftToRight, the control arranges its contents in rows from left to right. It positions its contents in a row until it runs out of room and then it starts a new row. FlowLayoutPanel is particularly useful for toolboxes and other situations where the goal is to display as many of the contained controls as possible at one time, and the exact arrangement of the controls isn't too important.

The TableLayoutPanel control displays its contents in a grid. All the cells in a particular row have the same height, and all the cells in a particular column have the same width. In contrast, the FlowLayoutPanel control simply places controls next to each other until it fills a row and then starts a new one.

A GroupBox control is good for visibly grouping related controls or for grouping RadioButton controls into a RadioButton group. (The RadioButton control is discussed later in this chapter in the section "Making Selections.") It provides a visible border and caption so that it can help the user make sense out of a very complicated form.

GREAT GROUPS

The rule of thumb in user interface design is that a user can evaluate around seven items (plus or minus two) at any given time. A list of five or six choices is manageable, but a list containing dozens of options can be confusing.

By placing choices into categories visibly separated in GroupBox controls, you can make the interface much easier for the user to understand. Rather than try to keep dozens of options straight all at once, the user can mentally break the problem into smaller pieces and consider each group of options separately.

Like the GroupBox, the Panel control can contain controls and define RadioButton groups, but its real advantage is its ability to automatically display scroll bars. If you set a Panel control's AutoScroll property to True and the Panel resizes so its content cannot fit, the control automatically displays scroll bars that the user can adjust to see different parts of the content. Scrolling back and forth can be cumbersome for the user, however, so this is not the best way to display data if the user must view it all frequently. If the user must jump back and forth between different controls inside a scrolling Panel, it may be better to use a TabControl.

A TabControl displays data grouped by pages. The tabs enable the user to quickly jump from page to page. The control can display scroll bars if the tabs don't all fit at once, although that makes using the control much more awkward. TabControl works well if the data falls into natural groupings that you can use for the tab pages. It doesn't work as well if the user must frequently compare values on one page with those on another, forcing the user to jump back and forth.

The SplitContainer control allows the user to divide an area between two adjacent regions. A SplitContainer contains two Panel controls in which you can place your own controls. When the user drags the splitter between the two panels, the control resizes the panels accordingly. You can set the Panels' AutoScroll properties to True to make them automatically provide scroll bars when necessary.

SplitContainer is helpful when the form isn't big enough to hold all the data the program must display, and the user should be able to trade area in one part of the form for area in another. It is particularly useful when the user must compare values in the two areas by viewing them at the same time.

Although you can nest SplitContainers inside other SplitContainers, they are easiest to use when they separate only two areas. Large groups of SplitContainers separating many areas are usually clumsy and confusing.

These container controls help arrange the controls they contain. The Anchor and Dock properties of any controls inside the containers work relative to the containers. For example, suppose you place a series of buttons with Anchor = Top, Left, Right inside a SplitContainer so that they are as wide as the Panel containing them. When you drag the splitter, the buttons automatically resize to fit the width of their Panel.

Making Selections

Selection controls enable the user to choose values. If you use them carefully, you can reduce the chances of the user making an invalid selection, so you can reduce the amount of error-handling code you need to write.

These controls include CheckBox, CheckedListBox, ComboBox, ListBox, RadioButton, DateTimePicker, MonthCalendar, DomainUpDown, NumericUpDown, TrackBar, HScrollBar, and VScrollBar.

CheckBox enables the user to select an option or not, independently of all other selections. If you want the user to select only one of a set of options, use a RadioButton instead. If a form requires more than, say, five to seven CheckBox controls that have related purposes, consider using a CheckedListBox instead.

The CheckedListBox control enables the user to select among several independent options. It is basically a series of CheckBox controls arranged in a list that provides scroll bars if necessary.

The ComboBox control enables the user to make one brief selection. This control is particularly useful when its DropDownStyle property is set to DropDownList because then the user must pick a value from a list. If you want to allow the user to select a value or enter one that is not on the list, set the control's DropDownStyle to Simple or DropDown. This control does roughly the same things as a simple ListBox but takes less space.

The ListBox control displays a list of items that the user can select. You can configure the control to let the user select one or more items. A ListBox takes more room than a ComboBox but can be easier to use if the list is very long.

LONG LISTS

If you have a long list and want to allow the user to select many items, it is relatively easy for the user to accidentally deselect all of the previous selections by clicking a new item. To make things easier for the user, you should consider using a CheckedListBox, which doesn't have that problem.

The RadioButton control lets the user pick one of a set of options. For example, three RadioButton controls might represent the choices Small, Medium, and Large. If the user selects one, Visual Basic automatically deselects the others. This control is useful when the list of choices is relatively small, and there is a benefit to allowing the user to see all of the choices at the same time. If the list of choices is long, consider using a ListBox or ComboBox.

The DateTimePicker and MonthCalendar controls enable the user to select dates and times. They validate the user's selections, so they are generally better than other controls for selecting dates and times. For example, if you use a TextBox to let the user enter month, date, and year, you must write extra validation code to ensure that the user doesn't enter February 29, 2013.

The DomainUpDown and NumericUpDown controls let the user scroll through a list of values. If the list is relatively short, a ListBox or ComboBox may be easier for the user. The DomainUpDown and NumericUpDown controls take very little space, however, so they may be helpful on very crowded forms. By holding down one of the controls' arrow buttons, the user can scroll very quickly through the values, so these controls can also be useful when they represent a long list of choices.

The TrackBar control lets the user drag a pointer to select an integer value. This is usually a more intuitive way to select a value than a NumericUpDown control, although it takes a lot more space on the form. It also requires some dexterity if the number of values allowed is large.

The HScrollBar and VScrollBar controls let the user drag a "thumb" across a bar to select an integral value much as the TrackBar does. HScrollBar, VScrollBar, and TrackBar even have similar properties. The main difference is in the controls' appearances. On one hand, the two scroll bar controls allow more flexible sizing (the TrackBar has definite ideas about how tall it should be for a given width), and they may seem more elegant to some users. On the other hand, most users are familiar with the scroll bars' normal purpose of scrolling an area on the form, so using them as numeric selection bars may sometimes be confusing.

Entering Data

Sometimes it is impractical to use the selection controls described in the previous section. For example, the user cannot reasonably enter a long work history or comments using a ComboBox or RadioButton.

The RichTextBox, TextBox, and MaskedTextBox controls let the user enter text with few restrictions. These controls are most useful when the user must enter a large amount of textual data that doesn't require any validation.

The TextBox control is less complex and easier to use than the RichTextBox control, so you may want to use it unless you need the RichTextBox control's extra features. If you need those features (such as multiple fonts, indentation, paragraph alignment, superscripting and subscripting, multiple colors, more than one level of undo/redo, and so forth), you need to use a RichTextBox.

The MaskedTextBox control is a TextBox control that requires the user to enter data in a particular format. For example, it can help the user enter a phone number of the form 234-567-8901. This is useful only for short fields where the format is tightly constrained. In those cases, however, it reduces the chances of the user making mistakes.

Displaying Data

These controls display data to the user: Label, DataGridView, ListView, TreeView, and PropertyGrid.

The Label control displays a simple piece of text that the user can view but not select or modify. Because you cannot select the text, you cannot copy it to the clipboard. If the text contains a value that you think the user might want to copy to the clipboard and paste into another application (for example, serial numbers, phone numbers, e-mail addresses, URLs, and so forth), you can use a TextBox control with its ReadOnly property set to True to allow the user to select and copy the text but not edit it.

The DataGridView control can display table-like data. The control can also display several tables linked with master/detail relationships and the user can quickly navigate through the data. You can also configure this control to allow the user to update the data.

The ListView control displays data that is naturally viewed as a series of icons or as a list of values with columns providing extra detail. With a little extra work, you can sort the data by item or by detail columns.

The TreeView control displays hierarchical data in a tree-like format similar to the directory display provided by Windows Explorer. You can determine whether the control allows the user to edit the nodes' labels.

The PropertyGrid control displays information about an object in a format similar to the one used by the Properties window at design time. The control enables the user to organize the properties alphabetically or by category and lets the user edit the property values.

Providing Feedback

These controls provide feedback to the user: ToolTip, HelpProvider, ErrorProvider, NotifyIcon, StatusStrip, and ProgressBar. Their general goal is to tell the user what is going on without being distracting. For example, the ErrorProvider flags a field as incorrect but doesn't prevent the user from continuing to enter data in other fields.

DISRUPTIVE VALIDATION

You can force users to fix errors by using a TextBox's Validating event handler. For example, if the event handler determines that a TextBox's value is invalid, it can set its e.Cancel parameter to True to prevent the user from moving out of the TextBox or closing the application.

I don't recommend this approach, however, particularly if the users are performing "heads down" data entry, because it interrupts their flow of work. Instead, use an ErrorProvider to flag the error and let the user fix the problem when it's convenient.

For more information on validation events, see the section "Validation Events" in Chapter 8.

The ToolTip control provides the user with a brief hint about a control's purpose when the user hovers the mouse over it. The HelpProvider gives the user more detailed help about a control's purpose when the user sets focus to the control and presses F1. A high-quality application provides both tooltips and F1 help for every control. These features are unobtrusive and appear only if the user needs them, so it is better to err on the side of providing too much help rather than not enough.

TOO MANY TOOLTIPS?

It may seem silly to place tooltips on every single control. For example, does it really make sense to place a tooltip on a TextBox that sits next to a label that says "Phone Number"? Surprisingly the answer is yes. It turns out that some screen reader applications for the visually impaired get important cues from tooltips. Giving that TextBox a tooltip can help some users figure out what data they should enter. The ErrorProvider control flags a control as containing invalid data. It is better to use selection controls that do not allow the user to enter invalid data, but this control is useful when that is not possible.

The NotifyIcon control can display a small icon in the taskbar notification area to let the user easily learn the application's status. This is particularly useful for applications that run in the background without the user's constant attention. If the application needs immediate action from the user, it should display a dialog or message box rather than rely on a NotifyIcon.

WHAT'S THE TRAY?

The *taskbar notification area*, also called the *Windows system tray*, is the small area in the taskbar, usually on the right, that displays the current time and icons indicating the status of various running applications.

The StatusStrip control displays an area (usually at the bottom of the form) where the program can give the user some information about its state. This information can be in the form of small images or short text messages. It can contain a lot more information than a NotifyIcon, although it is visible only when the form is displayed.

The ProgressBar indicates how much of a long task has been completed. Usually, the task is performed synchronously, so the user is left staring at the form while it completes. The ProgressBar lets the user know that the operation is not stuck.

Initiating Action

Every kind of control responds to events, so every control can initiate an action. Nevertheless, users expect only certain kinds of controls to perform significant actions. For example, users expect clicking a button to start an action, but they don't expect clicking a label or check box to start a long process.

To prevent confusion, you should start actions from the controls most often used to start actions. These controls include Button, MenuStrip, ContextMenuStrip, ToolStrip, LinkLabel, TrackBar, HScrollBar, VScrollBar, and Timer. All except the Timer control let the user initiate the action.

All of these controls interact with the program through event handlers. For example, the Button control's Click event handler normally makes the program perform some action when the user clicks the button.

Other controls also provide events that can initiate action. For example, the CheckBox control provides CheckChanged and Click events that you could use to perform some action. By catching the proper events, you can use almost any control to initiate an action. Because the main intent of those controls is not to execute code, they are not listed in this section.

The Button control enables the user to tell the program to execute a particular function. A button is normally always visible on its form, so it is most useful when the user must perform the action frequently or the action is part of the program's central purpose. For actions that are performed less often, use a MenuStrip or ContextMenuStrip control.

Items in a MenuStrip control also enable the user to make the program perform an action. You must perform more steps to open the menu, find the item, and select it than you must to click a button, so a Button control is faster and easier. On the other hand, menus take up less form real estate than buttons. You can also assign keyboard shortcuts (such as F5 or Ctrl+S) to frequently used menu items, making them even easier to invoke than buttons.

A ContextMenuStrip control provides the same advantages and disadvantages as a MenuStrip control. ContextMenuStrip is available only from certain controls on the form, however, so it is useful for commands that are appropriate only within specific contexts. For example, a Save command applies to all the data loaded by a program, so it makes sense to put it in a MenuStrip. A command that deletes a particular object in a drawing applies only to that object. By placing the command in a ContextMenuStrip control attached to the object, the program keeps the command hidden when the user is working on other things. It also makes the relationship between the action (delete) and the object clear to both the user and the program.

The ToolStrip control combines some of the best features of menus and buttons. It displays a series of buttons so they are easy to use without navigating through a menu. The buttons are small and grouped at the top of the form, so they don't take up as much space as a series of larger buttons.

It is common to place buttons or ToolStrip buttons on a form to duplicate frequently used menu commands. The menu commands provide keyboard shortcuts for more advanced users, and the buttons make it easy to invoke the commands for less-experienced users. More advanced applications such as Visual Studio may provide customizations that allow the user to decide which ToolStrips are visible.

The LinkLabel control displays text much as a Label control does. It also displays some text in blue with an underline, displays a special cursor when the user moves over that text, and raises an event if the user clicks the text. That makes the control appropriate when clicking a piece of text should perform some action. For example, on a web page, clicking a link typically navigates to the link's web page.

The TrackBar, HScrollBar, and VScrollBar controls let the user drag a "thumb" across a bar to select an integral value. As mentioned in the section "Making Selections" earlier in this chapter, you can use these controls to let the user select a numeric value. However, they can also be used to perform some action interactively. For example, the scroll bars are often used to scroll an area on the form. More generally, they are used to make the program take action based on some new value. For example, you could use a scroll bar to let the user select new red, green, and blue color components for an image. As the user changes a scroll bar's value, the program can update the image's colors.

The Timer control triggers some action at a regular interval. When the Timer control raises its Timer event, the program takes action.

Displaying Graphics

These controls display graphics, either on the screen or on a printout: Form, PictureBox, PrintPreviewControl, PrintDocument, and PrintPreviewDialog.

A Form provides methods for drawing, but it's often better to draw in a PictureBox control instead of on the form itself. That makes it easier to move the drawing if you later need to redesign the form. For example, if you decide that the picture might be too big, it is easy to move a PictureBox control into a scrolling Panel control. It would be much harder to rewrite the code to move the drawing from the Form into a PictureBox control later.

PrintPreviewControl displays a print preview for a PrintDocument object. The program responds to events raised by the PrintDocument object and generates the output to be printed. PrintPreviewControl displays the results within a control on one of the program's forms.

The PrintPreviewDialog control displays graphics from a PrintDocument object much as a PrintPreviewControl does, but it provides its own dialog box. Unless you need to arrange the print preview in some special way, it is easier to use a PrintPreviewDialog than it is to build your own preview dialog box with a PrintPreviewControl. The PrintPreviewDialog control provides many features that enable the user to zoom, scroll, and move through the pages of the preview document. Implementing those features yourself would be a lot of work.

Displaying Dialog Boxes

Visual Basic provides a rich assortment of dialog boxes that enable the user to make standard selections. Figuring out which of these dialog boxes to use is usually easy because each has a very specific purpose. The following table lists the dialog boxes and their purposes.

DIALOG	PURPOSE
ColorDialog	Select a color.
FolderBrowserDialog	Select a folder (directory).
FontDialog	Select a font.
OpenFileDialog	Select a file to open.
PageSetupDialog	Specify page setup for printing.
PrintDialog	Print a document.
PrintPreviewDialog	Display a print preview.
SaveFileDialog	Select a file for saving.

THIRD-PARTY CONTROLS

Visual Basic comes with a large number of useful controls all ready to go, but many other controls are available that you can use if you need them. If you right-click the Toolbox and select Choose Items, you can select from a huge list of .NET Framework and COM components available on your system.

You can obtain more controls provided by other companies and available for purchase and sometimes for free on the web. Many of these controls perform specialized tasks such as generating bar codes, making shaped forms, warping images, and providing special graphical effects.

Other controls extend the standard controls to provide more power or flexibility. Several controls are available that draw two- and three-dimensional charts and graphs. Other controls provide more powerful reporting services than those provided by Visual Studio's own tools.

If you search the web for "windows forms controls," you will find lots of websites where you can download controls for free or for a fee. A few places you might like to explore include:

➤ MVPs.org (`http://www.mvps.org`), a site leading to resources provided by people related to Microsoft's Most Valuable Professional (MVP) program. The Common Controls Replacement Project (`http://ccrp.mvps.org`) provides controls that duplicate and enhance standard Visual Basic 6 controls. Development on this project has stopped but some of the old Visual Basic 6 controls may give you some ideas for building controls of your own. MVPs.org is also a good general resource.

➤ Windows Forms .NET (`http://windowsclient.net`), Microsoft's official WPF and Windows Forms .NET community.

➤ ASP.NET (`http://www.asp.net`), Microsoft's official ASP.NET community.

➤ CNET (`http://download.cnet.com/windows`).

➤ Shareware.com (`http://www.shareware.com`).

➤ Shareware Connection (`http://www.sharewareconnection.com`).

You should use these as a starting point for your own search, not as a definitive list. You can download controls from hundreds (if not thousands) of websites.

CONTROL CHAOS

You should also show some restraint in downloading third-party controls and products in general. Every time you add another control to a project, you make the project depend on that control. If you later move the project to a newer version of Visual Basic, you must ensure that the control works with that version. Similarly, if the vendor makes a new version of the control, you must find out if it works with your version of Visual Basic. If it doesn't, you may be stuck using an older, unsupported version of the control.

continues

continued

If controls and tools interact with each other, the problem becomes much more difficult. If anything changes, you must find a set of versions for all of the tools that can work correctly together.

I try to keep my use of third-party controls to a bare minimum because, when I write a book, I generally cannot assume that you have a particular third-party control. I use tools such as WinZip (`http://www.WinZip.com`) and FileZilla (`http://filezilla-project.org`) outside of projects, but nothing inside them.

Use a third-party control if it will save you a lot of work. But, before you do, ask yourself how much work it would be to do without the control and how much work it will be to replace the control later if you need to move to a new version of Visual Basic.

And of course, if you download a control from a source that isn't trustworthy, you could be downloading a virus.

SUMMARY

Controls form the main connection between the user and the application. They allow the application to give information to the user, and they allow the user to control the application. Controls are everywhere in practically every Windows application. Only a tiny percentage of applications that run completely in the background can do without controls.

This chapter briefly described the purposes of the standard Visual Basic controls and provided a few tips for selecting the controls appropriate for different purposes.

Even knowing all about the controls doesn't guarantee that you can produce an adequate user interface. There's a whole science to designing user interfaces that are intuitive and easy to use. A good design enables the user to get a job done naturally and with a minimum of wasted work. A bad interface can encumber the user and turn even a simple job into an exercise in beating the application into submission.

For more information on building usable applications, read some books on user-interface design. They explain standard interface issues and solutions. You can also learn a lot by studying other successful applications. Look at the layout of their forms and dialog boxes. You shouldn't steal their designs outright, but you can try to understand why they arrange their controls in the ways they do. Look at applications that you like and find particularly easy to use. Compare them with applications that you find awkward and confusing.

This chapter provided an introduction to Windows Forms controls to help you decide which controls to use for different purposes. Chapter 8, "Using Windows Forms Controls," explains in greater detail how you can use the controls that you select. It tells how to add a control to a form at design time or run time, and explains how to use a control's properties, methods, and events.

Using Windows Forms Controls

WROX.COM CODE DOWNLOADS FOR THIS CHAPTER

The wrox.com code downloads for this chapter are found at `http://www.wrox.com/remtitle.cgi?isbn=9781118314074` on the Download Code tab. The code for this chapter is divided into the following major examples:

➤ AnchorButton

➤ DeferredValidation

➤ Docking

➤ MakeButtons

➤ UseTableLayoutPanel

USING CONTROLS AND COMPONENTS

As Chapter 7 mentioned, a *control* is a programming entity that has a graphical component. Text boxes, labels, list boxes, check boxes, menus, and practically everything else that you see in a Windows application is a control.

A *component* is similar to a control, except it is not visible at run time. When you add a component to a form at design time, it appears in the *component tray* below the bottom of the form. You can select the component and use the Properties window to view and change its properties just as you can with a control. At run time, the component is invisible to the user, although it may display a visible object such as a menu, dialog box, or status icon.

This chapter explains controls and components in general terms. It describes different kinds of controls and components. It explains how your program can use them at design time and run time to give the user information and to allow the user to control your application. It also explains in general terms how a control's properties, methods, and events work, and it lists some of the most useful properties, methods, and events provided by the Control class. Other controls that are derived from this class inherit those properties, methods, and events unless they are explicitly overridden.

CONTROLS AND COMPONENTS

Controls are graphic by nature. Buttons, text boxes, and labels provide graphical input and feedback for the user. They display data and let the user trigger program actions. Some controls (such as grid controls, tree view controls, and calendar controls) are quite powerful and provide a rich variety of tools for interacting with the user.

In contrast, components are represented by graphical icons at design time and are hidden at run time. They may display some other object (such as a dialog box, menu, or graphical indicator), but the component itself is hidden from the user.

Many components display information to the user. Others provide information needed by graphical controls. For example, a program can use connection, data adapter, and data set components to define data that should be selected from a database. Then a Grid control can display the data to the user. Because the connection, data adapter, and data set objects are components, you can define their properties at design time without writing code.

Figure 8-1 shows a form at design time that contains several components. The components appear in the component tray at the bottom of the form, not on the form's graphical surface.

This example contains four components. Timer1 fires an event periodically so the program can take some action at specified time intervals. ErrorProvider1 displays an error icon and error messages for certain controls on the form such as TextBoxes. BackgroundWorker1 performs tasks asynchronously while the main program works independently. ImageList1 contains a series of images for use by another control such as a Button, ListView, or TreeView.

Aside from the lack of a graphical component on the form, working with components is very similar to working with controls. You use the Properties window to set a component's properties, the code editor to define its event handlers, and code to call its methods. The rest of this chapter focuses on controls, but the same concepts apply just as well to components.

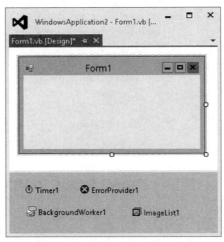

FIGURE 8-1: At design time components appear in the component tray below a form.

CREATING CONTROLS

Usually you add controls to a form graphically at design time. In some cases, however, you may want to add new controls to a form while the program is running. This gives you a bit more flexibility so that you can change the program's appearance at run time in response to the program's needs or the user's commands.

For example, you may not know how many pieces of data you will need to display until run time. Sometimes you can display unknown amounts of data using a list, grid, or other control that can hold a variable number of items, but other times you might like to display the data in a series of labels or text boxes. In cases such as these, you need to create new controls at run time.

The following code shows how a program might create a new Label control at run time. First it declares a variable of type Label and initializes it with the New keyword. It uses the label's SetBounds method to position the label on the form and sets its Text property to "Hello World!" The code then adds the label to the current form's Controls collection. ("Me" is a keyword that means "the object currently executing code," which in this case is the form.)

```
Dim lbl As New Label
lbl.SetBounds(10, 50, 100, 25)
lbl.Text = "Hello World!"
Me.Controls.Add(lbl)
```

CHANGING CONTAINERS

To place a control inside a container other than the form, add the control to the container's Controls collection. For example, to add the previous Label to a GroupBox named grpLabels, you would use the statement grpLabels.Controls .Add(lbl).

Usually, a label just displays a message so you don't need to catch its events. Other controls such as buttons and scroll bars, however, are not very useful if the program cannot respond to their events.

You can take two approaches to catching a new control's events. First, you can use the WithEvents keyword when you declare the control's variable. Then you can open the form in the code editor, select the variable's name from the left drop-down list, and select an event from the right drop-down list to give the control an event handler.

The following code demonstrates this approach. It declares a class-level variable btnHi using the WithEvents keyword. When you click the btnMakeHiButton button, its event handler initializes the variable to create the Hi button. It sets the control's position and text, and adds it to the form's

Controls collection. When the user clicks this button, the btnHi_Click event handler executes and displays a message.

```
' Declare the btnHi button WithEvents.
Private WithEvents btnHi As Button

' Make the new btnHi button.
Private Sub btnMakeHiButton_Click() Handles btnMakeHiButton.Click
    btnHi = New Button()
    btnHi.SetBounds(16, 16, 80, 23)
    btnHi.Text = "Say Hi"
    Me.Controls.Add(btnHi)
End Sub

' The user clicked the btnHi button.
Private Sub btnHi_Click() Handles btnHi.Click
    MessageBox.Show("Hi")
End Sub
```

This first approach works if you know the number and types of the controls you will need ahead of time. Then you can define variables for them all using the WithEvents keyword. If you don't know how many controls you need to create, however, this isn't practical. For example, suppose that you want to create a button for each file in a directory. When the user clicks a button, the file should open. If you don't know how many files the directory will hold, you don't know how many variables you'll need.

One solution to this dilemma is to use the AddHandler statement to add event handlers to the new controls. The following code demonstrates this approach. When you click the btnMakeHelloButton button, its Click event handler creates a new Button object, storing it in a locally declared variable. It sets the button's position and text and adds it to the form's Controls collection as before. Next, the program uses the AddHandler statement to make subroutine Hello_Click an event handler for the button's Click event. When the user clicks the new button, subroutine Hello_Click displays a message.

```
' Make a new Hello button.
Private Sub btnMakeHelloButton_Click() Handles btnMakeHelloButton.Click
    ' Make the button.
    Dim btnHello As New Button()
    btnHello.SetBounds(240, 64, 80, 23)
    btnHello.Text = "Say Hello"
    Me.Controls.Add(btnHello)

    ' Add a Click event handler to the button.
    AddHandler btnHello.Click, AddressOf Hello_Click
End Sub

' The user clicked the Hello button.
Private Sub Hello_Click()
    MessageBox.Show("Hello")
End Sub
```

> **TAG, YOU'RE IT**
>
> When you build controls at run time, particularly if you don't know how many controls you may create, the Tag property can be very useful. You can place something in a new control's Tag property to help identify it. For example, you might store a control number in each new control's Tag property and make them all use the same event handlers. The event handlers can check the Tag property to see which control raised the event.

You can use the same routine as an event handler for more than one button. In that case, the code can convert the sender parameter into a Button object and use the button's Name, Text, and other properties to determine which button was pressed.

To remove a control from the form, simply remove it from the form's Controls collection. To free the resources associated with the control, set any variables that refer to it to Nothing. For example, the following code removes the btnHi control created by the first example:

```
Me.Controls.Remove(btnHi)
btnHi = Nothing
```

This code can remove controls that you created interactively at design time, as well as controls you create during run time.

PROPERTIES

A *property* is some value associated with a control. Often, a property corresponds in an obvious way to the control's appearance or behavior. For example, the Text property represents the text that the control displays, BackColor represents the control's background color, Top and Left represent the control's position, and so forth.

Many properties, including Text, BackColor, Top, and Left, apply to many kinds of controls. Other properties work only with certain specific types of controls. For example, the ToolStrip control has an ImageList property that indicates the ImageList control containing the images the ToolStrip should display. Only a few controls such as Button and TabControl have an ImageList property.

The following sections explain how you can manipulate a control's properties interactively at design time or using code at run time.

Properties at Design Time

To modify a control's properties at design time, open its form in the Windows Forms Designer and click the control. The Properties window lets you view and edit the control's properties.

You can set many properties by clicking a property's value in the Properties window and then typing the new value. This works with simple string and numeric values such as the controls' Name and Text properties, and it works with some other properties where typing a value makes some sense.

For example, the HScrollBar control (horizontal scrollbar) has Minimum, Maximum, and Value properties that determine the control's minimum, maximum, and current values, respectively. You can click those properties in the Properties window and enter new values. When you press the Enter key or move to another property, the control validates the value you typed. If you entered a value that doesn't make sense (for example, if you typed ABC instead of a numeric value), the IDE reports the error and lets you fix it.

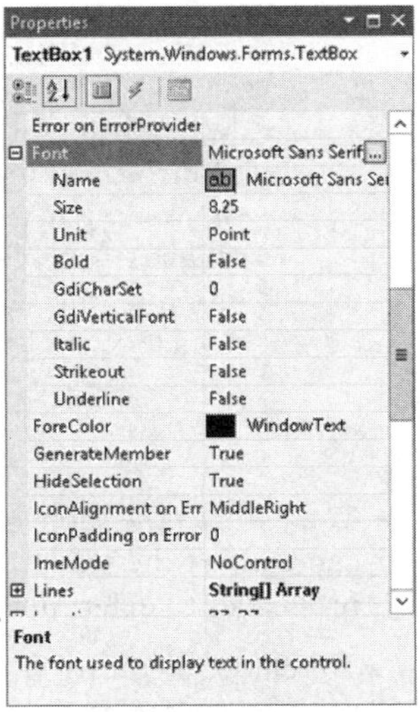

Compound Properties

A few properties have compound values. The Location property includes the X and Y coordinates of the control's upper-left corner. The Size property contains the control's width and height. The Font property is an object that has its own font name, size, boldness, and other font properties.

The Properties window displays these properties with a plus sign on the left. Figure 8-2 shows the Properties window displaying a TextBox's properties. Notice the plus sign next to the Lines property near the bottom.

FIGURE 8-2: The Properties window lets you change complex properties at design time.

When you click the plus sign, the window expands the property to show the values that it contains. Figure 8-2 shows the Font property expanded. You can click the Font property's subvalues and set them independently just as you can set any other property value.

When you expand a compound property, the plus sign changes to a minus sign (see the Font property in Figure 8-2). Click this minus sign to collapse the property and hide its members.

Some compound properties provide more sophisticated methods for setting the property's values. If you click the ellipsis button to the right of the Font property shown in Figure 8-2, the IDE presents a font selection dialog box that lets you set many of the font's properties.

Restricted Properties

Some properties allow more restricted values. For example, the Visible property is a Boolean, so it can only take the values True and False. When you click the property, a drop-down arrow appears on the right. If you click this arrow, a drop-down list lets you select one of the choices, True or False.

Many properties have enumerated values. The Button control's FlatStyle property allows the values Flat, Popup, Standard, and System. When you click the drop-down arrow to the right of this property, a drop-down list appears to let you select one of those values.

You can also double-click the property to cycle through its allowed values. After you select a property, you can use the up and down arrows to move through the values.

Some properties allow different values at different times. For example, some properties contain references to other controls. The Button control's ImageList property is a reference to an ImageList component that contains the picture that the Button should display. If you click the drop-down arrow to the right of this value, the Properties window displays a list of the ImageList components on the form that you might use for this property. This list also contains the entry (none), which you can select to remove any previous control reference in the property.

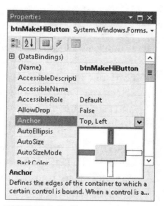

Many properties take very specialized values and provide specialized property editors to let you select values easily. For example, the Anchor property lets you anchor a control's edges to the edges of its container. Normally, a control is anchored to the top and left edges of the container so that it remains in the same position even if the container is resized. If you also anchor the control on the right, its right edge moves in or out as the container gets wider or narrower. This lets you make controls that resize with their containers in certain useful ways.

FIGURE 8-3: Some properties, such as Anchor, provide specialized editors to let you select their values.

If you select the Anchor property and click the drop-down arrow on the right, the Properties window displays the small graphical editor shown in Figure 8-3. Click the skinny rectangles on the left, top, right, or bottom to anchor or unanchor (sometimes called *float*) the control on those sides. Press the Enter key to accept your choices or press Esc to cancel them.

Other complex properties may provide other editors. These are generally self-explanatory. Click the ellipsis or drop-down arrow to the right of a property value to open the editor, and experiment to see how these editors work.

You can right-click any property's name and select Reset to reset the property to a default value. Many complex properties can take the value "(none)," and for those properties, selecting Reset usually sets the value to "(none)."

Collection Properties

Some properties represent collections of objects. For example, the ListBox control displays a list of items. Its Items property is a collection containing those items. The Properties window displays the value of this property as "(Collection)." If you select this property and click the ellipsis to the right, the Properties window displays a simple dialog box where you can edit the text displayed by the control's items. This dialog box is quite straightforward: Enter the items' text on separate lines and click OK.

Other properties are much more complex. For example, to create a TabControl that displays images on its tabs, you must also create an ImageList component. Select the ImageList component's Images property, and click the ellipsis to the right to display the dialog box shown in Figure 8-4. When you click the Add button, the dialog box displays a file selection dialog box that lets you add an image file to the control. The list on the left shows you the images you have loaded and includes a small thumbnail picture of each image. The values on the right show you the images' properties.

After you add pictures to the ImageList control, create a TabControl. Select its ImageList property, click the drop-down arrow on the right, and select the ImageList control that you created previously. Next, select the TabControl's TabPages property, and click the ellipsis on the right to see the dialog box shown in Figure 8-5.

Use the Add button to add tab pages to the control. To set a tab's image, select a tab page, click its ImageIndex property, click the drop-down arrow to the right, and pick the number of the image in the ImageList that you want to use for this tab.

Some properties even contain a collection of objects, each of which contains a collection of objects. For example, the ListView control has an Items property that is a collection of items. Each item is an object that has a SubItems property, which is itself a collection. When you display the ListView control as a list with details, an object in the Items collection represents a row in the view and its SubItems values represent the secondary values in the row.

To set these values at design time, select the ListView control and click the ellipsis to the right of its Items property in the Properties window. Create an item in the editor, and click the ellipsis to the right of the item's SubItems property.

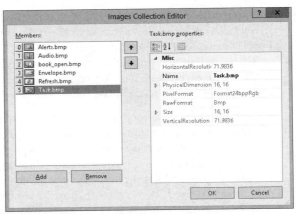

FIGURE 8-4: This dialog box lets you load images into an ImageList control at design time.

FIGURE 8-5: This dialog box lets you edit a TabControl's tab pages.

Other complicated properties provide similarly complex editors. Although they may implement involved relationships among various controls and components, they are usually easy enough to figure out with a little experimentation.

Properties at Run Time

Visual Basic lets you set most control properties at design time, but often you will need to get and modify property values at run time. For example, you might need to change a label's text to tell the user what is happening, disable a button because it is not allowed at a particular moment, or read the value selected by the user from a list.

As far as your code is concerned, a property is just like any other public variable defined by an object. You get or set a property by using the name of the control, followed by a dot, followed by the name of the property. For example, the following code examines the text in the TextBox named txtPath. If the text doesn't end with a / character, the code adds one. This code both reads and sets the Text property:

```
If Not txtPath.Text.EndsWith("/") Then txtPath.Text &= "/"
```

If a property contains a reference to an object, you can use that object's properties and methods in your code. The following code displays a message box indicating whether the txtPath control's font is bold. It examines the TextBox control's Font property. That property returns a reference to a Font object that has a Bold property.

```
If txtPath.Font.Bold Then
    MessageBox.Show("Bold")
Else
    MessageBox.Show("Not Bold")
End If
```

FINALIZED FONTS

A Font object's properties are read-only, so the code cannot set the value of txtPath .Font.Bold. To change the TextBox control's font, the code would need to create a new font as in the statement:

```
txtPath.Font = New Font(txtPath.Font, FontStyle.Bold)
```

This code passes the Font object's constructor a copy of the TextBox control's current font to use as a template, and a value indicating that the new font should be bold.

If a property represents a collection or array, you can loop through or iterate over the property just as if it were declared as a normal collection or array. The following code lists the items the user has selected in the ListBox control named lstChoices:

```
For Each selected_item As Object In lstChoices.SelectedItems()
    Debug.WriteLine(selected_item.ToString())
Next selected_item
```

A few properties are read-only at run time, so your code can examine them but not change their values. For example, a Panel's Controls property returns a collection holding references to the controls inside the Panel. This property is read-only at run time so you cannot set it equal to a new collection. (The collection provides methods for adding and removing controls so you don't really need to replace the whole collection; you can change the controls that it contains instead.)

Note also that at design time, this collection doesn't appear in the Properties window. Instead of explicitly working with the collection, you add and remove controls interactively by moving them in and out of the Panel control on the form.

A control's Bottom property is also read-only and not shown in the Properties window. It represents the distance between the top of the control's container and the control's bottom edge. This value is really just the control's Top property plus its Height property (control.Bottom = control.Top + control.Height), so you can modify it using those properties instead of setting the Bottom property directly.

THE ELUSIVE WRITE-ONLY PROPERTY

In theory, a property can also be write-only at run time. Such a property is really more like a subroutine than a property because it just passes a value to the control, so most controls use a subroutine instead. In practice, read/write properties are the norm, read-only properties are uncommon, and write-only properties are extremely rare.

Useful Control Properties

This section describes some of the most useful properties provided by the Control class. Appendix A, "Useful Control Properties, Methods, and Events," summarizes these and other Control properties for quick reference.

All controls (including the Form control) inherit directly or indirectly from the Control class. That means they inherit the Control class's properties, methods, and events (unless they take explicit action to override the Control class's behavior).

Although these properties are available to all controls that inherit from the Control class, many are considered advanced, so they are not shown by the IntelliSense pop-up's Common tab. For example, a program is intended to set a control's position by using its Location property not its Left and Top properties, so Location is in the Common tab whereas Left and Top are only in the Advanced tab.

Figure 8-6 shows the Common tab on the IntelliSense pop-up for a Label control. It shows the Location property but not the Left property. If you click the All tab, you can see Left and the other advanced properties.

When you type the control's name and enough of the string Left to differentiate it from the Location property (in this case "lblDirectory .Le"), the pop-up automatically switches to show

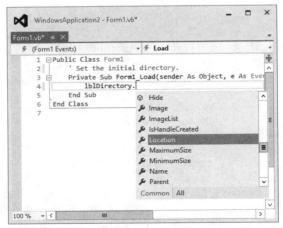

FIGURE 8-6: The Location property is on the IntelliSense Common tab but the Left property is not.

a smaller version of the IntelliSense pop-up listing only properties that contain "Le" such as Left, RightToLeft, and TopLevelControl.

Many of the Control class's properties are straightforward, but a few deserve special attention. The following sections describe some of the more confusing properties in greater detail.

Anchor

The Anchor property allows a control to automatically resize itself when its container is resized. Anchor determines which of the control's edges should remain a fixed distance from the corresponding edges of the container.

Normally a control's Anchor property is set to Top, Left. That means the control's top and left positions remain fixed when the container resizes. If the control's upper-left corner is at the point (8, 16) initially, it remains at the position (8, 16) when you resize the container. This is the normal control behavior, and it makes the control appear fixed on the container.

Now suppose that you set a control's Anchor property to Top, Right, and you place the control in the container's upper-right corner. When you resize the container, the control moves, so it remains in the upper-right corner.

If you set two opposite Anchor values, the control resizes itself to satisfy them both. For example, suppose that you make a button that starts 8 pixels from its container's left, right, and top edges. Then suppose that you set the control's Anchor property to Top, Left, Right. When you resize the container, the control resizes itself so that it is always 8 pixels from the container's left, right, and top edges.

In a more common scenario, many forms have Label controls on the left with Anchor set to Top, Left so they remain fixed on the form. On the right, the form holds TextBoxes and other controls with Anchor set to Top, Left, Right, so they resize themselves to take advantage of the resizing form's new width.

Similarly, you can make controls that stretch vertically as the form resizes. For example, if you set a ListBox control's Anchor property to Top, Left, Bottom, the control stretches vertically to take advantage of the form's height and display as much of its list of items as possible.

If you do not provide any Anchor value for either the vertical or the horizontal directions, the control anchors its center to the container's center. For example, suppose you position a Button control in the bottom middle of the form and you set its Anchor property to Bottom. Because you placed the control in the middle of the form, the control's center coincides with the form's center. When you resize the form, the control moves so it remains centered horizontally.

If you place other controls on either side of the centered one, they will all move so they remain together centered as a group as the form resizes. You may want to experiment with this property to see the effect.

At run time, you can set a control's Anchor property to AnchorStyles.None or to a Boolean combination of the values AnchorStyles.Top, AnchorStyles.Bottom, AnchorStyles.Left, and AnchorStyles.Right. For example, the example program AnchorButton, available for download on the book's website, uses the following code to move the btnAnchored control to the form's lower-right corner and set its Anchor property to Bottom, Right, so it stays there:

```
Private Sub Form1_Load() Handles MyBase.Load
    btnAnchored.Location = New Point(
        Me.ClientSize.Width - btnAnchored.Width,
        Me.ClientSize.Height - btnAnchored.Height)
    btnAnchored.Anchor = AnchorStyles.Bottom Or AnchorStyles.Right
End Sub
```

Dock

The Dock property determines whether a control attaches itself to one or more of its container's sides. For example, if you set a control's Dock property to Top, the control docks to the top of its container so it fills the container from left to right and is flush with the top of the container. If the container is resized, the control remains at the top, keeps its height, and resizes itself to fill the container's width. This is how a typical toolbar behaves. The effect is similar to placing the control at the top of the container so that it fills the container's width and then setting its Anchor property to Top, Left, Right.

You can set a control's Dock property to Top, Bottom, Left, Right, Fill, or None. The value Fill makes the control dock to all of its container's remaining interior space. If it is the only control in the container, then it fills the whole container.

If the container holds more than one control with Dock set to a value other than None, the controls are arranged according to their stacking order (also called the Z-order). The control that is first in the stacking order (the one that would normally be drawn first at the back) is positioned first using its Dock value. The control that comes next in the stacking order is arranged second in the remaining space, and so on until all of the controls are positioned.

Figure 8-7 shows example program Docking, which is available for download on the book's website. It contains four TextBoxes with Dock set to different values. The first in the stacking order has Dock set to Left, so it occupies the left edge of the form. The next control has Dock set to Top, so it occupies the top edge of the form's remaining area. The third control has Dock set to Right, so it occupies the right edge of the form's remaining area. Finally, the last control has Dock set to Fill, so it fills the rest of the form.

Controls docked to an edge resize to fill the container in one dimension. For example, a control with Dock set to Top fills whatever width the container has available. A control with Dock set to Fill resizes to fill all of the form's available space.

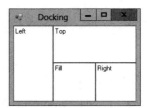

FIGURE 8-7: Docked controls are arranged according to their stacking order.

The Dock property does not arrange controls very intelligently when you resize the container. For example, suppose that you have two controls, one above the other. The first has Dock set to Top and the second has Dock set to Fill. You can arrange the controls so that they evenly divide the form vertically. When you make the form taller, however, the second control, with Dock set to Fill, takes up all of the new space, and the other control keeps its original size.

You cannot use the Dock or Anchor properties to make controls divide a form evenly when it is resized, but you can do that with a TableLayoutPanel control. For example, to make two TextBoxes divide a form horizontally, create TableLayoutPanel and dock it to fill the form. Give the control one row and two columns. Edit the Columns collection so each column is sized by percentage and the percent value is 50 percent. (This is the default for a new TableLayoutPanel so you don't need to change anything.) Now add the two TextBoxes to the TableLayoutPanel and dock them so they fill the two cells. Now when the user resizes the form, the TableLayoutPanel resizes, its columns divide the available space evenly, the TextBoxes resize to fill the columns.

Example program UseTableLayoutPanel, which is available for download on the book's website, demonstrates this method.

You can also use a SplitContainer to divide a form. The user can drag the divider between the two panels to adjust the size allocated to each.

Position and Size Properties

Controls contain many position and size properties, and the differences among them can be confusing. Some of the more bewildering aspects of controls are client area, non-client area, and display area.

A control's *client area* is the area inside the control where you can draw things or place other controls. A control's *non-client area* is everything else. In a typical form, the borders and title bar are the non-client area. The client area is the space inside the borders and below the title bar where you can place controls or draw graphics.

MENUS AND CLIENT AREA

A form's menus can make the client and non-client areas a bit confusing. Logically, you might think of the menus as part of the non-client area because you normally place controls below them. Nevertheless, the menus are themselves controls and you can even place other controls above or below the menus (although that would be very strange and confusing to the user), so they are really contained in the client area.

A control's *display area* is the client area minus any internal decoration. For example, a GroupBox displays an internal border and a title. Although you can place controls over these, you normally wouldn't. The display area contains the space inside the GroupBox's borders and below the space where the title sits.

The following table summarizes properties related to the control's size and position.

PROPERTY	DATA TYPE	READ/WRITE	PURPOSE
Bounds	Rectangle	Read/Write	The control's size and position within its container including non-client areas.
ClientRectangle	Rectangle	Read	The size and position of the client area within the control.
ClientSize	Size	Read/Write	The size of the client area. If you set this value, the control adjusts its size to make room for the non-client area, while giving you this client size.
DisplayRectangle	Rectangle	Read	The size and position of the area within the control where you would normally draw or place other controls.
Location	Point	Read/Write	The position of the control's upper-left corner within its container.
Size	Point	Read/Write	The control's size including non-client areas.
Left, Top, Width, Height	Integer	Read/Write	The control's size and position within its container including non-client areas.
Bottom, Right	Integer	Read	The position of the control's lower and right edges within its container.

METHODS

A *method* executes code associated with a control. The method can be a function that returns a value or a subroutine that does something without returning a value.

Because methods execute code, you cannot invoke them at design time. You can only invoke them by using code at run time.

Appendix A summarizes the Control class's most useful methods. Controls that inherit from the Control class also inherit these methods unless they have overridden the Control class's behavior.

EVENTS

A control or other object *raises* an *event* to let the program know about some change in circumstances. Sometimes raising an event is also called *firing* the event. Specific control classes provide events that are relevant to their special purposes. For example, the Button control provides a Click event to let the program know when the user clicks the button.

The program responds to an event by executing code in an *event handler* that *catches* the event and takes whatever action is appropriate. Each event defines its own event handler format and determines the parameters that the event handler will receive. Often, these parameters give additional information about the event.

For example, when part of the form is covered and exposed, the form raises its Paint event. The Paint event handler takes as a parameter an object of type PaintEventArgs named e. That object's Graphics property is a reference to a Graphics object that the program can use to redraw the form's contents.

Some event handlers take parameters that are used to send information about the event back to the object that raised it. For example, the Form class's FormClosing event handler has a parameter of type FormClosingEventArgs. That parameter is an object that has a property named Cancel. If the program sets Cancel to True, the Form cancels the FormClosing event and remains open. For example, the event handler can verify that the data entered by the user was properly formatted. If the values don't make sense, the program can display an error message and keep the form open.

Although many of a control's most useful events are specific to the control type, controls do inherit some common events from the Control class. Appendix A summarizes the Control class's most important events. Controls that inherit from the Control class also inherit these events unless they have overridden the Control class's behavior.

Creating Event Handlers at Design Time

You can create an event handler at design time in a couple of ways. If you open a form in the Windows Forms Designer and double-click a control, the code editor opens and displays the control's default event handler. For example, a TextBox control opens its TextChanged event handler, a Button control opens its Click event handler, and the form itself opens its Load event handler.

To create some other non-default event handler for a control, select the control and then click the Properties window's Events button (which looks like a lightning bolt). This makes the Properties window list the control's most commonly used events. If you have defined event handlers already, possibly for other controls, you can select them from the events' drop-down lists. Double-click an event's entry to create a new event handler.

To create event handlers inside the code editor, open the code window, select the control from the left drop-down list, and then select an event from the right drop-down list, as shown in Figure 8-8. To create an event handler for the form itself, select "(Form1 Events)" from the left drop-down and then select an event from the right drop-down.

The code window creates an event handler with the correct parameters and return value. For example, the following code shows an empty TextBox control's Click event handler. Now you just need to fill in the code that you want to execute when the event occurs.

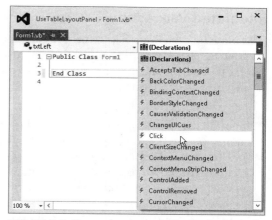

FIGURE 8-8: To create an event handler in the code window, select a control from the left drop-down, and then select an event from the right drop-down.

```
Private Sub txtLeft_Click(sender As Object, e As EventArgs) Handles txtLeft.Click

End Sub
```

RELAX

Visual Basic supports relaxed delegates, which allow you to omit the parameters from the event handler's declaration if you don't need to use them. Simply create the event handler as usual and then delete the parameters.

To make code easier to read, this book omits parameters wherever they are not needed. For example, the following code shows a relaxed version of the previous Click event handler:

```
Private Sub txtLeft_Click() Handles txtLeft.Click

End Sub
```

The section "Creating Controls" earlier in this chapter explains how you can use code to add and remove event handlers at run time.

Validation Events

Data validation is an important part of many applications. Visual Basic provides two events to make validating data easier: Validating and Validated. The following sections describe three approaches to using those events to validate data.

Integrated Validation

The Validating event fires when the code should validate a control's data. This happens when a control has the input focus and the form tries to close, or when focus moves to another control that has its CausesValidation property set to True. Integrated validation uses the Validating event to perform all validation.

The Validating event handler can verify that the data in a control has a legal value and take appropriate action if it doesn't. For example, the IntegratedValidation example program, which is available for download, is shown in Figure 8-9. Each of the program's TextBoxes has a Validating event handler that requires its value to be non-blank before the user can move to another control. In Figure 8-9 I entered the Name and Street values, and then tried to tab past the City field. The program used an ErrorProvider component named erroMissingData to display an error indicator beside the City field and prevented me from moving to a new control.

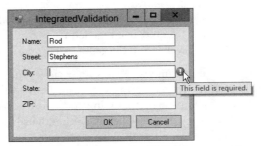

FIGURE 8-9: The IntegratedValidation example program displays an error indicator next to a TextBox if the user tries to leave that control without entering a value.

The following code shows the program's Validating event handler. Notice that the Handles clause lists all five TextBoxes' Validating events so this event handler catches the Validating event for all five controls.

```
' Verify that this field is not blank.
Private Sub txtValidating(sender As Object,
 e As System.ComponentModel.CancelEventArgs) Handles _
 txtName.Validating, txtStreet.Validating, txtCity.Validating,
 txtState.Validating, txtZip.Validating
    ' Convert sender into a TextBox.
    Dim txt As TextBox = DirectCast(sender, TextBox)

    ' See if it's blank.
    If (txt.Text.Length > 0) Then
        ' It's not blank. Clear any error.
        errMissingData.SetError(txt, "")
    Else
        ' It's blank. Show an error.
        errMissingData.SetError(txt, "This field is required.")

        ' Do not allow focus to leave the control.
        e.Cancel = True
    End If
End Sub
```

The event handler receives a reference to the control that raised the event in its sender parameter. The code uses DirectCast to convert that generic Object into a TextBox object. It then checks whether the TextBox's value is blank. If the text is non-blank, the code calls the ErrorProvider's SetError method to clear any error that was previously set for the TextBox. If the TextBox's value is blank, the code uses the ErrorProvider to display an error indicator. It then sets e.Cancel to prevent focus from leaving the TextBox.

Deferred Validation

By keeping focus in the control that contains the error, the previous approach forces the user to fix problems as soon as possible. In some applications, it may be better to let the user continue filling out other fields and fix the problems later. For example, a user who is touch-typing data into several fields may not look up to see the error until much later, after entering a series of invalid values in the first field and wasting a lot of time.

The DeferredValidation example program, which is available for download, uses the following code to let the user continue entering values in other fields and fix errors later:

```
' Verify that this field is not blank.
Private Sub txtValidating(sender As Object,
 e As System.ComponentModel.CancelEventArgs) Handles _
 txtName.Validating, txtStreet.Validating, txtCity.Validating,
 txtState.Validating, txtZip.Validating
    ' Convert sender into a TextBox.
    Dim txt As TextBox = DirectCast(sender, TextBox)

    ' See if it's blank.
    If (txt.Text.Length > 0) Then
```

```
            ' It's not blank. Clear any error.
            errMissingData.SetError(txt, "")
        Else
            ' It's blank. Show an error.
            errMissingData.SetError(txt, "This field is required.")
        End If
    End Sub

    ' See if any field is blank.
    Private Sub Form1_FormClosing(sender As Object,
      e As FormClosingEventArgs) Handles Me.FormClosing
        If (txtName.Text.Length = 0) Then e.Cancel = True
        If (txtStreet.Text.Length = 0) Then e.Cancel = True
        If (txtCity.Text.Length = 0) Then e.Cancel = True
        If (txtState.Text.Length = 0) Then e.Cancel = True
        If (txtZip.Text.Length = 0) Then e.Cancel = True
    End Sub
```

The Validating event handler is very similar to the one used by the IntegratedValidation program. If a value is missing, it still displays an error message but this version doesn't set e.Cancel to True so it doesn't prevent the user from moving to the next field.

When the user tries to close the form, the FormClosing event handler rechecks all of the TextBoxes and if any have blank values it sets e.Cancel to True to prevent the form from closing. (A more elaborate program might also display an error message telling the user which TextBox had an invalid value. It could even use that TextBox's Focus method to set focus to that control so the user can fix the problem more easily.)

> **VALIDATING BUTTONS**
>
> If the form is a dialog box, you could validate the form's data in an OK button's Click event handler instead of in the form's FormClosing event.
>
> Similarly, you may want to validate the data when the user clicks some other button. On a New Order form, you might validate all of the fields when the user clicks the Submit button.

SUMMARY

This chapter described controls, components, and objects in general terms. It told how to create controls and how to use their properties, methods, and events. It spent some extra time explaining two common data-validation strategies.

All controls inherit directly or indirectly from the Control class so any properties, methods, and events defined by the Control class are inherited by those other controls. The Form class also inherits from the Control class so it also inherits all of that class's properties, methods, and events. In some sense a Form is just another control but it does have special needs and provides special features that are not shared with other controls. To help you use these features effectively, Chapter 9, "Windows Forms," describes the Form class in greater detail.

Windows Forms

WROX.COM CODE DOWNLOADS FOR THIS CHAPTER

The wrox.com code downloads for this chapter are found at http://www.wrox.com/remtitle.cgi?isbn=9781118314074 on the Download Code tab. The code for this chapter is divided into the following major examples:

➤ CustomDialog

➤ Splash

➤ UseWaitCursor

➤ ViewWindowsMessages

USING FORMS

The Visual Basic Windows Form class is a descendant of the Control class. The inheritance trail is Control ⇨ ScrollableControl ⇨ ContainerControl ⇨ Form. That means a form *is* a type of control. Except where overridden, it inherits the properties, methods, and events defined by the Control class. In many ways, a form is just another kind of control like a TextBox or ComboBox.

At the same time, Forms have their own special features that set them apart from other kinds of controls. You usually place controls inside a form, but you rarely place a form inside another form. Forms also play a very central role in most Visual Basic applications. They are the largest graphical unit with which the user interacts directly. The user can minimize, restore, maximize, and close forms. They package the content provided by the other controls so that the user can manage them in a meaningful way.

This chapter describes some of the special features of Windows Forms not provided by other objects. It focuses on different ways that typical applications use forms. For example, it explains how to create shaped forms, build About dialog boxes, and set a form's icon.

The chapter covers the Form object's properties, methods, and events only in passing. For a detailed description of specific Form properties, methods, and events, see Appendix J, "Form Objects."

TRANSPARENCY

The Form object provides a couple of properties that you can use to make a form partially transparent. Opacity determines the form's opaqueness. At design time, the Properties window shows Opacity as a percentage where 100 percent means the form is completely opaque, and 0 percent means that the form is completely transparent. At run time, your program must treat Opacity as a floating-point value between 0 (completely transparent) and 1 (completely opaque).

A program can use an Opacity value less than 100 percent to let the user see what lies below the form. For example, you might build a partially transparent Search dialog box so the user could see the underlying document as a search progresses.

If Opacity is greater than 0 percent, the form behaves normally aside from its ghostlike appearance. The user can click it, interact with its controls, minimize and maximize it, and grab its borders to resize it.

If Opacity is 0 percent, the form is completely transparent and the user can interact with the form only through the keyboard. For example, the user can press the Tab key to move between the form's controls, type text, press the Spacebar to invoke a button that has the focus, and press Enter or Esc to fire the form's Accept and Cancel buttons; however, the form and its controls will not detect mouse clicks. The user also cannot see the form (obviously), so figuring out which control has the focus can be next to impossible.

> **TOO MUCH TRANSLUCENCY**
>
> Most applications don't need translucent forms. A well-designed application allows the user to move windows around so they don't obscure each other. Translucent forms can be confusing, may create extra confusion for users with special needs, and incur a performance penalty. They're an interesting special effect but are not generally necessary.

If Opacity is 2 percent, the form is still invisible, but it recognizes mouse clicks, so it can obscure the windows below.

A second property that helps determine the form's transparency is TransparencyKey. This property is a color that tells Visual Basic which parts of the form should be completely transparent. When the form is rendered, any areas with this color as their background colors are not drawn.

The most common use for TransparencyKey is to create shaped forms or skins. Set the form's FormBorderStyle property to None to remove the borders, title bar, and system buttons. Set the form's BackColor and TransparencyKey properties to a color that you don't want to appear on the form. Then draw the shape you want the form to have in some other color.

Figure 9-1 shows the Smiley example program, which has a form shaped like a smiley face. The form's TransparencyKey and BackColor properties are both red so the form is transparent. The Paint event handler draws the image on the form. These sorts of forms make interesting splash screens and About dialog boxes, although they are often too distracting for use in a program's main user interface.

If you use Opacity and TransparencyKey together, pixels that match TransparencyKey are completely removed and any remaining pixels are shown according to the Opacity value.

ABOUT, SPLASH, AND LOGIN FORMS

The TransparencyKey and Opacity properties enable you to build forms with unusual and interesting shapes. Although these would be distracting if used for the bulk of an application, they can add a little interest to About dialog boxes, splash screens, and login forms.

FIGURE 9-1: The TransparencyKey property lets you make shaped forms such as this one.

These three kinds of forms have quite a bit in common. Usually, they display the application's name, version number, copyright in formation, trademarks, and so forth. They may also display a serial number, the name of the registered user, and a website or phone number where the user can get customer support.

The main difference between these forms is in how the user dismisses them. A splash screen automatically disappears after a few seconds. The user closes an About dialog box by clicking an OK button. A login form closes when the user enters a valid username and password and then clicks OK. It also closes if the user clicks Cancel, although then it doesn't display the main application.

> **REMOVING THE SPLASH**
>
> Sometimes a splash screen is displayed while the application initializes, loads needed data, and otherwise prepares itself for work. In that case, the application removes the splash screen after initialization is complete or a few seconds have passed, whichever comes second.

The forms also differ slightly in the controls they contain. A splash screen needs a Timer to determine when it is time to close the form. An About dialog box needs a single OK button. A login form needs TextBoxes to hold the username and password, two Labels to identify them, and OK and Cancel buttons.

Splash screens and login forms greet the user, so there's no need to provide both in the same application. However, that still leaves you with the task of building two nearly identical forms: splash and About, or login and About. With a little planning, you can use a single form as a splash screen, About dialog box, and login form. At run time, you can add whichever set of controls is appropriate to the form's use. Alternatively, you can build the form with all three sets of controls at design time and then hide the ones you don't need for a particular purpose.

The following code shows how example program Splash, which is available for download on the book's website, displays a form either as a splash screen or as an About dialog box:

```
' Display as a splash screen.
Public Sub ShowSplash()
    Me.tmrUnload.Enabled = True ' The Timer closes the dialog.
    Me.TopMost = True           ' Keep on top of main form.
    Me.Show()                   ' Show non-modally.
End Sub

' Unload the splash screen.
Private Sub tmrUnload_Tick()  Handles tmrUnload.Tick
    Me.Close()
End Sub

' Display as an About dialog.
Public Sub ShowAbout()
    btnOK.Visible = True        ' The OK button closes the dialog.
    Me.ShowDialog()             ' Show modally.
End Sub

' Close the About dialog.
Private Sub btnOK_Click() Handles btnOK.Click
    Me.Close()
End Sub
```

The form contains both a Timer named tmrUnload and an OK button named btnAboutOk. The form's ShowSplash method enables the tmrUnload control and calls Show to display the form. The Timer's Interval property was set to 3,000 milliseconds at design time, so its Tick event fires after three seconds and closes the form.

The ShowAbout method makes the btnOk button visible and calls ShowDialog to display the form modally. A *modal* form holds the application's focus so the user cannot interact with other parts of the application until the modal form is dismissed. When the user clicks the button, the button's Click event handler closes the form.

MOUSE CURSORS

A form's Cursor property determines the kind of mouse cursor the form displays. The Form class inherits the Cursor property from the Control class, so other controls have a Cursor property, too. If you want to give a particular control a special cursor, you can set its Cursor property. For example, if you use a Label control as a hyperlink, you could make it display a pointing hand similar to those displayed by web browsers to let the user know that the control is a hyperlink.

The Cursors class provides several standard cursors as shared values. For example, the following statement sets a form's cursor to the system default cursor (normally an arrow pointing up and to the left):

```
Me.Cursor = Cursors.Default
```

Figure 9-2 shows example program ShowCursors, which is available for download on the book's website, displaying the names and images of the standard cursors defined by the Cursors class in Windows 8. In other versions of Windows, some of the cursors may appear differently.

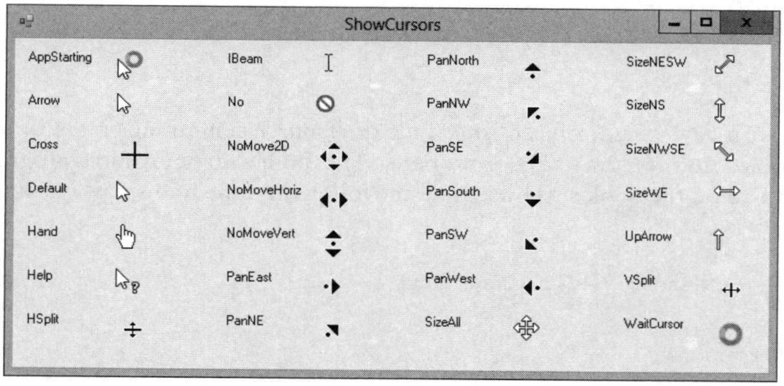

FIGURE 9-2: The Cursors class defines standard cursors.

Unless a control explicitly sets its own cursor, it inherits the cursor of its container. If the control is placed directly on the form, it displays whatever cursor the form is currently displaying. That means you can set the cursor for a form and all of its controls in a single step by setting the form's cursor.

Similarly, if a control is contained within a GroupBox, Panel, or other container control, it inherits the container's cursor. You can set the cursor for all the controls within a container by setting the cursor for the container.

One common use for cursors is to give the user a hint when the application is busy. The program sets its cursor to Cursors.WaitCursor when it begins a long task and then sets it back to Cursors .Default when it finishes. The UseWaitCursor example program, which is available for download on the book's website, uses the following code to display a wait cursor when you click its button:

```
Me.Cursor = Cursors.WaitCursor
' Perform the long task.
...
Me.Cursor = Cursors.Default
```

If the program displays more than one form, it must set the cursors for each form individually. It can set the cursors manually, or it can loop through the My.Application.OpenForms collection.

The UseMultipleWaitCursors example program, which is available for download on the book's website, uses the following SetAllCursors subroutine to display a wait cursor on each of its forms when you click its button:

```
Private Sub SetAllCursors(the_cursor As Cursor)
    For Each frm As Form In My.Application.OpenForms
        frm.Cursor = the_cursor
    Next frm
End Sub
```

The following code shows how the program uses the SetAllCursors subroutine while performing a long task:

```
SetAllCursors(Cursors.WaitCursor)
' Perform the long task.
...
SetAllCursors(Cursors.Default)
```

To use a custom cursor, create a new Cursor object using a file or resource containing cursor or icon data. Then assign the new object to the form's Cursor property. The SmileCursor example program, which is available for download on the book's website, uses the following code to display a custom cursor:

```
Me.Cursor = New Cursor(My.Resources.SmileIcon.Handle)
```

ICONS

Each form in a Visual Basic application has its own icon. A form's icon is displayed on the left side of its title bar, in the system's taskbar, and by applications such as the Task Manager and Windows Explorer.

Some of these applications display icons at different sizes. For example, Windows Explorer uses 32×32 pixel icons for its Large Icons view and 16×16 pixel icons for its other views. Toolbar icons come in 16×16, 24×24, and 32×32 pixel sizes. Windows uses still other sizes for different purposes. For more information on various pixel sizes used by Windows Vista, see http://msdn2 .microsoft.com/aa511280.aspx.

If an icon file doesn't provide whatever size Windows needs, the system shrinks or enlarges an existing image to fit. That may produce an ugly result. To get the best appearance, you should ensure that icon files include at least 16×16 and 32×32 pixel sizes. Depending on the characteristics of your system, you may also want to include other sizes.

The integrated Visual Studio icon editor enables you to define images for various color models ranging from monochrome to 24-bit color, and sizes ranging from 16×16 to 256×256 pixels. It even lets you build icon images with custom sizes such as 32×48 pixels, although it is unlikely that Windows will need to use those.

To use this editor, open Solution Explorer and double-click the My Project entry to open the Project Properties window. Select the Resources tab, open the Add Resource drop-down, and select Add

New Icon. Use the drawing tools to build the icons. Right-click the icon and use the Current Icon Image Types submenu to work with icons of different sizes. Right-click and select New Image type to add new image sizes or color formats.

ICON-A-THON

The integrated icon editor works and is free but it's fairly cumbersome. Many developers use other icon editors such as IconForge (`http://www.favicon.com/iconforge.html`), IconEdit (`http://www.iconedit.com`), IconEdit 2 (no relation between this and IconEdit, `http://www.iconedit2.com`), and RealWorld Cursor Editor (`http://www.rw-designer.com/cursor-maker`). Note that I don't endorse one over the others.

To assign an icon to a form at design time, open the Windows Forms Designer and select the Icon property in the Properties window. Click the ellipsis button on the right and select the icon file that you want to use.

To assign an icon to a form at run time, set the form's Icon property to an Icon object. The following code sets the form's Icon property to an icon resource named MainFormIcon:

```
Me.Icon = My.Resources.MainFormIcon
```

Some applications change their icons to provide an indication of their status. For example, a process-monitoring program might turn its icon red when it detects an error. It could even switch back and forth between two icons to make the icon blink in the taskbar.

Application Icons

Windows displays a form's icon in the form's title bar, in the taskbar, and in the Task Manager. Applications (such as Windows Explorer) that look at the application as a whole rather than at its individual forms display an icon assigned to the application, not to a particular form. To set the application's icon, open Solution Explorer and double-click the My Project entry to open the Project Properties window. On the Application tab, open the Icon drop-down list, and select the icon file that you want to use or select <Browse . . . > to look for the file you want to use.

Notification Icons

Visual Basic applications can display one other kind of icon by using the NotifyIcon control. This control can display an icon in the system tray. The *system tray* (also called the *status area*) is the little area holding small icons that is usually placed in the lower-left part of the taskbar.

The control's Icon property determines the icon that it displays. A typical application will change this icon to give information about the program's status. For example, a program that monitors the system's load could use its system tray icon to give the user an idea of the current load. Notification icons are particularly useful for programs that have no user interface or that run in the background so that the user isn't usually looking at the program's forms.

Notification icons also often include a context menu that appears when the user right-clicks the icon. The items in the menu enable the user to control the application. If the program has no other visible interface, this may be the only way the user can control it.

PROPERTIES ADOPTED BY CHILD CONTROLS

Some properties are adopted by many of the child controls contained in a parent control or in a form. For example, by default, a Label control uses the same background color as the form that contains it. If you change the form's BackColor property, its Label controls change to display the same color. Similarly if a GroupBox contains a Label and you change the GroupBox's BackColor property, its Label changes to match.

Some properties adopted by a form's controls include BackColor, ContextMenu, Cursor, Enabled, Font, and ForeColor. Not all controls use all of these properties, however. For example, a TextBox only matches its form's Enabled and Font properties.

If you explicitly set one of these properties for a control, its value takes precedence over the form's settings. For example, if you set a Label control's BackColor property to red, the control keeps its red background even if you change the Form's BackColor property.

Some of these properties are also not tremendously useful to the Form object itself, but they give guidance to the form's controls. For example, a form doesn't automatically display text on its surface, so it never really uses its Font property. Its Label, TextBox, ComboBox, List, RadioButton, CheckBox, and many other controls adopt the value of this property, however, so the form's Font property serves as a central location to define the font for all of these controls. If you change the form's Font property, even at run time, all of the form's controls change to match. The change applies to all of the form's controls, even those contained within GroupBoxes, Panels, and other container controls.

These properties can also help your application remain consistent both with the controls on the form and with other parts of the application. For example, the following code draws the string "Hello World!" on the form whenever the form needs to be repainted. This code explicitly creates the Comic Sans MS font.

```
Private Sub Form1_Paint(sender As Object, e As PaintEventArgs) Handles Me.Paint
    Using new_font As New Font("Comic Sans MS", 20)
        e.Graphics.DrawString("Hello World!",
            new_font, Brushes.Black, 10, 10)
    End Using
End Sub
```

Rather than making different parts of the program build their own fonts, you can use the forms' Font properties as shown in the following code. This makes the code simpler and ensures that different pieces of code use the same font.

```
Private Sub Form1_Paint(sender As Object, e As PaintEventArgs) Handles Me.Paint
    e.Graphics.DrawString("Hello World!", Me.Font, Brushes.Black, 10, 100)
End Sub
```

As a nice bonus, changing the form's Font property raises a Paint event, so, if the form's font changes, this code automatically runs again and redraws the text using the new font.

PROPERTY RESET METHODS

The Form class provides several methods that reset certain property values to their defaults. The most useful of those methods are ResetBackColor, ResetCursor, ResetFont, ResetForeColor, and ResetText.

If you change one of the corresponding form properties, either at design time or at run time, these methods restore them to their default values. The default values may vary from system to system, but currently on my computer BackColor is reset to Control, Cursor is reset to Default, Font is reset to 8.25-point regular (not bold or italic) Microsoft Sans Serif, ForeColor is reset to ControlText, and Text is reset to an empty string.

Because the controls on a form adopt many of these properties (all except Text), these methods also reset the controls on the form.

> **NOTE** *Of these methods, IntelliSense only shows ResetText even on its All tab. You have type them yourself.*

OVERRIDING WNDPROC

The Windows operating system sends all sorts of messages to applications that tell them about changes in the Windows environment. Messages tell forms to draw, move, resize, hide, minimize, close, respond to changes in the Windows environment, and do just about everything else related to Windows.

All Windows applications have a subroutine tucked away somewhere that responds to those messages. That routine is traditionally called a WindowProc. A Visual Basic .NET form processes these messages in a routine named WndProc. You can override that routine to take special actions when the form receives certain messages.

Example program FixedAspectRatio, which is available on the book's website, looks for WM_SIZING messages. When it finds those messages, it adjusts the form's new width and height so they always have the same aspect ratio (ratio of height to width).

> **WNDPROC WARNING**
>
> When you override the WndProc method, it is very important that the new method calls the base class's version of WndProc as shown in the following statement:
>
> ```
> MyBase.WndProc(m)
> ```
>
> If the program doesn't do this, it won't respond properly to events. For example, the form won't be able to draw itself correctly, resize or move itself, or even create itself properly.

When you override the WndProc method, you must also figure out what messages to intercept, what parameters those messages take, and what you can do to affect them safely. One way to learn about messages is to insert the following WndProc and then perform the action that you want to study (resizing the form, in this example):

```
Protected Overrides Sub WndProc(ByRef m As Message)
    Debug.WriteLine(m.ToString())
    MyBase.WndProc(m)
End Sub
```

Example program ViewWindowsMessages, which is available for download on the book's website, uses this code to display information about the messages it receives.

The following statement shows the result for the WM_SIZING message sent to the form while the user resizes it. It at least shows the message name (WM_SIZING) and its numeric value (hexadecimal 0x214).

```
msg=0x214 (WM_SIZING) hwnd=0x30b8c wparam=0x2 lparam=0x590e29c result=0x0
```

Searching for the message name on the Microsoft website and on other programming sites usually gives you the other information you need to know (such as what m.WParam and m.LParam mean).

Note also that the Form class inherits the WndProc subroutine from the Control class, so all other Windows Forms controls inherit it as well. That means you can override their WndProc routines to change their behaviors.

For example, the following code shows how the NoCtxMnuTextBox class works. This control is derived from the TextBox control. Its WndProc subroutine checks for WM_CONTEXTMENU messages and calls the base class's WndProc for all other messages. By failing to process the WM_CONTEXTMENU message, the control prevents itself from displaying the TextBox control's normal Copy/Cut/Paste context menu when you right-click it.

```
Public Class NoCtxMnuTextBox
    Inherits System.Windows.Forms.TextBox

    Protected Overrides Sub WndProc(ByRef m As Message)
        Const WM_CONTEXTMENU As Integer = &H7B

        If m.Msg <> WM_CONTEXTMENU Then
            MyBase.WndProc(m)
        End If
    End Sub
End Class
```

The NoContextMenu example program, which is available for download on the book's website, uses similar code to display a text box that does not display a context menu when you right-click it.

MRU LISTS

A *Most Recently Used list* (*MRU* list) is a series of menu items (usually at the bottom of an application's File menu) that displays the files most recently accessed by the user. If the user clicks one of these menu items, the program reopens the corresponding file.

By convention, these menu items begin with the accelerator characters 1, 2, 3, and so forth. If you opened the File menu and pressed 2, for example, the program would reopen the second file in the MRU list.

When the user opens a new file or saves a file with a new name, that file is placed at the top of the list. Most applications display up to four items in the MRU list and, if the list ever contains more items, the oldest are removed.

Most applications remove a file from the MRU list if the application tries to open it and fails. For example, if the user selects an MRU menu item but the corresponding file has been removed from the system, the program removes the file's menu item.

Building an MRU list isn't too difficult in Visual Basic. The MruList example program, which is available for download on the book's website, uses the MruList class to manage its MRU list. This class manages a menu that you want to use as an MRU list and updates the menu as the user opens and closes files. For example, if you configure the class to allow four MRU list entries and the user opens a fifth file, the class removes the oldest entry and adds the new one.

The class saves and restores the MRU list in the system's Registry. When the user selects a file from the MRU list, the class raises an event so the main program's code can open the corresponding file. The class also provides an Add method that the main program can use to add new files to the MRU list when the user opens a new file. Download the example and look at its code for more details.

The following code shows how the main MruList program uses the MruList class. This program is a simple text viewer that lets the user open and view files.

```
Public Class Form1
    Private WithEvents m_MruList As MruList

    ' Initialize the MRU list.
    Private Sub Form1_Load() Handles Me.Load
        m_MruList = New MruList("SdiMruList", mnuFile, 4)
    End Sub

    ' Let the user open a file.
    Private Sub mnuFileOpen_Click() Handles mnuFileOpen.Click
        If dlgOpen.ShowDialog() = Windows.Forms.DialogResult.OK Then
            OpenFile(dlgOpen.FileName)
        End If
    End Sub

    ' Open a file selected from the MRU list.
    Private Sub m_MruList_OpenFile(file_name As String) _
     Handles m_MruList.OpenFile
```

```
            OpenFile(file_name)
        End Sub

        ' Open a file and add it to the MRU list.
        Private Sub OpenFile(file_name As String)
            txtContents.Text = File.ReadAll(file_name)
            txtContents.Select(0, 0)
            m_MruList.Add(file_name)
            Me.Text = "[" & New FileInfo(file_name).Name & "]"
        End Sub
    End Class
```

The program declares an MruList variable named m_MruList. It uses the WithEvents keyword so that it is easy to catch the object's OpenFile event.

The form's New event handler initializes the MruList object, passing it the application's name, the File menu, and the number of items the MRU list should hold.

When the user selects the File menu's Open command, the program displays an open file dialog box. If the user selects a file and clicks OK, the program calls subroutine OpenFile, passing it the name of the selected file.

If the user selects a file from the MRU list, the m_MruList_OpenFile event handler executes and calls subroutine OpenFile, passing it the name of the selected file.

Subroutine OpenFile loads the file's contents into the txtContents TextBox control. It then calls the MruList object's Add method, passing it the file's name. It finishes by setting the form's caption to the file's name without its directory path.

You could easily convert the MruList class into a component so you could place it directly on the form. If you give the component ApplicationName, FileMenu, and MaxEntries properties, you can set those values at design time.

DIALOG BOXES

Using a form as a dialog box is easy. Create the form and give it whatever controls it needs to do its job. Add one or more buttons to let the user dismiss the dialog box. Many dialog boxes use OK and Cancel buttons, but you can also use Yes, No, Retry, and others.

You may also want to set the form's FormBorderStyle property to FixedDialog to make the form non-resizable, although that's not mandatory.

Set the form's AcceptButton property to the button that you want to invoke if the user presses the Enter key. Set its CancelButton property to the button you want to invoke when the user presses the Esc key.

The form's DialogResult property indicates the dialog box's return value. If the main program displays the dialog box by using its ShowDialog method, ShowDialog returns the DialogResult value.

The CustomDialog example program, which is available for download on the book's website, uses the following code to display a dialog box and react to its result.

```
Private Sub btnShowDialog_Click() Handles btnShowDialog.Click
    Dim dlg As New dlgEmployee
    If dlg.ShowDialog() = Windows.Forms.DialogResult.OK Then
        MessageBox.Show(
            dlg.txtFirstName.Text & " " &
            dlg.txtLastName.Text)
    Else
        MessageBox.Show("Canceled")
    End If
End Sub
```

This code creates a new instance of the dlgEmployee form and displays it by calling its ShowDialog method. If the user clicks OK, ShowDialog returns DialogResult.OK and the program displays the first and last names entered on the dialog box. If the user clicks the Cancel button, ShowDialog returns DialogResult.Cancel and the program displays the message "Canceled."

If the user clicks the Cancel button or closes the form by using the system menu (or the little "X" in the upper-right corner), the form automatically sets its DialogResult property to Cancel and closes the form.

If the user clicks some other button, your event handler should set DialogResult to an appropriate value. Setting this value automatically closes the form.

> **NOTE** *You can also set a button's DialogResult property to indicate the value that the dialog box should return when the user clicks that button. When the user clicks the button, Visual Basic sets the form's DialogResult property automatically.*

The following code shows how the dlgEmployee form reacts when the user clicks the OK button. It checks whether the first and last name TextBox controls contain non-blank values. If either value is blank, the event handler displays an error message and returns without setting the form's DialogResult property. If both values are non-blank, the code sets DialogResult to OK, and setting DialogResult closes the form.

```
Private Sub btnOk_Click() Handles btnOk.Click
    ' Verify that the first name is present.
    If txtFirstName.Text.Length = 0 Then
        MessageBox.Show(
            "Please enter a First Name",
            "First Name Required",
            MessageBoxButtons.OK,
            MessageBoxIcon.Exclamation)
        txtFirstName.Select()
        Exit Sub
    End If

    ' Verify that the last name is present.
    If txtLastName.Text.Length = 0 Then
        MessageBox.Show(
            "Please enter a Last Name",
```

```
            "Last Name Required",
            MessageBoxButtons.OK,
            MessageBoxIcon.Exclamation)
        txtLastName.Select()
        Exit Sub
    End If

    ' Accept the dialog.
    Me.DialogResult = Windows.Forms.DialogResult.OK
End Sub
```

CANCEL WITHOUT EVENTS

Note that the dialog box doesn't need an event handler for the Cancel button. If you set the form's CancelButton property to the button and if the user clicks it, Visual Basic automatically sets the form's DialogResult to Cancel and closes the form.

WIZARDS

One common type of dialog box is called a wizard. A *wizard* is a form that guides the user through a series of steps to do something. For example, building a database connection is complicated, so Visual Basic provides a data connection configuration wizard that helps the user enter the correct information for different kinds of databases. When it finishes, the wizard adds a connection object to the current form.

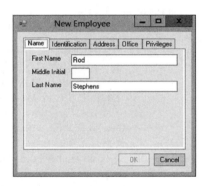

FIGURE 9-3: A wizard guides the user through the steps of some complicated task.

Figure 9-3 shows one kind of wizard. The user enters data on each tab and then moves on to the next one. This wizard asks the user to enter an employee's name, identification (Social Security number and Employee ID), address and phone number, office location and extension, and privileges. Many tabbed wizards also include Next and Previous buttons to help you move from one tab to another.

When the user has filled in all the fields, the wizard enables the OK button. When the user clicks the OK or Cancel button, control returns to the main program, which handles the result just as it handles any other dialog box.

Figure 9-4 shows a different style of wizard. Instead of tabs, it uses buttons to let the user move through pages of fields. The wizard enables a button only when the user has filled in the necessary information on the previous

FIGURE 9-4: This wizard uses buttons instead of tabs to move through its pages of data.

page. In Figure 9-4, the Office button is disabled because the user has not filled in all the fields on the Address page.

The button style is sometimes better at helping the user fill in all of the required fields because the user must finish filling in one page before moving on to the next. In a tabbed wizard, the user might leave a required field blank or use an incorrect format (for example, an invalid phone number) on the first tab and not realize it until clicking the OK button.

SUMMARY

Although forms are just one kind of control, they have some very special characteristics. They form the basic pieces of an application that sit on the desktop, and they have many properties, methods, and events that set them apart from other controls. Appendix J provides more information about form properties, methods, and events.

This chapter described some of the more typical uses of forms. It explained how to build About, splash, and login forms; manage a form's mouse cursor and icon; override WndProc to intercept a form's Windows messages; and make dialog boxes and wizards. After you master these tasks, you can build the forms that implement the large-scale pieces of an application.

Chapters 7, 8, and 9 described Windows Forms controls and the Form class. The next three chapters provide corresponding information for Windows Presentation Foundation (WPF) controls and forms. Chapter 10, "Selecting WPF Controls," starts by providing an overview of WPF controls and giving tips on which you might like to use for given purposes, much as Chapter 7 did for Windows Forms controls.

10

Selecting WPF Controls

WROX.COM CODE DOWNLOADS FOR THIS CHAPTER

The wrox.com code downloads for this chapter are found at `http://www.wrox.com/remtitle .cgi?isbn=9781118314074` on the Download Code tab. The code for this chapter includes several examples that demonstrate particularly useful WPF control features. These examples include the following:

➤ DrawingShapes

➤ EllipseClick

➤ FormImage

➤ UseExpander

➤ UseScrollViewer

WPF CONTROLS AND CODE

Windows Presentation Foundation (WPF) provides a whole new method for building user interfaces. Although it bears a superficial resemblance to Windows Forms, WPF provides new controls, a new event architecture, and a new foundation for building and interacting with properties.

WPF also provides tools for separating the user interface from the code behind the interface so that the two pieces can potentially be built by separate user interface designers and Visual Basic developers. It includes a new *eXtensible Application Markup Language (XAML,* pronounced "zammel") that lets you build a user interface by using declarative statements rather than executable code. XAML lets you determine the size, position, and other properties of the WPF controls on a form. It lets you define styles that can be shared among many controls, and it lets you define transformations and animations that affect the controls.

As is the case in Windows Forms applications, controls play a central role in WPF applications. Different kinds of controls give information to the user (Label, StatusBar, TreeView, ListView, Image) and organize the information so that it's easy to understand (Border, StackPanel, DockPanel, TabControl). They enable the user to enter data (TextBox, TextBlock, ComboBox, PasswordBox), select options (RadioButton, CheckBox, ListBox), and control the application (Button, Menu, Slider).

To make an application as effective as possible, you should match controls with your application's needs. Although many controls may work for a particular task, some controls usually work better than others. For example, you could display status information by changing a button's caption, but that's not really what buttons do best. A label in a status bar is usually a better way to give the user status information because the user will expect and understand it. Users generally don't expect to see status information in a button with changing text.

This chapter briefly describes the most common WPF controls so you can understand which controls work best for different purposes. To help you find the controls you need, the sections later in this chapter group controls by their general function. For example, if you need to display status to the user, look in the section "Providing Feedback."

I provide only brief descriptions of the WPF controls in this chapter, and some tips that can help you decide which control to use for different purposes. The following chapter, "Using WPF Controls," covers the controls in much greater detail, describing each control's most useful properties, methods, and events.

FOR MORE INFORMATION

This chapter and those that follow provide only the briefest glance at WPF. They explain enough to get you started, but for greater detail and more in-depth information, see a book about WPF such as my book *WPF Programmer's Reference: Windows Presentation Foundation with C# 2010 and .NET 4.0* (Wrox, Stephens, 2010, http://www.amazon.com/exec/obidos/ASIN/0470477229/vbhelper).

CONTROLS OVERVIEW

You can group WPF controls into several categories. Some of these correspond naturally to the purposes of Windows Forms controls. Other categories play a more important role in WPF than they do in Windows Forms applications.

In particular, WPF controls rely heavily on layout controls that arrange and organize the controls that they contain. Windows Forms developers often simply arrange controls on a form with fixed sizes and positions. A WPF application is more likely to arrange the controls in a hierarchy of StackPanel and Grid controls and let those controls arrange their contents.

The recent proliferation of screen formats makes this idea more important than ever. If you write programs running on everything from traditional desktop systems to Windows 8 tablets, your programs will need the ability to rearrange their controls automatically. A smartphone can even switch from portrait to landscape orientation while a program is running, so the program must respond to make effective use of the available space. I won't claim that most applications should be able to run on a tiny phone screen or a 17″ laptop without any changes, but good use of container controls can simplify some of the changes you'll need to make.

The following sections describe the main categories of WPF controls. The example programs for this chapter, which are available on the book's website, demonstrate many of the controls' basic uses.

CONCEALED CONTROLS

Not all of the controls described here are available by default when you create a new WPF application. You need to add some of these controls to the Toolbox before you can use them. To add a control that is missing, right-click a Toolbox section and select Choose Items. On the Choose Toolbox Items dialog box, select the WPF Components tab, check the boxes next to the controls that you want, and click OK.

Note, also, that some additional controls may be available in the Choose Toolbox Items dialog box that are not described here. The following sections describe only the most commonly used controls.

CONTAINING AND ARRANGING CONTROLS

Layout controls determine the arrangement of the controls that they contain. For example, they may arrange controls vertically, horizontally, or in rows and columns.

The preferred style for WPF control arrangement is to make container controls determine the positions of their children and let the children take advantage of whatever space is allowed. This can be particularly useful for localized applications where you cannot easily predict how much space a control will need in a particular language.

For example, suppose a form contains a StackPanel control. The StackPanel contains several buttons that launch application dialog boxes. If you remove the buttons' Width properties, the buttons automatically size themselves to fit the StackPanel horizontally. Now if you need to make the buttons wider to hold text for a new language, you can simply widen the form. The StackPanel widens to fill the form and the buttons widen to fit the StackPanel.

Example program ResizingButtons, which is available for download on the book's website, demonstrates buttons with fixed heights but widths that resize when their container resizes.

> **NOTE** *In a Windows Forms application, you can achieve a similar effect by using Anchor and Dock properties.*

Layout controls are also important because they can hold lots of other controls. Some of the WPF controls can hold only a single content item. For example, an Expander can hold only a single item. However, if you place another layout control such as a StackPanel inside the Expander, you can then place lots of other controls inside the StackPanel.

The following table briefly describes the WPF controls that are intended mainly to contain and arrange other controls.

CONTROL	PURPOSE
Border[1]	Provides a visible border or background to the contents.
BulletDecorator[2]	Contains two children. The first is used as a bullet and the second is aligned with the first. For example, you can use this to align bullet images next to labels. (See example program UseBulletDecorator, available for download on the book's website.)
Canvas	Creates an area in which you can explicitly position children by specifying their Width, Height, Canvas.Left, and Canvas.Top properties. (See example program UseCanvas, available for download on the book's website.)
DockPanel	Docks its children to its left, right, top, or bottom much as the Dock property does in a Windows Forms application. If the control's LastChildFill property is True, the control makes its last child control fill the remaining space. (See example program UseDockPanel, available for download on the book's website.)
Expander[1]	Displays a header with an expanded/collapsed indicator. The user can click the header or indicator to expand or collapse the control's single content item. (See example program UseExpander, available for download on the book's website.)
Grid	Displays children in rows and columns. This is somewhat similar to the Windows Forms TableLayoutPanel control. Grid is one of the most useful container controls.
GridSplitter	Enables the user to resize two rows or columns in a Grid control.
GridView	Displays data in columns within a ListView control.
GroupBox[1]	Displays a border and caption much as a Windows Forms GroupBox control does.

CONTROL	PURPOSE
Panel	Panel is the parent class for Canvas, DockPanel, Grid, TabPanel, ToolbarOverflowPanel, UniformGrid, StackPanel, VirtualizingPanel, and WrapPanel. Usually you should use one of those classes instead of Panel, but you can also use Panel to implement your own custom panel controls.
ScrollViewer[1]	Provides vertical and horizontal scroll bars for a single content element. (See example program UseScrollViewer, available for download on the book's website.)
Separator	Separates two controls inside a layout control. (See example program UseSeparator, available for download on the book's website.)
StackPanel	Arranges children in a single row or column. If there are too many controls, those that don't fit are clipped. StackPanel is one of the most useful container controls.
TabControl	Arranges children in tabs. TabItem controls contain the items that should be displayed in the tabs. (See example program UseTabControl, available for download on the book's website.)
TabItem[1]	Holds the content for one TabControl tab.
Viewbox[1]	Stretches its single child to fill the Viewbox. The Stretch property determines whether the control stretches its child uniformly (without changing the width-to-height ratio). (See example program UseViewbox, available for download on the book's website.)
Virtualizing StackPanel	Generates child items to hold items that can fit in the available area. For example, when working with a ListBox bound to a data source, the VirtualizingStackPanel generates only the items that will fit within the ListBox. If the control is not bound to a data source, this control behaves like a StackPanel.
WrapPanel	Arranges children in rows/columns depending on its Orientation property. When a row/column is full, the next child moves to a new row/column. This is similar to the Windows Forms FlowLayoutPanel control. (See example program UseWrapPanel, available for download on the book's website.)

[1]This control can hold only a single child.

[2]This control should hold exactly two children. Controls with no footnote can hold any number of children.

Many of the layout controls have the ability to resize their children if you let them. For example, if you place a Button inside a Grid control's first row and column, by default the Button resizes when its row and column resize. The control's Margin property determines how far from the cell's edges the Button's edges lie.

If a child control explicitly defines its Width and Height properties, those properties override the parent's arrangement policy. For example, if you set Width and Height for a Button inside a Grid, the Button does not resize when its Grid cell does.

To get the effect that you want, consider how the control's Margin, Width, and Height properties interact with the parent layout control.

MAKING SELECTIONS

Selection controls enable the user to choose values. If you use them carefully, you can reduce the chances of the user making an invalid selection, so you can reduce the amount of error-handling code you need to write.

The following table briefly describes the WPF controls that allow the user to select choices.

CONTROL	PURPOSE
CheckBox	Lets the user select an item or not. Each CheckBox choice is independent of all others.
ComboBox	Displays items in a drop-down list. ComboBoxItem controls contain the items displayed in the list. (See example program UseComboBox, available for download on the book's website.)
ComboBoxItem[1]	Holds the content for one ComboBox item.
ListBox	Displays items in a list. ListBoxItem controls contain the items displayed in the list. The control automatically displays scroll bars when needed. (See example program UseListBox, available for download on the book's website.)
ListBoxItem[1]	Holds the content for one ListBox item.
RadioButton	Lets the user pick from among a set of options. If the user checks one RadioButton, all others with the same parent become unchecked. (See example program UseRadioButtons, available for download on the book's website.)
ScrollBar	Allows the user to drag a "thumb" to select a numeric value. Usually scroll bars are used internally by other controls such as the ScrollViewer, and your applications should use a Slider instead. (See example program UseScrollBar, available for download on the book's website.)
Slider	Allows the user to drag a "thumb" to select a numeric value. Similar to the Windows Forms TrackBar control. (See example program UseSlider, available for download on the book's website.)

[1]This control can hold only a single child.

ENTERING DATA

Sometimes, it is impractical to use the selection controls described in the previous section. For example, the user cannot reasonably enter biographical data or comments using a Combo Box or RadioButton. In those cases, you can provide a text control where the user can type information.

The following table briefly describes the WPF controls that allow the user to enter text.

CONTROL	PURPOSE
PasswordBox	Similar to a TextBox but displays a mask character instead of the characters that the user types. (See example program UsePasswordBox, available for download on the book's website.)
RichTextBox	Similar to a TextBox but contains text in the form of a document object. See the section "Managing Documents" later in this chapter for more information on documents.
TextBox	Allows the user to enter simple text. Optionally can allow carriage returns and tabs, and can wrap text.

DISPLAYING DATA

These controls are used primarily to display data to the user. The following table briefly describes these WPF controls.

CONTROL	PURPOSE
Label	Displays non-editable text.
TextBlock	Displays more complex non-editable text. This control's contents can include inline tags to indicate special formatting. Tags can include AnchoredBlock, Bold, Hyperlink, InlineUIContainer, Italic, LineBreak, Run, Span, and Underline.
TreeView	Displays hierarchical data in a tree-like format similar to the directory display provided by Windows Explorer.

PROVIDING FEEDBACK

The following controls provide feedback to the user. Like the controls that display data in the previous section, these controls are intended to give information to the user and not to interact with the user. The following table briefly describes these WPF controls.

CONTROL	PURPOSE
Popup	Displays content in a window above another control. Usually you can use the Tooltip and ContextMenu controls instead of a Popup. (See example program UsePopup, available for download on the book's website.)
ProgressBar	Indicates the fraction of a long task that has been completed. If the task is performed synchronously, the user is left staring at the form while it completes. The ProgressBar lets the user know that the operation is not stuck. (See example program UseProgressBar, available for download on the book's website.)
StatusBar	Displays a container at the bottom of the form where you can place controls holding status information. Though you can place anything inside a StatusBar, this control is intended to hold summary status information, not tools. Generally, Menus, ComboBoxes, Buttons, Toolbars, and other controls that let the user manipulate the application do not belong in a StatusBar. (See example program UseStatusBar, available for download on the book's website.)
StatusBarItem[1]	Holds the content for one StatusBar item.
ToolTip	Displays a tooltip. To give a control a simple textual tooltip, set its Tooltip property. Use the Tooltip control to build more complex tooltips. For example, a Tooltip control might contain a StackPanel that holds other controls. (See example program UseToolTip, available for download on the book's website.)

[1]This control can hold only a single child.

INITIATING ACTION

Every kind of control responds to events, so every control can initiate an action. In practice, however, users expect only certain kinds of controls to perform actions. For example, they generally don't expect the application to launch into a time-consuming calculation when the mouse moves over a label.

The following table summarizes controls that normally initiate action.

CONTROL	PURPOSE
Button[1]	Raises a Click event that the program can catch to perform an action. (See example program UseButtonRepeatButton, available for download on the book's website.)
ContextMenu	Displays a context menu for other controls. Normally the ContextMenu contains MenuItem controls. (See example program UseMenuContextMenu, available for download on the book's website.)

CONTROL	PURPOSE
Menu	Displays a menu for the form. Normally, the Menu contains MenuItem controls representing the top-level menus. Those items contain other MenuItem controls representing commands. (See example program UseMenuContextMenu, available for download on the book's website.)
MenuItem	Contains an item in a ContextMenu or Menu.
PrintDialog	Displays a standard Windows print dialog. You shouldn't place a PrintDialog on a window. Instead use code to build and display the PrintDialog. (See example program UsePrintDialog, available for download on the book's website.)
RepeatButton[1]	Acts as a Button that raises its Click event repeatedly when it is pressed and held down. (See example program UseButtonRepeatButton, available for download on the book's website.)
ToolBar	Contains items. Normally, the control sits across the top of the form and contains command items such as buttons and combo boxes. (See example program UseToolBar, available for download on the book's website.)
ToolBarTray	Contains ToolBars and allows the user to drag them into new positions. (See example program UseToolBar, available for download on the book's website.)

[1]This control can hold only a single child.

PRESENTING GRAPHICS AND MEDIA

Any WPF control can display an image. Example program FormImage, which is available for download on the book's website, uses the following XAML code to fill a Grid control's background:

```
<Window x:Class="MainWindow"
 xmlns="http://schemas.microsoft.com/winfx/2006/xaml/presentation"
 xmlns:x=http://schemas.microsoft.com/winfx/2006/xaml
 Title="FormImage" Height="300" Width="300">
    <Window.Resources>
        <ImageBrush ImageSource="smile.bmp" x:Key="brSmile" />
    </Window.Resources>
    <Grid Background="{StaticResource brSmile}">

    </Grid>
</Window>
```

Although a Grid control can display an image or other graphic, its real purpose is to arrange other controls. The following table describes controls whose main purpose is to present graphics and media.

CONTROL	PURPOSE
Ellipse	Displays an ellipse.
Image	Displays a bitmap image, for example, from a .bmp, .jpg, or .png file. Can optionally stretch the image with or without distortion.
Line	Draws a line segment.
MediaElement	Presents audio and video. To let you control the media, it provides Play, Pause, and Stop methods, and Volume and SpeedRatio properties. (See example program UseMediaElement, available for download on the book's website.)
Path	Draws a series of drawing instructions.
Polygon	Draws a closed polygon.
Polyline	Draws a series of connected line segments.
Rectangle	Draws a rectangle, optionally with rounded corners.

The shape drawing objects (Ellipse, Line, Path, Polygon, Polyline, and Rectangle) all provide Stroke, StrokeThickness, and Fill properties to let you control their appearance. Although these controls are primarily intended to draw simple (or not so simple) shapes, like any other control they provide a full assortment of events. For example, they provide an IsMouseOver property and a MouseUp event that you can use to make these objects behave like simple buttons.

Example program DrawingShapes, which is available for download on the book's website, demonstrates several of these shape controls. Program EllipseClick, which is also available for download, uses triggers to change the color of an Ellipse when the mouse is over it, and displays a message when you click the Ellipse.

PROVIDING NAVIGATION

The Frame control provides support for navigation through external websites or the application's pages. Use the control's Navigate method to display a web page or a XAML page. The Frame provides back and forward arrows to let the user navigate through the pages visited.

Example program UseFrame, which is available for download on the book's website, uses a Frame control to provide navigation between two Page objects.

MANAGING DOCUMENTS

WPF includes three different kinds of documents: flow documents, fixed documents, and XPS documents. These different kinds of documents provide support for high-end text viewing and printing.

> **XPS EXPLAINED**
>
> XPS (XML Paper Specification) is a Microsoft standard that defines fixed-format documents similar to PDF files. An XPS reader can view an XPS file but will not reformat it as a web browser might rearrange the text on a web page. For more information, see the section "XPS Documents" in Chapter 11.

The following table summarizes the controls that WPF provides for viewing these kinds of documents.

CONTROL	PURPOSE
DocumentViewer	Displays fixed documents page by page.
FlowDocument PageViewer	Displays a flow document one page at a time. If the control is wide enough, it may display multiple columns although it still displays only one page at a time.
FlowDocument Reader	Displays flow documents in one of three modes. When in single page mode, it acts as a FlowDocumentReader. When in scrolling mode, it acts as a FlowDocumentScrollViewer. In book reading mode, it displays two pages side by side much as a real book does.
FlowDocument ScollViewer	Displays an entire flow document in a single long scrolling page and provides scroll bars to let the user move through the document.

DIGITAL INK

Digital ink controls provide support for stylus input from tablet PCs (where you use a plastic stylus similar to a pen to draw right on a tablet PC's touch screen). Normally you would only use digital ink in a tablet PC application where the user is expected to enter data by drawing on the screen with a stylus. These applications usually provide text recognition to understand what the user is writing. They also use the stylus to perform the same operations they would perform with the mouse on a desktop system. For example, they let you tap to click buttons, and tap and drag to move items.

Although ink controls are most useful for tablet PCs, WPF includes two ink controls that you can use in any Visual Basic application.

CONTROL	PURPOSE
InkCanvas	Displays or captures ink strokes.
InkPresenter	Displays ink strokes.

SUMMARY

Controls are the link between the user and the application. They allow the application to give information to the user, and they allow the user to control the application.

This chapter briefly described the most important WPF controls grouped by category. You can use the categories to help you decide which controls to use for a particular situation. If the user must select an item, consider the controls in the "Making Selections" section. If the application needs to display status information, look at the controls in the "Providing Feedback" section.

This chapter gave only a brief introduction to the WPF controls and provided some hints about each control's purpose. Chapter 11, "Using WPF Controls," describes the controls in greater detail. It explains the most important properties, methods, and events provided by the most useful WPF controls.

11

Using WPF Controls

WROX.COM CODE DOWNLOADS FOR THIS CHAPTER

The wrox.com code downloads for this chapter are found at http://www.wrox.com/remtitle
.cgi?isbn=9781118314074 on the Download Code tab. The code for this chapter includes several
examples that demonstrate particularly useful WPF features. These examples include the following:

- ➤ ButtonTemplate
- ➤ Calculator
- ➤ ProceduralAnimatedButton
- ➤ ProceduralCalculator
- ➤ SpinAndGrowButton

WPF CONTROLS

The code behind WPF controls is the same as the code behind Windows Forms controls. That means
that everything the earlier chapters have explained about applications, forms, controls, Visual Basic
code, error handling, drawing, printing, reports, and so forth still work almost exactly as before.

Chapter 10, "Selecting WPF Controls," briefly described the most common WPF controls, grouped
by category to help you pick the control that best suits a particular task. This chapter provides more
detail about WPF. It explains some of the more important concepts that underlie WPF. It also gives
more detail about how particular controls work and tells how you can use them in your applications.

WPF is a huge topic. It basically reproduces all of the functionality of Windows Forms programming, and then some. This chapter cannot hope to cover all of the concepts, tools, and techniques used by WPF. Instead, it introduces some of the more important concepts and explains how to build basic WPF forms.

WPF CONCEPTS

WPF applications are similar in concept to Windows Forms applications in many respects. Both display a form or window that contains controls. Controls in both systems provide properties, methods, and events that determine the control's appearance and behavior.

Windows Forms applications use a set of controls provided by the System.Windows.Forms namespace. WPF applications use a different set of controls in the System.Windows .Controls namespace. Many of these controls serve similar functions to those used by Windows Forms applications, but they provide a different set of capabilities. For example, both namespaces have buttons, labels, combo boxes, and check boxes, but their appearances and abilities are different.

WPF uses these similar, but different, controls for two main reasons:

➤ To take better advantage of the graphics capabilities of modern computer hardware and software. The new controls can more easily provide graphical effects such as transparent or translucent backgrounds, gradient shading, rotation, two- and three-dimensional appearance, multimedia, and other effects.

➤ To provide a greater separation between the user interface and the code behind it. The following sections describe this idea and some of the other key WPF concepts in greater detail.

Separation of User Interface and Code

The idea of separating the user interface from the code isn't new. Visual Basic developers have been building *thin user interface* applications for years. Here, the user interface contains as little code as possible, and calls routines written in libraries to do most of the work.

Unfortunately, the code that calls those libraries sits inside the same file that defines the user interface, at least in Windows Forms applications. That means you cannot completely separate the code from the user interface. For example, if one developer wants to modify the user interface, another developer cannot simultaneously modify the code behind it.

WPF separates the user interface from the code more completely. The program stores the user interface definition in a XAML file.

Associated with a XAML file is a code file containing Visual Basic code. It contains any code you write to respond to events and manipulate the controls much as Windows Forms code can. Unlike the case with Windows Forms, WPF keeps the user interface definition and the code behind it in two separate files so, in theory at least, different developers can work on the user interface and the code at the same time. For example, a graphics designer can use the Expression Blend design tool to build the user interface, defining the forms' labels, menus, buttons, and other controls. Then a Visual Basic developer can attach code to handle the controls' events.

> **NOTE** *Expression Blend is fairly expensive, although it's included in Expression Studio and is available to MSDN subscribers. It provides some useful tools that are missing from Visual Studio, however, such as tools to record animations. If you frequently need to build property animations, you should give it a try.*
>
> *You can learn more about Expression Blend and download a trial version at* `http://expression.microsoft.com`.

Because the user interface definition is separate from the code behind it, the graphic designer can later edit the XAML to rearrange controls, change their appearance, and otherwise modify the user interface while the code behind it should still work unchanged.

WPF Control Hierarchies

In a WPF application, the Window class plays a role similar to the one played by a Form in a Windows Forms application. However, a Form can contain any number of controls while a Window can contain only one. If you want a WPF form to display more than one control, you must first give it some kind of container control, and then place other controls inside that one.

For example, when you create a WPF application, its Window initially contains a Grid control that can hold any number of other controls, optionally arranged in rows and columns. Other container controls include Canvas, DockPanel, DocumentViewer, Frame, StackPanel, and TabControl.

The result is a tree-like control hierarchy with a single Window object serving as the root element. This matches the hierarchical nature of XAML. Because XAML is a form of XML, and XML files must have a single root element, XAML files must also have a single root element. When you look at XAML files later in this chapter, you will find that they begin with a Window element that contains all other elements.

Many non-container controls can hold only a single element, and that element is determined by the control's Content property. For example, you can set a Button control's Content property to the text that you want to display.

A control's Content property can have only a single value, but that value does not need to be something simple such as text. For example, Figure 11-1 shows a Button containing a Grid control that holds three labels.

FIGURE 11-1: This Button contains a Grid that holds three labels.

WPF IN THE IDE

The Visual Studio IDE includes editors for manipulating WPF Window classes and controls. Although many of the details are different, the basic operation of the IDE is the same whether you are building a Windows Forms application or a WPF application. For example, you can use the WPF Window Designer to edit a WPF window. You can select controls from the Toolbox and place them on the window much as you place controls on a Windows Form.

Despite their broad similarities, the Windows Forms Designer and the WPF Window Designer differ in detail. Although the Properties window displays properties for WPF controls much as it does for Windows Forms controls, many of the property values are not displayed in similar ways.

The window represents many Boolean properties with check boxes. It represents other properties that take enumerated values with combo boxes where you can select a value or type one in (if you know the allowed values).

Future Visual Studio releases may make Expression Blend more consistent with Visual Studio, although some more advanced features (such as animation recording) are likely to remain only in Expression Blend to encourage developers to buy it.

Note that the editors in the Properties window merely build the XAML code that defines the user interface. You can always edit the XAML manually to achieve effects that the Properties window does not support directly.

The following sections explain how to write XAML code and the Visual Basic code behind it.

Editing XAML

Figure 11-2 shows the IDE displaying a new WPF project. Most of the areas should look familiar from Windows Forms development. The Toolbox on the left contains tools that you can place on the window in the middle area. Solution Explorer on the right shows the files used by the application. The Properties window shows property values for the currently selected control in the middle. The selected object in Figure 11-2 is the main Window, so the top of the Properties window shows its type: Window.

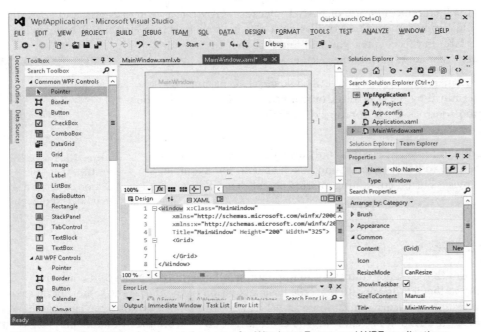

FIGURE 11-2: The IDE looks almost the same for Windows Forms and WPF applications.

One large difference between the IDE's appearance when building a WPF application versus a Windows Forms application is the central editor. In a Windows Forms application, you edit a form with the Windows Forms Designer. In a WPF application, you use the graphical XAML editor shown in Figure 11-2 to edit a Window object's XAML code. The upper half of this area shows a graphical editor where you can drag controls from the Toolbox much as you design a Windows Form. The lower part of the editor shows the resulting XAML code.

If you look closely at Figure 11-2, you can see the Window element that includes the rest of the file. When you first build an application, the Window object's element contains a single Grid control.

Usually, it is easiest to build WPF Window objects by using the graphical editor and the Toolbox. When you select a control in the graphical editor, you can view and modify its properties in the Properties window. If you can't get a desired effect by using the Properties window, you can use the XAML view at the bottom to edit the XAML code by hand. For example, the Properties window won't let you set a non-container control's Content property to another control, but you can do this easily with XAML code. For example, to place a Grid inside a Button control, simply type the Grid control's definition between the Button control's start and end tags.

The graphical editor and the Properties window don't give you access to all of XAML's features, but they do let you build a basic user interface for WPF applications. Once you have defined the window's basic structure, you can use XAML to fine-tune the result.

Editing Visual Basic Code

Each XAML file is associated with a Visual Basic code file. When you first create a WPF project, that file is opened by default. If you look closely at the central designer in Figure 11-2, you'll see that the XAML file MainWindow.xaml is open and visible in the designer. Another tab contains the corresponding Visual Basic file `MainWindow.xaml.vb`. Click that tab to view the Visual Basic source code.

The following text shows the Visual Basic source code initially created for a XAML file:

```
Class MainWindow

End Class
```

You can add event handlers to this file just as you can add event handlers to Windows Forms code. Use the left drop-down to select a control or MainWindow Events. Then use the right drop-down list to select an event for that object.

One difference between WPF and Windows Forms event programming is that WPF controls are not given names by default so they don't appear in the code editor's left drop-down list. If you want to use the editor's drop-downs to create an event handler for a control, you must give the control a name either by using the Properties window or by typing it into the XAML code.

Another way to create an event handler is to double-click a control on the WPF Window Designer.

In addition to event handlers, you can also add non-event handler subroutines and functions to the Visual Basic code file just as you can in any other Visual Basic file.

Inside the Visual Basic code file, you can get and set control properties and call control methods, just as you can in a Windows Forms project.

Anything you can do by using the WPF graphical designer or declaratively with XAML you can also do procedurally with Visual Basic code. The following section, "XAML Features," describes some of the things that you can do with XAML and shows examples. The section "Procedural WPF" later in this chapter explains how you can implement some of the same features with Visual Basic code instead of XAML.

XAML FEATURES

XAML is a form of XML that defines certain allowed combinations of XML elements. For example, a XAML file should have a single root element that represents a Window. That object can have a single child element that is normally a container. The container can hold several children with specifically defined properties such as Width and Height.

XAML is a very complicated language, and many of its features are available only in certain places within the file. For example, inside a Button element you can place attributes such as Background, BorderThickness, Margin, Width, Height, and Content. The XAML text editor provides IntelliSense that makes figuring out what is allowed in different places easier, but building a XAML file can still be quite challenging.

> **NOTE** *One good way to learn XAML is to go online and search for examples. The Microsoft website has lots of examples, as do several other sites. Although the documentation isn't always easy to use, the examples can help you learn specific techniques. Some good places to start include the XAML overview at* `http://msdn2.microsoft.com/ms752059.aspx` *and the Windows Presentation Foundation development page at* `http://msdn2.microsoft.com/ms754130 .aspx.` *My book* WPF Programmer's Reference *(Wrox, Stephens, 2010,* `http://www.amazon.com/exec/obidos/ASIN/0470477229/vbhelper`*) also provides lots of examples of useful techniques.*

The following sections describe some of the basic building blocks of a XAML application. They explain how to build objects; how to use resources, styles, and templates to make objects consistent and easier to modify; and how to use transformations and animations to make objects interactive. The section "Procedural WPF" later in this chapter explains how to do these things in Visual Basic code instead of XAML.

Objects

WPF objects are represented by XML elements in the XAML file. Their properties are represented either by attributes within the base elements or as separate elements within the main element.

For example, the following XAML code shows a Window containing a Grid object. The Grid element contains a Background attribute that makes the object's background red.

```
<Window x:Class="MainWindow"
 xmlns="http://schemas.microsoft.com/winfx/2006/xaml/presentation"
 xmlns:x="http://schemas.microsoft.com/winfx/2006/xaml"
 Title="MainWindow" Height="235" Width="300">
   <Grid Background="Red">

   </Grid>
</Window>
```

More complicated properties must be set in their own sub-elements. The following code shows a similar Grid that has a linear gradient background:

```
<Window x:Class="MainWindow"
 xmlns="http://schemas.microsoft.com/winfx/2006/xaml/presentation"
 xmlns:x="http://schemas.microsoft.com/winfx/2006/xaml"
 Title="MainWindow" Height="235" Width="300">
   <Grid>
     <Grid.Background>
       <LinearGradientBrush StartPoint="0,0" EndPoint="1,1">
       <GradientStop Color="Red" Offset="0.0" />
       <GradientStop Color="White" Offset="0.5" />
       <GradientStop Color="Blue" Offset="1.0" />
     </LinearGradientBrush>
   </Grid.Background>
   </Grid>
</Window>
```

Instead of using a Background attribute, the Grid element contains a Grid.Background element. That, in turn, contains a LinearGradientBrush element that defines the background. The StartPoint and EndPoint attributes indicate that the gradient should start at the upper-left corner of the grid (0, 0) and end at the lower right (1, 1). The GradientStop elements inside the brush's definition set the colors that the brush should display at different fractions of the way through the gradient. In this example, the gradient starts red, changes to white halfway through, and changes to blue at the end.

> **NOTE** *You cannot define an object's Background property more than once. If you include a Background attribute and a Grid.Background element for the same grid, the XAML editor complains.*

Object elements often contain other elements that further define the object. The following code defines a grid that has two rows and three columns. (From now on I'm leaving out the Window element to save space.) The rows each occupy 50 percent of the grid's height. The first column is 50 pixels wide and the other two columns each take up 50 percent of the remaining width.

```
<Grid>
  <Grid.RowDefinitions>
    <RowDefinition Height="50*" />
    <RowDefinition Height="50*" />
  </Grid.RowDefinitions>
  <Grid.ColumnDefinitions>
    <ColumnDefinition Width="50" />
    <ColumnDefinition Width="50*" />
    <ColumnDefinition Width="50*" />
  </Grid.ColumnDefinitions>
</Grid>
```

When you use a * in measurements, the control divides its height or width proportionally among items that contain a *. For example, if a grid has two rows with height 50*, they each get half of the control's height. If the two rows have heights 10* and 20*, the first is half as tall as the second.

If the control also contains items without a *, their space is taken out first. For example, suppose a grid defines rows with heights 10, 20*, and 30*. In that case the first row has height 10, the second row gets 20/50 of the remaining height, and the third row gets the rest.

An object element's body can also contain content for the object. In some cases, the content is simple text. The following example defines a Button object that has the caption Click Me:

```
<Button Margin="2,2,2,2" Name="btnClickMe">Click Me</Button>
```

An object's content may also contain other objects. The following code defines a grid with three rows and three columns holding nine buttons:

```
<Grid>
  <Grid.RowDefinitions>
    <RowDefinition Height="33*" />
    <RowDefinition Height="33*" />
    <RowDefinition Height="33*" />
  </Grid.RowDefinitions>
  <Grid.ColumnDefinitions>
    <ColumnDefinition Width="33*" />
    <ColumnDefinition Width="33*" />
    <ColumnDefinition Width="33*" />
  </Grid.ColumnDefinitions>
  <Button Grid.Row="0" Grid.Column="0" Margin="5">0, 0</Button>
  <Button Grid.Row="0" Grid.Column="1" Margin="5">0, 1</Button>
  <Button Grid.Row="0" Grid.Column="2" Margin="5">0, 2</Button>
  <Button Grid.Row="1" Grid.Column="0" Margin="5">1, 0</Button>
  <Button Grid.Row="1" Grid.Column="1" Margin="5">1, 1</Button>
  <Button Grid.Row="1" Grid.Column="2" Margin="5">1, 2</Button>
  <Button Grid.Row="2" Grid.Column="0" Margin="5">2, 0</Button>
  <Button Grid.Row="2" Grid.Column="1" Margin="5">2, 1</Button>
  <Button Grid.Row="2" Grid.Column="2" Margin="5">2, 2</Button>
</Grid>
```

Usually, it is easiest to start building a Window by using the graphical XAML editor, but you may eventually want to look at the XAML code to see what the editor has done. It often produces almost but not quite what you want. For example, if you size and position a control by using click and drag, the editor may set its Margin property to 10,10,11,9 when you really want 10,10,10,10 (or just 10).

It can also sometimes be hard to place controls exactly where you want them. You can fix some of these values in the Properties window, but sometimes it's just easier to edit the XAML code directly.

Resources

Example program Calculator, which is available for download on the book's website, is shown in Figure 11-3. This program contains three groups of buttons that use radial gradient backgrounds with similar colors. The number buttons, +/-, and the decimal point have yellow backgrounds drawn with RadialGradientBrush objects. The CE, C, and = buttons have blue backgrounds, and the operator buttons have green backgrounds.

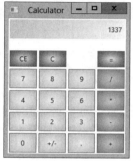

FIGURE 11-3: This program uses resources to simplify maintenance.

You could build each button separately, including the appropriate RadialGradientBrush objects to give each button the correct background. Suppose, however, you decide to change the color of all of the number buttons from yellow to red. You would have to edit each of their 12 RadialGradientBrush objects to give them their new colors. In addition to being a lot of work, those changes would give you plenty of chances to make mistakes. The changes would be even harder if you decide to change the numbers of colors used by the brushes (perhaps having the brush shade from yellow to red to orange), or if you want to use a completely different brush for the buttons such as a LinearGradientBrush.

One of the ways XAML makes maintaining projects such as this one easier is by letting you define resources. You can then use the resources when defining objects. In this example, you can define resources to represent button backgrounds and then use those resources to set each button's Background property. If you later need to change the backgrounds, you only need to update the resources.

The following code shows how the Calculator application shown in Figure 11-3 creates a LinearGradientBrush resource called brResult, which the program uses to draw the result text box at the top. Ellipses show where code has been omitted to make it easier to read.

```
<Window x:Class="Window1"
 xmlns="http://schemas.microsoft.com/winfx/2006/xaml/presentation"
 xmlns:x="http://schemas.microsoft.com/winfx/2006/xaml" Title="XamlCalculator"
 Height="292" Width="227" Focusable="True">
  <Window.Resources>
   ...
  <LinearGradientBrush x:Key="brResult" StartPoint="0,0" EndPoint="1,1">
   <GradientStop Color="LightBlue" Offset="0.0" />
   <GradientStop Color="AliceBlue" Offset="1.0" />
  </LinearGradientBrush>
   ...
  </Window.Resources>
  ...
</Window>
```

The Window element contains a Window.Resources tag that contains the resource definitions. The LinearGradientBrush element defines the brush. One of this element's more important attributes is x:Key, which identifies the brush for later use.

The following code shows how the Calculator program defines the Label that displays calculation results. The Background attribute refers to the resource brResult.

```
<Label Name="lblResult"
  Background="{StaticResource brResult}"
  Grid.ColumnSpan="4"
  Margin="2,2,2,2"
  HorizontalContentAlignment="Right"
  VerticalContentAlignment="Center">0</Label>
```

Later if you decide to change the background color for the result label, you only need to change the definition of the brResult resource. This example uses that resource for only one label so you don't save a huge amount of work by defining a resource. The program's buttons, however, reuse the same resources many times. Instead of reusing the background resources directly, however, the buttons use styles as described in the next section.

Styles

Resources make it easy to create many controls that share an attribute such as a background. Styles take attributes a step further by allowing you to bundle multiple attributes into one package. For example, you could define a style that includes background, width, height, and font properties. Then you could use the style to help define controls.

You can also use styles to define other styles. For example, you can make a base style to be applied to every button in an application. Then you can derive other styles for different kinds of buttons from the base style.

The following example defines a style named styAllButtons. It contains Setter elements that set control properties. This style sets a control's Focusable property to False and its Margin property to 2,2,2,2.

```
<Style x:Key="styAllButtons">
  <Setter Property="Control.Focusable" Value="false" />
  <Setter Property="Control.Margin" Value="2,2,2,2" />
</Style>
```

The following code defines a style named styClear for the calculator's C, CE, and = buttons:

```
<Style x:Key="styClear" BasedOn="{StaticResource styAllButtons}">
  <Setter Property="Control.Background" Value="{StaticResource brClear}" />
  <Setter Property="Grid.Row" Value="1" />
  <Setter Property="Control.Margin" Value="2,20,2,2" />
</Style>
```

The BasedOn attribute makes the new style start with the properties defined by styAllButtons. The new style then uses two Setter elements to add new values for the Background (set to the brush resource brClear) and Grid.Row properties (these buttons are all in row 1 in the calculator). It then overrides the styAllButtons style's value for the Margin property to increase the margin above these buttons.

The following code shows how the program defines its C button. By setting the button's style to styClear, the code sets most of the button's properties with a single statement. It then sets the button's Grid.Column property and its content (those values are different for the C, CE, and = buttons).

```
<Button Name="btnC"
  Style="{StaticResource styClear}"
  Grid.Column="1">C</Button>
```

Styles let the program keep all of the common properties for a set of controls in a single location. Now if you decided to change the color of the C, CE, and = buttons, you would need to change only the definition of the brClear brush. If you wanted to change the brushes' margins, you would need to change only the styClear style.

As the previous code shows, styles also keep the controls' definitions very simple.

Styles also let you easily change the controls' properties later. For example, if you later decide to specify the font family and font size for the calculator's C, CE, and = buttons, you only need to add the appropriate Setter elements to styClear instead of adding a new property to every button. If you want to set the font for every button in the program, you simply add the appropriate Setter elements to styAllButtons, and the other styles automatically pick up the changes.

Templates

Templates determine how controls are drawn and how they behave by default. For example, the default button template makes buttons turn light blue when the mouse hovers over them. When you press a button down, it grows slightly darker and shows a thin shadow along its upper and left edges. By using Template elements, you can override these default behaviors.

The following code contained in the Window.Resources section defines a button template:

```
<Style TargetType="Button">
  <Setter Property="Margin" Value="2,2,2,2" />
  <Setter Property="Template">
   <Setter.Value>
     <ControlTemplate TargetType="{x:Type Button}">
     <Grid>
       <Polygon x:Name="pgnBorder"
         Stroke="Purple"
         StrokeThickness="5"
         Points="0.2,0 0.8,0 1,0.2 1,0.8 0.8,1 0.2,1 0,0.8 0,0.2"
         Stretch="Fill"
         Fill="{StaticResource brOctagonUp}">
       </Polygon>
       <ContentPresenter HorizontalAlignment="Center"
         VerticalAlignment="Center" />
     </Grid>
```

```
        <!-- Triggers -->
        <ControlTemplate.Triggers>
          <Trigger Property="IsMouseOver" Value="true">
            <Setter TargetName="pgnBorder" Property="Stroke" Value="Black" />
            <Setter TargetName="pgnBorder" Property="Fill"
              Value="{StaticResource brOctagonOver}" />
          </Trigger>
        </ControlTemplate.Triggers>
      </ControlTemplate>
    </Setter.Value>
  </Setter>
</Style>
```

The code begins with a Style element that contains two Setter elements. The first Setter sets a button's Margin property to 2,2,2,2. The second Setter sets a Template property. The Setter's value is a ControlTemplate element targeted at Buttons.

The ControlTemplate contains a Grid that it uses to hold other elements. In this example, the Grid holds a Polygon element named pgnBorder. The Points attribute lists the points used to draw the polygon. Because the polygon's Fill attribute is set to Stretch, the polygon is stretched to fill its parent area, and Points coordinates are on a 0.0 to 1.0 scale within this area. The polygon's Fill attribute is set to the brOctagonUp brush defined elsewhere in the Window.Resources section and not shown here. This is a RadialGradientBrush that shades from white in the center to red at the edges.

The ControlTemplate element also contains a Triggers section. The single Trigger element in this section executes when the button's IsMouseOver condition is true. When that happens, a Setter changes the pgnBorder polygon's Stroke property to Black. A second Setter sets the polygon's Fill property to another brush named brOctagonOver. This brush (which also isn't shown here) shades from red in the center to white at the edges.

Because this style does not have an x:Key attribute, it applies to any button in the Window that doesn't have a Style set explicitly.

Example program ButtonTemplate uses the following code to create its controls:

```
<Grid>
  <Grid.ColumnDefinitions>
    <ColumnDefinition Width="0.25*" />
    <ColumnDefinition Width="0.25*" />
    <ColumnDefinition Width="0.25*" />
    <ColumnDefinition Width="0.25*" />
  </Grid.ColumnDefinitions>
  <Grid.RowDefinitions>
    <RowDefinition Height="0.50*" />
    <RowDefinition Height="0.50*" />
  </Grid.RowDefinitions>
  <Button Name="btnOne" Content="One" Grid.Row="1" Grid.Column="0" />
  <Button Name="btnTwo" Content="Two" Grid.Row="1" Grid.Column="1" />
  <Button Name="btnThree" Content="Three" Grid.Row="1" Grid.Column="2" />
  <Button Name="btnFour" Content="Four" Grid.Row="1" Grid.Column="3" />
```

```
<Button Name="btnClickMe" Content="Click Me"
  Style="{StaticResource styYellowButton}" />
<Button Name="btnYellow" Content="I'm Yellow"
  Style="{StaticResource styYellowButton}" Grid.Column="2" Grid.Row="0" />
</Grid>
```

The Window contains a Grid that holds six buttons. The first four buttons do not explicitly set their Style, so they use the previously defined octagonal style.

The final buttons set their Style attributes to styYellowButton (also defined in the Windows. Resources section, but not shown here) so they display a yellow background. That style also positions the button's text in the upper center. When you hover the mouse over these buttons, they switch to an orange background. If you press the mouse down on these buttons, they change to a red background with white text that says "Pushed!" Download the ButtonTemplate example program to see how the triggers work.

Figure 11-4 shows the result. The mouse is pressed on the upper-right button so it has turned red and is displaying the text "Pushed!"

FIGURE 11-4: Templates let you change the appearance and behavior of objects such as buttons.

TAME TEMPLATES

You can use templates to change the appearance and behavior of XAML objects to give your applications distinctive appearances, but you probably shouldn't get too carried away. Although you can make buttons radically change their colors, shapes, captions, and other characteristics when the user interacts with them, doing so may be very distracting. Use templates to make your applications distinctive, but not overwhelming.

Also be careful not to make controls hard for those with accessibility issues. For example, if you use subtle color differences to distinguish button states, users with impaired color vision, those who have trouble seeing small items, and even those using their computers under poor lighting conditions may have trouble using your program. Similarly using sounds to indicate state won't help hearing impaired users (and may annoy people sitting at nearby desks).

Transformations

Standard graphical properties such as Foreground and FontFamily determine a control's basic appearance, but you can further modify that appearance by using a RenderTransform element. The following code creates a button that has been rotated 270 degrees. The Button .RenderTransform element contains a RotateTransform element that represents the rotation.

```
<Button Name="btnSideways"
  Content="Sideways"
  Background="{StaticResource brButton}"
  Margin="-6,-6.5,0,0"
  Height="43"
  HorizontalAlignment="Left"
  VerticalAlignment="Top"
  Width="94">
  <Button.RenderTransform>
    <RotateTransform Angle="270" CenterX="75" CenterY="50" />
  </Button.RenderTransform>
</Button>
```

XAML also provides TranslateTransform and ScaleTransform elements that let you translate and scale an object. Example program RotatedButtons, which is available for download on the book's website and shown in Figure 11-5, uses transformations to draw several buttons that have been rotated and scaled vertically and horizontally.

XAML also defines a TransformGroup element that you can use to perform a series of transformations on an object. For example, a TransformGroup would let you translate, scale, rotate, and then translate an object again.

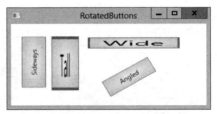

FIGURE 11-5: Buttons can be rotated and scaled vertically and horizontally by using RotateTransform and ScaleTransform.

Animations

The section "Templates" earlier in this chapter shows how to use Triggers to make an object change its appearance in response to events. For example, it shows how to make a button change its background and border color when the mouse moves over it.

XAML also provides methods for scripting more complicated actions that take place over a defined period of time. For example, you can make a button spin slowly for two seconds when the user clicks it.

You use a trigger to start the animation and a Storyboard object to control it. A Storyboard contains information about the state the animation should have at various times during the animation.

The SpinButton example program, which is available for download on the book's website, uses the following code to make a button rotate around its center when it is clicked:

```
<Button Name="btnSpinMe" Content="Spin Me"
  Width="150" Height="100">
  <Button.Background>
    <RadialGradientBrush
      Center="0.5,0.5"
      RadiusX="1.0" RadiusY="1.0">
      <GradientStop Color="Yellow" Offset="0.0" />
      <GradientStop Color="Orange" Offset="1.0" />
    </RadialGradientBrush>
  </Button.Background>
  <Button.RenderTransform>
    <RotateTransform x:Name="rotButton" Angle="0" CenterX="75" CenterY="50" />
  </Button.RenderTransform>
  <Button.Triggers>
    <EventTrigger RoutedEvent="Button.Click">
      <EventTrigger.Actions>
        <BeginStoryboard>
        <Storyboard
          Storyboard.TargetName="rotButton"
          Storyboard.TargetProperty="(RotateTransform.Angle)">
          <DoubleAnimationUsingKeyFrames>
          <SplineDoubleKeyFrame KeyTime="0:0:00.0" Value="0.0" />
          <SplineDoubleKeyFrame KeyTime="0:0:00.2" Value="30.0" />
          <SplineDoubleKeyFrame KeyTime="0:0:00.8" Value="330.0" />
          <SplineDoubleKeyFrame KeyTime="0:0:01.0" Value="360.0" />
          </DoubleAnimationUsingKeyFrames>
        </Storyboard>
        </BeginStoryboard>
      </EventTrigger.Actions>
    </EventTrigger>
  </Button.Triggers>
</Button>
```

Much of this code should seem familiar by now. The Button element's attributes set its name, contents, and size. A Background element fills the button with a RadialGradientBrush.

The Button element contains a RenderTransform element similar to the ones described in the previous section. In this case, the transform is a RotateTransform with angle of rotation initially set to 0 so that the button appears in its normal orientation. Its center is set to the middle of the button. The transform is named rotButton so that other code can refer to it later.

After the transform element, the code contains a Triggers section. This section holds an EventTrigger element that responds to the Button.Click routed event.

A *routed event* is a new kind of event developed for WPF. Routed events travel up and down through a WPF application's hierarchy of controls so interested controls can catch and process the events. For simple purposes, however, a routed event behaves much like a Windows Forms event does and you can catch it with a normal Visual Basic event handler. When the user clicks the button, the Button.Click event fires and this trigger springs into action.

The trigger's Actions element contains the tasks that the trigger should perform when it runs. In this example, the trigger performs the BeginStoryboard action. Inside the BeginStoryboard element is a Storyboard element that represents the things that the storyboard should do.

STORYBOARD START

When I see "BeginStoryboard," I think of the beginning of a storyboard. Actually, this element more properly means "start the storyboard." When this element executes, it starts the storyboard running. (The name "ExecuteStoryboard" or "PlayStoryboard" might have been more intuitive.)

The Storyboard element's TargetName attribute gives the target object on which the storyboard should act, in this case the RotateTransform object named rotButton. The TargetProperty attribute tells what property of the target button the storyboard should manipulate, in this example the object's RotateTransform.Angle property.

The Storyboard element contains a DoubleAnimationUsingKeyFrames element. A *key frame* is a specific point in an animation sequence with known values. The program automatically calculates values between the key frame values to make the animation smooth.

This DoubleAnimationUsingKeyFrames element holds a collection of SplineDoubleKeyFrame elements that define the animation's key values. Each key frame gives its time within the animation in hours, minutes, and seconds, and the value that the controlled property should have at that point in the animation. In this example, the rotation transformation's angle should have a value of 0 when the storyboard starts, a value of 30 when the animation is 20 percent complete, a value of 330 when the storyboard is 80 percent complete, and a value of 360 when the storyboard finishes. The result is that the button rotates slowly for the first 0.2 seconds, spins relatively quickly for the next 0.6 seconds, and then finishes rotating at a more leisurely pace.

Example program SpinButton animates a single property, the button's angle of rotation, but you can animate more than one property at the same time if you like. The SpinAndGrowButton example program, which is available for download on the book's website, simultaneously animates a button's angle of rotation and size. This example has two key differences from program SpinButton.

First, the new button's RenderTransform element contains a TransformGroup that contains two transformations, one that determines the button's angle of rotation and one that determines its scaling:

```
<Button.RenderTransform>
  <TransformGroup>
    <RotateTransform x:Name="rotButton" Angle="0" CenterX="50" CenterY="25" />
    <ScaleTransform x:Name="scaButton" ScaleX="1" ScaleY="1"
     CenterX="50" CenterY="25" />
  </TransformGroup>
</Button.RenderTransform>
```

The second difference is in the new button's Storyboard. The following code omits the animation's TargetName and TargetProperty from the Storyboard element's attributes. It includes three DoubleAnimationUsingKeyFrame elements inside the Storyboard, and it is there that it sets the

TargetName and TargetProperty. The three animations update the button's angle of rotation, horizontal scale, and vertical scale.

```xml
<Storyboard>
  <!-- Rotate -->
  <DoubleAnimationUsingKeyFrames
    Storyboard.TargetName="rotButton"
    Storyboard.TargetProperty="(RotateTransform.Angle)">
    <SplineDoubleKeyFrame KeyTime="0:0:00.0" Value="0.0" />
    <SplineDoubleKeyFrame KeyTime="0:0:01.0" Value="360.0" />
  </DoubleAnimationUsingKeyFrames>

  <!-- ScaleX -->
  <DoubleAnimationUsingKeyFrames
    Storyboard.TargetName="scaButton"
    Storyboard.TargetProperty="(ScaleTransform.ScaleX)">
    <SplineDoubleKeyFrame KeyTime="0:0:00.0" Value="1.0" />
    <SplineDoubleKeyFrame KeyTime="0:0:00.5" Value="2.0" />
    <SplineDoubleKeyFrame KeyTime="0:0:01.0" Value="1.0" />
  </DoubleAnimationUsingKeyFrames>

  <!-- ScaleY -->
  <DoubleAnimationUsingKeyFrames
    Storyboard.TargetName="scaButton"
    Storyboard.TargetProperty="(ScaleTransform.ScaleY)">
    <SplineDoubleKeyFrame KeyTime="0:0:00.0" Value="1.0" />
    <SplineDoubleKeyFrame KeyTime="0:0:00.5" Value="2.0" />
    <SplineDoubleKeyFrame KeyTime="0:0:01.0" Value="1.0" />
  </DoubleAnimationUsingKeyFrames>
</Storyboard>
```

By using XAML Storyboards, you can build complex animations that run when certain events occur. As with templates, however, you should use some restraint when building storyboard animations. A few small animations can make an application more interesting, but too many large animations can distract and annoy the user.

Drawing Objects

WPF provides several objects for drawing two-dimensional shapes, the most useful of which are Line, Ellipse, Rectangle, Polygon, Polyline, and Path.

Most of these are relatively straightforward and you can learn more about them by searching the online help. They all provide Stroke and StrokeThickness properties to determine the appearance and thickness of their borders and a Fill property to determine how a shape is filled (although Line ignores the Fill property because it doesn't draw a closed curve).

The Path object is the most confusing of these so it deserves some special attention. Instead of drawing a single simple shape, the Path object draws a series of shapes such as lines, arcs, and curves. A Path object can be incredibly complex, and can include any of the other drawing objects plus a few others that draw smooth curves.

You can define a Path object in two ways. First, you can make the Path element contain other elements (Line, Ellipse, and so forth) that define objects drawn by the path.

The second (and more concise) method is to use the Path element's Data attribute. This is a text attribute that contains a series of coded commands for drawing shapes. For example, the following code makes the Path move to the point (20, 20), and then draw to connect the following points (80, 20), (50, 60), (90, 100), and (50, 120):

```
<Path Stroke="Gray" StrokeThickness="5" Grid.Column="1" Grid.Row="1"
 Data="M 20,20 L 80,20 50,60 90,100 50,120" />
```

You can use spaces or commas to separate point coordinates. To make it easier to read the code, I use commas between a point's x and y coordinates and spaces between points, as in the previous example.

Some commands allow both uppercase and lowercase command letters. For those commands, the lowercase version means that the following points' coordinates are relative to the previous points' coordinates. For example, the following data makes the object move to the point (10, 20) and then draws to the absolute coordinates (30, 40):

```
Data="M 10,20 L 30,40"
```

In contrast, the following data moves to the point (10, 20) as before, but then moves distance (30, 40) relative to the current position. The result is that the line ends at point (10 + 30, 20 + 40) = (40, 60).

```
Data="M 10,20 l 30,40"
```

There isn't enough room for a complete discussion of the Path object, but the following table summarizes the commands that you can include in the Data attribute.

COMMAND	RESULT	EXAMPLE
F0	Sets the fill rule to the odd/even rule.	F0
F1	Sets the fill rule to the non-zero rule.	F1
M or m	Moves to the following point without drawing.	M 10,10
L or l	Draws a line to the following point(s).	L 10,10 20,20 30,10
H or h	Draws a horizontal line from the current point to the given X coordinate.	h 50
V or v	Draws a vertical line from the current point to the given Y coordinate.	v 30

COMMAND	RESULT	EXAMPLE
C or c	Draws a cubic Bezier curve. This command takes three points as parameters: two control points and an endpoint. The curve starts at the current point moving toward the first control point. It ends at the endpoint, coming from the direction of the second control point.	C 20,20 60,0 50,50
S or s	Draws a smooth cubic Bezier curve. This command takes two points as parameters: a control point and an endpoint. The curve defines an initial control point by reflecting the second control point used by the previous S command, and then uses it plus its two points to draw a cubic Bezier curve. This makes a series of Bezier curves join smoothly.	S 60,0 50,50 S 80,60 50,70
Q or q	Draws a quadratic Bezier curve. This command takes two points as parameters: a control point and an endpoint. The curve starts at the current point moving toward the control point. It ends at the endpoint, coming from the direction of the control point.	Q 80,20 50,60
T or t	Draws a smooth quadratic Bezier curve. This command takes one point as a parameter: an endpoint. The curve defines a control point by reflecting the control point used by the previous T command, and then uses it to draw a quadratic Bezier curve. The result is a smooth curve that passes through each of the points given as parameters to successive T commands.	T 80,20 T 50,60 T 90,100
A or a	Draws an elliptical arc. This command takes five parameters: size—The X and Y radii of the arc rotation_angle—The ellipse's angle of rotation large_angle—0 if the arc should span less than 180; 1 if the arc should span 180 degrees or more sweep_direction—0 if the arc should sweep counter-clockwise; 1 if it should sweep clockwise end_point—The point where the arc should end	A 50,20 0 1 0 60,80
Z or z	Closes the figure by drawing a line from the current point to the Path's starting point.	Z

Example program Shapes, which is shown in Figure 11-6 and which is available for download on the book's website, demonstrates several different Path objects.

Example program BezierCurves, which is shown in Figure 11-7 and is also available for download on the book's website, shows examples of the four different kinds of Bezier curves. This program also draws a gray polyline behind each to show the curves' parameters.

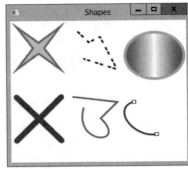

The cubic Bezier curve on the left connects the two endpoints using the two middle points to determine the curve's direction at the endpoints.

The smooth cubic Bezier curve shown next passes through the first, third, and fifth points. The second point determines the curve's direction as it leaves the first point and as it enters the third point. The curve automatically defines a control point to determine the direction leaving the third point, so the curve passes through the point smoothly. Finally, the fourth point determines the curve's direction as it ends at the fifth point.

FIGURE 11-6: Example program Shapes demonstrates the Polygon, Polyline, Ellipse, Line, and Path objects.

The next curve shows two quadratic Bezier curves. The first curve connects the first and third points, with the second point determining the curve's direction at both points. The second curve connects the third and fifth points, using the fourth to determine its direction.

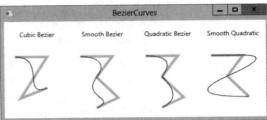

FIGURE 11-7: The Path object can draw Bezier curves.

The final curve in Figure 11-7 uses an M command to move to the point (20, 20). It then uses three smooth quadratic Bezier curves to connect the following three points. The curve automatically defines the control points it needs to connect the points smoothly.

With all of these drawing objects at your disposal, particularly the powerful Path object, you can draw just about anything you need. The graphical XAML editor does not provide interactive tools for drawing shapes, but you can draw them by using the XAML text editor. It may help to sketch out what you want to draw on graph paper first.

PROCEDURAL WPF

The previous sections explained how to use XAML to build WPF windows. By using XAML, you can define controls, resources, styles, templates, transformations, and even animations.

Behind the scenes, an application reads the XAML code, and then builds corresponding controls and other objects to make the user interface. Often, it's easiest to build forms by using the XAML editor, but if necessary, your Visual Basic code can build exactly the same objects.

> **NOTE** *Usually you should build the interface with XAML to increase the separation between the user interface and the code. However, it may sometimes be easier to build dynamic elements in code (for example, in response to data loaded at run time, inputs from the user, or errors).*

For example, the MakeButton example program, which is available for download on the book's website, uses the following Visual Basic code to add a button to its WPF window when you click the initial button:

```
' Add a new Button to the StackPanel.
Private Sub btnMakeButton_Click() Handles btnMakeButton.Click
    Dim btn As New Button()
    btn.Content = "Make Button"
    AddHandler btn.Click, AddressOf btnMakeButton_Click
    stkButtons.Children.Add(btn)
End Sub
```

The code starts by creating a new Button object and setting its Content property to the string Make Button. It uses an AddHandler statement to make the btnMakeButton_Click event handler catch the new button's Click event. Finally the code adds the new button to the stkButtons StackPanel control's Children collection.

Example program ProceduralAnimatedButton, which is available for download on the book's website, uses Visual Basic code to implement several of the techniques described earlier using XAML code. It creates a brush object and uses it to define a Style for buttons. It then creates three Buttons using that Style.

When the mouse moves over a button, the program's code builds and plays an animation to enlarge the button. When the mouse moves off of the button, the code restores the button to its original size.

The following code builds the user interface objects when the program's window loads:

```
Private WithEvents btnCenter As Button
Private Const BIG_SCALE As Double = 1.5

Private Sub Window1_Loaded() Handles Me.Loaded
    ' Make a style for the buttons.
    Dim br_button As New RadialGradientBrush(
        Colors.HotPink, Colors.Red)
    br_button.Center = New Point(0.5, 0.5)
    br_button.RadiusX = 1
    br_button.RadiusY = 1

    Dim style_button As New Style(GetType(Button))
    style_button.Setters.Add(New Setter(Control.BackgroundProperty,
        br_button))
    style_button.Setters.Add(New Setter(Control.WidthProperty, CDbl(70)))
    style_button.Setters.Add(New Setter(Control.HeightProperty, CDbl(40)))
```

```
style_button.Setters.Add(New Setter(Control.MarginProperty,
    New Thickness(5)))

' Set the transform origin to (0.5, 0.5).
style_button.Setters.Add(New Setter(
    Control.RenderTransformOriginProperty, New Point(0.5, 0.5)))

' Make a StackPanel to hold the buttons.
Dim stack_panel As New StackPanel()
stack_panel.Margin = New Thickness(20)

' Add the Left button.
Dim btn_left As Button
btn_left = New Button()
btn_left.Style = style_button
btn_left.Content = "Left"
btn_left.RenderTransform = New ScaleTransform(1, 1)
btn_left.SetValue(
    StackPanel.HorizontalAlignmentProperty,
    Windows.HorizontalAlignment.Left)
AddHandler btn_left.MouseEnter, AddressOf btn_MouseEnter
AddHandler btn_left.MouseLeave, AddressOf btn_MouseLeave
stack_panel.Children.Add(btn_left)

' Make the Center button.
btnCenter = New Button()
btnCenter.Style = style_button
btnCenter.Content = "Center"
btnCenter.RenderTransform = New ScaleTransform(1, 1)
btnCenter.SetValue(
    StackPanel.HorizontalAlignmentProperty,
    Windows.HorizontalAlignment.Center)
AddHandler btnCenter.MouseEnter, AddressOf btn_MouseEnter
AddHandler btnCenter.MouseLeave, AddressOf btn_MouseLeave
stack_panel.Children.Add(btnCenter)

' Make the Right button.
Dim btn_right As New Button
btn_right.Style = style_button
btn_right.Content = "Right"
btn_right.RenderTransform = New ScaleTransform(1, 1)
btn_right.SetValue(
    StackPanel.HorizontalAlignmentProperty,
    Windows.HorizontalAlignment.Right)
AddHandler btn_right.MouseEnter, AddressOf btn_MouseEnter
AddHandler btn_right.MouseLeave, AddressOf btn_MouseLeave
Stack_panel.Children.Add(btn_right)

    Me.Content = stack_panel
End Sub
```

This code starts by declaring a Button control using the WithEvents keyword. The program makes three buttons, but only catches the Click event for this one. The code also defines a constant that determines how large the button will grow when it enlarges.

When the window loads, the code creates a RadialGradientBrush and defines its properties. It then creates a Style object that can apply to Button objects. It adds several Setter objects to the Style to set a Button control's Background, Width, Height, Margin, and RenderTransformOrigin properties.

Next, the code creates a StackPanel object. This will be the window's main control and will replace the Grid control that Visual Studio creates by default.

The program then makes three Button objects. It sets various Button properties, including setting the Style property to the Style object created earlier. It also sets each Button control's RenderTransform property to a ScaleTransform object that initially scales the Button by a factor of 1 vertically and horizontally. It will later use this transformation to make the Button grow and shrink.

The code uses each Button control's SetValue method to set its HorizontalAlignment property for the StackPanel. The code uses AddHandler to give each Button an event handler for its MouseEnter and MouseLeave events. Finally, the code adds the Button controls to the StackPanel's Children collection.

The window's Loaded event handler finishes by setting the window's Content property to the new StackPanel containing the Button controls.

The following code shows how the program responds when the mouse moves over a Button:

```
' The mouse moved over the button.
' Make it larger.
Private Sub btn_MouseEnter(btn As Button, e As MouseEventArgs)
    ' Get the button's transformation.
    Dim scale_transform As ScaleTransform =
        DirectCast(btn.RenderTransform, ScaleTransform)

    ' Create a DoubleAnimation.
    Dim ani As New DoubleAnimation(1, BIG_SCALE,
        New Duration(TimeSpan.FromSeconds(0.15)))

    ' Create a clock for the animation.
    Dim ani_clock As AnimationClock = ani.CreateClock()

    ' Associate the clock with the transform's
    ' ScaleX and ScaleY properties.
    scale_transform.ApplyAnimationClock(
        ScaleTransform.ScaleXProperty, ani_clock)
    scale_transform.ApplyAnimationClock(
        ScaleTransform.ScaleYProperty, ani_clock)
End Sub
```

This code first gets the button's ScaleTransform object. It then creates a DoubleAnimation object to change a value from 1 to the BIG_SCALE value (defined as 1.5 in the earlier Const statement) over a period of 0.15 seconds. It uses the object's CreateClock statement to make an AnimationClock to control the animation. Finally, the code calls the ScaleTransformation object's ApplyAnimationClock method twice, once for its horizontal and vertical scales. The result is that the Button control's ScaleTransform object increases the Button control's scale vertically and horizontally.

The btn_MouseLeave event handler is very similar, except that it animates the Button controls' scale values shrinking from BIG_SCALE to 1.

Figure 11-8 shows example program ProceduralAnimatedButton in action with the mouse resting over the center button.

Other examples available for download on the book's website demonstrate other procedural WPF techniques. For example, program ProceduralCalculator builds a calculator similar to the one shown in Figure 11-3, but it builds its user interface in Visual Basic code. Example program GridButtonCode uses Visual Basic code to build a button that holds a grid similar to the one shown in Figure 11-1.

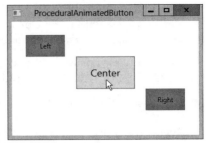

FIGURE 11-8: Program ProceduralAnimatedButton uses Visual Basic code to animate buttons.

DOCUMENTS

WPF includes three different kinds of documents: flow documents, fixed documents, and *XPS* (*XML Paper Specification*) documents. These different kinds of documents provide support for high-end text and printing capabilities.

For example, fixed documents allow you to generate a document that keeps the same layout whether it is viewed on a monitor, printed at low-resolution, or printed at a very high-resolution. On each device, the document uses the features available on that device to give the best result possible.

Each of these three kinds of documents is quite complex so there isn't room to do them justice here. However, the following three sections provide an overview and give brief examples.

Flow Documents

Flow documents are designed to display as much data as possible in the best way possible, depending on runtime constraints such as the size of the control displaying the document. If the control grows, the document rearranges its contents to take advantage of the new available space. If the control shrinks, the document again rearranges its contents to fit the available space. The effect sort of mimics the way a web browser behaves, rearranging the objects it displays as it is resized.

The WPF FlowDocument control represents flow document. The FlowDocument can contain four basic content elements: List, Section, Paragraph, and Table. These have rather obvious purposes: to display data in a list, group data in a section, group data in a paragraph, or display data in a table, respectively.

Although the main emphasis of these elements is on text, they can contain other objects. For example, a Paragraph can contain controls such as Button, Label, TextBox, and Grid. It can also contain shapes such as Polygon, Ellipse, and Path.

A fifth content element, BlockUIElement, can hold user interface controls such a Button, Label, and TextBox. A BlockUIElement can hold only one child, but if that child is a container such as a Grid or StackPanel, then the child can contain other controls.

WMF provides three types of objects for displaying FlowDocuments: FlowDocumentReader, FlowDocumentPageViewer, and FlowDocumentScrollViewer.

The *FlowDocumentReader* lets the user pick from three different viewing modes: single page, book reading, and scrolling. In *single page mode*, the reader displays the document one page at a time. The object determines how big to make a page based on its size. If the reader is wide enough, it will display the FlowDocument in two or more columns, although it still considers its surface to hold a single page at a time, even if that page uses several columns.

In *book reading mode*, the reader displays two pages at a time. The object divides its surface into left and right halves, and fills each with a "page" of data. The reader always displays two pages, no matter how big or small it is.

In *scrolling mode*, the reader displays all of the document's contents in a single long page, and it provides a scroll bar to allow the user to scroll down through the document. This is similar to the way web browsers handle a very tall web page.

Example program UseFlowDocumentReader, shown in Figure 11-9 and available for download on the book's website, shows a FlowDocumentReader object displaying a document in book reading mode. The program's View menu lets you change the viewing mode.

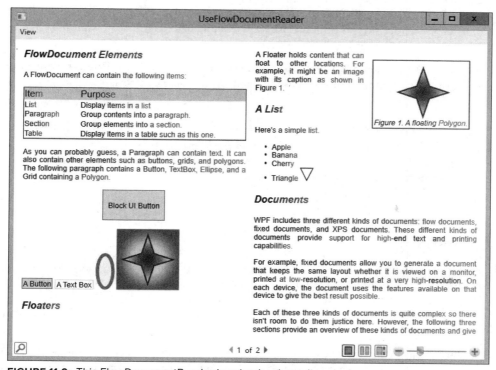

FIGURE 11-9: This FlowDocumentReader is using book reading mode.

This program demonstrates several useful features of FlowDocument objects. The section headers are contained in Paragraph objects that use a Style that defines their font. If you wanted to change the appearance of all of the headers, you would only need to change the Style.

The FlowDocument uses a LinearGradientBrush that shades from black to gray as the text moves left to right. (The effect is more striking on a monitor if you use a colored gradient.)

The document contains a table in its first section, Button and TextBox controls, an Ellipse, and a Grid that holds a Polygon. It uses the Floater element to allow another Grid containing a Polygon and a text caption to float to a position where it will fit nicely in the display. The document also holds a list, one item of which contains a Polygon drawing a triangle.

The bottom of the FlowDocumentReader displays a toolbar. If you click the magnifying glass button on the left, a search text box appears next to it. You can enter text to search for, and the reader will let you scroll back and forth through any matches.

In the middle of the toolbar, the reader displays the current page number and the total number of pages. The three buttons to the right let the user select the single page, book reading, and scrolling views. Finally, the slider on the lower right lets the user adjust the document's scale to zoom in or out.

The *FlowDocumentPageViewer* and *FlowDocumentScrollViewer* objects behave as the FlowDocumentReader does in its single page and scrolling modes, respectively. (The big difference is that FlowDocumentReader can display documents in several modes while the others use only one. If you want to offer the reader several options, use FlowDocumentReader. If you want to restrict the view available, use one of the other kinds of viewers.)

Example programs UseFlowDocumentPageViewer and UseFlowDocumentScrollViewer, which are both available for download on the book's website, demonstrate these controls.

> **NOTE** *If you display a FlowDocument element itself, it acts as a FlowDocumentReader. See example program UseFlowDocument, which is available for download on the book's website.*

Fixed Documents

A *FixedDocument* represents a document that should always be displayed exactly as it was originally composed. Whereas a FlowDocument rearranges its content to take advantage of its current size, all of the content in a FixedDocument remains where it was originally placed. If a FlowDocument is similar to a web browser, then a FixedDocument is similar to an Adobe Acrobat PDF document.

The FixedDocument object contains one or more PageContent objects, each containing a FixedPage object. It is in the FixedPage object that you place your content. You can use the usual assortment of containers to arrange controls and other objects inside the FixedPage object.

A program can use a *DocumentViewer* to display a FixedDocument. The DocumentViewer provides tools to let the user print, zoom in and out, size the document to fit the viewer, display the document in one- or two-page modes, and search for text within the document.

Example program UseFixedDocument, which is available for download on the book's website, displays a FixedDocument inside a DocumentViewer.

XPS Documents

In addition to flow documents and fixed documents, WPF also defines a third kind of document called *XML Paper Specification (XPS)* documents. XPS is an XML-based open standard used to represent fixed documents.

An XPS document is stored in a file called a *package*. The package is made up of pieces called *parts*. Physically, the parts are arranged as files and folders. When you save the document to disk, it is stored as a ZIP-compressed collection of these physical files and folders. If you change the file's extension from .xps to .zip, you can read the files using any ZIP-enabled viewer. For example, Windows Explorer will let you browse through the ZIP file.

Logically, the document's parts form a hierarchical representation of the document. (Remember that the document uses an XML format, and XML is hierarchical, so the document is also hierarchical.) The document itself may contain a FixedDocumentSequence object that contains one or more FixedDocument objects. The FixedDocument objects are similar to the ones described in the previous section, so they can hold container controls that contain any number of objects arranged in a hierarchical way.

In addition to the features provided by FixedDocuments, XPS documents also allow you to digitally sign the package. That tells others that you signed it, gives them the time and date that you signed it, and ensures that the document has not been modified since then. A document can contain more than one signature, and you can provide different levels of security on different parts of the document. For example, you could prevent others from changing the document's body, but allow them to add annotations.

Like the other WPF document objects, XPS documents are quite complex, and there isn't room to do them justice here. See Microsoft's online help (http://msdn2.microsoft.com/system .windows.xps and http://www.microsoft.com/whdc/xps/xpsspec.mspx are good places to start) and search the web for more detailed information and examples.

SUMMARY

One of the main goals of WPF is to separate the user interface more completely from the code behind it. XAML lets you declaratively build a user interface and then later add code to handle the events that the application needs to perform. Because the user interface is separate from the code, you can assign different developers to work on each of them. You can have a graphics designer use a graphical XAML editor to build the user interface and have a Visual Basic developer write the underlying code. Later, the graphical designer can modify the user interface without forcing you to rewrite the code.

WPF includes hundreds of new objects for defining user interfaces. These objects let you build windows that take advantage of modern computer graphics hardware and can provide advanced features such as rotated and scaled controls. New drawing objects let you produce complex graphics at design time such as polygons, Bezier curves, and complex paths.

Resources and styles let you customize objects so that they are easy to change in a central location. Triggers, animations, and storyboards let the interface interact with the user at a very high level, so the bulk of your code doesn't need to handle these more cosmetic chores.

New document objects let you display information that can flow to take best advantage of the available space, or that remain in fixed positions on any display device. Powerful document viewers let users scroll through documents, zoom in and out, print, and copy data to the clipboard.

WPF provides a huge number of powerful features, and this chapter barely scratched the surface.

In Windows Forms applications, Form objects play a special role. They represent the top-level user interface components in which all other controls reside.

In a WPF application, the situation is a little less obvious. A top-level object in a WPF application can be a Window, which roughly corresponds to a Form, but it can also be some other object such as a Page or FlowDocument that is designed to run inside a container such as a web browser. Chapter 12, "WPF Windows," describes the Windows class and these other top-level classes, and explains their special roles in WPF applications.

12

WPF Windows

WHAT'S IN THIS CHAPTER

➤ Window and Page applications

➤ Browser and Frame applications

WROX.COM CODE DOWNLOADS FOR THIS CHAPTER

The wrox.com code downloads for this chapter are found at `http://www.wrox.com/remtitle.cgi?isbn=9781118314074` on the Download Code tab. The code for this chapter is divided into the following major examples:

➤ BrowserApp

➤ FrameApp

➤ UseDialog

USING WPF WINDOWS

In Windows Forms applications, Form objects play a special role. They represent the top-level user interface components in which all other controls reside. Ignoring behind-the-scenes chores such as parsing command-line arguments and messing with the operating system, a typical Windows Forms application starts by displaying a Form object. That Form may provide buttons, menus, and other controls that open other Form objects, but all of the controls are contained in Form objects.

In WPF applications, you can display controls on a Window, an object that is basically the WPF version of a Form. Alternatively, you can display controls in a Page. A Page is a lot like a Window without decorations such as borders, title bar, and system menus (maximize, minimize, restore, close, and so forth). A Page must be hosted inside another object that provides these decorations. Usually, a Page is displayed in a web browser, but the WPF Frame control can also display Page objects.

This chapter explains how you can use these top-level objects, Window and Page, in your WPF applications. It explains how a program can display and manage multiple Window and Page objects, and provides some examples showing simple navigation schemes.

> **NOTE** *Metro-style applications display controls inside a UserControl object. Metro-style applications are described in Chapter 21.*

WINDOW APPLICATIONS

A typical desktop WPF application displays its controls in Window objects. To create this type of application, select the File menu's New Project command to display the New Project dialog box. On the Visual Basic ⇨ Windows tab, select WPF Application, enter a project name, and click OK.

The new application begins with a single Window class named Window1. Open the Solution Explorer and double-click the Window1.xaml entry to edit the Window's controls. Double-click the Window1.xaml.vb entry to edit the Visual Basic code behind the Window.

CODE-BEHIND

The code behind a Window is called its *code-behind*. It's not a very imaginative term, but it's easy to remember.

To add other Window classes, open the Project menu and select Add Window. Enter a name for the class and click OK.

To display a window in code, create a variable that refers to a new instance of the window. Call its Show method to display the window non-modally, or call its ShowDialog method to display the window modally. The following code creates a new window of type Window2 and displays it modally:

```
Dim win2 As New Window2()
win2.ShowDialog()
```

Although several similarities exist between the way a program uses a Window and the way it uses a Form, there are many significant differences.

For example, both classes have a DialogResult property that indicates how the user closed the form. Both classes' ShowDialog methods return this result, so the code can easily determine the form's DialogResult value. In a Form, the DialogResult property is a value of type DialogResult, an enumerated type that provides values such as OK, Cancel, Yes, and No to indicate which button the user clicked to close the form. If the code sets this value, the form automatically hides, so the calling ShowDialog method returns.

In contrast, a WPF Window's DialogResult value is a Boolean intended to indicate whether the user accepted or canceled the dialog box. If you need more detail (did the user click Yes, No, or Cancel?), you'll need to provide code in the dialog box to remember which button the user clicked. If the code sets DialogResult, the window automatically closes so the calling ShowDialog method returns. Unfortunately, the window closes rather than hides so you cannot display the dialog box again. (You cannot display a window after it has closed.) If you want to remember which button the user clicked and then hide the window without closing it, you'll need to implement your own property rather than DialogResult, and you'll need to hide the window explicitly.

The Windows Forms and WPF Button classes also both have properties that you can use to define a dialog box's default and cancel buttons, but they work in different ways.

You can set a Windows Forms Button object's DialogResult property to the value you want the button to give to the form's DialogResult property. If the user clicks the button, it assigns the form's DialogResult value and hides the form so the calling ShowDialog method returns that value.

In a WPF application, you can set a button's IsCancel property to True to indicate that the button is the form's cancel button. If the user presses the Escape key or clicks the button, the button sets the form's DialogResult property and closes the form so the calling ShowDialog method returns. Unfortunately, the button closes the form rather than merely hiding it so, as before, you cannot display the dialog box again.

You can also set a WPF button's IsDefault property to indicate that it should fire if the user presses the Enter key. Unfortunately, this does not automatically set the form's DialogResult property and does not close the dialog box.

Example program UseDialog, which is available for download on the book's website, shows one approach to solving this problem. The dialog class Window2 contains three buttons labeled Yes, No, and Cancel.

The following code shows how the dialog box handles button clicks. The single `btn_Click` event handler fires for all three of the buttons. It saves the button's text in the public variable `UserClicked` and then closes the form.

```
Partial Public Class Window2
    Public UserClicked As String = "Cancel"

    Private Sub btn_Click(btn As Button, e As RoutedEventArgs) _
     Handles btnYes.Click, btnNo.Click, btnCancel.Click
        UserClicked = btn.Content
        Me.Close()
    End Sub
End Class
```

The following code shows how the program's main window displays the dialog box and checks the result. When you click the Show Dialog button, the program creates a new dialog window and displays it modally. It then checks the dialog box's `UserClicked` property to see which button the user clicked.

```
Private Sub btnShowDialog_Click() Handles btnShowDialog.Click
    Dim win2 As New Window2()
    win2.ShowDialog()
    Select Case win2.UserClicked
        Case "Yes"
            MessageBox.Show("You clicked Yes", "Yes", MessageBoxButton.OK)
        Case "No"
            MessageBox.Show("You clicked No", "No", MessageBoxButton.OK)
        Case "Cancel"
            MessageBox.Show("You clicked Cancel", "Cancel", _
                MessageBoxButton.OK)
    End Select
End Sub
```

Most of the things that you can do with a Form you can do with a Window. For example, you can:

➤ Create new instances of Window classes.

➤ Display Windows modally or non-modally.

➤ Close or hide Windows.

➤ View and manipulate the properties of one Window from within the code of another Window.

Nevertheless, the details of Form and Window operations may be different. You may need to use slightly different properties, and you may need to take a slightly different approach, but Window is a fairly powerful class and with some perseverance you should be able to build usable interfaces with it.

PAGE APPLICATIONS

A Page is similar to a borderless Window. It doesn't provide its own decorations (border, title bar, and so forth), but instead relies on its container to provide those elements.

Often a Page is hosted by a web browser, although the WPF Frame control can also display Page objects.

The following sections explain how you can use Page objects to build WPF applications.

Browser Applications

To make a XAML Browser Application (XBAP, pronounced *ex-bap*), select the File menu's New Project command to display the New Project dialog box. On the Visual Basic ➪ Windows tab, select WPF Browser Application, enter a project name, and click OK.

EXCITING XBAPS

For an interesting site that has lots of information about XBAPs including a FAQ, tutorial, and samples, see XBap.org (http://www.xbap.org).

The new application begins with a single Page class named Page1. You can view and edit this Page exactly as you would view and edit a Window. Open the Solution Explorer and double-click the Page1.xaml entry to edit the Page's controls. Double-click the Page1.xaml.vb entry to edit the Visual Basic code behind the Page.

To run the application, open the Debug menu and select Start Debugging. Internet Explorer should open and display the initial Page. Visual Studio is nicely integrated with this instance of Internet Explorer so you can set breakpoints in the code to stop execution and debug the code just as you can debug a Windows Forms application or a WPF Window application.

To add other Page classes to the application, open the Project menu and select Add Page. Enter a name for the class and click OK.

To display a Page in code, create a variable that refers to a new instance of the Page. Then use the current Page's NavigationService object's Navigate method to display the new Page.

The following code creates a new page of type Page2, and then uses the NavigationService object to display it:

```
Dim p2 As New Page2()
NavigationService.Navigate(p2)
```

Because the application is hosted inside a browser, there are several differences in the ways the user will interact with the application. Rather than displaying new forms and dialog boxes, the application will generally display new material within the same browser.

This design has several consequences. For example, the previous code creates a new instance of the Page2 class and displays it. If the user were to execute this same code later, it would create a second instance of the class and display it. Because these are two instances of the class, they do not have the same controls, so any changes the user makes (entering text, checking radio buttons, and so forth) are not shared between the two pages. When the second instance appears, the user may wonder where all of the previous selections have gone.

The program can prevent this confusion by using a single application-global variable to hold references to the Page2 instance. Every time the program needs to show this page, it can display the same instance. That instance will display the same control values so the user's selections are preserved.

That approach solves one problem but leads to another. Because the application runs inside a browser, the browser's navigation and history tools work with it. If you press the browser's Back button, it will display the previous page. That part works relatively transparently, but every time the application uses NavigationService.Navigate to display a Page, that Page is added to the browser's history.

To see why this is an issue, suppose the application has an initial Page that contains a button leading to a second Page. That Page has a button that navigates back to the first page. If the user moves back and forth several times, the browser's history will be cluttered with entries such as Page 1, Page 2, Page 1, Page 2, and so forth. Although this represents the user's actual path through the Pages, it isn't very useful.

You can reduce clutter in the browser's history by using the NavigationService object's GoForward and GoBack methods whenever it makes sense. In this example, it would probably make sense for the second Page to use the GoBack method to return to the main page. Instead of creating a new entry in the history as the Navigate method does, GoBack moves back one position in the existing history. After several trips between the two Pages, the history will contain only those two Pages, one possibly available via the browser's Back button and one possibly available via the browser's Next button.

Example program BrowserApp demonstrates this technique. The program uses two Pages that provide buttons to navigate to each other. Both Pages also contain a text box where you can enter some text, just to verify that the values are preserved when you navigate between the pages.

The following code shows how the main Page navigates to the second Page. If the NavigationService can go forward, the code calls its GoForward method. If the NavigationService cannot go forward, the code uses its Navigate method to visit a new `Page2` object.

```
Private Sub btnPage2_Click() Handles btnPage2.Click
    If NavigationService.CanGoForward Then
        NavigationService.GoForward()
    Else
        NavigationService.Navigate(New Page2())
    End If
End Sub
```

The following code shows how the second Page returns to the first. This code simply calls the NavigationService object's GoBack method.

```
Private Sub btnBack_Click() Handles btnBack.Click
    Me.NavigationService.GoBack()
End Sub
```

Once you've built an XBAP, you can run it by pointing a web browser at the compiled xbap file. When I built the previous example program, the file `BrowserApp.xbap` was created in the project's `bin/Debug` directory and the file successfully loaded in both Internet Explorer and Firefox.

Building a Page class is almost exactly the same as building a Window class. You use the same XAML editor and Visual Basic code behind the scenes. The main difference is in how you navigate between the application's forms. In a WPF application, you create Window objects and use their Show or ShowDialog methods. In an XBAP, you create Page objects and use the NavigationService object's navigation methods.

Frame Applications

Although Page objects normally sit inside a browser, the WPF Frame control can also host them. The program simply navigates the Frame control to a Page, and the rest works exactly as it does for an XBAP.

Example program FrameApp, which is available for download on the book's website and shown in Figure 12-1, uses the following code to load a Page1 object into its Frame control:

FIGURE 12-1: The Frame control provides navigation between Page objects.

```
fraPages.Navigate(New Page1())
```

This example contains the same Page1 and Page2 classes used by the BrowserApp example program described in the previous section.

If an XBAP runs so easily in a browser, why would you want to host pages in a Frame control?

One reason is that you can place multiple frames within a Window to let the user view different pieces of information or perform different tasks at the same time. For example, you can display help in a separate frame, possibly in a separate Window.

If you build each frame's contents in a separate XBAP, you can load the frames at run time. That makes replacing XBAPs to upgrade or change their contents easy.

The Frame control also provides simple browser-style navigation that uses Next and Back buttons and that may be easier for users to navigate in some situations. Microsoft's web page "Top Rules for the Windows Vista User Experience" at `http://msdn2.microsoft.com/Aa511327.aspx` lists as Rule 7 "Use Windows Explorer-hosted, navigation-based user interfaces, provide a Back button." That page argues that this style of interaction simplifies navigation even in traditional applications.

> ### STRENGTH OR WEAKNESS?
>
> Personally I think Microsoft is claiming a weakness as a strength. Web browsers use this type of navigation because they have no context to provide more organized navigation other than the hyperlinks provided by web pages. There are certainly cases where this style of navigation is reasonable (for example, in wizards that lead the user through a series of steps), but many desktop applications are more natural if the user can open separate windows for different tasks. Let me know what you think at `RodStephens@vb-helper.com`.

The Frame control gives you more control than a browser does. For example, it provides easier access to Page history. You can also determine a Frame control's size, whereas you have no control over a browser's size and position.

Displaying Page objects within a Frame control won't make sense for every application, but for some it can be a useful technique.

SUMMARY

In a Windows Forms application, everything is contained in Form objects. Some of those Form classes may be dialog boxes or derived from the Form class, but ultimately everything is contained in a form.

In a WPF application, controls may be contained in Window objects or in Page objects. Window objects sit on the desktop much as Windows Forms do. Page objects must be hosted inside something else, usually a browser or a Frame control in a Window. The PageFunction class provides a modified version of a Page that makes it easier to pass values back and forth between coordinated Pages.

Chapters 7 through 12 give useful background on working with controls. They explain how to select and use both Windows Forms and WPF controls. They also explain the top-level user interface classes: Form for Windows Forms applications, and Window, Page, and PageFunction for WPF applications.

Although these are huge topics, there's even more to building a Visual Basic application than just controls. You also need to understand the code behind the Form or Window that lets the program take the controls' values, manipulate those values, and display a result in other controls. The next several chapters cover these topics in detail. Chapter 13, "Program and Module Structure," starts the process by explaining the files that make up a Visual Basic project and the structure contained within code files.

13

Program and Module Structure

WROX.COM CODE DOWNLOADS FOR THIS CHAPTER

The wrox.com code downloads for this chapter are found at `http://www.wrox.com/remtitle.cgi?isbn=9781118314074` on the Download Code tab. The code for this chapter is divided into the following major examples:

> ➤ CompilerConstantsInCode
> ➤ EmployeeAssert
> ➤ ShowAssemblyInfo
> ➤ WpfCompilerConstantsInCode

SOLUTIONS AND PROJECTS

A Visual Basic *solution* contains one or more related projects. A *project* contains files related to some topic. Usually, a project produces some kind of compiled output such as an executable program, class library, or control library. The project includes all the files related to the output, including source code files, resource files, documentation files, and whatever other kinds of files you decide to add to it.

This chapter describes the basic structure of a Visual Basic project. It explains the functions of some of the most common files and tells how you can use them to manage your applications.

This chapter also explains the basic structure of source code files. It explains regions, namespaces, and modules. It describes some simple typographic features provided by Visual Basic such as comments, line continuation, and line labels. These features do not execute programming commands themselves, but they are an important part of how you can structure your code.

HIDDEN FILES

Figure 13-1 shows the Solution Explorer window for a solution that contains two projects. The solution named MySolution contains two projects named WindowsApplication1 and WindowsApplication2. Each project contains a My Project item that represents the project's properties, various files containing project configuration settings, and a form named Form1.

In WindowsApplication2, the Show All Files button has been clicked (the highlighted button third from the right at the top of the picture) so that you can see all the project's files. WindowsApplication1 has similar files, but they are hidden by default.

These files are generated by Visual Basic for various purposes. For example, `Resources.resx` contains resources used by the project and `Settings.settings` contains project settings.

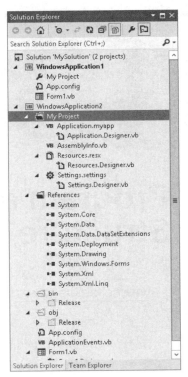

FIGURE 13-1: A solution contains one or more projects that contain files.

RESOURCES AND SETTINGS

Resources are chunks of data that are distributed with the application but that are not intended to be modified by the program. (Technically, you can change resource values, but then they are acting more as settings than resources, so I won't cover that here. In fact, changing resources in a strongly named resource file raises an alarm indicating that someone may have tampered with the file.) These might include prompt strings, error message strings, icons, and sound files.

For example, resources are commonly used for customizing applications for different languages. You build different resource files for different languages, and the program loads its prompts and error messages from the appropriate resource file. Chapter 28, "Configuration and Resources," has more to say about resources.

Settings are values that control the execution of the application. These might include flags telling the program what options to display or how to perform certain tasks. For example, you could build different profiles to provide settings that make the program run in a restricted demo mode or in a fully licensed mode. Normally, settings for .NET applications are stored in `.config` files, although an application can also store settings in the registry, XML, or `.ini` files. For example, this article discusses saving settings in XML files: `http://www.devsource.com/c/a/ Techniques/XML-Serialization-Better-than-the-Registry`.

The following list describes the files contained in WindowsApplication2 and shown in Figure 13-1. The exact files you see for an application may be different from those shown here, but this list should give you an idea of what's involved in building a project. Note that most of these files are generated automatically by Visual Studio and you shouldn't edit them manually. If you change them directly, you are likely to lose your changes when Visual Studio rebuilds them and you may even confuse Visual Studio.

➤ **WindowsApplication2** — This folder represents the entire project. You can expand or collapse it to show and hide the project's details.

➤ **My Project** — This folder represents the project's assembly information, application-level events, resources, and configuration settings. Double-click the My Project entry to view and edit these values.

➤ **Application.myapp** — This XML file defines application properties (such as whether it's a single instance program and whether its shutdown mode is AfterMainFormCloses or AfterAllFormsClose).

➤ **Application.Designer.vb** — This file contains code that works with the values defined in `Application.myapp`.

➤ **AssemblyInfo.vb** — This file contains information about the application's assembly such as copyright information, company name, trademark information, and assembly version.

➤ **Resources.resx** — This resource file contains the project's resources.

➤ **Resources.Designer.vb** — This file contains Visual Basic code for manipulating resources defined in `Resources.resx`. For example, if you define a string resource named Greeting in `Resources.resx`, Visual Basic adds a read-only property to this module so you can use the value of Greeting as shown in the following code:

```
MessageBox.Show(My.Resources.Greeting)
```

➤ **Settings.settings** — This file contains settings that you can define to control the application.

➤ **Settings.Designer.vb** — This file contains Visual Basic code for manipulating settings defined in `Settings.settings`, much as `Resources.Designer.vb` contains code for working with `Resources.resx`. For example, the following code uses the UserMode setting:

```
If My.Settings.UserMode = "Clerk" Then ...
```

➤ **References** — This folder lists references to external components such as DLLs and COM components.

➤ **bin** — This folder is used to build the application before it is executed. The Debug or Release subfolder contains the compiled `.exe` file (depending on whether this is a debug or release build).

➤ **obj** — This folder and its Debug and Release subfolders are used to build the application before it is executed.

➤ **ApplicationEvents.vb** — This code file contains application-level event handlers for the MyApplication object. For example, it contains the application's Startup, Shutdown, and NetworkAvailabilityChanged event handlers.

➤ **Form1.vb** — This is a form file. It contains the code you write for the form, its controls, their event handlers, and so forth. If you double-click this file in Solution Explorer, Visual Studio opens it in the Form Designer.

➤ **Form1.Designer.vb** — This file contains designer-generated Visual Basic code that builds the form. It initializes the form when it is created, adds the controls you placed on the form, and defines variables with the WithEvents keyword for the controls so that you can easily catch their events.

➤ **Form1** — This entry represents the code-behind that you add to the form. If you double-click this file in Solution Explorer, Visual Studio opens the form's code in the code editor. Alternatively, you can open the code by right-clicking the `Form.vb` entry and selecting View Code.

Some projects may have other hidden files. For example, when you add controls to a form, the designer adds a resource file to the form to hold any resources needed by the controls.

Normally, you do not need to work directly with the hidden files, and doing so can mess up your application. At best, the changes you make will be lost. At worst, you may confuse Visual Studio so it can no longer load your project.

Instead you should use other tools to modify the hidden files indirectly. For example, the files `Resources.Designer.vb`, `Settings.Designer.vb`, and `Form1.Designer.vb` are automatically generated when you modify their corresponding source files `Resources.resx`, `Settings.settings`, and `Form1.vb`.

You don't even need to work with all of those source files directly. For example, if you double-click the My Project item in Solution Explorer, the property pages shown in Figure 13-2 appear. The Application tab shown in this figure lets you set high-level application settings. The View Application Events button at the bottom right of the figure lets you edit the application-level events stored in `ApplicationEvents.vb`.

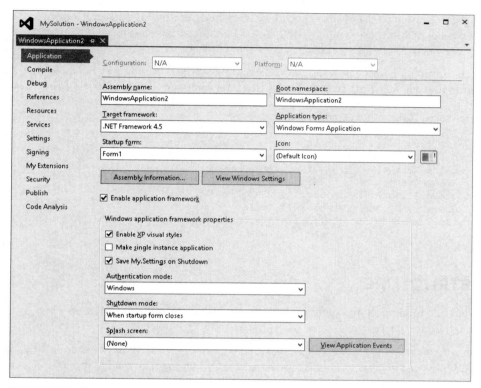

FIGURE 13-2: These property pages let you define the project's resources, settings, and general configuration.

The References tab shown in Figure 13-2 lets you view, add, and remove project references. As you can probably guess, the Resources and Settings tabs let you edit the project's resources and settings.

A particularly important section hidden away in these tabs is the assembly information. When you click the Assembly Information button shown in Figure 13-2, the dialog box shown in Figure 13-3 appears.

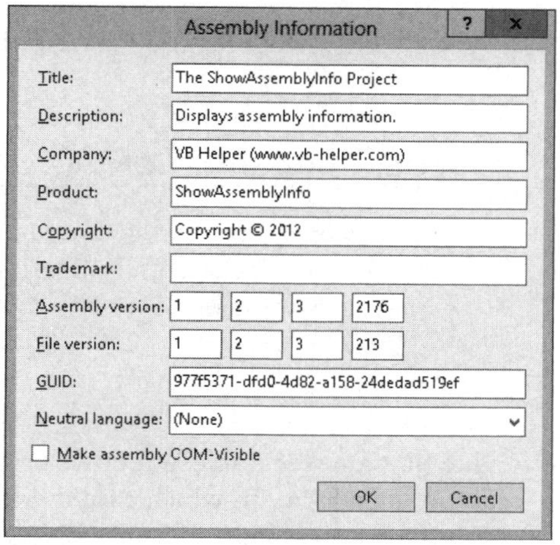

Many of the items in this dialog box, such as the application's title and description, are self-explanatory. They are simply strings that the assembly carries around for identification. The assembly and file versions are used by the Visual Studio run time to verify compatibility between an application's components. The GUID (which stands for "globally unique identifier" and is pronounced to rhyme with "squid") uniquely identifies the assembly and is generated by Visual

FIGURE 13-3: The Assembly Information dialog box lets you define basic project information such as title, copyright, and version number.

Studio. The Make Assembly COM-Visible check box lets you determine whether the assembly should make types defined in the assembly visible to COM applications. For more information on this dialog box, see `http://msdn2.microsoft.com/1h52t681.aspx`.

The My.Application.Info namespace provides easy access to these values at run time. Example program ShowAssemblyInfo uses the following code to display this information in a series of labels when it starts:

```
Private Sub Form1_Load() Handles MyBase.Load
    lblCompanyName.Text = My.Application.Info.CompanyName
    lblDescription.Text = My.Application.Info.Description
    lblCopyright.Text = My.Application.Info.Copyright
    lblTrademark.Text = My.Application.Info.Trademark
    lblDirectoryPath.Text = My.Application.Info.DirectoryPath
    lblProductName.Text = My.Application.Info.ProductName
    lblTitle.Text = My.Application.Info.Title
    lblVersion.Text = My.Application.Info.Version.ToString
End Sub
```

CODE FILE STRUCTURE

A form, class, or code module should contain the following sections in this order (if they are present — you can omit some):

➤   **Option statements** — Option Explicit, Option Strict, Option Compare, or Option Infer. By default, Option Explicit is on, Option Strict is off, Option Compare is binary, and Option Infer is on.

➤   **Imports statements** — These declare namespaces that the module will use.

➤   **A Main subroutine** — The routine that starts execution when the program runs.

➤   **Class, Module, and Namespace statements** — As needed.

> **DEBUGGING OPTIONS**
>
> To uncover potentially annoying and sometimes elusive bugs, turn Option Explicit on, Option Strict on, and Option Infer off. The section "Project" in Chapter 2 describes these options.

Some of these items may be missing. For example, Option and Imports statements are optional. Note that an executable Windows program can start from a Main subroutine or it can start by displaying a form, in which case it doesn't need a Main subroutine. (In that case, the program starts with the automatically generated New subroutine in the file `Application.Designer.vb`.) Classes and code modules don't need Main subroutines.

The following code shows a simple code module. It sets Option Explicit On (so variables must be declared before used), Option Strict On (so implicit type conversions cause an error), and Option

Infer Off (so you must give variables explicit data types). It imports the System.IO namespace so the program can easily use the classes defined there. It then defines the Employee class.

```
Option Explicit On
Option Strict On
Option Infer Off

Imports System.IO

Public Class Employee
    ...
End Class
```

Usually, you put each class or module in a separate file, but you can add multiple Class or Module statements to the same file if you like.

Class and Module statements define top-level nodes in the code hierarchy. Click the minus sign to the left of one of these statements in the code editor to collapse the code it contains. When the code is collapsed, click the plus sign to the left of it to expand the code.

The project can freely refer to any public class, or to any public variable or routine in a module. If two modules contain a variable or routine with the same name, the program can select the version it wants by prefixing the name with the module's name. For example, if the AccountingTools and BillingTools modules both have a subroutine named ConnectToDatabase, the following statement executes the version in the BillingTools module:

```
BillingTools.ConnectToDatabase()
```

Code Regions

Class and Module statements define regions of code that you can expand or collapse to make the code easier to understand. Subroutines and functions also define collapsible code sections. In addition to these, you can use the Region statement to create your own collapsible sections of code. You can place subroutines that have a common purpose in a region so you can collapse and expand the code as needed. The following code shows a simple region:

```
#Region "Drawing Routines"
    ...
#End Region
```

RENAME, DON'T REPLACE

Instead of using a global find and replace to rename a variable, class, or other programming entity, use Visual Basic's renaming feature. Right-click the entity you want to rename and select Rename. Enter the new name and click OK. Visual Basic will change all occurrences of the entity in every module as needed.

continues

continued

Using rename instead of global replace makes it easier to rename one variable while not renaming other variables with the same name in different scopes. It also prevents annoying replacement errors. For example, if you use global replace to change "man" to "person," you may accidentally change "manager" to "personager" and "command" to "compersond."

By itself, the End Region statement does not tell you which region it is ending. You can make your code easier to understand, particularly if you have many regions in the same module, by adding a comment after the End Region statement giving the name of the region, as shown in the following code:

```
#Region "Drawing Routines"
    ...
#End Region ' Drawing Routines
```

REAL-LIFE REGIONS

I use regions a lot in my code. They make it easy to collapse code that I'm not working on and they group related code into meaningful sections. Just building the regions helps me put related material together and makes reading the code easier.

Sometimes it may be easier to move related pieces of code into separate files. The Partial keyword allows you to place parts of a class in different files. For example, you could move a form's code for loading and saving data into a separate file and use the Partial keyword to indicate that the code was part of the form. Chapter 23, "Classes and Structures," describes the Partial keyword in detail.

However, you cannot use the Partial keyword with modules so a module's code must all go in one file. In that case, you can use regions to similarly separate a group of related routines and make the code easier to read.

Conditional Compilation

Conditional compilation statements allow you to include or exclude code from the program's compilation. The basic conditional compilation statement is similar to a multiline If-Then-Else statement. The following code shows a typical statement. If the value *condition1* is True, the code in *code_block_1* is included in the compiled program. If that value is False but the value *condition2* is True, the code in *code_block_2* becomes part of the compiled program. If neither condition is True, the code in *code_block_3* is included in the program.

```
#If condition1 Then
    code_block_1 ...
#ElseIf condition2 Then
```

```
    code_block_2 ...
#Else
    code_block_3 ...
#End if
```

It is important to understand that the code not included by the conditional compilation statements is *completely* omitted from the executable program. At compile time, Visual Studio decides whether or not a block of code should be included. That means any code that is omitted does not take up space in the executable program. It also means that you cannot set the execution statement to omitted lines in the debugger because those lines are not present.

In contrast, a normal If-Then-Else statement includes all the code in every code block in the executable program, and then decides which code to execute at run time.

Because the conditional compilation statement evaluates its conditions at compile time, those conditions must be expressions that can be evaluated at compile time. For example, they can be expressions containing values that you have defined using compiler directives (described shortly). They cannot include values generated at run time (such as the values of variables).

In fact, a conditional compilation statement actually evaluates its conditions at design time, not compile time, so it can give feedback while you are writing the code. For example, suppose Option Explicit is set to On. Because the first condition is True, the variable x is declared as a string. Option Explicit On disallows implicit conversion from an integer to a string, so the IDE flags the statement as an error.

```
#If True Then
    Dim X As String
#Else
    Dim X As Integer
#End If

    X = 10
```

That much makes sense, but it's also important to realize that the code not included in the compilation is *not* evaluated by the IDE. If the first condition in the previous code were False, the code would work properly because variable x would be declared as an integer. The IDE doesn't evaluate the other code, so it doesn't notice that there is an error if the condition is False. You probably won't notice the error until you try to actually use the other code.

You can set conditional compilation constants in two main ways: in code and in the project's compilation settings.

Setting Constants in Code

To set conditional compilation constants explicitly in your program, use a #Const statement, as shown in the following code:

```
#Const UserType = "Clerk"

#If UserType = "Clerk" Then
    ' Do stuff appropriate for clerks ...
```

```
    ...
#ElseIf UserType = "Supervisor" Then
    ' Do stuff appropriate for supervisors ...
    ...
#Else
    ' Do stuff appropriate for others ...
    ...
#End if
```

Note that these constants are defined only after the point at which they appear in the code. If you use a constant before it is defined, its value is False. (Unfortunately Option Explicit doesn't apply to these constants so the IDE doesn't notice that they are undefined at that point.)

To avoid possible confusion, many programmers define these constants at the beginning of the file so they don't need to worry about using a variable before it is defined.

Also note that your code can redefine a constant using a new #Const statement later. That means these are not really constants in the sense that their values are unchangeable.

Setting Constants with the Project's Compilation Settings

To set constants with the project's compilation settings, open Solution Explorer and double-click My Project. Select the Compile tab and click its Advanced Compile Options button to open the Advanced Compiler Settings dialog box shown in Figure 13-4. Enter the names and values of the constants in the Custom Constants text box. Enter each value in the form ConstantName=Value, separating multiple constants with commas.

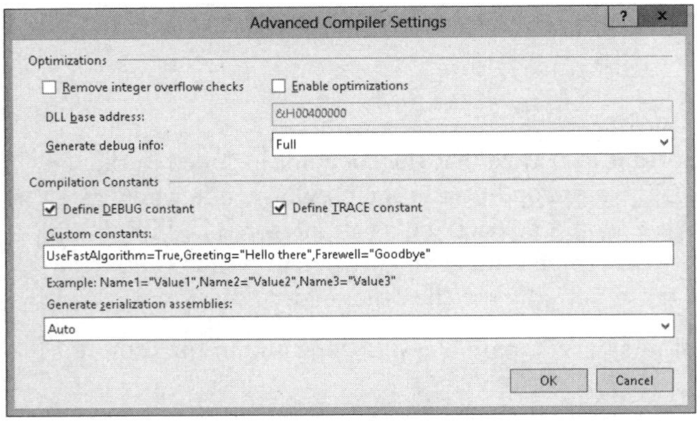

FIGURE 13-4: Use the Advanced Compiler Settings dialog box to define compilation constants.

Constants that you specify on the Advanced Compiler Settings dialog box are available everywhere in the project. However, your code can redefine the constant using a #Const directive. The constant has the new value until the end of the file or until you redefine it again.

Example program CompilerConstantsSettings, which is available for download on the book's website, includes constants set on this dialog box and code to check their values.

Predefined Constants

Visual Basic automatically defines several conditional compilation constants that you can use to determine the code that your application compiles. The following table describes these constants.

CONSTANT CASE

Compilation constant values are case-sensitive. For example, you should compare CONFIG to "Debug" not "debug" or "DEBUG."

CONSTANT	MEANING
CONFIG	A string that gives the name of the current build. Typically, this will be "Debug" or "Release."
DEBUG	A Boolean that indicates whether this is a debug build. By default, this value is True when you build a project's Debug configuration.
PLATFORM	A string that tells you the target platform for the application's current configuration. Unless you change this, the value is "AnyCPU."
TARGET	A string that tells the kind of application the project builds. This can be winexe (Windows Form or WPF application), exe (console application), library (class library), or module (code module).
TRACE	A Boolean that indicates whether the Trace object should generate output in the Output window.
VBC_VER	A number giving Visual Basic's major and minor version numbers. The value for Visual Basic 2005 is 8.0 and the value for Visual Basic 2008 is 9.0. The value for Visual Basic 2010 should logically be 10.0 but it was not updated so it remained 9.0. The value for Visual Basic 2012 is 11.0.
_MyType	A string that tells what kind of application this is. Typical values are "Console" for a console application, "Windows" for a class or Windows control library, and "WindowsForms" for a Windows Forms application.

MORE ON _MYTYPE

For more information on _MyType and how it relates to other special compilation constants, see http://msdn2.microsoft.com/ms233781.aspx.

Example program CompilerConstantsInCode, which is available for download on the book's website, shows how a program can check these compiler constants. Example program WpfCompilerConstantsInCode, which is also available for download, is a WPF version of the same program.

The following sections describe the DEBUG, TRACE, and CONFIG constants and their normal uses in more detail.

DEBUG

Normally when you make a debug build, Visual Basic sets the DEBUG constant to True. When you compile a release build, Visual Basic sets DEBUG to False. The Configuration Manager lets you select the Debug build, the Release build, or other builds that you define yourself.

After you have activated the Configuration Manager, you can open it by clicking the project in the Solution Explorer and then selecting the Build menu's Configuration Manager command. Figure 13-5 shows the Configuration Manager. Select Debug or Release from the drop-down list, and click Close.

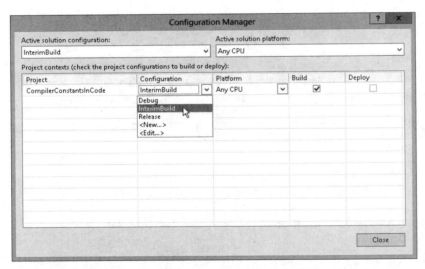

FIGURE 13-5: Use the Configuration Manager to select a Debug or Release build.

THE MISSING MANAGER MYSTERY

If the Configuration Manager is not available in the Build menu, open the Tools menu and select the Options command. Open the Projects and Solutions node's General entry, and select the Show Advanced Build Configurations check box.

When the DEBUG constant is True, the Debug object's methods send output to the Output window. When the DEBUG constant is not True, the Debug object's methods do not generate any code, so the object doesn't produce any output. This makes the Debug object useful for displaying diagnostic messages during development and then hiding the messages in release builds sent to customers.

The following sections describe some of the Debug object's most useful properties and methods.

Assert

The Debug.Assert method evaluates a Boolean expression and, if the expression is False, displays an error message. This method can optionally take as parameters an error message and a detailed message to display. The following code shows how a program might use Debug.Assert to verify that the variable NumEmployees is greater than zero:

```
Debug.Assert(NumEmployees > 0,
    "The number of employees must be greater than zero.",
    "The program cannot generate timesheets if no employees are defined")
```

Example program EmployeeAssert, which is available for download on the book's website, demonstrates this Debug.Assert statement.

If NumEmployees is less than or equal to zero, this statement displays an error dialog box that shows the error message and the detailed message. It also displays a long stack dump that shows exactly what code called what other code to reach this point of execution. Only the first few entries will make sense to practically anyone because the stack dump quickly moves out of the application's code and into the supporting Visual Basic libraries that execute the program.

The dialog box also displays three buttons labeled Abort, Retry, and Ignore. If you click the Abort button, the program immediately halts. If you click Retry, the program breaks into the debugger, so you can examine the code. If you click Ignore, the program continues as if the Assert statement's condition was True.

A good use for the Assert method is to verify that a routine's parameters or other variable values are reasonable before starting calculations. For example, suppose that the AssignJob subroutine assigns a repairperson to a job. The routine could begin with a series of Assert statements that verify that the person exists, the job exists, the person has the skills necessary to perform the job, and so forth. It is usually easier to fix code if you catch these sorts of errors before starting a long calculation or database modification that may later fail because, for example, the repairperson doesn't have the right kind of truck to perform the job.

If the DEBUG constant is not True, the Assert method does nothing. This lets you automatically remove these rather obscure error messages from the compiled executable that you send to customers. The dialog box with its messages and stack dump is so technical that it would terrify many users anyway, so there's no point inflicting it on them.

Fail

The Debug.Fail method displays an error message just as Debug.Assert does when its Boolean condition parameter is False.

IndentSize, Indent, Unindent, and IndentLevel

These properties and methods determine the amount of indentation used when the Debug object writes into the Output window. You can use them to indent the output produced by subroutines to show the program's structure more clearly.

The IndentSize property indicates the number of spaces that should be used for each level of indentation. The IndentLevel property determines the current indentation level. For example, if IndentSize is 4 and IndentLevel is 2, output is indented by eight spaces.

The Indent and Unindent methods increase and decrease the indentation level by one.

Write, WriteLine, WriteIf, and WriteLineIf

These routines send output to the Output window. The Write method prints text and stops without starting a new line. WriteLine prints text and follows it with a new line.

The WriteIf and WriteLineIf methods take a Boolean parameter and act the same as Write and WriteLine if the parameter's value is True.

TRACE

The Trace object is very similar to the Debug object and provides the same set of properties and methods. The difference is that it generates output when the TRACE constant is defined rather than when the DEBUG constant is defined.

Normally, the TRACE constant is defined for both debug and release builds so Trace.Assert and other Trace object methods work in both builds. By default, DEBUG is defined only for debug builds, so you get Debug messages for debug builds.

You can add *listener* objects to the Trace object (or the Debug object) to perform different actions on any Trace output. For example, a listener could write the Trace output into a log file.

CONFIG

The CONFIG constant's value is the name of the type of build. Normally, this is either Debug or Release, but you can also create your own build configurations. You can use these for interim builds, point releases, alpha and beta releases, or any other release category you can think of.

To create a new build type, click the project in the Solution Explorer and then select the Build menu's Configuration Manager command to display the dialog box shown in Figure 13-5. Open the Active Solution Configuration drop-down and select <New. . . > to display the New Project Configuration dialog box. Enter a name for the new configuration, select the existing configuration from which the new one should initially copy its settings, and click OK.

The following code shows how to use the CONFIG compiler constant to determine which build is being made and take different actions accordingly:

```
#If CONFIG = "Debug" Then
    ' Do stuff for a Debug build ...
#ElseIf CONFIG = "Release" Then
    ' Do stuff for a Release build ...
```

```
#ElseIf CONFIG = "InterimBuild" Then
    ' Do stuff for a custom InterimBuild ...
#Else
    MessageBox.Show("Unknown build type")
#End if
```

One reason you might want to make different configurations is to handle variations among operating systems. Your code can decide which configuration is in effect and then execute the appropriate code to handle the target operating system. For example, it might need to work around the reduced privileges that are granted by default on Vista.

Namespaces

Visual Studio uses *namespaces* to categorize code. A namespace can contain other namespaces, which can contain others, forming a hierarchy of namespaces.

You can define your own namespaces to help categorize your code. By placing different routines in separate namespaces, you can allow pieces of code to include only the namespaces they are actually using. That makes it easier to ignore the routines that the program isn't using. It also allows more than one namespace to define items that have the same names.

For example, you could define an Accounting namespace that contains the AccountsReceivable and AccountsPayable namespaces. Each of those might contain a subroutine named ListOutstandingInvoices. The program could select one version or the other by calling either Accounting.AccountsReceivable.ListOutstandingInvoices or Accounting.AccountsPayable .ListOutstandingInvoices.

You can use the Namespace statement only at the file level or inside another namespace, not within a class or module. Within a namespace, you can define nested namespaces, classes, or modules.

The following example defines the AccountingModules namespace. That namespace contains the two classes PayableItem and ReceivableItem, the module AccountingRoutines, and the nested namespace OrderEntryModules. The AccountingRoutines module defines the PayInvoice subroutine. All the classes, modules, and namespaces may define other items.

```
Namespace AccountingModules
    Public Class PayableItem
        ...
    End Class

    Public Class ReceivableItem
        ...
    End Class

    Module AccountingRoutines
        Public Sub PayInvoice(ByVal invoice_number As Long)
            ...
        End Sub
        ...
    End Module
```

```
Namespace OrderEntryModules
    Public Class OrderEntryClerk
        ...
    End Class
    ...
    End Namespace
End Namespace
```

Code using a module's namespace does not need to explicitly identify the module. If a module defines a variable or routine that has a unique name, you do not need to specify the module's name to use that item. In this example, there is only one subroutine named PayInvoice, so the code can invoke it as AccountingModules.PayInvoice. If the AccountingModules namespace contained another module that defined a PayInvoice subroutine, the code would need to indicate which version to use as in AccountingModules.AccountingRoutines.PayInvoice.

Although modules are transparent within their namespaces, nested namespaces are not. Because the nested OrderEntryModules namespace defines the OrderEntryClerk class, the code must specify the full namespace path to the class, as in the following code:

```
Dim oe_clerk As New AccountingModules.OrderEntryModules.OrderEntryClerk
```

NORMAL NAMESPACES

Note that a Visual Basic project defines its own namespace that contains everything else in the project. Normally, the namespace has the same name as the project. To view or modify this root namespace, double-click the Solution Explorer's My Project entry to open the project's property pages and select the Application tab. Enter the new root namespace name in the text box labeled Root Namespace in the upper right.

You can use an Imports statement to simplify access to a namespace inside a file. For example, suppose that you are working on the GeneralAccounting project that has the root namespace GeneralAccounting. The first statement in the following code allows the program to use items defined in the AccountingModules namespace without prefixing them with AccountingModules. The second statement lets the program use items defined in the AccountingModules nested namespace OrderEntryModules. The last two lines of code declare variables using classes defined in those namespaces.

```
Imports GeneralAccounting.AccountingModules
Imports GeneralAccounting.AccountingModules.OrderEntryModules
...
Private m_OverdueItem As PayableItem    ' In the AccountingModules namespace.
Private m_ThisClerk As OrderEntryClerk  ' In the namespace
                                        ' AccountingModules.OrderEntryModules.
```

TYPOGRAPHIC CODE ELEMENTS

A few typographic code elements can make a program's structure a bit easier to understand. They do not execute programming commands themselves, but they are an important part of how you can structure your code. These elements include comments, line continuation and joining characters, and line labels.

Comments

Comments can help other developers (or you at a later date) understand the program's purpose, structure, and method. You start a comment by typing a single quotation mark (') that is not inside a quoted string. All of the characters starting at the quote and continuing until the end of the line are part of the comment and are ignored by Visual Basic.

If a line with a comment ends with a line continuation character (described shortly), Visual Basic ignores that character. That means the line is *not* continued onto the next line, so the comment ends with the current line. In other words, you cannot use line continuation characters to make a multi-line comment.

To quickly comment or uncomment a large block of code, click and drag to select the code using the mouse and then open the Edit menu's Advanced submenu. Select the Comment Selection command to comment out the selection or select Uncomment Selection to remove the comment characters from the front of the selection. Those commands are also available more conveniently as buttons in the Standard toolbar. Use the View menu's Toolbars submenu to show or hide this toolbar.

Another way to quickly remove a chunk of code from the program is to surround it with compiler directives, as in the following code:

```
#If False Then
    Dim A As Integer
    Dim B As Integer
    Dim C As Integer
#End if
```

Use comments to make your code clear. Comments do not slow down the executable program (some superstitious developers think they must slow the code because they make the file bigger), so there's no good reason to avoid them.

XML Comments

A normal comment is just a piece of text that gives information to a developer trying to read your code. XML comments let you add some context to a comment. For example, you can mark a comment as a summary describing a subroutine.

Visual Studio automatically extracts XML comments to build an XML file describing the project. This file displays the hierarchical shape of the project, showing comments for the project's modules, namespaces, classes, and other elements.

The result is not particularly easy to read, but you can use it to automatically generate more useful documentation such as reports or web pages.

You can place a block of XML comments before code elements that are not contained in methods. Generally, you use them to describe a module, class, variable, property, method, or event.

To begin a comment block, place the cursor on the line before the element you want to describe and type three single quotes (' ' '). Visual Studio automatically inserts a template for an appropriate XML comment block. If the element that follows takes parameters, it includes sections describing the parameters, so it is in your best interest to completely define the parameters before you create the XML comment block. Otherwise you'll need to add the appropriate comment sections by hand later.

The following code shows the XML comment block created for a simple subroutine. It includes a summary area to describe the subroutine, two param sections to describe the subroutine's parameters, and a remarks section to provide additional detail.

```
''' <summary>
'''
''' </summary>
''' <param name="jobs"></param>
''' <param name="employees"></param>
''' <remarks></remarks>
Public Sub AssignJobs(ByVal jobs() As Job, ByVal employees() As Employee)

End Sub
```

Note that XML elements can span multiple lines, as the summary element does in this example.

You can add more XML comment sections to the block simply by typing them, following the convention that they should begin with three single quotes. For example, the following code adds some content for the comments in the previous code and an extra WrittenBy element that contains a date attribute:

```
''' <summary>
''' Assigns jobs to employees, maximizing the total value of jobs assigned.
''' </summary>
''' <param name="jobs">The array of Jobs to assign.</param>
''' <param name="employees">The array of Employees to assign.</param>
''' <remarks>The full assignment is not guaranteed to be unique.</remarks>
''' <WrittenBy date="4/1/12">Rod Stephens</WrittenBy>
Public Sub AssignJobs(ByVal jobs() As Job, ByVal employees() As Employee)

End Sub
```

COMMENT CONVENTIONS

Note that I just made up the WrittenBy element and its date attribute — they're not part of some XML comment standard. You can put anything you want in there, although the comments will be easiest to use if you use standard elements such as param and remarks whenever possible.

These XML comments are somewhat bulky and hard to read. In the previous example, it isn't easy to pick out the subroutine's most important summary information with a quick glance at the code. To make reading XML comments easier, Visual Basic defines an outlining section for each XML comment block. If you click the minus sign to the left of the first line in the block, the whole block collapses and shows only the summary information. If you then click the plus sign to the left of the summary, Visual Studio expands the comments to show them all.

The following code shows the beginning of an application that assigns jobs to employees. The project contains two files, a form named `Form1.vb` and a code module named `JobStuff.vb`. The form contains very little code. The code module defines the Job and Employee classes and the AssignJobs subroutine. Each of these has an XML comment block.

```
Public Class Form1
    Private Jobs() As Job
    Private Employees() As Employee
End Class

Module JobStuff
    Public Class Job
        Public JobNumber As Integer
        ''' <summary>
        ''' A list of skills required to perform this job.
        ''' </summary>
        ''' <remarks>Represent required equipment as skills.</remarks>
        Public SkillsRequired As New Collection
        ''' <summary>
        ''' The value of this job.
        ''' </summary>
        ''' <remarks>Higher numbers indicate more priority.</remarks>
         Public Priority As Integer
    End Class

Public Class Employee
    Public FirstName As String
    Public LastName As String
    ''' <summary>
    ''' A list of skills this employee has.
    ''' </summary>
    ''' <remarks>Represent special equipment as skills.</remarks>
    Public Skills As New Collection
    End Class

    ''' <summary>
    ''' Assigns jobs to employees.
    ''' </summary>
    ''' <param name="jobs">Array of Jobs to assign.</param>
    ''' <param name="employees">Array of Employees to assign jobs.</param>
    ''' <remarks>Maximizes total value of jobs assigned.</remarks>
```

```
''' <WrittenBy date="7/26/04">Rod Stephens</WrittenBy>
Public Sub AssignJobs(ByVal jobs() As Job, ByVal employees() As Employee)

    End Sub
End Module
```

In addition to providing documentation for your use, XML comments let IntelliSense provide additional information about your code. Figure 13-6 shows IntelliSense displaying information about the AssignJobs subroutine. It gets the description of the subroutine (Assigns jobs to employees) and the description of the jobs parameter (Array of jobs to assign) from the subroutine's XML comments.

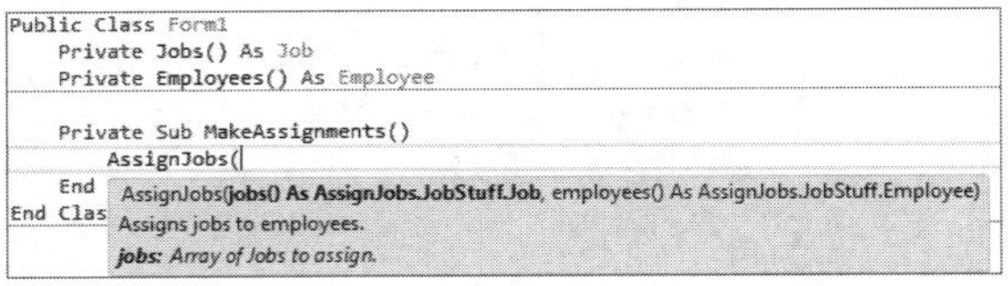

FIGURE 13-6: IntelliSense uses XML comments to display information about a subroutine and its parameters.

When you compile the application, Visual Studio extracts the XML comments and places them in an XML file with the same name as the executable file in the project's bin\Debug directory. The result isn't very readable but you can use it to generate more palatable documentation. Some third-party tools such as doxygen (http://www.doxygen.org) can also extract XML comments and build documentation.

Example program AssignJobs, which is available for download on the book's website, defines job assignment classes that you can view with the Object Browser. If you compile the program (which actually doesn't do any job assignment, it just defines the classes), you can examine its XML documentation.

Line Continuation

Line continuation characters let you break long lines across multiple shorter lines so that they are easier to read. To continue a line, end it with a space followed by an underscore (_). Visual Basic treats the following code as if it were all on one long line:

```
Dim background_color As Color = _
    Color.FromName( _
        My.Resources.ResourceManager.GetString( _
            "MainFormBackgroundColor"))
```

As the earlier section about comments explains, you cannot continue comments. A comment includes any space and underscore at the end of its line so the comment does not apply to the following line.

You can break a line just about anywhere that a space is allowed and between program elements. For example, you can break a line after the opening parenthesis in a parameter list, as shown in the following code:

```
AReallyReallyLongSubroutineNameThatTakesFiveParameters( _
    parameter1, parameter2, parameter3, parameter4, parameter5)
```

You cannot break a line inside a quoted string. If you want to break a string, end the string and concatenate it with the rest of the string on the next line, as in the following example:

```
Dim txt As String = "To break a long string across multiple lines, " & _
    "end the string and concatenate it with the rest of " & _
    "the string on the next line."
```

Visual Basic does not enforce its usual indentation rules on continued lines, so you can indent the lines in any way you like to make the code's structure more clear. For example, many programmers align parameters in long subroutine calls like this:

```
DoSomething( _
    parameter1, _
    parameter2, _
    parameter3)
```

Implicit Line Continuation

Visual Basic can also guess where you are continuing a line even if you don't use the line continuation character, at least sometimes. For example, Visual Basic can figure out that the statement shown in the following code isn't complete until the final line so it treats all of this code as if it were written on a single long line:

```
Dim background_color As Color =
    Color.FromName(
        My.Resources.ResourceManager.GetString(
            "MainFormBackgroundColor"
        )
    )
```

Visual Basic does not allow implicit line continuation in all cases, however. For example, in the following code the Next i statement is split across two lines. Because a Next statement's variable name is optional, Visual Basic doesn't know that the following i is required so it doesn't look for it.

```
For i As Integer = 1 To 10

Next
    i
```

In fact, the only place you can break the statement For i As Integer = 1 To 10 without a line continuation character and without confusing Visual Basic is after the equals sign. That's a pretty confusing place to break the code anyway so I would recommend against it.

Some places that Visual Basic *does* allow implicit line continuation include:

➤ After an equals sign

➤ After a binary operator such as + or *

➤ After commas

➤ After opening parentheses or brackets and before closing parentheses or brackets

The following code shows a few examples:

```
<
    ComClass()
>
Public Class Employee
    Public Function CalculateStuff(
        ByRef v1 As Integer,
        ByRef v2 As Integer
    )

        Dim a As Integer =
            Math.Max(
                v1,
                v2 +
                12
            )
        Return a
    End Function

    ...
End Class
```

Line Joining

Not only can you break a long statement across multiple lines, but you can also join short statements on a single line. To use two statements on a single line, separate them with a colon (:). The following line of code contains three statements that store the red, green, and blue components of a form's background color in the variables r, g, and b, respectively:

```
r = BackColor.R : g = BackColor.G : b = BackColor.B
```

Line joining is most useful when you have many lines in a row that all have a very similar structure. By scanning down the lines, you can tell if there are differences that may indicate a bug.

Use line joining with some caution. If the statements are long, or if you have a series of joined lines with dissimilar structure, combining lots of statements on a single line can make the code harder to read. If the code is easier to read with each statement on a separate line, write the code that way. Using more lines doesn't cost extra or make the code run any slower.

SUMMARY

A Visual Studio solution contains a hierarchical arrangement of items. At the top level, it contains one or more projects. Each project contains several standard items such as My Project (that represents the project as a whole), References (that records information about references to external objects), the bin and obj items (that are used by Visual Studio when building the application), and app.config (that holds configuration information). Projects also contain form, class, and other code modules.

Normally, many of these files are hidden, and you do not need to edit them directly. For example, if you double-click Solution Explorer's My Project entry, you can use the project's Properties pages to view and modify application values. Other hidden files store code and resources that determine a form's appearance, and you can modify them by altering the form with the Form Designer.

Within a code module, you can use modules, classes, regions, and namespaces to group related code into blocks. You can use conditional compilation statements and conditional compilation constants to determine which code is compiled into the executable program. The Debug and Trace objects let you generate messages and alerts, depending on whether certain predefined constants are defined.

Finally, typographic elements such as comments, line continuation, and line joining let you format the code so that it is easier to read and understand. XML comments provide additional information that is useful to IntelliSense and can help you automatically generate more readable documentation.

None of these components are required by Visual Basic but they can make the difference between understanding the code quickly and completely, and not understanding it at all. Over an application's lifetime of development, debugging, upgrading, and maintenance, this can determine a project's success or failure.

This chapter described structural elements that make up code files. Within those elements, you can place the code that gathers, manipulates, stores, and displays data. Chapter 14, "Data Types, Variables, and Constants," describes the variables that a program uses to hold data values. It explains how to declare variables, what types of data they can hold, and how Visual Basic converts from one data type to another.

14

Data Types, Variables, and Constants

WROX.COM CODE DOWNLOADS FOR THIS CHAPTER

The wrox.com code downloads for this chapter are found at `http://www.wrox`
`.com/remtitle.cgi?isbn=9781118314074` on the Download Code tab. The code for this
chapter is divided into the following major examples:

➤ AccessLevelEnum

➤ NullableTypes

➤ ShadowsTest

➤ UseDelegates

VARIABLES

Variables are among the most fundamental building blocks of a program. A *variable* is a
program object that stores a value. The value can be a number, letter, string, date, structure
containing other values, or an object representing both data and related actions.

When a variable contains a value, the program can manipulate it. It can perform arithmetic
operations on numbers, string operations on strings (concatenation, calculating substrings,
finding a target within a string), date operations (find the difference between two dates, add a
time period to a date), and so forth.

Four factors determine a variable's exact behavior:

➤ *Data type* determines the kind of data it can hold (integer, character, string, and so forth).

➤ *Scope* defines the code that can access the variable. For example, if you declare a variable inside a For loop, only other code inside the For loop can use the variable. If you declare a variable at the top of a subroutine, all the code in the subroutine can use the variable.

➤ *Accessibility* determines what code in other modules can access the variable. If you declare a variable at the module level (outside of any subroutine in the module) and you use the Private keyword, then only the code in the module can use the variable. If you use the Public keyword, then code in other modules can use the variable as well.

➤ *Lifetime* determines how long the variable's value is valid. A variable inside a subroutine that is declared with a normal Dim statement is created when the subroutine begins and is destroyed when it exits. If the subroutine runs again, it creates a new copy of the variable and its value is reset. If the variable is declared with the Static keyword, however, the same instance of the variable is used whenever the subroutine runs. That means the variable's value is preserved between calls to the subroutine.

For example, a variable declared within a subroutine has scope equal to the subroutine. Code outside of the subroutine cannot access the variable. If a variable is declared on a module level outside any subroutine, it has module scope. If it is declared with the Private keyword, it is accessible only to code within the module. If it is declared with the Public keyword, then it is also accessible to code outside of the module.

Visibility is a concept that combines scope, accessibility, and lifetime. It determines whether a certain piece of code can use a variable. If the variable is accessible to the code, the code is within the variable's scope, and the variable is within its lifetime (has been created and not yet destroyed), then the variable is visible to the code.

This chapter explains the syntax for declaring variables in Visual Basic. It explains how you can use different declarations to determine a variable's data type, scope, accessibility, and lifetime. It discusses some of the issues you should consider when selecting a type of declaration, and describes some concepts, such as anonymous and nullable types, which can complicate variable declarations. This chapter also explains ways you can initialize objects, arrays, and collections quickly and easily.

Constants, parameters, and property procedures all have concepts of scope and data type that are similar to those of variables, so they are also described here.

The chapter finishes with a brief explanation of naming conventions. Which naming rules you adopt isn't as important as the fact that you adopt some. This chapter discusses where you can find the conventions used by Microsoft Consulting Services. From those, you can build your own coding conventions.

DATA TYPES

The smallest piece of data a computer can handle is a *bit*, a single value that can be either 0 or 1. Eight bits are grouped into a *byte*. Computers typically measure disk space and memory space in kilobytes (1,024 bytes), megabytes (1,024 kilobytes), and gigabytes (1,024 megabytes).

Multiple bytes are grouped into *words* that may contain 2, 4, or more bytes depending on the computer hardware. Most computers these days use 4-byte (32-bit) words, although 8-byte (64-bit) computers are becoming more common.

Visual Basic also groups bytes in different ways to form data types with a higher logical meaning. For example, it uses 4 bytes to make an *integer*, a numeric data type that can hold values between –2,147,483,648 and 2,147,483,647.

The following table summarizes Visual Basic's elementary data types.

TYPE	SIZE	VALUES
Boolean	2 bytes	True or False
Byte	1 byte	0 to 255 (unsigned byte)
SByte	1 byte	–128 to 127 (signed byte)
Char	2 bytes	0 to 65,535 (unsigned character)
Short	2 bytes	–32,768 to 32,767
UShort	2 bytes	0 through 65,535 (unsigned short)
Integer	4 bytes	–2,147,483,648 to 2,147,483,647
UInteger	4 bytes	0 through 4,294,967,295 (unsigned integer)
Long	8 bytes	–9,223,372,036,854,775,808 to 9,223,372,036,854,775,807
ULong	8 bytes	0 through 18,446,744,073,709,551,615 (unsigned long)
Decimal	16 bytes	0 to +/–79,228,162,514,264,337,593,543,950,335 with no decimal point; 0 to +/–7.9228162514264337593543950335 with 28 places to the right of the decimal place
Single	4 bytes	–3.4028235E+38 to –1.401298E-45 (negative values) 1.401298E-45 to 3.4028235E+38 (positive values)
Double	8 bytes	–1.79769313486231570E+308 to –4.94065645841246544E-324 (negative values) 4.94065645841246544E-324 to 1.79769313486231570E+308 (positive values)
String	varies	Depending on the platform, a string can hold approximately 0 to 2 billion Unicode characters
Date	8 bytes	January 1, 0001 0:0:00 to December 31, 9999 11:59:59 pm
Object	4 bytes	Points to any type of data
Structure	varies	Structure members have their own ranges

Signed types such as Integer and Decimal can store positive and negative numbers. Unsigned types such as Byte and UInteger can only store positive values and they use the extra space that would have been used to store sign information to store larger values.

Normally in a program you think of the Char data type as holding a single character. That could be a simple Roman letter or digit, but Visual Basic uses 2-byte Unicode characters so the Char type can also hold more complex characters from other alphabets such as Kanji and Cyrillic.

The System namespace also provides integer data types that specify their numbers of bits explicitly. For example, Int32 represents a 32-bit integer. Using these values instead of Integer emphasizes the fact that the variable uses 32 bits. That can sometimes make code clearer. For example, suppose that you need to call an application programming interface (API) function that takes a 32-bit integer as a parameter. You can make it obvious that you are using a 32-bit integer by giving the parameter the Int32 type.

The data types that explicitly give their sizes are Int16, Int32, Int64, UInt16, UInt32, and UInt64.

The Integer data type is usually the fastest of the integral types. You will generally get better performance using Integers than you will with the Char, Byte, Short, Long, or Decimal data types. You should stick with the Integer data type unless you need the extra range provided by Long and Decimal, or you need to save space with the smaller Char and Byte data types. In many cases, the space savings you will get using the Char and Byte data types isn't worth the extra time and effort, unless you are working with a very large array of values.

Note that you cannot safely assume that a variable's storage requirements are exactly the same as its size. In some cases, the program may move a variable so that it begins on a boundary that is natural for the hardware platform. For example, if you make a structure containing several Short (2-byte) variables, the program may insert 2 extra bytes between them so they can all start on 4-byte boundaries because that may be more efficient for the hardware. For more information on structures, see Chapter 23, "Classes and Structures."

ALIGNMENT ATTRIBUTES

Actually, you can use the StructLayout attribute to change the way Visual Basic allocates the memory for a structure. In that case you may be able to determine exactly how the structure is laid out. This is a fairly advanced topic and is not covered in this book. For more information, see `http://msdn` `.microsoft.com/system.runtime.interopservices.structlayoutattribute` `.aspx`.

Some data types also come with some additional overhead. For example, an array stores some extra information about each of its dimensions.

TYPE CHARACTERS

Data type characters identify a value's data type. The following table lists the data type characters of Visual Basic.

CHARACTER	DATA TYPE
%	Integer
&	Long
@	Decimal
!	Single
#	Double
$	String

You can specify a variable's data type by adding a data type character after a variable's name when you declare it. When you use the variable later, you can omit the data type character if you like. For example, the following code declares variable num_desserts as a Long and satisfaction_quotient as a Double. It then assigns values to these variables.

```
Dim num_desserts&
Dim satisfaction_quotient#

num_desserts = 100
satisfaction_quotient# = 1.23
```

If you have Option Explicit turned off, you can include a data type character the first time you use the variable to determine its data type. If you omit the character, Visual Basic picks a default data type based on the value you assign to the variable.

If the value you assign is an integral value that will fit in an Integer, Visual Basic makes the variable an Integer. If the value is too big for an Integer, Visual Basic makes the variable a Long. If the value contains a decimal point, Visual Basic makes the variable a Double.

If you set a variable equal to a True or False, Visual Basic makes it a Boolean.

In Visual Basic, you surround date values with # characters. If you assign a variable to a date value, Visual Basic gives the variable the Date data type. The following code assigns Boolean and Date variables:

```
a_boolean = True
a_date = #12/31/2007#
```

In addition to data type characters, Visual Basic provides a set of *literal type characters* that determine the data type of literal values. These are values that you explicitly type into your code in statements such as assignment and initialization statements. The following table lists the literal type characters of Visual Basic.

CHARACTER	DATA TYPE
S	Short
US	UShort
I	Integer
UI	UInteger
L	Long
UL	ULong
D	Decimal
F	Single (F for floating point)
R	Double (R for real)
c	Char (note lowercase c)

A literal type character determines the data type of a literal value in your code and may indirectly determine the data type of a variable assigned to it. For example, suppose that the following code is the first use of the variables i and ch (with Option Explicit turned off):

```
i = 123L
ch = "X"c
```

Normally, Visual Basic would make i an Integer because the value 123 fits in an Integer. Because the literal value 123 ends with the L character, however, the value is a Long, so the variable i is also a Long.

Similarly, Visual Basic would normally make variable ch a String because the value "X" looks like a string. The c following the value tells Visual Basic to make this a Char variable instead.

Visual Basic also lets you precede a literal integer value with &H to indicate that it is hexadecimal (base 16) or &O to indicate that it is octal (base 8). For example, the following three statements set the variable flags to the same value. The first statement uses the decimal value 100, the second uses the hexadecimal value &H64, and the third uses the octal value &O144.

```
flags = 100   ' Decimal 100.
flags = &H64  ' Hexadecimal &H64 = 6 * 16 + 4 = 96 + 4 = 100.
flags = &O144 ' Octal &O144 = 1 * 64 + 4 * 8 + 4 = 64 + 32 + 4 = 100.
```

BASE CONVERSIONS

The Hex and Oct functions let you convert numeric values into hexadecimal and octal strings, respectively. In some sense, this is the opposite of what the &H and &O codes do: make Visual Basic interpret a string literal as hexadecimal or octal number.

The following code displays the value of the variable `flags` in decimal, hexadecimal, and octal:

```
Debug.WriteLine(flags)       ' Decimal.
Debug.WriteLine(Hex(flags))  ' Hexadecimal.
Debug.WriteLine(Oct(flags))  ' Octal.
```

Sometimes you must use literal type characters to make a value match a variable's data type. For example, consider the following code:

```
Dim ch As Char
ch = "X"  ' Error because "X" is a String.
ch = "X"c ' Okay because "X"c is a Char.

Dim amount As Decimal
amount = 12.34  ' Error because 12.34 is a Double.
amount = 12.34D ' Okay because 12.34D is a Decimal.
```

The first assignment tries to assign the value "X" to a Char variable. This throws an error because "X" is a String value so it won't fit in a Char variable. Although it is obvious to a programmer that this code is trying to assign the character X to the variable, Visual Basic thinks the types don't match.

The second assignment statement works because it assigns the Char value "X"c to the variable. The next assignment fails when it tries to assign the Double value 12.34 to a Decimal variable. The final assignment works because the value 12.34D is a Decimal literal.

The following code shows another way to accomplish these assignments. This version uses the data type conversion functions CChar and CDec to convert the values into the proper data types. The following section, "Data Type Conversion," has more to say about data type conversion functions.

```
ch = CChar("X")
amount = CDec(12.34)
```

Using data type characters, literal type characters, and the Visual Basic default data type assignments can lead to very confusing code. You cannot expect every programmer to notice that a particular variable is a Single because it is followed by ! in its first use but not in others. You can make your code less confusing by using variable declarations that include explicit data types.

DATA TYPE CONVERSION

Normally, you assign a value to a variable that has the same data type as the value. For example, you assign a string value to a String variable, you assign an integer value to an Integer variable, and so forth. Whether you can assign a value of one type to a variable of another type depends on whether the conversion is a narrowing or widening conversion.

Narrowing Conversions

A *narrowing conversion* is one where data is converted from one type to another type that cannot hold all of the possible values allowed by the original data type. For example, the following code copies the value from a Long variable into an Integer variable. A Long value can hold values that are too big to fit in an Integer, so this is a narrowing conversion. The value contained in the Long variable may or may not fit in the Integer.

```
Dim an_integer As Integer
Dim a_long As Long
...
an_integer = a_long
```

The following code shows a less obvious example. Here the code assigns the value in a String variable to an Integer variable. If the string happens to contain a number (for example, "10"), the assignment works. If the string contains a non-numeric value (such as "Hello"), the assignment fails with an error.

```
Dim an_integer As Integer
Dim a_string As String
...
an_integer = a_string
```

Another non-obvious narrowing conversion is from a class to a derived class. Suppose that the Employee class inherits from the Person class. Then setting an Employee variable equal to a Person object, as shown in the following code, is a narrowing conversion because you cannot know without additional information whether the Person is a valid Employee. All Employees are Persons, but not all Persons are Employees.

```
Dim an_employee As Employee
Dim a_person As Person
...
an_employee = a_person
```

If you have Option Strict turned on, Visual Basic will not allow implicit narrowing conversions. If Option Strict is off, Visual Basic will attempt an implicit narrowing conversion and generate an error at run time if the conversion fails.

To make a narrowing conversion with Option Strict turned on, you must explicitly use a data type conversion function. Visual Basic will attempt the conversion and generate an error if it fails. For example, the CByte function converts a numeric value into a Byte value, so you could use the following code to copy an Integer value into a Byte variable:

```
Dim an_integer As Integer
Dim a_byte As Byte
...
a_byte = CByte(an_integer)
```

If the Integer variable contains a value less than 0 or greater than 255, the value will not fit in a Byte variable so CByte throws an error.

The following table lists the data type conversion functions of Visual Basic.

FUNCTION	CONVERTS TO
CBool	Boolean
CByte	Byte
CChar	Char
CDate	Date
CDbl	Double
CDec	Decimal
CInt	Integer
CLng	Long
CObj	Object
CSByte	SByte
CShort	Short
CSng	Single
CStr	String
CUInt	UInteger
CULng	ULong
CUShort	UShort

The CInt and CLng functions round fractional values off to the nearest whole number. If the fractional part of a number is exactly 0.5, the functions round to the nearest even whole number. For example, 0.5 rounds down to 0, 0.6 rounds up to 1, and 1.5 rounds up to 2.

In contrast, the Fix and Int functions truncate fractional values. Fix truncates toward zero, so Fix(−0.9) is 0 and Fix(0.9) is 0. Int truncates downward, so Int(−0.9) is −1 and Int(0.9) is 0.

Fix and Int also differ from CInt and CLng because they return the same data type they are passed. CInt always returns an Integer no matter what type of value you pass it. If you pass a Long into Fix, Fix returns a Long. In fact, if you pass a Double into Fix, Fix returns a Double.

The CType function takes as parameters a value and a data type, and it converts the value into that type if possible. For example, the following code uses CType to perform a narrowing conversion from a Long to an Integer. Because the value of a_long can fit within an integer, the conversion succeeds.

```
Dim an_integer As Integer
Dim a_long As Long = 100
an_integer = CType(a_long, Integer)
```

The DirectCast statement changes value types much as CType does, except that it only works when the variable it is converting implements or inherits from the new type. For example, suppose the variable dessert_obj has the generic type Object and you know that it points to an object of type Dessert. Then the following code converts the generic Object into the specific Dessert type:

```
Dim dessert_obj As Object = New Dessert("Ice Cream")
Dim my_dessert As Dessert
my_dessert = DirectCast(dessert_obj, Dessert)
```

DirectCast throws an error if you try to use it to change the object's data type. For example, the following code doesn't work, even though you can always store an integer value in a Long variable:

```
Dim an_integer As Integer = 100
Dim a_long As Long
a_long = DirectCast(an_integer, Long)
```

The TryCast statement converts data types much as DirectCast does, except that it returns Nothing if there is an error, rather than throwing an error.

Data Type Parsing Methods

Each of the fundamental data types (except for String) has a Parse method that attempts to convert a string into the variable type. For example, the two final statements in the following code both try to convert the string value txt_entered into an Integer:

```
Dim txt_entered As String = "112358"
Dim num_entered As Integer
...
num_entered = CInt(txt_entered)          ' Use CInt.
num_entered = Integer.Parse(txt_entered) ' Use Integer.Parse.
```

Some of these parsing methods can take additional parameters to control the conversion. For example, the numeric methods can take a parameter that gives the international number style the string should have.

The class parsing methods have a more object-oriented feel than the conversion functions. They are also a bit faster. They only parse strings, however, so if you want to convert from a Long to an Integer, you need to use CInt rather than Integer.Parse or Int32.Parse.

Widening Conversions

In contrast to a narrowing conversion, a *widening conversion* is one where the new data type is always big enough to hold the old data type's values. For example, a Long is big enough to hold any Integer value, so copying an Integer value into a Long variable is a widening conversion.

Visual Basic allows widening conversions. Note that some widening conversions can still result in a loss of data. For example, a Decimal variable can store more significant digits than a Single variable can. A Single can hold any value that a Decimal can but not with the same precision, so if you assign a Decimal value to a Single variable, you may lose some precision.

The Convert Class

The Convert class provides an assortment of methods for converting a value from one data type to another. For example, the following code uses the ToInt32 method to convert the string "17" into a 32-bit integer:

```
Dim i As Integer = Convert.ToInt32("17")
```

These methods are easy to understand so they make code simple to read. Unfortunately they work with particular data type sizes such as 16- or 32-bit integer rather than with the system's default integer size so they may require you to change your code in the future. For example, if a later version of Visual Basic assumes 64-bit integers, then you may need to update your calls to Convert methods.

ToString

The ToString method is a conversion function that is so useful it deserves special mention. Every object has a ToString method that returns a string representation of the object. For example, the following code converts the integer value num_employees into a string:

```
Dim txt As String = num_employees.ToString()
```

Exactly what value ToString returns depends on the object. For example, a double's ToString method returns the double formatted as a string. More complicated objects tend to return their class names rather than their values (although you can change that behavior by overriding their ToString methods).

ToString can take as a parameter a format string to change the way it formats its result. For example, the following code displays the value of the double `angle` with two digits after the decimal point:

```
MessageBox.Show(angle.ToString("0.00"))
```

Appendix P, "Date and Time Format Specifiers," and Appendix Q, "Other Format Specifiers," describe format specifiers in greater detail.

VARIABLE DECLARATIONS

The complete syntax for a variable declaration is as follows:

```
[attribute_list] [accessibility] [Shared] [Shadows] [ReadOnly]
Dim [WithEvents] name [(bounds_list)] [As [New] type]
[= initialization_expression]
```

All declarations have only one thing in common: They contain a variable's name. Other than the name, different declarations may have nothing in common. Variable declarations with different forms can use or omit any other piece of the general declaration syntax. For example, the following two declarations don't share a single keyword:

```
Dim i = 1          ' Declare private Integer named i. (Option Explicit Off)
Public j As Integer ' Declare public Integer named j.
```

The many variations supported by a variable declaration make the general syntax rather intimidating. In most cases, however, declarations are straightforward. The previous two declarations are fairly easy to understand.

The following sections describe the pieces of the general declaration in detail.

Attribute_List

The optional attribute list is a comma-separated list of attributes that apply to the variable. An attribute further refines the definition of a variable to give more information to the compiler and the runtime system.

Attributes are rather specialized and address issues that arise when you perform very specific programming tasks. For example, when you write code to serialize and de-serialize data, you can use serialization attributes to gain more control over the process.

The following code defines the OrderItem class. This class declares three public variables: ItemName, Price, and Quantity. It uses attributes on its three variables to indicate that ItemName should be stored as text, Price should be stored as an attribute named Cost, and Quantity should be stored as an attribute with its default name, Quantity.

```
Public Class OrderItem
    <XmlText()>
    Public ItemName As String

    <XmlAttributeAttribute(AttributeName:="Cost")>
    Public Price As Decimal

    <XmlAttributeAttribute()>
    Public Quantity As Integer
End Class
```

The following code shows the XML serialization of an OrderItem object:

```
<OrderItem Cost="1.25" Quantity="12">Cookie</OrderItem>
```

Because attributes are so specialized, they are not described in more detail here. For more information, see the sections in the online help related to the tasks you need to perform. For more information on XML serialization attributes, for example, search for "System.Xml .Serialization Namespace," or look at these web pages:

➤ XML Serialization in the .NET Framework, http://msdn.microsoft.com/ms950721.aspx.

➤ Controlling XML Serialization Using Attributes, http://msdn.microsoft.com/2baksw0z .aspx.

➤ Attributes That Control XML Serialization, http://msdn.microsoft.com/83y7df3e.aspx.

For more information on attributes in general, see the "Attributes" section of the Visual Basic Language Reference or go to http://msdn.microsoft.com/39967861.aspx.

For a list of attributes you can use to modify variable declarations, search the online help for "Attribute Hierarchy," or see these web pages:

➤ Attributes Used in Visual Basic, http://msdn.microsoft.com/f51fe7sf.aspx.

➤ Attribute Class, http://msdn.microsoft.com/system.attribute.aspx. (Look for the "Inheritance Hierarchy" section to see what attributes inherit from the Attribute class.)

Accessibility

A variable declaration's *accessibility* clause can take one of the following values:

➤ Public — You can use the Public keyword only for variables declared at the module, class, structure, namespace, or file level but not inside a subroutine. Public indicates that the variable should be available to all code inside or outside of the variable's module. This allows the most access to the variable.

➤ Protected — You can use the Protected keyword only at the class level, not inside a module or inside a routine within a class. Protected indicates that the variable should be accessible only to code within the same class or a derived class. The variable is available to code in the same or a derived class, even if the instance of the class is different from the one containing the variable. For example, one Employee object can access a Protected variable inside another Employee object.

➤ Friend — You can use the Friend keyword only for variables declared at the module, class, namespace, or file level, not inside a subroutine. Friend indicates that the variable should be available to all code inside or outside of the variable's module within the same project. The difference between this and Public is that Public allows code outside of the project to access the variable. This is generally only an issue for code and control libraries where some other project may use the library. For example, suppose that you build a code library containing dozens of routines and then you write a program that uses the library. If the library declares a variable with the Public keyword, the code in the library and the code in the main program can use the variable. In contrast, if the library declares a variable with the Friend keyword, only the code in the library can access the variable, not the code in the main program.

➤ `Protected Friend` — You can use Protected Friend only at the class level, not inside a module or inside a routine within a class. Protected Friend is the union of the Protected and Friend keywords. A variable declared Protected Friend is accessible only to code within the same class or a derived class and only within the same project.

➤ `Private` — You can use the Private keyword only for variables declared at the module, class, or structure level, not inside a subroutine. A variable declared Private is accessible only to code in the same module, class, or structure. If the variable is in a class or structure, it is available to other instances of the class or structure. For example, one Customer object can access a Private variable inside another Customer object.

➤ `Static` — You can use the Static keyword only for variables declared within a subroutine or a block within a subroutine (for example, a For loop or Try Catch block). You cannot use Static with Shared or Shadows. A variable declared Static keeps its value between lifetimes. For example, if a subroutine sets a Static variable to 27 before it exits, the variable begins with the value 27 the next time the subroutine executes. The value is stored in memory, so it is not retained if you exit and restart the whole program. (Use a database, the System Registry, or some other means of permanent storage if you need to save values between program runs.)

Shared

You can use the Shared keyword at the class or structure level, not within a module or subroutine. This keyword means that all instances of the class or structure containing the variable share the same variable.

For example, suppose that the Order class declares the Shared variable `NumOrders` to represent the total number of orders in the application. Then all instances of the Order class share the same `NumOrders` variable. If one instance of an Order sets `NumOrders` to 10, all instances of Order see `NumOrders` equal 10.

You can access a Shared variable by using the class's name. For example, the following code sets the Orders class's shared `NumOrders` value to 101.

```
Order.NumOrders = 101      ' Use the class to set NumOrders = 101.
```

You cannot use the Shared keyword with the Static keyword. This makes sense because a Shared variable is in some fashion static to the class or structure that contains it. If one instance of the class modifies the variable, the value is available to all other instances. In fact, even if you destroy every instance of the class or never create any instances at all, the class itself still keeps the variable's value safe. That provides a persistence similar to that given by the Static keyword.

Shadows

You can use the Shadows keyword only for variables declared at the class or structure level, not inside a subroutine. Shadows indicates that the variable hides a variable with the same name in a base class or structure. In a typical example, a subclass provides a variable with the same name as a variable declared in one of its ancestor classes.

Example program ShadowTest, which is available for download on the book's website, uses the following code to demonstrate the Shadows keyword:

```
Public Class Person
    Public LastName As String
    Public EmployeeId As String
End Class

Public Class Employee
    Inherits Person
    Public Shadows EmployeeId As Long
End Class

Public Class Manager
    Inherits Employee
    Public Shadows LastName As String
End Class

Private Sub TestShadows()
    Dim txt As String = ""

    Dim mgr As New Manager
    mgr.LastName = "Manager Last Name"
    mgr.EmployeeId = 1

    Dim emp As Employee = CType(mgr, Employee)
    emp.LastName = "Employee Last Name"
    emp.EmployeeId = 2

    Dim per As Person = CType(mgr, Person)
    per.LastName = "Person Last Name"
    per.EmployeeId = "A"

    txt &= "Manager: " & mgr.EmployeeId & ": " & mgr.LastName & vbCrLf
    txt &= "Employee: " & emp.EmployeeId & ": " & emp.LastName & vbCrLf
    txt &= "Person: " & per.EmployeeId & ": " & per.LastName & vbCrLf

    txtResults.Text = txt
    txtResults.Select(0, 0)
End Sub
```

The code defines a Person class that contains public String variables `LastName` and `EmployeeId`. The Employee class inherits from Person and declares its own version of the `EmployeeId` variable. It uses the Shadows keyword so this version covers the version defined by the Person class. Note that Shadows works here even though the two versions of `EmployeeId` have different data types: Long versus String. An Employee object gets the Long version, and a Person object gets the String version.

The Manager class inherits from the Employee class and defines its own version of the `LastName` variable. A Manager object uses this version, and an Employee or Person object uses the version defined by the Person class.

Having defined these three classes, the program works with them to demonstrate shadowing. First it creates a Manager object, and sets its `LastName` variable to "Manager Last Name" and its

EmployeeId variable to 1. The LastName value is stored in the Manager class's version of the variable declared with the Shadows keyword. The EmployeeId value is stored in the EmployeeId variable declared with the Shadows keyword in the Employee class.

The program then creates an Employee variable and makes it point to the Manager object. This makes sense because Manager inherits from Employee. A Manager is a type of Employee so an Employee variable can point to a Manager object. The program sets the Employee object's LastName variable to "Employee Last Name" and its EmployeeId variable to 2. The LastName value is stored in the Person class's version of the variable. The EmployeeId value is stored in the EmployeeId variable declared with the Shadows keyword in the Employee class. Because the Manager class does not override this declaration with its own shadowing declaration of EmployeeId, this value overwrites the value stored by the Manager object.

Next, the program creates a Person variable and makes it point to the same Manager object. Again this makes sense because a Manager is a type of Person so a Person variable can point to a Manager object. The program sets the Person object's LastName variable to "Person Last Name" and its EmployeeId variable to "A." The Person class does not inherit, so the program stores the values in the versions of the variables defined by the Person class. Because the Employee class does not override the Person class's declaration of LastName with its own shadowing declaration, this value overwrites the value stored by the Employee object.

Finally, the program prints the values of the EmployeeId and LastName variables for each of the objects.

The following output shows the program's results. Notice that the Employee object's value for EmployeeId (2) overwrote the value saved by the Manager object (1) and that the Person object's value for LastName (Person Last Name) overwrote the value saved by the Employee object (Employee Last Name).

```
Manager: 2: Manager Last Name
Employee: 2: Person Last Name
Person: A: Person Last Name
```

Normally, you don't need to access shadowed versions of a variable. If you declare a version of LastName in the Employee class that shadows a declaration in the Person class, you presumably did it for a good reason and you don't need to access the shadowed version directly.

However, if you really do need to access the shadowed version, you can use variables from ancestor classes to do so. For example, the previous example creates Employee and Person objects pointing to a Manager object to access that object's shadowed variables.

Within a class, you can similarly cast the Me object to an ancestor class. For example, the following code in the Manager class makes a Person variable pointing to the same object and sets its shadowed LastName value:

```
Public Sub SetPersonEmployeeId(employee_id As String)
    Dim per As Person = CType(Me, Person)
    per.EmployeeId = employee_id
End Sub
```

Code in a class can also use the `MyBase` keyword to access the variables defined by the parent class. The following code in the Manager class sets the object's `LastName` variable declared by the Employee parent class:

```
Public Sub SetEmployeeLastName(last_name As String)
    MyBase.LastName = last_name
End Sub
```

ReadOnly

You can use the ReadOnly keyword only for variables declared at the module, class, or structure level, not inside a subroutine. ReadOnly indicates that the program can read, but not modify, the variable's value.

You can initialize the variable in one of two ways. First, you can include an initialization statement in the variable's declaration, as shown in the following code:

```
Public Class EmployeeCollection
    Public ReadOnly MaxEmployees As Integer = 100
    ...
End Class
```

Second, you can initialize the variable in the object's constructors. The following code declares the ReadOnly variable `MaxEmployees`. The empty constructor sets this variable to `100`. A second constructor takes an integer parameter and sets the `MaxEmployees` to its value.

```
Public Class EmployeeCollection
    Public ReadOnly MaxEmployees As Integer

    Public Sub New()
        MaxEmployees = 100
    End Sub

    Public Sub New(max_employees As Integer)
        MaxEmployees = max_employees
    End Sub
    ...
End Class
```

After the object is initialized, the program cannot modify the ReadOnly variable. This restriction applies to code inside the module that declared the variable, as well as code in other modules. If you want to allow code inside the same module to modify the value but want to prevent code in other modules from modifying the value, you should use a property procedure instead. See the section "Property Procedures" later in this chapter for more information.

Dim

The Dim keyword officially tells Visual Basic that you want to create a variable.

You can omit the Dim keyword if you specify Public, Protected, Friend, Protected Friend, Private, Static, or ReadOnly. In fact, if you include one of these keywords, the Visual Basic editor automatically removes the Dim keyword if you include it.

If you do not specify otherwise, variables you declare using a Dim statement are Private. The following two statements are equivalent:

```
Dim num_people As Integer
Private num_people As Integer
```

CERTAIN SCOPE

For certainty's sake, many programmers (including me) explicitly specify Private to declare private variables. Using Private means that programmers don't need to remember that the Dim keyword gives a private variable by default.

One place where the Dim keyword is common is when declaring variables inside subroutines. You cannot use the Public, Private, Protected, Friend, Protected Friend, or ReadOnly keywords inside a subroutine so you must use either Static or Dim.

WithEvents

The WithEvents keyword tells Visual Basic that the variable is of an object type that may raise events that you will want to catch. For example, the following code declares the variable Face as a PictureBox object that may raise events that you want to catch:

```
Private WithEvents Face As PictureBox
```

When you declare a variable with the WithEvents keyword, Visual Basic creates an entry for it in the left drop-down list in the module's code window, as shown in Figure 14-1.

If you select the object in the left drop-down list, Visual Basic fills the right drop-down list with the object's events that you might want to catch, as shown in Figure 14-2.

If you select an event, Visual Basic creates a corresponding empty event handler. Letting Visual Basic automatically generate the event handler in this way is easier than trying to type the event handler yourself, creating all of the required parameters by hand.

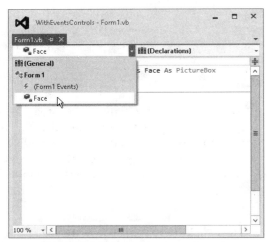

FIGURE 14-1: Visual Basic creates a drop-down entry for variables declared WithEvents.

Declaring variables using the WithEvents keyword is a powerful technique. You can make the variable point to an object to catch its events. Later, if you want to process events from some other object using the same event handlers, you can set the variable to point to the new object. If you no longer want to receive any events, you can set the variable to Nothing.

Unfortunately, you cannot declare an array using the WithEvents keyword. That means you cannot use a simple declaration to allow the same event handlers to process events from more than one object. However, you can achieve this by using the AddHandler method to explicitly set the event handler routines for a series of objects. For more information on this technique, see the section "Catching Events" in Chapter 23.

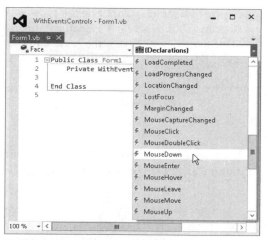

FIGURE 14-2: When you select an object declared WithEvents in the left drop-down list, Visual Basic fills the right drop-down list with events you might want to catch.

Name

A declaration's *name* clause gives the name of the variable. This must be a valid Visual Basic identifier. The rules for valid identifiers are a bit confusing, but generally an identifier should begin with a letter or underscore, followed by any number of letters, digits, or underscores.

If the identifier begins with an underscore (which is unusual), it must contain at least one other valid character (letter, digit, or underscore) so that Visual Basic doesn't confuse it with a line continuation character.

Identifier names cannot contain special characters such as &, %, #, and $, although some of these may be used as data type characters.

Here are some examples:

num_employees	Valid
NumEmployees	Valid
_manager	Valid (but unusual)
_	Invalid (contains only a single underscore)
__	Valid (two underscores is valid but could be very confusing)
1st_employee	Invalid (doesn't begin with a letter or underscore)
#employees	Invalid (contains the special character #)

Normal identifiers cannot be the same as a Visual Basic keyword. However, you can *escape* an identifier (mark it to give it a special meaning) by enclosing it in square brackets, and if you escape an identifier, you can give it the same name as a Visual Basic keyword. For example, in the following code, the `ParseString` subroutine takes a single parameter named `String` of type String:

```
Public Sub ParseString([String] As String)
    Dim values() As String = Split([String])
    . . .
End Sub
```

If you begin writing a call to this subroutine in the code editor, the IntelliSense pop-up describes this routine as ParseString(String As String).

These rules let you come up with some strange and potentially confusing identifier names. For example, you can make escaped variables named String, Boolean, ElseIf, and Case. Depending on your system's settings, underscores may be hard to read either on the screen or in printouts. That may make variables such as __ (two underscores) seem to vanish and may make it hard to tell the difference between _Name and Name.

Although these identifiers are all legal, they can be extremely confusing and may lead to long, frustrating debugging sessions. To avoid confusion, use escaped identifiers and identifiers beginning with an underscore sparingly.

Bounds_List

A variable declaration's *bounds_list* clause specifies bounds for an array. This should be a comma-separated list of non-negative integers that give the upper bounds for the array's dimensions. All dimensions have a lower bound of zero. You can optionally specify the lower bound, but it must always be zero.

LIMITED LOWER BOUNDS

Henry Ford once said, "Any customer can have a car painted any color that he wants so long as it is black." A similar rule applies here: You can specify any lower bound for an array as long as it's zero.

The following code declares two arrays in two different ways. The first statement declares a one-dimensional array of 101 Customer objects with indexes ranging from 0 to 100. The second statement defines a two-dimensional array of Order objects. The first dimension has bounds ranging from 0 to 100 and the second dimension has bounds ranging from 0 to 10. The array's entries are those between orders(0, 0) and orders(100, 10) giving a total of 101 * 11 = 1111 entries. The last two statements define similar arrays, while explicitly declaring the arrays' lower bounds.

```
Private customers(100) As Customer
Private orders(100, 10) As Order
Private customers2(0 To 100) As Customer
Private orders2(0 To 100, 0 To 10) As Order
```

You may find that specifying the lower bound makes the code easier to read because it gives the lower bound explicitly rather than requiring you to remember that lower bounds are always 0. It can be particularly helpful for those who have used Visual Basic 6 and earlier versions because those versions of Visual Basic allowed arrays to have lower bounds other than 0.

Note that declarations of this sort that use an object data type do not instantiate the objects. For example, the first declaration in the previous example defines 101 array entries that all point to Nothing. They do not initially point to instances of the Customer class. After this declaration, the program would need to create each object reference individually, as shown in the following code:

```
Private customers(100) As Customer
For i As Integer = 0 To 100
    customers(i) = New Customer()
Next i
```

Alternatively, the program can use an initialization statement to declare and initialize the objects in a single step. See the section "Initialization_Expression" coming up shortly for more information on initializing arrays in their declarations.

If you provide parentheses but no *bounds_list*, Visual Basic defines the array, but doesn't create it with specific bounds. Later, you can use the ReDim statement to give it bounds. Note that you can also use ReDim to change the bounds of an array that you initially give bounds. The following example declares two arrays named a1 and a2. Initially, the program allocates 11 items for array a1 but no items for array a2. The program then uses ReDim to allocate 21 entries for both arrays.

```
Dim a1(10) As Integer
Dim a2() As Integer

ReDim a1(20)
ReDim a2(0 To 20)
```

The ReDim statement cannot change the number of dimensions in an array. If you want to declare but not initialize a multidimensional array, include commas as if you were defining the bounds. The following code declares a three-dimensional array and initializes it in separate steps:

```
Dim a1(,,) As Integer

ReDim a1(10, 20, 30)
```

New

If you are declaring an object variable, the New keyword tells Visual Basic to create a new instance of the object. Without this keyword, Visual Basic makes an object variable that doesn't yet hold a reference to any object. It initially holds Nothing.

For example, the first line in the following code declares an Employee object variable named `emp1`. After that line, the variable is defined, but it doesn't point to anything. The second line sets `emp1` equal to a new Employee object. The last line creates an Employee object variable named `emp2` and assigns it to a new Employee object. This does the same thing as the first and second lines but in a single statement.

```
Dim emp1 As Employee
emp1 = New Employee()

Dim emp2 As New Employee()
```

If the object's class has constructors that take parameters, you can include the parameters after the class name. For example, suppose that the Employee class has two constructors: one that takes no parameters and a constructor that takes first and last name strings as parameters. Then the following code creates two Employee objects using the different constructors:

```
Dim emp1 As New Employee()
Dim emp2 As New Employee("Rod", "Stephens")
```

As Type and Inferred Types

The As clause tells Visual Basic what kind of variable you are declaring. For example, the following As statement indicates that the variable `cx` has type Single:

```
Dim cx As Single
```

If Option Infer is on, you do not need to declare a local variable's data type. If you omit the As clause, Visual Basic infers the variable's data type from the value that you assign to it. For example, the following code declares a variable named `message`. Because the code assigns a string value to the variable, Visual Basic infers that the variable should be a String.

```
Dim message = "Hello!"
```

Unfortunately, inferred data types make the code harder to understand later. You can figure out that the previous declaration makes a variable that is a String, but it is much more obvious if you explicitly include the As String clause. In this example, type inference only saves you a few keystrokes and makes the code slightly harder to understand. Now, consider the following statement:

```
Dim x = 1.234
```

Does this statement make variable `x` a Single, Double, Decimal, or some other data type? In this case, it's much less obvious what data type Visual Basic will decide to use. (It makes `x` a Double.)

MINIMIZE CONFUSION

To avoid confusion and make the code as easy to read as possible, I recommend that you turn Option Infer off. Then you can use an Option Infer statement at the top of any module where type inference would be helpful. Even in those modules, I recommend that you explicitly give variables data types whenever possible.

The only times when type inference is essential is when you cannot easily figure out the type needed by a variable. For example, LINQ lets a program generate results that have confusing data types, so type inference can be very handy when working with LINQ. For more information on LINQ, see Chapter 20, "LINQ."

INOFFENSIVE INFERENCE

When you create a new project, Option Infer is on by default. To restrict its scope, turn it off for the project as a whole and then turn it on only in the files that need it.

Initialization_Expression

The initialization_expression clause gives data that Visual Basic should use to initialize the variable. The most straightforward form of initialization assigns a simple value to a variable. The following code declares the variable num_employees and assigns it the initial value zero:

```
Dim num_employees As Integer = 0
```

More complicated data types may require more complex initialization clauses. If the declaration declares an object variable, you can use the New keyword to initialize the variable. For example, the first line in the following code declares an Employee variable named emp1 and sets it equal to a new Employee object. The second statement uses the As New form of declaration to do the same thing without a separate initialization clause. This version is slightly more compact, but you can use whichever version seems most natural to you.

```
Dim emp1 As Employee = New Employee("Rod", "Stephens")
Dim emp2 As New Employee("Rod", "Stephens")
```

The With keyword allows you to initialize an object without using a special constructor. This statement lets you assign values to an object's public properties and variables right after the object is created. The following code creates a new Employee object and sets its FirstName and LastName values much as the previous statements do:

```
Dim emp3 As New Employee With {.FirstName = "Rod", .LastName = "Stephens"}
```

Initializing Arrays

Arrays have their own special initialization syntax. To declare and initialize an array in one statement, you must omit the array's bounds. Visual Basic uses the initialization data to discover the bounds.

Place the array's values inside curly braces separated by commas. The following code initializes a one-dimensional array of integers:

```
Dim fibonacci() As Integer = {1, 1, 2, 3, 5, 8, 13, 21, 33, 54, 87}
```

If you have Option Infer on, you can omit the array's data type and Visual Basic will try to deduce it from the values that you use to initialize it. For example, the following code creates three arrays. Visual Basic can infer that the first contains Integers and the second contains Strings. The third array contains Strings, Integers, and Doubles so Visual Basic makes it an array of Objects.

```
Dim numbers() = {1, 2, 3}
Dim strings() = {"A", "B", "C"}
Dim objects() = {"A", 12, 1.23}
```

For a multidimensional array, put commas in the variable's parentheses to indicate the number of dimensions. Use curly braces to surround the array data. Nest each dimension of data inside the previous one, enclosing each dimension's data with braces and separating entries with commas.

This probably makes the most sense if you think of a multidimensional array as an array of arrays. For example, a three-dimensional array is an array of two-dimensional arrays. Each of the two-dimensional arrays is an array of one-dimensional arrays. You can use indentation to make the array's structure more obvious.

The following code declares and initializes a two-dimensional array of integers:

```
Dim int_values(,) As Integer =
    {
        {1, 2, 3},
        {4, 5, 6}
    }
```

The following code declares and initializes a three-dimensional array of strings. The text for each value gives its position in the array. For example, the value str_values(0, 1, 1) is "011."

```
Dim str_values(,,) As String =
    {
        {
            {"000", "001", "002"},
            {"010", "011", "012"}
        },
        {
            {"100", "101", "102"},
            {"110", "111", "112"}
        }
    }
```

Example program InitializeArrays, which is available for download on the book's website, uses similar code to demonstrate array initialization.

Note that you must provide the correct number of items for each of the array's dimensions. For example, the following declaration is invalid because the array's second row contains fewer elements than its first row:

```
Dim int_values(,) As Integer =
    {
        {1, 2, 3},
        {4, 5}
    }
```

Initializing Object Arrays

The basic syntax for initializing an array of objects is similar to the syntax you use to initialize any other array. You still omit the array bounds from the declaration and then include values inside curly braces. The values you use to initialize the array, however, are different because object variables do not take simple values such as 12 and "Test" that you would use to initialize integer or string arrays.

If you create an array of objects without an initialization clause, Visual Basic creates the object variables but does not create objects for them. Initially, all of the array's entries are Nothing.

The following code creates an array containing 11 references to Employee objects. Initially, all of the references are set to Nothing.

```
Dim employees(0 To 10) As Employee
```

If you want to initialize the objects, you must initialize each object in the array separately using the class's constructors. Optionally, you can add a With statement to set public properties and variables after creating the object. The following code declares an array of Employee objects. It initializes two entries using an Employee object constructor that takes as parameters the employees' first and last names, two entries with an empty constructor and a With statement, two with an empty constructor only, and two final entries with the value Nothing.

```
Dim employees() As Employee =
    {
        New Employee("Alice", "Andrews"),
        New Employee("Bart", "Brin"),
        New Employee With {.FirstName = "Cindy", .LastName="Cant"},
        New Employee With {.FirstName = "Dan", .LastName="Diver"},
        New Employee(),
        New Employee(),
        Nothing,
        Nothing
    }
```

To initialize higher-dimensional arrays of objects, use the syntax described in the previous section. Use Nothing or the New keyword and object constructors to initialize each array entry individually.

Initializing XML Variables

To initialize an XElement object, declare the XElement variable and set it equal to properly formatted XML code. Visual Basic reads the data's opening tag and then reads XML data until it reaches a corresponding closing tag so the XML data can include whitespace just as an XML document can. In particular, it can span multiple lines without line continuation characters.

In fact, if you use line continuation characters within the XML, the underscore characters become part of the XML data, which is probably not what you want.

For example, the following code declares a variable named `book_node` that contains XML data representing a book:

```
Dim book_node As XElement =
    <Book>
        <Title>The Bug That Was</Title>
        <Year>2012</Year>
        <Pages>376</Pages>
    </Book>
```

This type of declaration and initialization makes it easy to build XML data directly into your Visual Basic applications.

You can initialize XML literal values with much more complicated expressions. For example, you can use LINQ to select values from relational data sources and build results in the form of an XML document. For more information on LINQ, see Chapter 20.

INITIALIZING COLLECTIONS

Collection classes that provide an Add method such as List, Dictionary, and SortedDictionary have their own initialization syntax. Instead of using an equals sign as you would with an array initializer, use the From keyword followed by the values that should be added to the collection surrounded by curly braces.

For example, the following code initializes a new List(Of String):

```
Dim pies As New List(Of String) From
    {
        "Apple", "Banana", "Cherry", "Coconut Cream"
    }
```

The items inside the braces must include all of the values needed by the collection's Add method. For example, the Dictionary class's Add method takes two parameters giving the key and value that should be added so each entry in the initializer should include a key and value.

The following code initializes a Dictionary(Of String, String). The parameters to the class's Add method are an item's key and value so, for example, the value 940-283-1298 has the key Alice Artz. Later you could look up Alice's phone number by searching the Dictionary for the item with key "Alice Artz."

```
Dim phone_numbers As New Dictionary(Of String, String) From
    {
        {"Alice Artz", "940-283-1298"},
        {"Bill Bland", "940-237-3827"},
        {"Carla Careful", "940-237-1983"}
    }
```

ADDING ADD

Some collection classes such as Stack and Queue don't have an Add method, so From won't work for them. Fortunately, you can use extension methods (described in the "Extension Methods" section in Chapter 16, "Subroutines and Functions") to add one. The following code adds a simple extension method to the Stack (Of String) class:

```
<Extension()>
Public Sub Add(Of T)(the_stack As Stack(Of T), value As T)
    the_stack.Push(value)
End Sub
```

Now the program can initialize a Stack(Of String) as in the following code:

```
Dim orders As New Stack(Of String) From
    {
        "Art", "Beatrice", "Chuck"
    }
```

Multiple Variable Declarations

Visual Basic .NET allows you to declare more than one variable in a single declaration statement. For example, the following statement declares two Integer variables named num_employees and num_customers:

```
Private num_employees, num_customers As Integer
```

You can place accessibility keywords (Private, Public, and so on), Shared, Shadows, and ReadOnly only at the beginning of the declaration and they apply to all of the variables in the declaration. In the preceding statement, both num_employees and num_customers are Private.

You can declare variables with different data types by including more than one As clause separated by commas. The following statement declares two Integer variables and one String variable:

```
Private emps, custs As Integer, cust As String
```

You cannot use an initialization statement if multiple variables share the same As clause, but you can include an initialization statement for variables that have their own As clauses. In the preceding example, you cannot initialize the two Integer variables, but you can initialize the String variable as shown in the following statement:

```
Private emps, custs As Integer, cust As String = "Cozmo"
```

To initialize all three variables, you would need to give them each their own As clauses, as shown in the following example:

```
Private emps As Integer = 5, custs As Integer = 10, cust As String = "Cozmo"
```

You can also declare and initialize multiple objects, arrays, and arrays of objects all in the same statement.

While all of these combinations are legal, they quickly become too confusing to be of much practical use. Even the relatively simple statement that follows can lead to later misunderstandings. Quickly glancing at this statement, the programmer may think that all three variables are declared as Long.

```
Private num_employees, num_customers As Integer, num_orders As Long
```

You can reduce the possibility of confusion by using one As clause per declaration. Then a programmer can easily understand how the variables are defined by looking at the beginning and ending of the declaration. The beginning tells the programmer the variables' accessibility and whether they are shared, shadowing other variables, or read-only. The end gives the variables' data type.

You can also keep the code simple by giving variables with initialization statements their own declarations. Then a programmer reading the code won't need to decide whether an initialization statement applies to one or all of the variables.

There's nothing particularly wrong with declaring a series of relatively short variables in a single statement, as long as you don't find the code confusing. The following statements declare five Integer variables and three Single variables. Breaking this into eight separate Dim statements would not make it much clearer.

```
Dim i, j, k, R, C As Integer
Dim X, Y, Z As Single
```

OPTION EXPLICIT AND OPTION STRICT

The Option Explicit and Option Strict compiler options play an important role in variable declarations.

When Option Explicit is set to on, you must declare all variables before you use them. If Option Explicit is off, Visual Basic automatically creates a new variable whenever it sees a variable that it has not yet encountered. For example, the following code doesn't explicitly declare any variables. As it executes the code, Visual Basic sees the first statement, num_managers = 0. It doesn't recognize the variable num_managers, so it creates it. Similarly, it creates the variable i when it sees it in the For loop.

```
Option Explicit Off
Option Strict Off

Public Class Form1
    ...
    Public Sub CountManagers()
        num_managers = 0
        For i = 0 To m_Employees.GetUpperBound(0)
            If m_Employees(i).IsManager Then num_managrs += 1
        Next i

        MessageBox.Show(num_managers)
    End Sub
    ...
End Class
```

Keeping Option Explicit turned off can lead to two very bad problems. First, it silently hides typographical errors. If you look closely at the preceding code, you'll see that the statement inside the For loop increments the misspelled variable num_managrs instead of the correctly spelled variable num_managers. Because Option Explicit is off, Visual Basic assumes that you want to use a new variable, so it creates num_managrs. After the loop finishes, the program displays the value of num_managers, which is zero because it was never incremented.

The second problem that occurs when Option Explicit is off is that Visual Basic doesn't really know what you will want to do with the variables it creates for you. It doesn't know whether you will use a variable as an Integer, Double, String, or PictureBox. Even after you assign a value to the variable (say, an Integer), Visual Basic doesn't know whether you will always use the variable as an Integer or whether you might later want to save a String in it.

To keep its options open, Visual Basic creates undeclared variables as generic Objects. Then it can fill the variable with just about anything. Unfortunately, this can make the code much less efficient than it needs to be. For example, programs are much better at manipulating integers than they are at manipulating objects. If you are going to use a variable as an integer, creating it as an object makes the program run much slower.

IMPRECISE INFERENCE

If Option Infer is on, Visual Basic may be able to deduce an explicit data type for a variable declared without a type. In that case, the program may not incur a performance penalty. It won't be clear from the code whether that's the case, however, so it could lead to some confusion.

In more advanced terms, integers are value types, whereas objects are reference types. A reference type is really a fancy pointer that represents the location of the actual object in memory. When you treat a value type as a reference type, Visual Basic performs an operation called *boxing*, where it wraps the value in an object so it can use references to the boxed value. If you then perform an operation involving two boxed values, Visual Basic must unbox them, perform the operation, and then possibly box the result to store it in another reference variable. All of this boxing and unboxing has a significant overhead.

Example program TimeGenericObjects, which is available for download on the book's website, uses the following code to demonstrate the difference in speed between using variables with explicit types and using variables of the generic Object type:

```
Dim num_trials As Integer = Integer.Parse(txtNumTrials.Text)

Dim start_time As DateTime
Dim stop_time As DateTime
Dim elapsed_time As TimeSpan

start_time = Now
For i As Integer = 1 To num_trials

Next i
stop_time = Now
elapsed_time = stop_time.Subtract(start_time)
lblIntegers.Text = elapsed_time.TotalSeconds.ToString("0.000000")
Refresh()

start_time = Now
For j = 1 To num_trials

Next j
stop_time = Now
elapsed_time = stop_time.Subtract(start_time)
lblObjects.Text = elapsed_time.TotalSeconds.ToString("0.000000")
```

The code executes two For loops. In the first loop, it explicitly declares its looping variable to be of type Integer. In the second loop, the code doesn't declare its looping variable (an easy typo to make), so Visual Basic automatically makes it an Object when it is needed. In one test, the second loop took more than 60 times as long as the first loop.

The second compiler directive that influences variable declaration is Option Strict. When Option Strict is turned off, Visual Basic silently converts values from one data type to another, even if the types are not necessarily compatible. For example, Visual Basic will allow the following code to try to copy the string s into the integer i. If the value in the string happens to be a number (as in the first case), this works. If the string is not a number (as in the second case), this throws an error at run time.

```
Dim i As Integer
Dim s As String
s = "10"
i = s        ' This works.
s = "Hello"
i = s        ' This Fails.
```

If you turn Option Strict on, Visual Basic warns you of possibly illegal conversions at compile time. You can still use conversion functions such as CInt, Int, and Integer.Parse to convert a string into an Integer, but you must take explicit action to do so.

To avoid confusion and ensure total control of your variable declarations, you should always turn on Option Explicit and Option Strict.

For more information on Option Explicit and Option Strict (including instructions for turning these options on), see the "Project" section in Chapter 2, "Menus, Toolbars, and Windows."

SCOPE

A variable's *scope* determines which other pieces of code can access it. For example, if you declare a variable inside a subroutine, only code within that subroutine can access the variable. The four possible levels of scope are (in increasing size of scope) block, procedure, module, and namespace.

Block Scope

A *block* is a series of statements enclosed in a construct that ends with some sort of End, Else, Loop, or Next statement. If you declare a variable within a block of code, the variable has block scope, and only other code within that block can access the variable. Furthermore, only code that appears after the variable's declaration can see the variable.

Variables declared in the block's opening statement are also part of the block. Note that a variable is visible within any sub-block contained within the variable's scope.

For example, consider the following code snippet:

```
For i As Integer = 1 To 5
    Dim j As Integer = 3
    If i = j Then
        Dim M As Integer = i + j
        Debug.WriteLine("M: " & M)
    Else
        Dim N As Integer = i * j
        Debug.WriteLine("N: " & N)
    End If

    Dim k As Integer = 123
    Debug.WriteLine("k: " & k)
Next i
```

This code uses a For loop with the looping variable i declared in the For statement. The scope of variable i is block-defined by the For loop. Code inside the loop can see variable i, but code outside of the loop cannot.

Inside the loop, the code declares variable j. This variable's scope is also the For loop's block.

If i equals j, the program declares variable M and uses it. This variable's scope includes only the two lines between the If and Else statements.

If i doesn't equal j, the code declares variable N. This variable's scope includes only the two lines between the Else and End If statements.

The program then declares variable k. This variable also has block scope, but it is available only after it is declared, so the code could not have accessed it earlier in the For loop.

Other code constructs that define blocks include the following:

➤ `Select Case` **statements** — Each Case has its own block.

➤ `Try Catch` **statements** — The Try section and each Exception statement defines a block. Note also that the exception variable defined in each Exception statement is in its own block. (That means they can all have the same name.)

➤ **Single-line** `If Then` **statements** — These are strange and confusing enough that you should avoid them, but the following code is legal:

```
If is_manager Then Dim txt As String = "M" : MessageBox.Show(txt) Else _
Dim txt As String = "E" : MessageBox.Show(txt)
```

➤ `While` **loops** — Variables declared inside the loop are local to the loop.

➤ `Using` **statements** — Resources acquired by the block and variables declared inside the block are local to the block.

Because block scope is the most restrictive, you should use it whenever possible to reduce the chances for confusion. The section "Restricting Scope" later in this chapter talks more about restricting variable scope.

Procedure Scope

If you declare a variable inside a subroutine, function, or other procedure, but not within a block, the variable is visible to any code inside the procedure that follows the declaration. The variable is not visible outside of the procedure. In a sense, the variable has block scope where the block is the procedure.

A procedure's parameters also have procedure scope. For example, in the following code, the scope of the `order_object` and `order_item` parameters is the `AddOrderItem` subroutine:

```
Public Sub AddOrderItem(order_object As Order, order_item As OrderItem)
    order_object.OrderItems.Add(order_item)
End Sub
```

Module Scope

A variable with module scope is available to all code in its code module, class, or structure, even if the code appears before the variable's declaration. For example, the following code works even though the `DisplayLoanAmount` subroutine is declared before the `LoanAmount` variable that it displays:

```
Private Class Lender
    Public Sub DisplayLoanAmount()
        MessageBox.Show(LoanAmount)
    End Sub

    Private LoanAmount As Decimal
    ...
End Class
```

To give a variable module scope, you should declare it with the Private, Protected, or Protected Friend keyword. If you declare the variable Private, it is visible only to code within the same module.

If you declare the variable Protected, it is accessible only to code in its class or a derived class. (Remember that you can only use the Protected keyword in a class.)

A Protected Friend variable is both Protected and Friend, so it is available only to code that is inside the variable's class or a derived class (Protected) and within the same project (Friend).

These keywords apply to both variable and procedure declarations. For example, you can declare a subroutine, function, or property procedure Private, Protected, or Protected Friend.

For more information on accessibility keywords, see the section "Accessibility" earlier in this chapter.

Example program ScopeTest, which is available for download on the book's website, demonstrates module and procedure scope.

Namespace Scope

By default, a project defines a namespace that includes all the project's variables and code. However, you can use Namespace statements to create other namespaces if you like. This may be useful to help categorize the code in your application.

If you declare a variable with the Public keyword, it has namespace scope and is available to all code in its namespace, whether inside the project or in another project. It is also available to code in any namespaces nested inside the variable's namespace. If you do not create any namespaces of your own, the whole project lies in a single namespace, so you can think of Public variables as having global scope.

If you declare a variable with the Friend keyword, it has namespace scope and is available to all code in its namespace within the same project. It is also available to code in any namespaces nested inside the variable's namespace within the project. If you do not create any namespaces of your own, the whole project lies in a single namespace so you can think of Friend variables as having project scope.

For more information on the Public and Friend keywords, see the section "Accessibility" earlier in this chapter.

Restricting Scope

There are several reasons why you should give variables the most restrictive scope possible that still lets them do their jobs.

Limited scope keeps the variable localized so that programmers cannot use the variable incorrectly in far off code that is unrelated to the variable's main purpose.

Having fewer variables with global scope means programmers have less to remember when they are working on the code. They can concentrate on their current work, rather than worrying about whether variables r and c are declared globally and whether the current code will interfere with them.

Limiting scope keeps variables closer to their declarations, so it's easier for programmers to check the declaration. One of the best examples of this situation is when a For loop declares its looping variable right in the For statement. A programmer can easily see that the looping variable is an integer without scrolling to the top of the subroutine hunting for its declaration. It is also easy to see that the variable has block scope, so other variables with the same names can be used outside of the loop.

Limited scope means a programmer doesn't need to worry about whether a variable's old value will interfere with the current code, or whether the final value after the current code exits will later interfere with some other code. This is particularly true for looping variables. If a program declares variable i at the top of a subroutine, and then uses it many times in various loops, you might need to do a little thinking to be sure the variable's past values won't interfere with new loops. If you declare i separately in each For statement, each loop has its own version of i, so there's no way they can interfere with each other.

Finally, variables with larger scope tend to be allocated more often, so they take up memory more often. For example, block variables and non-static variables declared with procedure scope are allocated when they are needed and are destroyed when their scope ends, freeing their memory. A variable declared Static or with module or namespace scope is not freed until your application exits. If those variables are large arrays, they may take up a lot of memory the entire time your application is running.

PARAMETER DECLARATIONS

A *parameter declaration* for a subroutine, function, or property procedure defines the names and types of the parameters passed into it. Parameter declarations always have non-static procedure scope. Visual Basic creates parameter variables when a procedure begins and destroys them when the procedure ends. The subroutine's code can access the parameters, but code outside of the routine cannot.

For example, the following subroutine takes an integer as a parameter. The subroutine calls this value employee_id. Code within the subroutine can access employee_id and code outside of the subroutine cannot.

```
Public Sub DisplayEmployee(ByVal employee_id As Integer)
    ...
End Sub
```

A parameter's basic scope is straightforward (non-static procedure scope), but parameters have some special features that complicate the situation. Although this isn't exactly a scoping issue, it's related closely enough to scope that it's worth covering here.

You can declare a parameter ByRef or ByVal (ByVal is the default if you use neither keyword). If you declare the variable ByVal, which stands for "by value," the routine makes its own local parameter variable with procedure scope just as you would expect.

If you declare a parameter with the keyword ByRef, which stands for "by reference," the routine does not create a separate copy of the parameter variable. Instead, it uses a reference to the parameter you pass in, and any changes the routine makes to the value are reflected in the calling subroutine.

For example, consider the two routines in the following code that double their parameters:

```
Sub DoubleItByVal(ByVal X As Single)
    X *= 2
End Sub

Sub DoubleItByRef(ByRef X As Single)
    X *= 2
End Sub

Sub TestParameters()
    Dim value As Single

    value = 10
    DoubleItByVal(value)
    Debug.WriteLine(value)

    value = 10
    DoubleItByRef(value)
    Debug.WriteLine(value)
End Sub
```

Subroutine `DoubleItByVal` declares its parameter with the ByVal keyword. Behind the scenes, this routine makes a new variable named x and copies the value of its argument into that variable. The parameter X is available within the subroutine. The routine multiplies x by 2 and then exits. At that point, the parameter variable goes out of scope and is destroyed.

Subroutine `DoubleItByRef` declares its parameter with the ByRef keyword. This routine's variable x is a reference to the variable passed into the routine. The subroutine doubles X and that doubles the variable in the calling code.

Subroutine `TestParameters` calls each of these routines. It declares a variable named `value`, passes it to subroutine `DoubleItByVal`, and displays the result after `DoubleItByVal` returns. Because `DoubleItByVal` declares its parameter ByVal, the variable value is not changed so the result is 10.

Subroutine `TestParameters` then calls subroutine `DoubleItByRef` and displays the result after that call returns. Subroutine `DoubleItByRef` declares its parameter ByRef so the variable `value` is changed to 20.

Even this more complex view of how procedures handle parameters has exceptions. If you pass a literal value or the result of an expression into a procedure by reference, there is no variable to pass by reference, so Visual Basic creates its own temporary variable. In that case, any changes made to the ByRef parameter are not returned to the calling routine, because that code did not pass a variable into the procedure. The following code shows statements that pass a literal expression and the result of an expression into the `DoubleItByRef` subroutine:

```
DoubleItByRef(12)    ' Literal expression.
DoubleItByRef(X + Y) ' Result of an expression.
```

Another case where a ByRef parameter does not modify a variable in the calling code is when you omit an optional parameter. For example, the following subroutine takes an optional ByRef parameter. If you call this routine and omit the parameter, Visual Basic creates the `employee_id` parameter from scratch so the subroutine can use it in its calculations. Because you called the routine without passing it a variable, the subroutine does not update a variable.

```
Sub UpdateEmployee(Optional ByRef employee_id As Integer = 0)
    ...
End Sub
```

Probably the sneakiest way a ByRef variable can fail to update a variable in the calling routine is if you enclose the variable in parentheses. The parentheses tell Visual Basic to evaluate their contents as an expression, so Visual Basic creates a temporary variable to hold the result of the expression. It then passes the temporary variable into the procedure. If the procedure's parameter is declared ByRef, it updates the temporary variable, but not the original variable, so the calling routine doesn't see any change to its value.

The following code calls subroutine `DoubleItByRef`, passing the variable `value` into the routine surrounded with parentheses. The `DoubleItByRef` subroutine doubles the temporary variable Visual Basic creates, leaving `value` unchanged.

```
DoubleItByRef((value))
```

Keep these issues in mind when you work with parameters. Parameters have non-static procedure scope but the ByRef keyword can sometimes carry their values outside of the routine.

For more information on routines and their parameters, see Chapter 16.

PROPERTY PROCEDURES

Property procedures are routines that can represent a variable-like value. To other pieces of the program, property procedures look just like variables, so they deserve mention in this chapter.

The following code shows property procedures that implement a Name property. The Property Get procedure simply returns the value in the private variable m_Name. The Property Set procedure saves a new value in the m_Name variable.

```
Private m_Name As String

Property Name() As String
    Get
        Return m_Name
    End Get
    Set(ByVal Value As String)
        m_Name = Value
    End Set
End Property
```

A program could use these procedures exactly as if there were a single public `Name` variable. For example, if this code is in the Employee class, the following code shows how a program could set and then get the `Name` value for the Employee object named `emp`:

```
emp.Name = "Rod Stephens"
MessageBox.Show(emp.Name)
```

You might want to use property procedures rather than a public variable for several reasons. First, the routines give you extra control over the getting and setting of the value. For example, you could use code to validate the value before saving it in the variable. The code could verify that a postal code or phone number has the proper format and throw an error if the value is badly formatted.

You can also set breakpoints in property procedures. Suppose that your program is crashing because a piece of code is setting an incorrect value in a variable. If you implement the variable with property procedures, you can set a breakpoint in the Property Set procedure and stop whenever the program sets the value. This can help you find the problem relatively quickly.

Property procedures let you set and get values in formats other than those you want to actually use to store the value. For example, the following code defines `Name` property procedures that save a name in `m_FirstName` and `m_LastName` variables. If your code would often need to use the last and first names separately, you could also provide property procedures to give access to those values separately.

```
Private m_LastName As String
Private m_FirstName As String

Property MyName() As String
    Get
        Return m_FirstName & " " & m_LastName
    End Get
    Set(ByVal Value As String)
        m_FirstName = Value.Split(" "c)(0)
        m_LastName = Value.Split(" "c)(1)
    End Set
End Property
```

Finally, you can use property procedures to create read-only and write-only variables. The following code shows how to make a read-only `NumEmployees` property procedure and a write-only `NumCustomers` property procedure. (Write-only property procedures are unusual but legal.)

```
Public ReadOnly Property NumEmployees() As Integer
    Get
        . . .
    End Get
End Property

Public WriteOnly Property NumCustomers() As Integer
    Set(ByVal Value As Integer)
        . . .
    End Set
End Property
```

You don't need to remember all of the syntax for property procedures. If you type the first line and press Enter, Visual Basic fills in the rest of the empty property procedures. If you use the keyword ReadOnly or WriteOnly, Visual Basic only includes the appropriate procedure.

Visual Basic also allows you to make *auto-implemented properties*. These are simply properties that do not have separate property procedures. You declare the property's name, and Visual Basic automatically creates the necessary backing variables and property procedures behind the scenes.

The following code shows a simple `FirstName` property:

```
Public Property FirstName As String
```

You can give a property a default value as in the following code:

```
Public Property FirstName As String = "<missing>"
```

You cannot use the ReadOnly or WriteOnly keywords with auto-implemented properties. If you want to make a read-only or write-only property, you need to write Get and Set procedures as described earlier.

The advantage of auto-implemented properties is that you don't need to write as much code. The disadvantage is that you can't set breakpoints in the property procedures.

PROPERTY PROCEDURES AS YOU NEED THEM

To get the best of both worlds, you can initially use auto-implemented properties. Later if you need to set breakpoints in the property procedures, you can redefine the property to include them.

ENUMERATED DATA TYPES

An *enumerated type* is a discrete list of specific values. You define the enumerated type and the values allowed. Later, if you declare a variable of that data type, it can take only those values.

For example, suppose that you are building a large application where users can have one of three access levels: clerk, supervisor, and administrator. You could define an enumerated type named `AccessLevels` that allows the values `Clerk`, `Supervisor`, and `Administrator`. Now, if you declare a variable to be of type `AccessLevels`, Visual Basic will only allow the variable to take those values.

The following code shows a simple example. It defines the `AccessLevels` type and declares the variable `AccessLevel` using the type. Later the `MakeSupervisor` subroutine sets `AccessLevel` to the value `AccessLevels.Supervisor`. Note that the value is prefixed with the enumerated type's name.

```
Public Enum AccessLevels
    Clerk
    Supervisor
    Administrator
End Enum

Private AccessLevel As AccessLevels ' The user's access level.

' Set supervisor access level.
Public Sub MakeSupervisor()
    AccessLevel = AccessLevels.Supervisor
End Sub
```

The syntax for declaring an enumerated type is as follows:

```
[attribute_list] [accessibility] [Shadows] Enum name [As type]
    [attribute_list] value_name [= initialization_expression]
    [attribute_list] value_name [= initialization_expression]
    ...
End Enum
```

Most of these terms, including *attribute_list* and *accessibility*, are similar to those used by variable declarations. See the section "Variable Declarations" earlier in this chapter for more information.

The *type* value must be an integral type and can be Byte, Short, Integer, or Long. If you omit this value, Visual Basic stores the enumerated type values as integers.

The *value_name* pieces are the names you want to allow the enumerated type to have. You can include an initialization_expression for each value if you like. That value must be compatible with the underlying data type (Byte, Short, Integer, or Long). If you omit a value's initialization expression, the value is set to one greater than the previous value, with the first value equal to zero by default.

In the previous example, Clerk = 0, Supervisor = 1, and Administrator = 2. The following code changes the numeric assignments so Clerk = 10, Supervisor = 11, and Administrator = −1:

```
Public Enum AccessLevels
    Clerk = 10
    Supervisor
    Administrator = -1
End Enum
```

Usually, all that's important about an enumerated type is that its values are unique, so you don't need to explicitly initialize the values.

Note that you can give enumerated values the same integer value either explicitly or implicitly. For example, the following code defines several equivalent AccessLevels values. The first three values, Clerk, Supervisor, and Administrator, default to 0, 1, and 2, respectively. The code explicitly sets User to 0, so it is the same as Clerk. The values Manager and SysAdmin then default to the next two values, 1 and 2 (the same as Supervisor and Administrator). Finally, the code explicitly sets Superuser = SysAdmin.

```
Public Enum AccessLevels
    Clerk
    Supervisor
    Administrator
    User = 0
    Manager
    SysAdmin
    Superuser = SysAdmin
End Enum
```

This code is somewhat confusing. The following version makes it more obvious that some values are synonyms for others:

```
Public Enum AccessLevel
    Clerk
    Supervisor
    Administrator

    User = Clerk
    Manager = Supervisor
    SysAdmin = Administrator
    Superuser = Administrator
End Enum
```

If you really need to set an enumerated variable to a calculated value for some reason, you can use the CType function to convert an integer value into the enumerated type. For example, the following statement uses the value in the variable `integer_value` to set the value of the variable `AccessLevel`. Making you use CType to perform this type of conversion makes it less likely that you will set an enumerated value accidentally.

```
AccessLevel = CType(integer_value, AccessLevel)
```

Another benefit of enumerated types is that they allow Visual Basic to provide IntelliSense help. If you type `AccessLevel =`, Visual Basic provides a list of the allowed `AccessLevels` values.

A final benefit of enumerated types is that they provide a ToString method that returns the textual name of the value. For example, the following code displays the message "Clerk":

```
Dim access_level As AccessLevel = Clerk
MessageBox.Show(access_level.ToString())
```

Example program AccessLevelEnum, which is available for download on the book's website, makes an `AccessLevels` Enum and then displays the results returned by calling ToString for each of its values.

If you have a variable that can take only a fixed number of values, you should probably make it an enumerated type. Also, if you discover that you have defined a series of constants to represent related values, you should consider converting them into an enumerated type. Then you can gain the benefits of the improved Visual Basic type checking and IntelliSense.

ANONYMOUS TYPES

An *anonymous type* is an object data type that is built automatically by Visual Basic and never given a name for the program to use. The type is used implicitly by the code that needs it and is then discarded.

The following code uses LINQ to select data from an array of BookInfo objects named `BookInfos`. It begins by using a LINQ query to fill variable `book_query` with the selected books. It iterates through the results stored in `book_query`, adding information about the selected books to a string, and displays the result in a text box.

```
Dim book_query =
    From book As BookInfo In BookInfos
    Where book.Year > 1999
    Select book.Title, book.Pages, book.Year
    Order By Year

Dim txt As String = ""
For Each book_data In book_query
    txt &= book_data.Title & " (" & book_data.Year & ", " &
        book_data.Pages & " pages)" & vbCrLf
Next book_data
txtResult.Text = txt
```

The `book_query` variable is an ordered sequence containing objects that hold the data selected by the query: Title, Pages, and Year. This type of object doesn't have an explicit definition; it is an anonymous type created by Visual Basic to hold the selected values Title, Pages, and Year. If you hover the mouse over the `book_query` variable in the code editor, a tooltip appears giving the variable's data type as:

```
System.Linq.IOrderedEnumerable(Of <anonymous type>)
```

Later, the code uses a For Each loop to enumerate the objects in `book_query`. The looping variable `book_data` must have the same type as the items in the sequence. The code does not explicitly give the variable's data type, so Visual Basic can infer it. If you hover the mouse over the `book_data` variable in the code editor, a tooltip appears giving the variable's data type as:

```
<anonymous type>
```

You are not really intended to use anonymous types explicitly. For example, you shouldn't need to declare a new object of the anonymous type. They are intended to support LINQ. Although you won't use anonymous types explicitly, it's still helpful to understand what they are.

IMPORTANT INFERENCE

In this example, Visual Basic infers the data types for the `book_query` and `book` variables. This is important because they must use an anonymous type, so you cannot explicitly give them a type. Because these data types are inferred, the code will only work if Option Infer is on.

For more information on LINQ, see Chapter 20.

NULLABLE TYPES

Most relational databases have a concept of a null data value. A null value indicates that a field does not contain any data. It lets the database distinguish between valid zero or blank values and non-existing values. For example, a null bank balance would indicate that there is no known balance, while a 0 would indicate that the balance was 0.

You can create a nullable variable in Visual Basic by adding a question mark either to the variable's name or after its data type. You can also declare the variable to be of type Nullable(Of *type*). For example, the following code declares three nullable integers:

```
Dim i As Integer?
Dim j? As Integer
Dim k As Nullable(Of Integer)
```

To make a nullable variable "null," set it equal to Nothing. The following code makes variable num_choices null:

```
num_choices = Nothing
```

To see if a nullable variable contains a value, use the Is or IsNot operator to compare it to Nothing. The following code determines whether the nullable variable num_choices contains a value. If the variable contains a value, the code increments it. Otherwise the code sets the value to 1.

```
If num_choices IsNot Nothing Then
    num_choices += 1
Else
    num_choices = 1
End If
```

Calculations with nullable variables use "null-propagation" rules to ensure that the result makes sense. For example, if a nullable integer contains no value, it probably doesn't make sense to add another number to it. (What is null plus three?)

If one or more operands in an expression contains a null value, the result is a null value. For example, if num_choices in the previous example contains a null value, then num_choices + 1 is also a null value. (That's why the previous code checks explicitly to see whether num_choices is null before incrementing its value.)

Example program NullableTypes, which is available for download on the book's website, demonstrates nullable types.

CONSTANTS

In many respects, a constant is a lot like a read-only variable. Both variable and constant declarations may have attributes, accessibility keywords, and initialization expressions. Both read-only variables and constants represent a value that the code cannot change after it is assigned.

The syntax for declaring a constant is as follows:

```
[attribute_list] [accessibility] [Shadows]
Const name [As type] = initialization_expression
```

For the general meanings of the various parts of a constant declaration, see the section "Variable Declarations" earlier in this chapter. The following sections describe differences between read-only variable and constant declarations.

Accessibility

When you declare a variable, you can omit the Dim keyword if you use any of the keywords Public, Protected, Friend, Protected Friend, Private, Static, or ReadOnly. You cannot omit the Const keyword when you declare a constant, because it tells Visual Basic that you are declaring a constant rather than a variable.

You cannot use the Static, ReadOnly, or Shared keywords in a constant declaration. Static implies that the value will change over time and the value should be retained when the enclosing routine starts and stops. Because the code cannot change a constant's value, that doesn't make sense.

The ReadOnly keyword would be redundant because you already cannot change a constant's value.

You use the Shared keyword in a variable declaration within a class to indicate that the variable's value is shared by all instances of the class. If one object changes the value, all objects see the changed value. Because the program cannot change a constant's value, the value need not be shared. All objects have the same version of the constant at all times. You can think of a constant as always shared.

You can use the other accessibility keywords in a constant declaration: Public, Protected, Friend, Protected Friend, and Private.

As Type

If you have Option Strict turned on, you must include the constant's data type. A constant can only be an intrinsic type (Boolean, Byte, Short, Integer, Long, Decimal, Single, Double, Char, String, Date, or Object) or the name of an enumerated type. You cannot declare a constant that is a class, structure, or array.

If you declare the constant with the Object data type, the initialization_expression must set the object equal to Nothing. If you want a constant that represents some other object, or a class, structure, or array, use a read-only variable instead.

Because the generic Object class doesn't raise any events, and because you cannot make a constant of some other class type, it doesn't make sense to use the WithEvents keyword in a constant declaration.

> **INFER REQUIRED**
>
> Though Visual Basic has inferred types for local variables, it does not infer types of constants. If you have Option Strict on, you must explicitly give all constants a data type.

Initialization_Expression

The initialization_expression assigns the constant its never-changing value. You cannot use variables in the initialization_expression, but you can use conversion functions such as CInt. You can also use the values of previously defined constants and enumeration values. The expression can include type characters such as # or &H, and if the declaration doesn't include a type statement (and Option Explicit is off), the type of the value determines the type of the constant.

The following code demonstrates these capabilities. The first statement uses the CInt function to convert the value 123.45 into an integer constant. The second and third statements set the values of two Long constants to hexadecimal values. The next statement combines the values defined in the previous two using a bitwise Or. The final statement sets a constant to a value defined by the enumerated type AccessLevels.

```
Private Const MAX_VALUES As Integer = CInt(123.45)
Private Const MASK_READ As Long = &H1000&
Private Const MASK_WRITE As Long = &H2000&
Private Const MASK_READ_WRITE As Long = MASK_READ Or MASK_WRITE
Private Const MAX_ACCESS_LEVEL As AccessLevels = AccessLevels.SuperUser
```

DELEGATES

A *delegate* is a type that refers to a subroutine, function, or other method. The method can be an instance method provided by an object, a class's shared method, or a method defined in a code module. A delegate variable acts as a pointer to a subroutine or function. Delegate variables are sometimes called *type-safe function pointers*.

The Delegate keyword defines a delegate type and specifies the parameters and return type of the method to which the delegate will refer.

The following code demonstrates a delegate:

```
' Define a StringDisplayerType delegate to be a pointer to a subroutine
' that has a string parameter.
Private Delegate Sub StringDisplayerType(ByVal str As String)

' Declare a StringDisplayerType variable.
Dim DisplayStringRoutine As StringDisplayerType

' Assign the variable to a subroutine.
DisplayStringRoutine = AddressOf ShowStringInOutputWindow

' Invoke the delegate's subroutine.
DisplayStringRoutine("Hello world")
```

The code uses a Delegate statement to declare the StringDisplayerType to be a reference to a subroutine that takes a string as a parameter. Next, the code declares the variable DisplayStringRoutine to be of this type. This variable can hold a reference to a subroutine that takes a string parameter. The code then sets the variable equal to the ShowStringInOutputWindow subroutine. Finally, the code invokes the delegate's subroutine, passing it a string.

The delegate in the preceding example holds a reference to a subroutine defined in a code module. A delegate can also hold the address of a class's shared method or an instance method. For example, suppose the Employee class defines the shared function GetNumEmployees that returns the number of employees loaded. Suppose that it also defines the instance function ToString that returns an Employee object's first and last names.

Example program UseDelegates, which is available for download on the book's website, uses the following code to demonstrate delegates for both of these functions:

```
Dim emp As New Employee("Rod", "Stephens")

' Use a delegate pointing to a shared class method.
Private Delegate Function NumEmployeesDelegate() As Integer

Private Sub btnShared_Click() Handles btnShared.Click
    Dim show_num As NumEmployeesDelegate
    show_num = AddressOf Employee.GetNumEmployees
    MessageBox.Show(show_num().ToString, "# Employees")
End Sub

' Use a delegate pointing to a class instance method.
Private Delegate Function GetNameDelegate() As String
Private Sub btnInstance_Click() Handles btnInstance.Click
    Dim show_name As GetNameDelegate
    show_name = AddressOf emp.ToString
    MessageBox.Show(show_name(), "Name")
End Sub
```

First, the program declares and initializes an Employee object named emp. It then defines a delegate named NumEmployeesDelegate, which is a pointer to a function that returns an integer. The btnShared_Click event handler declares a variable of this type, sets it to the address of the Employee class's shared GetNumEmployees function, and calls the function. Then the code defines a delegate named GetNameDelegate, which is a pointer to a function that returns a string. The btnInstance_Click event handler declares a variable of this type, sets it to the address of the emp object's ToString function, and then calls the function.

These examples are somewhat contrived because the code could easily invoke the subroutines and functions directly without delegates, but they show how a program can save a delegate pointing to a subroutine or function and then call it later. A real application might set the delegate variable's value and only use it much later.

A particular delegate variable could hold references to different methods, depending on the program's situation. For example, different subroutines might generate output on a form, on the printer, or into a bitmap file. The program could set a delegate variable to any of these routines. Later, the program could invoke the variable's routine without needing to know which routine will actually execute.

Another useful technique is to pass a delegate variable into a subroutine or function. For example, suppose that you are writing a subroutine that sorts an array of Customer objects. This routine could take as a parameter a delegate variable that references the function to use when comparing the objects in the array. By passing different functions into the routine, you could make it sort customers by company name, contact name, customer ID, total past sales, or anything else you can imagine.

Delegates are particularly confusing to many programmers, but understanding them is worth a little extra effort. They can add an extra dimension to your programming by essentially allowing you to manipulate subroutines and functions as if they were data.

NAMING CONVENTIONS

Many development teams adopt naming conventions to make their code more consistent and easier to read. Different groups have developed their own conventions, and you cannot really say that one of them is best. It doesn't really matter which convention you adopt. What is important is that you develop some coding style that you use consistently.

One rather simple convention is to use `lowercase_letters_with_underscores` for variables with routine scope, `MixedCaseLetters` for variables with module and global scope, and `ALL_CAPS` for constants of any scope. For example, the following statement defines a module-scope PictureBox variable:

```
Private Canvas As PictureBox
```

Routine names are generally `MixedCase`.

Many developers carry these rules a bit further and add type prefix abbreviations to control names. For example, the following code declares a PictureBox variable:

```
Dim picCanvas As PictureBox
```

Some developers add scope prefixes (m for module, g for global), and some also add type prefixes to variables other than controls (such as `iNumEmployees` for an integer) and even to subroutine names (as in `gstrGetWebmasterName` for a global function that returns a string). Visual Studio's IntelliSense will tell you a variable's data type if you hover the mouse over it so these more complex prefixes are not as useful as they were before IntelliSense became so powerful. For that reason this type of prefix is much less common than it used to be.

No matter which convention you use, the most important piece of a name is the descriptive part. The name `mblnDL` tells you that the value is a module-scope Boolean, but it doesn't tell you what the value means (and variables with such terrible names are all too common). The name `DataIsLoaded` is much more descriptive.

WHAT'S IN A NAME?

I have never seen a project that suffered because it lacked variable prefixes such as `mbln`. However, I have seen developers waste huge amounts of time because the descriptive parts of variable names were confusing. Take a few seconds to think of a good, meaningful name.

Building an all-encompassing naming convention that defines abbreviations for every conceivable type of data, control, object, database component, menu, constant, and routine name takes a lot of time and more space than it's worth in a book such as this. For an article that describes the conventions used by Microsoft Consulting Services, go to `http://support.microsoft.com/kb/110264`. It explains everything, including data type abbreviations, making the first part of a function name contain a verb (`GetUserName` rather than `UserName`), and commenting conventions. That article was written in 2003 and common usage changes over time, but the article can give you a place to start in defining your own naming conventions.

Naming and coding conventions make it easier for other programmers to read your code. Look over the Microsoft Consulting Services conventions or search the web for others. Select the features that you think make the most sense and ignore the others. It's more important that you write consistent code than that you follow a particular set of rules.

SUMMARY

Two of the most important things you control with a variable declaration are its data type and its visibility. Visibility combines scope (the piece of code that contains the variable such as a For loop, subroutine, or module), accessibility (the code that is allowed to access the variable determined by keywords such as Private, Public, and Friend), and lifetime (when the variable has been created and not yet destroyed).

To avoid confusion, explicitly declare the data type whenever possible and use the most limited scope possible for the variable's purpose. Turn Option Explicit and Option Strict on to allow the IDE to help you spot potential scope and type errors before they become a problem.

Code that uses LINQ complicates matters somewhat. When you use LINQ, it is generally not possible to explicitly declare every variable's data type. A LINQ query can return a sequence of objects that have an anonymous type. If you enumerate over the sequence, the looping variable will be of the same anonymous type. In those cases, when you cannot explicitly declare a variable's type, use extra caution to make the code easy to understand so you can fix and maintain it later. For more information on LINQ, see Chapter 20.

Parameters, property procedures, and constants have similar data type and scope issues. Once you become comfortable with variable declarations, they should give you little trouble.

One of the most important steps you can take to make your code easier to debug and maintain is to make your code consistent. A good naming convention can help. Review the guidelines used by Microsoft Consulting Services, and adopt the pieces that make the most sense to you.

After you know how to declare variables, you are ready to learn how to combine them. Chapter 15, "Operators," explains the symbols (such as +, 2, and ^) that you can use to combine variables to produce new results.

15

Operators

WHAT'S IN THIS CHAPTER

➤ Arithmetic, concatenation, logical, and bitwise operators

➤ Operator precedence

➤ The StringBuilder class

➤ Operator overloading

WROX.COM CODE DOWNLOADS FOR THIS CHAPTER

The wrox.com code downloads for this chapter are found at `http://www.wrox.com/remtitle.cgi?isbn=9781118314074` on the Download Code tab. The code for this chapter is divided into the following major examples:

➤ ComplexNumbers

➤ MultiplyTimeSpan

➤ StringBuilderTest1

➤ StringBuilderTest2

UNDERSTANDING OPERATORS

An *operator* is a basic code element that performs some operation on one or more values to create a result. The values the operator acts upon are called *operands*. For example, in the following statement, the operator is + (addition), the operands are B and C, and the result is assigned to the variable A:

```
A = B + C
```

The Visual Basic operators fall into five categories: arithmetic, concatenation, comparison, logical, and bitwise. This chapter first explains these categories and the operators they contain, and then discusses other operator issues such as precedence, assignment operators, and operator overloading. Also included are discussions of some specialized issues that arise when you work with strings and dates.

ARITHMETIC OPERATORS

The following table lists the arithmetic operators provided by Visual Basic. Most programmers should be very familiar with most of them. The four operators that may need a little extra explanation are \, Mod, <<, and >>.

OPERATOR	PURPOSE	EXAMPLE	RESULT
^	Exponentiation	2 ^ 3	(2 to the power 3) = 2 * 2 * 2 = 8
–	Negation	–2	–2
*	Multiplication	2 * 3	6
/	Division	3 / 2	1.5
\	Integer division	17 \ 5	3
Mod	Modulus	17 Mod 5	2
+	Addition	2 + 3	5
–	Subtraction	3 – 2	1
<<	Bit left shift	10110111 << 1	01101110
>>	Bit right shift	10110111 >> 1	01011011

The \ operator performs integer division. It returns the result of dividing its first operand by the second, dropping any remainder. It's important to understand that the result is truncated toward zero, not rounded. For example, 7 \ 4 = 1 and –7 \ 4 = –1 rather than 2 and –2 as you might expect.

The Mod operator returns the remainder after dividing its first operand by its second. For example, 17 Mod 5 = 2 because 17 = 3 * 5 + 2.

The << operator shifts the bits of an Integer value to the left, padding the empty bits on the right with zeros. For example, the byte value with bits 10110111 shifted 1 bit to the left gives 01101110 and shifting 10110111 2 bits to the left gives 11011100.

The >> operator shifts the bits of a value to the right, padding the empty bits on the left with zeros. For example, the byte value with bits 10110111 shifted 1 bit to the right gives 01011011 and shifting 10110111 2 bits to the right gives 00101101.

Unfortunately, Visual Basic doesn't work easily with bit values, so you cannot use a binary value such as 10110111 in your code. Instead, you must write this value as the hexadecimal value &HB7 or the decimal value 183. The last two entries in the table show the values in binary, so it is easier to understand how the shifts work.

CALCULATOR CLEVERNESS

The Calculator application that comes with Windows lets you easily convert between binary, octal, hexadecimal, and decimal. To start the Calculator, open the Start menu and select Run. Type **calc** and click OK. In newer versions of the calculator, open the View menu and select Programmer. If your version doesn't have Programmer mode, open the View menu and select Scientific. Now you can click the Bin, Oct, Dec, or Hex radio buttons to select a base, enter a value, and select another base to convert the value.

CONCATENATION OPERATORS

Visual Basic provides two concatenation operators: + and &. Both join two strings together. Because the + symbol also represents an arithmetic operator, your code will be easier to read if you use the & symbol for concatenation. Using & can also make your code faster and lead to fewer problems because it lets Visual Basic know that the operands are strings.

COMPARISON OPERATORS

Comparison operators compare one value to another and return a Boolean value (True or False), depending on the result. The following table lists the comparison operators provided by Visual Basic. The first six (=, <>, <, <=, >, and >=) are relatively straightforward. Note that the Not operator is not a comparison operator, so it is not listed here. It is described in the next section, "Logical Operators."

OPERATOR	PURPOSE	EXAMPLE	RESULT
=	Equals	A = B	True if A equals B
<>	Not equals	A <> B	True if A does not equal B
<	Less than	A < B	True if A is less than B
<=	Less than or equal to	A <= B	True if A is less than or equal to B
>	Greater than	A > B	True if A is greater than B
>=	Greater than or equal to	A >= B	True if A is greater than or equal to B
Is	Equality of two objects	emp Is mgr	True if emp and mgr refer to the same object
IsNot	Inequality of two objects	emp IsNot mgr	True if emp and mgr refer to different objects

continues

(continued)

TypeOf ... Is	Object is of a certain type	TypeOf(obj) Is Manager	True if obj points to an object that inherits from Manager
Like	Matches a text pattern	A Like "###-####"	True if A contains three digits, a dash, and four digits

The Is operator returns True if its two operands refer to the same object. For example, if you create an Order object and make two different variables, A and B, point to it, the expression A Is B is True. Note that Is returns False if the two operands point to different Order objects that happen to have the same property values.

The IsNot operator is simply shorthand for a more awkward Not . . . Is construction. For example, the statement A IsNot Nothing is equivalent to Not (A Is Nothing).

The value *Nothing* is a special value that means *not an object*. If you have an object variable, you can use the Is or IsNot operator to compare it to Nothing to see if it represents anything. Note that you cannot use Is or IsNot to compare an object variable to 0 or some other numeric value. Is and IsNot work only with objects such as those stored in variables and the special value Nothing.

The TypeOf operator returns True if its operand is of a certain type or inherits from that type. This operator is particularly useful when a subroutine takes a parameter that could be of more than one object type. It can use TypeOf to see which type of object it has.

The Like operator returns True if its first operand matches a pattern specified by its second operand. Where the pattern includes normal characters, the string must match those characters exactly. The pattern can also include several special character sequences summarized in the following table.

CHARACTER(S)	MEANING
?	Matches any single character
*	Matches any zero or more characters
#	Matches any single digit
[characters]	Matches any of the characters between the brackets
[!characters]	Matches any character not between the brackets
A-Z	When inside brackets, matches any character in the range A to Z

You can combine ranges of characters and individual characters inside brackets. For example, the pattern [a-zA-Z] matches any letter between a and z or between A and Z. The following table lists some useful patterns for use with the Like operator.

PATTERN	MEANING
`[2-9]##-####`	Seven-digit U.S. phone number
`[2-9]##-[2-9]##-####`	Ten-digit phone number, including area code
`1-[2-9]##-[2-9]##-####`	Eleven-digit phone number, beginning with 1 and area code
`#####`	Five-digit ZIP code
`#####-####`	Nine-digit ZIP + 4 code
`?*@?*.?*`	E-mail address

For example, the following code checks whether the text box txtPhone contains something that looks like a 10-digit phone number:

```
If Not (txtPhone.Text Like "[2-9]##-[2-9]##-####") Then
    MessageBox.Show("Please enter a valid phone number")
End If
```

These patterns are not completely foolproof. For example, the e-mail address pattern verifies that the string contains at least one character, an @ character, at least one other character, a dot, and at least one more character. For example, it allows RodStephens@vb-helper.com. However, it does not verify that the extension makes sense, so it also allows RodStephens@vb-helper.commercial, and it allows more than one @ character, as in RodStephens@vb-helper.com@bad_value.

Regular expressions provide much more powerful pattern-matching capabilities. For an introduction to regular expressions, see http://www.codeproject.com/Articles/939/An-Introduction-to-Regular-Expressions.

LOGICAL OPERATORS

Logical operators combine two Boolean values and return True or False, depending on the result. The following table summarizes Visual Basic's logical operators.

OPERATOR	PURPOSE	EXAMPLE	RESULT
`Not`	Logical or bitwise negation	`Not A`	True if A is false
`And`	Logical or bitwise And	`A And B`	True if A and B are both true
`Or`	Logical or bitwise Or	`A Or B`	True if A or B or both are true
`Xor`	Logical or bitwise exclusive Or	`A Xor B`	True if A or B but not both is true
`AndAlso`	Logical or bitwise And with short-circuit evaluation	`A AndAlso B`	True if A and B are both true (see the following notes)
`OrElse`	Logical or bitwise Or with short-circuit evaluation	`A OrElse B`	True if A or B or both are true (see notes)

The operators Not, And, and Or are relatively straightforward.

"Xor" stands for "exclusive or," and the Xor operator returns True if one but not both of its operands is true. The expression A Xor B is true if A is true or B is true but both are not true.

Xor is useful for situations where exactly one of two things should be true. For example, suppose you're running a small software conference with two tracks so two talks are going on at any given time. Each attendee should sign up for one talk in each time slot but cannot sign up for both because they're at the same time. Then you might use code similar to the following to check whether an attendee has signed up for either talk 1a or talk 1b but not both:

```
If talk1a Xor talk1b Then
    ' This is okay
    ...
End If
```

The AndAlso and OrElse operators are similar to the And and Or operators, except that they provide short-circuit evaluation. In *short-circuit evaluation*, Visual Basic is allowed to stop evaluating operands if it can deduce the final result without them. For example, consider the expression A AndAlso B. If Visual Basic evaluates the value A and discovers that it is False, the program knows that the expression A AndAlso B is also False no matter what value B has, so it doesn't need to evaluate B.

Whether the program evaluates both operands doesn't matter much if A and B are simple Boolean variables. However, assume that they are time-consuming functions in the following code. For example, the TimeConsumingFunction routine might need to look up values in a database or download data from a website. In that case, not evaluating the second operand might save a lot of time.

```
If TimeConsumingFunction("A") AndAlso TimeConsumingFunction("B") Then ...
```

Just as AndAlso can stop evaluation if it discovers one of its operands is False, the OrElse operand can stop evaluating if it discovers that one of its operands is True. The expression A OrElse B is True if either A or B is True. If the program finds that A is True, it doesn't need to evaluate B.

Because AndAlso and OrElse do the same thing as And and Or but sometimes faster, you might wonder why you would ever use And and Or. The main reason is that the operands may have side effects. A *side effect* is some action a routine performs that is not obviously part of the routine. For example, suppose that the NumEmployees function opens an employee database and returns the number of employee records, leaving the database open. The fact that this function leaves the database open is a side effect.

Now, suppose that the NumCustomers function similarly opens the customer database, and then consider the following statement:

```
If (NumEmployees() > 0) AndAlso (NumCustomers() > 0) Then ...
```

After this code executes, you cannot be certain which databases are open. If NumEmployees returns 0, the AndAlso operator's first operand is False, so it doesn't evaluate the NumCustomers function and that function doesn't open the customer database.

The AndAlso and OrElse operators can improve application performance under some circumstances. However, to avoid possible confusion and long debugging sessions, do not use AndAlso or OrElse with operands that have side effects.

BITWISE OPERATORS

Bitwise operators work much like logical operators do, except they compare values one bit at a time. The bitwise negation operator Not flips the bits in its operand from 1 to 0 and vice versa. The following shows an example:

```
    10110111
Not 01001000
```

The And operator places a 1 in a result bit if both of the operands have a 1 in that position. The following shows the results of combining two binary values by using the bitwise And operator:

```
    10101010
And 00110110
    00100010
```

The bitwise Or operator places a 1 bit in the result if either of its operands has a 1 in the corresponding position. The following shows an example:

```
    10101010
Or  00110110
    10111110
```

The bitwise Xor operator places a 1 bit in the result if exactly one of its operands, but not both, has a 1 in the corresponding position. The following shows an example:

```
    10101010
Xor 00110110
    10011100
```

There are no bitwise equivalents for the AndAlso and OrElse operators.

OPERATOR PRECEDENCE

When Visual Basic evaluates a complex expression, it must decide the order in which to evaluate operators. For example, consider the expression 1 + 2 * 3 / 4 + 2. The following text shows three orders in which you might evaluate this expression to get three different results:

```
1 + (2 * 3) / (4 + 2) = 1 + 6 / 6 = 2
1 + (2 * 3 / 4) + 2 = 1 + 1.5 + 2 = 4.5
(1 + 2) * 3 / (4 + 2) = 3 * 3 / 6 = 1.5
```

Precedence determines which operator Visual Basic executes first. For example, the Visual Basic precedence rules say the program should evaluate multiplication and division before addition, so the second equation is correct.

The following table lists the operators in order of precedence. When evaluating an expression, the program evaluates an operator before it evaluates those lower than it in the list.

OPERATOR	DESCRIPTION
( )	Grouping (parentheses)
^	Exponentiation
-	Negation
*, /	Multiplication and division
\	Integer division
Mod	Modulus
+, -, +	Addition, subtraction, and concatenation
&	Concatenation
<<, >>	Bit shift
=, <>, <, <=, >, >=, Like, Is, IsNot, TypeOf ... Is	All comparisons
Not	Logical and bitwise negation
And, AndAlso	Logical and bitwise And with and without short-circuit evaluation
Xor, Or, OrElse	Logical and bitwise Xor, and Or with and without short-circuit evaluation

When operators are on the same line in the table, or if an expression contains more than one instance of the same operator, the program evaluates them in left-to-right order. For example, * and / are on the same line in the table so in the expression 12 * 4 / 20 Visual Basic would perform the multiplication first. (Of course, it wouldn't matter much in this example because the result should be the same either way, at least within the limits of the computer's precision.)

Parentheses are not really operators, but they do have a higher precedence than the true operators, so they're listed to make the table complete. You can always use parentheses to explicitly dictate the order in which Visual Basic will perform an evaluation.

If there's the slightest doubt about how Visual Basic will handle an expression, add parentheses to make it obvious. Even if you can easily figure out what an expression means, parentheses often make the code even easier to read and understand. There's no extra charge for using parentheses, and they may avoid some unnecessary confusion.

ASSIGNMENT OPERATORS

Visual Basic has always had the simple assignment operator =. Visual Basic .NET added several new assignment operators to handle some common statements where a value was set equal to itself combined with some other value. For example, the following two statements both add the value 10 to the variable `iterations`:

```
iterations = iterations + 10 ' Original syntax.
iterations += 10             ' New syntax.
```

All the other assignment operators work similarly by adding an equals sign to an arithmetic operator. For example, the statement A `^=` B is equivalent to A `=` A `^` B.

You can still use the original syntax if you like. However, the new syntax sometimes gives you better performance. If the left-hand side of the assignment is not a simple variable, Visual Basic may be able to save time by evaluating it only once. For example, the following code adds `0.1` to a customer order's discount value. By using +=, the code allows Visual Basic to find the location of this value only once.

```
Customers(cust_num).Orders(order_num).Discount += 0.1
```

> **PERFORMANCE ANXIETY**
>
> In most applications, performance is usually adequate whether you use += or the older syntax. Usually, you are best off if you use whichever version seems most natural and easiest to understand and only worry about performance when you are sure you have a problem.

The complete list of assignment operators is: =, ^=, *=, /=, \=, +=, -=, &=, <<=, and >>=.

If you have Option Strict set to On, the variables must have the appropriate data types. For example, /= returns a Double, so you cannot use that operator with an Integer, as in the following code:

```
Dim i As Integer = 100
i /= 2                       ' Not allowed.
```

To perform this operation, you must explicitly convert the result into an Integer, as shown in the following statement:

```
i = CInt(i / 2)
```

This makes sense because you are trying to assign the value of floating-point division to an Integer. It's less obvious why the following code is also illegal. Here the code is trying to assign an Integer result to a Single variable, so you might think it should work. After all, an Integer value will fit in a Single variable.

```
Dim x As Single
x \= 10                      ' Not allowed.
```

The problem isn't in the assignment but in performing the calculation. The following statement is equivalent to the previous one, and it is also illegal:

```
x = x \ 10                 ' Not allowed.
```

The problem with both of these statements is that the \ operator takes as arguments two Integers. If Option Strict is on, the program will not automatically convert a floating-point variable into an Integer for the \ operator. To make this statement work, you must manually convert the variable into an Integer data type, as shown in the following example:

```
x = CLng(x) \ 10 ' Allowed.
```

The += and &= operators both combine strings but &= is less ambiguous, so you should use it whenever possible. It may also give you better performance because it explicitly tells Visual Basic that the operands are strings.

THE STRINGBUILDER CLASS

The & and &= operators are useful for concatenating a few strings together. However, if you must combine a large number of strings, you may get better performance by using the StringBuilder class. This class is optimized for performing long sequences of concatenations to build big strings.

For small pieces of code, the difference between using a String and a StringBuilder is negligible. If you need to concatenate a dozen or so strings once, using a StringBuilder won't make much difference in run time and may even slow performance slightly.

However, if you make huge strings built up in pieces, or if you build simpler strings but many times in a loop, StringBuilder may make your program run faster.

Example program StringBuilderTest1, which is available for download on the book's website, concatenates the string 1234567890 a large number of times, first using a String variable and then using a StringBuilder. In one test that performed the concatenation 10,000 times to build strings 100,000 characters long, using a String took roughly 1.6 seconds. Using a StringBuilder, the program was able to build the string in roughly 0.001 seconds.

Admittedly, building such enormous strings is not a common programming task. Even when the strings are shorter, you can sometimes see a noticeable difference in performance, particularly if you must build a large number of such strings.

Example program StringBuilderTest2, which is also available for download, concatenates the string 1234567890 to itself 100 times, making a string 1,000 characters long. It builds the string repeatedly for a certain number of trials. In one test building the 1,000-character string 10,000 times, using a String took around 0.95 seconds but using a StringBuilder took only about 0.06 seconds.

Strings and string operations are a bit more intuitive than the StringBuilder class, so your code will usually be easier to read if you use String variables when performance isn't a big issue. If you are building enormous strings, or are building long strings a huge number of times, the performance edge given by the StringBuilder class may be worth slightly more complicated-looking code.

DATE AND TIMESPAN OPERATIONS

The Date data type is fundamentally different from other data types. When you perform an operation on most data types, you get a result that has the same data type or that is at least of some compatible data type. For example, if you subtract two Integer variables, the result is an Integer. If you divide two Integers using the / operator, the result is a Double. That's not another Integer, but it is a compatible numeric data type used because an Integer cannot always hold the result of a division.

If you subtract two Date variables, however, the result is not a Date. For example, what's August 7 minus July 20? It doesn't make sense to think of the result as a Date. Instead, Visual Basic defines the difference between two Dates as a TimeSpan. A TimeSpan measures the elapsed time between two Dates. In this example, August 7 minus July 20 is 18 days. (And yes, TimeSpans know all about leap years.)

The following equations define the arithmetic of Dates and TimeSpans:

➤ Date – Date = TimeSpan

➤ Date + TimeSpan = Date

➤ TimeSpan + TimeSpan = TimeSpan

➤ TimeSpan – TimeSpan = TimeSpan

The TimeSpan class also defines unary negation (ts2 = -ts1), but other operations (such as multiplying a TimeSpan by a number) are not defined. However, in some cases, you can still perform the calculation if you must.

Example program MultiplyTimeSpan, which is available for download on the book's website, uses the following statement to make the TimeSpan ts2 equal to 12 times the duration of TimeSpan ts1:

```
ts2 = New TimeSpan(ts1.Ticks * 12)
```

Sometimes using operators to combine Date and TimeSpan values can be a bit cumbersome. To make these kinds of calculations easier, the Date data type provides other methods for performing common operations that are a bit easier to read. Whereas the operator methods take both operands as parameters, these methods take a single operand as one parameter and use the current object as the other. For example, a Date object's Add method adds a TimeSpan to the date and returns the resulting date. The following table summarizes these methods.

SYNTAX	MEANING
`result_date = date1.Add(timespan1)`	Returns `date1` plus `timespan1`
`result_date = date1` `.AddYears(num_years)`	Returns the date plus the indicated number of years
`result_date = date1` `.AddMonths(num_months)`	Returns the date plus the indicated number of months
`result_date = date1` `.AddDays(num_days)`	Returns the date plus the indicated number of days
`result_date = date1` `.AddHours(num_hours)`	Returns the date plus the indicated number of hours
`result_date = date1` `.AddMinutes(num_minutes)`	Returns the date plus the indicated number of minutes
`result_date = date1` `.AddSeconds(num_seconds)`	Returns the date plus the indicated number of seconds
`result_date = date1` `.AddMilliseconds(num_milliseconds)`	Returns the date plus the indicated number of milliseconds
`result_date = date1` `.AddTicks(num_ticks)`	Returns the date plus the indicated number of ticks (100-nanosecond units)
`result_timespan = date1` `.Subtract(date2)`	Returns the time span between `date2` and `date1`
`result_integer = date1` `.CompareTo(date2)`	Returns a value indicating whether `date1` is greater than, less than, or equal to `date2`
`result_boolean = date1` `.Equals(date2)`	Returns True if `date1` equals `date2`

The CompareTo method returns a value less than zero if date1 < date2, greater than zero if date1 > date2, and equal to zero if date1 = date2.

OPERATOR OVERLOADING

Visual Basic defines operators for expressions that use standard data types such as Integers and Boolean values. It defines a few operators such as Is and IsNot for objects, but operators such as * and Mod don't make sense for objects in general.

Nevertheless, you can also define those operators for your structures and classes, if you like, by using the Operator statement. This is a more advanced topic, so if you're new to Visual Basic, you may want to skip this section and come back to it later, perhaps after you have read Chapter 23, "Classes and Structures."

The general syntax for operator overloading is:

```
[ <attributes> ] Public [ Overloads ] Shared [ Shadows ] _
[ Widening | Narrowing ] Operator symbol ( operands ) As type
    ...
End Operator
```

The parts of this declaration are:

➤ *attributes* — Attributes for the operator.

➤ Public — All operators must be Public and Shared.

➤ Overloads — You can use this only if the operator takes two parameters that are from a base class and a derived class as its two operators. In that case, it means the operator overrides the operator defined in the base class.

➤ Shared — All operators must be Public and Shared.

➤ Shadows — The operator replaces a similar operator defined in the base class.

➤ Widening — Indicates that the operator defines a widening conversion that always succeeds at run time. For example, an Integer always fits in a Single, so storing an Integer in a Single is a widening operation. This operator must catch and handle all errors. The CType operator must include either the Widening or the Narrowing keyword.

➤ Narrowing — Indicates that the operator defines a narrowing conversion that may fail at run time. For example, a Single does not necessarily fit in an Integer, so storing a Single in an Integer is a narrowing operation. The CType operator must include either the Widening or the Narrowing keyword.

➤ *symbol* — The operator's symbol. This can be +, −, *, /, \, ^, &, <<, >>, =, <>, <, >, <=, >=, Mod, Not, And, Or, Xor, Like, IsTrue, IsFalse, or CType.

➤ *operands* — Declarations of the objects to be manipulated by the operator. The unary operators +, −, Not, IsTrue, and IsFalse take a single operand. The binary operators +, −, *, /, \, ^, &, <<, >>, =, <>, <, >, <=, >=, Mod, And, Or, Xor, Like, and CType take two operands.

➤ *type* — All operators must have a return type and must return a value by using a Return statement.

Operator overloading is subject to several constraints:

➤ Some operands come in pairs, and if you define one you must define the other. The pairs are = and <>, < and >, <= and >=, and IsTrue and IsFalse.

➤ For the standard unary or binary operators, the class or structure that defines the operator must appear in an operand. For the CType conversion operator, the class or structure must appear in the operand or return type.

➤ The IsTrue and IsFalse operators must return Boolean values.

➤ The second operands for the << and >> operators must be Integers.

If you define an operator, Visual Basic automatically provides the corresponding assignment operator. For example, if you define the + operator, Visual Basic provides the += assignment operator.

Although you cannot use the IsTrue and IsFalse operators directly, you can use them indirectly. If you define IsTrue for a class, Visual Basic uses it to determine whether an object should be treated as True in a Boolean expression. For example, the following statement uses the IsTrue operator to decide whether the object c1 should be considered True:

```
if c1 Then ...
```

If you define the And and IsFalse operators, Visual Basic uses them to handle the AndAlso operator as well. For this to work, the And operator must return the same type of class or structure where you define it. For example, suppose you have defined And and IsFalse for the Composite class and suppose variables c1, c2, and c3 are all instances of this class. Then consider the following statement:

```
c3 = c1 AndAlso c2
```

Visual Basic uses IsFalse to evaluate c1. If IsFalse returns True, the program doesn't bother to evaluate c2. Instead it assumes the whole statement is False and returns a False value. Because IsFalse returned True for c1, Visual Basic knows that c1 is a False value, so it sets c3 equal to c1.

This is pretty confusing. It may make more sense if you think about how Visual Basic evaluates Boolean expressions that use the normal AndAlso operator.

Similarly, if you define the Or and IsTrue operators, Visual Basic automatically provides the OrElse operator.

Although you generally cannot make two versions of a function in Visual Basic that differ only in their return types, you can do that for CType conversion operators. When the program tries to make a conversion, Visual Basic can tell by the type of the result which conversion operator to use.

Example program ComplexNumbers, which is available for download on the book's website, uses the following code to define a Complex class that represents a complex number. It defines +, –, and * operators to implement normal addition, subtraction, and multiplication, respectively, on complex numbers. It also defines =, <>, and unary negation operators, and conversion operators that convert a Complex object into a Double and vice versa.

```
Public Class Complex
    Public Re As Double
    Public Im As Double

    ' Constructors.
    Public Sub New()
    End Sub
    Public Sub New(ByVal real_part As Double, ByVal imaginary_part As Double)
        Re = real_part
        Im = imaginary_part
    End Sub

    ' ToString.
    Public Overrides Function ToString() As String
```

```
        Dim txt As String = Re.ToString
        If Im < 0 Then
            txt &= " - " & Math.Abs(Im).ToString
        Else
            txt &= " + " & Im.ToString
        End If
        Return txt & "i"
    End Function

    ' Operators.
    Public Shared Operator *(ByVal c1 As Complex, ByVal c2 As Complex) _
     As Complex
        Return New Complex(
            c1.Re * c2.Re - c1.Im * c2.Im,
            c1.Re * c2.Im + c1.Im * c2.Re)
    End Operator
    Public Shared Operator +(ByVal c1 As Complex, ByVal c2 As Complex) _
     As Complex
        Return New Complex(
            c1.Re + c2.Re,
            c1.Im + c2.Im)
    End Operator
    Public Shared Operator -(ByVal c1 As Complex, ByVal c2 As Complex) _
     As Complex
        Return New Complex(
            c1.Re - c2.Re,
            c1.Im - c2.Im)
    End Operator
    Public Shared Operator =(ByVal c1 As Complex, ByVal c2 As Complex) _
     As Boolean
        Return (c1.Re = c2.Re) AndAlso (c1.Im = c2.Im)
    End Operator
    Public Shared Operator <>(ByVal c1 As Complex, ByVal c2 As Complex) _
     As Boolean
        Return (c1.Re <> c2.Re) OrElse (c1.Im <> c2.Im)
    End Operator
    Public Shared Operator -(ByVal c1 As Complex) As Complex
        Return New Complex(-c1.Re, -c1.Im)
    End Operator
    Public Shared Narrowing Operator CType(ByVal c1 As Complex) As Double
        Return System.Math.Sqrt(c1.Re * c1.Re + c1.Im * c1.Im)
    End Operator
    Public Shared Widening Operator CType(ByVal d As Double) As Complex
        Return New Complex(d, 0)
    End Operator
End Class
```

It is easy to get carried away with operator overloading. Just because you can define an operator for a class doesn't mean you should. For example, you might be able to concoct some meaning for addition with the Employee class, but it would probably be a counterintuitive operation. You would probably be better off writing a subroutine or function with a meaningful name instead of using an ambiguous operator such as + or >>.

SUMMARY

A program uses operators to manipulate variables, constants, and literal values to produce new results. The Visual Basic operators fall into five categories: arithmetic, concatenation, comparison, logical, and bitwise. In most cases, using operators is straightforward and intuitive.

Operator precedence determines the order in which Visual Basic applies operators when evaluating an expression. In cases where an expression's operator precedence is unclear, add parentheses to make the order obvious. Even if you don't change the way that Visual Basic handles the statement, you can make the code more understandable and avoid possibly time-consuming bugs.

The String data type has its own special needs. String manipulation plays a big role in many applications, so Visual Basic provides a StringBuilder class for manipulating strings more efficiently. If your program only works with a few short strings, it probably doesn't need to use a StringBuilder, and using the String data type will probably make your code easier to understand. However, if your application builds enormous strings or concatenates a huge number of strings, you may be able to save a noticeable amount of time by using the StringBuilder class.

The Date data type also behaves differently from other data types. The normal operators such as + and – have different meanings here from other data types. For example, a Date minus a Date gives a TimeSpan, not another Date. These operations generally make sense if you think carefully about what dates and time spans are.

Just as addition, subtraction, and the other operators have special meaning for Dates and TimeSpans, you can use operator overloading to define operators for your classes. Defining division or exponentiation may not make much sense for Employees, Customer, or Orders, but in some cases custom operators can make your code more readable. For example, you might imagine the following statement adding an OrderItem to a CustomerOrder:

```
the_order += new_item
```

This chapter explained how to use operators to combine variables to calculate new results. A typical program may perform the same set of calculations many times for different variable values. Although you might be able to perform those calculations in a long series, the resulting code would be cumbersome and hard to maintain. Chapter 16, "Subroutines and Functions," explains how you can use subroutines and functions to break a program into manageable pieces that you can then reuse to make performing the calculations easier and more consistent.

16

Subroutines and Functions

WROX.COM CODE DOWNLOADS FOR THIS CHAPTER

The wrox.com code downloads for this chapter are found at `http://www.wrox.com/remtitle.cgi?isbn=9781118314074` on the Download Code tab. The code for this chapter is divided into the following major examples:

- ➤ AsyncAwait
- ➤ AsyncCallEndInvoke
- ➤ LambaFunction
- ➤ RelaxedDelegates

MANAGING CODE

Subroutines and functions enable you to break an otherwise unwieldy chunk of code into manageable pieces. They allow you to extract code that you may need to use under more than one circumstance and place it in one location where you can call it as needed. This not only reduces repetition within your code but also enables you to maintain and update the code in a single location.

A *subroutine* performs a task for the code that invokes it. A *function* performs a task and then returns some value. The value may be the result of a calculation or a status code indicating whether the function succeeded or failed.

Together, subroutines and functions are sometimes called *routines* or *procedures*. They are also sometimes called *methods*, particularly when they are subroutines or functions belonging to a class. Subroutines are also occasionally called *sub procedures* or less formally *Subs*.

This chapter describes subroutines and functions. It explains the syntax for declaring and using each in a Visual Basic application. It also provides some tips for making routines more maintainable.

SUBROUTINES

A Sub statement defines the subroutine's name. It declares the parameters that the subroutine takes as arguments and defines the parameters' data types. Code between the Sub statement and an End Sub statement determines what the subroutine does when it runs.

The syntax for defining a subroutine is as follows:

```
[attribute_list] [inheritance_mode] [accessibility]
Sub subroutine_name([parameters]) [ Implements interface.subroutine ]
    [ statements ]
End Sub
```

The following sections describe the pieces of this declaration.

Attribute_List

The optional attribute list is a comma-separated list of attributes that apply to the subroutine. An attribute further refines the definition of a class, method, variable, or other item to give more information to the compiler and the runtime system.

> **DELIGHTFUL DECORATIONS**
>
> Applying an attribute to a class, variable, method, or other code entity is sometimes called *decorating* the entity.

Attributes are specialized and address issues that arise when you perform very specific programming tasks. For example, the Conditional attribute means the subroutine is conditional upon the definition of some compiler constant. Example program AttributeConditional uses the following code to demonstrate the Conditional attribute:

```
#Const DEBUG_LIST_CUSTOMERS = True
' #Const DEBUG_LIST_EMPLOYEES = True

Private Sub Form1_Load() Handles MyBase.Load
    ListCustomers()
    ListEmployees()

    txtResults.Select(0, 0)
End Sub

<Conditional("DEBUG_LIST_CUSTOMERS")>
```

```
Private Sub ListCustomers()
    txtResults.Text &= "ListCustomers" & vbCrLf
End Sub

<Conditional("DEBUG_LIST_EMPLOYEES")>
Private Sub ListEmployees()
    txtResults.Text &= "ListEmployees" & vbCrLf
End Sub
```

The code defines the compiler constant DEBUG_LIST_CUSTOMERS. The value DEBUG_LIST_EMPLOYEES is not defined because it is commented out.

This program's Form1_Load event handler calls subroutines ListCustomers and ListEmployees. ListCustomers is defined using the Conditional attribute with parameter DEBUG_LIST_CUSTOMERS. That tells the compiler to generate code for the routine only if DEBUG_LIST_CUSTOMERS is defined. Because that constant is defined, the compiler generates code for this subroutine.

Subroutine ListEmployees is defined using the Conditional attribute with parameter DEBUG_LIST_EMPLOYEES. Because that constant is not defined, the compiler does not generate code for this subroutine and, when Form1_Load calls it, the subroutine call is ignored.

The following text shows the output from this program:

```
ListCustomers
```

Visual Basic 2010 defines more than 400 attributes. Many have very specialized purposes that won't interest you most of the time, so only a few of the most useful are described here. For example, the Browsable attribute determines whether a property or event should be listed in the Properties window. It is fairly general and useful, so it's described shortly. In contrast, the System .EnterpriseServices.ApplicationQueuing attribute enables queuing for an assembly and allows it to read method calls from message queues. This attribute is useful only in very specialized circumstances, so it isn't described here.

The following list describes some of the most useful attributes. Most of them are in the System .ComponentModel namespace. Check the online help to find the namespaces for the others and to learn about each attribute's parameters. Even these most useful attributes are fairly specialized and advanced so you may not immediately see their usefulness. If one of them doesn't make sense, skip it and scan the list again after you have more experience with such topics as building custom controls.

> ➤ AttributeUsage — You can build your own custom attributes by inheriting from the Attribute class. You can give your attribute class the AttributeUsage attribute to specify how your attribute can be used. You can determine whether an item can have multiple instances of your attribute, whether your attribute can be inherited by a derived class, and the kinds of things that can have your attribute (assembly, class, method, and so forth).

> ➤ Browsable — This indicates whether a property or event should be displayed in an editor such as the Properties window or a PropertyGrid control. If you pass the attribute's constructor the value False, the Properties window and PropertyGrid controls do not display the property.

➤ `Category` — This indicates the grouping that should hold the property or event in a visual designer such as the Properties window or a PropertyGrid control. If the user clicks the Categorized button in the Properties window, the window groups the properties by category. This attribute tells which category should hold the property. Note that you can use any string you like and the Properties window will make a new category for you if necessary.

➤ `DefaultEvent` — This gives a class's default event name. If the class is a control or component and you double-click it in the Form Designer, the code editor opens to this event. For example, the default event for a Button is Click, so when you double-click a Button at design time, the code editor opens the control's Click event handler.

➤ `DefaultProperty` — This gives a class's default property name. Suppose that the Employee component has LastName set as its default property. Then suppose that you select the form and click the FormBorderStyle property in the Properties window. Now you click an Employee. Because Employee doesn't have a FormBorderStyle property, the Properties window displays its default property: LastName.

➤ `DefaultValue` — This gives a property a default value. If you right-click the property in the Properties window and select Reset, the property is reset to this value.

➤ `Description` — This gives a description of the item. If a property has a Description and you select the property in the Properties window, the window displays the description text at the bottom.

Visual Basic carries this one step further and also allows you to use XML comments to provide a description of routines and their parameters for use by IntelliSense. For more information, see the section "XML Comments" in Chapter 13, "Program and Module Structure."

➤ `Localizable` — This determines whether a property should be localizable so you can easily store different versions of the property for different languages and locales. If this is True, localized values are automatically stored in the appropriate resource files for different locales and automatically loaded at startup based on the user's computer settings. If this is False (the default), all locales share the same property value.

To try this out, set the form's Localizable property to True and enter a value for the property. Then set the form's Language property to another language and give the localizable property a new value.

➤ `MergableProperty` — This indicates whether or not the property can be merged with the same property provided by other components in the Properties window. If this is False and you select more than one instance of a control with the property, the Properties window does not display the property.

If this is True and you select more than one control with the property, the Properties window displays the value if the controls all have the same value. If you enter a new value, all of the controls are updated. This is the way the Text property works for TextBox, Label, and many other kinds of controls.

➤ `ParenthesizePropertyName` — This indicates whether editors such as the Properties window should display parentheses around the property's name. If the name has parentheses, the Properties window moves it to the top of the list when displaying properties alphabetically or to the top of its category when displaying properties by category.

➤ `ReadOnly` — This indicates whether designers should treat this property as read-only. The Properties window displays the property grayed out and doesn't let the user change its value. This attribute is a little strange in practice because ReadOnly is a Visual Basic keyword. If you enter just the attribute name ReadOnly, Visual Basic gets confused. Either use the full name System.ComponentModel.ReadOnly or enclose the name in square brackets as in <[ReadOnly](True)>. . . .

➤ `RecommendedAsConfigurable` — This indicates that a property should be tied to the configuration file. When you select the object at design time and expand the (Dynamic Properties) item, the property is listed. If you click the ellipsis to the right, a dialog box appears that lets you map the property to a key in the configuration file.

➤ `RefreshProperties` — This indicates how an editor should refresh the object's *other* properties if *this* property is changed. The value can be Default (do not refresh the other properties), Repaint (refresh all other properties), or All (re-query and refresh all properties).

➤ `Conditional` — This indicates that the method is callable if a compile-time constant such as DEBUG or MY_CONSTANT is defined. If the constant is not defined, code for the method is still generated and parameters in the method call are checked against the parameter types used by the method, but calls to the method are ignored at run time. If the method has more than one Conditional attribute, the method is callable if any of the specified compile-time constants is defined.

Note that the constant must be defined in the main program, not in the component if you are building a component. Select the main program, open the Project menu, select the Properties item at the bottom, open the Configuration Properties folder, click Build, and in the Custom constants text box enter a value such as IS_DEFINED=True.

You can also use the compiler directive #If to exclude code completely from compilation. However, if you eliminate a method in this way, any calls to the routine will generate compile-time errors because the method doesn't exist. The Conditional attribute lets you hide a method while still allowing the code to contain calls to it.

➤ `DebuggerHidden` — This tells debuggers whether a method should be debuggable. If DebuggerHidden is True, the debugger skips over the method and will not stop at breakpoints inside it.

➤ `DebuggerStepThrough` — This tells debuggers whether to let the developer step into a method in the debugger. If the DebuggerStepThrough attribute is present, the IDE will not step into the method.

➤ `ToolboxBitmap` — This tells the IDE where to find a control or component's Toolbox bitmap. This can be a file, or it can be a type in an assembly that contains the bitmap and the bitmap's name in the assembly. It's awkward but essential if you're developing controls or components.

➤ `NonSerializedAttribute` — This indicates that a member of a serializable class should not be serialized. This is useful for excluding values that need not be serialized.

➤ `Obsolete` — This indicates that the item (class, method, property, or whatever) is obsolete. Optionally, you can specify the message that the code editor should display to the developer if code uses the item (for example, "Use the NewMethod instead"). You can also indicate whether the IDE should treat using this item as a warning or an error.

➤ `Serializable` — This indicates that a class is serializable. All public and private fields are serialized by default. Attributes in the System.Xml.Serialization namespace can provide a lot of control over serializations.

FINDING ATTRIBUTES

Finding the attributes that are useful for a particular task can be tricky. It helps to realize that attribute classes inherit either directly or indirectly from the Attribute class. You can get information about the Attribute class at `http://msdn2 .microsoft.com/system.attribute.aspx`. You can see a list of classes that inherit from System.Attribute at `http://msdn2.microsoft.com/2e39z096.aspx`.

Inheritance_Mode

In a routine's declaration, the *inheritance_mode* can be one of the values Overloads, Overrides, Overridable, NotOverridable, MustOverride, Shadows, or Shared. These values determine how a subroutine declared within a class inherits from the parent class or how it allows inheritance in derived classes. The following list explains the meanings of these keywords:

➤ `Overloads` — Indicates that the subroutine has the same name as another subroutine defined for this class. The parameter list must be different in the different versions so that Visual Basic can tell them apart. (If they are the same, this works just like Overrides, described next.) If you are overloading a subroutine defined in a parent class, you must use this keyword. If you are overloading only subroutines in the same class, you can omit the keyword. If you use the keyword in any of the overloaded subroutines, however, you must include it for them all.

➤ `Overrides` — Indicates that this subroutine replaces a subroutine in the parent class that has the same name and parameters.

➤ `Overridable` — Indicates that a derived class can override this subroutine. This is the default for a subroutine that overrides another one.

➤ `NotOverridable` — Indicates that a derived class cannot override this subroutine. You can only use this with a subroutine that overrides another one.

➤ `MustOverride` — Indicates that any derived classes must override this subroutine. When you use this keyword, you omit all subroutine code and the End Sub statement, as in the following code:

```
MustOverride Sub Draw()
MustOverride Sub MoveMap(X As Integer, Y As Integer)
MustOverride Sub Delete()
...
```

If a class contains a subroutine declared MustOverride, you must declare the class using the MustInherit keyword. Otherwise, Visual Basic won't know what to do if you create an instance of the class and try to call this subroutine, because it contains no code.

MustOverride is handy for defining a subroutine that derived classes must implement, but for which a default implementation in the parent class doesn't make sense. For example, suppose that you make a Drawable class that represents a shape that can be drawn and that you will derive specific shape classes such as Rectangle, Ellipse, Line, and so forth. To let the program draw a generic shape, the Drawable class defines the Draw subroutine. Because Drawable doesn't have a particular shape, it cannot provide a default implementation of that subroutine. To require the derived classes to implement Draw, the Drawable class declares it MustOverride.

➤ Shadows — Indicates that this subroutine replaces an item (probably a subroutine) in the parent class that has the same name, but not necessarily the same parameters. If the parent class contains more than one overloaded version of the subroutine, this subroutine shadows them all. If the derived class defines more than one overloaded version of the subroutine, they must all be declared with the Shadows keyword.

➤ Shared — Indicates that this subroutine is associated with the class itself, rather than with a specific instance of the class. You should invoke the subroutine by using the class's name (ClassName.SharedSub) instead of an instance (class_instance.SharedSub). Because the subroutine is not associated with a specific class instance, it cannot use any properties or methods that are provided by a specific instance. The subroutine can only use other Shared properties and methods, as well as globally available variables.

Accessibility

A subroutine's *accessibility* clause can take one of these values: Public, Protected, Friend, Protected Friend, or Private. These values determine which pieces of code can invoke the subroutine. The following list explains these keywords:

➤ Public — Indicates that there are no restrictions on the subroutine. Code inside or outside of the subroutine's class or module can call it.

➤ Protected — Indicates that the subroutine is accessible only to code in the same class or in a derived class. You can only use the Protected keyword with subroutines declared inside a class.

➤ Friend — Indicates that the subroutine is available to all code inside or outside of the subroutine's module within the same project. The difference between this and Public is that Public allows code outside of the project to access the subroutine. This is generally only an issue for code and control libraries where some other project may use the library.

➤ `Protected Friend` — Indicates that the subroutine has both Protected and Friend status. The subroutine is available only within the same project and within the same class or a derived class.

➤ `Private` — Indicates that the subroutine is available only within the class or module that contains it.

To reduce the amount of information that developers must remember, you should generally declare subroutines with the most restricted accessibility that allows them to do their jobs. If you can, declare the subroutine Private. Then, developers working on other parts of the application don't even need to know that the subroutine exists. They can create other routines with the same name if necessary and won't accidentally misuse the subroutine.

Later, if you discover that you need to use the subroutine outside of its class or module, you can change its declaration to allow greater accessibility.

Subroutine_Name

The subroutine's name must be a valid Visual Basic identifier. That means it should begin with a letter or an underscore. It can then contain zero or more letters, numbers, and underscores. If the name begins with an underscore, it must include at least one other character so that Visual Basic can tell it apart from a line continuation character.

Many developers use *camel case* when naming subroutines so a subroutine's name consists of several descriptive words with their first letters capitalized. A good method for generating subroutine names is to use a short phrase beginning with a verb and describing what the subroutine does. Some examples include LoadData, SaveNetworkConfiguration, and PrintExpenseReport.

Subroutine names with leading underscores can be hard to read, so you should either save them for special purposes or avoid them entirely. Names such as _1 and __ (two underscores) are particularly confusing.

Parameters

The *parameters* section of the subroutine declaration defines the numbers and types of the parameters that the subroutine takes as arguments. This section also gives the names the subroutine will use to refer to the values.

Declaring parameters is very similar to declaring variables. See Chapter 14, "Data Types, Variables, and Constants," for information on variable declarations, data types, and other related topics.

The following sections describe some of the more important details related to subroutine parameter declarations.

ByVal

If you include the optional ByVal keyword before a parameter's declaration, the subroutine makes its own local copy of the argument. The subroutine can modify this value all it wants and the corresponding value in the calling procedure isn't changed.

ByRef

If you declare a parameter with the ByRef keyword, the subroutine does not create a separate copy of the argument. Instead, it uses a reference to the original argument passed into the subroutine and any changes the subroutine makes to the value are reflected in the calling subroutine.

For example, consider the following code. The main program initializes the variable A and prints its value in the Output window. It then calls subroutine DisplayDouble, which doubles its parameter X and displays the new value. Because X is declared ByRef, this doubles the value of the variable A that was passed by the main program into the subroutine. When the subroutine ends and the main program resumes, it displays the new doubled value of variable A.

```
Private Sub Main()
    Dim A As Integer = 12
    Debug.WriteLine("Main: " & A)
    DisplayDouble(A)
    Debug.WriteLine("Main: " & A)
End Sub

Private Sub DisplayDouble(ByRef X As Integer)
    X *= 2
    Debug.WriteLine("DisplayDouble: " & X)
End Sub
```

The following shows the results:

```
Main: 12
DisplayDouble: 24
Main: 24
```

Arrays Declared ByVal and ByRef

If you declare an array parameter using ByVal or ByRef, those keywords apply to the array itself, not to the array's values. In either case, the subroutine can modify the values inside the array.

If the array is declared ByRef, the subroutine can also change the memory to which the array points. It can set the parameter to a completely new array and the calling code will see the change in the array that it passed to the subroutine.

Parenthesized Parameters

A subroutine can fail to update a parameter declared using the ByRef keyword in a couple ways. The most confusing occurs if you enclose a variable in parentheses when you pass it to the subroutine. Parentheses tell Visual Basic to evaluate their contents as an expression. Visual Basic creates a temporary variable to hold the result of the expression and then passes the temporary variable into the procedure. If the procedure's parameter is declared ByRef, the subroutine updates the temporary variable but not the original variable, so the calling routine doesn't see any change to its value.

The following code calls subroutine DisplayDouble, passing it the variable A surrounded by parentheses. Subroutine DisplayDouble modifies its parameter's value, but the result doesn't get back to the variable A.

```
Private Sub Main()
    Dim A As Integer = 12
    Debug.WriteLine("Main: " & A)
    DisplayDouble((A))
    Debug.WriteLine("Main: " & A)
End Sub

Private Sub DisplayDouble(ByRef X As Integer)
    X *= 2
    Debug.WriteLine("DisplayDouble: " & X)
End Sub
```

The following text shows the results:

```
Main: 12
DisplayDouble: 24
Main: 12
```

Chapter 14 has more to say about parameters declared with the ByVal and ByRef keywords.

Optional

If you declare a parameter with the Optional keyword, the code that uses it may omit that parameter. When you declare an optional parameter, you must give it a default value for the subroutine to use if the parameter is omitted by the calling routine.

The DisplayError subroutine in the following code demonstrates an optional string parameter:

```
Private Sub DisplayError(Optional error_message As String =
 "An error occurred")
    MessageBox.Show(error_message)
End Sub

Private Sub PlaceOrder(the_customer As Customer, order_items() As OrderItem)
    ' See if the_customer exists.
    If the_customer Is Nothing Then
        DisplayError("Customer is Nothing in subroutine PlaceOrder")
        Exit Sub
    End If

    ' See if the_customer is valid.
    If Not the_customer.IsValid() Then
        DisplayError()
        Exit Sub
    End If

    ' Generate the order.
    ...
End Sub
```

If the calling routine provides the optional error_message parameter, the subroutine displays it. If the calling routine leaves this parameter out, DisplayError uses its default message "An error occurred."

The PlaceOrder subroutine checks its the_customer parameter. If this parameter is Nothing, PlaceOrder calls DisplayError to show the message "Customer is Nothing in subroutine PlaceOrder." Next, subroutine PlaceOrder calls the_customer's IsValid function. If IsValid returns False, the subroutine calls DisplayError this time without the parameter so DisplayError presents its default message.

Optional parameters must go at the end of the parameter list, so if one parameter uses the Optional keyword, all of the following parameters must use it, too.

OPTIONAL AND NULLABLE

Nullable parameters can also be optional. For example, the following code defines three subroutines that each take an optional nullable parameter. The first two give the parameter the default value Nothing, and the third uses the default value 0.

```
Public Sub Sub1(Optional ByVal x? As Integer = Nothing)
    ...
End Sub

Public Sub Sub2(Optional ByVal x As Integer? = Nothing)
    ...
End Sub

Public Sub Sub3(Optional ByVal x As Nullable(Of Integer) = 0)
    ...
End Sub
```

Optional parameters are particularly useful for initializing values in a class's constructor. The following code shows a DrawableRectangle class. Its constructor takes as parameters the rectangle's position and size. All the parameters are optional, so the main program can omit them if it desires. Because each parameter has default values, the constructor always knows it will have the four values, so it can always initialize the object's Bounds variable.

```
Public Class DrawableRectangle
    Public Bounds As Rectangle

    Public Sub New(
      Optional X As Integer = 0,
      Optional Y As Integer = 0,
      Optional Width As Integer = 100,
      Optional Height As Integer = 100
    )
        Bounds = New Rectangle(X, Y, Width, Height)
    End Sub
    ...
End Class
```

Note that overloaded subroutines cannot differ only in optional parameters. If a call to the subroutine omitted the optional parameters, Visual Basic would be unable to tell which version of the subroutine to use.

Optional versus Overloading

Different developers have varying opinions on whether you should use optional parameters or overloaded routines under various circumstances. For example, suppose that the FireEmployee method could take one or two parameters giving either the employee's name or the name and reason for dismissal. You could make this a subroutine with the reason parameter optional, or you could make one overloaded version of the FireEmployee method for each possible parameter list.

One argument in favor of optional parameters is that overloaded methods might duplicate a lot of code. However, it is easy to make each version of the method call another version that allows more parameters, passing in default values. For example, in the following code the first version of the FireEmployee method simply invokes the second version:

```
Public Sub FireEmployee(employee_name As String)
    FireEmployee(employee_name, "Unknown reason")
End Sub

Public Sub FireEmployee(employee_name As String, reason As String)
    ...
End Sub
```

Method overloading is generally superior when the different versions of the routine need to do something different. You might be able to make a single routine with optional parameters take different actions based on the values of its optional parameters, but separating the code into overloaded routines will probably produce a cleaner solution.

Parameter Arrays

Sometimes it is convenient to allow a subroutine to take a variable number of parameters. For example, a subroutine might take as parameters the addresses of people who should receive e-mail. It would loop through the names to send each a message.

One approach is to include a long list of optional parameters. For example, the e-mail subroutine might set the default value for each of its parameters to an empty string. Then it would need to send e-mail to every address parameter that was not empty.

Unfortunately, this type of subroutine would need to include code to deal with each optional parameter separately. This would also place an upper limit on the number of parameters the subroutine can take (however many you are willing to type in the subroutine's parameter list).

A better solution is to use the ParamArray keyword to make the subroutine's final argument a parameter array. A *parameter array* contains an arbitrary number of parameter values. At run time, the subroutine can loop through the array to process the parameter values.

The DisplayAverage subroutine shown in the following code takes a parameter array named values. It first checks the array's bounds to make sure it contains at least one value. If the array isn't empty, the subroutine adds the values it contains and divides by the number of values to calculate the average.

```
' Display the average of a series of values.
Private Sub DisplayAverage(ParamArray values() As Double)
    ' Do nothing if there are no parameters.
    If values Is Nothing Then Exit Sub
    If values.Length = 0 Then Exit Sub

    ' Display the average.
    MessageBox.Show((values.Sum()/ values.Length).ToString)
End Sub
```

The following code shows one way the program could use this subroutine. In this example, DisplayAverage would display the average of the integers 1 through 7, which is 4.

```
DisplayAverage(1, 2, 3, 4, 5, 6, 7)
```

Parameter arrays are subject to the following restrictions:

➤   A subroutine can have only one parameter array, and it must come last in the parameter list.

➤   All other parameters in the parameter list must *not* be optional.

➤   All parameter lists must be declared ByVal.

➤   The calling code may pass the value Nothing in the place of the parameter array. (That's why the code in the previous example checked whether values was Nothing before continuing.)

➤   The calling code can provide any number of values for the parameter array including zero. (That's why the code in the previous example checked whether values.Length was zero before continuing.)

➤   Even though the values passed into a parameter array are in a sense optional, you cannot use the Optional keyword when you declare the parameter array.

➤   All the items in the parameter array must have the same data type. However, you can use an array that contains the generic Object data type and then it can hold just about anything.

The program can also pass an array of the appropriate data type in place of a series of values. The following two calls to the DisplayAverage subroutine produce the same result inside the DisplayAverage subroutine:

```
DisplayAverage(1, 2, 3, 4, 5, 6, 7)

Dim values() As Double = {1, 2, 3, 4, 5, 6, 7}
DisplayAverage(values)
```

Implements interface.subroutine

An *interface* defines a set of properties, methods, and events that a class implementing the interface must provide. An interface is a lot like a class with all of its properties, methods, and events declared with the MustOverride keyword. Any class that inherits from the base class must provide implementations of those properties, methods, and events.

NAMING CONVENTION

Developers often begin the name of interfaces with a capital I so that it's obvious that it's an interface. In fact, it's such a common practice and has no disadvantages that it should practically be a requirement. Start interface names with "I" so other developers know they are interfaces.

The following code defines the IDrawable interface and the IDrawableRectangle that implements it:

```
Public Interface IDrawable
    Sub Draw(gr As Graphics)
    Function Bounds() As Rectangle
    Property IsVisible As Boolean
End Interface

Public Class DrawableRectangle
    Implements IDrawable

    Public Function Bounds() As Rectangle Implements IDrawable.Bounds

    End Function

    Public Sub Draw(gr As Graphics) Implements IDrawable.Draw

    End Sub

    Public Property IsVisible As Boolean Implements IDrawable.IsVisible
End Class
```

The IDrawable interface defines a Draw subroutine, a Bounds function, and a property named IsVisible.

The DrawableRectangle class begins with the statement Implements IDrawable. That tells Visual Basic that the class will implement the IDrawable interface. If you make the class declaration, type the Implements statement, and then press the Enter key, Visual Basic automatically fills in the declarations you need to satisfy the interface. In this example, it creates the empty Bounds function, Draw subroutine, and IsVisible property procedures shown here. All you need to do is fill in the details.

If you look at the preceding code, you can see where the subroutine declaration's Implements interface.subroutine clause comes into play. In this case, the Draw subroutine implements the IDrawable interface's Draw method.

When you type the Implements statement and press the Enter key, Visual Basic generates empty routines to satisfy the interface; then you don't need to type the Implements interface.subroutine clause yourself. Visual Basic enters this for you.

The only time you should need to modify this statement is if you change the interface's name or subroutine name or you want to use some other subroutine to satisfy the interface. For example, you could give the DrawableRectangle class a DrawRectangle method and add Implements IDrawable .Draw to its declaration. Visual Basic doesn't care what you call the routine, as long as some routine implements IDrawable.Draw.

Statements

A subroutine's *statements* section contains whatever Visual Basic code is needed to get the routine's job done. This can include all the usual variable declarations, For loops, If Then statements, and other Visual Basic paraphernalia.

The subroutine's body cannot include module, class, subroutine, function, structure, enumerated type, or other file-level statements. For example, you cannot define a subroutine within another subroutine.

One statement that I haven't mentioned before that you can use within a subroutine is Exit Sub. This command makes the subroutine immediately exit and return control to the calling routine. Within a subroutine, the Return statement is equivalent to Exit Sub.

You can use Exit Sub or Return as many times as you like to allow the subroutine to exit under different conditions. For example, the following subroutine checks whether a phone number has a 10-digit or 7-digit format. If the phone number matches a 10-digit format, the subroutine exits. Then if the phone number matches a 7-digit format, the subroutine exits. Finally if the number doesn't match either format, the subroutine displays an error message to the user.

```
Private Sub ValidatePhoneNumber(phone_number As String)
    ' Check for a 10-digit phone number.
    If phone_number Like "###-###-####" Then Exit Sub

    ' Check for a 7-digit phone number.
    If phone_number Like "###-####" Then Return

    ' The phone number is invalid.
    MessageBox.Show("Invalid phone number " & phone_number)
End Sub
```

FUNCTIONS

Functions are basically the same as subroutines, except that they return some sort of value. The syntax for defining a function is as follows:

```
[attribute_list] [inheritance_mode] [accessibility]
Function function_name([parameters]) [As return_type]
[ Implements interface.function ]
    [ statements ]
End function
```

This is almost the same as the syntax for defining a subroutine. See the section "Subroutines" earlier in this chapter for information about most of this declaration's clauses.

One difference is that a function ends with the End Function statement rather than End Sub. Similarly, a function can exit before reaching its end by using Exit Function rather than Exit Sub.

The one nontrivial difference between subroutine and function declarations is the clause As return_type that comes after the function's parameter list. This tells Visual Basic the type of value that the function returns.

The function can set its return value in one of two ways. First, it can set its own name equal to the value that it should return. The Factorial function shown in the following code calculates the factorial of a number. Written N!, the factorial of N is N * (N1) * (N2) . . .* 1. The function initializes its result variable to 1, and then loops over the values between 1 and the number parameter, multiplying these values to the result. It finishes by setting its name, Factorial, equal to the result value that it should return.

```
Private Function Factorial(number As Integer) As Double
    Dim result As Double = 1

    For i As Integer = 2 To number
        result *= i
    Next i

    Factorial = result
End function
```

A function can assign and reassign its return value as many times as it wants to before it returns. Whatever value is assigned last becomes the function's return value.

The second way a function can assign its return value is to use the Return keyword followed by the value that the function should return. The following code shows the Factorial function rewritten to use the Return statement:

```
Private Function Factorial(number As Integer) As Double
    Dim result As Double = 1

    For i As Integer = 2 To number
        result *= i
    Next i

    Return result
End function
```

The Return statement is roughly equivalent to setting the function's name equal to the return value, and then immediately using an Exit Function statement. The Return statement may allow the compiler to perform extra optimizations, however, so it is generally preferred to setting the function's name equal to the return value. (Return is also the more modern syntax and has become so common that some developers don't even recognize the other syntax anymore.)

PROPERTY PROCEDURES

Property procedures are routines that can represent a property value for a class. The simplest kind of property is an *auto-implemented property*. Simply add the Property keyword to a variable declaration as shown in the following code:

```
Public Property LastName As String
```

If you want, you can give the property a default value as in the following code:

```
Public Property LastName As String = "<missing>"
```

Behind the scenes, Visual Basic makes a hidden variable to hold the property's value. When other parts of the program get or set the value, Visual Basic uses the hidden variable.

This type of property is easy to make but it has few advantages over a simple variable. You can make the property more powerful if you write your own procedures to get and set the property's value. If you write your own procedures you can add validation code, perform complex calculations, save and restore values in a database, set breakpoints, and add other extras to the property.

A normal read-write property procedure contains a function for returning the property's value and a subroutine for assigning it.

The following code shows property procedures that implement a Value property. The Property Get procedure is a function that returns the value in the private variable m_Value. The Property Set subroutine saves a new value in the m_Value variable.

```
Private m_Value As Single

Property Value() As Single
    Get
        Return m_Value
    End Get

    Set(Value As Single)
        m_Value = Value
    End Set
End Property
```

Although the property is implemented as a pair of property procedures, the program can treat the value as a simple property. For example, suppose that the OrderItem class contains the preceding code. Then the following code sets the Value property for the OrderItem object named paper_item:

```
paper_item.Value = 19.95F
```

You can add property procedures to any type of object module. For example, you can use property procedures to implement a property for a form or for a class of your own.

It's less obvious that you can also use property procedures in a code module. The property procedures look like an ordinary variable to the routines that use them. If you place the previous example in a code module, the program could act as if there were a variable named `Value` defined in the module.

For more information on property procedures, see the section "Property Procedures" in Chapter 14.

EXTENSION METHODS

Extension methods allow you to add new methods to an existing class without rewriting it or deriving a new class from it. To make an extension method, place the method in a code module and decorate its declaration with the Extension attribute. The first parameter determines the class that the method extends. The method can use that parameter to learn about the item for which the method was called. The other parameters are passed into the method so it can use them to perform its chores.

EASIER EXTENSIONS

The Extension attribute is defined in the System.Runtime.CompilerServices namespace. Using an Imports statement to import that namespace makes it easier to write extensions.

For example, the following code adds a MatchesRegexp subroutine to the String class:

```
' Return True if a String matches a regular expression.
<Extension()>
Public Function MatchesRegexp(the_string As String,
 ByVal regular_expression As String) As Boolean
    Dim reg_exp As New Regex(regular_expression)
    Return reg_exp.IsMatch(the_string)
End function
```

The Extension attribute tells Visual Basic that this is an extension method. The method's first parameter is a String so this method extends the String class. The second parameter is a regular expression. The method returns True if the String matches the regular expression.

The following code shows how a program might use this method to decide whether the string stored in variable `phone_number` looks like a valid 7-digit United States phone number:

```
if Not phone_number.MatchesRegexp("^[2-9]\d{2}-\d{4}$") Then
    MessageBox.Show("Not a valid phone number")
End if
```

Example program ValidatePhone, which is available for download on the book's website, demonstrates the MatchesRegexp extension method. It also uses the MatchesRegexp method to define the following three additional extension methods that determine whether a string looks like a valid 7- or 10-digit United States phone number. These methods simply call the MatchesRegexp method, passing it appropriate regular expressions.

```
' Return True if a String looks like a 7-digit US phone number.
<Extension()>
Public Function IsValidPhoneNumber7digit(the_string As String) As Boolean
    Return the_string.MatchesRegexp("^[2-9]\d{2}-\d{4}$")
End Function

' Return True if a String looks like a 10-digit US phone number.
<Extension()>
Public Function IsValidPhoneNumber10digit(the_string As String) As Boolean
    Return the_string.MatchesRegexp("^([2-9]\d{2}-){2}\d{4}$")
End Function

' Return True if a String looks like a 7- or 10-digit US phone number.
<Extension()>
Public Function IsValidPhoneNumberUS(the_string As String) As Boolean
    Return IsValidPhoneNumber7digit(the_string) OrElse
            IsValidPhoneNumber10digit(the_string)
End function
```

If you build a class and later need to change its features, it's usually easiest to modify its code directly. That will cause less confusion than extension methods, which may lie in some obscure module that seems unrelated to the original class. If you need to add methods to existing classes that you cannot modify, such as String and other classes defined by Visual Basic and the .NET Framework, extension methods can be extremely useful.

LAMBDA FUNCTIONS

Lambda functions are functions that are defined within the flow of the program's code. Often they are defined, used, and forgotten in a single statement without ever being given a name.

To define a lambda function for later use, start with the Function keyword. Add the function's name and any parameters that it requires, followed by a single statement that evaluates to the value that the function should return.

Next include either (1) a single statement that evaluates to the value that the function should return, or (2) a function body that ends with an End Function statement.

The following code fragment shows examples of both of these styles:

```
Dim square_it = Function(n As Integer) n * n
Dim factorial = Function(n As Integer) As Integer
                Dim result As Integer = 1
                For i As Integer = 2 To n
                    result *= i
                Next i
                Return result
            End Function

Debug.WriteLine(square_it(5))
Debug.WriteLine(factorial(5))
```

The code first creates a lambda function named square_it that takes parameter n and returns n * n. It then creates a multiline lambda function named factorial that calculates and returns a number's factorial. The code finishes by calling both functions and displaying their results.

Example program LambdaFunction, which is available for download on the book's website, contains the following code fragment:

```
' Define a lambda function that adds two integers.
Dim plus = Function(i1 As Integer, i2 As Integer) i1 + i2

' Get A and B.
Dim A As Integer = Integer.Parse(txtA.Text)
Dim B As Integer = Integer.Parse(txtB.Text)

' Call the lambda function to calculate the result.
txtResult.Text = plus(A, B).ToString
```

This code starts by defining a variable named `plus`. This variable holds a reference to a lambda function that takes two integers as parameters and returns their sum. The code then gets input values from text boxes and calls the plus function, passing it those values. It converts the result into a string and displays it in the txtResult text box.

This example creates a variable to hold a reference to a lambda function and then invokes the function by using that variable. It could just as easily have invoked the lambda function itself while defining it.

Example program InlineFunction, which is also available for download on the book's website, demonstrates this in the following line of code. This line defines the function and invokes it without ever saving a reference to it.

```
txtResult.Text =
    (Function(i1 As Integer, i2 As Integer) i1 + i2)(A, B).ToString
```

Because lambda functions are declared in a single line of code, they are also called *inline functions*. A lambda function defined inside a subroutine or function is also sometimes called a *nested function*.

LAMBDA OR INLINE?

To the extent that anyone distinguishes between lambda and inline functions, the preceding example is more properly called an inline function because the function is contained within the line that uses it and is never given a name. The examples before that one are more properly called lambda functions because they create functions (square_it, factorial, and plus) with references that are used later.

No matter which method the program uses to define a lambda function, it could then pass the function to another routine that will later call the function. For example, suppose subroutine PerformCalculations takes as a parameter the function it should use to perform its calculations.

The following code shows how a program could call subroutine PerformCalculations while passing it the previous lambda functions:

```
' Define the plus function.
Dim plus = Function(i1 As Integer, i2 As Integer) i1 + i2

' Call PerformCalculations passing it the lambda function.
PerformCalculations(plus)

' Call PerformCalculations passing it an inline lambda function.
PerformCalculations(Function(i1 As Integer, i2 As Integer) i1 + i2)
```

Inline functions were invented for use by LINQ and are most often used with LINQ. For more information about LINQ, see Chapter 20, "LINQ."

In addition to lambda functions, you can write lambda subroutines that are similar to lambda functions except they don't return a value.

The following code defines two named lambda subroutines. The first does all of its work on a single line whereas the second uses the multiline format. After defining the subroutines, the code invokes them to display two messages.

```
Dim write_msg = Sub(msg As String) Debug.WriteLine("write_msg: " & msg)
Dim show_msg = Sub(msg As String)
                   MessageBox.Show("show_msg: " & msg)
               End Sub

write_msg("Hi")
show_msg("Hi again")
```

As with lambda functions, you can build and pass a lambda subroutine into another routine as a parameter.

RELAXED DELEGATES

If you assign a variable to the value in a variable of a different type, Visual Basic automatically converts the value into the correct type under some circumstances. If you set a Single variable equal to an Integer variable, Visual Basic automatically converts the Integer into a Single.

If Option Strict is off, you can also do the reverse: If you assign an Integer variable equal to a Single variable, Visual Basic converts the Single into an Integer (if it can).

In a similar manner, relaxed delegates let Visual Basic convert method parameters from one data type to another under certain circumstances. If the code invokes a subroutine by using a delegate, Visual Basic tries to convert parameters when it can. Probably the easiest way to understand how this works is to consider an example.

The following code declares a delegate type named TestDelegate. Methods that match this delegate should be subroutines that take a Control as a parameter.

```
' Declare the delegate type.
Private Delegate Sub TestDelegate(ctl As Control)
```

The following code defines three subroutines that take parameters of different types. The first takes an Object as a parameter, the second takes a TextBox, and the third takes no parameters. Note that the first subroutine cannot work if Option Strict is on. Option Strict disallows late binding, so the code cannot use a Text property provided by a generic Object.

```
' A more general parameter type.
Private Sub Test1(obj As Object)
    obj.Text = "Test1" ' Needs Option Strict off.
End Sub

' A more specific parameter type.
Private Sub Test2(text_box As TextBox)
    text_box.Text = "Test2"
End Sub

' Parameter omitted.
Private Sub Test3()
    txtField3.Text = "Test3"
End Sub
```

The following code declares three variables of the TestDelegate type and sets them equal to the addresses of the three test subroutines:

```
' Make variables of the delegate type hold references to the subroutines.
Private Sub1 As TestDelegate = AddressOf Test1
Private Sub2 As TestDelegate = AddressOf Test2 ' Needs Option Strict off.
Private Sub3 As TestDelegate = AddressOf Test3
```

The first assignment works even though subroutine Test1 does not exactly match the delegate type. Subroutine Test1 takes an Object as a parameter and TestDelegate takes a Control as a parameter. When Visual Basic invokes the Sub1 variable, it will pass the subroutine a Control object as a parameter because Sub1 has type TestDelegate, and that type takes a Control as a parameter. A Control is a type of Object, so Visual Basic can safely pass a Control in place of an Object parameter. That allows the code assigning Sub1 to the address of subroutine Test1 to work.

The second line of code that assigns variable Sub2 to subroutine Test2 works only if Option Strict is off. When Visual Basic invokes the Sub2 variable, it will pass the subroutine a Control object as a parameter because Sub1 has type TestDelegate, and that type takes a Control as a parameter. Subroutine Test2 takes a TextBox as a parameter, and not every Control is a TextBox. That means at design time Visual Basic cannot tell whether it can safely invoke the Sub2 delegate so, if Option Strict is on, Visual Basic flags this assignment as an error. If Option Strict is off, Visual Basic allows the assignment, although the program will crash if it tries to pass a control that is not a TextBox into Sub2 at run time.

STRICTLY SPEAKING

This is similar to setting a TextBox variable equal to the value in a Control variable. If Option Strict is on, Visual Basic will not allow that assignment.

The final assignment sets variable Sub3 to the address of subroutine Test3. Subroutine Test3 takes no parameters. This is a special case that Visual Basic allows: If the method does not need to use the parameters specified by the delegate, it can omit its parameters. Note that the method must omit all or none of the parameters; it cannot omit some and not others.

The following code invokes the subroutines pointed to by the three TestDelegate variables, passing each a reference to a different TextBox. Sub1 treats txtField1 as an Object, Sub2 treats txtField2 as a TextBox, and Sub3 ignores its parameter completely.

```
Sub1(txtField1)
Sub2(txtField2)
Sub3(txtField3)
' Test3(txtField3) ' This doesn't work.
```

The final line of code, that invokes subroutine Test3 directly, doesn't work. Omitting the parameter list from a method only works if you access the method from a delegate. If you call the method directly, the parameter list must match the one declared for the method.

Example program RelaxedDelegates, which is available for download on the book's website, demonstrates this code.

All of these relaxed delegate rules are somewhat confusing. They give you a little more flexibility, but they can make the code a lot more confusing. You may wonder why you should bother. In fact, if you use delegates such as those shown in this example, you might want to avoid using relaxed delegates to keep the code easier to understand.

These rules also apply to event handlers, and in that context they are much more useful. They let you change an event handler's parameter types to make them more general or more specific, or to omit them entirely.

The following code shows a simple, standard Button Click event handler. It takes two parameters of types Object and EventArgs. In this example, the code reads a text file into a text box.

```
Private Sub btnLoad_Click(sender As Object,
 ByVal e As EventArgs) Handles btnLoad.Click
    txtContents.Text = File.ReadAllText(txtFile.Text)
End Sub
```

Many event handlers must deal explicitly with the control that raised their event. In that case, the first thing the event handler usually does is convert the generic sender parameter from an Object into a more specific control type.

The following code defines a Button Click event handler similar to the previous one but this one declares its sender parameter to be of type Button. This works as long as the event is actually raised by a Button so the sender parameter really is a button. If you were to attach this event handler to a TextBox's TextChanged event, the program would crash when Visual Basic tried to convert the TextBox into a Button when it raises the event.

```
' Needs Option Strict off.
Private Sub btnLoad2_Click(btn As Button,
 ByVal e As Object) Handles btnLoad2.Click
    txtContents.Text = File.ReadAllText(txtFile.Text)
End Sub
```

Note that this version requires Option Strict off. If Option Strict is on, Visual Basic will not allow this subroutine to handle a Button's Click event. This is similar to the way Option Strict prevents you from setting a Button variable equal to a generic Object variable.

The previous code declares its parameters to have a more restrictive type than those passed into it by the control raising the event. You can also make the parameters more general. You could declare the e parameter to be of type Object instead of EventArgs. Usually, that doesn't help you much. It could be useful if you want to use the same event handler to catch different kinds of events that provide different types of arguments, but it's hard to imagine a really good example where that wouldn't be confusing.

A more common situation is where the event handler ignores its parameters completely. Usually each Button has a separate Click event handler so you don't need to look at the parameters to figure out which button was clicked.

The following code defines a Button Click event handler that takes no parameters. When the user clicks the btnLoad3 Button, Visual Basic doesn't pass the event handler any parameters. This code is easier to read than the previous versions, partly because the Sub statement fits all on one line.

```
Private Sub btnLoad3_Click() Handles btnLoad3.Click
    txtContents.Text = File.ReadAllText(txtFile.Text)
End Sub
```

Example program RelaxedEventHandlers, which is available for download on the book's website, demonstrates relaxed event handlers.

Relaxed delegates may add more confusion than they're worth if you use delegate variables, but they can be useful for simplifying event handlers. Declaring parameters with a more specific type (for example, Button instead of Object) can make the code easier to write and understand, although it has the large drawback of requiring Option Strict off. Omitting parameters when you don't need them is an even better technique. It simplifies the code without forcing you to turn Option Strict off.

ASYNCHRONOUS METHODS

Normally a program calls a routine and control passes to that routine. When the routine finishes executing, control returns to the calling code, which resumes executing its own code. All of this happens synchronously so the calling code waits until the called routine finishes all of its work before it continues.

Visual Basic provides several methods that you can use to execute code asynchronously. In those cases a calling piece of code can launch a routine in a separate thread and continue executing before the routine finishes. If your computer has multiple cores or CPUs, the calling code and the asynchronous routine may both be able to execute simultaneously on separate processors, potentially saving a lot of time.

Visual Basic provides several methods of various difficulties for executing code asynchronously. The following sections describe three of the more manageable approaches.

Calling EndInvoke Directly

This method uses a delegate's BeginInvoke method to start a routine executing asynchronously. Later the code calls EndInvoke to wait for the routine to finish and to process the result.

To use this method, first define a delegate that represents the routine that you want to run asynchronously. Call the delegate's BeginInvoke method, passing it whatever parameters the method needs plus two additional parameters: a callback method and a parameter to pass to the callback method. For this technique, set the extra parameters to Nothing so the routine does not invoke a callback when it completes. (The following section explains how to use the callback.)

The call to BeginInvoke launches the asynchronous code on its own thread and then returns immediately so the calling code can perform other tasks.

After the calling code has done as much as it can before the asynchronous thread finishes, it should invoke the delegate's EndInvoke method. That method waits until the asynchronous thread finishes (if it isn't already finished) and returns the result of the original method.

> **NOTE** *It is important that the code call EndInvoke even if the thread is executing a subroutine rather than a function and the code doesn't care about any returned result. The call to EndInvoke lets the program free resources used by the asynchronous thread.*

The AsyncCallEndInvoke example program, which is shown in Figure 16-1 and available for download on the book's website, uses this approach to generate embossed images for four different pictures.

The program uses an extension method named Emboss that allows a Bitmap object to return an embossed version of itself. The details of that method aren't important for this discussion so its code is not shown here. Download the example program to see how it works. The only feature of that method that is important right now is that it takes a long time to finish so running on multiple threads can make the program faster.

The following code shows how the AsyncCallEndInvoke program defines the delegate it uses to launch the Emboss extension method:

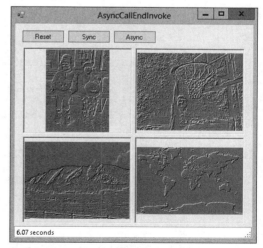

FIGURE 16-1: The AsyncCallEndInvoke example program generates embossed images asynchronously.

```
Private Delegate Function EmbossDelegate(bm As Bitmap) As Bitmap
```

The Emboss method takes a Bitmap as a parameter (the object that is calling the extension method) and returns a new Bitmap so the delegate takes a Bitmap as a parameter and returns a Bitmap as a result.

The following code shows how the program invokes the Emboss extension method asynchronously:

```
' Emboss the images asynchronously.
Private Sub btnAsync_Click(sender As Object, e As EventArgs) _
 Handles btnAsync.Click
    lblElapsedTime.Text = ""
    DisplayOriginalImages()
    Me.Cursor = Cursors.WaitCursor
    Application.DoEvents()

    Dim start_time As Date = Now

    ' Get all of the bitmaps.
    Dim bm1 As Bitmap = My.Resources.JackOLanterns
    Dim bm2 As Bitmap = My.Resources.Dunk
    Dim bm3 As Bitmap = My.Resources.Flatirons
    Dim bm4 As Bitmap = My.Resources.world

    ' Start the processes.
    Dim caller1 As EmbossDelegate = AddressOf bm1.Emboss
    Dim result1 As IAsyncResult =
        caller1.BeginInvoke(bm1, Nothing, Nothing)

    Dim caller2 As EmbossDelegate = AddressOf bm2.Emboss
    Dim result2 As IAsyncResult =
        caller2.BeginInvoke(bm2, Nothing, Nothing)

    Dim caller3 As EmbossDelegate = AddressOf bm3.Emboss
    Dim result3 As IAsyncResult =
        caller3.BeginInvoke(bm3, Nothing, Nothing)

    Dim caller4 As EmbossDelegate = AddressOf bm4.Emboss
    Dim result4 As IAsyncResult =
        caller4.BeginInvoke(bm4, Nothing, Nothing)

    ' Wait for the processes to complete.
    PictureBox1.Image = caller1.EndInvoke(result1)
    PictureBox2.Image = caller2.EndInvoke(result2)
    PictureBox3.Image = caller3.EndInvoke(result3)
    PictureBox4.Image = caller4.EndInvoke(result4)

    ' Display the elapsed time.
    Dim stop_time As Date = Now
    Dim elapsed_time As TimeSpan = stop_time - start_time
    lblElapsedTime.Text = elapsed_time.TotalSeconds.ToString("0.00") & " seconds"
    Me.Cursor = Cursors.Default
End Sub
```

After some preliminaries such as displaying the original images on the form and saving the start time, the program loads four bitmaps from its resources. Then for each bitmap it creates an

EmbossDelegate object that refers to the bitmap's instance of the Emboss extension method and calls that delegate's BeginInvoke method. At that point the method can begin executing asynchronously but the main program's code continues executing.

After it has called BeginInvoke for all four delegates, the program needs the results of the asynchronous methods so it calls EndInvoke for all four delegates. It passes EndInvoke the IAsyncResult object that it received when it called BeginInvoke to give the method information about the asynchronous call. EndInvoke returns the result of the function that the delegate represents, in this case the embossed images.

For example, the first delegate, named `caller1`, refers to the first bitmap's version of the Emboss extension method `bm1.Emboss`. That delegate's EndInvoke method returns the value returned by `bm1.Emboss`, which is an embossed version of the bitmap `bm1`.

The program assigns the returned bitmaps to the PictureBoxes' Image properties and displays the elapsed time.

In one set of tests on my dual-core computer, creating the four embossed images took roughly 12.9 seconds synchronously but only 7.2 seconds asynchronously. Because the computer has two cores, you might expect the asynchronous version to take only half the time used by the synchronous version, but there is some overhead in setting up and coordinating the threads. The result is still an impressive reduction in time, however, and would be even greater on a computer with more cores.

Handling a Callback

The technique described in the previous section directly calls EndInvoke to make the main UI thread wait until its asynchronous threads have finished before the main program continues.

Another approach is to let the main program continue without waiting for the threads to complete and then have the threads invoke a callback method when they finish.

This approach lets the main program ignore the asynchronous threads for most purposes but it does make the flow of execution less predictable. While the threads are running, the user can do other things, perhaps even starting new threads that duplicate those that are already running. When a thread finishes, the callback routine executes, possibly interrupting whatever the user is doing at the time.

There's one important catch to working with callbacks: Only the thread that created the user interface (called the *UI thread*) can directly interact with the controls in the user interface. That means the asynchronous threads cannot directly assign images to PictureBoxes, display text in Labels or TextBoxes, move controls around, or otherwise manipulate the controls. Because the threads invoke the callback methods, those methods cannot directly interact with the controls, either. In this example that means the callback methods cannot directly assign the PictureBox's Image properties.

You can get around this restriction by using the form's Invoke method. Invoke executes one of the form's methods on the UI thread.

The AsyncHandleCallback example program, which is available for download on the book's website, is similar to the AsyncCallEndInvoke example program but it uses callbacks instead of calling EndInvoke in the program's main flow of execution.

The AsyncHandleCallback program defines the Emboss delegate just as the AsyncCallEndInvoke program does. The following code shows how the program calls BeginInvoke for its first image:

```
Dim caller1 As EmbossDelegate = AddressOf bm1.Emboss
Dim result1 As IAsyncResult =
    caller1.BeginInvoke(bm1, AddressOf AsyncCallback, PictureBox1)
```

The code makes a delegate named caller1 that represents the bm1 object's Emboss method. It calls the delegate's BeginInvoke method, passing it the bitmap to process (bm1), the address of the callback routine (AsyncCallback), and the PictureBox that should display the embossed result (PictureBox1).

The code performs similar steps for the other images and then the btnAsync_Click event handler that contains this code ends without waiting for the threads to finish.

Later, when a thread finishes, it invokes the following callback routine:

```
' Handle a callback.
Private Sub AsyncCallback(result As AsyncResult)
    Dim caller As EmbossDelegate =
        DirectCast(result.AsyncDelegate, EmbossDelegate)

    ' Get the parameter we passed to the callback.
    Dim pic As PictureBox = DirectCast(result.AsyncState, PictureBox)

    ' Get the method's return value.
    Dim bm As Bitmap = caller.EndInvoke(result)

    ' Use Invoke to display the image on the PictureBox.
    Dim displayer As New SetPictureBoxImageDelegate(AddressOf SetPictureboxImage)
    Me.Invoke(displayer, pic, bm)
End Sub
```

This code receives as a parameter an AsyncResult object representing the thread's result. It uses that result's AsyncDelegate property to get a reference to the original delegate that the program used to call BeginInvoke.

The result's AsyncState property holds whatever value the program passed as the final parameter to BeginInvoke. In this example, that was the PictureBox that should display the embossed image. The callback code converts the AsyncState property into a PictureBox.

The code then calls the delegate's EndInvoke method and saves the result, which is the embossed bitmap created by the thread.

Because this code is executing in an asynchronous thread, it cannot directly set the PictureBox's Image property so it uses Invoke to run the SetPictureBoxImage method on the UI thread. To do that, it makes a delegate variable pointing to the method and then calls Invoke, passing it the delegate and the parameters to pass to the SetPictureBoxImage method.

The following code shows the definition of the SetPictureBoxImageDelegate and the SetPictureBoxImage method:

```
' Set a PictureBox's Image property.
Private Delegate Sub SetPictureBoxImageDelegate(pic As PictureBox, img As Image)
Private Sub SetPictureBoxImage(pic As PictureBox, img As Image)
    pic.Image = img
End Sub
```

This method simply sets the PictureBox's Image property. (I've removed some code that displays the elapsed time to keep the method simple. Download the example to see how that works.)

IGNORING INVOKE

Actually this program seems to work even if the callback sets the PictureBoxes' Image properties directly, but messing with controls from non-UI threads is a bad habit and doesn't work with all properties. Try setting the PictureBox's BorderStyle property to None directly in the callback and in subroutine SetPictureBoxImage to see what happens.

For more information on calling methods asynchronously by using BeginInvoke and EndInvoke, see the article "Calling Synchronous Methods Asynchronously" at `http://msdn.microsoft.com/library/2e08f6yc.aspx`.

Using Async and Await

Calling EndInvoke directly in the UI thread makes the code relatively simple but it means the program is blocked until all of the asynchronous threads finish running. Using a callback allows the main UI thread to finish before the threads do so the UI can interact with the user, but the code is somewhat more complex, particularly if the callback must manipulate controls, so it needs to use the form's Invoke method.

Visual Basic 2012 provides two new keywords that make it easier to use the callback approach without actually writing callbacks and calling Invoke yourself.

The Async keyword indicates that a routine may have parts that should run asynchronously. You should apply this keyword to your event handlers and other routines that will start tasks asynchronously and then wait for them.

The Await keyword makes the program wait until a particular task has finished running asynchronously. When it sees the Await keyword, Visual Basic essentially converts the rest of the routine into a callback that it invokes when the task has finished. One really nice feature of that "virtual callback" is that it executes on the UI thread so it can manipulate controls directly without using the form's Invoke method.

The AsyncAwait example program, which is available for download on the book's website, is very similar to the AsyncCallEndInvoke and AsyncHandleCallback example programs but it uses the Async and Await keywords.

The following code shows the `btnAsync_Click` event handler that executes when you click the program's Async button:

```
' Emboss the images asynchronously.
Private Async Sub btnAsync_Click(sender As Object, e As EventArgs) _
  Handles btnAsync.Click
    lblElapsedTime.Text = ""
    DisplayOriginalImages()
    Me.Cursor = Cursors.WaitCursor
    Application.DoEvents()

    Dim start_time As Date = Now

    ' Get all of the bitmaps.
    Dim bm1 As Bitmap = My.Resources.JackOLanterns
    Dim bm2 As Bitmap = My.Resources.Dunk
    Dim bm3 As Bitmap = My.Resources.Flatirons
    Dim bm4 As Bitmap = My.Resources.world

    'Start four embossing tasks running.
    Dim task1 As New Task(Of Bitmap)(AddressOf bm1.Emboss)
    task1.Start()
    Dim task2 As New Task(Of Bitmap)(AddressOf bm2.Emboss)
    task2.Start()
    Dim task3 As New Task(Of Bitmap)(AddressOf bm3.Emboss)
    task3.Start()
    Dim task4 As New Task(Of Bitmap)(AddressOf bm4.Emboss)
    task4.Start()

    ' Wait for the tasks to finish.
    PictureBox1.Image = Await task1
    PictureBox2.Image = Await task2
    PictureBox3.Image = Await task3
    PictureBox4.Image = Await task4

    ' Display the elapsed time.
    Dim stop_time As Date = Now
    Dim elapsed_time As TimeSpan = stop_time - start_time
    lblElapsedTime.Text = elapsed_time.TotalSeconds.ToString("0.00") & " seconds"
    Me.Cursor = Cursors.Default
End Sub
```

Because this event handler has parts that run asynchronously, its declaration includes the Async keyword.

The code begins as the previous versions do, saving the start time and retrieving the program's bitmaps. It then creates Task objects to make the embossed images on asynchronous threads. The `Of Bitmap` part of the Task declarations means that the Tasks return Bitmaps. For each Bitmap, the program creates a Task to execute the Bitmap's Emboss method and calls the Task's Start method to make it start running on its own thread.

After it has created and launched all four Tasks, the program calls Await for each Task. Each Task returns a Bitmap and the program displays the Bitmap in the corresponding PictureBox.

Calling Await is very similar to calling EndInvoke directly except that behind the scenes Visual Basic moves the code that follows into a callback so execution does not block until the Tasks return.

The btnAsync_Click event handler blocks until the Tasks finish, but the program's control returns to the event loop so the program can perform other tasks such as responding to the user. This is similar to the way control returns to the AsyncHandleCallback program's main code while the asynchronous threads continue executing.

When the Tasks finish, they invoke a behind-the-scenes callback that continues executing the btnAsync_Click event handler.

The result is a combination of the results of the two previous examples. As in program AsyncCallEndInvoke, the button's event handler doesn't finish until all of the Tasks have completed so you can write that code in a fairly linear fashion without worrying about callbacks. However, the program actually is using a callback behind the scenes so the button's event handler doesn't block the entire application while it is running. (And you don't need to create any callbacks yourself.)

To see the difference, run the example program and click the Async button to start building the embossed images. After one or two of the images are displayed, click the Reset button to display the original images. Repeat the same steps in the other two examples to see the differences.

For more information about using Async and Await, see the article "Asynchronous Programming with Async and Await" at `http://msdn.microsoft.com/library/hh191443(v=vs.110).aspx`.

SUMMARY

Subroutines and functions let you break an application into manageable, reusable pieces. A subroutine performs a series of commands. A function performs a series of commands and returns a value.

Property procedures use paired functions and subroutines to provide the appearance of a simple property.

These form the fundamental building blocks of the procedural part of an application. Chapters 22 through 26 explain the other half of an application's structure: the objects that encapsulate the application's behavior. Together, the program's objects and its procedural subroutines and functions define the application.

This chapter explained how to break an otherwise unwieldy expanse of code into subroutines and functions of manageable size. It also explained techniques related to subroutines and functions, such as extension methods and relaxed delegates, that let you use existing classes and events in new ways.

This chapter also explained three ways you can execute pieces of code simultaneously on different threads of execution. If your computer has multiple cores or CPUs, that may allow you to greatly improve performance.

The chapters so far have not explained how to write anything other than straight-line code that executes one statement after another with no deviation. Most programs need to follow more complex paths of execution, performing some statements only under certain conditions and repeating others many times. Chapter 17, "Program Control Statements," describes the statements that a Visual Basic program uses to control the flow of code execution. These include decision statements (If Then Else, Select Case, IIF, Choose) and looping statements (For Next, For Each, Do While, While Do, Repeat Until).

17

Program Control Statements

WROX.COM CODE DOWNLOADS FOR THIS CHAPTER

The wrox.com code downloads for this chapter are found at http://www.wrox.com/remtitle.cgi?isbn=9781118314074 on the Download Code tab. The code for this chapter is divided into the following major examples:

➤ EnumerateEmployees

➤ ExitAndContinue

➤ Loops

CONTROLLING PROGRAMS

Program control statements tell an application which other statements to execute under a particular set of circumstances. They control the path that execution takes through the code. They include commands that tell the program to execute some statements but not others and to execute certain statements repeatedly.

The two main categories of control statements are *decision statements* (or *conditional statements*) and *looping statements*. The following sections describe in detail the decision and looping statements provided by Visual Basic .NET.

DECISION STATEMENTS

A decision or conditional statement represents a branch in the program. It marks a place where the program can execute one set of statements or another, or possibly no statements at all, depending on some condition. These include several kinds of If statements, Choose statements, and Select Case statements.

Single-Line If Then

The single-line If Then statement has two basic forms. The first allows the program to execute a single statement if some condition is True. The syntax is as follows:

```
If condition Then statement
```

If the condition is True, the program executes the statement. In the most common form of single-line If Then statements, the statement is a single simple command (such as assigning a value to a variable or calling a subroutine).

The following example checks the `emp` object's `IsManager` property. If `IsManager` is True, the statement sets the `emp` object's `Salary` property to 90,000.

```
If emp.IsManager Then emp.Salary = 90000
```

The second form of the single-line If Then statement uses the Else keyword. The syntax is as follows:

```
If condition Then statement1 Else statement2
```

If the condition is True, the code executes the first statement. If the condition is False, the code executes the second statement. The decision about which statement to execute is an either-or decision; the code executes one statement or the other, but not both.

This type of single-line If Then Else statement can be confusing if it is too long to easily see in the code editor. For longer statements, a multiline If Then Else statement is easier to understand and debug. The performance of single-line and multiline If Then Else statements is comparable (in one test, the multiline version took only about 80 percent as long), so you should use the one that is easiest for you to read.

The single-line If Then statement can also include Else If clauses. For example, the following code examines the variable x. If x is 1, the program sets variable `txt` to "One." If x has the value 2, the program sets `txt` to "Two." If x is not 1 or 2, the program sets `txt` to a question mark.

```
Dim txt As String
If X = 1 Then txt = "One" Else If X = 2 Then txt = "Two" Else txt = "?"
```

The code can include as many Else If clauses as you like. However, confusing code such as the preceding example can lead to puzzling bugs that are easy to avoid if you use multiline If Then statements instead.

In summary, if you can write a simple single-line If Then statement with no Else If or Else clauses, and the whole thing fits nicely on the line so that it's easy to see the whole thing without confusion, go ahead. If the statement is too long to read easily, or contains Else If or Else clauses, you are usually better off using a multiline If Then statement. It may take more lines of code, but the code will be easier to read, debug, and maintain later.

Multiline If Then

A multiline If Then statement can execute more than one line of code when a condition is True. The syntax for the simplest form of the multiline If Then statement is as follows:

```
If condition Then
    statements ...
End If
```

If the condition is True, the program executes all the commands that come before the End If statement.

Like the single-line If Then statement, the multiline version can include Else If and Else clauses. For possibly historical reasons, ElseIf is spelled as a single word in the multiline If Then statement. The syntax is as follows:

```
If condition1 Then
    statements1 ...
ElseIf condition2
    statements2 ...
Else
    statements3 ...
End If
```

If the first condition is True, the program executes the first set of statements. If the first condition is False, the code examines the second condition and, if that one is True, the code executes the second set of statements. The program continues checking conditions until it finds one that is True and it executes the corresponding code.

If the program reaches an Else statement, it executes the corresponding code. If the program reaches the End If statement without finding a True condition or an Else clause, it doesn't execute any of the statement blocks.

It is important to understand that the program exits the If Then construction immediately after it has executed any block of statements. It does not examine the other conditions. This saves the program some time and is particularly important if the conditions involve functions. If each test calls a relatively slow function, skipping these later tests can save the program a significant amount of time.

Select Case

The Select Case statement lets a program execute one of several pieces of code depending on a single value. The basic syntax is as follows:

```
Select Case test_value
    Case comparison_expression1
        statements1
    Case comparison_expression2
        statements2
    Case comparison_expression3
        statements3
    ...
    Case Else
        else_statements
End Select
```

If test_value matches comparison_expression1, the program executes the statements in the block statements1. If test_value matches comparison_expression2, the program executes the statements in the block `statements2`. The program continues checking the expressions in the Case statements in order until it matches one, or it runs out of Case statements.

If `test_value` doesn't match any of the expressions in the Case statements, the program executes the code in the `else_statements` block. Note that you can omit the Case Else section. In that case, the program executes no code if `test_value` doesn't match any of the expressions.

Select Case is functionally equivalent to an If Then Else statement. The following code does the same thing as the previous Select Case code:

```
If test_value = comparison_expression1 Then
    statements1
ElseIf test_value = comparison_expression2 Then
    statements2
ElseIf test_value = comparison_expression3 Then
    statements3
...
Else
    else_statements
End If
```

Select Case is sometimes easier to understand than a long If Then Else statement. It is often faster as well, largely because Select Case doesn't need to reevaluate `test_value` for every Case statement. If `test_value` is a simple variable, the difference is insignificant, but if `test_value` represents a slow function call, the difference can be important. For example, suppose `test_value` represents a function that opens a database and looks up a value. The Select Case version will find the value once and use it in each comparison, whereas the If Then version would reopen the database for each comparison.

The previous If Then example assumes the comparison expressions are constants. A comparison expression can also specify ranges using the To and Is keywords, and include a comma-separated list of expressions. These forms are described in the following sections.

To

The To keyword specifies a range of values that `test_value` should match. The following code examines the variable `num_items`. If `num_items` is between 1 and 10, the program calls subroutine `ProcessSmallOrder`. If `num_items` is between 11 and 100, the program calls subroutine `ProcessLargeOrder`. If `num_items` is less than 1 or greater than 100, the program beeps.

```
Select Case num_items
    Case 1 To 10
        ProcessSmallOrder()
    Case 11 To 100
        ProcessLargeOrder()
    Case Else
        Beep()
End Select
```

Is

The Is keyword lets you perform logical comparisons using the test value. The word Is takes the place of the test value in the comparison expression. For example, the following code does almost the same things as the previous code. If the value `num_items` is less than or equal to 10, the program calls subroutine `ProcessSmallOrder`. If the first Case clause doesn't apply and `num_items` is less than or equal to 100, the program calls subroutine `ProcessLargeOrder`. If neither of these cases applies, the program beeps.

```
Select Case num_items
    Case Is <= 10
        ProcessSmallOrder()
    Case Is <= 100
        ProcessLargeOrder()
    Case Else
        Beep()
End Select
```

This version is slightly different from the previous one. If `num_items` is less than 1, this code calls subroutine `ProcessSmallOrder` whereas the previous version beeps.

You can use the operators =, <>, <, <=, >, and >= in an Is clause. (In fact, when you use a simple value in a Case clause as in `Case 7`, you are implicitly using `Is = ` as in `Case Is = 7`.)

Comma-Separated Expressions

A comparison expression can include a series of expressions separated by commas. If the test value matches any of the comparison values, the program executes the corresponding code.

For example, the following code examines the `department_name` variable. If `department_name` is "R & D," "Test," or "Computer Operations," the code adds the text "Building 10" to the `address_text` string. If `department_name` is "Finance," "Purchasing," or "Accounting," the code adds "Building 7" to the address. More Case clauses could check for other `department_name` values and the code could include an Else statement.

```
Select Case department_name
    Case "R & D", "Test", "Computer Operations"
        address_text &= "Building 10"
    Case "Finance", "Purchasing", "Accounting"
        address_text &= "Building 7"
    ...
End Select
```

Note that you cannot use comma-separated expressions in a Case Else clause. For example, the following code doesn't work:

```
Case Else, "Corporate" ' This doesn't work.
```

You can mix and match constants, To, and Is expressions in a single Case clause, as shown in the following example. This code checks the variable `item_code` and calls subroutine `DoSomething` if the value is less than 10, between 30 and 40 inclusive, exactly equal to 100, or greater than 200.

```
Select Case item_code
    Case Is < 10, 30 To 40, 100, Is > 200
        DoSomething()
    ...
End Select
```

Enumerated Values

Select Case statements work very naturally with lists of discrete values. You can have a separate Case statement for each value, or you can list multiple values for one Case statement in a comma-separated list.

Enumerated types defined by the Enum statement also work with discrete values, so they work well with Select Case statements. The enumerated type defines the values and the Select Case statement uses them, as shown in the following code fragment:

```
Private Enum JobStates
    Pending
    Assigned
    InProgress
    ReadyToTest
    Tested
    Released
End Enum
Private m_JobState As JobStates
...
Select Case m_JobState
    Case Pending
        ...
    Case Assigned
        ...
    Case InProgress
        ...
    Case ReadyToTest
        ...
    Case Tested
        ...
    Case Released
        ...
End Select
```

To catch bugs when changing an enumerated type, many developers include a Case Else statement that throws an exception. If you later add a new value to the enumerated type but forget to add corresponding code to the Select Case statement, the Select Case statement throws an error when it sees the new value, so you can fix the code.

For more information on enumerated types, see the section "Enumerated Data Types" in Chapter 14, "Data Types, Variables, and Constants."

IIf

The IIf statement evaluates a Boolean expression and then returns one of two values, depending on whether the expression is True or False. This statement may look more like an assignment statement or a function call than a decision statement such as If Then.

The syntax is as follows:

```
variable = IIf(condition, value_if_true, value_if_false)
```

For example, the following code examines an Employee object's IsManager property. If IsManager is True, the code sets the employee's Salary to 90,000. If IsManager is False, the code sets the employee's Salary to 10,000.

```
emp.Salary = IIf(emp.IsManager, 90000, 10000)
```

Note that the IIf statement returns an Object data type. If you have Option Strict turned on, Visual Basic will not allow this statement, because it assigns a result of type Object to an Integer variable. To satisfy Visual Basic, you must explicitly convert the value into an Integer, as in the following code:

```
emp.Salary = CInt(IIf(emp.IsManager, 90000, 10000))
```

The IIf statement has several drawbacks. First, it is confusing. When you type an IIf statement, IntelliSense will remind you that its parameters give a condition, a True value, and a False value. When you are reading the code, however, you must remember what the different parts of the statement mean. If you use IIf in some other statement, the chances for confusion increase. For example, consider the following code:

```
For i = 1 To CInt(IIf(employees_loaded, num_employees, 0))
    ' Process employee i.
    ...
Next i
```

Code is generally much easier to understand if you replace IIf with an appropriate If Then statement.

Another drawback to IIf is that it evaluates both the True and False values whether the condition is True or False. For example, consider the following code:

```
num_objects = CInt(IIf(use_groups, CountGroups(), CountIndividuals()))
```

If the Boolean use_groups is True, this code sets num_objects to the result of the CountGroups function. If use_groups is False, the code sets num_objects to the result of the CountIndividuals function. In either case, IIf evaluates both functions no matter which value it actually needs. If the functions are time-consuming or executed inside a large loop, using IIf can waste a lot of time.

For an even more dangerous example, consider the following code:

```
num_loaded = CInt(IIf(data_loaded, num_employees, LoadEmployees()))
```

If data_loaded is True, this statement sets num_loaded = num_employees. If data_loaded is False, the code sets num_loaded to the value returned by the LoadEmployees function (which loads the employees and returns the number of employees it loaded).

IIf evaluates both the value num_employees and the value LoadEmployees() no matter what. If the employees are already loaded, IIf calls LoadEmployees() to load the employees again, ignores the returned result, and sets `num_loaded = num_employees`. `LoadEmployees` may waste quite a lot of time loading the data that is already loaded. Even worse, the program may not be able to handle loading the data when it is already loaded.

A final drawback to IIf is that it is slower than a comparable If Then Else statement. In one test, IIf took roughly twice as long as a comparable If Then statement.

One case where you can argue that IIf is easier to understand is when you have a long series of very simple statements. In that case, IIf statements may allow you to easily see the common features in the code and notice if anything looks wrong. For example, the following code initializes several text boxes using strings. It uses an IIf statement to set a text box's value to `<Missing>` if the string is not yet initialized.

```
txtLastName.Text = IIf(last_name Is Nothing, "<Missing>", last_name)
txtFirstName.Text = IIf(first_name Is Nothing, "<Missing>", first_name)
txtStreet.Text = IIf(street Is Nothing, "<Missing>", street)
txtCity.Text = IIf(city Is Nothing, "<Missing>", city)
txtState.Text = IIf(state Is Nothing, "<Missing>", state)
txtZip.Text = IIf(zip Is Nothing, "<Missing>", zip)
```

To avoid confusing side effects, use IIf only if it makes the code easier to understand.

If

The If statement, not to be confused with an If Then statement, resolves some of the problems with the IIf statement. It evaluates a Boolean expression and then returns one of two values, depending on whether the expression is True or False, as IIf does. The difference is that If only evaluates the return value that it actually returns.

For example, the following code examines an Employee object's `IsManager` property. If `IsManager` is True, the code sets the employee's `Salary` to the result returned by the `GetManagerSalary` function and never calls function `GetEmployeeSalary`. If `IsManager` is False, the code sets the employee's `Salary` to the result of the `GetEmployeeSalary` function and never calls function `GetManagerSalary`.

```
emp.Salary = If(emp.IsManager, GetManagerSalary(), GetEmployeeSalary())
```

Other than the fact that If doesn't evaluate both of its possible return values, it behaves just as IIf does.

Choose

The IIf and If statements use a Boolean expression to pick between two values. The Choose statement uses an integer to decide among any number of options. The syntax is as follows:

```
variable = Choose(index, value1, value2, value3, value4, ... )
```

If the `index` parameter is 1, Choose returns the first value, `value1`; if `index` is 2, Choose returns `value2`; and so forth. If `index` is less than 1 or greater than the number of values in the parameter list, Choose returns Nothing.

This statement has the same drawbacks as IIf. Choose evaluates all of the result values no matter which one is selected, so it can slow performance. It can be particularly confusing if the values are functions with side effects.

Often Choose is more confusing than a comparable Select Case statement. If the values look dissimilar (mixing integers, objects, function calls, and so forth), involve complicated functions, or are wrapped across multiple lines, a Select Case statement may be easier to read.

However, if the Choose statement's values are short and easy to understand, and the statement contains many values, the Choose statement may be easier to read. For example, the following Choose and Select Case statements do the same thing. Because the Choose statement's values are short and easy to understand, this statement is easy to read. The Select Case statement is rather long. If the program had more choices, the Select Case statement would be even longer, making it more difficult to read.

```
fruit = Choose(index, "apple", "banana", "cherry", "date")

Select Case index
    Case 1
        fruit = "apple"
    Case 2
        fruit = "banana"
    Case 3
        fruit = "cherry"
    Case 4
        fruit = "date"
End Select
```

Although it's not always clear whether a Choose statement or a Select Case statement will be easier to read, Select Case is certainly faster. In one test, Choose took more than five times as long as Select Case. If the code lies inside a frequently executed loop, the speed difference may be an issue.

Choose and Select Case are not your only options. You can also store the program's choices in an array, and then use the index to pick an item from the array. For example, the following code stores the strings from the previous example in the values array. It then uses the index to pick the right choice from the array.

```
Dim fruit_names() As String = {"apple", "banana", "cherry", "date"}

fruit = fruit_names(index - 1)
```

INTELLIGENT INDEXING

Notice that the code subtracts 1 from the index when using it to pick the right choice. The Choose statement indexes its values starting with 1, but arrays in Visual Basic .NET start with index 0. Subtracting 1 allows the program to use the same index values used in the previous example.

This version makes you think about the code in a different way. It requires that you know that the `fruit_names` array contains the names of the fruits that the program needs. If you understand the array's purpose, then the assignment statement is easy to understand.

The assignment code is even slightly faster than Select Case, at least if you can initialize the `fruit_names` array ahead of time.

If you find Choose easy to understand and it doesn't make your code more difficult to read in your particular circumstances, by all means use it. If Select Case seems clearer, use that. If you will need to perform the assignment many times and pre-building an array of values makes sense, using a value array might improve your performance.

LOOPING STATEMENTS

Looping statements make the program execute a series of statements repeatedly. The loop can run for a fixed number of repetitions, run while some condition is True, or run while some condition is False.

Broadly speaking, there are two types of looping statements. For Next loops execute a certain number of times that (in theory at least) is known. For example, a For Next loop may execute a series of statements exactly 10 times. Or, it may execute the statements once for each object in a certain collection. If you know how many items are in the collection, you know the number of times the loop will execute.

A While loop executes while a condition is True or until a condition is met. Without a lot more information about the application, it is impossible to tell how many times the code will execute. For example, suppose a program uses the InputBox function to get names from the user until the user clicks the Cancel button. In that case, there's no way for the program to guess how many values the user will enter before canceling.

The following sections describe the looping statements supported by Visual Basic .NET. The next two sections describe For Next loops, and the sections after those describe While loops. (Example program Loops, which is available for download on the book's website, demonstrates some of these kinds of loops.)

For Next

The For Next loop is the most common type of looping statement in Visual Basic. The syntax is as follows:

```
For variable [As data_type] = start_value To stop_value [Step increment]
    statements
    [Exit For]
    statements
    [Continue For]
    statements
Next [variable]
```

The value `variable` is the looping variable that controls the loop. When the program reaches the For statement, it sets `variable` equal to `start_value`. It then compares `variable` to `stop_value`.

If `variable` has passed `stop_value`, the loop exits. Note that the loop may not execute even once depending on the start and stop values.

For example, the following loop runs for the values `employee_num = 1`, `employee_num = 2`, . . ., `employee_num = num_employees`. If the program has not loaded any employees so `num_employees = 0`, the code inside the loop is not executed at all.

```
For employee_num = As Integer 1 To num_employees
    ProcessEmployee(employee_num)
Next employee_num
```

After it compares `variable` to `stop_value`, the program executes the statements inside the loop. It then adds `increment` to `variable` and starts the process over, again comparing `variable` to `stop_value`. If you omit `increment`, the program uses an increment of 1.

Note that `increment` can be negative or a fractional number, as in the following example:

```
For i As Integer = 3 To 1 Step -0.5
    Debug.WriteLine(i)
Next i
```

If `increment` is positive, the program executes as long as `variable <= stop_value`. If `increment` is negative, the program executes as long as `variable >= stop_value`. This means that the loop would not execute infinitely if `increment` were to move `variable` away from `stop_value`. For example, in the following code `start_value = 1` and `increment = −1`. The variable `i` would take the values `i = 1`, `i = 0`, `i = −1`, and so forth, so `i` will never reach the `stop_value` of 2. However, because `increment` is negative, the loop only executes while `i >= 2`. Because `i` starts with the value 1, the program immediately exits and the loop doesn't execute at all.

```
For i As Integer = 1 To 2 Step -1
    Debug.WriteLine(i)
Next i
```

Visual Basic doesn't require that you include the variable's name in the Next statement, although this makes the code easier to read. If you do specify the name in the Next statement, it must match the name you use in the For statement.

If you do not specify the looping variable's data type in the For statement and Option Explicit is on and Option Infer is off, then you must declare the variable before the loop. For example, the following loop declares the variable `i` outside of the loop:

```
Dim i As Integer

For i = 1 To 10
    Debug.WriteLine(i)
Next i
```

Declaring the looping variable in the For statement is a good practice for several reasons. It limits the scope of the variable so you don't need to remember what the variable is for in other pieces of code. It keeps the variable's declaration close to the code where it is used, so it's easier to remember the variable's data type. It also lets you more easily reuse counter variables without fear of confusion. If you have several loops that need an arbitrarily named looping variable, they can all declare and use the variable i without interfering with each other.

The program calculates its start_value and stop_value before the loop begins and it never recalculates them, even if their values change. For example, the following code loops from 1 to this_customer.Orders(1).NumItems. The program calculates this_customer.Orders(1).NumItems before executing the loop and doesn't recalculate that value even if it later changes. This saves the program time, particularly for long expressions such as this one, which could take a noticeable amount of time to reevaluate each time through a long loop.

```
For item_num As Integer = 1 To this_customer.Orders(1).NumItems
    this_customer.ProcessItem(item_num)
Next item_num
```

If you must reevaluate stop_value every time the loop executes, use a While loop instead of a For Next loop.

The Exit For statement allows the program to leave a For Next loop before it would normally finish. For example, the following code loops through the employees array. When it finds an entry with the IsManager property set to True, it saves the employee's index and uses Exit For to immediately stop looping.

```
Dim manager_index As Integer

For i As Integer = employees.GetLowerBound(0) To employees.GetUpperBound(0)
    If employees(i).IsManager Then
        manager_index = i
        Exit For
    End If
Next i
```

The Exit For statement exits only the For Next loop immediately surrounding the statement. If a For Next loop is nested within another For Next loop, the Exit For statement exits only the inner loop.

The Continue For statement makes the loop jump back to its For statement, increment its looping variable, and start the loop over again. This is particularly useful if the program doesn't need to execute the rest of the steps within the loop's body and wants to start the next iteration quickly.

OUT OF CONTROL

Your code can change the value of the control variable inside the loop, but that's generally not a good idea. The For Next loop has a very specific intent, and modifying the control variable inside the loop violates that intent, making the code more difficult to understand and debug. If you must modify the control variable in more complicated ways than are provided by a For Next loop, use a While loop instead. Then programmers reading the code won't expect a simple incrementing loop.

Non-Integer For Next Loops

Usually a For Next loop's control variable is an integral data type such as an Integer or Long but it can be any of the fundamental Visual Basic numeric data types. For example, the following code uses a variable declared as Single to display the values 1.0, 1.5, 2.0, 2.5, and 3.0:

```
For x As Single = 1 To 3 Step 0.5
    Debug.WriteLine(x.ToString("0.0"))
Next x
```

Because floating-point numbers cannot exactly represent every possible value, these data types are subject to rounding errors that can lead to unexpected results in For Next loops. The preceding code works as you would expect, at least on my computer. The following code, however, has problems. Ideally, this code would display values between 1 and 2, incrementing them by 1/7. Because of rounding errors, however, the value of x after seven trips through the loop is approximately 1.85714316. The program adds 1/7 to this and gets 2.0000003065381731. This is greater than the stopping value 2, so the program exits the loop and the Debug statement does not execute for x = 2.

```
For x As Single = 1 To 2 Step 1 / 7
    Debug.WriteLine(x)
Next x
```

One solution to this type of problem is to convert the code into a loop that uses an Integer control variable. Integer variables do not have the same problems with rounding errors that floating-point numbers do, so you have more precise control over the values used in the loop.

The following code does roughly the same thing as the previous code. It uses an Integer control variable, however, so this loop executes exactly eight times as desired. The final value printed into the Output window by the program is 2.

```
Dim x As Single

x = 1
For i As Integer = 1 To 8
    Debug.WriteLine(x)
    x += CSng(1 / 7)
Next i
```

If you look at the value of variable x in the debugger, you will find that its real value during the last trip through the loop is roughly 2.0000001702989851. If this variable were controlling the For loop, the program would see that this value is greater than 2, so it would not display its final value.

For Each

A For Each loop iterates over the items in a collection, array, or other container class that supports For Each loops. The syntax is as follows:

```
For Each variable [As object_type] In group
    statements
    [Exit For]
    statements
```

```
      [Continue For]
      statements
  Next [variable]
```

Here, `group` is a collection, array, or other object that supports For Each. As in For Next loops, the control variable must be declared either in or before the For statement if you have Option Explicit on and Option Infer off.

ENABLING ENUMERATORS

To support For Each, the `group` object must implement the System.Collections .IEnumerable interface. This interface defines a GetEnumerator method that returns an enumerator. For more information, see the next section, "Enumerators."

The control variable must be of a data type compatible with the objects contained in the group. If the group contains Employee objects, the variable could be an Employee object. It could also be a generic Object or any other class that readily converts into an Employee object. For example, if Employee inherits from the Person class, then the variable could be of type Person.

Visual Basic doesn't automatically understand what kinds of objects are stored in a collection or array until it tries to use them. If the control variable's type is not compatible with an object's type, the program generates an error when the For Each loop tries to assign the control variable to that object's value.

That means if a collection or array contains more than one type of object, the control variable must be of a type that can hold all of the objects. If the objects in a collection do not inherit from a common ancestor class, the code must use a control variable of type Object.

Like For Next loops, For Each loops support the Exit For and Continue For statements.

As is the case with For Next loops, declaring the looping variable in the For Each statement is a good practice. It limits the scope of the variable, so you don't need to remember what the variable is for in other pieces of code. It keeps the variable's declaration close to the code where it is used, so it's easier to remember the variable's data type. It also lets you more easily reuse counter variables without fear of confusion. If you have several loops that need an arbitrarily named looping variable, they can all declare and use the variable `obj`, `person`, or whatever else makes sense without interfering with each other.

Your code can change the value of the control variable inside the loop, but that has no effect on the loop's progress through the collection or array. The loop resets the variable to the next object inside the group and continues as if you had never changed the variable's value. To avoid confusion, don't bother.

Changes to a collection are immediately reflected in the loop. For example, if the statements inside the loop add a new object to the end of the collection, then the loop continues until it processes the new item. Similarly, if the loop's code removes an item from the end of the collection (that it has not yet reached), the loop does not process that item.

The exact effect on the loop depends on whether the item added or removed comes before or after the object the loop is currently processing. For example, if you remove an item before the current item, the loop has already examined that item, so there is no change to the loop's behavior. If you remove an item after the current one, the loop doesn't examine it. If you remove the current item, the loop seems to get confused and exits without raising an error.

Additions and deletions to an array are *not* reflected in the loop. If you use a ReDim statement to add items to the end of the array, the loop does not process them. If you try to access those objects, however, the program generates an "Index was outside the bounds of the array" error.

If you use ReDim to remove items from the end of the array, the loop processes those items anyway! If you modify the values in the array, for example, you change an object's properties or set an array entry to an entirely new object, the loop sees the changes.

To avoid all these possible sources of confusion, don't modify a collection or array while a For Each loop is examining its contents.

CREATIVE COLLECTIONS

If you really must modify a collection while looping through it, create a new collection and modify that one instead. For example, suppose you want to loop through the original collection and remove some items. Make the new collection and then loop through the original, copying the items that you want to keep into the new collection.

In really complicated situations, you may need to use a While loop and some careful indexing instead of a For Each loop.

One common scenario when dealing with collections is examining every item in the collection and removing some of them. If you use a For Each loop, removing the loop's current item makes the loop exit prematurely.

Another approach that seems like it might work (but doesn't) is to use a For Next loop, as shown in the following code. If the code removes an object from the collection, the loop skips the next item because its index has been reduced by one and the loop has already passed that position in the collection. Worse still, the control variable i will increase until it reaches the original value of employees.Count. If the loop has removed any objects, the collection no longer holds that many items. The code tries to access an index beyond the end of the collection and throws an error.

```
Dim emp As Employee

For i As Integer = 1 To employees.Count
    emp = employees(i)
    If emp.IsManager Then employees.Remove(i)
Next i
```

One solution to this problem is to use a For Next loop to examine the collection's objects in reverse order, as shown in the following example. In this version, the code never needs to use an index after it has been deleted because it is counting backward. The index of an object in the collection also doesn't change unless that object has already been examined by the loop. The loop examines every item exactly once, no matter which objects are removed.

```
For i As Integer = employees.Count To 1 Step -1
    emp = employees(i)
    If emp.IsManager Then employees.Remove(i)
Next i
```

Enumerators

An *enumerator* is an object that lets you move through the objects contained by some sort of container class. For example, collections, arrays, and hash tables provide enumerators. This section discusses enumerators for collections, but the same ideas apply for these other classes.

You can use an enumerator to view the objects in a collection but not to modify the collection itself. You can use the enumerator to alter the objects in the collection (for example, to change their properties), but you can generally not use it to add, remove, or rearrange the objects in the collection.

Initially, an enumerator is positioned before the first item in the collection. Your code can use the enumerator's MoveNext method to step to the next object in the collection. MoveNext returns True if it successfully moves to a new object or False if there are no more objects in the collection.

The Reset method restores the enumerator to its original position before the first object, so you can step through the collection again.

The Current method returns the object that the enumerator is currently reading. Note that Current returns a generic Object, so you will probably need to convert the result into a more specific data type before you use it. Invoking Current throws an error if the enumerator is not currently reading any object. That happens if the enumerator is before the first object or after the last object.

The following example uses an enumerator to loop through the items in a collection named Employees:

```
Dim emp As Employee
Dim employee_enumerator As IEnumerator
employee_enumerator = Employees.GetEnumerator()
Do While (employee_enumerator.MoveNext)
    emp = CType(employee_enumerator.Current, Employee)
    Debug.WriteLine(emp.Title & " " &.FirstName & " " & emp.LastName)
Loop
```

This code declares an Employee variable named emp and an IEnumerator object named employee_enumerator. It uses the collection's GetEnumerator method to obtain an enumerator for the collection. The program then enters a While loop. If employee_enumerator.MoveNext returns True, the enumerator has successfully moved to the next object in the collection. As long as it has read an object, the program uses CType to convert the generic object returned by Current into an Employee object, and it displays the Employee object's `Title`, `FirstName`, and `LastName` values. When it has finished processing all of the objects in the collection, `employee_enumerator.MoveNext` returns False and the While loop ends.

EXACT ENUMERATORS

Some containers support enumerators that use more specific data types. For example, a program can use a generic List that contains a specific kind of object such as Employee. Then it can use a generic enumerator of the correct type, in this case `IEnumerator(Of Employee)`. In that case, the enumerator's Current property returns an Employee instead of an Object so the code does not need to convert it into an Employee before using its methods.

Example program EnumerateEmployees, which is available for download on the book's website, creates a generic `List(Of Employee)`. It then creates a generic `IEnumerator(Of Employee)` for the list and uses it to loop through the list. For more information on generics, see Chapter 26, "Generics."

A For Each loop provides roughly the same access to the items in a container class as an enumerator. Under some circumstances, however, an enumerator may provide a more natural way to loop through a container class than a For Each loop. For example, an enumerator can skip several items without examining them closely. You can also use an enumerator's Reset method to restart the enumeration. To restart a For Each loop, you would need to repeat the loop, possibly by placing it inside yet another loop that determines when to stop looping.

The Visual Basic documentation states that an enumerator is valid only as long as you do not modify the collection. If you add or remove an object to or from the collection, the enumerator throws an "invalid operation" exception the next time you use it. In at least some cases, however, this doesn't seem to be true, and an enumerator can still work even if you modify its collection. This could lead to extremely confusing situations, however. To avoid unnecessary confusion, do not modify a collection while you are accessing it with an enumerator.

The IEnumerable interface defines the features needed for enumerators so any class that implements the IEnumerable interface provides enumerators. Any class that supports For Each must also implement the IEnumerable interface, so any class that supports For Each also supports enumerators. A few of the classes that implement IEnumerable include the following:

Array	HybridDictionary	SqlDataReader
ArrayList	ListDictionary	Stack
Collection	MessageQueue	String

continues

(continued)

CollectionBase	OdbcDataReader	StringCollection
ControlCollection	OleDbDataReader	StringDictionary
DataView	OracleDataReader	TableCellCollection
DictionaryBase	Queue	TableRowCollection
DictionaryEntries	ReadOnlyCollectionBase	XmlNode
Hashtable	SortedList	XmlNodeList

Iterators

An *iterator* is similar in concept to an enumerator. It also provides methods that allow you to step through the objects in some sort of container object. Iterators are more specialized than enumerators and work with a particular kind of class. Although you can use a nonspecific IEnumerator object to step through the items contained in any class that implements IEnumerable (an array, collection, hash table, or whatever), a certain iterator class is associated with a specific container class.

For example, a GraphicsPath object represents a series of connected lines and curves. A GraphicsPathIterator object can step through the line and curve data contained in a GraphicsPath object.

Iterators are much more specialized than enumerators. How you use them depends on what you need to do and on the kind of iterator, so they are not described in detail here.

Do Loop Statements

Visual Basic .NET supports three basic forms of Do Loop statements. The first form is a loop that repeats forever. The syntax is as follows:

```
Do
    statements
    [Exit Do]
    statements
    [Continue Do]
    statements
Loop
```

This kind of Do Loop executes the code it contains until the program somehow ends the loop. The following loop processes work orders. It calls the WorkOrderAvailable function to see if a work order is available. If an order is available, the code calls ProcessWorkOrder to process it. The code then repeats the loop to look for another work order.

```
Do
    ' See if a work order is available.
    If WorkOrderAvailable() Then
        ' Process the next work order.
        ProcessWorkOrder()
    End If
Loop
```

This example keeps checking for work orders forever. Most programs include some method for the loop to end so that the program can eventually stop. For example, the loop might use the Exit Do statement described shortly to end the loop if the user clicks a Stop button.

The second and third forms of Do Loop statements both include a test to determine whether they should continue looping. The difference between the two versions is where they place the test.

The next version of Do Loop places its test at the beginning, so the test is evaluated before the code is executed. If the test initially indicates that the loop should not continue, the statements inside the loop are never executed. The syntax is as follows:

```
Do {While | Until} condition
    statements
    [Exit Do]
    statements
    [Continue Do]
    statements
Loop
```

The final version of Do Loop places its test at the end. In this version, the statements inside the loop are executed before the loop performs its test. That means that the code is always executed at least once. The syntax is as follows:

```
Do
    statements
    [Exit Do]
    statements
    [Continue Do]
    statements
Loop {While | Until} condition
```

If the code uses the While keyword, the loop executes as long as the condition is True. If the code uses the Until keyword, the loop executes as long as the condition is False. Note that the statement Until condition is equivalent to While Not condition. Visual Basic provides these two variations so that you can pick the one that makes your code more readable. Use the one that makes the most sense to you.

The Exit Do statement allows the program to leave the nearest enclosing Do loop before it would normally finish. The Continue Do statement makes the loop jump back to its Do statement and start the loop over again. This is particularly useful if the program doesn't need to execute the rest of the steps within the loop and wants to quickly start the next iteration.

> **NOTE** *Example program ExitAndContinue, which is available for download on the book's website, demonstrates the Exit and Continue statements for Do and For loops.*

Unlike a For Next or For Each loop, the Do Loop does not automatically increment a looping variable or move to the next object in a collection. The code must explicitly change the loop's condition before reaching the Loop statement or calling Continue Do or else the loop will continue forever.

While End

A While End loop is equivalent to a Do While Loop. The syntax is as follows:

```
While condition
    statements
    [Exit While]
    statements
    [Continue While]
    statements
End While
```

This is equivalent to the following Do While Loop:

```
Do While condition
    statements
    [Exit Do]
    statements
    [Continue Do]
    statements
Loop
```

The Exit While statement exits a While End Loop just as an Exit Do statement exits a Do While Loop. Similarly, Continue While makes the program return to the top of the loop just as Continue Do does for Do loops.

The difference between While End and Do While Loop is stylistic, and you can use whichever seems clearer to you. Because Do Loop provides more flexibility, having four different versions using While or Until at the start or finish of the loop, you might want to stick to them for consistency's sake.

SUMMARY

Control statements form the heart of any program. Decision statements determine what commands are executed, and looping statements determine how many times they are executed.

Single-line and multiline If Then statements, as well as Select Case statements, are the most commonly used decision statements. IIf and Choose statements are often more confusing and sometimes slower, so usually you should use If Then and Select Case statements instead. Under some specific circumstances, however, IIf and Choose may make your code more readable. Use your judgment and pick the method that makes the most sense in your application.

For Next, For Each, and Do Loop are the most common looping statements. Some container classes also support enumerators that let you step through the items in the container. An enumerator can be more natural than a For Each loop under some circumstances.

A While End loop is equivalent to Do While Loop. You can use whichever you think makes more sense, although you might want to use Do While because it is more consistent with the other forms of Do Loop.

Using the control statements described in this chapter, you can build extremely complex and powerful applications. In fact, you can build applications that are so complex that it is difficult to ensure that they work correctly. Even a relatively simple application sometimes encounters errors. Chapter 18, "Error Handling," explains how you can protect an application from unexpected errors and let it take action to correct any problems, or at least to avoid crashing.

18

Error Handling

WHAT'S IN THIS CHAPTER

- ➤ Global exception handling
- ➤ Try Catch Finally statements
- ➤ Throwing and re-throwing exceptions
- ➤ Custom exceptions

WROX.COM CODE DOWNLOADS FOR THIS CHAPTER

The wrox.com code downloads for this chapter are found at `http://www.wrox.com/remtitle.cgi?isbn=9781118314074` on the Download Code tab. The code for this chapter is divided into the following major examples:

- ➤ CustomException
- ➤ GlobalException
- ➤ ShowExceptionInfo
- ➤ ThrowError
- ➤ ValidateInteger

THE STRUGGLE FOR PERFECTION

Although it is theoretically possible to write a program that perfectly predicts every possible situation that it might encounter, in practice that's very difficult for nontrivial programs. For large applications, it is extremely difficult to plan for every eventuality. Errors in the program's design and implementation can introduce bugs that give unexpected results. Users and corrupted databases may give the application values that it doesn't expect.

Similarly, changing requirements over time may introduce data that the application was never intended to handle. The Y2K bug is a good example. When engineers wrote accounting, auto registration, financial, inventory, and other systems in the 1960s and 1970s, they never dreamed their programs would still be running in the year 2000. At the time, disk storage and memory were relatively expensive, so they stored years as 2-byte values (for example, 89 meant 1989). When the year 2000 rolled around, the applications couldn't tell whether the value 01 meant the year 1901 or 2001. In one humorous case, an auto registration system started issuing horseless carriage license plates to new cars because it thought cars built in 00 must be antiques.

The Y2K problem wasn't really a bug. It was a case of software used with data that wasn't part of its original design.

This chapter explains different kinds of exceptional conditions that can arise in an application. These range from unplanned data (as in the Y2K problem) to bugs where the code is just plain wrong. With some advance planning, you can build a robust application that can keep running gracefully, even when the unexpected happens.

BUGS VERSUS UNPLANNED CONDITIONS

Several different types of unplanned conditions can derail an otherwise high-quality application. How you should handle these conditions depends on their nature.

For this discussion, a *bug* is a mistake in the application code. Some bugs become apparent right away and are easy to fix. These usually include simple typographic errors in the code and cases where you misuse an object (for example, by using the wrong control property). Other bugs are subtler and may only be detected long after they occur. For example, a data-entry routine might place invalid characters into a rarely used field in a Customer object. Only later when the program tries to access that field will you discover the problem. This kind of bug is difficult to track down and fix, but you can take some proactive steps to make these sorts of bugs easier to find.

> ### BUGS THROUGHOUT HISTORY
>
> On a historical note, the term "bug" has been used since at least the time of the telegraph to mean some sort of defect. Probably the origin of the term in computer science was an actual moth that was caught between two relays in an early computer in 1947. For a bit more information, including a picture of this first computer bug, see http://www.jamesshuggins.com/h/tek1/first_computer_bug.htm.

An *unplanned condition* is some predictable condition that you don't want to happen, but that you know could happen despite your best efforts. For example, there are many ways that a simple printing operation can fail. The printer might be unplugged, disconnected from its computer, disconnected from the network, out of toner, out of paper, experiencing a memory fault, clogged by a paper jam, or just plain broken. These are not bugs, because the application software is not at fault. There is some condition outside of the program's control that must be fixed.

Another common unplanned condition occurs when the user enters invalid data. You may want the user to enter a value between 1 and 10 in a text box, but the user might enter 0, 9999, or "lunch" instead.

You can't *fix* unplanned conditions but you can try to make your program handle them gracefully and produce some meaningful result instead of crashing.

Catching Bugs

By definition, bugs are unplanned. No reasonable programmer sits down and thinks, "Perhaps I'll put a bug in this variable declaration."

Because bugs are unpredictable, you cannot know ahead of time where a bug will lie. However, you can watch for behavior in the program that indicates that a bug may be present. For example, suppose that you have a subroutine that sorts a purchase order's items by cost. If the routine receives an order with 100,000 items, something is probably wrong. If one of the items is a computer keyboard with a price of $73 trillion, something is probably wrong. If the customer who placed the order doesn't exist, something is probably wrong.

This routine could go ahead and sort the 100,000 items with prices ranging from a few cents to $73 trillion. Later, the program would try to print a 5,000-page invoice with no shipping or billing address. Only then would the developers realize that there was a problem.

Rather than trying to work around the problematic data, it would be better if the sorting routine immediately told developers that something was wrong so they could start trying to find the cause of the problem. Bugs are easier to find the sooner they are detected. This bug will be easier to find if the sorting routine notices it, rather than waiting until the application tries to print an invalid invoice. Your routines can protect themselves and the program as a whole by proactively validating inputs and outputs, and reporting anything suspicious to developers.

Some developers object to making routines spend considerable effort validating data that they know is correct. After all, one routine generated this data and passed it to another, so you *know* that it is correct because the first routine did its job properly. That's only true if every routine that touches the data works perfectly. Because bugs are by definition unexpected, you cannot safely assume that all the routines are perfect and that the data remains uncorrupted.

> ### AUTOMATED BUG CATCHERS
>
> Many companies use automated testing tools to try to flush out problems early. Regression testing tools can execute code to verify that its outcome isn't changed after you have made modifications to other parts of the application. If you build a suite of testing routines to validate data and subroutines' results, you may be able to work them into an automated testing system, too.

To prevent validation code from slowing down the application, you can use the Debug object's Assert method to check for strange conditions. When you are debugging the program, these statements throw an error if they detect something suspicious. When you make a release build to send to customers, the Debug.Assert code is automatically removed from the application. That makes the application faster and doesn't inflict cryptic error messages on the user.

You can also use the DEBUG, TRACE, and CONFIG compiler constants to add other input and output validation code.

Example program SortOrders, which is available for download from the book's website, uses the following code to validate a subroutine's inputs. (This program doesn't actually do anything; it just shows how to write input validation code.)

```
Private Sub SortOrderItems(ByVal the_order As Order)
    ' Validate input.
    Debug.Assert(the_order.Items IsNot Nothing, "No items in order")
    Debug.Assert(the_order.Customer IsNot Nothing, "No customer in order")
    Debug.Assert(the_order.Items.Count < 100, "Too many order items")
    ...

    ' Sort the items.
    ...

    ' Validate output.
#If DEBUG Then
    ' Verify that the items are sorted.
    For i As Integer = 2 To the_order.Items.Count
        Dim order_item1 = the_order.Items(i - 1)
        Dim order_item2 = the_order.Items(i)
        Debug.Assert(order_item1.Price <= order_item2.Price,
            "Order items not properly sorted")
    Next i
#End If
End Sub
```

The subroutine starts by validating its input. It verifies that the Order object that it received has an Items collection and that its Customer property is not Nothing. It also verifies that the order contains fewer than 100 items. If a larger order comes along during testing, developers can increase this number to 200 or whatever value makes sense, but there's no need to start with an unreasonably large default.

Before the subroutine exits, it loops through the sorted items to verify that they are correctly sorted. If any item has cost less than the one before it, the program throws an error. Because this test is contained within an #If DEBUG Then statement, this code is removed from release builds.

After you have tested the application long enough, you should have discovered most of these types of errors. When you make the release build, the compiler automatically removes the validation code, making the finished executable smaller and faster.

Catching Unplanned Conditions

Although you don't want an unplanned condition to happen, with some careful thought, you can often predict where one might occur. Typically, these situations arise when the program must work with something outside of its own code. For example, when the program needs to access a file, printer, web page, floppy disk, or CD-ROM, that item may be unavailable. Similarly, whenever the program takes input from the user, the user may enter invalid data.

Notice how this differs from the bugs described in the previous section. After sufficient testing, you should have found and fixed most of the bugs. No amount of testing can remove the possibility of unplanned conditions. No matter what code you use, the user may still remove a flash drive from the drive before the program is ready or unplug the printer while your program is using it.

Whenever you know that an unplanned condition might occur, you should write code to protect the program from dangerous conditions. It is generally better to test for these conditions ahead of time before you perform an action that might fail rather than simply attempting to perform the action and then catching the error when you fail. Testing for problem conditions generally gives you more complete information about what's wrong. It's also usually faster than catching an error because structured error handling (described shortly) comes with considerable overhead.

For example, the following statement sets an integer variable using the value the user entered in a text box:

```
Dim num_items As Integer = Integer.Parse(txtNumItems.Text)
```

The user might enter a valid value in the text box. Unfortunately, the user may also enter something that is not a number, a value that is too big to fit in an integer, or a negative number when you are expecting a positive one. The user may even leave the field blank.

Example program ValidateInteger uses the following code to validate integer input:

```
' Check for blank entry.
Dim num_items_txt As String = txtNumItems.Text
If num_items_txt.Length < 1 Then
    MessageBox.Show("Please enter Num Items")
    txtNumItems.Focus()
    Exit Sub
End If

' See if it's numeric.
If Not IsNumeric(num_items_txt) Then
    MessageBox.Show("Num Items must be a number")
    txtNumItems.Select(0, num_items_txt.Length)
    txtNumItems.Focus()
    Exit Sub
End If

' Assign the value.
Dim num_items As Integer
Try
    num_items = Integer.Parse(txtNumItems.Text)
Catch ex As Exception
    MessageBox.Show("Error in Num Items." & vbCrLf & ex.Message)
    txtNumItems.Select(0, num_items_txt.Length)
    txtNumItems.Focus()
    Exit Sub
End Try
```

```
' Check that the value is between 1 and 100.
If num_items < 1 Or num_items > 100 Then
    MessageBox.Show("Num Items must be between 1 and 100")
    txtNumItems.Select(0, num_items_txt.Length)
    txtNumItems.Focus()
    Exit Sub
End If
```

The code checks that the field is not blank and uses the IsNumeric function to verify that the field contains a numeric value.

Unfortunately, the IsNumeric function doesn't exactly match the behavior of functions such as Integer.Parse. IsNumeric returns False for values such as &H10, which is a valid hexadecimal value that Integer.Parse can correctly interpret. IsNumeric also returns True for values such as 123456789012345 that lie outside of the values allowed by integers and 1.2, which is numeric but not an integer. Because IsNumeric doesn't exactly match Integer.Parse, the program still needs to use a Try Catch block (bolded in the previous code) to protect itself when it actually tries to convert the string into an integer.

The code finishes by verifying that the value lies within a reasonable bound. If the value passes all of these checks, the code uses the value.

> **NOTE** *These checks must always occur so you cannot replace them with Debug .Assert statements, which are removed from release builds.*

A typical program might need to read and validate many values, and retyping this code for each value would be cumbersome. A better solution is to move it into an `IsValidInteger` function and then call the function as needed.

You can write similar routines to validate other types of data fields such as phone numbers, e-mail addresses, street addresses, and so on.

Global Exception Handling

Normally, you should try to catch an error as close as possible to the place where it occurs. If an error occurs in a particular subroutine, it will be easiest to fix the bug if you catch it in that subroutine.

However, bugs often arise in unexpected places. Unless you protect every subroutine with error-handling code (a fairly common strategy), a bug may arise in code that you have not protected.

In early versions of Visual Basic, you could not catch that kind of bug, so the application crashed. In the most recent versions of Visual Basic, however, you can define a global error handler to catch any bug that isn't caught by other error-handling code.

ERRORS, ERRORS, EVERYWHERE

In fact, some sources of errors are completely beyond your control. For example, power surges, static electricity, intermittent short circuits, or even stray radiation striking exactly the right part of a chip can make the computer's hardware misbehave so code that should work correctly fails. There's little you can do to anticipate these kinds of errors but you can use global error handling to try to recover from them.

Of course that doesn't excuse you from rigorously checking your code for errors. The vast majority of bugs are due to real mistakes in the code or data rather than to magical cosmic rays flipping a single bit on a memory chip.

To define application-level event handlers, double-click My Project in the Project Explorer. Open the Application tab and click the View Application Events button. This opens a code window for application-level events.

In the left drop-down list, select (MyApplication Events). Then in the right drop-down list, you can select one of several events including NetworkAvailabilityChanged, Shutdown, Startup, StartupNextInstance, and UnhandledException. Select the last of these commands to open the UnhandledException event handler.

In the event handler, you can take whatever action is appropriate for the error. Because you probably didn't anticipate the error, there's usually little chance that the program can correct it properly. However, you can at least log the error and possibly save data before shutting down the application.

The event parameter e has an ExitApplication property that you can set to True or False to tell Visual Basic whether the application should terminate.

KEEP RUNNING

Usually it's better for an application to do the best it can to recover and keep running instead of exiting. Even if the program must reset itself to a default state, that at least saves the user the trouble of restarting the application, reopening forms, arranging toolbars, and otherwise getting the program ready to work. Before you decide, compare the difficulty of making the program reset and continue with the trouble the user will have restarting and getting back to work.

Example program GlobalException uses the following code to display a message giving the unhandled exception's error message. It then sets e.ExitApplication to False, so the program keeps running.

```
Private Sub MyApplication_UnhandledException(sender As Object,
 e As ApplicationServices.UnhandledExceptionEventArgs) _
 Handles Me.UnhandledException
    MessageBox.Show("Exception caught globally" & vbCrLf & e.Exception.Message)
    e.ExitApplication = False
End Sub
```

When you run the application in the IDE, Visual Basic stops execution in the debugger when it reaches the statement that causes the error, so the UnhandledException event handler never executes. If you run the compiled executable, however, the UnhandledException event fires and the global error handler runs.

STRUCTURED ERROR HANDLING

Visual Basic .NET uses the Try Catch block to provide structured error handling. The syntax is as follows:

```
Try
    try_statements ...
[Catch ex As exception_type_1
    exception_statements_1 ...
]
[Catch ex As exception_type_2
    exception_statements_2 ...
]
...
[Catch
    final_exception_statements ...
]
[Finally
    finally_statements ...
]
End Try
```

The program executes the code in the try_statements block. If any of that code throws an exception, the program jumps to the first Catch statement.

If the exception matches exception_type_1, the program executes the code in exception_statements_1. The exception type might match the Catch statement's exception class exactly, or it might be a subclass of the listed class. For example, suppose that the code in the try_statements block performs a calculation that divides by zero. That raises a DivideByZeroException. That class inherits from the ArithmeticException class, which inherits from SystemException, which inherits from Exception. That means the code would stop at the first Catch statement it finds that looks for DivideByZeroException, ArithmeticException, SystemException, or Exception.

If the raised exception does not match the first exception type, the program checks the next Catch statement. The program keeps comparing the exception to Catch statements until it finds one that applies, or it runs out of Catch statements.

CATCH CONTROL

Arrange Catch statements so the most specific come first. Otherwise, a more general statement will catch errors before a more specific statement has a chance. For example, the generic Exception class matches all other exceptions, so if the first Catch statement catches Exception, no other Catch statements will ever execute.

If two Catch statements are unrelated, neither will catch the other's exceptions, so put the exception more likely to occur first. That will make the code more efficient because it looks for the most common problems first. It also keeps the code that is most likely to execute near the top where it is easier to read.

If no Catch statement matches the exception, the exception "bubbles up" to the next level in the call stack and Visual Basic moves to the routine that called the current one. If that routine has appropriate error-handling code, it deals with the error. If that routine can't catch the error, the exception bubbles up again until Visual Basic eventually either finds error-handling code that can catch the exception or runs off the top of the call stack. If it runs off the call stack, Visual Basic calls the global UnhandledException event handler described in the previous section, if one exists. If there is no UnhandledException event handler, the program crashes.

If you include a Catch statement with no exception type, that block matches any exception. If the raised exception doesn't match any of the previous exception types, the program executes the final_exception_statements block of code. Note that the statement Catch ex As Exception also matches all exceptions, so it's just as good as Catch by itself. It also gives you easy access to the exception object's properties and methods.

You can figure out what exception classes to use in Catch statements in several ways. First, you can spend a lot of time digging through the online help. An easier method is to let the program crash and then look at the error message it produces. Figure 18-1 shows the error message a program throws when it tries to convert the non-numeric string Hello into an integer with Integer.Parse. From the exception dialog box's title, it's easy to see that the program should look for a FormatException.

Another way to decide what types of exceptions to catch is to place a final generic Catch ex As Exception statement at the end of the Catch list. Place code inside that Catch block that displays either the exception's type name (use TypeName) or the result of its ToString method. When you encounter new exception types, you can give them their own Catch statements and take action that's appropriate to that exception type.

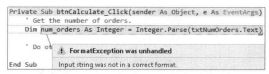

FIGURE 18-1: When a program crashes, the message it generates tells you the type of exception it raised.

CATCH CATASTROPHES

It may not be possible to take meaningful action when you catch certain exceptions. For example, if a program uses up all of the available memory, Visual Basic throws an OutOfMemoryException. If there is no memory available, you may have trouble doing anything useful. Similarly, if there's a problem with the filesystem, you may be unable to write error descriptions into a log file.

After it has finished running the code in try_statements and it has executed any necessary exception code in a Catch block, the program executes the code in finally_statements. The statements in the Finally section execute whether the code in try_statements succeeds or fails.

You do not need to include any Catch statements in a Try block, but leaving them all out defeats the Try block's purpose. If the try_statements raise an error, the program doesn't have any error code to execute, so it sends the error up the call stack. Eventually, the program finds an active error handler or the error pops off the top of the stack and the program crashes. You may as well not bother with the Try block if you aren't going to use any Catch sections.

A Try block must include at least one Catch or Finally section, although those sections do not need to contain any code. For example, the following Try block calls subroutine DoSomething and uses an empty Catch section to ignore any errors that occur:

```
Try
    DoSomething()
Catch
End Try
```

Example program ThrowError, which is available for download on the book's website, shows how a program can use a Try Catch block to handle errors.

Exception Objects

When a Catch statement catches an exception, its exception variable contains information about the error that raised the exception. Different exception classes may provide different features, but they all provide the basic features defined by the Exception class from which they are all derived. The following table lists the most commonly used Exception class properties and methods.

ITEM	PURPOSE
InnerException	The exception that caused the current exception. For example, suppose that you write a tool library that catches an exception and then throws a new custom exception describing the problem in terms of your library. You should set InnerException to the exception that you caught before you threw the new exception.
Message	Returns a brief message that describes the exception.

Source	Returns the name of the application or object that threw the exception.
StackTrace	Returns a string containing a stack trace giving the program's location when the error occurred.
TargetSite	Returns the name of the method that threw the exception.
ToString	Returns a string describing the exception and including the stack trace.

Example program ShowExceptionInfo, which is available for download on the book's website, displays an exception's Message, StackTrace, and ToString values.

At a minimum, the program should log or display the Message value for any unexpected exceptions so you know what exception occurred. It might also log the StackTrace or the result of ToString so you can see where the exception occurred.

The StackTrace and ToString values can help developers find a bug, but they can be intimidating to end users. Even the abbreviated format used by the exception's Message property is usually not very useful to a user. When the user clicks the Find Outstanding Invoices button, the message "Attempted to divide by zero" doesn't really tell the user what the problem is or what to do about it.

When a program catches an error, a good strategy is to record the full ToString message in a log file or e-mail it to a developer. Then display a message that restates the error message in terms that the user can understand. For example, the program might say the following: "Unable to total outstanding invoices. A bug report has been sent to the development team." The program should then try to continue as gracefully as possible. It may not be able to finish this calculation, but it should not crash, and it should allow the user to continue working on other tasks if possible.

Throwing Exceptions

In addition to catching exceptions, your program may need to generate its own exceptions. Because handling an exception is called *catching* it, raising an exception is called *throwing* it. (This is just a silly pun. People also catch lions and colds, but I don't think many people throw them. It's as good a term as any, however.)

To throw an exception, the program creates an instance of the type of exception it wants to generate, passing the constructor additional information describing the problem. The program can then set other exception fields if you like. For example, it might set the exception's Source property to tell any other code that catches the error where it originated. The program then uses the Throw statement to raise the error. If an error handler is active somewhere in the call stack, Visual Basic jumps to that point and the error handler processes the exception.

Example program DrawableRect, which is available for download on the book's website, uses the following code to show how the DrawableRectangle class can protect itself against invalid input:

```
Public Class DrawableRectangle
    Public Sub New(new_x As Integer, new_y As Integer,
    new_width As Integer, new_height As Integer)
        ' Verify that new_width > 0.
```

```
        If new_width <= 0 Then
            Dim ex As New ArgumentException(
                "DrawableRectangle must have a width greater than zero",
                "new_width")
            Throw ex
        End If

        ' Verify that new_height> 0.
        If new_height < = 0 Then
            Throw New ArgumentException(
                "DrawableRectangle must have a height greater than zero",
                "new_height")
        End If
        ' Save the parameter values.
        ...
    End Sub
    ...
End Class
```

The class's constructor takes four arguments: an X and Y position, and a width and height. If the width is less than or equal to zero, the program creates a new ArgumentException object. It passes the exception's constructor a description string and the name of the argument that is invalid. After creating the exception object, the program uses the Throw statement to raise the error. The code checks the object's new height similarly, but it creates and throws the exception in a single statement to demonstrate another style for throwing an error.

The following code shows how a program might use a Try block to protect itself while creating a new DrawableRectangle object:

```
Try
    Dim rect As New DrawableRectangle(10, 20, 0, 100)
Catch ex As Exception
    MessageBox.Show(ex.Message)
End Try
```

When your application needs to throw an exception, it's easiest to use an existing exception class. There are a few ways to get lists of exception classes so that you can find one that makes sense for your application. Appendix O, "Useful Exception Classes," lists some of the more useful exception classes. The online help topic, "Introduction to Exception Handling in Visual Basic .NET" at http://msdn.microsoft.com/aa289505.aspx also has a good list of exception classes at the end. Microsoft's web page http://msdn.microsoft.com/system .exception_derivedtypelist.aspx provides a very long list of exception classes that are derived from the System.Exception class.

Another method for finding exception classes is to open the Object Browser (select the View menu's Object Browser command) and search for "Exception."

When you throw exceptions, you must use your judgment about selecting these classes. For example, Visual Basic uses the System.Reflection.AmbiguousMatchException class when it tries to bind a subroutine call to an object's method and it cannot determine which overloaded method to use. This happens at a lower level than your program will act, so you won't use that class for exactly the same purpose but it still may be useful to throw that exception. For example, if your program parses a string and, based on the string, cannot decide what action to take, you might use this class to represent the error, even though you're not using it exactly as it was originally intended.

Be sure to use the most specific exception class possible. Using more generic classes such as Exception makes it much harder for developers to understand and locate an error. If you cannot find a good, specific fit, create your own exception class as described in the section "Custom Exceptions" later in this chapter.

Re-throwing Exceptions

Sometimes when you catch an exception, you cannot completely handle the problem. In that case, it may make sense to re-throw the exception so a routine higher up in the call stack can take a crack at it.

To re-throw an error exactly as you caught it, simply use the Throw keyword as in the following example:

```
Try
    ' Do something hard here.
    . . .

Catch ex As ArithmeticException
    ' We can handle this exception. Fix it.
    . . .

Catch ex As Exception
    ' We don't know what to do with this one. Re-throw it.
    Throw
End Try
```

If your code can figure out more or less why an error is happening but it cannot fix it, it's sometimes a good idea to re-throw the error as a different exception type. For example, suppose a piece of code causes an ArithmeticException but the underlying cause of the exception is an invalid argument. In that case it is better to throw an ArgumentException instead of an ArithmeticException because that will provide more specific information higher up in the call stack.

At the same time, however, you don't want to lose the information contained in the original ArithmeticException.

The solution is to throw a new ArgumentException but place the original ArithmeticException in its InnerException property so code that catches the new exception has access to the original information.

The following code demonstrates this technique:

```
Try
    ' Do something hard here.
    ...

Catch ex As ArithmeticException
    ' This was caused by an invalid argument.
    ' Re-throw it as an ArgumentException.
    Throw New ArgumentException("Invalid argument X in function Whatever.", ex)

Catch ex As Exception
    ' We don't know what to do with this one. Re-throw it.
    Throw
End Try
```

Custom Exceptions

When your application needs to raise an exception, it's easiest to use an existing exception class. Reusing existing exception classes makes it easier for developers to understand what the exception means. It also prevents exception proliferation, where the developer needs to watch for dozens or hundreds of types of exceptions.

Sometimes, however, the predefined exceptions don't fit your needs. For example, suppose that you build a class that contains data that may exist for a long time. If the program tries to use an object that has not refreshed its data for a while, you want to raise some sort of "data expired" exception. You could squeeze this into the System.TimeoutException class, but that exception doesn't quite fit this use.

Building a custom exception class is easy. Make a new class that inherits from the System.ApplicationException class. Then, provide constructor methods to let the program create instances of the class. That's all there is to it.

By convention, an exception class's name should end with the word Exception. Also by convention, you should provide at least three overloaded constructors for developers to use when creating new instances of the class. (For more information on what constructors are and how to define them, see the section "Class Instantiation Details" in Chapter 23, "Classes and Structures.")

The first constructor takes no parameters and initializes the exception with a default message describing the general type of error.

The other two versions take as parameters an error message, and an error message plus an inner exception object. These constructors pass their parameters to the base class's constructors to initialize the object appropriately.

For completeness, you can also make a constructor that takes as parameters a SerializationInfo object and a StreamingContext object. This version can also pass its parameters to a base class constructor to initialize the exception object, so you don't need to do anything special with the parameters. This constructor is useful if the exception will be serialized and deserialized. If you're not sure whether you need this constructor, you probably don't. If you do include it, however, you will need to import the System.Runtime.Serialization namespace in the exception class's file to define the SerializationInfo and StreamingContext classes.

Example program CustomException, which is available for download on the book's website, uses the following code to define the ObjectExpiredException class:

```
Imports System.Runtime.Serialization

Public Class ObjectExpiredException
    Inherits System.ApplicationException

    ' No parameters. Use a default message.
    Public Sub New()
        MyBase.New("This object has expired")
    End Sub

    ' Set the message.
    Public Sub New(new_message As String)
        MyBase.New(new_message)
    End Sub

    ' Set the message and inner exception.
    Public Sub New(new_message As String,
     ByVal inner_exception As Exception)
        MyBase.New(new_message, inner_exception)
    End Sub

    ' Include SerializationInfo object and StreamingContext objects.
    Public Sub New(info As SerializationInfo, context As StreamingContext)
        MyBase.New(info, context)
    End Sub
End Class
```

After you have defined the exception class, you can throw and catch it just as you can throw and catch any exception class defined by Visual Basic. For example, the following code throws an ObjectExpiredException error:

```
Throw New ObjectExpiredException("This Customer object has expired.")
```

The parent class System.ApplicationException automatically handles the object's Message, StackTrace, and ToString properties so you don't need to implement them yourself.

DEBUGGING

Visual Basic provides a rich set of tools for debugging an application. Using the development environment, you can stop the program at different lines of code and examine variables, change variable values, look at the call stack, and call routines to exercise different pieces of the application. You can step through the program, executing the code one statement at a time to see what it is doing. You can even make some modifications to the source code and let the program continue running.

Chapter 6, "Debugging," describes tools that the development environment provides to help you debug an application. These include tools for stepping through the code, breakpoints, and windows such as the Immediate, Locals, and Call Stack windows. See Chapter 6 for details.

In addition to setting breakpoints in the code, you can use the Stop statement to pause execution at a particular line. This can be particularly useful for detecting unexpected values during testing. For example, the following statement stops execution if the variable m_NumEmployees is less than 1 or greater than 100:

```
If (m_NumEmployees < 1) Or (m_NumEmployees > 100) Then Stop
```

SUMMARY

In practice, it's extremely difficult to anticipate every condition that might occur within a large application. You should try to predict as many incorrect situations as possible, but you should also plan for unforeseen errors. You should write error-checking code that makes bugs obvious when they occur and recovers from them if possible. You may not be able to anticipate every possible bug, but with a little thought you can make the program detect and report obviously incorrect values.

You should also look for unplanned conditions (such as the user entering a phone number in a Social Security number field) and make the program react gracefully. Your program cannot control everything in its environment (such as the user's actions, printer status, and network connectivity), but it should be prepared to work when things aren't exactly the way they should be.

When you do encounter an error, you can use tools such as breakpoints, watches, and the development environment's Locals, Auto, Immediate, and Call Stack windows to figure out where the problem begins and how to fix it. You may never be able to remove every last bug from a 100,000-line program, but you can make any remaining bugs relatively harmless and appear so rarely that the users can do their jobs in relative safety.

Chapters 7 through 12 focused on controls, forms, and other user interface objects. Chapters 13 through 17 focused on the code that lies behind the user interface. Chapter 19, "Database Controls and Objects," covers database topics that fall into both the user interface and code-behind categories. It describes database controls that you can use to build an application's user interface, as well as components and other objects that you can use behind the scenes to manipulate databases.

19

Database Controls and Objects

WROX.COM CODE DOWNLOADS FOR THIS CHAPTER

The wrox.com code downloads for this chapter are found at http://www.wrox.com/
remtitle.cgi?isbn=9781118314074 on the Download Code tab. The code for this chapter
is divided into the following major examples:

DATA SOURCES

The Windows Forms controls described in Chapter 7, "Selecting Windows Forms Controls,"
allow the application and the user to communicate. They let the application display data to the
user, and they let the user control the application.

Visual Basic's database controls play roughly the same role between the application and a
database. They move data from the database to the application, and they allow the application
to send data back to the database.

Database programming is an enormous topic, and many books have been written that focus exclusively on database programming. This is such a huge field that no general Visual Basic book can adequately cover it in any real depth. However, database programming is also a very important topic, and every Visual Basic programmer should know at least something about using databases in applications.

This chapter explains how to build data sources and use drag-and-drop to create simple table- and record-oriented displays. It also explains the most useful controls and objects that Visual Basic provides for working with databases. Although this chapter is far from the end of the story, it will help you get started building basic database applications.

> **DATA DESTINATIONS**
>
> Note that the example programs described in this chapter refer to database locations as they are set up on my test computer. If you download them from the book's website (`http://www.vb-helper.com/vb_prog_ref.htm`), you will have to modify many of them to work with the database locations on your computer.

AUTOMATICALLY CONNECTING TO DATA

Visual Studio provides tools that make getting started with databases remarkably easy. Although the process is relatively straightforward, it does involve a lot of steps. The steps also allow several variations, so describing every possible way to build a database connection takes a long time. To make the process more manageable, the following two sections group the steps in two pieces: connecting to the data source and adding data controls to the form.

Connecting to the Data Source

To build a simple database program, start a new application and select the Data menu's Add New Data Source command to display the Data Source Configuration Wizard shown in Figure 19-1.

Visual Studio allows you to use databases, web services, and objects as data sources for your application. The most straightforward choice is Database. Select the type of data source you want to add (this example assumes it's a database) and click Next to select a data model. The data model determines the kinds of objects your code can use to manipulate the data. This example assumes you will use a DataSet, which provides objects to represent tables and rows in the database. Pick the data model type and click Next to select a data connection on the page shown in Figure 19-2.

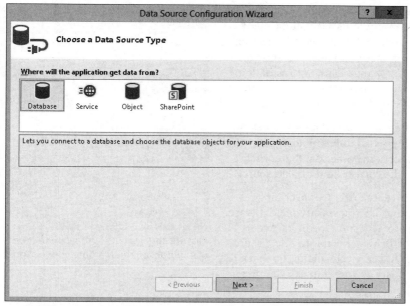

FIGURE 19-1: Select the data source type for a new connection.

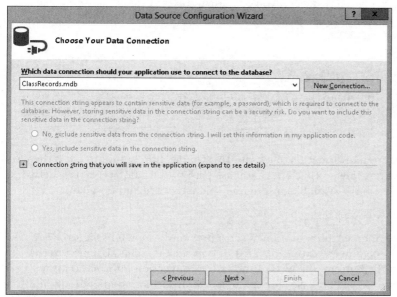

FIGURE 19-2: Pick the data connection or click New Connection to create a new one.

If you have previously created data connections, you can select one from the drop-down list. If you have not created any data connections, click the New Connection button to open the Add Connection dialog box shown in Figure 19-3. (If you see a Change Data Source dialog box at this point, pick a data source type and click OK to see the Add Connection dialog box.)

In Figure 19-3 I was selecting an Access database so Data Source is set to Microsoft Access Database File. If you want to use SQL Server, Oracle, or some other database, click the Change button to pick the correct kind of data source.

After you select a data source, the Add Connection dialog box rearranges itself to let you specify the database. In Figure 19-3 the dialog box lets you type in an Access database's path or click the Browse button to select the file. If the data source is SQL Server, the dialog box lets you pick the server from a list of those that are running.

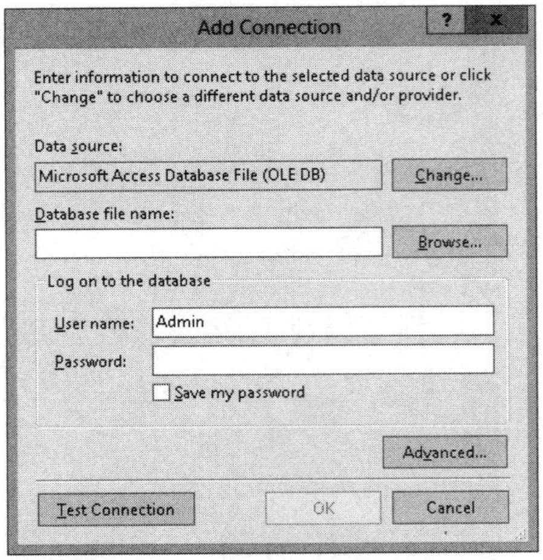

FIGURE 19-3: Use the Add Connection dialog box to create a data connection.

DOWNLOADING DATABASES

You don't need to have Access to use an Access database in Visual Basic. However, if you want to give Access a try, you can download a 60-day trial version at `http://office.microsoft.com/en-us/products /get-microsoft-access-FX102159812.aspx`.

Another popular database choice is SQL Server. You can download the free Express Edition at `http://www.microsoft.com/express/sql`.

You can also download the open source MySQL database at `http://www .mysql.com`.

After you enter all of the required information, click the Test Connection button to see if the wizard can open the database. If the test fails, recheck the database path (if the database is on a network, make sure the network connection is available), username, and password and try again.

Once you can test the database connection, click OK.

When you return to the Data Source Configuration Wizard previously shown in Figure 19-2, the new connection should be selected in the drop-down list. If you click the plus sign next to the "Connection string" label at the bottom, the wizard shows the connection information it will use to connect the data source to the database. For example, this information might look like the following:

```
Provider=Microsoft.Jet.OLEDB.4.0;
DataSource=|DataDirectory|\ClassRecords.mdb
```

When you click Next, the wizard tells you that you have selected a local database file that is not part of the project and it asks if you want to add it to the project. If you click Yes, the wizard adds the database to the project so it shows up in Project Explorer. If you plan to distribute the database with the application, you may want to do this to make it easier to manage the database and the Visual Basic source code together.

Next, the wizard asks whether you want to save the connection string in the project's configuration file. If you leave this check box selected, the wizard adds the string to the project's `app.config` file.

The following shows the part of the configuration file containing the connection string:

```
<connectionStrings>
    <add name="Students.My.MySettings.ClassRecordsConnectionString"
        connectionString="Provider=Microsoft.Jet.OLEDB.4.0;
Data Source=|DataDirectory|\ClassRecords.mdb;
        providerName="System.Data.OleDb" />
</connectionStrings>
```

Later, the program uses that value to connect to the database. You can easily make the program connect to another data source by changing this configuration setting and then restarting the application.

PASSWORD PRECAUTION

You should never save real database passwords in the configuration file. The file is stored in plaintext and anyone can read it. If you need to use a password, store a connection string that contains a placeholder for the real password. At run time, load the connection string and replace the placeholder with a real password entered by the user.

You can store an encrypted password in a configuration file, but then the program must contain the key needed to decrypt the password at run time and a determined hacker might be able to dig the password out of the code. The best place to store passwords is in the user's head.

Adding Data Controls to the Form

At this point you have defined the basic connection to the database. Visual Studio knows where the database is and how to build an appropriate connection string to open it. Now you must decide what data to pull out of the database and how to display it on the form.

Click Next to display the dialog box shown in Figure 19-4. This page shows the objects available in the database. In this example, the database contains two tables named Students and TestScores. By clicking the triangles to the left of the objects, you can expand them to see what they contain. In Figure 19-4, the tables are expanded so you can see the fields they contain.

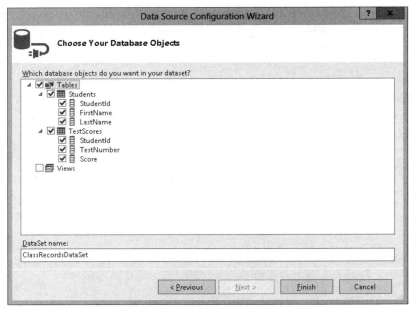

FIGURE 19-4: Select the database objects that you want included in the data source.

Select the database objects that you want to include in the data source. In Figure 19-4, both of the tables are selected.

When you click Finish, the wizard adds a couple of objects to the application. The Solution Explorer now lists the new file `ClassRecordsDataSet.xsd`. This is a schema definition file that describes the data source.

When you double-click the schema file, Visual Basic opens it in the editor shown in Figure 19-5. This display shows the tables

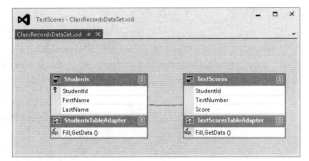

FIGURE 19-5: The Schema Editor shows the tables defined by the schema and their relationships.

defined by the schema, their fields, and any relationships defined between the tables.

The line between the files with the little key on the left and the infinity symbol on the right indicates that the tables are joined by a one-to-many relationship. In this example, the Students .StudentId field and TestScores.StudentId field form a foreign key relationship. That means every StudentId value in the TestScores table must correspond to some StudentId value in the Students table. In other words, a test score must be associated with a student who exists.

When you double-click the relationship link or right-click it and select Edit Relation, the editor displays a dialog box that you can use to modify the relation.

At the bottom of the tables shown in Figure 19-5, you can see two table adapter objects containing the labels Fill, GetData(). These represent data adapter objects that the program will later use to move data from and to the data source.

In addition to adding the schema file to Solution Explorer, the Data Source Configuration Wizard also added a new DataSet object to the Data Sources window shown in Figure 19-6. (If this window is not visible, select the Data menu's Show Data Sources command.)

You can use the triangles to the left of the entries to expand and collapse the objects in the DataSet. In Figure 19-6, the DataSet is expanded to show its tables, and the tables are expanded to show their fields. Notice that the TestScores table is listed within the Students table's entries because it has a parent/child relationship with that table.

FIGURE 19-6: The Data Sources window lists the new data source.

It takes a lot of words and pictures to describe this process, but using the wizard to build the data source is actually quite fast. After you have created the data source, you can build a simple user interface with almost no extra work. Simply drag objects from the Data Sources window onto the form.

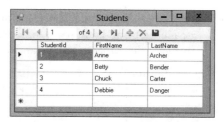

When you click and drag a table from the Data Sources window onto the form, Visual Basic automatically creates BindingNavigator and DataGridView controls, and other components to display the data from the table. Figure 19-7 shows the result at run time.

FIGURE 19-7: Drag and drop a table from the Data Sources window onto the form to create a simple DataGridView.

Instead of dragging an entire table onto the form, you can drag individual database columns. In that case, Visual Basic adds controls to the form to represent the column. Figure 19-8 shows the columns from the Students table dragged onto a form.

If you select a table in the Data Sources window, a drop-down arrow appears on the right. Open the drop-down to give the table a different display style. For example, if you set a table's style to Details and drag the table onto a form, Visual Basic displays the table's data using a record detail view similar to the one shown in Figure 19-8. Set the table's style to DataGridView and drag it onto the form to get a grid similar to the one shown in Figure 19-7.

FIGURE 19-8: Drag and drop table columns onto a form to create a record-oriented view instead of a grid.

Similarly, you can change the display styles for specific columns. Select a column in the Data Sources window and click its drop-down arrow to make it display in a text box, label, link label, combo box, or other control. Now, when you drag the column onto a form, or when you drag the table onto the form to build a record view, Visual Basic uses this type of control to display the column's values.

AUTOMATICALLY CREATED OBJECTS

When you drag database tables and columns from the Data Sources window onto a form, Visual Basic does a lot more than simply place a DataGridView control on a form. It also creates about two dozen other controls and components. Five of the more important of these objects are the DataSet, TableAdapter, TableAdapterManager, BindingSource, and BindingNavigator.

The program stores data in a DataSet object. A single DataSet object can represent an entire database. It contains DataTable objects that represent database tables. Each DataTable contains DataRow objects that represent rows in a table, and each DataRow contains DataColumn objects representing column values for the row.

The TableAdapter object copies data between the database and the DataSet. It has methods for performing operations on the database such as selecting, inserting, updating, and deleting records. Hidden inside the TableAdapter is a connection object that contains information on the database so that the TableAdapter knows where to find it.

The TableAdapterManager coordinates updates among different TableAdapters. This is most useful for hierarchical data sets, a topic that is outside the scope of this book. The wizard-generated code also uses the TableAdapterManager to update the single data set it creates.

The BindingSource object encapsulates all of the DataSet object's data and provides programmatic control functions. These perform such actions as moving through the data, adding and deleting items, and so forth.

The BindingNavigator provides a user interface so the user can control the BindingSource.

Figure 19-9 shows the relationships among the DataSet, TableAdapter, BindingSource, and BindingNavigator objects. The BindingNavigator is the only one of these components that has a presence on the form. It is connected to the BindingSource with a dotted arrow to indicate that it controls the BindingSource but does not actually transfer data back and forth. The other arrows represent data moving between objects.

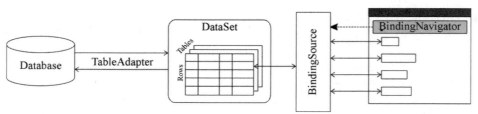

FIGURE 19-9: Visual Basic uses TableAdapter, DataSet, BindingSource, and BindingNavigator objects to display data.

Even working together, all these objects don't quite do everything you need to make the program display data. When it creates these objects, Visual Basic also adds the following code to the form:

```
public Class Form1
    Private Sub StudentsBindingNavigatorSaveItem_Click(
    sender As Object, e As EventArgs) _
    Handles StudentsBindingNavigatorSaveItem.Click
        Me.Validate()
        Me.StudentsBindingSource.EndEdit()
        Me.TableAdapterManager.UpdateAll(Me.ClassRecordsDataSet)
    End Sub

    Private Sub Form1_Load(sender As Object, e As EventArgs) _
    Handles MyBase.Load
        'TODO: This line of code loads data into the 'ClassRecordsDataSet.Students'
        ' table. You can move, or remove it, as needed.
        Me.StudentsTableAdapter.Fill(Me.ClassRecordsDataSet.Students)
    End Sub
End Class
```

The StudentsBindingNavigatorSaveItem_Click event handler fires when the user clicks the BindingNavigator object's Save tool. This routine makes the TableAdapter save any changes to the Students table in the database.

The Form1_Load event handler makes the TableAdapter copy data from the database into the DataSet when the form loads.

Visual Basic builds all this automatically, and if you ran the program at this point, it would display data and let you manipulate it. It's still not perfect, however. It doesn't perform any data validation, and it will let you close the application without saving any changes you have made to the data. It's a pretty good start for such a small amount of work, however.

OTHER DATA OBJECTS

If you want a simple program that can display and modify data, then the solution described in the previous sections may be good enough. In that case, you can let Visual Basic do most of the work for you, and you don't need to dig into the lower-level details of database access.

You can also use objects similar to those created by Visual Basic to build your own solutions. You can create your own DataSet, TableAdapter, BindingSource, and BindingNavigator objects to bind controls to a database. (You can even modify the controls supplied by Visual Basic by overriding their properties and methods, although that's a very advanced topic so it isn't covered here.)

If you need to manipulate the database directly with code, it doesn't necessarily make sense to create all these objects. If you simply want to modify a record programmatically, it certainly doesn't make sense to create DataGridView, BindingNavigator, and BindingSource objects.

For cases such as this, Visual Basic provides several other kinds of objects that you can use to interact with databases. These objects fall into the following four categories:

➤ *Data containers* hold data after it has been loaded from the database into the application much as a DataSet does. You can bind controls to these objects to automatically display and manipulate the data.

➤ *Connections* provide information that lets the program connect to the database.

➤ *Data adapters* move data between a database and a data container.

➤ *Command objects* provide instructions for manipulating data. A command object can select, update, insert, or delete data in the database. It can also execute stored procedures in the database.

Data container and adapter classes are generic and work with different kinds of databases, but different types of connection and command objects are specific to different kinds of databases. For example, the connection objects OleDbConnection, SqlConnection, OdbcConnection, and OracleConnection work with Object Linking and Embedding Database (OLE DB); SQL Server, including SQL Server Express; Open Database Connectivity (ODBC); and Oracle databases, respectively. The SQL Server and Oracle objects work only with their specific brand of database, but they are more completely optimized for those databases and may give better performance.

Aside from the different database types they support, the various objects work in more or less the same way. The following sections explain how an application uses those objects to move data to and from the database. They describe the most useful properties, methods, and events provided by the connection, transaction, data adapter, and command objects.

Later sections describe the DataSet and DataView objects and tell how you can use them to bind controls to display data automatically.

DATA OVERVIEW

An application uses three basic objects to move data to and from a database: a connection, a data adapter, and a data container such as a DataSet.

The connection object defines the connection to the database. It contains information about the database's name and location, any username and password needed to access the data, database engine information, and flags that determine the kinds of access the program will need.

The data adapter object defines a mapping from the database to the DataSet. It determines what data is selected from the database, and which database columns are mapped to which DataSet columns.

The DataSet object stores the data within the application. It can hold more than one table and can define and enforce relationships among the tables. For example, the database used in the earlier examples in this chapter has a TestScores table that has a StudentId field. The values in this field must be values listed in the Students table. This is called a *foreign key constraint*. The DataSet can represent this constraint and raise an error if the program tries to create a TestScores record with a StudentId value that does not appear in the Students table. The section "Constraints" later in this chapter says more about constraints.

When the connection, data adapter, and DataSet objects are initialized, the program can call the data adapter's Fill method to copy data from the database into the DataSet. Later it can call the data adapter's Update method to copy any changes to the data from the DataSet back into the database.

CONNECTION OBJECTS

The connection object manages the application's connection to the database. It allows a data adapter to move data in and out of a DataSet.

The different flavors of connection object (OleDbConnection, SqlConnection, OdbcConnection, OracleConnection, and so on) provide roughly the same features, but there are some differences. Check the online help to see if a particular property, method, or event is supported by one of the flavors. The web page `http://msdn.microsoft.com/32c5dh3b.aspx` provides links to pages that explain how to connect to SQL Server, OLE DB, ODBC, and Oracle data sources. Other links lead to information on the SqlConnection, OleDbConnection, and OdbcConnection classes.

If you will be working extensively with a particular type of database (for example, SQL Server), you should also review the features provided by its type of connection object to see if it has special features for that type of database.

Some connection objects can work with more than one type of database. For example, the OleDbConnection object works with any database that has an OLE DB (Object Linking and Embedding Database) provider. Similarly the OdbcConnection object works with databases that have ODBC (Open Database Connectivity) providers such as MySQL.

Generally, connections that work with a specific kind of database (such as SqlConnection and OracleConnection) give better performance. If you think you might later need to change databases, you can minimize the amount of work required by sticking to features that are shared by all the types of connection objects.

> **NOTE** *The Toolbox window does not automatically display tools for these objects. To add them, right-click the Toolbox tab where you want them and select Choose Items. Select the check boxes next to the tools you want to add (for example, OracleCommand or OdbcConnection) and click OK.*

The following table describes the most useful properties provided by the OleDbConnection and SqlConnection classes.

PROPERTY	PURPOSE
ConnectionString	Gets or sets the string that defines the connection to the database.
ConnectionTimeout	Gets or sets the time the object waits while trying to connect to the database. If this timeout expires, the object gives up and raises an error.
Database	Returns the name of the current database.
DataSource	Returns the name of the current database file or database server.

continues

(continued)

PROPERTY	PURPOSE
Provider	(OleDbConnection only) Returns the name of the OLE DB database provider (for example, Microsoft.Jet.OLEDB.4.0).
ServerVersion	Returns the database server's version number. This value is available only when the connection is open and may look like 04.00.0000.
State	Returns the connection's current state. This value can be Closed, Connecting, Open, Executing (executing a command), Fetching (fetching data), or Broken (the connection was open but then broke; you can close and reopen the connection).

The ConnectionString property includes many fields separated by semicolons. The following text shows a typical ConnectionString value for an OleDbConnection object that will open an Access database. The text here shows each embedded field on a separate line, but the actual string would be all run together in one long line.

```
Jet OLEDB:Global Partial Bulk Ops=2;
Jet OLEDB:Registry Path=;
Jet OLEDB:Database Locking Mode=1;
Data Source="C:\Personnel\Data\Personnel.mdb";
Mode=Share Deny None;
Jet OLEDB:Engine Type=5;
Provider="Microsoft.Jet.OLEDB.4.0";
Jet OLEDB:System database=;
Jet OLEDB:SFP=False;
persist security info=False;
Extended Properties=;
Jet OLEDB:Compact Without Replica Repair=False;
Jet OLEDB:Encrypt Database=False;
Jet OLEDB:Create System Database=False;
Jet OLEDB:Don't Copy Locale on Compact=False;
User ID=Admin;
Jet OLEDB:Global Bulk Transactions=1"
```

> **NOTE** *The data source value will be different on your system. In this example, the database is at* C:\Personnel\Data\Personnel.mdb. *You would need to change it to match the location of the data on your system.*

Many of these properties are optional and you can omit them. Remembering which ones are optional (or even which fields are allowed for a particular type of connection object) is not always easy. Fortunately, it's also not necessary. Instead of typing all these fields into your code or in the connection control's ConnectString property in the Properties window, you can let Visual Basic build the string for you.

Simply follow the steps described in the section "Connecting to the Data Source" earlier in this chapter. After you build or select the database connection, look at the connection string at the bottom of the dialog box shown in Figure 19-2. Use the mouse to highlight the connection string and then press Ctrl+C to copy it to the clipboard.

The following code fragment shows how a program can create, open, use, and close an OleDbConnection object. The code assumes the database name is in the text box txtDatabase.

```
' Make the connect string.
Dim connect_string As String =
    "Provider=Microsoft.Jet.OLEDB.4.0;" &
    "Data Source=""" & txtDatabase.Text & """;" &
    "Persist Security Info=False"

' Open a database connection.
Using conn_people As New OleDb.OleDbConnection(connect_string)
    conn_people.Open()

    ' Do stuff with the connection.
    '...

    ' Close the connection.
    conn_people.Close()
End Using
```

Example program CommandInsert, which is available for download on the book's website, uses similar code to open a connection before inserting new data into the database.

The following table describes the most useful methods provided by the OleDbConnection and SqlConnection classes.

METHOD	PURPOSE
BeginTransaction	Begins a database transaction and returns a transaction object representing it. A transaction lets the program ensure that a series of commands are either all performed or all canceled as a group. See the section "Transaction Objects" later in this chapter for more information.
ChangeDatabase	Changes the currently open database.
Close	Closes the database connection.
CreateCommand	Creates a command object that can perform some action on the database. The action might select records, create a table, update a record, and so forth.
Open	Opens the connection using the values specified in the ConnectionString property.

The connection object's most useful events are InfoMessage and StateChange. The InfoMessage event occurs when the database provider issues a warning or informational message. The program can read the message and take action or display it to the user. The StateChange event occurs when the database connection's state changes.

Note that you don't need to open and close a connection directly when you use a data adapter's Fill and Update methods. Fill and Update automatically open the connection, perform their tasks, and then close the connection so that you don't need to manage the connection object yourself.

TRANSACTION OBJECTS

A transaction defines a set of database actions that should be executed "atomically" as a single unit. Either all of them should occur or none of them should occur, but no action should execute without all of the others.

The classic example is a transfer of money from one account to another. Suppose a program tries to subtract money from one account and add it to another. After it subtracts the money from the first account, however, the program crashes. The database has lost money — a bad situation for the owners of the accounts.

On the other hand, suppose that the program performs the operations in the reverse order: First it adds money to the second account and then subtracts it from the first. This time if the program gets halfway through the operation before crashing, the database has created new money — a bad situation for the bank.

The solution is to wrap these two operations in a transaction. If the program gets halfway through the transaction and then crashes, the database engine unwinds the transaction when the database restarts, so the data looks as if nothing had happened. This isn't as good as performing the whole transaction flawlessly, but at least the database is consistent and the money has been conserved.

To use transactions in Visual Basic, the program uses a connection object's BeginTransaction method to open a transaction. It then creates command objects associated with the connection and the transaction, and it executes them. When it has finished, the program can call the transaction object's Commit method to make all the actions occur, or it can call Rollback to cancel them all.

Example program Transactions, which is available for download on the book's website, uses the following code to perform two operations within a single transaction. This code removes an amount of money from one account and adds the same amount to another account.

```
' Make a transfer.
Private Sub btnUpdate_Click() Handles btnUpdate.Click
    ' Open the connection.
    Using conn_accounts As New OleDbConnection(MakeConnectString())
        conn_accounts.Open()

        ' Make the transaction.
        Dim trans As OleDbTransaction =
            conn_accounts.BeginTransaction(IsolationLevel.ReadCommitted)

        ' Make a Command for this connection.
```

```
' and this transaction.
Dim cmd As New OleDbCommand(
    "UPDATE Accounts SET Balance=Balance + ? WHERE AccountName=?",
    conn_accounts,
    trans)

' Create parameters for the first command.
cmd.Parameters.Add(New OleDbParameter("Balance",
    Decimal.Parse(txtAmount.Text)))
cmd.Parameters.Add(New OleDbParameter("AccountName",
    "Alice's Software Emporium"))

' Execute the second command.
cmd.ExecuteNonQuery()

' Create parameters for the second command.
cmd.Parameters.Clear()
cmd.Parameters.Add(New OleDbParameter("Balance",
    -Decimal.Parse(txtAmount.Text)))
cmd.Parameters.Add(New OleDbParameter("AccountName",
    "Bob's Consulting"))

' Execute the second command.
cmd.ExecuteNonQuery()

' Commit the transaction.
If MessageBox.Show(
    "Commit transaction?",
    "Commit?",
    MessageBoxButtons.YesNo,
    MessageBoxIcon.Question) = Windows.Forms.DialogResult.Yes _
Then
    ' Commit the transaction.
    trans.Commit()
Else
    ' Rollback the transaction.
    trans.Rollback()
End If

' Display the current balances.
ShowValues(conn_accounts)

' Close the connection.
conn_accounts.Close()
    End Using
End Sub
```

The code first creates a connection. It uses the MakeConnectString function to build an appropriate connection string.

Next the code uses the connection's BeginTransaction method to make the transaction object trans.

The code then defines an OleDbCommand object named cmd, setting its command text to the following text:

```
UPDATE Accounts SET Balance=Balance + ? WHERE AccountName=?
```

Note that it passes the transaction object into the command object's constructor to make the command part of the transaction.

The question marks in the command text represent parameters to the command. The program defines the parameters' values by adding two parameter objects to the command object. It then calls the command's ExecuteNonQuery method to perform the query.

The code clears the command's parameters, adds two parameters with different values, and calls the command's ExecuteNonQuery method again.

Now the program displays a message box asking whether you want to commit the transaction. If you click Yes, the program calls the transaction's Commit method and both of the update operations occur. If you click No, the program calls the transaction's Rollback method and both of the update operations are canceled.

The program finishes by calling ShowValues to display the updated data and by closing the connection.

Instead of clicking Yes or No when the program asks if it should commit the transaction, you can use the IDE to stop the program. When you then restart the program, you will see that neither update was processed.

In addition to the Commit and Rollback methods, transaction objects may provide other methods for performing more complex transactions. For example, the OleDbTransaction class has a Begin method that enables you to create a nested transaction. Similarly, the SqlTransaction class has a Save method that creates a "savepoint" that you can use to roll back part of the transaction. See the online help for the type of transaction object you are using to learn about these methods. The web page http://msdn.microsoft.com/2k2hy99x.aspx gives an overview of using transactions.

DATA ADAPTERS

A data adapter transfers data between a connection and a DataSet. This object's most important methods are Fill and Update, which move data from and to the database, respectively. A data adapter also provides properties and other methods that can be useful. The following table describes the object's most useful properties.

PROPERTY	PURPOSE
DeleteCommand	The command object that the adapter uses to delete rows.
InsertCommand	The command object that the adapter uses to insert rows.
SelectCommand	The command object that the adapter uses to select rows.

PROPERTY	PURPOSE
TableMappings	A collection of DataTableMapping objects that determine how tables in the database are mapped to tables in the DataSet. Each DataTableMapping object has a ColumnMappings collection that determines how the columns in the database table are mapped to columns in the DataSet table.
UpdateCommand	The command object that the adapter uses to update rows.

You can create the command objects in a couple of ways. For example, if you use the Data Adapter Configuration Wizard (described shortly) to build the adapter at design time, the wizard automatically creates these objects. You can select the adapter and expand these objects in the Properties window to read their properties, including the CommandText property that defines the commands.

Another way to create these commands is to use a command builder object. If you attach a command builder to a data adapter, the adapter uses the command builder to generate the commands it needs automatically.

Example program GenerateCommands uses the following code to determine the commands used by a data adapter. The code creates a new OleDbCommandBuilder, passing its constructor the data adapter. It then uses the command builder's GetDeleteCommand, GetInsertCommand, and GetUpdateCommand methods to learn about the automatically generated commands.

```
' Attach a command builder to the data adapter
' and display the generated commands.
Dim command_builder As New OleDbCommandBuilder(OleDbDataAdapter1)

Dim txt As String = ""

txt &= command_builder.GetDeleteCommand.CommandText & vbCrLf & vbCrLf
txt &= command_builder.GetInsertCommand.CommandText & vbCrLf & vbCrLf
txt &= command_builder.GetUpdateCommand.CommandText & vbCrLf & vbCrLf

txtCommands.Text = txt
txtCommands.Select(0, 0)
```

The following text shows the results of the previous Debug statements. The DELETE and UPDATE statements are wrapped across multiple lines. The command builder generated these commands based on the select statement SELECT * From Books that was used to load the DataSet.

```
DELETE FROM Books WHERE ((Title = ?) AND ((? = 1 AND URL IS NULL) OR (URL = ?))
AND ((? = 1 AND Year IS NULL) OR (Year = ?)) AND ((? = 1 AND ISBN IS NULL) OR
(ISBN = ?)) AND ((? = 1 AND Pages IS NULL) OR (Pages = ?)))

INSERT INTO Books (Title, URL, Year, ISBN, Pages) VALUES (?, ?, ?, ?, ?)

UPDATE Books SET Title = ?, URL = ?, Year = ?, ISBN = ?, Pages = ? WHERE
((Title = ?) AND ((? = 1 AND URL IS NULL) OR (URL = ?)) AND ((? = 1 AND Year IS
NULL) OR (Year = ?)) AND ((? = 1 AND ISBN IS NULL) OR (ISBN = ?)) AND ((? = 1
AND Pages IS NULL) OR (Pages = ?)))
```

A data adapter's TableMappings property enables you to change how the adapter maps data in the database to the DataSet. For example, you could make it copy the Employees table in the database into a DataSet table named People. You don't usually need to change the table and column names, however, and you can make these changes interactively at design time more easily than you can do this in code, so you will usually leave these values alone at run time.

To create a data adapter control at design time, open a form in the Windows Forms Designer, select the Toolbox's Data tab, and double-click the appropriate data adapter control. (If the data adapter you want doesn't appear in the Toolbox, right-click the Toolbox, select Choose Items, and pick the data adapter that you want to use.)

When you create a data adapter, the Data Adapter Configuration Wizard appears. The wizard's first page lets you select or build a data connection much as the Data Source Configuration Wizard does in Figure 19-2. Select or create a connection as described in the section "Connecting to the Data Source" earlier in this chapter.

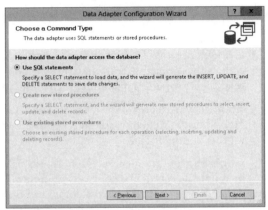

Click Next to display the page shown in Figure 19-10. Use the option buttons to select the method the adapter should use to work with the data source. This determines how the data adapter will fetch, update, delete, and insert data in the database.

FIGURE 19-10: Select the method the data adapter will use to manipulate database data.

Your options are:

➤ **Use SQL Statements** — Makes the adapter use simple SQL statements to manipulate the data

➤ **Create New Stored Procedures** — Makes the wizard generate stored procedures in the database to manipulate the data

➤ **Use Existing Stored Procedures** — Makes the wizard use procedures you have already created to manipulate the data

In Figure 19-10, only the first option is enabled because it is the only option available to the OleDbDataAdapter used in this example.

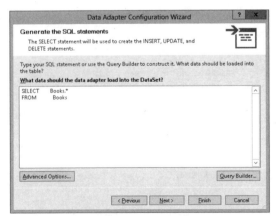

When you select the Use SQL Statements option and click Next, the form shown in Figure 19-11 appears. If you are experienced at writing SQL statements, enter the SELECT statement that you want the data adapter to use to select its data.

FIGURE 19-11: Enter a SQL SELECT statement or click the Query Builder button.

If you have less experience or are not familiar with the database's structure, click the Query Builder button to use the Query Builder shown in Figure 19-12. The area in the upper left shows the tables currently selected for use by the

SQL query. Check boxes indicate which fields in the tables are selected. To add new tables to the query, right-click in this area and select Add Table.

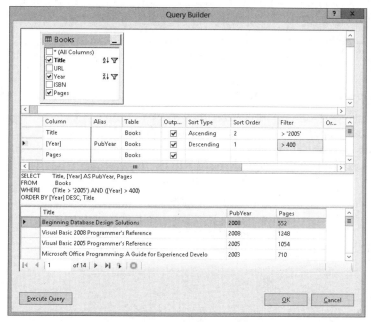

FIGURE 19-12: You can use the Query Builder to interactively define the data that a data adapter selects.

Figure 19-12 shows the Query Builder. The top part shows that the Books table is included in the query and that its Title, Year, and Pages fields are selected.

Below the table and field selection area is a grid that lists the selected fields. Columns let you specify modifiers for each field. A field's Alias indicates the name the field is known by when it is returned by the query. In Figure 19-12, the Year field will be returned with the alias PubYear.

The Output check box determines whether the field is selected. This check box does the same thing as the one in the upper field selection area.

The Sort Type column lets you indicate that the results should be sorted in either ascending or descending order. Sort Order determines the order in which the fields are sorted. The query shown in Figure 19-12 sorts first by Year in descending order. If more than one book has the same Year, they are ordered by Title in ascending order.

The Filter column lets you add conditions to the fields. The values in Figure 19-12 make the query select records only where the Year is greater than 2005. Additional fields scrolled off to the right in Figure 19-12 let you add more filters combined with OR. For example, you could select books where the Year is greater than 2005 OR less than 1990.

If you place filters on more than one field, their conditions are combined with AND. For example, the values shown in Figure 19-12 select records where Year is greater than 2005 AND Pages is greater than 400.

Below the grid is a text box that shows the SQL code for the query. If you look at the query, you can see that it selects the fields checked in the field selection area at the top, uses an appropriate WHERE clause, and orders the results properly.

Click the Execute Query button to make the Query Builder run the query and display the results in the bottom grid. You can use this button to test the query to verify that it makes sense before you finish creating the data adapter.

Click OK to close the Query Builder and return to the Data Adapter Configuration Wizard.

When you click Next, the Data Adapter Configuration Wizard displays a summary page indicating what it did and did not do while creating the data adapter. Depending on the query you use to select data, the wizard may not generate all of the commands to select, update, insert, and delete data. For example, if the query joins more than one table, the wizard will be unable to figure out how to update the tables, so it won't generate insert, update, or delete commands.

Click Finish to close the wizard and see the new data adapter and its new connection object. You can see the adapter's DeleteCommand, InsertCommand, SelectCommand, and UpdateCommand objects in the Properties window. These objects' CommandText values show the corresponding SQL statements used by the objects. The wizard also generates default table mappings to transform database values into DataSet values.

COMMAND OBJECTS

The command object classes (OleDbCommand, SqlCommand, OdbcCommand, and OracleCommand) define database commands. The command can be a SQL query, or some non-query statement such as an INSERT, UPDATE, DELETE, or CREATE TABLE statement.

The object's Connection property gives the database connection object on which it will execute its command. CommandText gives the SQL text that the command represents.

The CommandType property tells the database the type of command text the command holds. This can be StoredProcedure (CommandText is the name of a stored procedure), TableDirect (CommandText is the name of one or more tables from which the database should return data), or Text (CommandText is a SQL statement).

The command object's Parameters collection contains parameter objects that define any values needed to execute the command text.

Example program CommandInsert, which is available for download on the book's website, uses the following code to create an OleDbCommand object that executes the bolded SQL statement `INSERT INTO PeopleNames (FirstName, LastName) VALUES (?, ?)`. The question marks are placeholders for parameters that will be added later. The code then adds two new OleDbParameter objects to the command's Parameters collection. When the code invokes the command's ExecuteNonQuery method, the adapter replaces the question marks with these parameter values in the order in which they appear in the Parameters collection. In this example, the value of `txtFirstName.Text` replaces the first question mark and `txtLastName.Text` replaces the second.

```vb
Private Sub btnAdd_Click() Handles btnAdd.Click
    ' Make the connect string.
    Dim connect_string As String =
        "Provider=Microsoft.Jet.OLEDB.4.0;" &
        "Data Source=""" & txtDatabase.Text & """;" &
        "Persist Security Info=False"

    ' Open a database connection.
    Using conn_people As New OleDb.OleDbConnection(connect_string)
        conn_people.Open()

        ' Make a Command to insert data.
        Dim cmd As New OleDbCommand(
            "INSERT INTO PeopleNames (FirstName, LastName) VALUES (?, ?)",
            conn_people)

        ' Create parameters for the command.
        cmd.Parameters.Add(New OleDbParameter("FirstName", txtFirstName.Text))
        cmd.Parameters.Add(New OleDbParameter("LastName", txtLastName.Text))

        ' Execute the command.
        Try
            cmd.ExecuteNonQuery()
        Catch ex As Exception
            MessageBox.Show(ex.Message)
        End Try

        ' Show the current values.
        ShowValues(conn_people)

        ' Close the connection.
        conn_people.Close()
    End Using
End Sub
```

The command object's Transaction property gives the transaction object with which it is associated. See the section "Transaction Objects" earlier in this chapter for more information about transactions.

The command object provides three methods for executing its CommandText. ExecuteNonQuery executes a command that is not a query and that doesn't return any values. For example, CREATE TABLE, UPDATE, and INSERT statements do not return any values.

ExecuteScalar executes a command and returns the first column in the first row selected. This is useful for commands that return a single value such as SELECT COUNT * FROM Users.

ExecuteReader executes a SELECT statement and returns a data reader object (for example, OleDbDataReader). The program can use this object to navigate through the returned rows of data.

The command object's two other most useful methods are CreateParameter and Prepare. As you may be able to guess, CreateParameter adds a new object to the command's Parameters collection. The Prepare method compiles the command into a form that the database may be able to execute more quickly. It is often faster to execute a compiled command many times using different parameter values than it is to execute many new commands.

DataSet

DataSet is the flagship object when it comes to holding data in memory. It provides all the features you need to build, load, store, manipulate, and save data similar to that stored in a relational database. It can hold multiple tables related with complex parent/child relationships and uniqueness constraints. It provides methods for merging DataSet objects, searching for records that satisfy criteria, and saving data in different ways (such as into a relational database or an XML file). In many ways, it is like a complete database stored in memory rather than on a disk.

One of the most common ways to use a DataSet object is to load it from a relational database when the program starts, use various controls to display the data and let the user manipulate it interactively, and then save the changes back into the database when the program ends.

In variations on this basic theme, the program can load its data from an XML file or build a DataSet in memory without using a database. The program can use controls bound to the DataSet to let the user view and manipulate complex data with little extra programming.

The following table describes the DataSet object's most useful properties.

PROPERTY	PURPOSE
CaseSensitive	Determines whether string comparisons inside DataTable objects are case-sensitive.
DataSetName	The DataSet object's name. Often, you don't need to use this for much. If you need to use the DataSet object's XML representation, however, this determines the name of the root element.
DefaultViewManager	Returns a DataViewManager object that you can use to determine the default settings (sort order, filter) of DataView objects you create later.
EnforceConstraints	Determines whether the DataSet should enforce constraints when updating data. For example, if you want to add records to a child table before the master records have been created, you can set EnforceConstraints to False while you add the data. You should be able to avoid this sort of problem by adding the records in the correct order.
HasErrors	Returns True if any of the DataSet object's DataTable objects contains errors.
Namespace	The DataSet's namespace. If this is nonblank, the DataSet object's XML data's root node includes an xmlns attribute as in <Scores xmlns="my_namespace">.
Prefix	Determines the XML prefix that the DataSet uses as an alias for its namespace.
Relations	A collection of DataRelation objects that represent parent/child relations among the columns in different tables.
Tables	A collection of DataTable objects representing the tables stored in the DataSet.

The DataSet object's XML properties affect the way the object reads and writes its data in XML form. For example, if the Namespace property is `my_namespace` and the Prefix property is `pfx`, the DataSet object's XML data might look like the following:

```
<pfx:Scores xmlns:pfx="my_namespace">
  <Students xmlns="my_namespace">
    <FirstName>Art</FirstName>
    <LastName>Ant</LastName>
    <StudentId>1</StudentId>
  </Students>
  <Students xmlns="my_namespace">
    <FirstName>Bev</FirstName>
    <LastName>Bug</LastName>
    <StudentId>2</StudentId>
  </Students>
  ...
  <TestScores xmlns="my_namespace">
    <StudentId>1</StudentId>
    <TestNumber>1</TestNumber>
    <Score>78</Score>
  </TestScores>
  <TestScores xmlns="my_namespace">
    <StudentId>1</StudentId>
    <TestNumber>2</TestNumber>
    <Score>81</Score>
  </TestScores>
  ...
</pfx:Scores>
```

The following table describes the DataSet object's most useful methods.

METHOD	PURPOSE
AcceptChanges	Accepts all changes to the data that were made since the data was loaded, or since the last call to AcceptChanges. When you modify a row in the DataSet, the row is flagged as modified. If you delete a row, the row is marked as deleted but not actually removed. When you call AcceptChanges, new and modified rows are marked as Unchanged instead of Added or Modified, and deleted rows are permanently removed.
Clear	Removes all rows from the DataSet object's tables.
Clone	Makes a copy of the DataSet including all tables, relations, and constraints, but not including the data.
Copy	Makes a copy of the DataSet including all tables, relations, constraints, and the data.

continues

(continued)

METHOD	PURPOSE
GetChanges	Makes a copy of the DataSet containing only the rows that have been modified. This method's optional parameter indicates the type of changes that the new DataSet should contain (added, modified, deleted, or unchanged).
GetXml	Returns a string containing the DataSet object's XML representation.
GetXmlSchema	Returns the DataSet object's XML schema definition (XSD).
HasChanges	Returns True if any of the DataSet object's tables contains new, modified, or deleted rows.
Merge	Merges a DataSet, DataTable, or array of DataRow objects into this DataSet.
ReadXml	Reads XML data from a stream or file into the DataSet.
ReadXmlSchema	Reads an XML schema from a stream or file into the DataSet.
RejectChanges	Undoes any changes made since the DataSet was loaded or since the last call to AcceptChanges.
WriteXml	Writes the DataSet object's XML data into a file or stream. It can optionally include the DataSet object's schema.
WriteXmlSchema	Writes the DataSet object's XSD schema into an XML file or stream.

Several of these methods mirror methods provided by other finer-grained data objects. For example, HasChanges returns True if any of the DataSet object's tables contains changes. The DataTable and DataRow objects also have HasChanges methods that return True if their more limited scope contains changes.

These mirrored methods include AcceptChanges, Clear, Clone, Copy, GetChanges, and RejectChanges. See the following sections that describe the DataTable and DataRow objects for more information.

DataTable

The DataTable class represents the data in one table within a DataSet. A DataTable contains DataRow objects representing its data, DataColumn objects that define the table's columns, constraint objects that define constraints on the table's data (for example, a uniqueness constraint requires that only one row may contain the same value in a particular column), and objects representing relationships between the table's columns and the columns in other tables. This object also provides methods and events for manipulating rows.

The following table describes the DataTable object's most useful properties.

PROPERTY	PURPOSE
CaseSensitive	Determines whether string comparisons inside the DataTable are case-sensitive.
ChildRelations	A collection of DataRelation objects that define parent/child relationships where this table is the parent.
Columns	A collection of DataColumn objects that define the table's columns (column name, data type, default value, maximum length, and so forth).
Constraints	A collection of Constraint objects that represent restrictions on the table's data. A ForeignKeyConstraint requires that the values in some of the table's columns must be present in another table. A UniqueConstraint requires that the values in a set of columns must be unique within the table.
DataSet	The DataSet object that contains this DataTable.
DefaultView	Returns a DataView object that you can use to view, sort, and filter the table's rows.
HasErrors	Returns True if any of the DataTable object's rows contains an error.
MinimumCapacity	The initial capacity of the table.
Namespace	The DataTable object's namespace. If this is nonblank, the DataTable object's XML records' root nodes include an xmlns attribute as in <Students xmlns="my_namespace">.
ParentRelations	A collection of DataRelation objects that defines parent/child relationships where this table is the child.
Prefix	Determines the XML prefix that the DataTable uses as an alias for its namespace.
PrimaryKey	Gets or sets an array of DataColumn objects that define the table's primary key. The primary key is always unique and provides the fastest access to the records.
Rows	A collection of DataRow objects containing the table's data.
TableName	The table's name.

The DataTable object's XML properties affect the way the object reads and writes its data in XML form. For example, if the Namespace property is my_namespace and the Prefix property is tbl1, one of the DataTable object's XML records might look like the following:

```
<tbl1:Students xmlns:tbl1="my_namespace">
  <FirstName xmlns="my_namespace">Art</FirstName>
  <LastName xmlns="my_namespace">Ant</LastName>
  <StudentId xmlns="my_namespace">1</StudentId>
</pfx:Students>
```

The following table describes the DataTable object's most useful methods.

METHOD	PURPOSE
AcceptChanges	Accepts all changes to the table's rows that were made since the data was loaded or since the last call to AcceptChanges.
Clear	Removes all rows from the table.
Clone	Makes a copy of the DataTable, including all relations and constraints, but not including the data.
Compute	Computes the value of an expression using the rows that satisfy a filter condition.
Copy	Makes a copy of the DataTable including all relations, constraints, and data.
GetChanges	Makes a copy of the DataTable containing only the rows that have been modified. This method's optional parameter indicates the type of changes that the new DataSet should contain (added, modified, deleted, or unchanged).
GetErrors	Gets an array of DataRow objects that contain errors.
ImportRow	Copies the data in a DataRow object into the DataTable.
LoadDataRow	This method takes an array of values as a parameter. It searches the table for a row with values that match the array's primary key values. If it doesn't find such a row, it uses the values to create the row. The method returns the DataRow object it found or created.
NewRow	Creates a new DataRow object that matches the table's schema. To add the new row to the table, you create a new DataRow, fill in its fields, and use the table's Rows.Add method.
RejectChanges	Undoes any changes made since the DataTable was loaded or since the last call to AcceptChanges.
Select	Returns an array of DataRow objects selected from the table. Optional parameters indicate a filter expression that the selected rows must match, sort columns and sort order, and the row states to select (new, modified, deleted, and so forth).

The DataTable object also provides several useful events, which are listed in the following table.

EVENT	PURPOSE
ColumnChanged	Occurs after a value has been changed in a column.
ColumnChanging	Occurs when a value is being changed in a column.

EVENT	PURPOSE
RowChanged	Occurs after a row has changed. A user might change several of a row's columns and ColumnChanged will fire for each one. RowChanged fires only once when the user moves to a new row.
RowChanging	Occurs when a row is being changed.
RowDeleted	Occurs after a row has been deleted.
RowDeleting	Occurs when a row is being deleted.

DataRow

A DataRow object represents the data in one record in a DataTable. This object is relatively simple. It basically just holds data for the DataTable, and the DataTable object does most of the interesting work.

The following table describes the DataRow object's most useful properties.

PROPERTY	PURPOSE
HasErrors	Returns True if the row's data has errors.
Item	Gets or sets one of the row's item values by column index or name. Optionally you can indicate the version of the row that you want so, for example, you can read the original value in a row that has been modified.
ItemArray	Gets or sets all of the row's values by using an array of generic Objects.
RowError	Gets or sets the row's error message text.
RowState	Returns the row's current state: Added, Deleted, Modified, or Unchanged.
Table	Returns a reference to the DataTable containing the row.

If a row has an error message defined by its RowError property, the DataGrid control displays a red circle containing a white exclamation point to the left of the row as an error indicator. If you hover the mouse over the error indicator, a tooltip displays the RowError text. In Figure 19-13, the third row has RowError set to "Missing registration."

Example program MemoryDataSetWithErrors, which is available for download on the book's website, uses the following code to set errors on the second row's third column (remember, indexes start at zero) and on the third row. The result is shown in Figure 19-13.

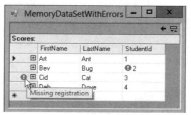

FIGURE 19-13: The DataGrid control marks a DataRow that has a nonblank RowError.

```
students_table.Rows(1).SetColumnError(2, "Bad name format")
students_table.Rows(2).RowError = "Missing registration"
```

The following table describes the DataRow object's most useful methods.

METHOD	PURPOSE
AcceptChanges	Accepts all changes to the row that were made since the data was loaded or since the last call to AcceptChanges.
BeginEdit	Puts the row in data-editing mode. This suspends events for the row, so your code or the user can change several fields without triggering validation events. BeginEdit is implicitly called when the user modifies a bound control's value and EndEdit is implicitly called when you invoke AcceptChanges.
CancelEdit	Cancels the current edit on the row and restores its original values.
ClearErrors	Clears the row's column and row errors.
Delete	Deletes the row from its table.
GetChildRows	Returns an array of DataRow objects representing this row's child rows as specified by a parent/child data relation.
GetColumnError	Returns the error text assigned to a column.
GetParentRow	Returns a DataRow object representing this row's parent record as specified by a parent/child data relation.
GetParentRows	Returns an array of DataRow objects representing this row's parent records as specified by a data relation.
HasVersion	Returns True if the row has a particular version (Current, Default, Original, or Proposed). For example, while a row is being edited, it has Current and Proposed versions.
IsNull	Indicates whether a particular column contains a NULL value.
RejectChanges	Removes any changes made to the row since the data was loaded or since the last call to AcceptChanges.
SetColumnError	Sets the error text for one of the row's columns. This is similar to a row's error text but it applies to a particular column.
SetParentRow	Sets the row's parent row according to a data relation.

DataColumn

The DataColumn object represents a column in a DataTable. It defines the column's name and data type, and your code can use it to define relationships among different columns.

The following table describes the DataColumn object's most useful properties.

PROPERTY	PURPOSE
AllowDBNull	Determines whether the column allows NULL values.
AutoIncrement	Determines whether new rows automatically generate auto-incremented values for the column.
AutoIncrementSeed	Determines the starting value for an auto-increment column.
AutoIncrementStep	Determines the amount by which an auto-incrementing column's value is incremented for new rows.
Caption	Gets or sets a caption for the column. Note that some controls may not use this value. For example, the DataGrid control displays the column's ColumnName, not its Caption.
ColumnMapping	Determines how the column is saved in the table's XML data. This property can have one of the values Attribute (save the column as an attribute of the row's element), Element (save the column as a subelement), Hidden (don't save the column), and SimpleContent (save the column as XmlText inside the row's element). If a column is hidden, the DataGrid control doesn't display its value. See the text following this table for an example.
ColumnName	Determines the name of the column in the DataTable. Note that data adapters use the column name to map database columns to DataSet columns, so, if you change this property without updating the table mapping, the column will probably not be filled.
DataType	Determines the column's data type. Visual Basic supports the data types Boolean, Byte, Char, DateTime, Decimal, Double, Int16, Int32, Int64, SByte, Single, String, TimeSpan, UInt16, UInt32, and UInt64.
DefaultValue	Determines the default value assigned to the column in new rows.
Expression	Sets an expression for the column. You can use this to create calculated columns. For example, the expression Quantity * Price makes the column display the value of the Quantity column times the value of the Price column.
MaxLength	Determines the maximum length of a text column.

continues

(continued)

PROPERTY	PURPOSE
Namespace	The column's namespace. If this is nonblank, the rows' XML root nodes include an xmlns attribute as in <StudentId xmlns="my_namespace">12</StudentId>.
Ordinal	Returns the column's index in the DataTable object's Columns collection.
Prefix	Determines the XML prefix that the DataColumn uses as an alias for its namespace. For example, if Namespace is my_namespace and Prefix is pfx, then a row's StudentId field might be encoded in XML as <pfx:StudentId xmlns:pfx="my_namespace">12</pfx:StudentId>.
ReadOnly	Determines whether the column allows changes after a record is created.
Table	Returns a reference to the DataTable containing the column.
Unique	Determines whether different rows in the table can have the same value for this column.

Example program MemoryDataSetXmlMappedColumns, which is available for download on the book's website, uses the following code to define XML column mappings for the Students table. It indicates that the table's FirstName and LastName columns should be saved as attributes of the row elements, and that the StudentId column should be saved as XmlText.

```
students_table.Columns("FirstName").ColumnMapping = MappingType.Attribute
students_table.Columns("LastName").ColumnMapping = MappingType.Attribute
students_table.Columns("StudentId").ColumnMapping = MappingType.SimpleContent
```

The following text shows some of the resulting XML Students records:

```
<Students FirstName="Art" LastName="Ant">1</Students>
<Students FirstName="Bev" LastName="Bug">2</Students>
<Students FirstName="Cid" LastName="Cat">3</Students>
<Students FirstName="Deb" LastName="Dove">4</Students>
```

DataRelation

A DataRelation object represents a parent/child relationship between sets of columns in different tables. For example, suppose that a database contains a Students table containing FirstName, LastName, and StudentId fields. The TestScores table has the fields StudentId, TestNumber, and Score. The StudentId fields connect the two tables in a parent/child relationship. Each Students record may correspond to any number of TestScores records. In this example, Students is the parent table, and TestScores is the child table.

The following code defines this relationship. It uses the Students.StudentId field as the parent field and the TestScores.StudentId field as the child field.

```
' Make a relationship linking the two tables' StudentId fields.
scores_dataset.Relations.Add(
    "Student Test Scores",
    students_table.Columns("StudentId"),
    test_scores_table.Columns("StudentId"))
```

A DataRelation can also relate more than one column in the two tables. For example, two tables might be linked by the combination of the LastName and FirstName fields.

Most programs don't need to manipulate a relation after it is created. The DataSet object's Relations. Add method shown in the previous code creates a relation and thereafter the program can usually leave it alone. However, the DataRelation object does provide properties and methods in case you do need to modify one. The following table describes the DataRelation object's most useful properties.

PROPERTY	PURPOSE
ChildColumns	Returns an array of DataColumn objects representing the child columns.
ChildKeyConstraint	Returns the ForeignKeyConstraint object for this relation.
ChildTable	Returns a DataTable object representing the relation's child table.
DataSet	Returns a reference to the DataSet containing the relation.
Nested	Determines whether the child data should be nested within parent rows in the DataSet's XML representation.
ParentColumns	Returns an array of DataColumn objects representing the parent columns.
ParentKeyConstraint	Returns the UniqueConstraint object for this relation. This object requires that the values in the parent's columns are unique within the parent table.
ParentTable	Returns a DataTable object representing the relation's parent table.
RelationName	Determines the relation's name.

Normally, tables are stored separately in a DataSet object's XML representation, but you can use the Nested property to make the XML include one table's records inside another's. For example, suppose that the Students and TestScores tables are linked by a common StudentId field. If you set this relation's Nested property to True, the XML data would include the TestScores for a student within the Students record, as shown in the following:

```
<Students>
  <FirstName>Deb</FirstName>
  <LastName>Dove</LastName>
  <StudentId>4</StudentId>
  <TestScores>
    <StudentId>4</StudentId>
    <TestNumber>1</TestNumber>
```

```
        <Score>81</Score>
      </TestScores>
      <TestScores>
        <StudentId>4</StudentId>
        <TestNumber>2</TestNumber>
        <Score>68</Score>
      </TestScores>
      ...
    </Students>
```

Example program MemoryDataSetNestedXml, which is available for download on the book's website, demonstrates this nested XML structure.

Note that in this representation the TestScores table's StudentId value is redundant because the same value is contained in the Students element's StudentId subelement.

Constraints

A constraint imposes a restriction on the data in a table's columns. DataSets support two kinds of constraint objects:

➤ *ForeignKeyConstraint* restricts the values in one table based on the values in another table. For example, you could require that values in the Addresses table's State field must exist in the States table's StateName field.

➤ *UniqueConstraint* requires that the combination of one or more fields within the same table must be unique. For example, an Employee table might require that the combination of the FirstName and LastName values be unique.

The following sections describe each of these types of constraint objects in greater detail.

ForeignKeyConstraint

In addition to requiring that values in one table must exist in another table, a ForeignKeyConstraint can determine how changes to one table propagate to the other. For example, suppose that the Addresses table has a ForeignKeyConstraint requiring that its State field contain a value that is present in the States table's StateName field. If you delete the States table's record for Colorado, the constraint could automatically delete all of the Addresses records that used that state's name.

The following table describes the ForeignKeyConstraint object's most useful properties.

PROPERTY	PURPOSE
AcceptRejectRule	Determines the action taken when the AcceptChanges method executes. This value can be None (do nothing) or Cascade (update the child fields' values to match the new parent field values).
Columns	Returns an array containing references to the constraint's child columns.
ConstraintName	Determines the constraint's name.

PROPERTY	PURPOSE
DeleteRule	Determines the action taken when a row is deleted. This value can be Cascade (delete the child rows), None (do nothing), SetDefault (change child field values to their default values), or SetNull (change child field values to NULL).
RelatedColumns	Returns an array containing references to the constraint's parent columns.
RelatedTable	Returns a reference to the constraint's parent table.
Table	Returns a reference to the constraint's child table.
UpdateRule	Determines the action taken when a row is updated. This value can be Cascade (update the child rows' values to match), None (do nothing), SetDefault (change child field values to their default values), or SetNull (change child field values to NULL).

UniqueConstraint

If you want to require the values in a single column to be unique, you can set the column's Unique property to True. This automatically creates a UniqueConstraint object and adds it to the DataTable. The following code shows how a program can make the Students table's StudentId column require unique values:

```
students_table.Columns("StudentId").Unique = True
```

You can use the UniqueConstraint object's constructors to require that a group of fields has a unique combined value. The following code demonstrates that technique:

```
' Make the combined FirstName/LastName unique.
Dim first_last_columns() As DataColumn = {
    students_table.Columns("FirstName"),
    students_table.Columns("LastName")
}
students_table.Constraints.Add(New UniqueConstraint(first_last_columns))
```

This code makes an array of DataColumn objects representing the Students table's FirstName and LastName fields. It passes the array into the UniqueConstraint object's constructor to require that the FirstName/LastName pair be unique in the table.

After executing this code, the program could add two records with the same FirstName and different LastNames, or with the same LastName and different FirstNames, but it could not create two records with the same FirstName and LastName values.

The following table describes the UniqueConstraint object's properties.

PROPERTY	PURPOSE
Columns	Returns an array of DataColumn objects representing the columns that must be unique.
IsPrimaryKey	Returns True if the columns form the table's primary key.
Table	Returns a reference to the DataTable that contains the constraint.

Example program MemoryDataSet, which is available for download on the book's website, defines several uniqueness constraints including a constraint requiring that StudentId be unique and a constraint requiring that the FirstName and LastName combination be unique.

DATAVIEW

A DataView object represents a customizable view of the data contained in a DataTable. You can use the DataView to select some or all of the DataTable's data and display it sorted in some manner without affecting the underlying DataTable.

A program can use multiple DataViews to select and order a table's data in different ways. You can then bind the DataViews to controls such as the DataGrid control to display the different views. If any of the views modifies its data, for example, by adding or deleting a row, the underlying DataTable object's data is updated and any other views that need to see the change are updated as well.

Example program DataGrids, which is available for download on the book's website, uses the following code to demonstrate DataViews:

```
Private Sub Form1_Load() Handles MyBase.Load
    ' Make a DataTable.
    Dim contacts_table As New DataTable("Contacts")

    ' Add columns.
    contacts_table.Columns.Add("FirstName", GetType(String))
    contacts_table.Columns.Add("LastName", GetType(String))
    contacts_table.Columns.Add("Street", GetType(String))
    contacts_table.Columns.Add("City", GetType(String))
    contacts_table.Columns.Add("State", GetType(String))
    contacts_table.Columns.Add("Zip", GetType(String))

    ' Make the combined FirstName/LastName unique.
    Dim first_last_columns() As DataColumn =
    {
        contacts_table.Columns("FirstName"),
        contacts_table.Columns("LastName")
    }
    contacts_table.Constraints.Add(New UniqueConstraint(first_last_columns))

    ' Make some contact data.
```

```
contacts_table.Rows.Add(New Object() {"Art", "Ant",
    "1234 Ash Pl", "Bugville", "CO", "11111"})
contacts_table.Rows.Add(New Object() {"Bev", "Bug",
    "22 Beach St", "Bugville", "CO", "22222"})
contacts_table.Rows.Add(New Object() {"Cid", "Cat",
    "3 Road Place Lane", "Programmeria", "KS", "33333"})
contacts_table.Rows.Add(New Object() {"Deb", "Dove",
    "414 Debugger Way", "Programmeria", "KS", "44444"})
contacts_table.Rows.Add(New Object() {"Ed", "Eager",
    "5746 Elm Blvd", "Bugville", "CO", "55555"})
contacts_table.Rows.Add(New Object() {"Fran", "Fix",
    "647 Foxglove Ct", "Bugville", "CO", "66666"})
contacts_table.Rows.Add(New Object() {"Gus", "Gantry",
    "71762-B Gooseberry Ave", "Programmeria", "KS", "77777"})
contacts_table.Rows.Add(New Object() {"Hil", "Harris",
    "828 Hurryup St", "Programmeria", "KS", "88888"})

' Attach grdAll to the DataTable.
grdAll.DataSource = contacts_table
grdAll.CaptionText = "All Records"

' Make a DataView for State = CO.
Dim dv_co As New DataView(contacts_table)
dv_co.RowFilter = "State = 'CO'"
grdCO.DataSource = dv_co
grdCO.CaptionText = "CO Records"

' Make a DataView for FirstName >= E.
Dim dv_name As New DataView(contacts_table)
dv_name.RowFilter = "FirstName >= 'E'"
grdName.DataSource = dv_name
grdName.CaptionText = "LastName >= E"
End Sub
```

The code builds a DataTable named Contacts containing the fields FirstName, LastName, Street, City, State, and Zip. It places a uniqueness constraint on the FirstName/LastName pair and adds some rows of data to the table. It then binds the DataTable to the DataGrid control named grdAll. Next the program makes a DataView named dv_co based on the table, sets its RowFilter property to make it select rows where the State field has the value CO, and binds the DataView to the DataGrid named grdCO. Finally, the code makes another DataView with RowFilter set to select records where the FirstName field is greater than or equal to E and binds that DataView to the grdName DataGrid. Figure 19-14 shows the result.

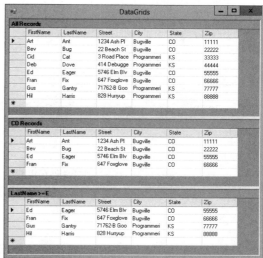

FIGURE 19-14: Different DataView objects can show different views of the same data.

The following table describes the DataView object's most useful properties.

PROPERTY	PURPOSE
AllowDelete	Determines whether the DataView allows row deletion. If this is False, any bound controls such as the DataGrid will not allow the user to delete rows.
AllowEdit	Determines whether the DataView allows row editing. If this is False, any bound controls will not allow the user to edit rows.
AllowNew	Determines whether the DataView allows new rows. If this is False, any bound controls will not allow the user to add rows.
Count	Returns the number of rows selected by the view.
Item	Returns a DataRowView object representing a row in the view.
RowFilter	A string that determines the records selected by the view.
RowStateFilter	The state of the records that should be selected by the view. This can be Added, CurrentRows (unchanged, new, and modified rows), Deleted, ModifiedCurrent (current version of modified rows), ModifiedOriginal (original version of modified rows), None, OriginalRows (original, unchanged, and deleted rows), and Unchanged.
Sort	A string giving the columns that should be used to sort the data.
Table	Specifies the underlying DataTable object.

The following table describes some of the most useful DataView methods.

METHOD	PURPOSE
AddNew	Adds a new row to the underlying DataTable.
Delete	Deletes the row with a specific index from the underlying DataTable.
Find	Returns the index of a row that matches the view's sort key columns. This method returns −1 if no row matches the values it is passed.
FindRows	Returns an array of DataRowView objects representing rows that match the view's sort key columns.

The DataView object's Sort property determines not only the fields by which the data is sorted but also the key fields used by the Find method. The following code makes the dv_name DataView sort by FirstName and LastName. It then uses the Find method to display the index of a row with FirstName = Hil and LastName = Harris.

```
dv_name.Sort = "FirstName, LastName"
MessageBox.Show(dv_name.Find(New String() {"Hil", "Harris"}).ToString)
```

DATAROWVIEW

A DataRow object can hold data for more than one state. For example, if a DataTable row has been modified, its DataRow object contains the row's original data and the modified values.

A DataRowView object represents a view of a DataRow object in a particular state. That state can be Current (the current value), Default (if columns have defined default values), Original (the original values), or Proposed (new values during an edit before EndEdit or CancelEdit is called).

A DataView object holds DataRowView objects representing a view of a DataTable selecting particular rows in a particular state.

The DataRowView object's purpose is to represent a row in a specific state so this object is relatively simple. It basically indicates the chosen state and refers to a DataRow.

The following table describes the DataRowView object's most useful properties.

PROPERTY	PURPOSE
DataView	The DataView that contains the DataRowView.
IsEdit	Returns True if the row is in editing mode.
IsNew	Returns True if the row is new.
Item	Gets or sets the value of one of the row's fields.
Row	The DataRow object that this DataRowView represents.
RowVersion	The version of the DataRow represented by this object (Current, Default, Original, or Proposed).

SIMPLE DATA BINDING

Binding a simple property such as Text to a data source is relatively easy. First, create a DataSet, DataTable, or DataView to act as the data source. You can create this object at design time using controls or at run time using object variables.

If you build the data source at design time, you can also bind the property at design time. Select the control that you want to bind and open the Properties window. Expand the (DataBindings) entry and find the property that you want to bind (for example, Text). Click the drop-down arrow on the right, and use the pop-up display to select the data source item that you want to bind to the property.

Figure 19-15 shows the pop-up binding the txtTitle control's Text property to the dsBooks DataSet object's Books table's Title field.

At run time, your code can bind a simple property to a data source by using the control's DataBindings collection. This collection's Add method takes as parameters the name of the property to bind, the data source, and the name of the item in the data source to bind.

The following statement binds the txtUrl control's Text property to the dsBooks DataSet object's Books table's URL field:

FIGURE 19-15: You can bind a simple control property to a data source at design time.

```
txtUrl.DataBindings.Add("Text", dsBooks.Books, "URL")
```

BINDING BASICS

When you bind the first property, Visual Basic adds a BindingSource to the form. You can reuse this BindingSource to bind other properties. When you open the drop-down shown in Figure 19-15, expand the existing BindingSource to reuse it rather than create a new one.

That's all there is to binding simple properties. By itself, however, this binding doesn't provide any form of navigation. If you were to bind the Text properties of a bunch of TextBox controls and run the program, you would see the data for the data source's first record and nothing else. To allow the user to navigate through the data source, you must use a CurrencyManager object.

CURRENCYMANAGER

Some controls such as the DataGrid control provide their own forms of navigation. If you bind a DataGrid to a DataSet, it allows the user to examine the DataSet object's tables, view and edit data, and follow links between the tables. The DataGrid provides its own methods for navigating through the data. For simpler controls, such as the TextBox, which can display only one data value at a time, you must provide some means for the program to navigate through the data source's records.

A data source manages its position within its data by using a CurrencyManager object. The CurrencyManager supervises the list of Binding objects that bind the data source to controls such as TextBoxes.

> **NOTE** *The name CurrencyManager has nothing to do with money. Here "currency" refers to the current record, not cash.*

The following table describes the CurrencyManager object's most useful properties.

PROPERTY	PURPOSE
Bindings	A collection of the bindings that the object manages.
Count	Returns the number of rows associated with the CurrencyManager.
Current	Returns a reference to the current data object (row).
List	Returns an object that implements the IList interface that provides the data for the CurrencyManager. For example, if the data source is a DataSet or DataTable, this object is a DataView.
Position	Gets or sets the current position within the data. For example, in a DataTable this is the row number.

The CurrencyManager also provides some methods for manipulating the data. The following table describes the CurrencyManager object's most useful methods.

METHOD	PURPOSE
AddNew	Adds a new item to the data source
CancelCurrentEdit	Cancels the current editing operation
EndCurrentEdit	Ends the current editing operation, accepting any changes
Refresh	Refills the bound controls
RemoveAt	Removes the data source item at a specified index

The CurrencyManager class raises a PositionChanged event when its position in the data changes.

Example program BindSimple, which is available for download on the book's website, uses the following code to navigate through a DataSet:

```
Public Class Form1
    Private WithEvents MyCurrencyManager As CurrencyManager

    Private Sub Form1_Load() Handles MyBase.Load
        Me.BooksTableAdapter.Fill(Me.BooksDataSet.Books)

        ' Get the CurrencyManager.
        MyCurrencyManager = DirectCast(Me.BindingContext(
            BooksBindingSource), CurrencyManager)

        ' Display the record number.
        MyCurrencyManager_PositionChanged()
    End Sub

    ' Move to the previous record.
    Private Sub btnPrev_Click() Handles btnPrev.Click
        If MyCurrencyManager.Position = 0 Then
            Beep()
        Else
            MyCurrencyManager.Position -= 1
        End If
    End Sub

    ' Move to the next record.
    Private Sub btnNext_Click() Handles btnNext.Click
        If MyCurrencyManager.Position >= MyCurrencyManager.Count - 1 Then
            Beep()
        Else
            MyCurrencyManager.Position += 1
        End If
    End Sub

    ' Go to the first record.
    Private Sub btnFirst_Click() Handles btnFirst.Click
        MyCurrencyManager.Position = 0
    End Sub

    ' Go to the last record.
    Private Sub btnLast_Click() Handles btnLast.Click
        MyCurrencyManager.Position = MyCurrencyManager.Count - 1
    End Sub

    Private Sub MyCurrencyManager_PositionChanged() _
    Handles MyCurrencyManager.PositionChanged
        lblPosition.Text =
            (MyCurrencyManager.Position + 1) & " of " & MyCurrencyManager.Count
    End Sub

    ' Add a record.
```

```
Private Sub btnAdd_Click() Handles btnAdd.Click
    MyCurrencyManager.AddNew()
    txtTitle.Focus()
End Sub

' Delete the current record.
Private Sub btnDelete_Click() Handles btnDelete.Click
    If MessageBox.Show("Are you sure you want to remove this record?",
        "Confirm?", MessageBoxButtons.YesNo, MessageBoxIcon.Question) =
        Windows.Forms.DialogResult.Yes _
    Then
        MyCurrencyManager.RemoveAt(MyCurrencyManager.Position)
    End If
End Sub
End Class
```

When the form loads, the program fills its data set and saves a reference to a CurrencyManager object that controls the data set's Books table. It then calls subroutine MyCurrency Manager_PositionChanged to display the current record's index (this is described shortly).

The first, last, previous, and next record buttons all work by changing the CurrencyManager's Position property. For example, the previous record button's event handler checks whether the current position is greater than zero, and if it is the code decreases the position by one.

Similarly, the next record button increases the current position by one if the CurrencyManager is not already displaying the last record.

The first and last record buttons set the position to the indexes of the first and last records, respectively.

Whenever the CurrencyManager's position changes, its PositionChanged event handler executes. This code displays the current record's index in a label for the user to see.

When the user clicks the add record button, the code calls the CurrencyManager's AddNew method to make a new record. It also sets focus to the first text box to make filling in the new record easier.

Finally, when the user clicks the delete record button, the code confirms the deletion and then calls the CurrencyManager's RemoveAt method to delete the record.

FIGURE 19-16: This program's buttons use a CurrencyManager to let the user add, delete, and navigate through a table's records.

Figure 19-16 shows the BindSimple program in action.

Example program BindSimpleMemoryDataSet, which is available for download on the book's website, is similar to program BindSimple except it uses a DataSet built-in memory rather than one loaded from a database.

COMPLEX DATA BINDING

For some controls (such as the TextBox and Label) binding the Text property is good enough. Other controls, however, do not display a simple textual value.

For example, suppose that you have a database containing a Users table with fields FirstName, LastName, and UserType. The UserTypes table has fields UserTypeId and UserTypeName. The Users.UserType field contains a value that should match UserTypes.UserTypeId. The UserTypes .UserTypeName field contains values such as Programmer, Project Manager, Department Manager, Program Manager, and Lab Director.

When you build a form to display the Users table data, you would like to use a ComboBox to allow the user to select only the allowed choices Programmer, Project Manager, and so on. However, the Users table doesn't store those string values. Instead it stores the UserTypeId value corresponding to the UserTypeName value that the user selects. When the user picks a UserTypes.UserTypeName value, the ComboBox should look up the corresponding UserTypes.UserTypeId value and save it in the Users.UserType field.

Clearly, the simple binding strategy used for TextBoxes won't work here. Binding this control requires two rather complicated steps: defining the DataSet and binding the control. Each piece of the operation is easy, but you must do everything correctly. If you miss any detail, the ComboBox won't work, and Visual Basic's error messages probably won't give you enough information to figure out how to fix the problem.

> **NOTE** *Example program BindComboBox, which is available for download on the book's website, demonstrates this technique. You may want to download this example and copy the included database ComputerUsers.mdb into a new directory so you can follow along.*

The first step is building a data connection. Select the Data menu's Add New Data Source command. Use the Data Source Configuration Wizard to make a data source that selects both the Users and the UserTypes tables from the database.

Next, add a ComboBox named **cboUserType** to the form. In the Properties window, select the control's DataSource property and click the drop-down arrow on the right. Select the UserTypes table as shown in Figure 19-17. This tells the ComboBox where to look up values.

When you set this property, Visual Basic also adds a DataSet, BindingSource, and TableAdapter to the form. These components provide access to the UserTypes table.

FIGURE 19-17: Set the ComboBox's DataSource property to the UserTypes table.

Set the ComboBox's DisplayMember property to the field in the lookup table (specified by the DataSource property) that the control will display to the user. In this example, the field is UserTypeName.

Set the ComboBox's ValueMember property to the field in the lookup table that represents the value that the ComboBox will need to read and write from the database. In this example, that's the UserTypeId field.

That takes care of telling the ComboBox how to relate display values with IDs. Next, you need to bind the ComboBox to the field that it must read and write in the database. In this example, that's the Users table's UserType field. To simplify this binding, use the Toolbox to add a new BindingSource to the form. Change its name to UsersBindingSource and set its DataSource property to the ComputerUsersDataSet as shown in Figure 19-18. Then set the BindingSource object's DataMember property to the Users table.

The last ComboBox property you need to set is SelectedValue. Click the ComboBox, open the Properties window, and expand the (DataBindings) entry at the top. Click the drop-down arrow to the right of the SelectedValue property and select the field that the control must read and write in the database. For this example, that's the UsersBindingSource object's UserType field.

Next, create TextBox controls to display the Users table's FirstName and LastName fields. In the Properties window, open their (Data Bindings) items and set their Text properties to the UsersBindingSource object's FirstName and LastName fields.

Finally, to give the user a way to navigate through the data, add a BindingNavigator to the form. Set this component's BindingSource property to UsersBindingSource and the program is ready to run. Figure 19-19 shows the BindComboBox example program, which is available for download on the book's website, in action. (I also added a save button to the BindingNavigator and some code to save changes when the user clicks it.)

The steps for binding a ListBox control are exactly the same as those for binding a ComboBox. Example program BindListBox, which is available for download on the book's website, works much as program BindComboBox does, except it uses a ListBox instead of a ComboBox. As you move through the records, the ListBox selects the appropriate user type for each user record.

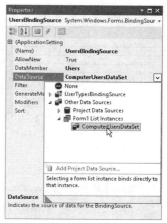

FIGURE 19-18: Set the BindingSource object's DataSource to the ComputerUsersDataSet.

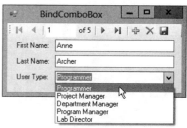

FIGURE 19-19: At run time, the ComboBox displays the field bound to its DisplayMember property while updating the field bound to its SelectedValue property.

SUMMARY

Working with databases in Visual Basic is an enormous topic. This chapter did not cover every detail of database programming, but it did explain the basics. It told how to build data sources and how to drag and drop tables and fields from the Data Sources window onto a form. It described the most important database controls and objects, such as connection, data adapter, DataSet, and DataTable objects. It also explained the fundamentals of simple and complex data binding, and using CurrencyManager objects to navigate through data.

For more information on database programming in Visual Basic .NET, see one or more books about database programming. This is a very broad field so you may want to look at several books about database design, database maintenance using your particular database (for example, Access or SQL Server), Visual Basic database programming, and so forth.

If you must build and maintain large databases, you should also read books about database management. These can tell you how to design, build, and maintain a database throughout the application's lifetime. My book *Beginning Database Design Solutions* (Rod Stephens, Wrox, 2008) explains how to analyze database needs and build a robust and efficient database design.

You should also read about the particular kinds of databases that you need to use. For example, if you are working with SQL Server databases, get a good book on using SQL Server, such as *Professional Microsoft SQL Server 2008 Programming* by Robert Viera (Wrox, 2009).

Becoming an expert database developer is a big task, but the techniques described in this chapter should at least get you started.

The controls and other objects described in this chapter let a program filter, select, and arrange data taken from a database. Chapter 20, "LINQ," explains how a program can use LINQ queries to filter, select, and arrange data taken from lists, collections, arrays, and other data structures within the program's code.

20

LINQ

WHAT'S IN THIS CHAPTER

➤ LINQ to Objects, LINQ to XML, and LINQ to ADO.NET

➤ LINQ query syntax

➤ LINQ functions and extension methods

➤ Extending LINQ

WROX.COM CODE DOWNLOADS FOR THIS CHAPTER

The wrox.com downloads for this chapter are found at http://www.wrox.com/remtitle
.cgi?isbn=9781118314074 on the Download Code tab. The code for this chapter is divided
into the following major examples:

➤ GroupByWithTotals

➤ JoinExamples

➤ LinqFunctions

➤ LinqLambda

➤ OrderByExamples

THE MANY FACES OF LINQ

LINQ (*Language Integrated Query*, pronounced "link") is a data-selection mechanism
designed to give programs the ability to select data in the same way from *any* data source.
Ideally the program would be able to use exactly the same method to fetch data whether it's
stored in arrays, lists, relational databases, XML data, Excel worksheets, or some other data
store. Currently the LINQ API supports data stored in relational databases, objects within the
program stored in arrays or lists, and XML data.

LOTS OF LINQ

This chapter covers only the default LINQ providers included with Visual Basic, but you can build providers to make LINQ work with just about anything. For a list of some third-party LINQ providers to Google, Amazon, Excel, Active Directory, and more, see `http://rshelton.com/archive/2008/07/11/list-of-linq-providers.aspx`.

Microsoft also has created a LINQ provider for SharePoint. For more information, see `http://msdn.microsoft.com/library/ee535491.aspx`.

LINQ queries often let a program make complex data selections with very little code. For example, suppose you're writing a billing program and you want to list customers with outstanding balances ordered by their balances. You could certainly use Visual Basic code to loop through a customer list to find the customers and then sort the results, but a LINQ query can find and order them in a few simple lines. The result isn't always as fast as optimized Visual Basic code but it is often much simpler for complicated queries such as this one.

LINQ provides dozens of extension methods that apply to all sorts of data-holding objects such as arrays, dictionaries, and lists. Visual Basic provides a LINQ query syntax that converts SQL-like queries into calls to the LINQ extension methods to select data.

LINQ tools are divided into the three categories summarized in the following list:

➤   *LINQ to Objects* refers to LINQ functions that interact with Visual Basic objects such as arrays, dictionaries, and lists. Most of this chapter presents examples using these kinds of objects to demonstrate LINQ concepts.

➤   *LINQ to XML* refers to LINQ features that read and write XML data. Using LINQ, you can easily move data between XML hierarchies and other Visual Basic objects.

➤   *LINQ to ADO.NET* refers to LINQ features that let you write LINQ-style queries to extract data from relational databases.

The first section in this chapter, "Introduction to LINQ," provides an intuitive introduction to LINQ. Many of the details about LINQ functions are so complex and technical that they can be hard to understand, but the basic ideas are really quite simple. The introduction gives examples that demonstrate the essential concepts to try to give you an understanding of the basics.

The section "Basic LINQ Query Syntax" describes the most useful LINQ query commands. These let you perform complex queries that select, filter, and arrange data taken from program objects. The next section, "Advanced LINQ Query Syntax," describes additional LINQ query commands.

"LINQ Functions" describes functions that are provided by LINQ but that are not supported by Visual Basic's LINQ query syntax. To use these functions, you must apply them to the arrays, dictionaries, lists, and other objects that they extend.

"LINQ Extension Methods" explains how LINQ extends objects such as arrays, dictionaries, and lists. It describes method-based queries and explains how you can write your own extensions to increase the power of method-based queries.

After describing the tools provided by LINQ, most of the rest of the chapter describes the three main categories of LINQ usage: LINQ to Objects, LINQ to XML, and LINQ to ADO.NET. The chapter finishes by describing Parallel LINQ (PLINQ).

LINQ to Objects is a bit easier to cover effectively than LINQ to XML and LINQ to ADO.NET because it doesn't require that you have any special knowledge beyond Visual Basic itself. To understand LINQ to XML properly, you need to understand XML, which is a complex topic in its own right. Similarly, to get the most out of LINQ to ADO.NET, you need to understand relational databases such as SQL Server, a huge topic about which many books have been written.

Because LINQ to Objects is easiest to cover, this chapter focuses mostly on it, and most of the examples throughout the chapter deal with LINQ to Objects. The final sections of the chapter do provide some information about LINQ to XML and LINQ to ADO.NET, however, to give you an idea of what is possible in those arenas.

INTRODUCTION TO LINQ

The LINQ API provides relatively low-level access to data in various storage formats. Visual Basic provides a higher-level layer above the LINQ API that makes querying data sources easier. This higher-level layer uses *query expressions* to define the data that should be selected from a data source. These expressions use a SQL-like syntax so they will be familiar to developers who have worked with relational databases.

For example, suppose a program defines a Customer class that provides typical customer properties such as Name, Phone, StreetAddress, AccountBalance, and so forth. Suppose also that the list all_customers holds all of the application's Customer objects. Then the following expression defines a query that selects customers with negative account balances. The results are ordered by balance in ascending order so customers with the most negative balances (who owe the most) are listed first. (Example program LinqLambda, which is available for download on the book's website, defines a simple Customer class and performs a similar query.)

```
Dim overdue_custs =
    From cust In all_customers
    Where cust.AccountBalance < 0
    Order By cust.AccountBalance Ascending
    Select cust.Name, cust.AccountBalance
```

Behind the scenes, Visual Basic transforms the query expression into calls to the LINQ API and fetches the selected data. The program can then loop through the results as shown in the following code:

```
For Each cust In overdue_custs
    Debug.WriteLine(cust.Name & ": " & cust.AccountBalance)
Next cust
```

There are a couple of interesting things to note about this code. First, the previous code fragments do not declare data types for the overdue_custs expression or the looping variable cust in the For Each loop. The data types for both of these variables are inferred automatically by Visual Basic.

If you stop the program while it is executing and use the TypeName function to see what types these variables have, you'll find that they have the following ungainly names:

```
WhereSelectEnumerableIterator`2
VB$AnonymousType_0`2
```

Because these data types have such awkward names, you don't really want to try to guess them. It's much easier to leave Option Infer on and let Visual Basic infer them for you.

In fact, as the previous code fragments show, you never even need to know what these data types are. The code can define the query without declaring its types, and the For Each loop can iterate through the results without knowing the data type of the looping variable.

Because the code doesn't need to know what these data types really are, they are called *anonymous types*.

A second interesting fact about this code is that the program doesn't actually fetch any data when the query expression is defined. It only accesses the data source (in this case the all_customers list) when the code tries to access the result in the For Each loop. Many programs don't really need to distinguish between when the expression is declared and when it is executed. For example, if the code iterates through the results right after defining the query, there isn't much difference. However, if it may be a long time between defining the query and using it or if the query takes a long time to execute, the difference may matter.

Third, if you have any experience with relational databases, you'll notice that the Select clause is in a different position from where it would be in a SQL statement. In SQL the Select clause comes first whereas in LINQ it comes at the end. This placement is due to implementation issues Microsoft encountered while implementing IntelliSense for LINQ. The concept is similar in SQL and LINQ. In both cases the Select clause tells which "fields" you want to select from the data. As long as you remember the difference in position (or let IntelliSense help you remember), it shouldn't be too confusing.

> **INTELLISENSE DEFERRED**
>
> Basically IntelliSense doesn't know what "fields" you can select until it knows what fields are available. In the preceding example, the From clause indicates that the data will be selected from all_customers, a list of Customer objects. It isn't until after the From clause that IntelliSense knows that the Select statement can pick from the Customer class's properties.

The following sections explain the most useful LINQ keywords that are supported by Visual Basic.

BASIC LINQ QUERY SYNTAX

The following text shows the typical syntax for a LINQ query:

```
From ... Where ... Order By ... Select ...
```

The following sections describe these four basic clauses. The sections after those describe some of the other most useful LINQ clauses.

From

The From clause is the only one that is required. It tells where the data comes from and defines the name by which it is known within the LINQ query. Its basic form is:

```
From query_variable In data_source
```

Here `query_variable` is a variable that you are declaring to manipulate the items selected from the `data_source`. This is similar to declaring a looping variable in a For or For Each statement.

You can supply a data type for `query_variable` if you know its type, although because of the anonymous types used by LINQ, it's often easiest to let LINQ infer the data type automatically. For example, the following query explicitly indicates that the query variable `cust` is from the Customer class:

```
Dim query = From cust As Customer In all_customers
```

The From clause can include more than one query variable and data source. In that case, the query selects data from all of the data sources. For example, the following query selects objects from the `all_customers` and `all_orders` lists:

```
Dim query = From cust In all_customers, ord In all_orders
```

This query returns the cross-product of the objects in the two lists. In other words, for every object in the `all_customers` list, the query returns that object paired with every object in the `all_orders` list. If `all_customers` contains Ann, Bob, and Cindy, and `all_orders` contains orders numbered 1, 2, 3, then the following text shows the results returned by this query:

```
Ann       Order 1
Ann       Order 2
Ann       Order 3
Bob       Order 1
Bob       Order 2
Bob       Order 3
Cindy     Order 1
Cindy     Order 2
Cindy     Order 3
```

Usually, you will want to use a Where clause to join the objects selected from the two lists. For example, if customers and orders are related by a common CustomerId property, you might use the following query to select customers together with their corresponding orders rather than all orders:

```
Dim query = From cust In all_customers, ord In all_orders
    Where cut.CustomerId = ord.CustomerId
```

If Ann, Bob, and Cindy have CustomerId values 1, 2, 3, and the three orders have the corresponding CustomerId values, the preceding query would return the following results:

```
Ann        Order 1
Bob        Order 2
Cindy      Order 3
```

Where

The Where clause applies filters to the records selected by the From clause. It can include tests involving the objects selected and properties of those objects. The last example in the preceding section shows a particularly useful kind of query that *joins* objects from two data sources that are related by common property values. Although the Where clause is often used for simple joins, it can also execute functions on the selected objects and their properties.

For example, suppose the GoodCustomer class inherits from Customer, a class that has AccountBalance and PaymentIsLate properties. Also suppose the `all_customers` list contains Customer and GoodCustomer objects.

The OwesALot function defined in the following code returns True if a Customer owes more than $50. The query that follows selects objects from `all_customers` where the object is not a GoodCustomer and has a PaymentIsLate property of True and for which function OwesALot returns True.

```
Private Function OwesALot(ByVal cust As Customer) As Boolean
    Return cust.AccountBalance < -50
End Function

Dim query = From cust In all_customers
    Where Not (TypeOf cust Is GoodCustomer) _
        AndAlso cust.PaymentIsLate _
        AndAlso OwesALot(cust)
```

The Where clause can include just about any Boolean expression, usually involving the selected objects and their properties. As the preceding example shows, it can include Not, Is, AndAlso, and function calls. It can also include And, Or, OrElse, Mod, and Like.

Expressions can use any of the arithmetic, date, string, or other comparison operators. The following query selects Order objects from `all_orderitems` where the OrderDate property is after April 5, 2012:

```
Dim query = From ord In all_orders
    Where ord.OrderDate > #4/5/2012#
```

Order By

The Order By clause makes a query sort the objects selected according to one or more values. Usually the values are properties of the objects selected. For example, the following query selects Customer objects from the `all_customers` list and sorts them by their LastName and FirstName properties:

```
Dim query = From cust In all_customers
    Order By cust.LastName, cust.FirstName
```

In this example, customers are sorted first by last name. If two customers have the same last name, they are sorted by first name.

An Order By clause can also sort objects based on calculated values. For example, suppose some customers' names are surrounded by parentheses. Because "(" comes alphabetically before letters, those customers would normally end up at the beginning of the sorted list. The following query uses a String class's Replace method to remove parentheses from the values used in sorting so all names are positioned in the list as if they did not contain parentheses:

```
Dim query = From cust In all_customers
    Order By cust.LastName.Replace("(", "").Replace(")", ""),
        cust.FirstName.Replace("(", "").Replace(")", "")
```

Note that the values used for ordering results are not the values selected by the query. The two preceding queries do not specify what results they select so LINQ takes its default action and selects the Customer objects in the `all_customers` list. See the next section, "Select," for information on determining the values that the query selects.

To arrange items in descending order, simply add the keyword Descending after an ordering expression. Each expression can have its own Descending keyword so you can arrange them independently.

Select

The Select clause lists the fields that the query should select into its result. This can be an entire record taken from a data source or it can be one or more fields taken from the data sources. It can include the results of functions and calculations on the fields. It can even include more complicated results such as the results of nested queries.

You can add an alias to any of the items that the query selects. This is particularly useful for calculated results.

The following query selects objects from `all_customers`. It gives the first selected field the alias Name. That field's value is the customer's first and last name separated by a space. The query also selects the customer's AccountBalance property, giving it the alias Balance.

```
Dim query = From cust In all_customers
    Select Name = cust.FirstName & " " & cust.LastName,
        Balance = Cust.AccountBalance
```

The result of the query is an IEnumerable that contains objects of an anonymous type that holds two fields: Name and Balance. The following code shows how you might display the results:

```
For obj In query
    Debug.WriteLine(obj.Name & " " & FormatCurrency(obj.Balance))
Next obj
```

You can also use the New keyword to create objects of an anonymous type. The following query builds a result similar to the earlier query but uses New:

```
Dim query = From cust In all_customers
    Select New With
    {
        .Name = cust.FirstName & " " & cust.LastName,
        .Balance = Cust.AccountBalance
    }
```

This version emphasizes that you are creating new objects, but it is more verbose.

The earlier queries return objects of an anonymous type. If you like, you can define a type to hold the results and then create new objects of that type in the Select clause. For example, suppose the CustInfo class has Name and Balance properties. The following query selects the same data as the preceding query but this time saves the results in a new CustInfo object:

```
Dim query = From cust In all_customers
    Select New CustInfo With
    {
        .Name = cust.FirstName & " " & cust.LastName,
        .Balance = Cust.AccountBalance
    }
```

The result of this query contains CustInfo objects, not objects of an anonymous type. The following code shows how a program can use an explicitly typed looping variable to display these results:

```
For ci As CustInfo In query
    Debug.WriteLine(ci.Name & " " & FormatCurrency(ci.Balance))
Next ci
```

If the CustInfo class provides a constructor that takes a name and account balance as parameters, you can achieve a similar result by using the constructor instead of the With keyword. The following query provides a result similar to the preceding one:

```
Dim query = From cust In all_customers
    Select New CustInfo(
        cust.FirstName & " " & cust.LastName,
        cust.AccountBalance)
```

From all of these different kinds of examples, you can see the power of LINQ. You can also see the potential for confusion. The Select clause in particular can take a number of different forms and can return a complicated set of results.

The following example shows one of the more complicated queries that uses only basic LINQ syntax. It selects data from multiple sources, uses a common field to join them, adds a Where filter, uses multiple values to order the results, and returns the Customer and Order objects that meet its criteria.

```
Dim query = From cust In all_customers, ord In all_orders
    Where cust.CustId = ord.CustId AndAlso
```

```
         cust.AccountBalance < 0
    Order By cust.CustId, ord.OrderDate
    Select cust, ord
```

Note that the Select clause changes the scope of the variables involved in the query. Statements that come after the Select clause can only refer to items in that clause.

For example, the following query selects customer first and last names. The Order By clause comes after the Select clause so it can only refer to items included in the Select clause. This example orders the results by the LastName and FirstName fields picked by the Select clause.

```
Dim query = From cust In all_customers
    Select cust.FirstName, cust.LastName
    Order By LastName, FirstName
```

Because the original `cust` variable is not chosen by the Select clause, the Order By clause cannot refer to it.

Note also that if the Select clause gives a result an alias, then any later clause must refer to the alias. For example, the following query selects the customers' last and first names concatenated into a field known by the alias FullName so the Order By clause must use the alias FullName:

```
Dim query = From cust In all_customers
    Select FullName = cust.LastName & ", " & cust.FirstName
    Order By FullName
```

Usually, it is easiest to place Order By and other clauses before the Select clause to avoid confusion.

Using LINQ Results

A LINQ query expression returns an IEnumerable containing the query's results. A program can iterate through this result and process the items that it contains.

To determine what objects are contained in the IEnumerable result, you need to look carefully at the Select clause. If this clause chooses a simple value such as a string or integer, then the result contains those simple values.

For example, the following query selects customer first and last names concatenated into a single string. The result is a string, so the query's IEnumerable result contains strings and the For Each loop treats them as strings.

```
Dim query = From cust In all_customers
    Select cust.FirstName & " " & cust.LastName

For Each cust_name As String In query
    Debug.WriteLine(cust_name)
Next cust_name
```

Often the Select clause chooses some sort of object. The following query selects the Customer objects contained in the `all_customers` list. The result contains Customer objects, so the code can explicitly type its looping variable and treat it as a Customer.

```
Dim query = From cust In all_customers
    Select cust

For Each cust As Customer In query
    Debug.WriteLine(cust.LastName & " owes " & cust.AccountBalance)
Next cust
```

ADVANCED LINQ QUERY SYNTAX

The earlier sections described the basic LINQ commands that you might expect to use regularly, but there's much more to LINQ than these simple queries. The following sections describe some of the more advanced LINQ commands that are less intuitive and that you probably won't need to use as often.

Join

The Join keyword selects data from multiple data sources matching up corresponding fields. The following pseudo-code shows the Join command's syntax:

```
From variable1 In data source1
Join variable2 In data source2
On variable1.field1 Equals variable2.field2
```

For example, the following query selects objects from the all_customers list. For each object it finds, it also selects objects from the all_orders list where the two records have the same CustId value.

```
Dim query = From cust As Customer In all_customers
    Join ord In all_orders
    On cust.CustId Equals ord.CustId
```

A LINQ Join is similar to a SQL join except the On clause only allows you to select objects where fields are equal and the Equals keyword is required.

The following query selects a similar set of objects without using the Join keyword. Here the Where clause makes the link between the all_customers and all_orders lists:

```
Dim query = From cust As Customer In all_customers, ord In all_orders
    Where cust.CustId = ord.CustId
```

This is slightly more flexible because the Where clause can make tests that are more complicated than the Join statement's Equals clause.

The Group Join statement selects data much as a Join statement does, but it returns the results differently. The Join statement returns an IEnumerable object that holds whatever is selected by the query (the cust and ord objects in this example).

The Group Join statement returns the same objects but in a different arrangement. Each item in the IEnumerable result contains an object of the first type (cust in this example) plus another IEnumerable that holds the corresponding objects of the second type (ord in this example).

> **NOTE** *Actually, the main result is a GroupJoinIterator, but that inherits from IEnumerable, so you can treat it as such.*

For example, the following query selects customers and their corresponding orders much as the earlier examples do. The new clause `Into CustomerOrders` means the IEnumerable containing the orders for each customer should be called CustomerOrders. The `= Group` part means CustomerOrders should contain the results of the grouping.

```
Dim query =
    From cust In all_customers
        Group Join ord In all_orders
        On cust.CustId Equals ord.CustId
        Into CustomerOrders = Group
```

The following code shows how a program might display these results:

```
For Each c In query
    ' Display the customer.
    Debug.WriteLine(c.cust.ToString())

    ' Display the customer's orders.
    For Each o In c.CustomerOrders
        Debug.WriteLine(Space$(4) & "OrderId: " & o.OrderId &
            ", Date: " & o.OrderDate & vbCrLf
    Next o
Next c
```

Each item in the main IEnumerable contains a `cust` object and an IEnumerable named CustomerOrders. Each CustomerOrders object contains `ord` objects corresponding to the `cust` object.

This code loops through the query's results. Each time through the loop, it displays the `cust` object's information and then loops through its CustomerOrders, displaying each `ord` object's information indented.

Example program JoinExamples, which is available for download on the book's website, demonstrates these types of Join queries.

Group By

Like the Group Join clause, the Group By clause lets a program select data from a flat, relational style format and build a hierarchical arrangement of objects. It also returns an IEnumerable that holds objects, each containing another IEnumerable.

The following code shows the basic Group By syntax:

```
From variable1 In datasource1
Group items By value Into groupname = Group
```

Here, `items` is a list of items whose properties you want selected into the group. In other words, the properties of the `items` variables are added to the objects in the nested IEnumerable.

If you omit the `items` parameter, the query places the objects selected by the rest of the query into the nested IEnumerable.

The `value` property tells LINQ on what field to group objects. This value is also stored in the top-level IEnumerable values.

The `groupname` parameter gives a name for the group. The objects contained in the top-level IEnumerable get a property with this name that is an IEnumerable containing the grouped values.

Finally, the = Group clause indicates that the group should contain the fields selected by the query.

If this definition seems a bit confusing, an example should help. The following query selects objects from the `all_orders` list. The Group By statement makes the query group orders with the same CustId value.

```
Dim query1 = From ord In all_orders
    Order By ord.CustId, ord.OrderId
    Group ord By ord.CustId Into CustOrders = Group
```

The result is an IEnumerable that contains objects with two fields. The first field is the CustId value used to define the groups. The second field is an IEnumerable named CustOrders that contains the group of order objects for each CustId value.

The following code shows how a program might display the results in a TreeView control:

```
Dim root1 As TreeNode = trvResults.Nodes.Add("Orders grouped by CustId")
For Each obj In query1
    ' Display the customer id.
    Dim cust_node As TreeNode = root1.Nodes.Add("Cust Id: " & obj.CustId)

    ' List this customer's orders.
    For Each ord In obj.CustOrders cust_node.Nodes.Add("OrderId: " & ord.OrderId &
        ", Date: " & ord.OrderDate)
    Next ord
Next obj
```

The code loops through the top-level IEnumerable. Each time through the loop, it displays the group's CustId and then loops through the group's CustOrders IEnumerable displaying each order's ID and date.

Example program SimpleGroupBy, which is available for download on the book's website, demonstrates this type of Group By statement.

Another common type of query uses the Group By clause to apply some aggregate function to the items selected in a group. The following query selects order and order item objects, grouping each order's items and displaying each order's total price:

```
Dim query1 = From ord In all_orders, ord_item In all_order_items
    Order By ord.CustId, ord.OrderId
    Where ord.OrderId = ord_item.OrderId
    Group ord_item By ord Into
        TotalPrice = Sum(ord_item.Quantity * ord_item.UnitPrice),
        OrderItems = Group
```

The query selects objects from the `all_orders` and `all_order_items` lists using a Where clause to join them.

The `Group ord_item` piece places the fields of the `ord_item` object in the group. The `By ord` piece makes each group hold items for a particular `ord` object.

The Into clause selects two values. The first is a sum over all of the group's `ord_item` objects adding up the `ord_items`' Quantity times UnitPrice fields. The second value selected is the group named OrderItems.

The following code shows how a program might display the results in a TreeView control named `trvResults`:

```
Dim root1 As TreeNode = trvResults.Nodes.Add("Orders")
For Each obj In query1
    ' Display the order id.
    Dim cust_node As TreeNode =
        root1.Nodes.Add("Order Id: " & obj.ord.OrderId &
            ", Total Price: " & FormatCurrency(obj.TotalPrice))
    ' List this order's items.
    For Each ord_item In obj.OrderItems
        cust_node.Nodes.Add(ord_item.Description & ": " &
            ord_item.Quantity & " @ " & FormatCurrency(ord_item.UnitPrice))
    Next ord_item
Next obj
```

Each loop through the query results represents an order. For each order, the program creates a tree node showing the order's ID and the TotalPrice value that the query calculated for it.

Next, the code loops through the order's items stored in the OrderItems group. For each item, it creates a tree node showing the item's Description, Quantity, and TotalPrice fields.

Example program GroupByWithTotals, which is available for download on the book's website, demonstrates this Group By statement.

Aggregate Functions

The preceding section explained how a Group By query can use the Sum aggregate function. LINQ also supports the reasonably self-explanatory aggregate functions Average, Count, LongCount, Max, and Min.

The following query selects order objects and their corresponding order items. It uses a Group By clause to calculate aggregates for each of the orders' items.

```
Dim query1 = From ord In all_orders, ord_item In all_order_items
    Order By ord.CustId, ord.OrderId
    Where ord.OrderId = ord_item.OrderId
    Group ord_item By ord Into
        TheAverage = Average(ord_item.UnitPrice * ord_item.Quantity),
        TheCount = Count(ord_item.UnitPrice * ord_item.Quantity),
        TheLongCount = LongCount(ord_item.UnitPrice * ord_item.Quantity),
        TheMax = Max(ord_item.UnitPrice * ord_item.Quantity),
        TheMin = Min(ord_item.UnitPrice * ord_item.Quantity),
        TheSum = Sum(ord_item.Quantity * ord_item.UnitPrice)
```

The following code loops through the query's results and adds each order's aggregate values to a string named txt. It displays the final results in a text box named txtResults.

```
For Each obj In query1
    ' Display the order info.
    txt &= "Order " & obj.ord.OrderId &
        ", Average: " & obj.TheAverage &
        ", Count: " & obj.TheCount &
        ", LongCount: " & obj.TheLongCount &
        ", Max: " & obj.TheMax &
        ", Min: " & obj.TheMin &
        ", Sum: " & obj.TheSum &
        vbCrLf
Next obj
txtResults.Text = txt
```

Set Operations

If you add the Distinct keyword to a query, LINQ keeps only one instance of each value selected. For example, the following query returns a list of IDs for customers who placed an order before 4/15/2012:

```
Dim query = From ord In all_orders
    Where ord.OrderDate < #4/15/2012#
    Select ord.CustId
    Distinct
```

The code examines objects in the all_orders list with OrderDate fields before 4/15/2012. It selects those objects' CustId fields and uses the Distinct keyword to remove duplicates. If a particular customer placed several orders before 4/15/2012, this query lists that customer's ID only once.

LINQ also provides Union, Intersection, and Except extension methods, but they are not supported by Visual Basic's LINQ syntax. See the section "LINQ Functions" later in this chapter for more information.

Example program SetExamples, which is available for download on the book's website, demonstrates these set operations.

Limiting Results

LINQ includes several keywords for limiting the results returned by a query.

➤ *Take* makes the query keep a specified number of results and discard the rest.

➤ *Take While* makes the query keep selected results as long as some condition holds and then discard the rest.

➤ *Skip* makes the query discard a specified number of results and keep the rest.

➤ *Skip While* makes the query discard selected results as long as some condition holds and then keep the rest.

The following code demonstrates each of these commands:

```
Dim q1 = From cust In all_customers Take 5
Dim q2 = From cust In all_customers Take While cust.FirstName.Contains("n")
Dim q3 = From cust In all_customers Skip 3
Dim q4 = From cust In all_customers Skip While cust.FirstName.Contains("n")
```

The first query selects the first five customers and ignores the rest.

The second query selects customers as long as the FirstName field contains the letter "n." It then discards any remaining results, even if a later customer's FirstName contains an "n."

The third query discards the first three customers and then selects the rest.

The final query skips customers as long as their FirstName values contain the letter "n" and then keeps the rest.

Example program LimitingExamples, which is available for download on the book's website, demonstrates these commands.

LINQ FUNCTIONS

LINQ provides several functions (implemented as extension methods) that are not supported by Visual Basic's LINQ syntax. Though you cannot use these in LINQ queries, you can apply them to the results of queries to perform useful operations.

For example, the following code defines a query that looks for customers named Rod Stephens. It then applies the FirstOrDefault extension method to the query to return either the first object selected by the query or Nothing if the query selects no objects.

```
Dim rod_query = From cust In all_customers
    Where cust.LastName = "Stephens" AndAlso cust.FirstName = "Rod"
Dim rod As Person = rod_query.FirstOrDefault()
```

The following list describes some of the more useful of these extension methods:

➤ **Aggregate** — Uses a function specified by the code to calculate a custom aggregate.

➤ **Concat** — Concatenates two sequences into a new sequence.

➤ **Contains** — Determines whether the result contains a specific value.

➤ **DefaultIfEmpty** — If the query's result is not empty, returns the result. If the result is empty, returns an IEnumerable containing a default value. Optionally can also specify the default value (for example, a new object rather than Nothing) to use if the query's result is empty.

➤ **ElementAt** — Returns an element at a specific position in the query's result. If there is no element at that position, it throws an exception.

➤ **ElementAtOrDefault** — Returns an element at a specific position in the query's result. If there is no element at that position, it returns a default value for the data type.

➤ **Empty** — Creates an empty IEnumerable.

➤ **Except** — Returns the items in one IEnumerable that are not in a second IEnumerable.

➤ **First** — Returns the first item in the query's result. If the query contains no results, it throws an exception.

➤ **FirstOrDefault** — Returns the first item in the query's result. If the query contains no results, it returns a default value for the data type.

➤ **Intersection** — Returns the intersection of two IEnumerable objects. In other words, it returns an IEnumerable containing items that are in both of the original IEnumerable objects.

➤ **Last** — Returns the last item in the query's result. If the query contains no results, it throws an exception.

➤ **LastOrDefault** — Returns the last item in the query's result. If the query contains no results, it returns a default value for the data type.

➤ **Range** — Creates an IEnumerable containing a range of integer values.

➤ **Repeat** — Creates an IEnumerable containing a value of a given type repeated a specific number of times.

➤ **SequenceEqual** — Returns True if two sequences are identical.

➤ **Single** — Returns the single item selected by the query. If the query does not contain exactly one result, it throws an exception.

➤ **SingleOrDefault** — Returns the single item selected by the query. If the query contains no results, it returns a default value for the data type. If the query contains more than one item, it throws an exception.

➤ **Union** — Returns the union of two IEnumerable objects. In other words, it returns an IEnumerable containing items that are in either of the original IEnumerable objects.

Example program FunctionExamples, which is available for download on the book's website, demonstrates most of these functions. Example program SetExamples demonstrates Except, Intersection, and Union.

LINQ also provides functions that convert results into new data types. The following list describes these methods:

➤ **AsEnumerable** — Converts the result into a typed IEnumerable(Of T).

➤ **AsQueryable** — Converts an IEnumerable into an IQueryable.

➤ **OfType** — Removes items that cannot be cast into a specific type.

➤ **ToArray** — Places the results in an array.

➤ **ToDictionary** — Places the results in a Dictionary using a selector function to set each item's key.

➤ **ToList** — Converts the result into a List(Of T).

➤ **ToLookup** — Places the results in a Lookup (one-to-many dictionary) using a selector function to set each item's key.

Note that the ToArray, ToDictionary, ToList, and ToLookup functions force the query to execute immediately instead of waiting until the program accesses the results.

LINQ EXTENSION METHODS

Visual Basic doesn't *really* execute LINQ queries. Instead it converts them into a series of function calls (provided by extension methods) that perform the query. Though the LINQ query syntax is generally easier to use, it is sometimes helpful to understand what those function calls look like.

The following sections explain the general form of these function calls. They explain how the function calls are built, how you can use these functions directly in your code, and how you can extend LINQ to add your own LINQ query methods.

Method-Based Queries

Suppose a program defines a List(Of Customer) named `all_customers` and then defines the following query expression:

```
Dim q1 =
    From cust In all_customers
    Where cust.AccountBalance < 0
    Order By cust.AccountBalance
    Select cust.Name, cust.AccountBalance
```

This query finds customers that have AccountBalance values less than zero, orders them by AccountBalance, and returns an IEnumerable object that can enumerate their names and balances. (Example program `LinqLambda`, which is available for download on the book's website, defines a simple Customer class and performs a similar query.)

To perform this selection, Visual Basic converts the query into a series of function calls to form a *method-based query* that performs the same tasks as the original query. For example, the following method-based query returns roughly the same results as the original LINQ query:

```
Dim q2 = all_customers.
    Where(AddressOf OwesMoney).
    OrderBy(AddressOf OrderByAmount).
    Select(AddressOf SelectFields)
```

This code calls the `all_customers` list's Where method. It passes that method the address of the function OqesMoney, which returns True if a Customer object has a negative account balance.

The code then calls the OrderBy method of the result returned by Where. It passes the OrderBy method the address of the function OrderByAmount, which returns a Decimal value that OrderBy can use to order the results of Where.

Finally, the code calls the Select method of the result returned by OrderBy. It passes Select the address of a function that returns a CustInfo object representing each of the selected Customer objects. The CustInfo class contains the Customer's Name and AccountBalance values.

The exact series of method calls generated by Visual Studio to evaluate the LINQ query is somewhat different from the one shown here. The version shown here uses the OwesMoney, OrderByAmount, and SelectFields methods that I defined in the program to help pick, order, and select data. The method-based query generated by Visual Basic uses automatically generated anonymous types and lambda expressions, so it is much uglier.

The following code shows the OwesMoney, OrderByAmount, and SelectFields methods:

```
Private Function OwesMoney(ByVal c As Customer) As Boolean
    Return c.AccountBalance < 0
End Function

Private Function OrderByAmount(ByVal c As Customer) As Decimal
    Return c.AccountBalance
End Function

Private Function SelectFields(ByVal c As Customer, ByVal index As Integer) _
 As CustInfo
    Return New CustInfo() With
    {
        .CustName = c.Name, .Balance = c.AccountBalance
    }
End Function
```

Function OwesMoney simply returns True if a Customer's balance is less than zero. The Where method calls OwesMoney to see if it should pick a particular Customer for output.

Function OrderByAmount returns a Customer's balance. The OrderBy method calls OrderByAmount to order Customer objects.

Function SelectFields returns a CustInfo object representing a Customer.

That explains where the functions passed as parameters come from, but what are Where, OrderBy, and Select? After all, Where is called as if it were a method provided by the `all_customers` object. But `all_customers` is a List(Of Customer) and that has no such method.

In fact, Where is an extension method added to the IEnumerable interface by the LINQ library. The generic List class implements IEnumerable so it gains the Where extension method.

Similarly, LINQ adds other extension methods to the IEnumerable interface including Any, All, Average, Count, Distinct, First, GroupBy, OfType, Repeat, Sum, Union, and many more.

Method-Based Queries with Lambda Functions

Lambda functions, or anonymous functions, make building method-based queries somewhat easier. When you use lambda functions, you don't need to define separate functions to pass as parameters to LINQ methods such as Where, OrderBy, and Select. Instead, you can pass a lambda function directly into the method.

The following code shows a revised version of the previous method-based query. Here the method bodies have been included as lambda functions.

```
Dim q3 = all_customers.
    Where(Function(c As Customer) c.AccountBalance < 0).
    OrderBy(Of Decimal)(Function(c As Customer) c.AccountBalance).
    Select(Of CustInfo)(Function(c As Customer, index As Integer) _
        New CustInfo() With
        {
            .CustName = c.Name, .Balance = c.AccountBalance
        }
    )
```

Although this is more concise, not requiring you to build separate functions, it can also be a lot harder to read and understand. Passing a simple lambda function to the Where or OrderBy method may not be too confusing, but if you need to use a very complex function you may be better off making it a separate routine.

The following code shows a reasonable compromise. This code defines three lambda functions but saves them in delegate variables. It then uses the variables in the calls to the LINQ functions. This version is more concise than the original version and doesn't require separate functions, but it is easier to read than the preceding version, which uses purely inline lambda functions.

```
' Query with LINQ and inline function delegates.
Dim owes_money = Function(c As Customer) c.AccountBalance < 0
Dim cust_balance = Function(c As Customer) c.AccountBalance
Dim new_custinfo = Function(c As Customer) New CustInfo() With
    {.Name = c.Name, .Balance = c.AccountBalance}
Dim q4 = all_customers.
    Where(owes_money).
    OrderBy(Of Decimal)(cust_balance).
    Select(Of CustInfo)(new_custinfo)
```

Note that LINQ cannot always infer a lambda function's type exactly, so sometimes you need to give it some hints. The Of Decimal and Of CustInfo clauses in this code tell LINQ the data types returned by the `cust_balance` and `new_custinfo` functions.

> **HIDDEN GENERICS**
>
> The Of Decimal and Of CustInfo clauses use generic versions of the OrderBy and Select functions. Generics let a function take a data type as a parameter, allowing it to work more closely with objects of that type. For more information on generics, see Chapter 26, "Generics," or http://msdn.microsoft.com/w256ka79.aspx.

Instead of using these clauses, you could define the functions' return types in their declarations. The Func delegate types defined in the System namespace let you explicitly define parameters and return types for functions taking between zero and four parameters. For example, the following code shows how you might define the cust_balance function, indicating that it takes a Customer as a parameter and returns a Decimal:

```
Dim cust_balance As Func(Of Customer, Decimal) =
    Function(c As Customer) c.AccountBalance
```

If you use this version of cust_balance, you can leave out the Of Decimal clause in the previous query.

No matter which version of the method-based queries you use, the standard LINQ query syntax is usually easier to understand, so you may prefer to use that version whenever possible. Unfortunately, many references describe the LINQ extension methods as if you are going to use them in method-based queries rather than in LINQ queries. For example, the description of the OrderBy method at http://msdn.microsoft.com/library/bb534966.aspx includes the following definition:

```
<ExtensionAttribute()>
Public Shared Function OrderBy(Of TSource, TKey)( _
    source As IEnumerable(Of TSource), _
    key_selector As Func(Of TSource, TKey) _
) As IOrderedEnumerable(Of TSource)
```

Here, ExtensionAttribute indicates that this is a function that extends another class. The type of the first parameter, in this case the parameter source has type IEnumerable(Of TSource), gives the class that this method extends. The other parameters are passed to this method. In other words, this code allows you to call the OrderBy function for an object of type IEnumerable(Of TSource), passing it a key_selector of type Func(Of TSource, TKey). Confusing enough for you? For more information on extension methods, see the section "Extension Methods" in Chapter 16, "Subroutines and Functions."

This online description of how the method's parameters work is technically correct but may be a bit too esoteric to be intuitive. It may be easier to understand if you consider a concrete example.

If you look closely at the examples in the preceding section, you can see how this definition matches up with the use of the OrderBy method and the OrderByAmount function. In those examples, TSource corresponds to the Customer class and TKey corresponds to the Decimal type. In the definition of OrderBy shown here, the source parameter has type IEnumerable(Of Customer). The key_selector parameter is the OrderByAmount function, which takes a Customer (TSource) parameter and returns a Decimal (TKey). The OrderBy method itself returns an IEnumerable(Customer), corresponding to IEnumerable(TSource).

It all works but it's a mess. The following syntax is much more intuitive:

```
Order By <value1> [Ascending/Descending],
        <value2> [Ascending/Descending],
    ...
```

Generally, you should try to use the LINQ query syntax whenever possible, so most of the rest of this chapter assumes you will do so and describes LINQ methods in this manner rather than with confusing method specifications.

One time when you cannot easily use this type of syntax specification is when you want to extend the results of a LINQ query to add new features. The following section explains how you can write extension methods to provide new features for LINQ results.

Extending LINQ

LINQ queries return some sort of IEnumerable object. (Actually they return some sort of SelectIterator creature but the result implements IEnumerable.) The items in the result may be simple types such as Customer objects or strings, or they may be of some bizarre anonymous type that groups several selected fields together, but whatever the items are, the result is some sort of IEnumerable.

Because the result is an IEnumerable, you can add new methods to the result by creating extension methods for IEnumerable.

For example, the following code defines a standard deviation function. It extends the IEnumerable(Of Decimal) interface so the method applies to the results of a LINQ query that fetches Decimal values.

```
' Return the standard deviation of
' the values in an IEnumerable(Of Decimal).
<Extension()>
Public Function StdDev(source As IEnumerable(Of Decimal)) As Decimal
    ' Get the total.
    Dim total As Decimal = 0
    For Each value As Decimal In source
        total += value
    Next value

    ' Calculate the mean.
    Dim mean As Decimal = total / source.Count

    ' Calculate the sums of the deviations squared.
    Dim total_devs As Decimal = 0
    For Each value As Decimal In source
        Dim dev As Decimal = value - mean
        total_devs += dev * dev
    Next value

    ' Return the standard deviation.
    Return Math.Sqrt(total_devs / (source.Count - 1))
End Function
```

NON-STANDARD STANDARDS

There are a couple of different definitions for standard deviation. This topic is outside the scope of this book so it isn't explored here. For more information, see http://mathworld.wolfram.com/StandardDeviation.html.

Now, the program can apply this method to the result of a LINQ query that selects Decimal values. The following code uses a LINQ query to select AccountBalance values from the `all_customers` list where the AccountBalance is less than zero. It then calls the query's StdDev extension method and displays the result.

```
Dim bal_due =
    From cust In all_customers
    Where cust.AccountBalance < 0
    Select cust.AccountBalance
MessageBox.Show(bal_due.StdDev())
```

The following code performs the same operations without storing the query in an intermediate variable:

```
MessageBox.Show(
    (From cust In all_customers
     Where cust.AccountBalance < 0
     Select cust.AccountBalance).StdDev())
```

Similarly, you can make other extension methods for IEnumerable to perform other calculations on the results of LINQ queries.

The following version of the StdDev extension method extends IEnumerable(Of T). To process an IEnumerable(Of T), this version also takes as a parameter a selector function that returns a Decimal value for each of the objects in the IEnumerable(Of T).

```
<Extension()>
Public Function StdDev(Of T)( source As IEnumerable(Of T),
 selector As Func(Of T, Decimal)) As Decimal
    ' Get the total.
    Dim total As Decimal = 0
    For Each value As T In source
        total += selector(value)
    Next value

    ' Calculate the mean.
    Dim mean As Decimal = total / source.Count

    ' Calculate the sums of the deviations squared.
    Dim total_devs As Decimal = 0
    For Each value As T In source
        Dim dev As Decimal = selector(value) - mean
        total_devs += dev * dev
    Next value
```

```
    ' Return the standard deviation.
    Return Math.Sqrt(total_devs / (source.Count - 1))
End Function
```

For example, if a LINQ query selects Customer objects, the result implements IEnumerable (Of Customer). In that case, the selector function should take as a parameter a Customer object and it should return a Decimal. The following code shows a simple selector function that returns a Customer's AccountBalance:

```
Private Function TotalBalance(ByVal c As Customer) As Decimal
    Return c.AccountBalance
End Function
```

The following code shows how a program can use this version of StdDev with this selector function. The LINQ query selects Customer objects with AccountBalance values less than zero. The code then calls the query's StdDev method, passing it the address of the selector function. The new version of StdDev uses the selector to calculate the standard deviation of the selected Customer objects' AccountBalance values, and then the code displays the result.

```
Dim stddev_due =
    From cust In all_customers
    Where cust.AccountBalance < 0
    Select cust
Dim result As Decimal = stddev_due.StdDev(AddressOf TotalBalance)
MessageBox.Show(result)
```

LINQ TO OBJECTS

LINQ to Objects refers to methods that let a program extract data from objects that are extended by LINQ extension methods. These methods extend IEnumerable(Of T) so that they apply to any class that implements IEnumerable(Of T) including Dictionary(Of T), HashSet(Of T), LinkedList (Of T), Queue(Of T), SortedDictionary(Of T), SortedList(Of T), Stack(Of T), and others.

For example, the following code searches the all_customers list for customers with negative account balances. It orders them by account balance and returns their names and balances.

```
Dim overdue_custs =
    From cust In all_customers
    Where cust.AccountBalance < 0
    Order By cust.AccountBalance Ascending
    Select cust.Name, cust.AccountBalance
```

The result of this query is an IEnumerable object that the program can iterate through to take action for the selected customers.

All of the examples shown previously in this chapter use LINQ to Objects, so this section says no more about them. See the previous sections for more information and examples.

LINQ TO XML

LINQ to XML refers to methods that let a program move data between XML objects and other data-containing objects. For example, using LINQ to XML you can select customer data and use it to build an XML document.

LINQ provides a new selection of XML elements. These classes contained in the System.Xml .Linq namespace correspond to the classes in the System.Xml namespace. The names of the new classes begin with "X" instead of "Xml." For example, the LINQ class representing an element is XElement whereas the System.Xml class is XmlElement.

The LINQ versions of the XML classes provide many of the same features as the System.Xml versions, but they also provide support for new LINQ features.

The following section describes one of the most visible features of the LINQ XML classes: XML literals. The two sections after that introduce methods for using LINQ to move data into and out of XML objects.

XML Literals

In addition to features similar to those provided by the System.Xml classes, the System.Xml.Linq classes provide new LINQ-oriented features. One of the most visible of those features is the ability to use XML literal values. For example, the following code creates an XDocument object that contains three Customer elements:

```
Dim xml_literal As XElement =
    <AllCustomers>
        <Customer FirstName="Ann" LastName="Archer">100.00</Customer>
        <Customer FirstName="Ben" LastName="Best">-24.54</Customer>
        <Customer FirstName="Carly" LastName="Cant">62.40</Customer>
    </AllCustomers>
```

Visual Basic LINQ translates this literal into an XML object hierarchy holding a root element named AllCustomers that contains three Customer elements. Each Customer element has two attributes, FirstName and LastName.

To build the same hierarchy using System.Xml objects would take a lot more work. The CustomersToXml example program, which is available for download on the book's website, includes a System.Xml version in addition to the previous LINQ literal version. The System.Xml version takes 26 lines of code and is much harder to read than the LINQ literal version.

Other LINQ XML classes such as XDocument, XComment, XCdata, and XProcessingInstruction also have literal formats, although usually it's easier to use an XElement instead of an XDocument, and the others are usually contained in an XElement or XDocument.

The Visual Basic code editor also provides some extra enhancements to make writing XML literals easier. For example, if you type a new XML tag, when you type the closing ">" character the editor automatically adds a corresponding closing tag. If you type "<Customer>" the editor adds the "</Customer>" tag. Later if you change a tag's name, the code editor automatically changes the corresponding closing tag.

Together these LINQ XML literal tools make building hard-coded XML data much easier than it is using the System.Xml objects.

LINQ into XML

To select data into XML objects, you can use syntax similar to the syntax you use to build an XML literal. You then add the special characters <%= ... %> to indicate a "hole" within the literal. Inside the hole, you replace the ellipsis with a LINQ query that extracts data from Visual Basic objects and uses them to build new XML objects.

For example, suppose the `all_customers` list contains Customer objects. The following code builds an XElement object that contains Customer XML elements for all of the Customer objects:

```
Dim x_all As XElement = _
    <AllCustomers>
        <%= From cust In all_customers
            Select New XElement("Customer",
            New XAttribute("FirstName", cust.FirstName),
            New XAttribute("LastName", cust.LastName),
            New XText(cust.Balance.ToString("0.00")))
        %>
    </AllCustomers>
```

The following text shows a sample of the resulting XML element:

```
<AllCustomers>
  <Customer FirstName="Ann" LastName="Archer">100.00</Customer>
  <Customer FirstName="Ben" LastName="Best">-24.54</Customer>
  <Customer FirstName="Carly" LastName="Cant">62.40</Customer>
</AllCustomers>
```

You can have more than one hole in the XML literal. The following code uses an XML literal that contains two holes. The first uses a Where clause to select customers with non-negative balances, and the second selects customers with negative balances. It places these two groups of customers inside different sub-elements within the resulting XML.

```
' Separate customers with positive and negative balances.
Dim separated As XElement = _
    <AllCustomers>
        <PositiveBalances>
            <%= From cust In x_all.Descendants("Customer")
                Where CDec(cust.Value) >= 0
                Order By CDec(cust.Value) Descending
                Select New XElement("Customer",
                New XAttribute("FirstName",
                    CStr(cust.Attribute("FirstName"))),
                New XAttribute("LastName",
                    CStr(cust.Attribute("LastName"))),
                New XText(cust.Value))
            %>
        </PositiveBalances>
        <NegativeBalances>
```

```
        <%= From cust In x_all.Descendants("Customer")
            Where CDec(cust.Value) < 0
            Order By CDec(cust.Value) Descending
            Select New XElement("Customer",
            New XAttribute("FirstName",
                CStr(cust.Attribute("FirstName"))),
            New XAttribute("LastName",
                CStr(cust.Attribute("LastName"))),
            New XText(cust.Value))
        %>
    </NegativeBalances>
  </AllCustomers>
```

The following text shows the resulting XML element:

```
<AllCustomers>
  <PositiveBalances>
    <Customer FirstName="Dan" LastName="Dump">117.95</Customer>
    <Customer FirstName="Ann" LastName="Archer">100.00</Customer>
    <Customer FirstName="Carly" LastName="Cant">62.40</Customer>
  </PositiveBalances>
  <NegativeBalances>
    <Customer FirstName="Ben" LastName="Best">-24.54</Customer>
    <Customer FirstName="Frank" LastName="Fix">-150.90</Customer>
    <Customer FirstName="Edna" LastName="Ever">-192.75</Customer>
  </NegativeBalances>
</AllCustomers>
```

Example program LinqToXml, which is available for download on the book's website, demonstrates these XML literals containing holes.

LINQ out of XML

The LINQ XML objects provide a standard assortment of LINQ functions that make moving data from those objects into IEnumerable objects simple. Using these functions, it's about as easy to select data from the XML objects as it is from IEnumerable objects such as arrays and lists.

Because the XML objects represent special hierarchical data structures, they also provide methods to help you search those data structures. For example, the XElement object provides a Descendants function that searches the object's descendants for elements of a certain type.

The following code extracts the x_all XElement object's Customer descendants. It selects their FirstName and LastName attributes, and the balance saved as each element's value.

```
Dim select_all = From cust In x_all.Descendants("Customer")
    Order By CDec(cust.Value)
    Select FName = cust.Attribute("FirstName").Value,
           LName = cust.Attribute("LastName").Value,
           Balance = cust.Value
```

The program can now loop through the select_all object just as it can loop through any other IEnumerable selected by a LINQ query.

The following query selects only customers with a negative balance:

```
Dim x_neg = From cust In x_all.Descendants("Customer")
    Where CDec(cust.Value) < 0
    Select FName = cust.Attribute("FirstName").Value,
           LName = cust.Attribute("LastName").Value,
           Balance = cust.Value
```

Example program LinqToXml, which is available for download on the book's website, demonstrates these XML literals containing holes.

The following table describes other methods supported by XElement that a program can use to navigate through an XML hierarchy. Most of the functions return IEnumerable objects that you can then use in LINQ queries.

FUNCTION	RETURNS
Ancestors	IEnumerable containing all ancestors of the element.
AncestorsAndSelf	IEnumerable containing this element followed by all of its ancestors.
Attribute	The element's attribute with a specific name.
Attributes	IEnumerable containing the element's attributes.
Descendants	IEnumerable containing all descendants of the element.
DescendantsAndSelf	IEnumerable containing this element followed by all of its descendants.
DescendantNodes	IEnumerable containing all descendant nodes of the element. These include all nodes such as XElement and XText.
DescendantNodesAndSelf	IEnumerable containing this element followed by all of its descendant nodes.
Element	The first child element with a specific name.
Elements	IEnumerable containing the immediate children of the element.
ElementsAfterSelf	IEnumerable containing the siblings of the element that come after this element.
ElementsBeforeSelf	IEnumerable containing the siblings of the element that come before this element.
Nodes	IEnumerable containing the nodes that are immediate children of the element. These include all nodes such as XElement and XText.
NodesAfterSelf	IEnumerable containing the sibling nodes of the element that come after this element.
NodesBeforeSelf	IEnumerable containing the sibling nodes of the element that come before this element.

Most of these functions that return an IEnumerable take an optional parameter that you can use to indicate the names of the elements to select. For example, if you pass the Descendants function the parameter "Customer," the function returns only the descendants of the element that are named Customer.

Example program LinqToXmlFunctions, which is available for download on the book's website, demonstrates these XML functions.

In addition to these functions, Visual Basic's LINQ query syntax recognizes several axis selectors. In XML, an *axis* is a "direction" in which you can move from a particular node. These include such directions as the node's descendants, the node's immediate children, and the node's attributes.

The following table gives examples of shorthand expressions for node axes and their functional equivalents.

SHORTHAND	MEANING	EQUIVALENT
x...<Customer>	Descendants named Customer	x.Descendants("Customer")
x.<Child>	An element named Child that is a child of this node	x.Element("Child")
x.@<FirstName>	The value of the FirstName attribute	x.Attribute("FirstName").Value
x.@FirstName	The value of the FirstName attribute	x.Attribute("FirstName").Value

For example, consider the following XElement literal:

```
Dim x_all As XElement =
    <AllCustomers>
        <PositiveBalances>
            <Customer FirstName="Dan" LastName="Dump">117.95</Customer>
            <Customer FirstName="Ann" LastName="Archer">100.00</Customer>
            <Customer FirstName="Carly" LastName="Cant">62.40</Customer>
        </PositiveBalances>
        <NegativeBalances>
            <Customer FirstName="Ben" LastName="Best">-24.54</Customer>
            <Customer FirstName="Frank" LastName="Fix">-150.90</Customer>
            <Customer FirstName="Edna" LastName="Ever">-192.75</Customer>
        </NegativeBalances>
    </AllCustomers>
```

The following code uses axis shorthand to make several different selections:

```
' Select all Customer descendants of x_all.
Dim desc = x_all.Descendants("Customer") ' Functional version.
Dim desc2 = x_all.<Customer>              ' LINQ query version.

' Select Customer descendants of x_all where FirstName attribute is Ben.
```

```
Dim ben = From cust In x_all.Descendants("Customer")
    Where cust.@FirstName = "Ben"

' Select Customer descendants of x_all where FirstName attribute is Ann.
Dim ann = From cust In x_all.<Customer>
    Where cust.@<FirstName> = "Ann"

' Starting at x_all, go to the NegativeBalances node and find
' its descendants that are Customer elements. Select those with
' value less than -50.
Dim neg_desc2 = From cust In x_all.<NegativeBalances>...<Customer>
    Where CDec(cust.Value) < -50
```

Example program LinqAxes, which is available for download on the book's website, demonstrates these LINQ query XML axes.

Note that IEnumerable objects allow indexing so you can use an index to select a particular item from the results of any of these functions that returns an IEnumerable. For example, the following statement starts at element x_all, goes to descendants named NegativeBalances, gets that element's Customer children, and then selects the second of them (indexes are numbered starting with zero):

```
Dim neg_cust1 = x_all.<NegativeBalances>.<Customer>(1)
```

Together the LINQ XML functions and query axes operators let you explore XML hierarchies quite effectively.

In addition to all of these navigational features, the LINQ XML classes provide the usual assortment of methods for manipulating XML hierarchies. Those functions let you find an element's parent, add and remove elements, and so forth. For more information, see the online help or the MSDN website.

LINQ TO ADO.NET

LINQ to ADO.NET provides tools that let your applications apply LINQ-style queries to objects used by ADO.NET to store and interact with relational data.

LINQ to ADO.NET includes three components: LINQ to SQL, LINQ to Entities, and LINQ to DataSet. The following sections briefly give additional details about these three pieces.

LINQ to SQL and LINQ to Entities

LINQ to SQL and LINQ to Entities are object-relational mapping (O/RM) tools that build strongly typed classes for modeling databases. They generate classes to represent the database and the tables that it contains. LINQ features provided by these classes allow a program to query the database model objects.

For example, to build a database model for use by LINQ to SQL, select the Project menu's Add New Item command and add a new "LINQ to SQL Classes" item to the project. This opens a designer where you can define the database's structure.

Now you can drag SQL Server database objects from the Server Explorer to build the database model. If you drag all of the database's tables onto the designer, you should be able to see all of the tables and their fields, primary keys, relationships, and other structural information.

LINQ to SQL defines a DataContext class to represent the database. Suppose a program defines a DataContext class named dcTestScores and creates an instance of it named db. Then the following code selects all of the records from the Students table ordered by first and last name:

```
Dim query = From stu In db.Students
    Order By stu.FirstName, stu.LastName
```

Microsoft intends LINQ to SQL to be a quick tool for building LINQ-enabled classes for use with SQL Server databases. The designer can quickly take a SQL Server database, build a model for it, and then create the necessary classes.

The Entity Framework that includes LINQ to Entities is designed for use in more complicated enterprise scenarios. It allows extra abstraction that decouples a data object model from the underlying database. For example, the Entity Framework allows you to store pieces of a single conceptual object in more than one database table.

Building and managing SQL Server databases and the Entity Framework are topics too large to cover in this book so LINQ to SQL and LINQ to Entities are not described in more detail here. For more information, consult the online help or Microsoft's website. Some of Microsoft's relevant websites include:

➤ LINQ to SQL (http://msdn.microsoft.com/bb386976.aspx)

➤ LINQ to SQL: .NET Language-Integrated Query for Relational Data (http://msdn .microsoft.com/bb425822.aspx)

➤ The ADO.NET Entity Framework Overview (http://msdn.microsoft.com/aa697427 .aspx)

LINQ to DataSet

LINQ to DataSet lets a program use LINQ-style queries to select data from DataSet objects. A DataSet contains an in-memory representation of data contained in tables. Although a DataSet represents data in a more concrete format than is used by the object models used in LINQ to SQL and LINQ to Entities, DataSets are useful because they make few assumptions about how the data was loaded. A DataSet can hold data and provide query capabilities whether the data was loaded from SQL Server, from some other relational database, or by the program's code.

The DataSet object itself doesn't provide many LINQ features. It is mostly useful because it holds DataTable objects that represent groupings of items, much as IEnumerable objects do.

The DataTable class does not directly support LINQ either, but it has an AsEnumerable method that converts the DataTable into an IEnumerable, which you already know supports LINQ.

> **WHERE'S IENUMERABLE?**
>
> Actually, the AsEnumerable method converts the DataTable into an EnumerableRowCollection object but that object implements IEnumerable.

Example program LinqToDataSetScores, which is available for download on the book's website, demonstrates LINQ to DataSet concepts. This program builds a DataSet that contains two tables. The Students table has fields StudentId, FirstName, and LastName. The Scores table has fields StudentId, TestNumber, and Score.

The example program defines class-level variables `DtStudents` and `DtScores` that hold references to the two DataTable objects inside the DataSet.

The program uses the following code to select Students records where the LastName field comes before "D" alphabetically:

```
Dim before_d =
    From stu In DtStudents.AsEnumerable()
    Where stu!LastName < "D"
    Order By stu.Field(Of String)("LastName")
    Select First = stu!FirstName, Last = stu!LastName

dgStudentsBeforeD.DataSource = before_d.ToList
```

There are only a few differences between this query and previous LINQ queries. First, the From clause calls the DataTable object's AsEnumerable method to convert the table into something that supports LINQ.

Second, the syntax `stu!LastName` lets the query access the LastName field in the `stu` object. The `stu` object is a DataRow within the DataTable.

Third, the Order By clause uses the `stu` object's Field(Of T) method. The Field(Of T) method provides strongly typed access to the DataRow object's fields. In this example the LastName field contains string values. You could just as well have used `stu!LastName` in the Order By clause, but Visual Basic wouldn't provide strong typing.

Finally, the last line of code in this example sets a DataGrid control's DataSource property equal to the result returned by the query so the control will display the results. The DataGrid control cannot display the result directly so the code calls the ToList method to convert the result into a list, which the DataGrid can use.

The following list summarizes the key differences between a LINQ to DataSet query and a normal LINQ to Objects query:

➤ The LINQ to DataSet query must use the DataTable object's AsEnumerable method to make the object queryable.

➤ The code can access the fields in a DataRow, as in `stu!LastName` or as in `stu.Field(Of String)("LastName")`.

➤ If you want to display the results in a bound control such as a DataGrid or ListBox, use the query's ToList method.

If you understand these key differences, the rest of the query is similar to those used by LINQ to Objects. The following code shows two other examples:

```
' Select all students and their scores.
Dim joined =
    From stu In DtStudents.AsEnumerable()
    Join score In DtScores.AsEnumerable()
    On stu!StudentId Equals score!StudentId
    Order By stu!StudentId, score!TestNumber
    Select
        ID = stu!StudentId,
        Name = stu!FirstName & stu!LastName,
        Test = score!TestNumber,
        score!Score
dgJoined.DataSource = joined.ToList

' Select students with average scores >= 90.
Dim letter_grade =
    Function(num_score As Double)
        Return Choose(num_score \ 10,
            New Object() {"F", "F", "F", "F", "F", "D", "C", "B", "A", "A"})
    End Function

' Add "Where Ave >= 90" after the Group By statement
' to select students getting an A.
Dim grade_a =
    From stu In DtStudents.AsEnumerable()
        Join score In DtScores.AsEnumerable()
        On stu!StudentId Equals score!StudentId
    Group score By stu Into
        Ave = Average(CInt(score!Score)), Group
    Order By Ave
    Select Ave,
        Name = stu!FirstName & stu!LastName,
        ID = stu!StudentId,
        Grade = letter_grade(Ave)
dgAverages.DataSource = grade_a.ToList
```

The first query selects records from the Students table and joins them with the corresponding records in the Scores table. It displays the results in the dgJoined DataGrid control.

Next, the code defines an inline function and saves a reference to it in the variable letter_grade. This function returns a letter grade for numeric scores between 0 and 100.

The next LINQ query selects corresponding Students and Scores records, and groups them by the Students records, calculating each Student's average score at the same time. The query orders the results by average and selects the students' averages, names, IDs, and letter grades. Finally, the code displays the result in the dgAverages DataGrid.

LINQ to DataSet not only allows you to pull data out of a DataSet but also provides a way to put data into a DataSet. If the query selects DataRow objects, then its CopyToDataTable method converts the query results into a new DataTable object that you can then add to a DataSet.

The following code selects records from the Students table for students with last name less than "D." It then uses CopyToDataTable to convert the result into a DataTable and displays the results in the dgNewTable DataGrid control. It sets the new table's name and adds it to the DsScores DataSet object's collection of tables.

```
' Make a new table.
Dim before_d_rows =
    From stu In DtStudents.AsEnumerable()
    Where stu!LastName < "D"
    Select stu
Dim new_table As DataTable = before_d_rows.CopyToDataTable()
dgNewTable.DataSource = new_table

new_table.TableName = "NewTable"
DsScores.Tables.Add(new_table)
```

The LinqToDataSetScores example program displays a tab control. The first tab holds a DataGrid control that uses the DsScores DataSet as its data source, so you can see all of the DataSet's tables including the new table. Other tabs show the results of other queries described in this section.

PLINQ

PLINQ (Parallel LINQ, pronounced "plink") allows a program to execute LINQ queries across multiple processors or cores in a multi-core system. If you have a multi-core CPU and a nicely parallelizable query, PLINQ may improve your performance considerably.

So what kinds of queries are "nicely parallelizable"? The short, glib answer is, it doesn't really matter. Microsoft has gone to great lengths to minimize the overhead of PLINQ, so using PLINQ may help for some queries and shouldn't hurt you too much for queries that don't parallelize nicely.

Simple queries that select items from a data source often work well. If the items in the source can be examined, selected, and otherwise processed independently, then the query is parallelizable.

Queries that must use multiple items at the same time do not parallelize nicely. For example, adding an OrderBy function to the query forces the program to gather all of the results before sorting them so that part of the query at least will not benefit from PLINQ.

THE NEED FOR SPEED

Some feel that adding parallelism to LINQ is kind of like giving caffeine to a snail. A snail is slow. Giving it caffeine might speed it up a bit, but you'd get a much bigger performance gain if you got rid of the snail and got a cheetah instead.

Similarly, LINQ isn't all that fast. Adding parallelism will speed it up but you will probably get a larger speed improvement by moving the data into a database or using special-purpose algorithms designed to manage your particular data.

continues

continued

This argument is true, but you don't use LINQ because it's fast; you use it because it's convenient, easy to use, and flexible. Adding parallelism makes it a bit faster and, as you'll see shortly, is so easy that it doesn't cost you much effort.

If you really need significant performance improvements, you should consider moving the data into a database or more sophisticated data structure, but if you're using LINQ anyway, you may as well take advantage of PLINQ when you can.

Adding parallelism to LINQ is remarkably simple. First, add a reference to the System.Threading library to your program. Then add a call to AsParallel to the enumerable object that you're searching. For example, the following code uses AsParallel to select the even numbers from the array numbers:

```
Dim evens =
    From num In numbers.AsParallel()
    Where num Mod 2 = 0
```

PUZZLING PARALLELISM

Note that for small enumerable objects (lists containing only a few items) and on computers that have only a single CPU, the overhead of using AsParallel may actually slow down execution slightly.

SUMMARY

LINQ provides the ability to perform SQL-like queries within Visual Basic. Depending on which form of LINQ you are using, the development environment may provide strong type checking and IntelliSense support.

LINQ to Objects allows a program to query arrays, lists, and other objects that implement the IEnumerable interface. LINQ to XML and the LINQ XML classes allow a program to extract data from XML objects and to use LINQ to generate XML hierarchies. LINQ to ADO.NET (which includes LINQ to SQL, LINQ to Entities, and LINQ to DataSet) allows a program to perform queries on objects representing data in a relational database. Together these LINQ tools allow a program to select data in powerful new ways.

Visual Basic includes many features that support LINQ. Extension methods, inline or lambda functions, anonymous types, type inference, and object initializers all help make LINQ possible. If misused, some of these features can make code harder to read and understand, but used judiciously, they give you new options for program development.

For much more information on the various LINQ technologies, see the online help and the web. The following list includes several useful Microsoft web pages that you can follow to learn more about LINQ. Some are a bit old but they still provide valuable information.

➤ **Getting Started with LINQ in Visual Basic** — `http://msdn.microsoft.com/bb397910.aspx`.

➤ **Hooked on LINQ (a wiki with some useful information, particularly its "5 Minute Overviews")** — `http://www.hookedonlinq.com/LINQtoSQL5MinuteOverview.ashx`.

➤ **LINQ to SQL** — `http://msdn.microsoft.com/bb386976.aspx`.

➤ **LINQ to SQL: .NET Language-Integrated Query for Relational Data** — `http://msdn.microsoft.com/bb425822.aspx`.

➤ **101 Visual Basic LINQ Samples** — `http://msdn.microsoft.com/vstudio/bb688088`.

➤ **LINQ jump page** — `http://msdn.microsoft.com/bb397926.aspx`.

➤ **Visual Studio 2008 Code Samples** — `http://msdn.microsoft.com/vbasic/bb330936.aspx`.

➤ **Visual Studio 2010 Code Samples** — `http://msdn.microsoft.com/vstudio/dd238515.aspx`.

➤ **The .NET Standard Query Operators** — `http://msdn.microsoft.com/bb394939.aspx`.

➤ **Querying DataSets — Introduction to LINQ to DataSet (by Erick Thompson, ADO.NET Program Manager, in the ADO.NET team blog)** — `http://blogs.msdn.com/adonet/archive/2007/01/26/querying-datasets-introduction-to-linq-to-dataset.aspx`.

➤ **LINQ to SQL: .NET Language-Integrated Query for Relational Data** — `http://msdn.microsoft.com/bb425822.aspx`.

➤ **The ADO.NET Entity Framework Overview** — `http://msdn.microsoft.com/aa697427.aspx`.

➤ **Parallel LINQ (PLINQ)** — `http://msdn.microsoft.com/dd460688.aspx`.

The last several chapters have explained how to build Visual Basic applications that run on the Microsoft Windows desktop, but Visual Basic programs can also run on the Windows Metro platform. Chapter 21 provides an introduction to building Metro-style applications. These applications use the same WPF ideas described in several earlier chapters.

21

Metro-Style Applications

BUILDING METRO-STYLE APPLICATIONS

The Windows 8 operating system is quite different from other Windows operating systems such as Vista and Windows 7. Windows 8's Metro interface doesn't provide Windows Explorer to let you browse through the system's directory structure, doesn't display a desktop where you can arrange folders and icons, and doesn't let you have many programs all running and visible at the same time. Because the Metro interface is so different from those of previous operating systems, Metro-style programs must be written in a new way to work properly.

This chapter explains the basic process of building a Metro-style application. It explains how to create a Metro-style application and give it the images it needs to display properly in the Windows 8 Metro interface.

To help you get started, this chapter walks through the most important parts of the MetroBones application shown in Figure 21-1. This program is a "hangman" game where you try to guess the letters in a randomly chosen word. When you click a letter button on the bottom, the program displays it in the top spaces if the letter is part of the current word. If the letter is not part of the current word, the program displays a new piece of the skeleton on the left. If you guess all of the word's letters before you build the complete skeleton, you win.

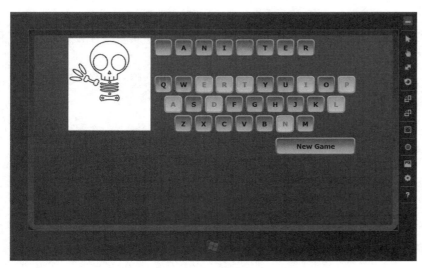

FIGURE 21-1: This chapter explains how to build the MetroBones "hangman" game.

> **NOTE** *The artwork for MetroBones was kindly provided by Jeff Scarterfield, the webmaster of DrawCartoonsOnline.com, a site that provides step-by-step instructions for drawing a huge variety of cartoons.*

STARTING A NEW PROJECT

To start a new Metro-style project, select the File menu's New Project command as usual. In the New Project dialog box shown in Figure 21-2, expand the project-type tree on the left to find the category Installed ⇨ Templates ⇨ Visual Basic ⇨ Windows Metro Style and select the type of application that you want to create. Enter a project name and click OK.

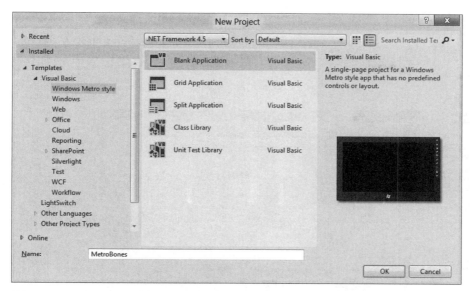

FIGURE 21-2: Select the Windows Metro-style template category to create a Metro-style application.

This version of Visual Studio stores new projects in a temporary location until you save the project. That means if Visual Studio crashes before you save the project, you may lose all of the work you have done. To prevent that, save the project into a directory right after you create it by using the File menu's Save All command. After that, Visual Studio automatically saves any changes you make every time you run the program so your changes should be safe.

SPECIAL IMAGE FILES

A Metro-style application includes several image files that are used for splash screens, icons, and the like. These files are `Logo.png`, `WideLogo.png`, `SmallLogo.png`, and `SplashScreen.png`.

`Logo.png` is a 150 × 150 pixel image file that is displayed on the Metro interface if you pin your application to the Metro start window. Normally the system adds the name of the application at the bottom of the image in white so you should leave that area blank and fill it with a dark color so the name is visible. Figure 21-3 shows the MetroBones application in the Metro start window. (The shaded strip at the bottom of the icon is part of the `Logo.png` file. The system automatically added the program's name on top of the shaded strip in white text.)

`WideLogo.png` is a 310 × 150 pixel image file that Windows uses if the application is shown in two columns in the Metro interface.

`SmallLogo.png` is a 30 × 30 pixel image file that the operating system can use as a smaller representation of the application.

FIGURE 21-3: The file Logo .png determines how the program appears in the Metro start window.

`SplashScreen.png` is a 620 × 300 pixel image file that is displayed while the program is loading.

The locations of these files are set in the application's manifest. If you open Solution Explorer and double-click the file `Package.appxmanifest`, you can change these settings in the Manifest Designer shown in Figure 21-4.

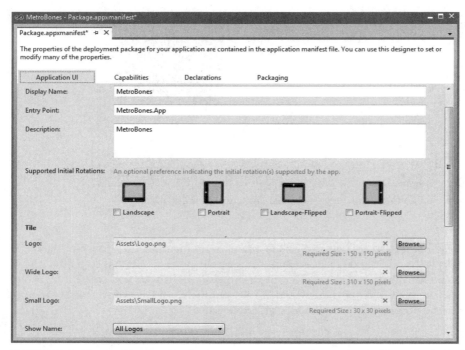

FIGURE 21-4: Use the Manifest Designer to change the application's logo files and other fundamental properties.

The Manifest Designer also lets you set other application properties such as a wide logo file (in which case the Metro start window displays the application double wide), whether the system automatically adds the application's name to its icons, and the application's initial orientation.

For more information on the Manifest Designer, see the article "Manifest Designer" at `http://msdn.microsoft.com/library/windows/apps/br230259.aspx`.

BUILDING METROBONES

Much of the work of building an application such as MetroBones is in creating and arranging its controls. To save space, I won't discuss where every control is positioned for MetroBones. You can look at Figure 21-1 to see the general arrangement and you can download the example program to see the details.

While I don't want to cover the code in complete detail, there are a few points worth mentioning.

Control Layout

The program's left side holds a stack of Image controls holding skeleton images in various states. The program hides and displays these controls to show the game's current state.

The program's right side contains a vertical StackPanel that holds a series of other controls. Those controls include:

➤ A horizontal StackPanel holding the current word's letters

➤ A TextBlock that can indicate when the user wins or loses

➤ Three horizontal StackPanels holding the letter buttons

➤ The New Game button

The current word's letters are displayed as Border controls that hold TextBlocks. They are created at run time when the program picks a word.

Those controls and the program's buttons use styles defined in the program's resources to give them their sizes and appearance. The following section describes the program's styles.

XAML Code

The most interesting part of XAML code is the definition of the resources that determine the appearance of the program's buttons. The following code shows the application's resources. Those resources are available to the later XAML code to set the controls' appearance.

```xaml
<Page.Resources>
    <LinearGradientBrush x:Key="EnabledBorderBrush"
      StartPoint="0,0" EndPoint="0,1">
        <GradientStop Color="LightGreen" Offset="0"/>
        <GradientStop Color="DarkGreen" Offset="1"/>
    </LinearGradientBrush>
    <LinearGradientBrush x:Key="EnabledFillBrush"
      StartPoint="0,0" EndPoint="0,1">
        <GradientStop Color="DarkGreen" Offset="0"/>
        <GradientStop Color="LightGreen" Offset="1"/>
    </LinearGradientBrush>
    <LinearGradientBrush x:Key="DisabledFillBrush"
      StartPoint="0,0" EndPoint="0,1">
        <GradientStop Color="DarkGray" Offset="0"/>
        <GradientStop Color="LightGray" Offset="1"/>
    </LinearGradientBrush>
    <LinearGradientBrush x:Key="DisabledBorderBrush"
      StartPoint="0,0" EndPoint="0,1">
        <GradientStop Color="LightGray" Offset="0"/>
        <GradientStop Color="DarkGray" Offset="1"/>
    </LinearGradientBrush>

    <Style x:Key="BasicButton" TargetType="Button">
        <Setter Property="Foreground" Value="Black"/>
        <Setter Property="Width" Value="45"/>
        <Setter Property="Height" Value="45"/>
        <Setter Property="Margin" Value="3"/>
```

```xml
            <Setter Property="FontFamily" Value="Verdana"/>
            <Setter Property="FontSize" Value="16"/>
            <Setter Property="FontWeight" Value="Bold"/>
            <Setter Property="Background" Value="{StaticResource EnabledFillBrush}"/>
            <Setter Property="BorderBrush"
                Value="{StaticResource EnabledBorderBrush}"/>
            <Setter Property="Template">
                <Setter.Value>
                    <ControlTemplate TargetType="Button">
                        <Border
                            BorderThickness="3"
                            CornerRadius="7"
                            Background="{TemplateBinding Background}"
                           BorderBrush="{TemplateBinding BorderBrush}">
                            <Grid>
                                <ContentPresenter HorizontalAlignment="Center"
                                 VerticalAlignment="Center" Name="content"/>
                            </Grid>
                        </Border>
                    </ControlTemplate>
                </Setter.Value>
            </Setter>
        </Style>

        <Style x:Key="EnabledButton" TargetType="Button"
         BasedOn="{StaticResource BasicButton}"/>
        <Style x:Key="DisabledButton" TargetType="Button"
         BasedOn="{StaticResource BasicButton}">
            <Setter Property="Background" Value="{StaticResource DisabledFillBrush}"/>
            <Setter Property="BorderBrush"
                Value="{StaticResource DisabledBorderBrush}"/>
            <Setter Property="Foreground" Value="Gray"/>
            <Setter Property="IsEnabled" Value="False"/>
        </Style>

        <Style x:Key="LetterBorder" TargetType="Border">
            <Setter Property="BorderBrush"
                Value="{StaticResource EnabledBorderBrush}"/>
            <Setter Property="BorderThickness" Value="3"/>
            <Setter Property="CornerRadius" Value="7"/>
            <Setter Property="Width" Value="45"/>
            <Setter Property="Height" Value="45"/>
            <Setter Property="Margin" Value="3"/>
            <Setter Property="Background"
                Value="{StaticResource EnabledFillBrush}"/>
        </Style>
        <Style x:Key="LetterTextBlock" TargetType="TextBlock">
            <Setter Property="FontFamily" Value="Verdana"/>
            <Setter Property="FontSize" Value="16"/>
            <Setter Property="FontWeight" Value="Bold"/>
            <Setter Property="Foreground" Value="Black"/>
            <Setter Property="HorizontalAlignment" Value="Center"/>
            <Setter Property="VerticalAlignment" Value="Center"/>
        </Style>
    </Page.Resources>
```

The resources start by defining several LinearGradientBrushes. The program uses the EnabledBorderBrush and EnabledFillBrush to determine how the buttons are outlined and filled when they are enabled. Similarly the DisabledBorderBrush and DisabledFillBrush determine the buttons' appearance when they are disabled.

The BasicButton style defines the basic characteristics of the program's buttons. It sets the buttons' default text color, size, and font. It sets the border and fill colors to the EnabledBorderBrush and EnabledFillBrush.

The BasicButton style also sets the buttons' template to determine the controls that make up the button. This template uses a Border control with rounded corners that holds a Grid that contains the buttons' content. I created this template because the normal button template includes a lot of interior space and this program didn't have enough room to fit in all of the letter buttons when using that template.

Unfortunately, when you use a new template the buttons forfeit all of the features of the default template. In particular, they lose the ability to respond to events so, for example, they don't flash when the user taps them. I could have added new behaviors to the new template to make the buttons behave in that way but it would have been more work and didn't seem necessary for this example.

After defining the BasicButton style, the code then defines two styles named EnabledButton and DisabledButton that are based on the BasicButton. EnabledButton simply copies the features of BasicButton.

DisabledButton copies the features of BasicButton and then overrides some of its properties to make the button look disabled. It sets the buttons' border and fill brushes to DisabledBorderBrush and DisabledFillBrush. It also sets the buttons' foreground color (which is used to draw text) to Gray and sets the IsEnabled property to False so the buttons won't respond to user taps.

The resources finish by defining styles for the controls that display the current word's letters. The LetterBorder and LetterTextBlock styles define the appearances of the Border and TextBlock controls that display the letters.

The later XAML code uses some of these styles to determine the controls' appearance. For example, the following code shows how the program defines the first row of letter buttons:

```
<StackPanel Orientation="Horizontal">
    <Button Style="{StaticResource DisabledButton}" Name="btnQ" Content="Q"/>
    <Button Style="{StaticResource DisabledButton}" Name="btnW" Content="W"/>
    <Button Style="{StaticResource DisabledButton}" Name="btnE" Content="E"/>
    <Button Style="{StaticResource DisabledButton}" Name="btnR" Content="R"/>
    <Button Style="{StaticResource DisabledButton}" Name="btnT" Content="T"/>
    <Button Style="{StaticResource DisabledButton}" Name="btnY" Content="Y"/>
    <Button Style="{StaticResource DisabledButton}" Name="btnU" Content="U"/>
    <Button Style="{StaticResource DisabledButton}" Name="btnI" Content="I"/>
    <Button Style="{StaticResource DisabledButton}" Name="btnO" Content="O"/>
    <Button Style="{StaticResource DisabledButton}" Name="btnP" Content="P"/>
</StackPanel>
```

The buttons are contained in a horizontal StackPanel. Each button uses the DisabledButton style so they are initially disabled. The program's Visual Basic code enables the buttons when they are needed. Each button has a name that is used by the Visual Basic code and displays a single letter.

Zooming in on the Controls

The XAML code that arranges the MetroBones controls create a Grid that is 728 pixels wide and 480 pixels tall. I picked that size because it fits nicely on a Windows phone. A Windows Phone device is required to provide an 800 × 480 pixel screen so that made sense for those devices. (There have long been rumors of new devices with different screen sizes coming, but they haven't appeared yet.)

In contrast, a Windows 8 system running Metro applications could have a large number of screen sizes with varying pixel densities. Anticipated sizes range from 10.1" to 27" screens with pixel densities ranging from 96 dpi to 291 dpi. (See "Scaling to Different Screens" at http://blogs.msdn.com/b/b8/archive/2012/03/21/scaling-to-different-screens.aspx for a discussion of screen size issues.)

You could simply use this 800 × 480 pixel size. The application would fit on most Windows 8 devices but the result would be a relatively small program centered in the middle of a large screen for many devices.

A better approach is to use Silverlight's arranging controls such as Grid, StackPanel, and WrapGrid to make the application take best advantage of whatever space is available.

For MetroBones I used a simpler approach. Because the program doesn't really need more space to display more information, I just enlarged it. I put the program's main Grid control inside a Viewbox. The Viewbox enlarges its contents to fill the space occupied by the Viewbox.

One of the nice things about WPF controls, including those used by Silverlight, is that they use the DirectX graphic library to make themselves scalable. That means you can enlarge the controls as much as you like and they will remain smooth and not become grainy like a greatly enlarged bitmap does. The result in MetroBones is that the image of the skeleton and all of the buttons simply get bigger to fill the available space.

The following code shows the part of the MetroBones program's XAML code that contains the Viewbox. I've omitted most of the code to save space.

```
<!-- The Viewbox enlarges the basic layout to fill the available area. -->
<Viewbox Margin="30">
    <!-- Content area -->
    <Grid Width="728" Height="480">
    ...
    </Grid> <!-- End of content area -->
</Viewbox>
```

The following section explains how the Visual Basic code uses the styles defined in the XAML code at run time.

Visual Basic Code

The MetroBones program's Visual Basic code is relatively straightforward but it does demonstrate a few useful tricks. The code includes only three event handlers, which are described in the following sections.

The Page_Loaded Event Handler

The Page_Loaded event handler executes when the page is loaded. The following code shows how this event handler initializes the application so it is ready for use:

```vb
' Array of letter buttons.
Private LetterButtons() As Button

' Array of skeleton Image controls.
Private SkeletonImages() As Image

' The index of the current skeleton picture.
Private CurrentPictureIndex As Integer = 0

' Words.
Private Words() As String

' The current word.
Private CurrentWord As String = ""

' Controls used to display letters.
Private LetterTextBlocks As New List(Of TextBlock)()

' Prepare the program for use.
Private Async Sub Page_Loaded(sender As Object, e As RoutedEventArgs) _
Handles MyBase.Loaded
    ' Make the array of letter Buttons.
    LetterButtons = New Button() _
    {
        btnQ, btnW, btnE, btnR, btnT, btnY, btnU, btnI, btnO, btnP,
        btnA, btnS, btnD, btnF, btnG, btnH, btnJ, btnK, btnL,
        btnZ, btnX, btnC, btnV, btnB, btnN, btnM
    }

    ' Make the array of skeleton Images.
    SkeletonImages = New Image() _
    {
        img0, img1, img2, img3, img4, img5, img6
    }

    ' Prepare the letter buttons.
    For Each btn As Button In LetterButtons
        AddHandler btn.Click, AddressOf btnLetter_Click
        btn.Tag = btn.Content.ToString()
    Next btn

    ' Load the words.
    Words = Await ReadAssetFileLinesAsync("Words.txt")
End Sub
```

The code starts by declaring several class-level variables that are used to keep track of the program's state. These variables include:

➤ LetterButtons — The Button controls that the user can click to guess a letter

➤ SkeletonImages — The Image controls that represent the skeleton in various stages of completion

➤ CurrentPictureIndex — The index of the currently visible skeleton Image control

➤ Words — An array of words from which the game randomly picks

➤ CurrentWord — The currently selected word

➤ LetterTextBlocks — The TextBlock controls that hold the current word's letters

The Page_Loaded event handler initializes some of these variables. It starts by creating the LetterButtons and SkeletonImages arrays, filling them with references to the appropriate controls.

Next the code prepares the letter buttons. It loops over the buttons in the LetterButtons array to add the btnLetter_Click event handler to each button and to set each button's Tag property to the letter it displays.

The code then loads the dictionary file Words.txt. Loading a file in a Metro-style application is somewhat complicated so it's described separately in the following section.

Loading Files

Loading a file is a bit more complicated in a Metro-style application than it is in a desktop application. A Metro-style application doesn't have access to the full filesystem. It also doesn't have access to the very convenient My namespace so it can't use My.Computer.FileSystem.ReadAllText to easily read the file. Even the System.IO.File class that is provided for Windows Phone applications doesn't include the ReadAllText or ReadAllLines methods.

Metro-style applications also assume you will often be downloading files over the Internet. To make that kind of download more efficient, the Metro-style tools assume downloads will be made asynchronously, and that complicates the program's code.

You can make it a little easier to handle the asynchronous download of Words.txt in the MetroBones program by using the Async and Await keywords described in the section "Using Async and Await" in Chapter 16. When the program should wait for an asynchronous operation to complete, it adds the Await keyword. Any method that uses Await must be declared with the Async keyword so code that calls it can use Await to wait for it to complete. Notice that the Page_Loaded event handler shown in the code in the previous section is declared with the Async keyword.

To load the dictionary file, the MetroBones application uses a resource file. At design time, I used the Project menu's Add Existing Item command to add the file Words.txt to the project. I selected the file in Solution Explorer and set its Builds Action property to Resource.

The following code shows how the Page_Loaded event handler loads the dictionary file:

```
Words = Await ReadAssetFileLinesAsync("Words.txt")
```

This code simply calls the ReadAssetFileLinesAsync method and uses the Await keyword to wait for that method to return. (By convention, the names of asynchronous methods end with "Async.")

The following code shows the ReadAssetFileLinesAsync method:

```
' Return the file's contents as an array of lines.
Public Async Function ReadAssetFileLinesAsync(filename As String) _
  As Task(Of String())
    Dim txt As String = Await ReadAssetFileAsync(filename)
    Return txt.Replace(vbCrLf, vbCr).Split(vbCr)
End Function
```

The ReadAssetFileLinesAsync method also uses the Await keyword so it is declared Async. It returns a Task(Of String()). That means it returns a task that returns an array of strings. The calling code (the Page_Loaded event handler) uses Await to wait for the task to finish so it can collect the resulting string array.

The ReadAssetFileLinesAsync method calls the ReadAssetFileAsync method described next to get the contents of an asset file, using the Await keyword to wait for ReadAssetFileAsync to finish. It then splits the file into lines as before.

The following code shows the ReadAssetFileAsync method:

```
' Return the file's contents as a string.
Public Async Function ReadAssetFileAsync(filename As String) As Task(Of String)
    ' Get the installed location.
    Dim storage_folder As StorageFolder =
        ApplicationModel.Package.Current.InstalledLocation
    storage_folder = Await storage_folder.GetFolderAsync("Assets")

    ' Get the file.
    Dim storage_file As StorageFile =
        Await storage_folder.GetFileAsync(filename)

    ' Use a StreamReader to read the file.
    Using stream_reader As
     New StreamReader(Await storage_file.OpenStreamForReadAsync())
        Return stream_reader.ReadToEnd()
    End Using
End Function
```

This method also uses the Await keyword so it is declared Async. It returns a Task(Of String): a task that returns a string.

The code creates a StorageFolder object that represents the program's installed location. It uses the GetFolderAsync method to get the installation folder's Assets subfolder, which is where the Words.txt file is stored. It uses Await to wait for GetFolderAsync to finish.

Next the code uses the folder object's GetFileAsync method to get a StorageFile object representing the file, again using the Await keyword to wait for the operation to finish.

The code then creates a StreamReader object associated with the file, passing the StreamReader's constructor the result of the StorageFile object's OpenStreamForReadAsync method, using the Await keyword yet again.

Finally, the code uses the StreamReader's ReadToEnd method to read the file's contents into a string and returns the result.

This is a very roundabout method for loading a file that is installed with the application. In an application that loaded large files over the Internet, handling files asynchronously would be much more important.

TESTING

After you have created a Metro-style application, you can use Visual Studio to test it. As is the case with Windows Phone development, you have a couple of testing options.

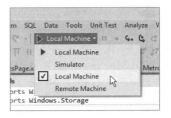

Visual Studio's Standard toolbar has a drop-down that lets you select where you want to test the program. Figure 21-5 shows the drop-down expanded to show its choices: Local Machine, Simulator, and Remote Machine. Click the drop-down arrow on the right to make a selection and then click the body of the drop-down to start testing.

FIGURE 21-5: Use this drop-down in the Standard toolbar to determine where the application runs and to start it.

The Local Machine option makes the application fill your computer's Metro interface. This is useful for testing the program as it would appear on your system.

The Simulator option makes the program run in the Microsoft Windows Simulator shown in Figure 21-6.

FIGURE 21-6: The Microsoft Windows Simulator lets you test Metro applications at different sizes and orientations.

You can resize the simulator to see what your application would look like on different hardware platforms and you can use the simulator's tools to test the application in different orientations.

The Microsoft Windows Simulator takes a while to start. When you try to close the simulator, it actually hides so Visual Studio can use it again when you test the program later.

The Remote Machine option lets you test an application on a machine other than the one where you are running Visual Studio. This is particularly useful for testing features that are not supported by your development machine. For example, you might be programming on a typical desktop system but want to test the program on a tablet that has a touch screen.

SUMMARY

This chapter explained how to create the MetroBones Metro-style application. It explained the purposes of the `Logo.png`, `SmallLogo.png`, `SplashScreen.png`, and `StoreLogo.png` files, and explained how to modify them for your applications. The chapter also explained how to use the Manifest Designer to set application properties such as its initial orientation and a wide logo file.

The chapter then explained how to use a Viewbox to enlarge a basic fixed-size interface so it can fill Metro devices of various sizes. This technique is not as flexible as using Grid and other arranging controls to fill the available space on different devices, but it is much easier and works quite well for an application such as MetroBones, which doesn't display large amounts of data.

The chapter explained how to read resource files in Metro-style applications. Because many Metro file processing methods work asynchronously, the program uses the Await keyword to wait for them to complete.

Finally, the chapter explained how to test Metro applications in the Microsoft Windows Simulator or on the local machine.

The MetroBones program demonstrates some useful techniques but it barely touches on the things you can do with Metro-style applications. Some devices that support Metro provide all sorts of other features such as cameras, accelerometers, orientation sensors, geolocation, and multi-touch input. The MetroBones program doesn't demonstrate any of that. Those topics and many others are outside the scope of this book. For more information, search the Internet or look for a book that focuses on Windows Metro programming. Many of these concepts are also supported by Windows Phone programs so you may also get useful information by learning about Windows Phone programming.

The following list gives some links that you may find helpful in Metro-style programming:

➤   Metro Style Apps
    `http://msdn.microsoft.com/windows/apps`

➤   Create your first Metro style app using C# or Visual Basic
    `http://msdn.microsoft.com/library/windows/apps/br211380.aspx`

➤   Metro style apps, downloads for developers
    `http://msdn.microsoft.com/windows/apps/br229516`

➤   Windows 8 Metro style app samples
    `http://code.msdn.microsoft.com/windowsapps/site/search`

The chapters in Part II of this book deal mostly with basic programming tasks. They explain how to select and use controls, use Visual Basic syntax to perform tasks such as looping and error handling, and use LINQ to simplify complex selection and ordering tasks.

The chapters in Part III deal with the higher-level concepts of object-oriented programming (OOP). Chapter 22, "OOP Concepts," introduces fundamental object-oriented concepts that make it easier to build and maintain complex applications.

PART III
Object-Oriented Programming

22

OOP Concepts

WROX.COM CODE DOWNLOADS FOR THIS CHAPTER

There are no code downloads for this chapter.

INTRODUCING OOP

This chapter explains the fundamental ideas behind object-oriented programming (OOP). It describes the three main features of OOP languages: encapsulation, inheritance, and polymorphism. It explains the benefits of these features and describes how you can take advantage of them in Visual Basic.

This chapter also describes method overloading. In a sense, overloading provides another form of polymorphism. It lets you create more than one definition of the same class method, and Visual Basic decides which version to use based on the parameters the program passes to the method.

Many of the techniques described in this chapter help you define a new class, but extension methods let you modify an existing class. For example, you could use extension methods to add new features to the String class, perhaps to make it encrypt and decrypt text.

Many of the ideas described in this chapter will be familiar to you from your experiences with forms, controls, and other building blocks of the Visual Basic language. Those building blocks are object-oriented constructs in their own rights, so they provide you with the benefits of encapsulation, inheritance, and polymorphism whether you knew about them or not.

CLASSES

A *class* is a programming entity that gathers together all of the data and behavior that characterizes some sort of programming abstraction. It wraps the abstraction in a nice, neat package with well-defined interfaces to outside code. Those interfaces determine exactly how code outside of the class can interact with the class. A class determines which data values are visible outside of the class and which are hidden. It determines the routines that the class supports and their availability (visible or hidden).

A class defines properties, methods, and events that let the program work with the class:

➤ A *property* is some sort of data value. It may be a simple value (such as a name or number), or it may be a more complex item (such as an array, collection, or object containing its own properties, methods, and events).

➤ A *method* is a subroutine or function. It is a piece of code that makes the object defined by the class do something.

➤ An *event* is a notification defined by the class. An event calls some other piece of code to tell it that some condition in a class object has occurred.

For a concrete example, imagine a Job class that represents a piece of work to be done by an employee. This class might have the properties shown in the following table.

PROPERTY	PURPOSE
JobDescription	A string describing the job
EstimatedHours	The number of hours initially estimated for the job
ActualHours	The actual number of hours spent on the job
Status	The job's status (New, Assigned, In Progress, or Done)
ActionTaken	A string describing the work performed, parts installed, and so forth
JobCustomer	An object of the Customer class that describes the customer for whom the job is performed (name, address, phone number, service contract number, and so on)
AssignedEmployee	An object of the Employee class that describes the employee assigned to the job (name, employee ID, Social Security number, and so on)

The JobDescription, EstimatedHours, ActualHours, Status, and ActionTaken properties are relatively simple string and numeric values. The JobCustomer and AssignedEmployee properties are objects themselves with their own properties, methods, and events.

This class might provide the methods shown in the following table.

METHOD	PURPOSE
AssignJob	Assign the job to an employee
PrintInvoice	Print an invoice for the customer after the job is finished
EstimatedCost	Calculate and return an estimated cost based on the customer's service contract type and EstimatedHours

The class could provide the events shown in the following table to keep the main program informed about the job's progress.

EVENT	PURPOSE
Created	Occurs when the job is first created
Assigned	Occurs when the job is assigned to an employee
Rejected	Occurs if an employee refuses to do the job, perhaps because the employee doesn't have the right skills or equipment to do the work
Canceled	Occurs if the customer cancels the job before it is worked
Finished	Occurs when the job is finished

In a nutshell, a class is an entity that encapsulates the data and behavior of some programming abstraction such as a Job, Employee, Customer, LegalAction, TestResult, Report, or just about anything else you could reasonably want to manipulate as a single entity.

After you have defined a class, you can create instances of the class. An *instance* of the class is an object of the class type. For example, if you define a Job class, you can then make an instance of the class that represents a specific job, perhaps installing a new computer for a particular customer. The process of creating an instance of a class is called *instantiation*.

There are a couple of common analogies to describe instantiation. One compares the class to a blueprint. After you define the class, you can use it to create any number of instances of the class, much as you can use the blueprint to make any number of similar houses (instances).

Another analogy compares a class definition to a cookie cutter. When you define the cookie cutter, you can use it to make any number of cookies (instances).

Note that Visual Basic is jam-packed with classes. Every type of control and component (Form, TextBox, Label, Timer, ErrorProvider, and so forth) is a class. The parent classes Control and Component are classes. Even Object, from which all other classes derive, is a class. Whenever you work with any of these (getting or setting properties, calling methods, and responding to events), you are working with instances of classes.

Because all of these ultimately derive from the Object class, they are often simply called *objects*. If you don't know or don't care about an item's class, you can simply refer to it as an object.

> **OUTSTANDING OBJECTS**
>
> When you read the section "Polymorphism" later in this chapter, you'll see that this makes technical, as well as intuitive, sense. Because all classes eventually derive from the Object class, all instances of all classes are in fact Objects.

The following sections, which describe some of the features that OOP languages in general and Visual Basic in particular, add to this bare-bones definition of a class.

ENCAPSULATION

A class's *public interface* is the set of properties, methods, and events that are visible to code outside of the class. The class may also have private properties, methods, and events that it uses to do its job. For example, the Job class described in the previous section provides an AssignJob method. That method might call a private FindQualifiedEmployee function that looks through an employee database to find someone who has the skills and equipment necessary to do the job. That routine is not used outside of the class, so it can be declared private.

The class may also include properties and events hidden from code outside of the class. These hidden properties, methods, and events are not part of the class's public interface.

The class *encapsulates* the programming abstraction that it represents (a Job in this ongoing example). Its public interface determines what is visible to the application outside of the class. It hides the ugly details of the class's implementation from the rest of the world. Because the class hides its internals in this way, encapsulation is also sometimes called *information hiding.*

By hiding its internals from the outside world, a class prevents exterior code from messing around with those internals. It reduces the dependencies between different parts of the application, allowing only those dependencies that are explicitly permitted by its public interface.

Removing dependencies between different pieces of code makes the code easier to modify and maintain. If you must change the way the Job class assigns a job to an employee, you can modify the AssignJob method appropriately. The code that calls the AssignJob routine doesn't need to know that the details have changed. It simply continues to call the method and leaves the details up to the Job class.

Removing dependencies also helps break the application into smaller, more manageable pieces. A developer who calls the AssignJob method can concentrate on the job at hand, rather than on how the routine works. This makes developers more productive and less likely to make mistakes while modifying the encapsulated code.

The simpler and cleaner a class's public interface is, the easier it is to use. You should try to hide as much information and behavior inside a class as possible while still allowing the rest of the program to do its job. Keep properties, methods, and events as simple and focused as possible. When you write code that the class needs to use to perform its duties, do not expose that code to the outside program unless it is really necessary. Adding extra features complicates the class's public interface and makes the programmer's job more difficult.

This can be a troublesome concept for beginning programmers. Exposing more features for developers to use gives them more power, so you might think it would make their jobs easier. Actually, it makes development more difficult. Rather than thinking in terms of giving the developer more power, you should think about giving the developer more things to worry about and more ways to make mistakes. Ideally, you should not expose any more features than the developer will actually need.

INHERITANCE

Inheritance is the process of deriving a child class from a parent class. The child class inherits all of the properties, methods, and events of the parent class. It can then modify, add to, or subtract from the parent class. Making a child class inherit from a parent class is also called *deriving* the child class from the parent, and *subclassing* the parent class to form the child class.

For example, suppose you define a Person class that includes variables named FirstName, LastName, Street, City, State, Zip, Phone, and Email. It might also include a DialPhone method that dials the person's phone number on the phone attached to the computer's modem or on a voice over Internet protocol (VoIP) provider.

You could then derive the Employee class from the Person class. The Employee class inherits the FirstName, LastName, Street, City, State, Zip, Phone, and Email variables. It then adds new EmployeeId, SocialSecurityNumber, OfficeNumber, Extension, and Salary variables. This class might override the Person class's DialPhone method, so it dials the employee's office extension instead of the home phone number.

You can continue deriving classes from these classes to make as many types of objects as you need. For example, you could derive the Manager class from the Employee class and add fields such as Secretary that would refer to another Employee object that represents the manager's secretary. Similarly, you could derive a Secretary class from Employee that includes a reference to a Manager object. You could derive ProjectManager, DepartmentManager, and DivisionManager from the Manager class, Customer from the Person class, and so on for other types of people that the application needs to use. Figure 22-1 shows these inheritance relationships.

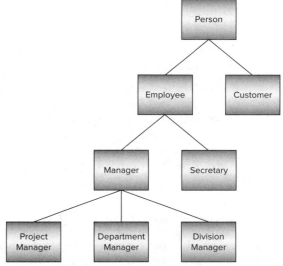

FIGURE 22-1: You can derive classes from other classes to form quite complex inheritance relationships.

Inheritance Hierarchies

One of the key benefits of inheritance is code reuse. When you derive a class from a parent class, the child class inherits the parent's properties, methods, and events, so the child class gets to reuse the parent's code. That means you don't need to implement separate FirstName and LastName properties for the Person, Employee, Manager, Secretary, and other classes shown in Figure 22-1. These properties are defined only in the Person class, and all of the other classes inherit them.

Code reuse not only saves you the trouble of writing more code but also makes maintenance of the code easier. Suppose that you build the hierarchy shown in Figure 22-1 and then decide that everyone needs a new BirthDate property. Instead of adding a new property to every class, you can simply add it to the Person class, and all of the other classes inherit it.

Similarly, if you need to modify or delete a property or method, you need to make the change only in the class where it is defined, not in all of the classes that inherit it. If the Person class defines a SendEmail method and you must modify it so that it uses a particular e-mail protocol, you need to change the routine only in the Person class, not in all the classes that inherit it.

MULTIPLE INHERITANCE

Some languages allow *multiple inheritance*, where one class can be derived from more than one parent class. For example, suppose that you create a Vehicle class that defines properties of vehicles (number of wheels, horsepower, maximum speed, acceleration, and so forth) and a House class that defines properties of living spaces (square feet, number of bedrooms, number of bathrooms, and so forth). Using multiple inheritance, you could derive a MotorHome class from both the Vehicle and House classes. This class would have the features of both Vehicles and Houses.

Visual Basic does not allow multiple inheritance, so a class can have at most one parent class. That means relationships such as those shown in Figure 22-1 are treelike and form an inheritance hierarchy.

If you think you need multiple inheritance, you can use interface inheritance. Instead of defining multiple parent classes, define parent interfaces. Then you can make the child class implement as many interfaces as you like. The class doesn't inherit any code from the interfaces, but at least its behavior is defined by the interfaces. See the section "Implements interface" in Chapter 23, "Classes and Structures," for more information on interfaces.

Refinement and Abstraction

You can think about the relationship between a parent class and its child classes in two different ways. First, using a top-down view of inheritance, you can think of the child classes as *refining* the parent class. They provide extra detail that differentiates among different types of the parent class.

For example, suppose that you start with a broadly defined class such as Person. The Person class would need general fields such as name, address, and phone number. It would also need more specific fields that do not apply to all types of people. For example, employees would need employee ID, Social Security number, office number, and department fields. In contrast customers would need customer ID, company name, and discount code fields. You could dump all these fields in the Person class, but that would mean stretching the class to make it play two very different roles. A Person acting as an Employee would not use the Customer fields, and vice versa.

A better solution is to derive new Employee and Customer classes that refine the Person class and differentiate between the types of Person.

A bottom-up view of inheritance considers the parent class as *abstracting* common features out of the child classes into the parent class. Common elements in the child classes are removed and placed in the parent class. Because the parent class is more general than the child classes (it includes a larger group of objects), abstraction is sometimes called *generalization*.

Suppose that you are building a drawing application and you define classes to represent various drawing objects such as Circle, Ellipse, Polygon, Rectangle, and DrawingGroup (a group of objects that should be drawn together). After you work with the code for a while, you may discover that these classes share a lot of functionality. Some, such as Ellipse, Circle, and Rectangle, are defined by bounding rectangles. All the classes need methods for drawing the object with different pens and brushes on the screen or on a printer.

You could abstract these classes and create a new parent class named Drawable. That class might provide basic functionality such as a simple variable to hold a bounding rectangle. This class would also define a DrawObject routine for drawing the object on the screen or printer. It would declare that routine with the MustOverride keyword, so each child class would need to provide its own DrawObject implementation, but the Drawable class would define its parameters.

Sometimes you can pull variables and methods from the child classes into the parent class. In this example, the Drawable class might include Pen and Brush variables that the objects would use to draw themselves. Putting code in the parent class reduces the amount of redundant code in the child classes, making debugging and maintenance easier.

To make the classes more consistent, you could even change their names to reflect their shared ancestry. You might change their names to DrawableEllipse, DrawablePolygon, and so forth. This not only makes it easier to remember that they are all related to the Drawable class but also helps avoid confusion with class names such as Rectangle that are already used by Visual Basic.

The Drawable parent class also allows the program to handle the drawing objects more uniformly. It can define a collection named AllDrawables that contains references to all of the current drawing's objects. It could then loop through the collection, treating the objects as Drawables, and calling their DrawObject methods. The section "Polymorphism" later in this chapter provides more details.

Often application architects define class hierarchies using refinement. They start with broad general classes and then refine them as necessary to differentiate among the kinds of objects that the application will need to use. These classes tend to be relatively intuitive, so you can easily imagine their relationships.

Abstraction often arises during development. As you build the application's classes, you notice that some have common features. You abstract the classes and pull the common features into a parent class to reduce redundant code and make the application more maintainable.

Refinement and abstraction are useful techniques for building inheritance hierarchies, but they have their dangers. Designers should be careful not to get carried away with *unnecessary refinement* or *over refinement*. For example, suppose that you define a Vehicle class. You then refine this class by creating Auto, Truck, and Boat classes. You refine the Auto class into Wagon and Sedan classes and further refine those for different drive types (four-wheel drive, automatic, and so forth). If you really go crazy, you could define classes for specific manufacturers, body styles, and color.

The problem with this hierarchy is that it captures more detail than the application needs. If the program is a repair dispatch application, it might need to know whether a vehicle is a car or truck. It will not need to differentiate between wagons and sedans, different manufacturers, or colors. Vehicles with different colors have the same behaviors as far as this application is concerned. Creating many unnecessary classes makes the object model harder to understand and can lead to confusion and mistakes. (I worked on one project that failed because of an overly complicated object model.)

Avoid unnecessary refinement by refining a class only when doing so lets you capture new information that the application actually needs to know.

Just as you can take refinement to ridiculous extremes, you can also overdo class abstraction. Because abstraction is driven by code rather than intuition, it sometimes leads to unintuitive inheritance hierarchies. For example, suppose that your application needs to mail work orders to remote employees and invoices to customers. If the WorkOrder and Invoice classes have enough code in common, you might decide to give them a common parent class named MailableItem that contains the code needed to mail a document to someone.

This type of unintuitive relationship can confuse developers. Because Visual Basic doesn't allow multiple inheritance, it can also cause problems if the classes are already members of other inheritance hierarchies. You can avoid some of those problems by moving the common code into a library and having the classes call the library code. In this example, the WorkOrder and Invoice classes would call a common set of routines for mailing documents and would not need to be derived from a common parent class.

Unnecessary refinement and overabstracted classes lead to overinflated inheritance hierarchies. Sometimes the hierarchy grows very tall and thin. Other times, it may include several root classes (with no parents) on top of only one or two small classes each. Either of these can be symptoms of poor designs that include more classes than necessary. If your inheritance hierarchy starts to take on one of these forms, you should spend some time reevaluating the classes. Ensure that each adds something meaningful to the application and that the relationships are reasonably intuitive. Too many classes with confusing relationships can drag a project to a halt as developers spend more time trying to understand the hierarchy than they spend implementing the individual classes.

If you are unsure whether to add a new class, leave it out. It's usually easier to add a new class later if you discover that it is necessary than it is to remove an unnecessary class after developers start using it.

"Has-a" and "Is-a" Relationships

Refinement and abstraction are two useful techniques for generating inheritance hierarchies. The "has-a" and "is-a" relationships can help you understand whether it makes sense to make a new class using refinement or abstraction.

The "is-a" relationship means one object is a specific type of another class. For example, an Employee "is-a" specific type of Person object. The "is-a" relation maps naturally into inheritance hierarchies. Because an Employee "is-a" Person, it makes sense to derive the Employee class from the Person class.

The "has-a" relationship means that one object has some item as an attribute. For example, a Person object "has-a" street address, city, state, and ZIP code. The "has-a" relation maps most naturally to embedded objects. For example, you could give the Person class Street, City, State, and Zip properties.

Suppose that the program also works with WorkOrder, Invoice, and other classes that also have street, city, state, and ZIP code information. Using abstraction, you might make a HasPostalAddress class that contains those values. Then you could derive Person, WorkOrder, and Invoice as child classes. Unfortunately, that makes a rather unintuitive inheritance hierarchy. Deriving the Person, WorkOrder, and Invoice classes from HasPostalAddress makes those classes seem closely related when they are actually related almost coincidentally.

A better solution would be to encapsulate the postal address data in its own PostalAddress class and then include an instance of that class in the Person, WorkOrder, and Invoice classes.

You make a parent class through abstraction in part to avoid duplication of code. The parent class contains a single copy of the common variables and code, so the child classes don't need to have their own separate versions for you to debug and maintain. Placing an instance of the PostalAddress class in each of the other classes provides the same benefit without complicating the inheritance hierarchy.

You can often view a particular relationship as either an "is-a" or a "has-a" relationship. A Person "has-a" postal address. At the same time, a Person "is-a" thing that has a postal address. Use your intuition to decide which view makes more sense. One hint is that *postal address* is easy to describe whereas *thing that has a postal address* is more awkward and ill-defined. Also, think about how the relationship might affect other classes. Do you really want Person, WorkOrder, and Invoice to be siblings in the inheritance hierarchy? Or would it make more sense for them to just share an embedded class?

Adding and Modifying Class Features

Adding new properties, methods, and events to a child class is easy. You simply declare them as you would in any other class. The parent class knows nothing about them, so the new items are added only to the child class.

The following code shows how you could implement the Person and Employee classes in Visual Basic:

```
Public Class Person
    Public FirstName As String
    Public LastName As String
    Public Street As String
    Public City As String
    Public State As String
    Public Zip As String
    Public Phone As String
    Public Email As String

    ' Dial the phone using Phone property.
    Public Overridable Sub DialPhone()
        MessageBox.Show("Dial " & Me.Phone)
    End Sub
End Class

Public Class Employee
    Inherits Person
    Public EmployeeId As Integer
    Public SocialSecurityNumber As String
    Public OfficeNumber As String
    Public Extension As String
    Public Salary As Single

    ' Dial the phone using Extension property.
    Public Overrides Sub DialPhone()
        MessageBox.Show("Dial " & Me.Extension)
    End Sub
End Class
```

The Person class includes variables that define the FirstName, LastName, Street, City, State, Zip, Phone, and Email values. It also defines the DialPhone method. The version shown here simply displays the Person object's Phone value.

The Employee class inherits from the Person class. It declares its own EmployeeId, SocialSecurityNumber, OfficeNumber, Extension, and Salary variables. It also defines a new version of the DialPhone method that displays the Employee object's Extension value rather than its Phone value.

The DialPhone method in the Person class is declared with the Overridable keyword to allow derived classes to override it. The version defined in the Employee class is declared with the Overrides keyword to indicate that it should replace the version defined by the parent class.

A class can also *shadow* a feature defined in a parent class. When you declare a property, method, or event with the Shadows keyword, it hides any item in the parent that has the same name. This is very similar to overriding, except that the parent class does not have to declare the item as overridable and the child item needs only to match the parent item's name.

For example, the parent might define a SendMail subroutine that takes no parameters. If the child class defines a SendMail method that takes some parameters and uses the Shadows keyword, the child's version hides the parent's version.

In fact, the child and parent items don't even need to be the same kind of item. For example, the child class could make a *subroutine* named FirstName that shadows the parent class's FirstName *variable*. This type of change can be confusing, however, so usually you should only shadow items with similar items.

The following code shows how the Employee class might shadow the Person class's SendMail subroutine:

```
Public Class Person
    ...
    ' Send some mail to the person's address.
    Public Sub SendMail()
        MessageBox.Show("Mail " & Street & ", " & City & ", " &
            State & " " & Zip)
    End Sub
End Class

Public Class Employee
    Inherits Person
    ...
    ' Send some mail to the person's office.
    Public Shadows Sub SendMail()
        MessageBox.Show("Mail " & OfficeNumber)
    End Sub
End Class
```

The Person class displays the mailing address where it would send a letter. A real application might print a letter on a specific printer for someone to mail. The Employee class shadows this routine with one of its own, which displays the employee's office number instead of a mailing address.

Interface Inheritance

When you derive one class from another, the child class inherits the properties, methods, and events defined by the parent class. It inherits both the definition of those items and the code that implements them.

Visual Basic also enables you to define an interface. An *interface* defines a class's behaviors, but does not provide an implementation. After you have defined an interface, a class can use the Implements keyword to indicate that it provides the behaviors specified by the interface. It's then up to you to provide the code that implements the interface.

For example, consider again the MotorHome class. Visual Basic does not allow a class to inherit from more than one parent class, but a class can implement as many interfaces as you like. You could define an IVehicle interface (by convention, interface names begin with the capital letter I) that defines properties of vehicles (number of wheels, horsepower, maximum speed, acceleration, and so forth) and an IHouse interface that defines properties of living spaces (square feet, number of bedrooms, number of bathrooms, and so forth). Now, you can make the MotorHome class implement both of those interfaces. The interfaces do not provide any code, but they do declare that the MotorHome class implements the interface's features.

Like true inheritance, interface inheritance provides polymorphism (see the next section, "Polymorphism," for more details on this topic). You can use a variable having the type of the interface to refer to objects that define the interface. For example, suppose that the Employee, Manager, and Customer classes implement the IPerson interface. Then you can use a variable of type IPerson to refer to an object of type Employee, Manager, or Customer.

Suppose that the people collection contains Employee, Manager, and Customer objects. The following code uses a variable of type IPerson to display the objects' names:

```
For Each person As IPerson In people
    Debug.WriteLine(person.FirstName & " " & person.LastName)
Next person
```

POLYMORPHISM

Roughly speaking, *polymorphism* means treating one object as another. In OOP terms, it means that you can treat an object of one class as if it were from a parent class.

For example, suppose that Employee and Customer are both derived from the Person class. Then you can treat Employee and Customer objects as if they were Person objects because, in a sense, they are Person objects. They are specific types of Person objects. After all, they provide all of the properties, methods, and events of a Person object.

Visual Basic enables you to assign a value from a child class to a variable of the parent class. In this example, you can place an Employee or Customer object in a Person variable, as shown in the following code:

```
Dim emp As New Employee    ' Create an Employee.
Dim cust As New Customer   ' Create a Customer.
Dim per As Person          ' Declare a Person variable.
per = emp                  ' Okay. An Employee is a Person.
per = cust                 ' Okay. A Customer is a Person.
emp = per                  ' Not okay. A Person is not necessarily an Employee.
```

One common reason to use polymorphism is to treat a collection of objects in a uniform way that makes sense in the parent class. For example, suppose that the Person class defines the FirstName and LastName fields. The program could define a collection named AllPeople and add references to Customer and Employee objects to represent all the people that the program needs to work with. The code could then iterate through the collection, treating each object as a Person, as shown in the following code:

```
For Each per As Person In AllPeople
    Debug.WriteLine(per.FirstName & " " & per.LastName)
Next Per
```

You can only access the features defined for the type of variable you actually use to refer to an object. For example, if you use a Person variable to refer to an Employee object, you can only use the features defined by the Person class, not those added by the Employee class.

If you know that a particular object is of a specific subclass, you can convert the variable into a more specific variable type. The following code loops through the AllPeople collection and uses the TypeOf statement to test each object's type. It uses DirectCast to convert the more general Person variable into a variable with a more specific class and then uses the new variable to perform class-specific tasks.

```
For Each per As Person In AllPeople
    If TypeOf per Is Employee Then
        Dim emp As Employee = DirectCast(per, Employee)
        ' Do something Employee-specific.
        ...
    ElseIf TypeOf per Is Customer Then
        Dim cust As Customer = DirectCast(per, Customer)
        ' Do something Customer-specific.
        ...
    End If
Next per
```

METHOD OVERLOADING

Visual Basic .NET enables you to give a class more than one method with the same name but with different parameters. The program decides which version of the method to use based on the parameters being passed to the method.

For example, the Person class shown in the following code has two constructors named New. The first takes no parameters and initializes the object's FirstName and LastName variables to default values. The second overloaded constructor takes two strings as parameters and uses them to initialize FirstName and LastName.

```
Public Class Person
    Public FirstName As String
    Public LastName As String

    Public Sub New()
        FirstName = "<first>"
        LastName = "<last>"
    End Sub

    Public Sub New(first_name As String, last_name As String)
        FirstName = first_name
        LastName = last_name
    End Sub
End Class
```

The following code uses these constructors. The first statement passes no parameters to the constructor, so Visual Basic uses the first version of the New method. The second statement passes two strings to the constructor, so Visual Basic uses the second constructor.

```
Dim person1 As New Person()
Dim person2 As New Person("Rod", "Stephens")
```

A common technique for providing constructors that take different numbers of arguments is to make the simpler constructors call those with more parameters passing them default values. In the following code, the parameterless constructor calls a constructor that takes two parameters:

```
Public Class Person
    Public FirstName As String
    Public LastName As String

    Public Sub New()
        Me.New("<first>", "<last>")
    End Sub

    Public Sub New(first_name As String, last_name As String)
        FirstName = first_name
        LastName = last_name
    End Sub
End Class
```

Two overloaded methods cannot differ only by optional parameters. For example, the `first_name` and `last_name` parameters in the previous constructor could not both be optional. If they were, Visual Basic .NET could not tell which version of the New subroutine to call if the program passed it no parameters. Although you cannot make the parameters optional in the second constructor, you can get a similar result by combining the two constructors, as shown in the following code:

```
Public Class Person
    Public FirstName As String
    Public LastName As String

    Public Sub New(
     Optional first_name As String = "<first>",
     Optional last_name As String = "<last>")
        FirstName = first_name
        LastName = last_name
    End Sub
End Class
```

Overloaded functions also cannot differ only in their return types. In other words, you cannot have two versions of a function with the same name and parameters but different return types.

EXTENSION METHODS

Extension methods let you add new subroutines or functions to an existing class without rewriting it or deriving a new class from it even if you don't have access to the class's source code.

To make an extension method, create a new method in a code module and place the System .Runtime.CompilerServices.Extension attribute before the method's declaration. (If you like, you can add the statement "Imports System.Runtime.CompilerServices" at the top of the file so you only need to use the name Extension for the attribute.)

Then make a normal subroutine or function that takes one or more parameters. The first parameter determines the class that the method extends. The method can use that parameter to learn about the item for which the method was called. The other parameters are passed into the method so it can use them to do its work.

For example, the following code adds a MatchesRegexp subroutine to the String class:

```
' Return True if a String matches a regular expression.
<Extension()>
Public Function MatchesRegexp(the_string As String,
 regular_expression As String) As Boolean
    Dim reg_exp As New Regex(regular_expression)
    Return reg_exp.IsMatch(the_string)
End Function
```

The Extension attribute tells Visual Basic that this is an extension method. The method's first parameter is a String so this method extends the String class. The second parameter is a regular expression. The method returns True if the String matches the regular expression.

The program can use the extension method just as if it were part of the String class. The following code uses the MatchesRegexp method to decide whether the phone_number variable contains a value that looks like a valid United States phone number:

```
If Not phone_number.MatchesRegexp("^[2-9]\d{2}-\d{4}$") Then
    MessageBox.Show("Not a valid phone number")
End If
```

If used haphazardly, extension methods can blur the purpose of a class. They can make the class do things for which it was never intended. They add behaviors that the class's original authors did not have in mind. The result may be a class that does too many poorly defined or unrelated things, and that is confusing and hard to use properly. They weaken the class's encapsulation by adding new features that are not hidden within the control's code.

If you have access to the class's source code, make changes to the class within that code. Then if there is a problem, at least all of the code is together within the class. If you really need to add new methods to a class that is outside of your control, such as adding new methods to String and other classes defined by Visual Basic and the .NET Framework, you can use extension methods.

SUMMARY

Classes are programming abstractions that group data and related behavior in tightly encapsulated packages. After you define a class, you can instantiate it to create an instance of the class. You can interact with the new object by using its properties, methods, and events.

Inheritance enables you to derive one class from another. You can then add, remove, or modify the behavior that the child class inherits from the parent class. Sometimes it makes sense to think of the classes in inheritance hierarchies in a top-down manner, so child classes refine the features of their parents. At other times, it makes sense to use a bottom-up view and think of a parent class as abstracting the features of its children.

Interface inheritance lets you define some of the features of a class without using true class inheritance. This gives you another method for using polymorphism and lets you build classes that, in a sense, appear to inherit from multiple parents.

Polymorphism enables you to treat an object as if it were of an ancestor's type. For example, if the Manager class inherits from Employee and Employee inherits from Person, then you can treat a Manager object as if it were a Manager, Employee, or Person.

In addition to these features, Visual Basic .NET enables you to overload a class's subroutines, functions, and operators. It lets you create different methods with the same name but different parameters. The compiler selects the right version of the method based on the parameters you pass to it. Extension methods even let you add new subroutines and functions to existing classes when you don't have access to the class's source code.

These object-oriented concepts provide the general background you need to understand classes in Visual Basic. Chapter 23, "Classes and Structures," describes the specifics of classes and structures in Visual Basic .NET. It shows how to declare and instantiate classes and structures and explains the differences between the two.

23

Classes and Structures

WHAT'S IN THIS CHAPTER

- ➤ Creating classes
- ➤ Differences between structures and classes
- ➤ Garbage collection and finalization
- ➤ Properties, methods, and events
- ➤ Shared variables and methods

WROX.COM CODE DOWNLOADS FOR THIS CHAPTER

The wrox.com code downloads for this chapter are found at http://www.wrox.com/remtitle.cgi?isbn=9781118314074 on the Download Code tab. The code for this chapter is divided into the following major examples:

- ➤ FinalizeObjects
- ➤ GarbageCollection
- ➤ StructuresAndClasses
- ➤ UseDispose

PACKAGING DATA

A variable holds a single value. It may be a simple value such as an integer or string, or a reference that points to a more complex entity. Two kinds of more complex entities are classes and structures.

Classes and structures are both *container types*. They group several related data values into a convenient package that you can manipulate as a group.

For example, an EmployeeInfo structure might contain fields that hold information about an employee (such as first name, last name, employee ID, office number, extension, and so on). If you make an EmployeeInfo structure and fill it with the data for a particular employee, you can then move the structure around as a single unit instead of passing around a bunch of separate variables holding the first name, last name, and the rest.

This chapter explains how to declare classes and structures, and how to create instances of them (*instantiate* them). It explains the differences between classes and structures and provides some advice about which to use under different circumstances.

Finally, this chapter describes some of the mechanical issues that you'll face when building classes. It explains how garbage collection affects objects. It finishes by explaining how to implement some of the most basic features of classes: constants, properties, methods, and events.

CLASSES

A class packages data and related behavior. For example, a WorkOrder class might store data describing a customer's work order in its properties. It could contain methods (subroutines and functions) for manipulating the work order. It might provide methods for scheduling the work, modifying the order's requirements, and setting the order's priority.

Here is the syntax for declaring a class:

```
[attribute_list] [Partial] [accessibility] [Shadows] [inheritance] _
Class name[(Of type_list)]
    [Inherits parent_class]
    [Implements interface]
    statements
End Class
```

The only things that all class declarations must include are the Class clause (including the class's name) and the End Class statement. Everything else is optional. The following code describes a valid (albeit not very interesting) class:

```
Class EmptyClass
End Class
```

The following sections describe the pieces of the general declaration in detail.

Attribute_list

The optional *attribute_list* is a comma-separated list of attributes that apply to the class. An attribute further refines the definition of a class to give more information to the compiler and the runtime system.

AVOID COMMA DRAMA

Instead of using commas to separate multiple attributes inside one set of brackets, you can place each attribute inside its own brackets. For example, the following code defines two classes, each having two attributes: Serializable and Obsolete.

```
<Serializable(), Obsolete("No longer supported. Use Sku instead")>
Public Class SkuNumber
    ...
End Class

<Serializable()>
<Obsolete("No longer supported. Use ProductType instead")>
Public Class Product
    ...
End Class
```

Which style you should use is a matter of personal preference, although it's slightly easier to insert or remove attributes with the second style because you can add or remove whole lines at a time without messing up the commas.

Attributes are rather specialized. They address issues that arise when you perform very specific programming tasks. For example, if your application must use drag-and-drop support to copy instances of the class from one application to another, you must mark the class with the Serializable attribute.

Some attributes are particular to specific kinds of classes. For example, the DefaultEvent attribute gives the Windows Form Designer extra information about component classes. If you double-click a component on a form, the code designer opens to the component's default event.

Because attributes are so specialized, they are not described in more detail here. For more information, see the sections in the online help that are related to the tasks you need to perform.

For more information on attributes, see Microsoft's "Attributes in Visual Basic" web page at `http://msdn.microsoft.com/39967861.aspx`. For a list of attributes that you can use, go to Microsoft's "Attribute Class" web page at `http://msdn.microsoft.com/system.attribute.aspx` and look at the "Inheritance Hierarchy" section.

Partial

The Partial keyword tells Visual Basic that the current declaration defines only part of the class. The following code shows the Employee class broken into two pieces:

```
Partial Public Class Employee
    Public FirstName As String
    Public LastName As String
    ...
End Class
```

```
... other code, possibly unrelated to the Employee class ...

Partial Public Class Employee
    Public Email As String
    ...
End Class
```

The program could contain any number of other pieces of the Employee class, possibly in different code modules. At compile time, Visual Basic finds these pieces and combines them to define the class.

One of the primary benefits of classes is that they hold the code and data associated with the class together in a nice package. Scattering the pieces of a class in this way makes the package less self-contained and may lead to confusion. To prevent confusion, you should avoid splitting a class unless you have a good reason to (for example, to allow different developers to work on different pieces of the class at the same time or if one piece must have Option Strict turned off).

At least one of the pieces of the class must be declared with the Partial keyword, but in the other pieces it is optional. Explicitly providing the keyword in all of the class's partial definitions emphasizes the fact that the class is broken into pieces and may reduce confusion.

Accessibility

A class's *accessibility* clause takes one of the following values: Public, Protected, Friend, Protected Friend, or Private.

Public indicates that the class should be available to all code inside or outside of the class's module. This enables the most access to the class. Any code can create and manipulate instances of the class.

You can use the Protected keyword only if the class you are declaring is contained inside another class. For example, the following code defines an Employee class that contains a protected EmployeeAddress class:

```
Public Class Employee
    Public FirstName As String
    Public LastName As String
    Protected Address As EmployeeAddress

    Protected Class EmployeeAddress
        Public Street As String
        Public City As String
        Public State As String
        Public Zip As String
    End Class

    ... other code ...
End Class
```

Because the EmployeeAddress class is declared with the Protected keyword, it is visible only within the enclosing Employee class and any derived classes. For example, if the Manager class inherits from the Employee class, code within the Manager class can access the Address variable.

The Friend keyword indicates that the class should be available to all code inside or outside of the class's module *within the same project*. The difference between this and Public is that Public allows code outside of the project to access the class. This is generally only an issue for code libraries (.dll files) and control libraries. For example, suppose that you build a code library containing dozens of routines and then you write a program that uses the library. If the library declares a class with the Public keyword, the code in the library and the code in the main program can use the class. If the library declares a class with the Friend keyword, only the code in the library can access the class, not the code in the main program.

Protected Friend is the union of the Protected and Friend keywords. A class declared Protected Friend is accessible only to code within the enclosing class or a derived class and only within the same project.

A class declared Private is accessible only to code in the enclosing module, class, or structure. If the EmployeeAddress class were declared Private, only code within the Employee class could use that class.

If you do not specify an accessibility level, it defaults to Friend.

Shadows

The Shadows keyword indicates that the class hides the definition of some other entity in an ancestor class.

The following code shows an Employee class that declares a public class OfficeInfo and defines an instance of that class named Office. The derived class Manager inherits from Employee. It declares a new version of the OfficeInfo class with the Shadows keyword. It defines an instance of this class named ManagerOffice.

```
Public Class Employee
    Public Class OfficeInfo
        Public OfficeNumber As String
        Public Extension As String
    End Class

    Public FirstName As String
    Public LastName As String
    Public Office As New OfficeInfo
End Class

Public Class Manager
    Inherits Employee

    Public Shadows Class OfficeInfo
        Public OfficeNumber As String
        Public Extension As String
        Public SecretaryOfficeNumber As String
        Public SecretaryExtension As String
    End Class

    Public ManagerOffice As New OfficeInfo
End Class
```

The following code uses the Employee and Manager classes. It creates instances of the two classes and sets their Office.Extension properties. Both of those values are part of the Employee class's version of the OfficeInfo class. Next, the code sets the Manager object's ManagerOffice .SecretaryExtension value.

```
Dim emp As New Employee
Dim mgr As New Manager
emp.Office.Extension = "1111"
mgr.Office.Extension = "2222"
mgr.ManagerOffice.SecretaryExtension = "3333"
```

Note that the Manager class contains two different objects of type OfficeInfo. Its Office property is the Employee class's flavor of OfficeInfo class. Its ManagerOffice value is the Manager class's version of OfficeInfo.

The presence of these different classes with the same name can be confusing. Usually, you are better off not using the Shadows keyword in the declarations and giving the classes different names. In this case, you could call the Manager class's included class ManagerOfficeInfo.

Inheritance

A class's *inheritance* clause can take the value MustInherit or NotInheritable.

MustInherit prohibits the program from creating instances of the class. The program should create an instance of a derived class instead. This kind of class is sometimes called an *abstract* class.

By using MustInherit, you can make a parent class that defines some of the behavior that should be implemented by derived classes without implementing the functionality itself. The parent class is not intended to be used itself, just to help define the derived classes.

The NotInheritable keyword does the opposite of the MustInherit keyword. MustInherit says that a class must be inherited to be instantiated. NotInheritable says no class can inherit from this one.

You can use NotInheritable to stop other developers from making new versions of the classes you have built. This isn't really necessary if you design a well-defined object model before you start programming and if everyone obeys it. NotInheritable can prevent unnecessary proliferation of classes if developers don't pay attention, however. For example, declaring the Car class NotInheritable would prevent overeager developers from deriving FrontWheelDriveCar, RedCar, and Subaru classes from the Car class.

> **EXTENSION TENSION**
>
> Extension methods allow developers to add new subroutines and functions to a class even if it is marked NotInheritable. This can ruin the class's focus of purpose, making it harder to understand and use safely. It also violates the intent of the NotInheritable keyword so you should avoid it if possible. For more information, see the section "Extension Methods" in Chapter 22, "OOP Concepts."

Of type_list

The *Of type_list* clause makes the class generic. It allows the program to create instances of the class that work with different data types. For example, the following code defines a generic Tree class. The class includes a public variable named RootObject that has the data type given in the class's Of data_type clause.

```
Public Class Tree(Of data_type)
    Public RootObject As data_type
    . . .
End Class
```

When you read this declaration, you should think "Tree of *something*," where *something* is defined later when you make an instance of the class.

The following code fragment declares and instantiates the variable my_tree to be a "Tree of Employee." It then sets its RootObject variable to a new Employee object.

```
Dim my_tree As New Tree(Of Employee)
my_tree.RootObject = New Employee
. . .
```

Chapter 26, "Generics," discusses generic classes further.

Inherits parent_class

The Inherits statement indicates that the class (the child class) is derived from another class (the parent class). The child class automatically inherits the parent's properties, methods, and events.

The following code defines an Employee class that contains LastName, FirstName, OfficeNumber, and Phone variables. It then derives the Manager class from the Employee class. The Manager class adds new SecretaryOfficeNumber and SecretaryPhone variables. These are available to instances of the Manager class but not to the Employee class.

```
Public Class Employee
    Public FirstName As String
    Public LastName As String
    Public OfficeNumber As String
    Public Phone As String
End Class

Public Class Manager
    Inherits Employee

    Public SecretaryOfficeNumber As String
    Public SecretaryPhone As String
End Class
```

If a class inherits from another class, the Inherits statement must be the first statement after the Class statement that is not blank or a comment. Also note that a class can inherit from at most one parent class, so a class definition can include at most one Inherits statement.

For more information on inheritance, see the section "Inheritance" in Chapter 22.

Implements interface

The Implements keyword indicates that a class will implement an interface. An interface defines behaviors that the implementing class must provide, but it does not provide any implementation for the behaviors.

For example, the following code defines the IDomicile interface. (By convention, the names of interfaces should begin with the capital letter I.)

```
Public Interface IDomicile
    Property SquareFeet As Integer
    ReadOnly Property NeedsFireSystem As Boolean
    Sub Clean()
End Interface
```

The House class shown in the following code implements the IDomicile interface. When you type the Implements statement and press Enter, Visual Basic automatically generates empty routines to provide the features defined by the interface.

```
Public Class House
    Implements IDomicile

    Public Sub Clean() Implements IDomicile.Clean

    End Sub

    Public ReadOnly Property NeedsFireSystem As Boolean _
     Implements IDomicile.NeedsFireSystem
        Get

        End Get
    End Property

    Public Property SquareFeet As Integer Implements IDomicile.SquareFeet
End Class
```

If a class declaration uses any Implements statements, they must come after any Inherits statement and before any other statements (other than blank lines and comments).

For more information on interfaces and how you can use them to mimic inheritance, see the section "Interface Inheritance" in Chapter 22.

STRUCTURES

Structures are very similar to classes. The syntax for declaring a structure is as follows:

```
[attribute_list] [Partial] [accessibility] [Shadows] _
Structure name[(Of type_list)]
    [Implements interface]
    statements
End Structure
```

The only thing that all structure declarations must include is the Structure clause (including the structure's name) and the End Structure statement. The rest is optional.

Unlike a class, however, a structure cannot be empty. It must contain at least one variable or event declaration. The following code defines a valid structure. Its only member is a Private variable, so this structure wouldn't be of much use, but it is valid.

```
Structure EmptyStructure
    Private Num As Integer
End Structure
```

The structure's *attribute_list* and *accessibility* clauses, Shadows and Partial keywords, and the Implements statement are the same as those for classes. See the earlier sections discussing these keywords for details.

There are two main differences between a structure and a class: Structures cannot inherit, and structures are value types rather than reference types.

Structures Cannot Inherit

Unlike a class, a structure cannot inherit so it cannot use the MustInherit, NotInheritable, or Inherits keywords; however, like a class, a structure can implement any number of interfaces. You can use interface inheritance to define inheritance-mimicking hierarchies of structures, and you can simulate multiple inheritance by making a structure implement multiple interfaces.

Structures Are Value Types

The biggest difference between a structure and a class is in how each allocates memory for its data. Classes are *reference types*. That means an instance of a class is actually a reference to the object's storage in memory. When you create an instance of a class, Visual Basic creates a reference that points to the object's actual location in memory.

In contrast, structures are *value types*. An instance of a structure contains the data inside the structure rather than simply points to it. Figure 23-1 illustrates the difference.

The difference between reference and value type has several important consequences that are described in the following sections.

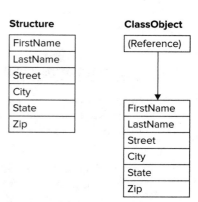

FIGURE 23-1: A structure contains the data, whereas a class object contains a reference that points to data.

Memory Required

The difference in memory required by classes and structures is small when you consider only a single object. If you look at an array, however, the distinction is more important. An array of class objects contains references to data in some other part of memory. When you first declare the array, the references all have the value Nothing, so they don't point to any data and no memory is allocated for the data. The references take 4 bytes each, so the array uses only 4 bytes per array entry.

An array of structure instances, on the other hand, allocates space for the data inside the array. If each structure object takes up 1000 bytes of memory, then an array containing N items uses 1000 * N bytes of memory. Each structure instance's memory is allocated, whether or not its fields contain meaningful data.

Figure 23-2 illustrates this situation. The array of class objects on the left uses very little memory when the references are Nothing. The array of structure objects on the right uses a lot of memory even if its elements have not been initialized.

If you must use a large array of objects where only a few at a time will have values other than Nothing, using a class may save the program a considerable amount of memory. If you will need most of the objects to have values other than Nothing at the same time, it may be faster to allocate all the memory at once using a structure. This will also use slightly less memory, because an array of class references requires 4 extra bytes per entry to hold the references.

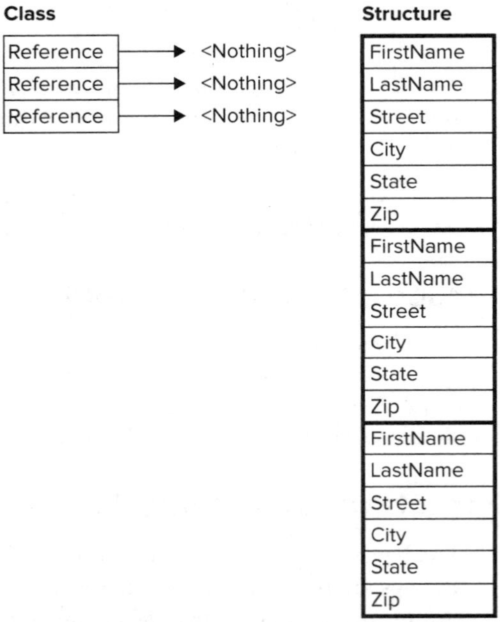

Class		Structure
Reference	→ <Nothing>	FirstName
Reference	→ <Nothing>	LastName
Reference	→ <Nothing>	Street
		City
		State
		Zip
		FirstName
		LastName
		Street
		City
		State
		Zip
		FirstName
		LastName
		Street
		City
		State
		Zip

FIGURE 23-2: An array of class objects contains small references to data, many of which may be Nothing. An array of structures takes up a significant amount of memory.

Heap and Stack Performance

Visual Basic programs allocate variables from two pools of memory called the *stack* and the *heap*. Programs take memory for value types (such as integers and dates) from the stack.

Space for reference types comes from the heap. More than one reference can point to the same chunk of memory allocated on the heap. That makes garbage collection and other heap-management issues more complex than using the stack, so using the heap is generally slower than using the stack.

Because structures are value types and classes are reference types, structures are allocated on the stack and class objects are allocated on the heap. That makes structures faster than classes. The exact difference for a particular program depends on the application.

Note that arrays are themselves reference types, so all arrays are allocated from the heap whether they contain structures or references to class objects. The memory for an array of structures is allocated all at once, however, so there is still some benefit to using structures. All the memory in an array of structures is contiguous, so the program can access its elements more quickly than it would if the memory were scattered throughout the heap.

Object Assignment

When you assign one reference type variable to another, you make a new reference to an existing object. When you are finished, the two variables point to the same object. If you change the object's fields using one variable, the fields shown by the other are also changed.

In contrast, if you set one value type variable equal to another, Visual Basic copies the data from one to the other. If you later change the fields in one object, the fields in the other remain unchanged. Figure 23-3 illustrates the difference for classes and structures.

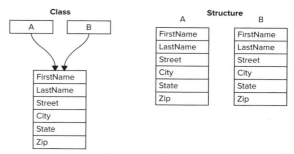

FIGURE 23-3: Assigning one class reference to another makes them both point to the same object. Assigning one structure variable to another makes a new copy of the data.

Example program StructuresAndClasses uses the following code to demonstrate this difference:

```
Dim cperson1 As New CPerson
Dim cperson2 As CPerson
cperson1.FirstName = "Alice"
cperson2 = cperson1
cperson2.FirstName = "Ben"
MessageBox.Show(cperson1.FirstName & vbCrLf & cperson2.FirstName)

Dim sperson1 As New SPerson
Dim sperson2 As SPerson
sperson1.FirstName = "Alice"
sperson2 = sperson1
sperson2.FirstName = "Ben"
MessageBox.Show(sperson1.FirstName & vbCrLf & sperson2.FirstName)
```

The code creates a CPerson class object and sets its first name value. It then assigns another CPerson variable to the same object. Because CPerson is a class, the two variables refer to the same piece of memory so when the code sets the new variable's first name value it overwrites the previous variable's first name value. The message box displays the name Ben twice.

The code performs the same steps again but this time it uses structure variables instead of class variables. The code makes an SPerson structure and sets its first name value. When it sets the second SPerson variable equal to the first one, that makes a copy of the structure. Now when the code sets the second variable's first name to Ben, it does not overwrite the previous variable's first name value. The message box displays the names Alice and Ben.

Parameter Passing

When you pass a parameter to a function or subroutine, you can pass it by reference using the ByRef keyword or by value using the ByVal keyword. If you pass a parameter by reference, any changes that the routine makes are reflected in the original parameter passed into the routine.

For example, consider the following code.

```
Public Sub TestByRef()
    Dim i As Integer = 1

    PassByVal(i)
    MessageBox.Show(i.ToString) ' i = 1.

    PassByRef(i)
    MessageBox.Show(i.ToString) ' i = 2.
End Sub

Public Sub PassByVal(ByVal the_value As Integer)
    the_value *= 2
End Sub

Public Sub PassByRef(ByRef the_value As Integer)
    the_value *= 2
End Sub
```

Subroutine TestByRef creates an integer named i and sets its value to 1. It then calls subroutine PassByVal. That routine declares its parameter with the ByVal keyword, so i is passed by value. PassByVal multiplies its parameter by 2 and ends. Because the parameter was declared ByVal, the original variable i is unchanged, so the message box displays the value 1.

Next the program calls subroutine PassByRef, passing it the variable i. Subroutine PassByRef declares its parameter with the ByRef keyword, so a reference to the variable is passed into the routine. PassByRef doubles its parameter and ends. Because the parameter is declared with the ByRef keyword, the value of variable i is modified so the message box displays the value 2.

When you work with class references and structures, you must think a bit harder about how ByRef and ByVal work. There are four possible combinations: class ByVal, structure ByVal, class ByRef, and structure ByRef.

If you pass a class reference to a routine by value, the routine receives a *copy of the reference*. If it changes the reference (perhaps making it point to a new object), the original reference passed into the routine remains unchanged. It still points to the same object it did when it was passed to the routine. However, the routine can change the values in the object to which the reference points. If the reference points to a Person object, the routine can change the object's FirstName, LastName, and other fields. It cannot change the reference itself to make it point to a different Person object, but it can change the object's data.

In contrast, suppose that you pass a structure into a routine by value. In that case, the routine receives a *copy of the entire structure*. The routine can change the values contained in its copy of the structure, but the original structure's values remain unchanged. It cannot change the original structure's fields the way it could if the parameter were a reference type.

If you pass a class reference variable by reference, the routine can not only modify the values in the reference's object but also make the reference point to a different object. For example, the routine could use the New keyword to make the variable point to a completely new object.

If you pass a structure by reference, the routine receives a pointer to the structure's data. If it changes the structure's data, the fields in the original variable passed into the routine are modified. (The result is similar to what happens if you pass a class reference by value.)

In addition to these differences in behavior, passing class references and structures by reference or by value can make differences in performance. When you pass a reference to data, Visual Basic only needs to send the routine a 4-byte value. If you pass a structure into a routine by value, Visual Basic must duplicate the entire structure, so the routine can use its own copy. If the structure is very large, that may take a little extra time.

Boxing and Unboxing

Visual Basic allows a program to treat any variable as an object. For example, a collection class stores objects. If you add a simple value type such as an Integer to a collection, Visual Basic wraps the Integer in an object and adds that object to the collection.

The process of wrapping the Integer in an object is called *boxing*. Later, if you need to use the Integer as a value type again, the program *unboxes* it. Because structures are value types, the program must box and unbox them whenever it treats them as objects, and that adds some extra overhead.

Some operations that require boxing and possibly unboxing include assigning a structure to an Object variable, passing a structure to a routine that takes an Object as a parameter, or adding a structure to a collection class. Note that this last operation includes adding a structure to a collection used by a control or other object. For example, adding a structure to a ListBox control's Items collection requires boxing.

Note that arrays are themselves reference types, so treating an array as an object doesn't require boxing.

CLASS INSTANTIATION DETAILS

When you declare a reference variable, Visual Basic allocates space for the reference. Initially, that reference is set to Nothing, so it doesn't point to anything and no memory is allocated for an actual object.

You create an object by using the New keyword. Creating an actual object is called *instantiating* the class.

The following code shows a simple object declaration and instantiation. The first line declares the reference variable. The second line makes the variable point to a new Employee object.

```
Dim emp As Employee ' Declare a reference to an Employee object.
emp = New Employee  ' Make a new Employee object and make emp point to it.
```

Visual Basic also enables you to declare and initialize a variable in a single statement. The following code shows how to declare and initialize an object reference in one statement:

```
Dim emp As Employee = New Employee ' Declare and instantiate an object.
```

Visual Basic lets you declare a variable to be of a new object type, as shown in the following statement. This version has the same effect as the preceding one but is slightly more compact.

```
Dim emp As New Employee ' Declare and instantiate an object.
```

Both of these versions that define and initialize an object in a single statement ensure that the variable is initialized right away. They guarantee that the object is instantiated before you try to use it. If you place these kinds of declarations immediately before the code where the object is used, they also make it easy to see where the object is defined.

Although you can declare and instantiate a reference variable separately, value type variables are allocated when they are declared. Because structures are value types, when you declare one you also allocate space for its data, so you don't need to use the New keyword to initialize a structure variable.

Both classes and structures can provide special subroutines called *constructors*. A constructor is a special subroutine named New that Visual Basic calls when a new instance of the class or structure is created. The constructor can perform initialization tasks to get the new object ready for use.

A constructor can optionally take parameters to help in initializing the object. For example, the Person class shown in the following code has a constructor that takes as parameters first and last names and saves them in the control's FirstName and LastName variables:

```
Public Class Person
    Public FirstName As String
    Public LastName As String

    Public Sub New(ByVal first_name As String, ByVal last_name As String)
        FirstName = first_name
        LastName = last_name
    End Sub
End Class
```

The following code shows how a program might use this constructor to create a new Person object:

```
Dim author As New Person("Rod", "Stephens")
```

You can overload the New method just as you can overload other class methods. The different overloaded versions of the constructor must have different parameter lists so that Visual Basic can decide which one to use when it creates a new object.

The following code shows a Person class that provides two constructors. The first takes two strings as parameters and copies them into the object's FirstName and LastName values. The second version takes no parameters and invokes the first constructor to set the object's FirstName and LastName values to <unknown>.

```
Public Class Person
    Public FirstName As String
    Public LastName As String

    Public Sub New(first_name As String, last_name As String)
        FirstName = first_name
        LastName = last_name
    End Sub

    Public Sub New()
        Me.New("<unknown>", "<unknown>")
    End Sub
End Class
```

The following code uses each of these constructors:

```
Dim person1 As New Person                     ' <unknown> <unknown>.
Dim person2 As New Person("Olga", "O'Toole") ' Olga O'Toole.
```

If you do not provide any constructors for a class, Visual Basic allows the program to use the New keyword with no parameters. If you create any constructor, however, Visual Basic does not allow the program to use this default empty constructor (without parameters) unless you build one explicitly. For example, if the previous version of the Person class did not include a parameterless constructor, the program could not use the first declaration in the previous code that doesn't include any parameters.

You can use this feature to ensure that the program assigns required values to an object. In this case, it would mean that the program could not create a Person object without assigning FirstName and LastName values.

If you want to allow an empty constructor in addition to other constructors, an alternative is to create a single constructor with optional parameters. The following code shows this approach. With this class, the program could create a new Person object, passing its constructor zero, one, or two parameters.

```
Public Class Person
    Public FirstName As String
    Public LastName As String

    Public Sub New(
```

```
        Optional first_name As String = "<unknown>",
        Optional last_name As String = "<unknown>")
            FirstName = first_name
            LastName = last_name
        End Sub
    End Class
```

When you use a class's parameterless constructor to create an object, you can also include a With clause to initialize the object's properties. The following code uses the Person class's parameterless constructor to make a new Person object. The With statement then sets values for the object's FirstName and LastName values.

```
Dim author As New Person() With {.FirstName = "Rod", .LastName = "Stephens"}
```

STRUCTURE INSTANTIATION DETAILS

Structures handle instantiation somewhat differently from object references. When you declare a reference variable, Visual Basic does not automatically allocate the object to which the variable points. In contrast, when you declare a value type such as a structure, Visual Basic automatically allocates space for the variable's data. That means you never need to use the New keyword to instantiate a structure.

However, the Visual Basic compiler warns you if you do not explicitly initialize a structure variable before using it. To satisfy the compiler, you can use the New keyword to initialize the variable when you declare it.

A structure can also provide constructors, and you can use those constructors to initialize the structure. The following code defines the SPerson structure and gives it a constructor that takes two parameters, the second optional:

```
Public Structure SPerson
    Public FirstName As String
    Public LastName As String

    Public Sub New(
     ByVal first_name As String,
     Optional ByVal last_name As String = "<unknown>")
        FirstName = first_name
        LastName = last_name
    End Sub
End Structure
```

To use a structure's constructor, you initialize the structure with the New keyword much as you initialize a reference variable. The following code allocates an SPerson structure variable using the two-parameter constructor:

```
Dim artist As New SPerson("Sergio", "Aragones")
```

You can also use structure constructors later to reinitialize a variable or set its values, as shown here:

```
' Allocate the artist variable.
Dim artist As SPerson

' Do something with artist.
...

' Reset FirstName and LastName to Nothing.
artist = New SPerson
...

' Set FirstName and LastName to Bill Amend.
artist = New SPerson("Bill", "Amend")
```

As is the case with classes, you can use a With clause to set structure values when you initialize a structure variable. For example, the following code creates a new SPerson structure and sets its FirstName and LastName values:

```
Dim artist As New SPerson() With {.FirstName = "Anna", .LastName = "Aux"}
```

> **NEW NEEDED**
>
> Although you can create a structure without using the New keyword, you cannot include a With clause unless you use New.

Structure and class constructors are very similar, but there are some major differences:

➤ A structure cannot declare a constructor that takes no parameters.

➤ A structure cannot provide a constructor with all optional parameters, because that would allow the program to call it with no parameters.

➤ Visual Basic always allows the program to use a default parameterless constructor to declare a structure variable, but you cannot make it use *your* parameterless constructor. Unfortunately, that means you cannot use a default constructor to guarantee that the program always initializes the structure's values as you can with a class. If you need that feature, you should use a class instead of a structure.

➤ You also cannot provide initialization values for variables declared within a structure as you can with a class. That means you cannot use this technique to provide default values for the structure's variables.

The following code demonstrates these differences. The CPerson class defines initial values for its FirstName and LastName variables, provides an empty constructor, and provides a two-parameter constructor. The SPerson structure cannot define initial values for FirstName and LastName and cannot provide an empty constructor.

```
' Class.
Public Class CPerson
    Public FirstName As String = "<unknown>" ' Initialization value allowed.
    Public LastName As String = "<unknown>"  ' Initialization value allowed.

    ' Empty constructor allowed.
    Public Sub New()
    End Sub

    ' Two-parameter constructor allowed.
    Public Sub New(first_name As String, last_name As String)
        FirstName = first_name
        LastName = last_name
    End Sub
End Class

' Structure.
Public Structure SPerson
    Public FirstName As String ' = "<unknown>" ' Initialization NOT allowed.
    Public LastName As String ' = "<unknown>" ' Initialization NOT allowed.

    '' Empty constructor NOT allowed.
    'Public Sub New()
    'End Sub

    ' Two-parameter constructor allowed.
    Public Sub New(first_name As String, last_name As String)
        FirstName = first_name
        LastName = last_name
    End Sub
End Structure
```

GARBAGE COLLECTION

When a program starts, the system allocates a chunk of memory for the program called the *managed heap*. When it allocates data for reference types (class objects), Visual Basic uses memory from this heap. (For more information about the stack and heap and their relative performance, see the section "Heap and Stack Performance" earlier in this chapter.)

When the program no longer needs to use a reference object, Visual Basic does *not* mark the heap memory as free for later use. If you set a reference variable to Nothing so that no variable points to the object, the object's memory is no longer available to the program, but Visual Basic does not reuse the object's heap memory, at least not right away.

The optimizing engine of the *garbage collector* (GC) determines when it needs to clean up the heap. If the program allocates and frees many reference objects, a lot of the heap may be full of memory that is no longer used. In that case, the garbage collector will decide to clean house.

When it runs, the garbage collector examines all the program's reference variables, parameters that are object references, CPU registers, and other items that might point to heap objects. It uses those values to build a graph describing the heap memory that the program can still access. It then compacts the objects in the heap and updates the program's references so they can find any moved items. The garbage collector then updates the heap itself so that the program can allocate memory from the unused portion.

When it destroys an object, the garbage collector frees the object's memory and any managed resources it contains. It may not free unmanaged resources, however. You can determine when and how an object frees its managed and unmanaged resources by using the Finalize and Dispose methods.

Finalize

When it destroys an object, the garbage collector frees any managed resources used by that object. For example, suppose that an unused object contains a reference to an open file stream. When the garbage collector runs, it notices that the file stream is inaccessible to the program, so it destroys the file stream, as well as the object that contains its reference.

However, suppose that the object uses an *unmanaged resource* that is outside of the scope of objects that Visual Basic understands. For example, suppose the object holds an integer representing a file handle, network connection, or channel to a hardware device that Visual Basic doesn't understand. In that case, the garbage collector doesn't know how to free that resource.

You can tell the garbage collector what to do by overriding the class's Finalize method, which is inherited from the Object class. The garbage collector calls an object's Finalize method before permanently removing the object from the heap. Note that there are no guarantees about exactly when the garbage collector calls this method, or the order in which different objects' Finalize methods are called. Two objects' Finalize methods may be called in either order even if one contains a reference to the other or if one was freed long before the other. If you must guarantee a specific order, you must provide more specific cleanup methods of your own.

Example program GarbageCollection uses the following code to demonstrate the Finalize method:

```
Public Class Form1
    Public Running As Boolean

    Private Class Junk
        Public MyForm As Form1

        Public Sub New(my_form As Form1)
            MyForm = my_form
        End Sub

        ' Garbage collection started.
        Protected Overrides Sub Finalize()
            ' Stop making objects.
            MyForm.Running = False
        End Sub
    End Class

    ' Make objects until garbage collection starts.
    Private Sub btnCreateObjects_Click() Handles btnCreateObjects.Click
        Running = True
```

```
            Dim new_obj As Junk
            Dim max_i As Long
            For i As Long = 1 To 1000000
                new_obj = New Junk(Me)

                If Not Running Then
                    max_i = i
                    Exit For
                End If
            Next i
            MessageBox.Show("Allocated " & max_i.ToString & " objects")
        End Sub
    End Class
```

The Form1 class defines the public variable Running. It then defines the Junk class, which contains a variable referring to the Form1 class. This class's constructor saves a reference to the Form1 object that created it. Its Finalize method sets the Form1 object's Running value to False.

When the user clicks the form's Create Objects button, the btnCreateObjects_Click event handler sets Running to True and starts creating Junk objects, passing the constructor this form as a parameter. The routine keeps creating new objects as long as Running is True. Note that each time the routine creates a new object, the old object that the variable new_obj used to point to becomes inaccessible to the program so it is available for garbage collection.

Eventually the program's heap runs low, so the garbage collector executes. When it destroys one of the Junk objects, the object's Finalize subroutine executes and sets the form's Running value to False. When the garbage collector finishes, the btnCreateObjects_Click event handler sees that Running is False, so it stops creating new Junk objects. It displays the number of the last Junk object it created and is done.

In one test, this program created 30,456 Junk objects before the garbage collector ran. In a second trial run immediately after the first, the program created 59,150 objects, and in a third it created 26,191. The garbage collector gives you little control over when it finalizes objects.

Visual Basic also calls every object's Finalize method when the program ends. Again, there are no guarantees about the exact timing or order of the calls to different objects' Finalize methods.

Example program FinalizeObjects, which is available for download on the book's website, uses the following code to test the Finalize method when the program ends:

```
Public Class Form1
    Private Class Numbered
        Private Number As Integer
        Public Sub New(my_number As Integer)
            Number = my_number
        End Sub

        ' Garbage collection started.
        Protected Overrides Sub Finalize()
            ' Display the object's number.
            Debug.WriteLine("Finalized object " & Number)
        End Sub
```

```
        End Class

        ' Make objects until garbage collection starts.
        Private Sub btnGo_Click() Handles btnGo.Click
            Static i As Integer = 0
            i += 1
            Dim new_numbered As New Numbered(i)
            Debug.WriteLine("Created object " & i.ToString)
        End Sub
    End Class
```

The Numbered class contains a variable Number and initializes that value in its constructor. Its Finalize method writes the object's number in the Output window.

The btnGo_Click event handler creates a new Numbered object, giving it a new number. When the event handler ends, the new_numbered variable referring to the Numbered object goes out of scope, so the object is no longer available to the program. If you look at the Output window at this time, you will probably find that the program has not bothered to finalize the object yet. If you click the button several times and then close the application, Visual Basic calls each object's Finalize method. If you click the button five times, you should see five messages displayed by the objects' Finalize methods.

If your class allocates unmanaged resources, you should give it a Finalize method to free them.

MEMORY MADNESS

Better still, use and free unmanaged resources as quickly as possible, not even waiting for finalization if you can. Unmanaged resources, in particular memory allocated in strange ways such as by using Marshal, can cause strange behaviors and leaks if you don't free them properly and promptly.

Dispose

Because Visual Basic doesn't keep track of whether an object is reachable at any given moment, it doesn't know when it can permanently destroy an object until the program ends or the garbage collector reclaims it. That means the object's memory and resources may remain unused for quite a while. The memory itself isn't a big issue. If the program's heap runs out of space, the garbage collector runs to reclaim some of the unused memory.

If the object contains a reference to a resource, however, that resource is not freed until the object is finalized, and that can have dire consequences. You generally don't want control of a file, network connection, scanner, or other scarce system resource left to the whims of the garbage collector.

By convention, the Dispose subroutine frees an object's resources. Before a program frees an object that contains important resources, it can call that object's Dispose method to free the resources explicitly.

To handle the case where the program does not call Dispose, the class should also free any unmanaged resources that it holds in its Finalize subroutine. Because Finalize is executed whether or not the program calls Dispose, the class must also be able to execute both the Dispose and the Finalize subroutines without harm. For example, if the program shuts down some piece of unusual hardware, it probably should not shut down the device twice.

To make building a Dispose method a little easier, Visual Basic defines the IDisposable interface, which declares the Dispose method. If you enter the statement Implements IDisposable and press Enter, Visual Basic creates an empty Dispose method for you.

Example program UseDispose, which is available for download on the book's website, uses the following code to demonstrate the Dispose and Finalize methods:

```
Public Class Form1
    Private Class Named
        Implements IDisposable

        ' Save our name.
        Public Name As String
        Public Sub New(new_name As String)
            Name = new_name
        End Sub

        ' Free resources.
        Protected Overrides Sub Finalize()
            Dispose()
        End Sub

        ' Display our name.
        Public Sub Dispose() Implements System.IDisposable.Dispose
            Static done_before As Boolean = False
            If done_before Then Exit Sub
            done_before = True

            Debug.WriteLine(Name)
        End Sub
    End Class

    ' Make an object and dispose it.
    Private Sub btnDispose_Click() Handles btnDispose.Click
        Static i As Integer = 0
        i += 1
        Dim obj As New Named("Dispose " & i)
        obj.Dispose()
    End Sub

    ' Make an object and do not dispose it.
    Private Sub btnNoDispose_Click() Handles btnNoDispose.Click
        Static i As Integer = 0
        i += 1
        Dim obj As New Named("No Dispose " & i)
    End Sub
End Class
```

The Named class has a Name variable that contains a string identifying an object. Its Finalize method simply calls its Dispose method. Dispose uses a static variable named `done_before` to ensure that it performs its task only once. If it has not already run, the Dispose method displays the object's name. In a real application, this method would free whatever resources the object holds. Whether the program explicitly calls Dispose, or whether the garbage collector calls the object's Finalize method, this code is executed exactly once.

The main program has two buttons labeled Dispose and No Dispose. When you click the Dispose button, the btnDispose_Click event handler makes a Named object, giving it a new name, and then calls the object's Dispose method, which immediately displays the object's name.

When you click the No Dispose button, the btnNoDispose_Click event handler makes a new Named object with a new name and then ends without calling the object's Dispose method. Later, when the garbage collector runs or when the program ends, the object's Finalize method executes and calls Dispose, which displays the object's name.

If your class allocates managed or unmanaged resources and you don't want to wait for the garbage collector to get around to freeing them, you should implement a Dispose method and use it when you no longer need an object.

CONSTANTS, PROPERTIES, AND METHODS

The way you declare constants, properties, and methods within a class is the same as the way you declare them outside a class. The main difference is that the context of the declaration is the class rather than a namespace. For example, a variable declared Private within a class is available only to code within the class.

For information on declaring variables and constants, see Chapter 14, "Data Types, Variables, and Constants." For information on declaring methods, see Chapter 16, "Subroutines and Functions," which also describes property procedures, special routines that implement a property for a class.

One issue that is sometimes confusing is that the unit of scope of a class is the class's *code*, not the code within a specific instance of the class. If you declare a variable within a class Private, then all code within the class can access the variable, whether or not that code belongs to the instance of the object that contains the variable.

For example, consider the following Student class. The Scores array is Private to the class, so you might think that a Student object could only access its own scores. In fact, any Student object can access any other Student object's Scores array as well. The CompareToStudent subroutine calculates the total score for the current Student object. It then calculates the total score for another student and displays the results.

```
Public Class Student
    Public FirstName As String
    Public LastName As String
    Private Scores() As Integer
    ...
    Public Sub CompareToStudent(other_student As Student)
        Dim my_score As Integer = 0
```

```
        For i As Integer = 0 To Scores.GetUpperBound(0)
            my_score += Scores(i)
        Next i

        Dim other_score As Integer = 0
        For i As Integer = 0 To other_student.Scores.GetUpperBound(0)
            other_score += other_student.Scores(i)
        Next i

        Debug.WriteLine("My score: " & my_score)
        Debug.WriteLine("Other score: " & other_score)
    End Sub
    ...
End Class
```

Breaking the encapsulation provided by the objects in this way can lead to unnecessary confusion. It is generally better to try to access an object's Private data only from within that object. You can provide access routines that make using the object's data easier.

The following version of the Student class includes a TotalScore function that returns the total of a Student object's scores. This function works only with its own object's scores, so it does not pry into another object's data. The CompareToStudent subroutine uses the TotalScore function to display the total score for its object and for a comparison object.

```
Public Class Student
    Public FirstName As String
    Public LastName As String
    Private Scores() As Integer
    ...
    Public Sub CompareToStudent(other_student As Student)
        Debug.WriteLine("My score: " & TotalScore())
        Debug.WriteLine("Other score: " & other_student.TotalScore())
    End Sub

    ' Return the total of this student's scores.
    Private Function TotalScore() As Integer
        Dim total_score As Integer = 0
        For i As Integer = 0 To Scores.GetUpperBound(0)
            total_score += Scores(i)
        Next i

        Return total_score
    End Function
    ...
End Class
```

Function TotalScore is itself declared Private, so only code within the class can use it. In this example, the CompareToStudent subroutine calls another object's Private TotalScore function, so the separation between the two objects is not absolute, but at least CompareToStudent doesn't need to look directly at the other object's data.

EVENTS

Properties let the application view and modify an object's data. Methods let the program invoke the object's behaviors and perform actions. Together, properties and methods let the program send information (data values or commands) to the object.

In a sense, events do the reverse: They let the object send information to the program. When something noteworthy occurs in an object's code, the object can raise an event to tell the main program about it. The main program can then decide what to do about the event.

For example, the most commonly used event is probably a Button's Click event. When the user presses and releases the mouse over a Button object, the object raises its Click event to tell the program that this has happened. Normally the program performs some action in response.

The following sections describe events. They explain how a class declares events and how other parts of the program can catch events.

Declaring Events

A class object can raise events whenever it needs to notify the program of changing circumstances. Normally, the class declares the event using the Event keyword. The following text shows the Event statement's syntax:

```
[attribute_list] [accessibility] [Shadows] _
Event event_name([parameters]) [Implements interface.event]
```

The following sections describe the pieces of this declaration. Some of these are similar to earlier sections that describe constant, variable, and class declarations. By now, you should notice some similarity in the use of the *attribute_list* and *accessibility* clauses. For more information on constant and variable declarations, see Chapter 14. For more information on class declarations, refer to the section "Classes" earlier in this chapter.

attribute_list

The *attribute_list* defines attributes that apply to the event. For example, the following declaration defines a description that the code editor should display for the ScoreAdded event:

```
Imports System.ComponentModel

Public Class Student
    <Description("Occurs when a score is added to the object")>
    Public Event ScoreAdded(test_number As Integer)
    ...
End Class
```

accessibility

The *accessibility* value can take one of the following values: Public, Protected, Friend, Protected Friend, or Private. These values determine which pieces of code can catch the event.

The meanings of these keywords are very similar to those of the class accessibility keywords described earlier in this chapter. See the section "Accessibility" earlier in this chapter for details.

Shadows

The Shadows keyword indicates that this event replaces an event in the parent class that has the same name but not necessarily the same parameters.

parameters

The *parameters* clause gives the parameters that the event will pass to event handlers. The syntax for the parameter list is the same as the syntax for declaring the parameter list for a subroutine or function.

If an event declares a parameter with the ByRef keyword, the code that catches the event can modify that parameter's value. When the event handler ends, the class code that raised the event can read the new parameter value.

Implements interface.event

If the class implements an interface and the interface defines an event, this clause identifies this event as the one defined by the interface. For example, the IStudent interface shown in the following code defines the ScoreChanged event handler. The Student class implements the IStudent interface. The declaration of the ScoreChanged event handler uses the Implements keyword to indicate that this event handler provides the event handler defined by the IStudent interface.

```
Public Interface IStudent
    Event ScoreChanged()
    ...

End Interface

Public Class Student
    Implements IStudent

    Public Event ScoreChanged() Implements IStudent.ScoreChanged
    ...
End Class
```

Raising Events

After it has declared an event, a class raises it with the RaiseEvent keyword. It should pass the event whatever parameters were defined in the Event statement.

For example, the Student class shown in the following code declares a ScoreChange event. The AddScore method shown in the following code makes room for a new score, adds the score to the Scores array, and then raises the ScoreChanged event, passing the event handler the index of the score in the Scores array.

```
Public Class Student
    Private Scores() As Integer
    ...
    Public Event ScoreChanged(ByVal test_number As Integer)
    ...
    Public Sub AddScore(ByVal new_score As Integer)
        ReDim Preserve Scores(Scores.Length)
        Scores(Scores.Length - 1) = new_score
        RaiseEvent ScoreChanged(Scores.Length - 1)
    End Sub
    ...
End Class
```

Catching Events

You can catch an object's events in two ways. First, you can declare the object variable using the WithEvents keyword, as shown in the following code:

```
Private WithEvents TopStudent As Student
```

Then in the code editor, click the left drop-down list and select the variable's name. In the right drop-down list, select the event. This makes the code editor create an empty event handler similar to the following one. When the object raises its ScoreChanged event, the event handler executes.

```
Private Sub TopStudent_ScoreChanged(test_number As Integer) _
 Handles TopStudent.ScoreChanged

End Sub
```

The second method for catching events is to use the AddHandler statement to define an event handler for the event at run time. First, write the event handler subroutine. This subroutine must take parameters of the proper type to match those defined by the event's declaration in the class.

The following code shows a subroutine that can handle the ScoreChanged event. Note that the parameter's name has been changed, but its accessibility (ByRef or ByVal) and data type must match those declared for the ScoreChanged event.

```
Private Sub HandleScoreChanged(quiz_num As Integer)

End Sub
```

After you build the event handler routine, use the AddHandler statement to assign the routine to a particular object's event. The following statement makes the HandleScoreChanged event handler catch the TopStudent object's ScoreChanged event:

```
AddHandler TopStudent.ScoreChanged, AddressOf HandleScoreChanged
```

AddHandler is particularly convenient if you want to work with an array of objects. The following code shows how a program might create an array of Student objects and then use the HandleScoreChanged subroutine to catch the ScoreChanged event for all of them:

```
' Create an array of Student objects.
Const MAX_STUDENT As Integer = 30
Dim students(0 To MAX_STUDENT) As Student
For i As Integer = 0 To MAX_STUDENT
    students(i) = New Student
    AddHandler students(i).ScoreChanged, AddressOf HandleScoreChanged
Next i
...
```

If you plan to use AddHandler in this way, you may want to ensure that the events provide enough information for the event handler to figure out which object raised the event. For example, you might modify the ScoreChanged event so that it passes a reference to the object raising the event into the event handler. Then the shared event handler can determine which Student object had a score change.

AddHandler lets you add an event handler to an event. Conversely, RemoveHandler lets you remove an event handler from an event. The syntax is similar to the syntax for AddHandler, as shown here:

```
RemoveHandler TopStudent.ScoreChanged, AddressOf HandleScoreChanged
```

Note that relaxed delegates allow an event handler to declare its parameters to have different data types from those provided by the event, as long as the new data types are compatible, or to omit the parameters entirely.

For example, suppose the Student class defines a ScoreChanged event that takes an Integer parameter. The following three subroutines could all catch this event. The first matches the event's parameters precisely. The second version declares its `quiz_num` parameter to be a Long. Long is compatible with Integer so, when it invokes the event handler, Visual Basic can convert the Integer value into a Long parameter safely. The third version of the event handler declares no parameters so the event's Integer value is ignored.

```
Private Sub HandleScoreChanged1(quiz_num As Integer)

End Sub

Private Sub HandleScoreChanged2(quiz_num As Long)

End Sub

Private Sub HandleScoreChanged3()

End Sub
```

STRICTLY SPEAKING

The second version works because you can always store an Integer value in a Long parameter. The reverse is not always true: A Long value won't necessarily fit in an Integer. If the event is declared with a Long parameter but the event handler is declared with an Integer parameter, the result depends on the Option Strict setting. If Option Strict is off, Visual Basic allows the code and tries to convert the Long value into an Integer parameter, possibly crashing at runtime. If Option Strict is on, Visual Basic flags this as an error.

For more information, see the section "Relaxed Delegates" in Chapter 16.

Shared Variables

If you declare a variable in a class with the Shared keyword, all objects of the class share a single instance of that variable. Any instance of the class can get or set the variable's value. Code outside of the class can use the class itself to get or set the variable's value.

For example, suppose the Student class declares a shared NumStudents variable and uses it, as shown in the following code:

```
Public Class Student
    Shared NumStudents As Integer

    Public Sub ShowNumStudents()
        MessageBox.Show("# Students: " & NumStudents)
    End Sub
    ...
End Class
```

In this case, all instances of the Student class share the same NumStudents value. The following code creates a Student object. It uses the class to set the shared NumStudents value and then calls the student's ShowNumStudents method.

```
Dim student1 As New Student
Student.NumStudents = 100
student1.ShowNumStudents()
```

Because all instances of the class share the same variable, any changes to the value that you make using one object are visible to all the others. Figure 23-4 illustrates this idea. Each Student class instance has its own FirstName, LastName, Scores, and other individual data values, but they all share the same NumStudents value.

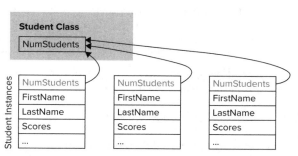

FIGURE 23-4: If a variable in a class is declared Shared, all instances of a class share the same value.

Shared Methods

Shared methods are a little less intuitive than shared variables. Like shared variables, shared methods are accessible using the class's name. For example, the NewStudent function shown in the following code is declared with the Shared keyword. This function creates a new Student object, initializes it by adding it to some sort of database, and then returns the new object.

```
Public Class Student
    ...
    ' Return a new Student.
    Public Shared Function NewStudent() As Student
        ' Instantiate the Student.
```

```
        Dim new_student As New Student

        ' Add the new student to the database.
        ' ...

        ' Return the new student.
        Return new_student
    End Function
    ...
End Class
```

This type of function that creates a new instance of a class is sometimes called a *factory method*. In some cases, you can use an appropriate constructor instead of a factory method. One time when a factory method is useful is when object creation might fail. If data passed to the method is invalid, some resource (such as a database) prohibits the new object (perhaps a new Student has the same name as an existing Student), or the object may come from more than one place (for example, it may be either a new object or one taken from a pool of existing objects). In those cases, a factory method can return Nothing. A constructor could raise an error, but it cannot return Nothing if it fails.

If you want to force the program to use a factory method rather than create an instance of the object directly, give the class a private constructor. Code that lies outside of the class cannot use the constructor because it is private. It also cannot use the default constructor associated with the New statement because the class has an explicitly defined constructor. The code must create new objects by using the factory method, which can use the private constructor because it's inside the class.

As is the case with shared variables, you access a shared method by using the class's name.

The following code declares the student1 variable and initializes it by calling the NewStudent factory method using the class's name:

```
    Dim student1 As Student = Student.NewStudent()
```

One oddity of shared methods is that they can use class variables and methods only if they are also shared. If you think about accessing a shared method through the class name, this makes sense. Because you don't use an instance of the class to call the method, there is no instance to give the method data.

Figure 23-5 illustrates the situation. The shared NewStudent method is contained within the class itself and has access to the NumStudents variable. If it wanted to use a FirstName, LastName, or Scores value, however, it needs to use an instance of the class.

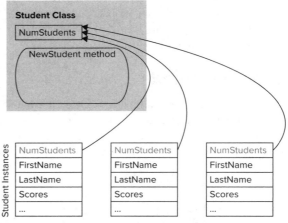

FIGURE 23-5: A shared method can only access other shared variables and methods.

SUMMARY

Classes and structures are very similar. Both are container types that group related variables, methods, and events in a single entity.

Most developers use classes exclusively, primarily because structures are relatively new and developers are more familiar with classes. Structures also cannot take advantage of inheritance.

Another significant factor when picking between classes and structures, however, is their difference in variable type. Classes are reference types, whereas structures are value types. This gives them different behaviors when defining and initializing objects and when passing objects to routines by value and by reference.

When you understand the differences between classes and structures, you can select the one that is more appropriate for your application.

If you build enough classes and structures, you may start to have naming collisions. It is common for developers working on different projects to define similar business classes such as Employee, Customer, Order, and InventoryItem. Although these objects may be similar, they may differ in important details. The Customer class defined for a billing application might include lots of account and billing address information, whereas a repair assignment application might focus on the customer's equipment and needs.

Having two Customer classes around can result in confusion and programs that cannot easily interact with each other. Namespaces can help categorize code and differentiate among classes. You can define separate namespaces for the billing and repair assignment applications, and use them to tell which version of the Customer class you need for a particular purpose.

Chapter 24, "Namespaces," describes namespaces in detail. It explains how to create namespaces and how to use them to refer to classes created in other modules.

24

Namespaces

WROX.COM CODE DOWNLOADS FOR THIS CHAPTER

The wrox.com code downloads for this chapter are found at `http://www.wrox.com/remtitle.cgi?isbn=9781118314074` on the Download Code tab. The code for this chapter is divided into the following major examples:

➤ DrawDashes

➤ DrawDashesImportsDashStyle

➤ DrawDashesWithImports

➤ JobNamespaces

➤ NamespaceHierarchy

HANDLING NAME CONFLICTS

In large applications, it is fairly common to have name collisions. One developer might create an Employee class, while another makes a function named Employee that returns the employee ID for a particular person's name. Or two developers might build different Employee classes that have different properties and different purposes. When multiple items have the same name, this is called a *namespace collision* or *namespace pollution*.

These sorts of name conflicts are most common when programmers are not working closely together. For example, different developers working on the payroll and human resources systems might both define Employee classes with slightly different purposes.

Namespaces enable you to classify and distinguish among programming entities that have the same name. For example, you might build the payroll system in the Payroll namespace and the human resources system in the HumanResources namespace. Then, the two Employee classes would have the fully qualified names Payroll.Employee and HumanResources.Employee, so they could coexist peacefully and the program could tell them apart.

The following code shows how an application would declare objects of these two types:

```
Dim payroll_emp As Payroll.Employee
Dim hr_emp As HumanResources.Employee
```

Namespaces can contain other namespaces, so you can build a hierarchical structure that groups different entities. You can divide the Payroll namespace into pieces to give developers working on that project some isolation from each other.

Namespaces can be confusing at first, but they are really fairly simple. They just break up the code into manageable pieces so that you can group parts of the program and tell different parts from each other.

This chapter describes namespaces. It explains how to use namespaces to categorize programming items and how to use them to select the right versions of items with the same name.

THE IMPORTS STATEMENT

Visual Studio defines thousands of variables, classes, routines, and other entities to provide tools for your applications. It categorizes them in namespaces to prevent name collisions and to make it easier for you to find the items you need.

The .NET Framework root namespaces are named Microsoft and System. The Microsoft namespace includes namespaces that support different programming languages and tools. For example, typical namespaces include CSharp, JScript, and VisualBasic, which contain types and other tools that support the C#, JScript, and Visual Basic languages. The Microsoft namespace also includes the Win32 namespace, which provides classes that handle operating system events and that manipulate the registry.

The System namespace contains a huge number of useful programming items, including many nested namespaces. For example, the System.Drawing namespace contains classes related to drawing, System.Data contains classes related to databases, System.Threading holds classes dealing with multithreading, and System.Security includes classes for working with security and cryptography.

Note that these namespaces are not necessarily available to your program at all times. For example, by default, the Microsoft.JScript namespace is not available to Visual Basic programs. To use it, you must first add a reference to the Microsoft.JScript.dll library.

Visual Studio includes so many programming tools that the namespace hierarchy is truly enormous. Namespaces are refined into sub-namespaces, which may be further broken into more namespaces until they reach a manageable size. Although this makes it easier to differentiate among all of the different programming entities, it makes the fully qualified names of some classes rather cumbersome.

Example program DrawDashes, which is available for download on the book's website, uses the following code to draw a rectangle inside its form. Fully qualified names such as System.Drawing .Drawing2D.DashStyle.DashDotDot are so long that they make the code hard to read.

```
Private Sub DrawDashedBox(gr As System.Drawing.Graphics)
    gr.Clear(Me.BackColor)

    Dim rect As System.Drawing.Rectangle = Me.ClientRectangle
    rect.X += 10
    rect.Y += 10
    rect.Width -= 20
    rect.Height -= 20

    Using my_pen As New System.Drawing.Pen(System.Drawing.Color.Blue, 5)
        my_pen.DashStyle = System.Drawing.Drawing2D.DashStyle.DashDotDot
        gr.DrawRectangle(my_pen, rect)
    End Using
End Sub
```

You can use the Imports statement at the top of the file to make using namespaces easier. After you import a namespace, your code can use the items it contains without specifying the namespace.

Example program DrawDashesWithImports, which is also available for download on the book's website, uses the following code. It imports the System.Drawing and System.Drawing.Drawing2D namespaces so it doesn't need to mention the namespaces in its object declarations. This version is much easier to read.

```
Imports System.Drawing
Imports System.Drawing.Drawing2D
...
Private Sub DrawDashedBox(gr As Graphics)
    gr.Clear(Me.BackColor)

    Dim rect As Rectangle = Me.ClientRectangle
    rect.X += 10
    rect.Y += 10
    rect.Width -= 20
    rect.Height -= 20

    Using my_pen As New Pen(Color.Blue, 5)
        my_pen.DashStyle = DashStyle.DashDotDot
        gr.DrawRectangle(my_pen, rect)
    End Using
End Sub
```

> **DRAWING DEFAULTS**
>
> System.Drawing is automatically imported by default in Windows Forms applications so you normally don't need to import it. See the following section for more information on automatic imports.

A file can include any number of Imports statements. The statements must appear at the beginning of the file, and they define namespace shortcuts for the entire file. If you want different pieces of code to use different sets of Imports statements, you must place the pieces of code in different files. If the pieces of code are in the same class, use the Partial keyword so you can split the class into multiple files.

> **COLLISION PROVISION**
>
> If a program imports two namespaces that define classes with the same names, Visual Basic may become confused and give you an *ambiguous reference* error. To fix the problem, the code must use fully qualified names to select the right versions.
>
> For example, suppose that the Payroll and HumanResources modules both define Employee classes. Then you must use the fully qualified names Payroll.Employee and HumanResources.Employee to differentiate between the two within the same file.

The complete syntax for the Imports statement is as follows:

```
Imports [alias =] namespace[.element]
```

Later sections in this chapter describe namespace aliases and elements in detail.

Automatic Imports

Visual Basic lets you quickly import a namespace for all of the modules in a project. In Solution Explorer, double-click My Project. Click the References tab to display the page shown in Figure 24-1.

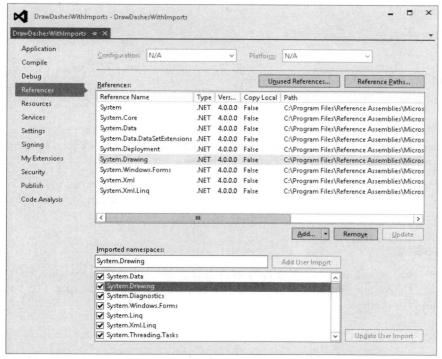

FIGURE 24-1: Use the My Project References tab to import namespaces for every module in a project.

In the Imported namespaces list at the bottom, select the check boxes next to the namespaces that you want to import. The program's files will be able to use the objects defined in these namespaces without including Imports statements.

This is most useful when most of the program's modules need to import the same namespaces. Including the Imports statement in the files makes it easier for developers to see which namespaces are available, however, so you might want to do this instead, particularly if you use unusual namespaces.

By default, Visual Basic imports namespaces for the type of application you are building. For example, when you start a Windows Form application, Visual Basic imports the following namespaces:

➤ Microsoft.VisualBasic

➤ System

➤ System.Collections

➤ System.Collections.Generic

➤ System.Data

- ➤ System.Drawing

- ➤ System.Diagnostics

- ➤ System.Windows.Forms

- ➤ System.Linq

- ➤ System.Xml.Linq

- ➤ System.Threading.Tasks

You can use the upper half of the References property page to manage project references. Use the Add and Remove buttons to add and remove references to libraries.

Click the Unused References button near the top in Figure 24-1 to see a list of libraries that are referenced but not currently used by the project. Before you distribute the program, you can remove the unused references.

Namespace Aliases

You can use the *alias* clause to define a shorthand notation for the namespace. For instance, the following code imports the System.Drawing.Drawing2D namespace and gives it the alias D2. Later, it uses D2 as shorthand for the fully qualified namespace.

```
Imports D2 = System.Drawing.Drawing2D
...
Dim dash_style As D2.DashStyle = D2.DashStyle.DashDotDot
```

This technique is handy if you need to use two namespaces that define different classes with the same name. Normally, if two namespaces define classes with the same name, you must use the fully qualified class names so that Visual Basic can tell them apart. You can use aliases to indicate the namespaces more concisely.

Namespace Elements

In addition to importing a namespace, you can import an element within the namespace. This is particularly useful for enumerated types.

For example, the following code imports the System.Drawing.Drawing2D namespace, which defines the DrawStyle enumeration. It declares the variable dash_style to be of the DashStyle type and sets its value to DashStyle.DashDotDot.

```
Imports System.Drawing.Drawing2D
...
Dim dash_style As DashStyle = DashStyle.DashDotDot
...
```

Example program DrawDashesImportsDashStyle, which is available for download on the book's website, uses the following code to import the System.Drawing.Drawing2D.DashStyle enumeration. That allows it to set the value of my_pen.DashStyle to DashDotDot without needing to specify the name of the enumeration (DashStyle).

```
Imports System.Drawing.Drawing2D
Imports System.Drawing.Drawing2D.DashStyle
...
my_pen.DashStyle = DashDotDot
...
```

THE ROOT NAMESPACE

Every project has a root namespace, and every item in the project is contained directly or indirectly within that namespace. To view or change the project's root namespace, open Solution Explorer and double-click the My Projects entry. View or modify the root namespace in the Application tab's Root Namespace text box.

MAKING NAMESPACES

You can create new namespaces nested within the root namespace to further categorize your code. The easiest way to create a namespace is by using the Namespace statement. The following code declares a namespace called SchedulingClasses. It includes the definition of the TimeSlot class and possibly other classes.

```
Namespace SchedulingClasses
    Public Class TimeSlot
        ...
    End Class
    ...
End Namespace
```

Code inside the namespace can refer to the TimeSlot class as simply TimeSlot. Code outside of the namespace can refer to the class using the namespace as shown in the following code (assuming MyApplication is the project's root namespace):

```
Dim time_slot As New MyApplication.SchedulingClasses.TimeSlot
```

You can nest namespaces within other namespaces to any depth. In fact, because all of your application's code is contained within the root namespace, any namespace you create is already contained within another namespace. There is no way to make a namespace that is not contained within the root namespace.

If you want to make a namespace that lies outside of the application's root namespace, you must create a library project. Then the code in that project lies within its own root namespace.

A Namespace statement can appear only at the namespace level. You cannot create a namespace within a module, class, structure, or method.

Inside a namespace, you can define other namespaces, classes, structures, modules, enumerated types, and interfaces. You cannot directly define variables, properties, subroutines, functions, or events. Those items must be contained within some other entity (such as a class, structure, module, or interface).

You can use more than one Namespace statement to define pieces of the same namespace. For example, the following code uses a Namespace statement to make the OrderEntryClasses namespace, and it defines the Employee class inside it. Later, the code uses another Namespace statement to add the Customer class to the same namespace. In this case, the single namespace contains both classes.

```
Namespace OrderEntryClasses
    Public Class Employee
        ...
    End Class
End Namespace
...
Namespace OrderEntryClasses
    Public Class Customer
        ...
    End Class
End Namespace
```

Example program NamespaceHierarchy, which is available for download on the book's website, defines several nested namespaces.

Scattering pieces of a namespace throughout your code will probably confuse other developers. One case where it might make sense to break a namespace into pieces would be if you want to put different classes in different code files, either to prevent any one file from becoming too big or to allow different programmers to work on the files at the same time. In that case, it might make sense to place related pieces of the application in the same namespace but in different files.

CLASSES, STRUCTURES, AND MODULES

Classes, structures, and modules create their own name contexts that are similar in some ways to namespaces. For example, a class or structure can contain the definition of another class or structure, as shown in the following code:

```
Public Class Class1
    Public Class Class2
        ...
    End Class

    Public Structure Struct1
        Public Name As String

        Public Structure Struct2
            Public Name As String
        End Structure
    End Structure
End Class
```

You can access public module members and shared class or structure members using a fully qualified syntax similar to the one used by namespaces. For example, the following code creates the GlobalValues module and defines the public variable MaxJobs within it. Later, the program can set MaxJobs using its fully qualified name.

```
Module GlobalValues
    Public MaxJobs As Integer
    ...
End Module
...
MyApplication.GlobalValues.MaxJobs = 100
```

Although these cases look very similar to namespaces, they really are not. One big difference is that you cannot use a Namespace statement inside a class, structure, or module.

IntelliSense gives another clue that Visual Basic treats classes, structures, and modules differently from namespaces. The IntelliSense pop-up shown in Figure 24-2 displays curly braces { } next to the FinanceStuff and JobClasses namespaces, but it displays different icons for the classes Employer and Form1, and the module Module1. When you select a namespace, IntelliSense also displays a tooltip (on the right in Figure 24-2) indicating that it is a namespace and giving its name.

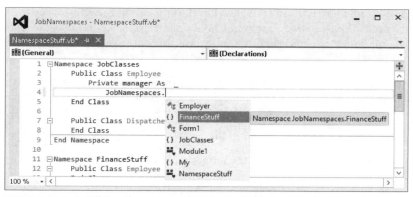

FIGURE 24-2: IntelliSense displays curly braces { } to the left of namespaces such as FinanceStuff and Job Classes.

RESOLVING NAMESPACES

Normally, Visual Basic does a pretty good job of resolving namespaces, so you don't need to worry too much about the process. If you import a namespace, you can omit the namespace in any declarations that you use. If you have not imported a namespace, you can fully qualify declarations that use the namespace and you're done. There are some in-between cases, however, that can be confusing. To understand them, you will find it helpful to know a bit more about how Visual Basic resolves namespaces.

When Visual Basic sees a reference that uses a fully qualified namespace, it looks in that namespace for the item it needs and that's that. It either succeeds or fails. For example, the following code declares a variable of type System.Collections.Hashtable. Visual Basic looks in the System.Collections namespace and tries to find the Hashtable class. If the class is not there, the declaration fails.

```
Dim hash_table As New System.Collections.Hashtable
```

When Visual Basic encounters a qualified namespace, it first assumes that it is fully qualified. If it cannot resolve the reference as described in the previous paragraph, it tries to treat the reference as partially qualified and it looks in the current namespace for a resolution. For example, suppose you declare a variable as shown in the following code:

```
Dim emp As JobClasses.Employee
```

In this case, Visual Basic searches the current namespace for a nested namespace called JobClasses. If it finds such a namespace, it looks for the Employee class in that namespace.

If Visual Basic cannot resolve a namespace using these methods, it moves up the namespace hierarchy and tries again. For example, suppose that the current code is in the MyApplication.JobStuff .EmployeeClasses.TimeSheetRoutines namespace. Now, suppose that the SalaryLevel class is defined in the MyApplication.JobStuff namespace and consider the following code:

```
Dim salary_level As New SalaryLevel
```

Visual Basic examines the current namespace MyApplication.JobStuff.EmployeeClasses .TimeSheetRoutines and doesn't find a definition for SalaryLevel. It moves up the namespace hierarchy and searches the MyApplication.JobStuff.EmployeeClasses namespace, again failing to find SalaryLevel. It moves up the hierarchy again to the MyApplication.JobStuff namespace, and there it finally finds the SalaryLevel class.

Movement up the namespace hierarchy can sometimes be a bit confusing. It may lead Visual Basic to resolve references in an ancestor of the current namespace, in some sort of "uncle/aunt" namespace, or in a "cousin" namespace.

For example, consider the namespace hierarchy shown in Figure 24-3.

➤ The root namespace MyApplication contains the namespaces BusinessClasses and AssignmentStuff.

➤ The BusinessClasses namespace defines the Employee and Customer classes.

➤ The AssignmentStuff namespace contains the AssignmentGlobals module, which defines the MakeAssignment subroutine and a different version of the Employee class.

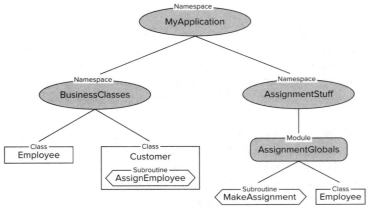

FIGURE 24-3: Visual Basic may search all over the namespace hierarchy to resolve a declaration.

Now, suppose that the Customer class contains the following subroutine:

```
Public Sub AssignEmployee()
    AssignmentStuff.AssignmentGlobals.MakeAssignment(Me)
    ...
End Sub
```

This code lies in the MyApplication.BusinessClasses namespace. Visual Basic cannot find a meaning for the AssignmentStuff namespace locally in that context, so it moves up the namespace hierarchy to MyApplication, where it finds the AssignmentStuff namespace. Within that namespace, it finds the AssignmentGlobals module and the MakeAssignment subroutine that it contains.

Visual Basic can also peer into modules as if their public contents were part of the namespace itself. That means you can rewrite the previous code in the following slightly simpler version:

```
Public Sub AssignEmployee()
    AssignmentStuff.MakeAssignment(Me)
    ...
End Sub
```

In this example, there is only one MakeAssignment subroutine, so there's little doubt that Visual Basic has found the correct one. If different namespaces define items with the same names, the situation can be more confusing. Suppose that the Customer class declares an object that is from the Employee class defined in the MyApplication.AssignmentStuff namespace, as shown in the following code:

```
Dim emp As New AssignmentStuff.Employee
```

If you understand how Visual Basic performs namespace resolution, you can figure out that the object is of the Employee class defined in the MyApplication.AssignmentStuff namespace. This isn't completely obvious, however.

If you add an Imports statements to the program, the situation gets more confusing. Suppose that the program imports the AssignmentStuff namespace and then the Customer class declares a variable of type Employee. Because this code is in the BusinessClasses namespace, Visual Basic uses that namespace's version of Employee. If the code is in some other namespace (such as MyApplication), the program uses the imported AssignmentStuff version of the class.

Finally, suppose that the program imports both BusinessClasses and AssignmentStuff .AssignmentGlobals and then makes the following declaration in another namespace. In this case, Visual Basic cannot decide which version of the class to use, so it generates an error.

```
Dim emp As Employee
```

This example is so confusing, however, that you would probably be better off restructuring the namespaces and possibly renaming one of the versions of the Employee class rather than trying to figure out how Visual Basic is resolving the namespaces.

You can simplify these issues by avoiding duplicate names across all namespaces. When you do use duplicate names, you can use fully qualified namespaces to avoid ambiguity. You can also use Imports statements to make namespace aliases and then use the aliases to avoid ambiguity more concisely.

SUMMARY

Namespaces are everywhere in Visual Basic. Every piece of code you write is contained in some namespace, even if it is only the application's root namespace. Despite the pervasiveness of namespaces, many developers never need to use them explicitly, so they find them somewhat mystifying.

Namespaces are really quite simple, however. They merely divide programming items into a hierarchy. They enable you to categorize related items and resolve name collisions in different parts of the application.

You can use the Imports statement to allow the program to refer to items in a namespace without giving fully qualified names. A namespace alias lets you explicitly specify an item's namespace in an abbreviated form. This is particularly useful for resolving ambiguous names that appear in more than one namespace included by Imports statements.

This chapter described namespaces in general. Chapter 25, "Collection Classes," describes some of the useful classes for grouping object classes, including those in the System.Collections and System .Collections.Generic namespaces.

25

Collection Classes

WROX.COM CODE DOWNLOADS FOR THIS CHAPTER

The wrox.com code downloads for this chapter are found at `http://www.wrox.com/remtitle.cgi?isbn=9781118314074` on the Download Code tab. The code for this chapter is divided into the following major examples:

➤ ArraySpeeds

➤ GenericEmployeeList

➤ GenericStringList

➤ UseCaseInsensitiveSortedList

➤ UseQueue

GROUPING DATA

Visual Basic .NET includes a large assortment of prebuilt classes that store and manage groups of objects. These collection classes provide a wide variety of different features, so the right class for a particular purpose depends on your application.

This chapter describes these different kinds of collection classes and provides tips for selecting the right one for various purposes.

WHAT IS A COLLECTION?

The word *collection* means a group of objects that should be kept together. For example, a coin collection is a group of coins that you keep together because they are rare, valuable, or otherwise interesting.

Unfortunately, the idea of a collection is such a useful concept that Visual Basic adopted the word and made a specific class named Collection. The Collection class *does* keep a group of objects together, but it reserves for its own use the perfect word for other similar kinds of groups of objects.

That leads to some semantic ambiguity when you talk about collection classes. Do you mean the Collection class? Or do you mean some other class that groups objects? Even the Visual Basic documentation has this problem and sometimes uses *collection classes* to mean classes that group things together.

This chapter describes the Collection class, as well as other collection classes.

One of the most basic Visual Basic entities that groups objects is an *array*. An array stores data values or references to objects in a simple block of memory with one entry directly following another. The Array *class* provides some special methods for manipulating arrays (such as reversing, sorting, or searching an array).

The Collection class provides a few specific features for working with its group of objects. It enables you to add an item to the Collection, optionally specifying a key for the item. You can then search for the item or remove the item using its key or its index in the Collection.

One of the most useful features of the Collection class is that it supports enumerators and For Each loops. That lets you easily loop over the objects in a Collection without worrying about the number of objects it contains.

Other classes derived from the Collection class provide additional features. For example, the Hashtable class can store a large number of objects with associated keys very efficiently. Dictionary is essentially a strongly typed generic Hashtable. The Hashtable class uses the Object data type for its key/value pairs and the Dictionary class uses more specific data types that you specify such as Strings or Employees. The section "Dictionaries" later in this chapter describes the Dictionary class in more detail.

The Queue class makes it easy to work with objects in first-in-first-out (FIFO) order. In contrast the Stack class helps you work with objects in a last-in-first-out order (LIFO).

The remainder of this chapter describes these classes in greater detail.

ARRAYS

Visual Basic .NET provides two basic kinds of arrays. First, it provides the normal arrays that you get when you declare a variable by using parentheses. For example, the following code declares an array of Integers named "squares":

```
Private Sub ShowSquaresNormalArray()
    Dim squares(10) As Integer

    For i As Integer = 0 To 10
        squares(i) = i * i
    Next i

    Dim txt As String = ""
    For i As Integer = 0 To 10
        txt &= squares(i).ToString & vbCrLf
    Next i
    MessageBox.Show(txt)
End Sub
```

The array contains 11 items with indexes ranging from 0 to 10. The code loops over the items, setting each one's value. Next, it loops over the values again, adding them to a string. When it has finished building the string, the program displays the result.

INITIALIZING ARRAYS

You can initialize an array as in the following code:

```
Dim fibonacci() As Integer = {1, 1, 2, 3, 5, 8, 13, 21, 33, 54, 87}
```

If you have Option Infer turned on, you can omit the data type as in the following:

```
Dim numbers() = {1, 2, 3}
```

For more information on array initialization, see the section "Initializing Arrays" in Chapter 14, "Data Types, Variables, and Constants."

The Visual Basic Array class provides another kind of array. This kind of array is actually an object that provides methods for managing the items stored in the array.

The following code shows the previous version of the code rewritten to use an Array object:

```
Private Sub ShowSquaresArrayObject()
    Dim squares As Array =
        Array.CreateInstance(GetType(Integer), 11)

    For i As Integer = 0 To 10
        squares.SetValue(i * i, i)
    Next i
```

```
        Dim txt As String = ""
        For i As Integer = 0 To 10
            txt &= squares.GetValue(i).ToString & vbCrLf
        Next i
        MessageBox.Show(txt)
    End Sub
```

This version creates the array by using the Array class's shared CreateInstance method, passing it the data type that the array should contain and the number of items that it should hold. The code then loops over the items using the array's SetValue method to set the items' values. If you have Option Strict turned off, the code can set the items' values exactly as before by using the statement `squares(i) = i * i`. If Option Strict is on, you need to use SetValue.

Next, the program loops over the items again, using the array's GetValue method to add the item values to a string. If Option Strict is off, you can use the same syntax as before: `txt &= squares(i).ToString & vbCrLf`. If Option Strict is on, you need to use the array's GetValue method. After building the string, the program displays it in a message box as before.

Example program ShowSquares uses similar code to build a list of squares by using a normal array and by using an Array object.

The following sections describe the similarities and differences between normal arrays and Array objects.

Array Dimensions

Both normal variable arrays and Array objects can support multiple dimensions. The following statement declares a three-dimensional array with 11 items in the first dimension, 11 in the second, and 21 in the third. It then sets the value for the item in position (1, 2, 3).

```
Dim values(10, 10, 20) As Integer
values(1, 2, 3) = 100
```

The following code does the same thing with an Array object:

```
Dim values As Array =
    Array.CreateInstance(GetType(Integer), 11, 21, 31)
values.SetValue(100, 1, 2, 3)
```

If Option Strict is off, the code can use the same syntax for getting and setting the Array item's value. The following code sets the (1, 2, 3) item's value to 100 and then displays its value:

```
Option Strict Off
...
values(1, 2, 3) = 100
Debug.WriteLine(values(1, 2, 3))
```

Lower Bounds

A normal array of variables always has lower bound 0 in every dimension. The following code declares an array with indexes ranging from 0 to 10:

```
Dim values(10) As Integer
```

You can fake a variable array that has nonzero lower bounds, but it requires extra work on your part. You must add or subtract an appropriate amount from each index to map the indexes you want to use to the underlying zero-based indexes.

Array objects can handle nonzero lower bounds for you. The following code creates a two-dimensional array with indexes ranging from 1 to 10 in the first dimension, and 101 to 120 in the second dimension:

```
Dim dimension_lengths() As Integer = {10, 20}
Dim lower_bounds() As Integer = {1, 101}
Dim values As Array =
    Array.CreateInstance(GetType(Integer), dimension_lengths, lower_bounds)
```

The code first defines an array containing the number of elements it wants for each dimension (10 in the first dimension and 20 in the second dimension). It then creates an array containing the lower bounds it wants to use for each dimension (the first dimension starts with index 1 and the second dimension starts with index 101).

The code then calls the Array class's shared CreateInstance method, passing it the data type of the array's objects, the array of dimension lengths, and the array of lower bounds. The CreateInstance method uses the arrays of lower bounds and dimensions to create an Array object with the appropriate bounds.

Resizing

You can use the ReDim statement to change a normal array's dimensions. Add the Preserve keyword if you want the array to keep its existing values, as shown here:

```
Dim values(100) As Integer
...
ReDim Preserve values(200)
```

An Array object cannot resize itself, but it is relatively easy to copy an Array object's items to another Array object. The following code creates a values array containing 101 items with indexes ranging from 0 to 100. Later, it creates a new Array object containing 201 items and uses the values array's CopyTo method to copy its values into the new array. The second parameter to CopyTo gives the index in the destination array where the copy should start placing values.

```
Dim values As Array =
    Array.CreateInstance(GetType(Integer), 101)
...
Dim new_array As Array =
```

```
        Array.CreateInstance(GetType(Integer), 201)
    values.CopyTo(new_array, 0)
    values = new_array
```

The Array class's shared Copy method allows you greater control. It lets you specify the index in the source array where the copy should start, the index in the destination array where the items should be copied, and the number of items to be copied.

Although building a new Array object and copying items into it is more cumbersome than using ReDim to resize a variable array, the process is surprisingly fast.

Speed

There's no doubt that arrays of variables are much faster than Array objects. In one test, setting and getting values in an Array object took more than 100 times as long as performing the same operations in a variable array.

If your application performs only a few hundred array operations, the difference is unimportant. If your application must access array values many millions of times, you may need to consider using an array of variables even if the Array class would be more convenient for other reasons (such as non-zero lower bounds).

Microsoft has also optimized one-dimensional variable arrays, so they are faster than multidimensional arrays. The difference is much less dramatic than the difference between variable arrays and Array classes, however.

Example program ArraySpeeds, which is available for download on the book's website, compares the speeds of variable arrays and Array objects. Enter the number of items that you want to use in the arrays and click Go. The program builds one- and two-dimensional arrays and Array objects holding integers. It then fills the arrays and displays the elapsed time.

FIGURE 25-1: Variable arrays are faster than Array classes.

Figure 25-1 shows the results. Variable arrays are much faster than array classes, and one-dimensional variable arrays generally seem to be slightly faster than two-dimensional arrays.

Other Array Class Features

The Array class provides several other useful shared methods. For example, the IndexOf and LastIndexOf methods return the position of a particular item in an Array.

Methods such as IndexOf and LastIndexOf would be a strong argument supporting Array objects over normal arrays of variables if it weren't for one somewhat surprising fact: Those same methods work with regular arrays of variables, too! The following code fills an array of integers and then uses Array methods to display the indexes of the first item with value 6 and the last item with value 3:

```
Dim values(10) As Integer
For i As Integer = 0 To 10
    values(i) = i
Next i

MessageBox.Show(Array.IndexOf(values, 6).ToString)
MessageBox.Show(Array.LastIndexOf(values, 3).ToString)
```

The following table summarizes some other useful Array class methods.

PROPERTY/METHOD	PURPOSE
BinarySearch	Returns the index of an item in the previously sorted array. The items must implement the IComparable interface, or you must provide an IComparer object.
Clear	Removes all of the items from the array.
ConvertAll	Converts an array of one type into an array of another type.
Exists	Determines whether the array contains a particular item.
Reverse	Reverses the order of the items in the array.
Sort	Sorts the items in the array. The items must implement the IComparable interface, or you must provide an IComparer object.

Example program ArrayTests, which is available for download on the book's website, demonstrates the Array class's IndexOf, LastIndexOf, Reverse, and BinarySearch methods. It also demonstrates the Sort method for arrays containing integers, objects that implement the IComparable interface, and objects that can be sorted with IComparer objects.

COLLECTIONS

The Visual Basic collection classes basically hold items and don't provide a lot of extra functionality. Other classes described later in this chapter provide more features.

The following sections describe the simple collection classes in Visual Basic: ArrayList, StringCollection, and NameValueCollection. They also describe strongly typed collections that you can build to make code that uses these classes a bit easier to debug and maintain.

ArrayList

The ArrayList class is a resizable array. You can add and remove items from any position in the list and it resizes itself accordingly. The following table describes some of the class's more useful properties and methods.

PROPERTY/METHOD	PURPOSE
Add	Adds an item at the end of the list.
AddRange	Adds the items in an object implementing the ICollection interface to the end of the list.
BinarySearch	Returns the index of an item in the list. The items must implement the IComparable interface, or you must provide the Sort method with an IComparer object.
Capacity	Gets or sets the number of items that the list can hold.
Clear	Removes all of the items from the list.
Contains	Returns True if a specified item is in the list.
CopyTo	Copies some of the list or the entire list into a one-dimensional Array object.
Count	Returns the number of items currently in the list. This is always less than or equal to Capacity.
GetRange	Returns an ArrayList containing the items in part of the list.
IndexOf	Returns the zero-based index of the first occurrence of a specified item in the list.
Insert	Adds an item at a particular position in the list.
InsertRange	Adds the items in an object implementing the ICollection interface to a particular position in the list.
Item	Returns the item at a particular position in the list.
LastIndexOf	Returns the zero-based index of the last occurrence of a specified item in the list.
Remove	Removes the first occurrence of a specified item from the list.
RemoveAt	Removes the item at the specified position in the list.
RemoveRange	Removes the items in the specified positions from the list.
Reverse	Reverses the order of the items in the list.
SetRange	Replaces the items in part of the list with new items taken from an ICollection object.
Sort	Sorts the items in the list. The items must implement the IComparable interface, or you must provide the Sort method with an IComparer object.

PROPERTY/METHOD	PURPOSE
ToArray	Copies the list's items into a one-dimensional array. The array can be an array of objects, an array of a specific type, or an Array object (holding objects).
TrimToSize	Reduces the list's allocated space so that it is just big enough to hold its items. This sets Capacity = Count.

A single ArrayList object can hold objects of many different kinds. The following code creates an ArrayList and adds a string, Form object, integer, and Bitmap to it. It then loops through the items in the list and displays their types.

```
Dim array_list As New ArrayList
array_list.Add("What?")
array_list.Add(Me)
array_list.Add(1001)
array_list.Add(New Bitmap(10, 10))
For Each obj As Object In array_list
    Debug.WriteLine(obj.GetType.ToString)
Next obj
```

The following text shows the results:

```
System.String
UseArrayList.Form1
System.Int32
System.Drawing.Bitmap
```

The value displayed for the second item depends on the name of the project (in this case, UseArrayList).

StringCollection

A StringCollection is similar to an ArrayList, except that it can hold only strings. Because it works only with strings, this class provides some extra type checking that the ArrayList does not. For example, if your program tries to add an Employee object to a StringCollection, the collection raises an error.

To take advantage of this extra error checking, you should always use a StringCollection instead of an ArrayList if you are working with strings. Of course, if you need other features (such as the fast lookups provided by a Hashtable), you should use one of the classes described in the following sections.

NameValueCollection

The NameValueCollection class is a collection that can hold more than one string value for a particular key (name). For example, you might use employee names as keys. The string values associated with a particular key could include extension, job title, employee ID, and so forth. Of course, you could also store the same information by putting extension, job title, employee ID, and the other fields in an object or structure, and then storing the objects or structures in some sort of collection class such as an ArrayList. A NameValueCollection, however, is useful if you don't know ahead of time how many strings will be associated with each key.

The following table describes some of the NameValueCollection's most useful properties and methods.

PROPERTY/METHOD	DESCRIPTION
Add	Adds a new name/value pair to the collection. If the collection already holds an entry for the name, it adds the new value to that name's values.
AllKeys	Returns a string array holding all of the key values.
Clear	Removes all names and values from the collection.
CopyTo	Copies items starting at a particular index into a one-dimensional Array object. This copies only the items (see the Item property), not the keys.
Count	Returns the number of key/value pairs in the collection.
Get	Gets the items for a particular index or name as a comma-separated list of values.
GetKey	Returns the key for a specific index.
GetValues	Returns a string array containing the values for a specific name or index.
HasKeys	Returns True if the collection contains any non-null keys.
Item	Gets or sets the item for a particular index or name as a comma-separated list of values.
Keys	Returns a collection containing the keys.
Remove	Removes a particular name and all of its values.
Set	Sets the item for a particular index or name as a comma-separated list of values.

Note that there is no easy way to remove a particular value from a name. For example, if a person's name is associated with extension, job title, and employee ID, it is not easy to remove only the job title.

Example program UseNameValueCollection, which is available for download on the book's website, demonstrates NameValueCollection class features.

DICTIONARIES

A *dictionary* is a collection that associates keys with values. You look up a key, and the dictionary provides you with the corresponding value. This is similar to the way a NameValueCollection works, except that a dictionary's keys and values need not be strings, and a dictionary associates each key with a single value object.

Visual Studio provides several different kinds of dictionary classes that are optimized for different uses. Their differences come largely from the ways in which they store data internally. Although you don't need to understand the details of how the dictionaries work internally, you do need to know how they behave so that you can pick the best one for a particular purpose.

Because all of the dictionary classes provide the same service (associating keys with values), they have roughly the same properties and methods. The following table describes some of the most useful of these.

PROPERTY/METHOD	DESCRIPTION
Add	Adds a key/value pair to the dictionary.
Clear	Removes all key/value pairs from the dictionary.
Contains	Returns True if the dictionary contains a specific key.
CopyTo	Copies the dictionary's data starting at a particular position into a one-dimensional array of DictionaryEntry objects. The DictionaryEntry class has Key and Value properties.
Count	Returns the number of key/value pairs in the dictionary.
Item	Gets or sets the value associated with a key.
Keys	Returns a collection containing all of the dictionary's keys.
Remove	Removes the key/value pair with a specific key.
Values	Returns a collection containing all of the dictionary's values.

The following sections describe different Visual Studio dictionary classes in more detail.

ListDictionary

A ListDictionary stores its data in a linked list. In a linked list, each item is held in an object that contains its data plus a reference or *link* to the next item in the list.

Figure 25-2 illustrates a linked list. This list contains the key/value pairs Appetizer/Salad, Entrée/Sandwich, Drink/Water, and Dessert/Cupcake. The link out of the Dessert/Cupcake item is set to Nothing, so the program can tell when it has reached the end of the list. A reference variable inside the ListDictionary class, labeled Top in Figure 25-2, points to the first item in the list.

The links in a linked list make adding and removing items relatively easy. The ListDictionary simply moves the links to point to new objects, add objects, remove objects, or insert objects between two others. For example, to add a new item at the top of the list, you create the new item, set its link to point to the item that is currently at the top, and then make the list's Top variable point to the new item. Other rearrangements are almost as easy. For more information on how linked lists work, see a book on algorithms and data structures such as *Data Structures and Algorithms Using Visual Basic.NET* (McMillan, Cambridge University Press, 2005).

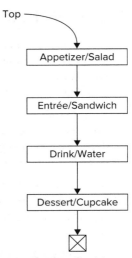

FIGURE 25-2: Each item in a linked list keeps a reference to the next item in the list.

Unfortunately, if the list grows long, finding items in it can take a long time. To find an item in the list, the program starts at the top and works its way down, following the links between items, until it finds the one it wants. If the list is short, that doesn't take very long. If the list holds 100,000 items, this means potentially a 100,000-item crawl from top to bottom. That means a ListDictionary object's performance degrades if it contains too many items.

If you need to store only a few hundred items in the dictionary and you don't need to access them frequently, a ListDictionary is fine. If you need to store 100,000 entries, or if you need to access the dictionary's entries a huge number of times, you may get better performance using a "heavier" object such as a Hashtable. A Hashtable has more overhead than a ListDictionary but is faster at accessing its entries.

Hashtable

A Hashtable looks a lot like a ListDictionary on the outside, but internally it stores its data in a very different way. Rather than using a linked list, this class uses a hash table to hold data.

A hash table is a data structure that allows extremely fast access to items using their keys. Exactly how hash tables work is interesting but outside the scope of this book. For more information, see a book on algorithms and data structures such as *Data Structures and Algorithms Using Visual Basic.NET* (McMillan, Cambridge University Press, 2005).

To use a hash table, however, you should know a few of their external characteristics.

Hash tables provide extremely fast lookup but they require a fair amount of extra space. If a hash table becomes too full, it must resize itself and rearrange the items it contains to remain efficient.

Resizing a hash table can take some time so the Hashtable class provides some extra tools to help you avoid resizing.

One overloaded version of the Hashtable class's constructor takes a parameter that tells how many items the table should initially be able to hold. If you know you are going to load 1000 items into the Hashtable, you might initially give it enough room to hold 1500 items. Then the program could add all 1000 items without filling the table too much, so it would still give good performance. If you don't set an initial size, the hash table might start out too small and need to resize itself many times before it could hold 1000 items, and that will slow it down.

Another version of the constructor lets you specify the hash table's *load factor*. The load factor is a number between 0.1 and 1.0 that gives the largest ratio of elements to spots in the table that the Hashtable will allow before it enlarges its internal table. You can use the load factor to prevent a Hashtable from becoming too full, which degrades its performance. For example, suppose that the Hashtable's capacity is 100 and its load factor is 0.8. Then when it holds 80 elements, the Hashtable will enlarge its internal table to make more room.

For high-performance lookups, the Hashtable class is a great solution as long as it doesn't resize too often and doesn't become too full.

HybridDictionary

A HybridDictionary is a cross between a ListDictionary and a Hashtable. If the dictionary is small, the HybridDictionary stores its data in a ListDictionary. If the dictionary grows too large, HybridDictionary switches to a Hashtable.

If you know that you will only need a few items, use a ListDictionary. If you know you will need to use a very large number of items, use a Hashtable. If you are unsure whether you will have few or many items, you can hedge your bet with a HybridDictionary. It'll take a bit of extra time to switch from a list to a Hashtable if you add a lot of items, but you'll save time in the long run if the list does turn out to be enormous.

StringDictionary

The StringDictionary class uses a hash table to manage keys and values that are all strings. Because it uses a hash table, it can handle very large data sets quickly.

Its methods are strongly typed to require strings, so they provide extra type checking that can make finding potential bugs easier. For that reason, you should use a StringDictionary instead of a generic ListDictionary or Hashtable if you want to work exclusively with strings.

SortedList

The SortedList class acts as a Hashtable/Array hybrid. When you access a value by key, it acts as a hash table. When you access a value by index, it acts as an array containing items sorted by key value. For example, suppose that you add a number of Job objects to a SortedList named jobs using their priorities as keys. Then jobs(0) always returns the job with the smallest priority value.

Example program UseSortedList, which is available for download on the book's website, demonstrates the SortedList class.

A SortedList is more complicated than a Hashtable or an array, so you should only use it if you need its special properties.

COLLECTIONSUTIL

Normally Hashtables and SortedLists are case-sensitive. The CollectionsUtil class provides two shared methods, CreateCaseInsensitiveHashtable and CreateCaseInsensitiveSortedList, that create Hashtables and SortedLists objects that are case-insensitive.

Example program UseCaseInsensitiveSortedList, which is available for download on the book's website, uses code similar to the following to create a normal case-sensitive SortedList. It then adds two items with keys that differ only in their capitalization. This works because a case-sensitive SortedList treats the two keys as different values. The code then creates a case-insensitive SortedList. When it tries to add the same two items, the list raises an exception, complaining that it already has an object with key value Sport.

```
Dim sorted_list As SortedList

' Use a normal, case-sensitive SortedList.
sorted_list = New SortedList
sorted_list.Add("Sport", "Volleyball")
sorted_list.Add("sport", "Golf") ' Okay because Sport <> sport.

' Use a case-insensitive SortedList.
sorted_list = CollectionsUtil.CreateCaseInsensitiveSortedList()
sorted_list.Add("Sport", "Volleyball")
sorted_list.Add("sport", "Golf") ' Error because Sport = sport.
```

If you can use case-insensitive Hashtables and SortedLists, you may want to do so to prevent the program from adding two entries that are supposed to be the same but have different capitalization. For example, if one routine spells a key value "Law Suit" and another spells it "law suit," the case-insensitive Hashtable or SortedList will quickly catch the error. Neither will notice an error if part of your program spells this "LawSuit." (You could also add extra logic to remove spaces and special symbols to increase the chances of finding similar terms that should be the same, but a discussion of these sorts of methods is beyond the scope of this book.)

STACKS AND QUEUES

Stacks and queues are specialized data structures that are useful in many programming applications that need to add and remove items in a particular order. The Visual Basic Stack and Queue classes implement stacks and queues.

The difference between a stack and a queue is the order in which they return the items stored in them. The following two sections describe stacks and queues and explain the ways in which they return items.

Stack

A *stack* returns items in last-in-first-out (LIFO, pronounced *life-o*) order. Because of the LIFO behavior, a stack is sometimes called a *LIFO list* or simply a *LIFO*.

Adding an item to the stack is called *pushing the item onto the stack* and removing an item is called *popping the item off of the stack*. These operations have the names push and pop because a stack is like a spring-loaded stack of plates in a cafeteria or buffet. You push new plates down onto the top of the stack and the plates sink into the counter. You pop the top plate off and the stack rises to give you the next plate.

Figure 25-3 illustrates this kind of stack. If you haven't seen this sort of thing before, don't worry about it. Just remember that push adds an item and pop removes the top item.

Normally, you use a Stack object's Push and Pop methods to add and remove items, but the Stack class also provides some cheating methods that let you peek at the Stack's top object or convert the Stack into an array. The following table describes the Stack class's most useful properties and methods.

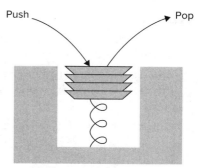

FIGURE 25-3: A Stack lets you remove items in last-in-first-out (LIFO) order.

PROPERTY/METHOD	PURPOSE
Clear	Removes all items from the Stack.
Contains	Returns True if the Stack contains a particular object.
CopyTo	Copies some or all of the Stack class's objects into a one-dimensional array.
Count	Returns the number of items in the Stack.
Peek	Returns a reference to the Stack class's top item without removing it from the Stack.
Pop	Returns the Stack class's top item and removes it from the Stack.
Push	Adds an item to the top of the Stack.
ToArray	Returns a one-dimensional array containing references to the objects in the Stack. The Stack class's top item is placed first in the array.

A Stack allocates memory to store its items. If you Push an object onto a Stack that is completely full, the Stack must resize itself to make more room and that slows down the operation.

To make memory management more efficient, the Stack class provides three overloaded constructors. The first takes no parameters and allocates a default initial capacity. The second takes as a parameter the number of items the Stack should initially be able to hold. If you know that you will add 10,000 items to the Stack, you can avoid a lot of resizing by initially allocating room for 10,000 items.

The third version of the constructor takes as a parameter an object that implements the ICollection interface. The constructor allocates enough room to hold the items in the collection and copies them into the Stack.

Example program UseStack, which is available for download on the book's website, uses a Stack to reverse the characters in a string.

Queue

A *queue* returns items in first-in-first-out (FIFO, pronounced *fife-o*) order. Because of the FIFO behavior, a queue is sometimes called a *FIFO list* or simply a *FIFO*.

A queue is similar to a line at a customer service desk. The first person in line is the first person to leave it when the service desk is free. Figure 25-4 shows the idea graphically.

FIGURE 25-4: Customers leave a queue in first-in-first-out (FIFO) order.

Queues are particularly useful for processing items in the order in which they were created. For example, an order-processing application might keep orders in a queue so that customers who place orders first are satisfied first (or at least their order is shipped first, whether they are satisfied or not).

Historically, the routines that add and remove items from a queue are called Enqueue and Dequeue. The following table describes these methods and the Queue class's other most useful properties and methods.

PROPERTY/METHOD	PURPOSE
Clear	Removes all items from the Queue.
Contains	Returns True if the Queue contains a particular object.
CopyTo	Copies some or all of the Queue class's objects into a one-dimensional array.
Count	Returns the number of items in the Queue.
Dequeue	Returns the item that has been in the Queue the longest and removes it from the Queue.
Enqueue	Adds an item to the back of the Queue.
Peek	Returns a reference to the Queue class's oldest item without removing it from the Queue.
ToArray	Returns a one-dimensional array containing references to the objects in the Queue. The Queue class's oldest item is placed first in the array.
TrimToSize	Frees empty space in the Queue to set its capacity equal to the number of items it actually contains.

A Queue allocates memory to store its items. If you Enqueue an object while the queue's memory is full, the Queue must resize itself to make more room, and that slows down the operation.

To make memory management more efficient, the Queue class provides four overloaded constructors. The first takes no parameters and allocates a default initial capacity. If the Queue is full, it enlarges itself by a default growth factor.

The second constructor takes as a parameter its initial capacity. If you know that you will add 600 items to the Queue, you can save some time by initially allocating room for 600 items. With this constructor, the Queue also uses a default growth factor.

The third constructor takes as a parameter an object that implements the ICollection interface. The constructor allocates enough room to hold the items in the collection and copies them into the Queue. It also uses a default growth factor.

The final version of the constructor takes as parameters an initial capacity and a growth factor between 1.0 and 10.0. A larger growth factor will mean that the Queue resizes itself less often, but it may contain a lot of unused space.

Example program UseQueue, which is available for download on the book's website, demonstrates a Queue.

GENERICS

Chapter 26 explains how you can build and use generic classes to perform similar actions for objects of various types. For example, you could build a Tree class that can build a tree of any specific kind of object. Your program could then make a tree of Employees, a tree of Customers, a tree of Punchlines, or even a tree of trees. Visual Basic comes with a useful assortment of prebuilt generic collection classes.

The System.Collections.Generic namespace provides several generic collection classes that you can use to build strongly typed collections. These collections work with a specific data type that you supply in a variable's declaration. For example, the following code makes a List that holds strings:

```
Imports System.Collections.Generic

...
Dim places As New List(Of String)
places.Add("Chicago")
```

The places object's methods are strongly typed and work only with strings, so they provide extra error protection that a less specialized collection doesn't provide. To take advantage of this extra protection, you should use generic collections whenever possible.

You cannot directly modify a generic collection class, but you can add extension methods to it. For example, the following code adds an AddPerson method to the generic List(Of Person) class. This method takes as parameters a first and last name, uses those values to make a Person object, and adds it to the list.

```
Module PersonListExtensions
    <Extension()>
    Public Sub AddPerson(person_list As List(Of Person),
     first_name As String, last_name As String)
        Dim per As New Person() With _
            {.FirstName = first_name, .LastName = last_name}
        person_list.Add(per)
    End Sub
End Module
```

For more information on extension methods, see the section "Extension Methods" in Chapter 16, "Subroutines and Functions."

In addition to adding extension methods to a generic class, you can also derive an enhanced collection from a generic class. For example, the following code defines an EmployeeList class that inherits from the generic List(Of Employee). It then adds an overloaded version of the Add method that takes first and last names as parameters.

```
Imports System.Collections.Generic

Public Class EmployeeList
    Inherits List(Of Employee)

    Public Overloads Sub Add(
     first_name As String, last_name As String)
        Dim emp As New Employee(first_name, last_name)
        MyBase.Add(emp)
    End Sub
End Class
```

NO OVERLOADS ALLOWED

Note that extension methods cannot overload a class's methods. If you want multiple versions of the Add method as in this example, you need to use a derived class.

The following table lists some of the most useful collection classes defined by the System .Collections.Generic namespace.

COLLECTION	PURPOSE
Comparer	Compares two objects of the specific type and returns −1, 0, or 1 to indicate whether the first is less than, equal to, or greater than the second
Dictionary	A strongly typed dictionary
LinkedList	A strongly typed linked list

COLLECTION	PURPOSE
LinkedListNode	A strongly typed node in a linked list
List	A strongly typed list
Queue	A strongly typed queue
SortedDictionary	A strongly typed sorted dictionary
SortedList	A strongly typed sorted list
Stack	A strongly typed stack

Example program GenericStringList, which is available for download on the book's website, demonstrates a generic List(Of String). Example program GenericEmployeeList, which is also available for download, derives a strongly typed EmployeeList class from a generic List(Of Employee).

For more information on generics (including instructions for writing your own generic classes), see Chapter 26.

COLLECTION INITIALIZERS

Initializers allow you to easily initialize collection classes that have an Add method. To initialize a collection, follow the variable's instantiation with the keyword From and then a series of comma-separated values inside braces.

For example, the following code snippet initializes an ArrayList, StringCollection, and generic List(Of Person). Notice how the generic List's initializer includes a series of new Person objects that are initialized with the With keyword.

```
Dim numbers As New ArrayList() From {1, 2, 3}
Dim names As New StringCollection() From {"Alice", "Bob", "Cynthia"}
Dim authors As New List(Of Person) From {
    New Person() With {.FirstName = "Simon", .LastName = "Green"},
    New Person() With {.FirstName = "Christopher", .LastName = "Moore"},
    New Person() With {.FirstName = "Terry", .LastName = "Pratchett"}
}
```

If a collection's Add method takes more than one parameter, simply include the appropriate values for each item inside their own sets of braces. The following code uses this method to initialize a NameValueCollection and a Dictionary with Integer keys and String values:

```
Dim phone_numbers As New NameValueCollection() From {
    {"Ashley", "502-253-3748"},
    {"Jane", "505-847-2984"},
```

```
        {"Mike", "505-847-3984"},
        {"Shebly", "502-487-4939"}
    }
    Dim greetings As New Dictionary(Of Integer, String) From {
        {1, "Hi"},
        {2, "Hello"},
        {3, "Holla"}
    }
```

The same technique works for other collections that need two values such as ListDictionary, Hashtable, HybridDictionary, StringDictionary, and SortedList.

Unfortunately, you cannot use this method to initialize the Stack and Queue classes. For historical reasons, the methods in those classes that add new items are called Push and Enqueue rather than Add, and this method requires the class to have an Add method.

Fortunately, you can write extension methods to give those classes Add methods. The following code creates Add methods for the Stack and Queue classes:

```
Module Extensions
    <Extension()>
    Public Sub Add(the_stack As Stack, value As Object)
        the_stack.Push(value)
    End Sub

    <Extension()>
    Public Sub Add(the_queue As Queue, value As Object)
        the_queue.Enqueue(value)
    End Sub
End Module
```

After you create these extension methods, you can initialize Stacks and Queues as in the following code:

```
Dim people_stack As New Stack() From {"Electra", "Storm", "Rogue"}
Dim people_queue As New Queue() From {"Xavier", "Anakin", "Zaphod"}
```

ITERATORS

One of the benefits of collection classes is that they allow you to use a For Each loop to iterate through the items they contain. Visual Basic lets you write your own iterator function to provide access to items in a group. Then other code can loop over those items by using a For Each loop.

To make an iterator, create a function that uses the keyword Iterator before its Function keyword. Then make the function return the type IEnumerable or a generic version of IEnumerable such as IEnumerable(Of String). Finally, inside the function, use the Yield statement to return a value in the enumeration.

For example, the following function enumerates a list of prime numbers:

```
Private Iterator Function Primes(
    start_number As Integer, end_number As Integer) As IEnumerable(Of Integer)
      ' Define an inline function that returns True if a number is prime.
    Dim is_prime = Function(i)
                If i = 1 Then Return False        ' 1 is not prime.
                If i = 2 Then Return True         ' 2 is prime.
                If i Mod 2 = 0 Then Return False  ' Other even numbers are not prime.
                For test As Integer = 3 To Math.Sqr(i) Step 2
                    If i Mod test = 0 Then Return False
                Next test
                Return True
            End Function

    For i As Integer = start_number To end_number
        ' If this number is prime, enumerate it.
        If is_prime(i) Then Yield i
    Next i
End Function
```

The following code shows how a program might use the Primes iterator:

```
For Each prime As Integer In Primes(1, 1000)
    Debug.WriteLine(prime)
Next prime
Debug.WriteLine("# Primes: " & Primes(1, 1000).Count)
```

SUMMARY

This chapter explained several types of collection classes.

Variable arrays store objects sequentially. They allow fast access at any point in the array. The Array class lets you make arrays indexed with nonzero lower bounds, although they provide slower performance than arrays of variables, which require lower bounds of zero. The Array class provides several useful methods for working with Array objects and normal variable arrays, including Sort, Reverse, IndexOf, LastIndexOf, and BinarySearch.

Collections store data in ways that are different from those used by arrays. An ArrayList stores items in a linked list. That works well for short lists, but slows down when the list grows large. A StringCollection holds a collection of strings. StringCollection is an example of a strongly typed collection (it holds only strings). The NameValueCollection class is a specialized collection that can hold more than one string value for a given key value.

Dictionaries associate key values with corresponding data values. You look up the key to find the data much as you might look up a word in the dictionary to find its definition. The ListDictionary class stores its data in a linked list. It is fast for small data sets but slow when it contains too much data. In contrast a Hashtable has substantial overhead but is extremely fast for large dictionaries. A HybridDictionary acts as a ListDictionary if it doesn't contain too much data and switches to a Hashtable when it gets too big. The StringDictionary class is basically a Hashtable that is strongly typed to work with strings. The SortedList class is a Hashtable/Array hybrid that lets you access values by key or in sorted order.

Stack classes provide access to items in last-in-first-out (LIFO) order. Queue classes give access to their items in first-in-first-out (FIFO) order.

The generic Dictionary, LinkedList, List, Queue, SortedDictionary, SortedList, and Stack classes enable you to use strongly typed data structures.

Although these classes have very different features for adding, removing, finding, and ordering objects, they share some common traits. For example, those that provide an Add method support collection initialization. They also all support enumeration by For Each statements.

These classes provide many useful features so you can pick the class that best satisfies your needs. Deciding which class is best can be tricky, but making the right choice can mean the difference between programs that process a large data set in seconds, hours, or not at all. Spend some time reviewing the different characteristics of the classes so that you can make the best choice possible.

This chapter explained how you can use the generic collection classes provided by the System .Collections.Generic namespace. Chapter 26, "Generics," explains how you can build generic classes of your own. Using generics, you can build strongly typed classes that manipulate objects of any data type.

26

Generics

WHAT'S IN THIS CHAPTER

- ➤ Vantages of generics
- ➤ Defining generics
- ➤ Using generics
- ➤ Generic methods
- ➤ Generics and extension methods

WROX.COM CODE DOWNLOADS FOR THIS CHAPTER

The wrox.com code downloads for this chapter are found at `http://www.wrox.com/rem title.cgi?isbn=9781118314074` on the Download Code tab. The code for this chapter is divided into the following major examples:

- ➤ GenericBinaryTree
- ➤ GenericPairDictionary
- ➤ GenericTreeImportsAlias
- ➤ SortedBinaryTree
- ➤ UseSwitcher

CLASS CREATORS

Classes are often described as cookie cutters for creating objects. You define a class, and then you can use it to make any number of objects that are instances of the class.

Similarly, a *generic* is like a cookie cutter for creating classes. You define a generic, and then you can use it to create any number of classes that have similar features.

For example, Visual Basic comes with a generic List class. You can use it to make lists of strings, lists of integers, lists of Employee objects, or lists of just about anything else.

This chapter explains generics. It shows how you can define generics of your own and how you can use them.

ADVANTAGES OF GENERICS

A generic class takes one or more data types as parameters. An instance of a generic class has those parameters filled in with specific data types such as String, TextBox, or Employee.

For example, you can build a list of OrderItem objects, a hash table containing PurchaseOrders identified by number, or a Queue that contains Customer objects.

Tying generics to specific data types gives them several advantages over non-generic classes:

➤ **Strong typing** — Methods can take parameters and return values that have the class's instance type. For example, a List(Of String) can hold only String values, its Add method can only add Strings to the list, and its Item method returns String values. This makes it more difficult to accidentally add the wrong type of object to the collection.

➤ **IntelliSense** — By providing strong typing, a class built from a generic lets Visual Studio provide IntelliSense. If you make a List(Of Employee), Visual Studio knows that the items in the collection are Employee objects, so it can give you appropriate IntelliSense.

➤ **No boxing** — Because the class manipulates objects with a specific data type, Visual Basic doesn't need to convert items to and from the plain Object data type. For example, if a program stores TextBox controls in a normal collection, the program must convert the TextBox controls to and from the Object class when it adds and uses items in the collection. Avoiding these steps makes the code more efficient.

➤ **Code reuse** — You can use a generic class with more than one data type. For example, if you have built a generic PriorityQueue class, you can make a PriorityQueue holding Employee, Customer, Order, or Objection objects. Without generics, you would need to build four separate classes to build strongly typed priority queues for each of these types of objects. Reusing this code makes it easier to write, test, debug, and maintain the code.

The main disadvantage to generics is that they are slightly more complicated and confusing than non-generic classes. If you know that you will only ever need to provide a class that works with a single type, you can simplify things slightly by not using a generic class. If you think you might want to reuse the code later for another data type, it's easier to just build the class generically from the start.

DEFINING GENERICS

Visual Basic allows you to define generic classes, structures, interfaces, procedures, and delegates. The basic syntax for all of those is similar, so once you know how to make generic classes, making generic structures, interfaces, and the others is fairly easy.

To define a generic class, make a class declaration as usual. After the class name, add a parenthesis, the keyword Of, a placeholder for a data type, and a closing parenthesis. The data type placeholder is similar to a parameter name that you would give to a subroutine except it is a type, not a simple value. The class's code can use the name ItemType to refer to the type associated with the instance of the generic class.

For example, suppose you want to build a binary tree that could hold any kind of data. The following code shows how you could define a BinaryNode class to hold the tree's data:

```
Public Class BinaryNode(Of T)
    Public Value As T
    Public LeftChild As BinaryNode(Of T)
    Public RightChild As BinaryNode(Of T)
End Class
```

The class's declaration takes a type parameter named T. (Many developers use the name T for the type parameter. If the class takes more than one type parameter separated by commas, they start each name with T as in TKey and TData.)

The class defines a public field named Data that has type T. This is where the node's data is stored.

The class also defines two fields that refer to the node's left and right children in the binary tree. Those fields hold references to objects from this same class: BinaryNode(Of T).

The following code shows how a program could use this class to build a small binary tree of Employee objects:

```
' Define the tree's root node.
Dim root As New BinaryNode(Of Employee)
root.Value = New Employee("Ben", "Baker")

' Create the root's left child.
root.LeftChild = New BinaryNode(Of Employee)
root.LeftChild.Value = New Employee("Ann", "Archer")

' Create the root's right child.
root.RightChild = New BinaryNode(Of Employee)
root.RightChild.Value = New Employee("Cindy", "Carter")
```

Generic Constructors

Generic classes can have constructors just as any other class can. For example, the following constructor initializes a BinaryNode object's LeftChild and RightChild references:

```
' Assign this node's left and right children.
Public Sub New(new_value As T,
 Optional left_child As BinaryNode(Of T) = Nothing,
 Optional right_child As BinaryNode(Of T) = Nothing)
    Value = new_value
    LeftChild = left_child
    RightChild = right_child
End Sub
```

To use the constructor, the main program adds normal parameters after the type parameters in the object declaration. The following code uses the new constructor to create a binary tree similar to the previous one:

```
' Define the child nodes.
Dim left_child As New BinaryNode(Of Employee)(New Employee("Ann", "Archer"))
Dim right_child As New BinaryNode(Of Employee)(New Employee("Cindy", "Carter"))

' Define the tree's root node.
Dim root As New BinaryNode(Of Employee)(
    New Employee("Ben", "Baker"),
    left_child, right_child)
```

Multiple Types

If you want the class to work with more than one type, you can add other types to the declaration separated by commas. For example, suppose that you want to create a dictionary that associates keys with pairs of data items. Example program GenericPairDictionary uses the following code to define the generic PairDictionary class. This class acts as a dictionary that associates a key value with a pair of data values. The class declaration includes three data types named TKey, TValue1, and TValue2.

```
' A Dictionary that associates a pair of data values with each key.
Public Class PairDictionary(Of TKey, TValue1, TValue2)
    ' A structure to hold paired data.
    Private Structure ValuePair
        Public Value1 As TValue1
        Public Value2 As TValue2
        Public Sub New(new_value1 As TValue1, new_value2 As TValue2)
            Value1 = new_value1
            Value2 = new_value2
        End Sub
    End Structure

    ' A Dictionary to hold the paired data.
    Private ValueDictionary As New Dictionary(Of TKey, ValuePair)

    ' Return the number of data pairs.
    Public ReadOnly Property Count() As Integer
        Get
            Return ValueDictionary.Count
        End Get
    End Property

    ' Add a key and value pair.
    Public Sub Add(ByVal key As TKey,
     new_value1 As TValue1,
     new_value2 As TValue2)
        ValueDictionary.Add(key, New ValuePair(new_value1, new_value2))
    End Sub
```

```
' Remove all data.
Public Sub Clear()
    ValueDictionary.Clear()
End Sub

' Return True if PairDictionary contains this key.
Public Function ContainsKey(key As TKey) As Boolean
    Return ValueDictionary.ContainsKey(key)
End Function

' Return a data pair.
Public Sub GetItem(ByVal key As TKey,
 ByRef data_value1 As TValue1,
 ByRef data_value2 As TValue2)
   Dim data_pair As DataPair = ValueDictionary.Item(key)
   data_value1 = data_pair.Value1
   data_value2 = data_pair.Value2
End Sub

' Set a data pair.
Public Sub SetItem(key As TKey,
 data_value1 As TValue1,
 data_value2 As TValue2)
    ValueDictionary.Item(key) = New DataPair(data_value1, data_value2)
End Sub

' Return a collection containing the keys.
Public ReadOnly Property Keys() As System.Collections.ICollection
    Get
        Return ValueDictionary.Keys()
    End Get
End Property

' Remove a particular entry.
    Public Sub Remove(key As TKey) ValueDictionary.Remove(key)
End Sub
End Class
```

The PairDictionary class defines its own private ValuePair class to hold pairs of data values. The ValuePair class has two public variables of types TValue1 and TValue2. Its only method is a constructor that makes initializing the two variables easier.

After defining the ValuePair class, the PairDictionary class declares a generic Dictionary object named ValueDictionary using the key type TKey and data type ValuePair.

PairDictionary provides Count, Add, Clear, ContainsKey, GetItem, SetItem, Keys, and Remove methods. Notice how it delegates these to the ValueDictionary object and how it uses the ValuePair class to store values in ValueDictionary.

The following code creates an instance of the generic PairDictionary class that uses integers as keys and strings for both data values. It adds three entries to the PairDictionary and then retrieves and displays the entry with key value 32.

```
' Create the PairDictionary and add some data.
Dim pair_dictionary As New PairDictionary(Of Integer, String, String)
pair_dictionary.Add(10, "Ann", "Archer")
pair_dictionary.Add(32, "Bill", "Beach")
pair_dictionary.Add(17, "Cynthia", "Campos")

' Print the values for index 32.
Dim value1 As String = ""
Dim value2 As String = ""
pair_dictionary.GetItem(32, value1, value2)
Debug.WriteLine(value1 & ", " & value2)
```

Constrained Types

To get the most out of your generic classes, you should make them as flexible as possible. Depending on what the class will do, however, you may need to constrain the class's generic types.

For example, suppose you want to make a generic SortedBinaryNode class similar to the BinaryNode class described earlier but that keeps its values sorted. When you add a new value to a node, the program compares the new value to the node's value and places the new node in the left or right subtree depending on whether the new value is less than or greater than the node's value.

For example, suppose node A contains the value 7 and you want to add the value 5 to its subtree. The new value 5 is less than 7 so node A would put the new value in its left subtree. If node A has no left child node then it places the new value in a new node and makes that node its left child. If node A already has a left child, Node A calls that child's Add method to add the child somewhere in its subtree.

Figuring out whether a new value belongs in a node's left or right subtree is relatively straightforward if the node holds integers or strings, but there's no obvious way to determine whether one Employee object should be placed before another. The SortedBinaryNode class will only work if the data type of the objects it holds supports comparison.

One way to allow the nodes to compare items is to require that the items they contain implement the IComparable interface. Then the program can use their CompareTo methods to see whether one item is greater than or less than another item.

To require that a generic class's type implements an interface, add an "As inferface" clause after the type's declaration. Example program SortedBinaryTree uses the following SortedBinaryNode class:

```
Public Class SortedBinaryNode(Of T As IComparable)
    Public Value As T
    Public LeftChild As SortedBinaryNode(Of T)
    Public RightChild As SortedBinaryNode(Of T)

    Public Sub New(new_value As T)
        Value = new_value
    End Sub

    ' Add a new value to this node's subtree.
    Public Sub Add(new_value As T)
        ' See if it belongs in the left or right child's subtree.
        If (new_value.CompareTo(Value) < 0) Then
            ' Left subtree.
```

```
            If (LeftChild Is Nothing) Then
                ' Add it as the new left child.
                LeftChild = New SortedBinaryNode(Of T)(new_value)
            Else
                ' Add it in the left subtree.
                LeftChild.Add(new_value)
            End If
        Else
            ' Right subtree.
            If (RightChild Is Nothing) Then
                ' Add it as the new right child.
                RightChild = New SortedBinaryNode(Of T)(new_value)
            Else
                ' Add it in the right subtree.
                RightChild.Add(new_value)
            End If
        End If
    End Sub
End Class
```

A type's As clause can specify any number of interfaces and at most one class from which the type must be derived. It can also include the keyword New to indicate that the type used must provide a constructor that takes no parameters. If you include more than one constraint, the constraints should be separated by commas and enclosed in brackets.

The following code defines the StrangeGeneric class that takes three type parameters. The first type must implement the IComparable interface and must provide an empty constructor. The second type has no constraints, and the third type must be a class that inherits from Control.

```
Public Class StrangeGeneric(Of T1 As {IComparable, New}, T2, T3 As Control)
    ...
End Class
```

The following code declares an instance of the StrangeGeneric class:

```
Dim strange_generic As New StrangeGeneric(Of Integer, Employee, Button)
```

Constraining a type gives Visual Basic more information about that type, so it lets you use the properties and methods defined by the type. In the previous code, for example, if a variable is of type T3, then Visual Basic knows that it inherits from the Control class, so you can use Control properties and methods such as Anchor, BackColor, and Font.

INSTANTIATING GENERIC CLASSES

The previous sections have already shown a few examples of how to use a generic class. The program declares the class and includes whatever data types are required in an Of clause. The following code shows how a program might create a generic list of strings:

```
Imports System.Collections.Generic
...
Dim names As New List(Of String)
```

To pass parameters to a generic class's constructor, add a second set of parentheses and any parameters after the type specifications. The following statement creates an IntStringList object, passing it the types Integer, String, and Employee. It calls the class's constructor, passing it the value 100.

```
Dim the_employees As New IntStringList(Of Integer, String, Employee)(100)
```

If the program needs to use only a few generic classes (for example, a single collection of strings), this isn't too bad. If the program needs to use many instances of the class, however, the code becomes cluttered.

For example, suppose that the TreeNode class shown in the following code represents a node in a tree. Its MyData field holds some piece of data, and its Children list holds references to child nodes.

```
Public Class TreeNode(Of T)
    Public MyData As T
    Public Children As New List(Of TreeNode(Of T))

    Public Sub New(ByVal new_data As T)
        MyData = new_data
    End Sub
End Class
```

The following code uses this class to build a small tree of Employee objects:

```
Dim root As New TreeNode(Of Employee)(New Employee("Annabelle", "Ant"))
Dim child1 As New TreeNode(Of Employee)(New Employee("Bert", "Bear"))
Dim child2 As New TreeNode(Of Employee)(New Employee("Candice", "Cat"))

root.Children.Add(child1)
root.Children.Add(child2)
```

Example program GenericTree, which is available for download on the book's website, uses similar code to build a generic Tree(Of T) class.

Repeating the nodes' data types in the first three lines makes the code rather cluttered. Two techniques that you can use to make the code a bit simpler are using an imports alias and deriving a new class. Both of these let you create a simpler name for the awkward class name TreeNode (Of Employee).

Imports Aliases

Normally, you use an Imports statement to make it easier to refer to namespaces and the symbols they contain. However, the Imports statement also lets you define an alias for a namespace entity. To use this to make using generics easier, create an Imports statement that refers to the type of generic class you want to use and give it a simple alias.

For example, the following code is in the DataTreeTest namespace. It uses an Imports statement to refer to a TreeNode of Employee. It gives this entity the alias EmployeeNode. Later, the program can use the name EmployeeNode instead of the more cumbersome TreeNode (Of Employee).

```
Imports EmployeeNode = DataTreeTest.TreeNode(Of DataTreeTest.Employee)
...
Dim root As New EmployeeNode(New Employee("Annabelle", "Ant"))
Dim child1 As New EmployeeNode(New Employee("Bert", "Bear"))
Dim child2 As New EmployeeNode(New Employee("Candice", "Cat"))

root.Children.Add(child1)
root.Children.Add(child2)
...
```

Example program GenericTreeImportsAlias demonstrates this approach.

Derived Classes

A second method that simplifies using generics is to derive a class from the generic class. The following code derives the EmployeeNode class from TreeNode(Of Employee). Later, it creates instances of this class to build the tree.

```
Public Class EmployeeNode
    Inherits TreeNode(Of Employee)
    Public Sub New(new_data As Employee)
        MyBase.New(new_data)
    End Sub
End Class
...
Dim root As New EmployeeNode(New Employee("Annabelle", "Ant"))
Dim child1 As New EmployeeNode(New Employee("Bert", "Bear"))
Dim child2 As New EmployeeNode(New Employee("Candice", "Cat"))

root.Children.Add(child1)
root.Children.Add(child2)
...
```

Example program GenericTreeSubclass demonstrates this approach.

If you use this technique, you can also add extra convenience functions to the derived class. For example, the following code shows a new EmployeeNode constructor that creates the Employee object that it holds:

```
Public Sub New(first_name As String, last_name As String)
    MyBase.New(New Employee(first_name, last_name))
End Sub
```

GENERIC COLLECTION CLASSES

The System.Collections.Generic namespace defines several generic classes. These are basically collection classes that use generics to work with the data type you specify. See the section "Generics" near the end of Chapter 25, "Collection Classes," for more information and a list of the more useful predefined generic collection classes.

GENERIC METHODS

Generics are usually used to build classes that are not data type–specific such as the generic collection classes. You can also give a class (generic or otherwise) a generic method. Just as a generic class is not tied to a particular data type, the parameters of a generic method are not tied to a specific data type.

The method's declaration includes an Of clause similar to the one used by generic classes, followed by the method's parameter list.

Example program UseSwitcher uses the following code to define a generic Switch subroutine. This subroutine defines the generic type T and takes two parameters of type T. If this were a function, you could use the type T for its return value if you wanted. Subroutine Switch declares a variable temp of type T and uses it to switch the values of its parameters.

```
Public Class Switcher
    Public Sub Switch(Of T)(ByRef thing1 As T, ByRef thing2 As T)
        Dim temp As T = thing1
        thing1 = thing2
        thing2 = temp
    End Sub
End Class
```

GENERIC CLASSES AND METHODS

The Switcher class is not generic but it contains a generic method. Note that a generic class can also contain generic and non-generic methods. You can also create generic methods in code modules.

The following code uses a Switcher object to switch the values of two Person variables. In the call to the Switch method, Visual Basic uses the first parameter to infer that the type T is Person and then requires the second parameter to have the same type.

```
Dim person1 As New Person("Anna")
Dim person2 As New Person("Bill")
Dim a_switcher As New Switcher()
a_switcher.Switch(person1, person2)
```

GENERICS AND EXTENSION METHODS

Just as extension methods allow you to add new features to existing classes, they also allow you to add new features to generic classes. For example, suppose you have an application that uses a List(Of Person). This List class is a generic collection class defined in the System.Collections .Generic namespace.

The generic class is not defined in your code so you cannot modify it, but you can add extension methods to it. The following code adds an AddPerson method to List(Of Person) that takes as parameters a first and last name, uses those values to make a Person object, and adds it to the list:

```
Module PersonListExtensions
    <Extension()>
    Public Sub AddPerson(person_list As List(Of Person),
     first_name As String, last_name As String)
        Dim per As New Person() With _
            {.FirstName = first_name, .LastName = last_name}
        person_list.Add(per)
    End Sub
End Module
```

This example adds an extension method to a specific instance of a generic class. In this example, the code adds the method to List(Of Person). With a little more work, you can add a generic extension method to a generic class itself instead of adding it to an instance of the class.

Example program GenericNumDistinct uses the following code to add a NumDistinct function to the generic List(Of T) class for any type T. The declaration identifies its generic type T. The first parameter has type List(Of T) so this method extends List(Of T). The function has an Integer return type.

```
Module ListExtensions
    <Extension()>
    Public Function NumDistinct(Of T)(the_list As List(Of T)) As Integer
        Return the_list.Distinct().Count()
    End Function
End Module
```

The generic List(Of T) class provides a Distinct method that returns a new list containing the distinct objects in the original list. The NumDistinct function calls that method and returns the new list's Count value.

The following code shows how a program could call this function. It creates a new List(Of String) and gives it some data. It then calls the list's NumDistinct function.

```
Dim name_list As New List(Of String)
name_list.Add("Llamaar Aarchibald")
name_list.Add("Dudley Eversol")
...

MessageBox.Show("The list contains " &
    name_list.Count() & " entries and " &
    name_list.NumDistinct() &    " distinct entries")
```

For more information on extension methods, see the section "Extension Methods" in Chapter 16, "Subroutines and Functions."

SUMMARY

A class abstracts the properties and behaviors of a set of objects to form a template that you can use to make objects that implement those properties and behaviors. After you define the class, you can make many instances of it, and they will all have the features defined by the class.

Generics take abstraction one level higher. A generic class abstracts the features of a set of classes defined for any given data types. It determines the properties and methods that any class in the generic group provides. After you define the generic class, you can easily make classes that work with different data types but that all provide the common set of features defined by the generic.

By defining common functionality, generic classes let you reuse code to perform similar actions for different data types. By allowing you to parameterize the class instances with a data type, they let you build strongly typed classes quickly and easily. That, in turn, lets Visual Basic provide IntelliSense to make programming faster and easier.

Together these benefits — easier code reuse, strong typing, and IntelliSense support — help you write, test, debug, and maintain code more easily.

The programs described in this book so far are relatively self-contained. They take input from the user, perform some calculations, and display the results on the program's forms.

The chapters in the next part of the book explain ways a program can interact with the system. Chapter 27, "Printing," explains how to generate output on a printer.

PART IV
Interacting with the Environment

27

Printing

WROX.COM CODE DOWNLOADS FOR THIS CHAPTER

The wrox.com code downloads for this chapter are found at `http://www.wrox.com/remtitle .cgi?isbn=9781118314074` on the Download Code tab. The code for this chapter is divided into the following major examples:

- ➤ BrushSamples
- ➤ DrawInPaintEvent
- ➤ DrawOnBitmap
- ➤ PrintBooklet
- ➤ UsePrintPreviewDialog

PRINTING CONCEPTS

Visual Basic .NET provides several good tools for printing. String formatting objects enable you to determine how text is wrapped and truncated if it won't fit in a printing area. Methods provided by Graphics objects enable you to easily scale, rotate, and translate drawing commands.

The basic process, however, seems somewhat backward to many programmers. Rather than issuing commands to a printer object, a program responds to requests to draw pages generated by a PrintDocument object. Instead of telling the printer what to do, the program responds to the PrintDocument object's requests for data.

The following section describes the basic process and explains this backward-seeming approach. The sections after that explain how to print specific items such as shapes and text, and how to scale, center, and otherwise arrange the results.

BASIC PRINTING

The PrintDocument class sits at the heart of Visual Basic's printing process. The program creates an instance of this class and installs event handlers to catch its events. When the object must perform printing-related tasks, it raises events to ask the program for help.

The PrintDocument object raises four key events:

➤ **BeginPrint** — The PrintDocument raises its BeginPrint event when it is about to start printing. The program can initialize data structures, load data, connect to databases, and perform any other chores it must do to get ready to print.

➤ **QueryPageSettings** — Before it prints a page, the PrintDocument object raises its QueryPageSettings event. A program can catch this event and modify the document's margins for the page that it is about to print.

➤ **PrintPage** — The PrintDocument object raises its PrintPage event to generate a page. The program must catch this event and use the Graphics object provided by the event handler's parameters to generate output. When it is finished, the event handler should set the value e.HasMorePages to True or False to tell the PrintDocument whether there are more pages to generate after this one.

➤ **EndPrint** — When it has finished printing, the PrintDocument object raises its EndPrint event. The program can catch this event to clean up any resources it used while printing. It can free data structures, close data files and database connections, and perform any other necessary cleanup chores.

Having created a PrintDocument object and its event handlers, you can do three things with it. First you can call the object's Print method to immediately send a printout to the currently selected printer. The PrintDocument object raises its events as necessary as it generates the printout.

Second, you can set a PrintPreviewDialog control's Document property to the PrintDocument object and then call the dialog box's ShowDialog method. The PrintPreviewDialog displays the print preview window shown in Figure 27-1, using the PrintDocument object to generate the output it displays.

The preview dialog box's printer button on the left sends the printout to the printer. Note that this makes the PrintDocument object regenerate the printout using its events, this time sending the results to the printer instead of to the print preview dialog box. The magnifying glass button displays a drop-down list

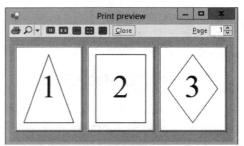

FIGURE 27-1: The PrintPreviewDialog control lets the user zoom in and out and view the printout's various pages.

where the user can select various scales for viewing the printout. The next five buttons let the user display one, two, three, four, or six of the printout's pages at the same time. The Close button closes the dialog box and the Page up/down arrows let the user move through the printout's pages.

The PrintPreviewControl displays a print preview much as the PrintPreviewDialog control does, except that it sits on your form. It does not provide all the buttons that the dialog box does, but it does provide methods that let you implement similar features. For example, it lets your program set the zoom level, the number of columns in the display, and so forth.

The third thing you can do with a PrintDocument is assign it to a PrintDialog object's Document property and then call the dialog box's ShowDialog method. This displays a dialog box that lets the user select the printer and set its properties (for example, selecting landscape or portrait orientation). When the user clicks the dialog box's Print button, the dialog box uses the PrintDocument object to send the printout to the printer.

> **PREVIEW POSSIBILITIES**
>
> Your results could look different from those shown here. The print preview adjusts its appearance based on such factors as the type of printer you are using, its settings, the size of the paper you are using, and the paper's orientation.

Example program UsePrintPreviewDialog uses the following code to preview and print a page showing the page's bounds and margin bounds. This is just about the smallest program that demonstrates all three uses for a PrintDocument object: printing immediately, displaying a print preview dialog box, and displaying a print dialog box.

```
Imports System.Drawing.Printing

Public Class Form1
    Private WithEvents MyPrintDocument As PrintDocument

    Private PageNumber As Integer

    ' Display a print preview dialog.
    Private Sub btnPrintPreview_Click() Handles btnPrintPreview.Click
        PageNumber = 1
        MyPrintDocument = New PrintDocument
        dlgPrintPreview.Document = MyPrintDocument
        dlgPrintPreview.ShowDialog()
    End Sub

    ' Display a print dialog.
    Private Sub btnPrintDialog_Click() Handles btnPrintDialog.Click
        PageNumber = 1
        MyPrintDocument = New PrintDocument
        dlgPrint.Document = MyPrintDocument
        dlgPrint.ShowDialog()
    End Sub
```

```vb
' Print now.
Private Sub btnPrintNow_Click() Handles btnPrintNow.Click
    PageNumber = 1
    MyPrintDocument = New PrintDocument
    MyPrintDocument.Print()
End Sub

' Print a page with a diamond on it.
Private Sub MyPrintDocument_PrintPage(
 sender As Object, e As PrintPageEventArgs) Handles MyPrintDocument.PrintPage
    e.Graphics.SmoothingMode = Drawing2D.SmoothingMode.AntiAlias
    e.Graphics.TextRenderingHint =
        Drawing.Text.TextRenderingHint.AntiAliasGridFit

    Using the_font As New Font("Times New Roman", 300)
        Using string_format As New StringFormat
            string_format.Alignment = StringAlignment.Center
            string_format.LineAlignment = StringAlignment.Center

            e.Graphics.DrawString(PageNumber.ToString,
                the_font, Brushes.Black,
                e.MarginBounds, string_format)
        End Using ' string_format
    End Using ' the_font

    Using the_pen As New Pen(Color.Black, 10)
        Select Case PageNumber
            Case 1  ' Draw a triangle.
                Dim points() As Point =
                {
                    New Point(e.MarginBounds.Left + e.MarginBounds.Width \ 2,
                        e.MarginBounds.Top),
                    New Point(e.MarginBounds.Right, e.MarginBounds.Bottom),
                    New Point(e.MarginBounds.Left, e.MarginBounds.Bottom)
                }
                e.Graphics.DrawPolygon(the_pen, points)

            Case 2  ' Draw a rectangle.
                e.Graphics.DrawRectangle(the_pen, e.MarginBounds)

            Case 3  ' Draw a diamond.
                Dim points() As Point = {
                    New Point(e.MarginBounds.Left + e.MarginBounds.Width \ 2,
                        e.MarginBounds.Top),
                    New Point(e.MarginBounds.Right,
                        e.MarginBounds.Top + e.MarginBounds.Height \ 2),
                    New Point(e.MarginBounds.Left + e.MarginBounds.Width \ 2,
                        e.MarginBounds.Bottom),
                    New Point(e.MarginBounds.Left,
                        e.MarginBounds.Top + e.MarginBounds.Height \ 2)
                }
                e.Graphics.DrawPolygon(the_pen, points)
```

```
            End Select
        End Using ' the_pen

        PageNumber += 1
        e.HasMorePages = PageNumber <= 3
    End Sub
End Class
```

The code declares a PrintDocument object named MyPrintDocument. It uses the WithEvents keyword, so it can easily catch the object's events.

Next, the code defines the variable PageNumber. It uses this variable later to keep track of the page it is printing.

If the user clicks the Print Preview button, the btnPrintPreview_Click event handler resets PageNumber to 1, assigns MyPrintDocument to a new PrintDocument object, sets the PrintPreviewDialog object's Document property equal to the new PrintDocument object, and invokes the dialog box's ShowDialog method.

If the user clicks the Print Dialog button, the btnPrintDialog_Click event handler resets PageNumber to 1, assigns MyPrintDocument to a new PrintDocument object, sets the PrintDialog object's Document property equal to the new PrintDocument object, and calls the dialog box's ShowDialog method.

If the user clicks the Print Now button, the btnPrintNow_Click event handler resets PageNumber to 1, assigns MyPrintDocument to a new PrintDocument object, and calls its Print method.

In all three cases, the PrintDocument object raises its PrintPage event when it is ready to print a page. The PrintPage event handler shown here demonstrates several techniques that are worth mentioning briefly.

The e.Graphics parameter holds a reference to the Graphics object that the event handler should use to produce the printed page. The section "Graphics Objects" later in this chapter says more about Graphics objects.

The event handler starts by setting the Graphics object's SmoothingMode property to AntiAlias. That makes the object produce smoother results when it draws lines, ellipses, and other shapes. This slows drawing slightly but, unless the shapes you're drawing are extremely complex, it doesn't take too much extra time and the result is usually worth it.

Next, the event handler sets the Graphics object's TextRenderingHint property to AntiAliasGridFit. This also slows drawing somewhat but usually makes text appear smoother (except for very small fonts).

The event handler then creates a large 300-point font. Like many graphical classes including pens and brushes, the Font class implements the IDisposable method so the program creates the font in a Using statement so its resources are automatically freed when the Using block ends.

Inside the Using block, the program creates a StringFormat object. It sets that object's Alignment and LineAlignment properties to Center to center text vertically and horizontally. The code then calls the Graphics object's DrawString method to draw the current page number. It passes

DrawString the page's MarginBounds so it knows to place the text inside the page's margins. It also passes DrawString the StringFormat object to make it center the text vertically and horizontally within the MarginBounds.

The event handler then creates a 10-pixel-wide black pen. Depending on the current page number, the code draws a triangle, rectangle, or diamond. The following sections provide a bit more information about how the Graphics object's drawing methods work.

After it has drawn the page, the code increments PageNumber and sets e.HasMorePages to True if it has not yet printed all three pages. Figure 27-1 shows the program displaying its print preview dialog box.

DRAWING BASICS

The previous section describes the UsePrintPreview example program, which draws some simple shapes and text. It focuses mostly on the PrintDocument events that support the printing process, however, and glosses over exactly how the graphics are drawn.

A program uses three things to produce graphics: a Graphics object, pens, and brushes. It uses those things whether the output should be printed on a printer, displayed on the screen, or drawn into an image file such as a bitmap or JPG file.

The following sections describe Graphics objects, pens, and brushes.

Graphics Objects

A Graphics object represents a drawing surface. You can think of it as the canvas or paper on which the program will draw.

The Graphics class provides many methods for drawing lines, rectangles, curves, and other shapes. The following table summarizes these methods.

METHOD	DESCRIPTION
DrawArc	Draws an arc of an ellipse.
DrawBezier	Draws a Bézier curve.
DrawBeziers	Draws a series of Bézier curves.
DrawClosedCurve	Draws a smooth closed curve that joins a series of points, connecting the final point to the first point.
DrawCurve	Draws a smooth curve that joins a series of points. This is similar to a DrawClosedCurve, except that it doesn't connect the final point to the first point.
DrawEllipse	Draws an ellipse. (To draw a circle, draw an ellipse with equal width and height.)

METHOD	DESCRIPTION
DrawIcon	Draws an icon.
DrawIconUnstretched	Draws an icon without scaling. If you know that you will not resize the icon, this may be faster than the DrawIcon method.
DrawImage	Draws an image. Bitmap is a subclass of Image, so you can use this method to draw a Bitmap.
DrawImageUnscaled	Draws an image without scaling. If you know that you will not resize the image, this may be faster than the DrawImage method.
DrawLine	Draws a line.
DrawLines	Draws a series of connected lines. If you need to draw a series of connected lines, this is much faster than using DrawLine repeatedly.
DrawPath	Draws a GraphicsPath object.
DrawPie	Draws a pie slice taken from an ellipse.
DrawPolygon	Draws a polygon. This is similar to DrawLines, except that it connects the last point to the first point.
DrawRectangle	Draws a rectangle with horizontal and vertical sides.
DrawRectangles	Draws a series of rectangles. If you need to draw a series of rectangles, this is much faster than using DrawRectangle repeatedly.
DrawString	Draws text.

The methods listed in the preceding table draw the outline of something such as a line, rectangle, or ellipse. The Graphics class also provides corresponding methods that fill many of these shapes. For example, the DrawRectangle method outlines a rectangle, and the corresponding FillRectangle method fills a rectangle. The filling methods include FillClosedCurve, FillEllipse, FillPath, FillPie, FillPolygon, FillRectangle, and FillRectangles.

The "Draw" methods take a pen as a parameter and use that pen to determine how the outline is drawn. In contrast, the "Fill" methods take a brush as a parameter and use the brush to decide how to fill the area.

The one exception is the DrawString method. Even though its name begins with "Draw," this method takes a brush as a parameter and uses it to fill the text. The following two sections describe pens and brushes in greater detail.

See the online help for specific information about the Graphics class's drawing and filling methods. You can find links to the pages describing these methods at the Graphics class's web page http://msdn.microsoft.com/library/system.drawing.graphics.

There are several ways a program can obtain a Graphics object on which to draw. For example, a PrintDocument's PrintPage event handler provides a parameter named e that has a property named Graphics that is a Graphics object that represents the printout being generated. The UsePrintPreviewDialog example program described earlier uses the following code to draw the triangle shown on its first printed page:

```
Dim points() As Point =
{
    New Point(e.MarginBounds.Left + e.MarginBounds.Width \ 2,
        e.MarginBounds.Top),
    New Point(e.MarginBounds.Right, e.MarginBounds.Bottom),
    New Point(e.MarginBounds.Left, e.MarginBounds.Bottom)
}
e.Graphics.DrawPolygon(the_pen, points)
```

This code creates an array of Points that define the triangle's corners. It then calls the e.Graphics object's DrawPolygon method, passing it a Pen object (pens are described in the next section) and the Points.

Just as the PrintPage event provides a Graphics object on which a program can draw, so too does the Paint event. When a form, PictureBox, or other control is hidden and then exposed, it raises a Paint event. The e.Graphics parameter gives the program a Graphics object that it can use to redraw the control's contents. The DrawInPaintEvent example program, which is available for download on the book's website, demonstrates this technique.

The last common way to obtain a Graphics object is to create one that is associated with a Bitmap. The program can then use the Graphics object to draw on the Bitmap. The DrawOnBitmap example program, which is also available for download on the book's website, uses the following code to draw on a Bitmap and display it on the form's background:

```
' Draw on a bitmap and use it as the form's background.
Private Sub Form1_Load() Handles MyBase.Load
    Dim bm As New Bitmap(16, 16)
    Using gr As Graphics = Graphics.FromImage(bm)
        gr.DrawEllipse(Pens.Blue, 2, 2, 12, 12)
    End Using
    Me.BackgroundImage = bm
End Sub
```

When the program starts, this code creates a 16 × 16 pixel Bitmap and associates a Graphics object with it. It draws a circle on the Bitmap and then sets the form's BackgroundImage property to the Bitmap.

Pens

The Pen object determines how lines are drawn. It determines the lines' color, thickness, dash style, join style, and end cap style.

A program can explicitly create Pen objects, but often it can simply use one of the more than 280 pens that are predefined by the Pens class. For example, the following code draws a rectangle using a hot pink line that's one pixel wide:

```
gr.DrawRectangle(Pens.HotPink, 10, 10, 50, 50)
```

The following table summarizes the Pen class's constructors:

CONSTRUCTORS	DESCRIPTION
Pen(brush)	Creates a pen of thickness 1 using the indicated Brush.
Pen(color)	Creates a pen of thickness 1 using the indicated color.
Pen(brush, thickness)	Creates a pen with the indicated thickness (a Single) using a Brush.
Pen(color, thickness)	Creates a pen with the indicated thickness (a Single) using the indicated color.

The following table describes some of the Pen class's most useful properties and methods:

PROPERTY OR METHOD	PURPOSE
Brush	Determines the Brush used to fill lines.
Color	Determines the lines' color.
CompoundArray	Lets you draw lines that are striped lengthwise.
CustomEndCap	Determines the line's end cap.
CustomStartCap	Determines the line's start cap.
DashCap	Determines the cap drawn at the ends of dashes. This can be Flat, Round, or Triangle.
DashOffset	Determines the distance from the start of the line to the start of the first dash.
DashPattern	An array of Singles that specifies a custom dash pattern. The array entries tell how many pixels to draw, skip, draw, skip, and so forth. Note that these values are scaled if the pen is not one pixel wide.
DashStyle	Determines the line's dash style. This value can be Dash, DashDot, DashDotDot, Dot, Solid, or Custom. If you set the DashPattern property, this value is set to Custom. Note that the dashes and gaps between them are scaled if the pen is not one pixel wide.
EndCap	Determines the cap used at the end of the line. This value can be ArrowAnchor, DiamondAnchor, Flat, NoAnchor, Round, RoundAnchor, Square, SquareAnchor, Triangle, and Custom. If LineCap is Custom, you should use a CustomLineCap object to define the cap.
LineJoin	Determines how lines are joined by methods that draws connected lines such as DrawLines or DrawPolygon. This value can be Bevel, Miter, and Round.

continues

(continued)

PROPERTY OR METHOD	PURPOSE
SetLineCap	Specifies the Pen class's StartCap, EndCap, and LineJoin properties at the same time.
StartCap	Determines the cap used at the start of the line.
Width	The width of the pen.

The DrawInPaintEvent example program, which is available for download on the book's website, uses the following code to draw two shapes on the program's form:

```
Private Sub Form1_Paint(sender As Object, e As PaintEventArgs) Handles Me.Paint
    e.Graphics.SmoothingMode = Drawing2D.SmoothingMode.AntiAlias

    ' Draw a dashed ellipse.
    Using ellipse_pen As New Pen(Color.Black, 5)
        ellipse_pen.DashStyle = Drawing2D.DashStyle.DashDotDot
        e.Graphics.DrawEllipse(ellipse_pen, 50, 50, 150, 100)
    End Using

    ' Draw a polygon.
    Using polygon_pen As New Pen(Color.Gray, 10)
        polygon_pen.LineJoin = Drawing2D.LineJoin.Bevel
        Dim points() As Point =
        {
            New Point(20, 20),
            New Point(200, 20),
            New Point(100, 50),
            New Point(230, 190),
            New Point(20, 150)
        }
        e.Graphics.DrawPolygon(polygon_pen, points)
    End Using
End Sub
```

The code creates a black pen of thickness 5. It sets the pen's DashStyle property to DashDotDot and then draws an ellipse with it.

The code then creates a gray pen of thickness 10. It sets the pen's LineJoin property to Bevel so line joins are beveled and draws a polygon with it. Figure 27-2 shows the result.

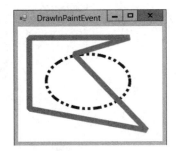

FIGURE 27-2: The DrawIn-PaintEvent program demonstrates dashed lines and beveled line joins.

Brushes

The Brush object determines how areas are filled when you draw them using the Graphics object's methods FillClosedCurve, FillEllipse, FillPath, FillPie, FillPolygon, FillRectangle, and FillRectangles. Different types of Brushes fill areas with solid colors, hatch patterns, and color gradients.

The Brush class is an abstract or MustInherit class, so you cannot make instances of the Brush class itself. Instead, you can create instances of one of the derived classes SolidBrush, TextureBrush, HatchBrush, LinearGradientBrush, and PathGradientBrush. The following table briefly describes these classes:

CLASS	PURPOSE
SolidBrush	Fills areas with a single solid color
TextureBrush	Fills areas with a repeating image
HatchBrush	Fills areas with a repeating hatch pattern
LinearGradientBrush	Fills areas with a linear gradient of two or more colors
PathGradientBrush	Fills areas with a color gradient that follows a path

The BrushSamples example program, which is available for download on the book's website, uses the following code to demonstrate four kinds of brushes:

```
' Draw some brush samples.
Private Sub Form1_Paint(sender As Object, e As PaintEventArgs) Handles Me.Paint
    Dim rect As New Rectangle(10, 10, 100, 50)
    Using solid_brush As New SolidBrush(Color.Gray)
        e.Graphics.FillRectangle(solid_brush, rect)
    End Using
    rect.Y += 60

    Using gradient_brush As New LinearGradientBrush(
     rect, Color.Black, Color.Gray, 0)
        e.Graphics.FillRectangle(gradient_brush, rect)
    End Using

    rect = New Rectangle(120, 10, 100, 50)
    Using texture_brush As New TextureBrush(My.Resources.smile)
        e.Graphics.FillRectangle(texture_brush, rect)
    End Using
    rect.Y += 60

    Using hatch_brush As New HatchBrush(
     HatchStyle.DiagonalBrick, Color.Black, Color.White)
        e.Graphics.FillRectangle(hatch_brush, rect)
    End Using
End Sub
```

This example uses SolidBrush, LinearGradientBrush, TextureBrush, and HatchBrush objects to fill four rectangles. You can see the result in Figure 27-3.

You can find more information about the brush classes at http://msdn .microsoft.com/library/system.drawing.brush.aspx.

FIGURE 27-3: The BrushSamples program fills four rectangles with different kinds of brushes.

A BOOKLET EXAMPLE

The UsePrintPreviewDialog example program described earlier draws some text centered on the program's three pages of printout. This section describes a more useful example that prints a long series of paragraphs that may each use a different font size.

The PrintBooklet example program, which is available for download on the book's website, figures out how to break the text into pages. It assumes that you will print the pages double-sided and then later staple the results into a booklet. To allow extra room for the staples, the program adds a *gutter* to the margin of each page on the side where the staples will be. The program assumes that you will place the first page on the outside of the booklet, so it adds the gutter to the left margin on odd-numbered pages and to the right margin on even-numbered pages. Finally, the program displays a page number in the upper corner opposite the gutter.

In addition to demonstrating event handlers for the PrintDocument class's events, this example shows how to use StringFormat objects to align text and break lines at word boundaries, wrap text within a target rectangle, and measure text to see how much will fit in a target rectangle.

Figure 27-4 shows the PrintBooklet program's print preview dialog box, so you can understand the goals. If you look closely, you can see that the left margins on the first and third pages and the right margin on the second page are enlarged to allow room for the gutter. (Imagine the second page printed on the back of the first, so their gutters lie on the same edge of the paper.) You can also see that the page numbers are in the upper corner on the side that doesn't have the gutter.

The program's Print Preview, Print Dialog, and Print Now buttons work much as the UsePrintPreviewDialog program's buttons do, displaying the appropriate dialog boxes or calling the PrintDocument object's Print method. The most interesting differences between this program and the UsePrintPreviewDialog program are in how this program stores its text to print and how it generates pages of printout.

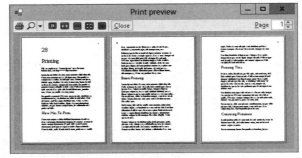

FIGURE 27-4: This preview shows text broken across pages with a gutter and displaying page numbers along the outside edges.

The program uses the following ParagraphInfo structure to store information about the text it will print:

```
' Information about the paragraphs to print.
Private Structure ParagraphInfo
    Public FontSize As Integer
    Public Text As String
    Public Sub New(font_size As Integer, txt As String)
        FontSize = font_size
        Text = txt
    End Sub
End Structure
```

The following code shows how the program prepares the text it will print:

```
' The PrintDocument.
Private WithEvents MyPrintDocument As New PrintDocument

' The paragraphs.
Private AllParagraphs As List(Of ParagraphInfo)
Private ParagraphsToPrint As List(Of ParagraphInfo)
Private PagesPrinted As Integer

' Load the paragraph info.
Private Sub Form1_Load() Handles MyBase.Load
    ' Attach the PrintDocument to the
    ' PrintDialog and PrintPreviewDialog.
    dlgPrint.Document = MyPrintDocument
    dlgPrintPreview.Document = MyPrintDocument

    ' Make the text to print.
    AllParagraphs = New List(Of ParagraphInfo)
    AllParagraphs.Add(New ParagraphInfo(45, "28"))
    AllParagraphs.Add(New ParagraphInfo(36, "Printing"))
    ... Code to create other ParagraphInfo structures omitted...
End Sub
```

This code declares a PrintDocument object named MyPrintDocument. It uses the WithEvents keyword so it will be easy to catch the object's events.

The code then declares lists to hold all of the ParagraphInfo structures that it will print and those that have not yet been printed.

When the program's form loads, the code initializes these variables and adds a series of ParagraphInfo structures containing the text it will print to the AllParagraphs collection.

When the PrintDocument object starts drawing a printout, the BeginPrint event handler shown in the following code executes:

```
' Get ready to print pages.
Private Sub MyPrintDocument_BeginPrint() Handles MyPrintDocument.BeginPrint
    ' We have not yet printed any pages.
    PagesPrinted = 0

    ' Make a copy of the text to print.
    ParagraphsToPrint = New List(Of ParagraphInfo)
    For Each para_info As ParagraphInfo In AllParagraphs
        ParagraphsToPrint.Add(
            New ParagraphInfo(para_info.FontSize, para_info.Text))
    Next para_info
End Sub
```

This code resets the page number variable PagesPrinted. It then copies the ParagraphInfo structures from the AllParagraphs list (which holds all of the data) into the ParagraphsToPrint list (which holds those paragraphs that have not yet been printed).

After the BeginPrint event handler finishes, the PrintDocument object starts printing pages. Before it prints each page, the object raises its QueryPageSettings event. The program uses the following code to catch this event and prepare the next page for printing:

```
' Set the margins for the following page.
Private Sub MyPrintDocument_QueryPageSettings(
 sender As Object, e As QueryPageSettingsEventArgs) _
 Handles MyPrintDocument.QueryPageSettings
    ' Use a 1 inch gutter (printer units are 100 per inch).
    Const gutter As Integer = 100

    ' See if the next page will be the first, odd, or even.
    If PagesPrinted = 0 Then
        ' First page. Increase the left margin.
        e.PageSettings.Margins.Left += gutter
    ElseIf (PagesPrinted Mod 2) = 0 Then
        ' Odd page. Shift the margins right.
        e.PageSettings.Margins.Left += gutter
        e.PageSettings.Margins.Right -= gutter
    Else
        ' Even page. Shift the margins left.
        e.PageSettings.Margins.Left -= gutter
        e.PageSettings.Margins.Right += gutter
    End If
End Sub
```

This code determines whether the next page will be odd or even numbered and adjusts the page's margin appropriately to create the gutter.

After each QueryPageSettings event, the PrintDocument object raises its PrintPage event to generate the corresponding page. The following code shows the most complicated part of the program, the PrintPage event handler:

```
' Print the next page.
Private Sub MyPrintDocument_PrintPage(sender As Object, e As PrintPageEventArgs) _
 Handles MyPrintDocument.PrintPage
    ' Increment the page number.
    PagesPrinted += 1

    ' Draw the margins (for debugging).
    'e.Graphics.DrawRectangle(Pens.Red, e.MarginBounds)

    ' Print the page number right justified
    ' in the upper corner opposite the gutter
    ' and outside of the margin.
    Dim x As Integer
    Using string_format As New StringFormat
        ' See if this is an odd or even page.
        If (PagesPrinted Mod 2) = 0 Then
            ' This is an even page.
            ' The gutter is on the right and
            ' the page number is on the left.
            x = (e.MarginBounds.Left + e.PageBounds.Left) \ 2
            string_format.Alignment = StringAlignment.Near
```

```
        Else
            ' This is an odd page.
            ' The gutter is on the left and
            ' the page number is on the right.
            x = (e.MarginBounds.Right + e.PageBounds.Right) \ 2
            string_format.Alignment = StringAlignment.Far
        End If

        ' Print the page number.
        Using the_font As New Font("Times New Roman", 20,
         FontStyle.Regular, GraphicsUnit.Point)
            e.Graphics.DrawString(PagesPrinted.ToString,
                the_font, Brushes.Black, x,
                (e.MarginBounds.Top + e.PageBounds.Top) \ 2,
                string_format)
        End Using ' the_font

        ' Draw the rest of the text left justified,
        ' wrap at words, and don't draw partial lines.
        string_format.Alignment = StringAlignment.Near
        string_format.FormatFlags = StringFormatFlags.LineLimit
        string_format.Trimming = StringTrimming.Word

        ' Draw some text.
        Dim paragraph_info As ParagraphInfo
        Dim ymin As Integer = e.MarginBounds.Top
        Dim layout_rect As RectangleF
        Dim text_size As SizeF
        Dim characters_fitted As Integer
        Dim lines_filled As Integer
        Do While ParagraphsToPrint.Count > 0
            ' Print the next paragraph.
            paragraph_info = ParagraphsToPrint(0)
            ParagraphsToPrint.RemoveAt(0)

            ' Get the area available for this paragraph.
            layout_rect = New RectangleF(
                e.MarginBounds.Left, ymin,
                e.MarginBounds.Width,
                e.MarginBounds.Bottom - ymin)
            ' Work around bug where MeasureString
            ' thinks characters fit if height <= 0.
            If layout_rect.Height < 1 Then layout_rect.Height = 1

            ' See how big the text will be and
            ' how many characters will fit.
            ' Get the font.
            Using the_font As New Font("Times New Roman",
             paragraph_info.FontSize, FontStyle.Regular, GraphicsUnit.Point)
                text_size = e.Graphics.MeasureString(
                    paragraph_info.Text, the_font,
                    New SizeF(layout_rect.Width, layout_rect.Height),
                    string_format, characters_fitted, lines_filled)
```

```
                    ' See if any characters will fit.
                    If characters_fitted > 0 Then
                        ' Draw the text.
                        e.Graphics.DrawString(paragraph_info.Text,
                            the_font, Brushes.Black,
                            layout_rect, string_format)

                        ' Debugging: Draw a rectangle around the text.
                        'e.Graphics.DrawRectangle(Pens.Green,
                        '    layout_rect.Left,
                        '    layout_rect.Top,
                        '    text_size.Width,
                        '    text_size.Height)

                        ' Increase the location where we can start.
                        ' Add a little interparagraph spacing.
                        ymin += CInt(text_size.Height +
                            e.Graphics.MeasureString("M", the_font).Height / 2)
                    End If
                End Using ' the_font

                ' See if some of the paragraph didn't fit on the page.
                If characters_fitted < Len(paragraph_info.Text) Then
                    ' Some of the paragraph didn't fit.
                    ' Prepare to print the rest on the next page.
                    paragraph_info.Text = paragraph_info.Text.
                        Substring(characters_fitted)
                    ParagraphsToPrint.Insert(0, paragraph_info)

                    ' That's all that will fit on this page.
                    Exit Do
                End If
            Loop
        End Using ' string_format

        ' If we have more paragraphs, we have more pages.
        e.HasMorePages = (ParagraphsToPrint.Count > 0)
    End Sub
```

The PrintPage event handler starts by incrementing the number of pages printed. It then includes commented code to draw a rectangle around the page's margins. When you are debugging a printing routine, drawing this rectangle can help you see where your drawing is in relation to the page's margins.

Next, the routine creates a font for the page number. Depending on whether this page is odd or even numbered, it calculates an x coordinate halfway between the non-gutter margin and the edge of the printable page. It sets a StringFormat object's Alignment property to make numbers in the left margin left-justified and to make numbers in the right margin right-justified. It then draws the page number at the calculated x position, halfway between the top margin and the paper's top printable boundary.

The program then prepares to draw the text for this page. It sets the StringFormat object's properties so that the text is left-justified and lines wrap at word boundaries instead of in the middle of words.

It then sets the FormatFlags property to LineLimit. If only part of a line of text would fit vertically on the page, this makes Visual Basic not draw the line rather than draw just the top halves of its letters.

After this preparation, the program sets variable ymin to the minimum Y coordinate where the routine can draw text. Initially, this is the page's top margin. It then enters a Do loop to process as much text as will fit on the page.

Inside the loop, the program takes the first ParagraphInfo structure from the ParagraphsToPrint list and makes a font that has the right size for that paragraph. It creates a RectangleF structure representing the remaining area on the page. This includes the area between the left and right margins horizontally, and between ymin and the bottom margin vertically.

The program then uses the e.Graphics object's MeasureString method to see how much space the next piece of text will need. It passes MeasureString the layout rectangle's size and the StringFormat object so Visual Basic can decide how it will need to wrap the paragraph's text when it draws it. The code also passes in the variables `characters_fitted` and `lines_filled`. These parameters are passed by reference so MeasureString can fill in the number of characters and lines it could draw within the target rectangle.

The routine then checks characters_fitted to see if any characters will fit in the available area. If any characters can fit, the program draws the paragraph. Commented code draws a rectangle around the text to help with debugging. The program increases ymin by the paragraph's printed height plus half of the font's height to provide a break between paragraphs.

Next, the program determines whether the entire paragraph fits in the target rectangle. If some of the paragraph did not fit, the program stores the remaining text in the ParagraphInfo structure and puts the structure back at the beginning of the ParagraphsToPrint list so it can be printed on the next page. The code then exits the Do loop because the current page is full.

When the page is full or the ParagraphsToPrint list is empty, the PrintPage event handler is finished. The code sets e.HasMorePages to True if m_ParagraphsToPrint is not empty.

Finally, when the PrintDocument has finished printing the whole document, the following EndPrint event handler executes:

```
' Clean up.
Private Sub MyPrintDocument_EndPrint() Handles MyPrintDocument.EndPrint
    ParagraphsToPrint = Nothing
End Sub
```

The EndPrint event handler cleans up by setting the ParagraphsToPrint variable to Nothing, freeing up the list's memory. In this program, freeing the list is a small matter. In a program that allocated more elaborate data structures, cleaning up in this event handler might be more important.

SUMMARY

The PrintDocument object sits at the heart of the Visual Basic printing process. A program makes a PrintDocument object and then responds to its BeginPrint, QueryPageSettings, PrintPage, and EndPrint events to generate a printout.

The PrintDocument object's Print method immediately generates a printout. You can also attach the PrintDocument to a PrintDialog, PrintPreviewDialog, or PrintPreviewControl and use those objects to display previews and generate printouts.

This chapter described printing in general. Using the Graphics object provided by the PrintDocument object's PrintPage event, you can print lines, curves, text, images, and anything else you can draw to the screen.

Appendix I, "Visual Basic Power Packs," describes some additional tools that you can download for free. The Printer Compatibility Library and the PrintForm component give you new options for printing. See Appendix I for more information.

Most of the programs described in this book so far are relatively self-contained. They take input from the user, perform some calculations, and display the results. Only a few chapters have interacted much with the outside system. The two exceptions are Chapter 22, which explained how to use drag and drop and the clipboard to interact with other programs, and this chapter, which explained how to interact with printers.

The programs described earlier in this book interact only with the user. Printing is one way a program can interact with some other part of the system. The next chapter, "Configuration and Resources," describes some other ways that a Visual Basic program can interact with the system by storing configuration and resource values for use at run time. Some of the most useful of these methods include environment variables, the Registry, configuration files, and resource files.

28

Configuration and Resources

WROX.COM CODE DOWNLOADS FOR THIS CHAPTER

The wrox.com downloads for this chapter are found at `http://www.wrox.com/remtitle` `.cgi?isbn=9781118314074` on the Download Code tab. The code for this chapter is divided into the following major examples:

➤ ListEnviron

➤ ConfigFile

➤ UseResources

➤ EmbeddedResources

➤ LocalizedUseGerman

THE NEED FOR CONFIGURATION

A very simple application performs a well-defined task that changes minimally over time. You may not need to configure such an application for different circumstances.

More complex applications, however, must be configured to meet different conditions. For example, the application might display different data for different kinds of users (such as data-entry clerks, supervisors, managers, and developers). Similarly, you might configure an application for various levels of support. You might have different configurations for trial, basic, professional, and enterprise versions.

The application may also need to save state information between sessions. It might remember the types of forms that were last running, their positions, and their contents. The next time the program runs, it can restore those forms so the user can get back to work as quickly as possible.

The .NET Framework provides many tools for storing and using application configuration and resource information. This chapter describes some of these tools. It starts by describing the My namespace that was invented to make these tools easier to find. It then tells how an application can use environment variables, the registry, configuration files, resource files, and the Application object to save and restore configuration information.

This chapter does not explain how to work with disk files more directly. Databases, XML files, text files, and other disk files are generally intended for storage of larger amounts of data, rather than simple configuration and resource information. Those topics are described more thoroughly in Chapters 19, "Database Controls and Objects," and 30, "Filesystem Objects."

MY

In older versions of Visual Basic .NET, programmers discovered that many common tasks were difficult to perform. For example, many programs get the name of the user logged on to the computer, read a text file into a string, get the program's version number, or examine all of the application's currently loaded forms. Although you could accomplish all of these tasks in early versions of Visual Basic .NET, doing so was awkward.

To make these common tasks easier, the My namespace was introduced to provide shortcuts for basic chores. For example, to read the text in a file in Visual Basic .NET 2003, you must create some sort of object that can work with a file such as a StreamReader, use the object to read the file (the ReadToEnd method for a StreamReader), and then dispose of the object. The following code shows how you might do this in Visual Basic .NET 2003:

```
Dim stream_reader As New IO.StreamReader(file_name)
Dim file_contents As String = stream_reader.ReadToEnd()
stream_reader.Close()
```

This isn't too difficult, but it does seem more complicated than such a simple everyday task should be.

The My namespace provides a simpler method for reading a file's contents. The My.Computer .FileSystem.ReadAllText method reads a text file in a single statement. The following statement reads the text in the file C:\Temp\Test.txt:

```
Dim file_contents As String =
    My.Computer.FileSystem.ReadAllText("C:\Temp\Test.txt")
```

There is nothing new in the My namespace. All the tasks it performs you can already handle using other methods. The My namespace just makes some things easier.

This section describes the My namespace and the shortcuts it provides.

Me and My

Some programmers confuse the Me object and the My namespace. Me is a reference to the object that is currently executing code. If a piece of code is inside a particular class, Me is a reference to the class object that is running.

For example, if the class is a form, then within the form's code, Me returns a reference to the running form. If the form's code must change the form's BackColor property, it can use the Me object to explicitly refer to its own form. It can also omit the keyword to refer to its form implicitly. That means the following two statements are equivalent:

```
Me.BackColor = SystemColors.Control
BackColor = SystemColors.Control
```

If you build several instances of a class, the code in each instance gets a different value for Me. Each instance's Me object returns a reference to that instance.

On the other hand, My isn't an object at all. It is a namespace that contains objects, values, routines, and other namespaces that implement common functions. The My namespace is a single unique entity shared by all of the code throughout the application.

It may help if you try not to think of the My namespace as a thing in and of itself. The My namespace doesn't do anything all alone. It needs to be paired with something within the namespace. Think of My.Application, My.User, My.Computer, and so forth.

My Sections

The following table briefly outlines the major sections within the My namespace. Other sections of this chapter and Appendix S, "The My Namespace," describe these sections in greater detail.

SECTION	PURPOSE
My.Application	Provides information about the current application: current directory, culture, and assembly information (such as program version number, log, splash screen, and forms)
My.Computer	Controls the computer hardware and system software: audio, clock, keyboard, clipboard, mouse, network, printers, registry, and filesystem
My.Forms	Provides access to an instance of each type of Windows Form defined in the application
My.Resources	Provides access to the application's resources: strings, images, audio, and so forth
My.Settings	Provides access to the application's settings
My.User	Provides access to information about the current user
My.WebServices	Provides access to an instance of each XML web service referenced by the application

ENVIRONMENT

Environment variables are values that a program can use to learn information about the system. There are three types of environment variables that apply at the system, user, and process levels. As you may guess from their names, system-level variables apply to all processes started on the system, user-level variables apply to processes started by a particular user, and process-level variables apply to a particular process and any other processes that it starts.

Environment variables may indicate such things as the name of the operating system, the location of temporary directories, the user's name, and the number of processors the system has. You can also store configuration information in environment variables for your programs to use.

Environment variables are loaded when a process starts, and they are inherited by any process launched by the initial process. During Visual Basic development, that means the variables are loaded when you start Visual Studio and they are inherited by the program you are working on when you start it. If you make changes to the system's environment variables, you need to close and reopen Visual Studio before your program will see the changes.

A program can also create temporary process-level variables that are inherited by launched processes and that disappear when the original process ends.

Visual Basic provides a couple of tools for working with the application's environment. The following sections describe two: the Environ function and the System.Environment object. Before you can read environment variables, however, you should know how to set their values.

Setting Environment Variables

Environment variables are normally set on a systemwide basis before the program begins. In older operating systems, batch files such as autoexec.bat set these values. More recent systems provide Control Panel tools to set environment variables.

Newer systems also use an autoexec.nt file to set environment variables that apply only to command-line (console) applications so they don't affect GUI applications. Sometimes you can use this fact to your advantage by giving different kinds of applications different environment settings.

To set environment variables in newer versions of Windows, open the Control Panel and search for the keyword "environment." In Windows 8, open the search tool and search the Settings category for "environment."

You should find two links with titles similar to "Edit environment variables for your account" and "Edit the system environment variables." Click one of those links to display the System Properties dialog box's Advanced tab. Click the Environment Variables button to add, remove, and modify environment variables.

Be careful to use the variables properly. Use system variables when a value should apply to all processes started by all users, user variables when a value should apply to all processes started by a particular user, and process variables when a value should apply to a process and any processes that it starts.

> **REMEMBER TO REFRESH**
>
> Remember that Visual Studio won't see environment variable changes that you make after it is running. You need to close and reopen Visual Studio before your program will see the changes.

Using Environ

At run time, a Visual Basic application can use the Environ function to retrieve environment variable values. If you pass this function a number, it returns a string giving the statement that assigns the corresponding environment variable. For example, Environ(1) might return the following string:

```
ALLUSERSPROFILE=C:\ProgramData
```

You should pass the function a number between 1 and 255. Environ returns a zero-length string if the number does not correspond to an environment variable. The following code uses this fact to list all of the application's environment variables. When it finds a variable that has zero length, it knows it has read all of the variables with values.

```
For i As Integer = 1 To 255
    If Environ(i).Length = 0 Then Exit For
    Debug.WriteLine(i & ": " & Environ(i))
Next i
```

Example program ListEnviron uses similar code to display all of the environment variables' assignment statements. Example program ListEnvironValues uses the String class's Split method to separate the environment variables' names and values and displays them in separate columns in a ListView control.

If you pass the Environ function the name of an environment variable, the function returns the variable's value or Nothing if the variable does not exist. For example, the following code displays a greeting that includes the names of the user and the computer:

```
MessageBox.Show("Welcome " & Environ("USERNAME") & " on " & Environ("COMPUTERNAME"))
```

Using System.Environment

The Environ function is easy to use, but it's not very flexible. It can read environment variable values but it cannot create or modify them.

The System.Environment object provides methods for getting and setting process-level environment variables. It also provides properties and methods for working with many other items in the application's environment. The following table describes the Environment object's most useful properties.

PROPERTY	PURPOSE
CommandLine	Returns the process's command line.
CurrentDirectory	Gets or sets the fully qualified path to the current directory.
ExitCode	Gets or sets the process's exit code. If the program starts from a Main function, that function's return value also sets the exit code.
HasShutdownStarted	Returns True if the Common Language Runtime is shutting down.
MachineName	Returns the computer's NetBIOS name.
NewLine	Returns the environment's defined new line string. For example, this might be a carriage return followed by a line feed.
OSVersion	Returns an OperatingSystem object containing information about the operating system. This object provides the properties ServicePack (name of the most recent service pack installed), Version (includes Major, Minor, Build, and Revision; ToString combines them all), VersionString (combines the operating system name, version, and most recent service pack), and Platform, which can be UNIX, Win32NT (Windows NT or later), Win32S (runs on 16-bit Windows to provide access to 32-bit applications), Win32Windows (Windows 95 or later), or WinCE.
ProcessorCount	Returns the number of processors on the computer.
StackTrace	Returns a string describing the current stack trace.
SystemDirectory	Returns the system directory's fully qualified path.
TickCount	Returns the number of milliseconds that have elapsed since the system started.
UserDomainName	Returns the current user's network domain name.
UserInteractive	Returns True if the process is interactive. This only returns False if the application is a service process or web service.
UserName	Returns the name of the user who started the process.
Version	Returns a Version object describing the Common Language Runtime. This object provides the properties Major, Minor, Build, and Revision. Its ToString method combines them all.
WorkingSet	Returns the amount of physical memory mapped to this process in bytes.

Example program SystemEnvironment displays the values of many of the Environment object's properties.

The following table describes the Environment object's most useful methods.

METHOD	PURPOSE
Exit	Ends the process immediately. Form Closing and Closed event handlers do not execute.
ExpandEnvironmentVariables	Replaces environment variable names in a string with their values. For example, the following code displays the current user's name: `MessageBox.Show(Environment.ExpandEnvironmentVariables("I am %username%."))`.
GetCommandLineArgs	Returns an array of strings containing the application's command-line arguments. The first entry (with index 0) is the name of the program's executable file.
GetEnvironmentVariable	Returns an environment variable's value.
GetEnvironmentVariables	Returns an IDictionary object containing the names and values of all environment variables.
GetFolderPath	Returns the path to a system folder. This method's parameter is a SpecialFolder enumeration value such as Cookies, Desktop, SendTo, or Recent. See the online help for a complete list of available folders.
GetLogicalDrives	Returns an array of strings containing the names of the logical drives on the current computer.
SetEnvironmentVariable	Creates, modifies, or deletes an environment variable.

The SetEnvironmentVariable method lets you set environment variables at the system, user, and process level. If you set a variable's value to Nothing, this method deletes the variable. For system and user values, it updates the registry appropriately to set the values. Example program EnvironmentVariableLevels uses SetEnvironmentVariable to get and set variable values. For more information on the SetEnvironmentVariable method, see `http://msdn2.microsoft.com/library/96xafkes.aspx`.

> **NOTE** *Note that a program needs privilege to write to the registry to set a system-level environment variable.*

REGISTRY

The system registry is a hierarchical database that stores values for applications on the system. The hierarchy's root is named MyComputer and is divided into the several subtrees that are also called *hives*. Which hives are available depends on your operating system. The following table summarizes the most commonly available hives. (The "HKEY" part of each name stands for "hive key.")

REGISTRY BRANCH	CONTAINS
HKEY_CLASSES_ROOT	Definitions of types or classes, and properties associated with those types.
HKEY_CURRENT_CONFIG	Information about the system's current hardware configuration.
HKEY_CURRENT_USER	The current user's preferences (such as environment variable settings, program group information, desktop settings, colors, printers, network connections, and preferences specific to applications). Each user has separate HKEY_CURRENT_USER values. This is usually the subtree where a Visual Basic application stores and retrieves its settings.
HKEY_DYN_DATA	Performance data for Windows 95, 98, and Me. (Yes, this is a bit outdated but this hive is still there.)
HKEY_LOCAL_MACHINE	Information about the computer's physical state including bus type, system memory, installed hardware and software, and network logon and security information.
HKEY_USERS	Default configuration information for new users and the current user's configuration.

Depending on your operating system, the registry may also contain the unsupported keys HKEY_PERFORMANCE_DATA, HKEY_PERFORMANCE_NLSTEXT, and HKEY_PERFORMANCE_TEXT.

Many applications store information in the registry. The HKEY_CURRENT_USER subtree is particularly useful for storing individual users' preferences and other configuration information.

Lately, the registry has gone out of style for saving configuration information. Microsoft now recommends that you store this kind of data locally within a user's data storage area. This makes sense because it makes it easier to copy the settings (they're just files), helps reduce clutter in the registry, and reduces the chances that mistakes will corrupt the registry. You can store this information in configuration files (see the section "Configuration Files" later in this chapter) or XML files.

Visual Basic provides two main ways to access the registry. First, you can use the Visual Basic native registry methods. Second, you can use the tools in the My.Computer.Registry namespace. These two methods are described in the following sections.

You can also use API functions to manipulate the registry. These are more complicated and not generally necessary because the My.Computer.Registry namespace contains some very powerful tools, so they are not described here.

Native Visual Basic Registry Methods

Visual Basic provides four methods for saving and reading registry values for a particular application: SaveSetting, GetSetting, GetAllSettings, and DeleteSetting.

The SaveSetting method saves a value into a registry key. This routine takes as parameters the name of the application, a section name, the setting's name, and the setting's value. For example, the following code saves the value stored in the MapDirectory variable in the RegistrySettings application's Config section with the name MapDirectory:

```
SaveSetting("RegistrySettings", "Config", "MapDirectory",
    MapDirectory)
```

SaveSetting automatically creates the application and section areas in the registry if they don't already exist.

This value is saved at the following registry location. This is all one name; it just doesn't fit on one line here:

```
HKEY_CURRENT_USER\Software\VB and VBA Program Settings\
    RegistrySettings\Config\MapDirectory
```

If you use the Visual Basic SaveSetting, GetSetting, GetAllSettings, and DeleteSetting methods, you don't need to worry about the first part of this registry path. You only need to remember the application name, section name, and setting name.

> **POWERFUL PRIVILEGES**
>
> Windows protects the registry so that you cannot inadvertently damage critical values. If you mess up some values, you can wreak havoc on the operating system, and even make the system unbootable.
>
> To prevent possible chaos, newer versions of Windows don't let you edit some parts of the registry without elevated privileges. Fortunately, the part of the registry used by these routines is accessible to normal users, so you don't need elevated privileges to use SaveSetting, GetSetting, GetAllSettings, or DeleteSetting.

The GetSetting function retrieves a registry value. It takes as parameters the application name, section name, and setting name you used to save the value. It can optionally take a default value to return if the setting doesn't exist in the registry. The following code displays the value saved by the previous call to SaveSetting. If no value is saved in the registry, it displays the string <none>.

```
MessageBox.Show(GetSetting("RegistrySettings", "Config", "MapDirectory",
    "<none>"))
```

The GetAllSettings function returns a two-dimensional array of name and value pairs for a registry section. The following code uses GetAllSettings to fetch the values stored in the RegistrySettings application's Config section. It loops through the results, displaying the setting names and values.

```
Dim settings As String(,) = GetAllSettings("RegistrySettings", "Config")
For i As Integer = 0 To settings.GetUpperBound(0)
    Debug.WriteLine(settings(i, 0) & " = " & settings(i, 1))
Next i
```

If an application needs to use all of the settings in a section, GetAllSettings may be faster than using GetSetting repeatedly.

The DeleteSetting method removes a setting, a section, or an entire application's setting area from the registry. The following code shows how to remove each of those kinds of items:

```
' Remove the RegistrySettings/Config/CurrentDirectory setting.
DeleteSetting("RegistrySettings", "Config", "CurrentDirectory")

' Remove the RegistrySettings/Config section.
DeleteSetting("RegistrySettings", "Config")

' Remove all of the RegistrySettings application's settings.
DeleteSetting("RegistrySettings")
```

NEATNESS COUNTS

As part of its uninstallation procedure, a program should remove any registry entries it has made. All too often, programs leave the registry cluttered with garbage. This not only makes it harder to figure out what real values the registry contains but can also slow the system down.

In an attempt to combat this problem, Microsoft is promoting XCopy compatibility, where applications store values in configuration files instead of the registry. Then you can easily copy and remove these files rather than modify the registry.

Example program RegistrySettings demonstrates each of Visual Basic's Registry commands.

My.Computer.Registry

The My.Computer.Registry namespace provides objects that manipulate the registry. My.Computer .Registry has seven properties that refer to objects of type RegistryKey. The following table lists these objects and the corresponding registry subtrees:

MY.COMPUTER.REGISTRY PROPERTY	REGISTRY SUBTREE
ClassesRoot	HKEY_CLASSES_ROOT
CurrentConfig	HKEY_CURRENT_CONFIG
CurrentUser	HKEY_CURRENT_USER
DynData	HKEY_DYNAMIC_DATA
LocalMachine	HKEY_LOCAL_MACHINE
PerformanceData	HKEY_PERFORMANCE_DATA
Users	HKEY_USERS

REGISTRY RESTRICTIONS

Some parts of the registry are off limits to programs running as normal users in recent versions of Windows. Normal users can modify values in HKEY_ CURRENT_USER, but to do more than look in other areas, a program would probably need to run with elevated privileges. For more information on privilege elevation, see Microsoft's article "User Account Control Step-by-Step Guide" at `http://technet.microsoft.com/library/cc709691.aspx`.

The program can use these RegistryKey objects to work with the corresponding registry subtree. The following table describes the most useful properties and methods provided by the RegistryKey class:

PROPERTY OR METHOD	PURPOSE
Close	Closes the key and writes it to disk if it has been modified.
CreateSubKey	Creates a new subkey or opens an existing subkey within this key.
DeleteSubKey	Deletes the specified subkey. This method will delete the subkey if it contains values, but not if it contains other subkeys. The subkey to be deleted need not be a direct child of this key. For example, the following code uses the CurrentUser RegistryKey object to delete the descendant key Software\VB and VBA Program Settings\MyComputerRegistry\Config: `My.Computer.Registry.CurrentUser.DeleteSubKey("Software\ VB and VBA Program Settings\RegistrySettings\Config")`
DeleteSubKeyTree	Recursively deletes a subkey and any child subkeys it contains. The sub-key to be deleted need not be a direct child of this key.
DeleteValue	Deletes a value from the key.
Flush	Writes any changes to the key into the registry.
GetSubKeyNames	Returns an array of strings giving subkey names.
GetValue	Returns the value of a specified value within this key.
GetValueKind	Returns the type of a specified value within this key. This can be Binary, DWord, ExpandString, MultiString, QWord, String, or Unknown.
GetValueNames	Returns an array of strings giving the names of all of the values contained within the key.
Name	Returns the key's registry path.
OpenSubKey	Returns a RegistryKey object representing a descendant key. Parameters give the subkey name, and indicate whether the returned RegistryKey should allow you to modify the subkey.

continues

(continued)

PROPERTY OR METHOD	PURPOSE
SetValue	Sets a value within the key.
SubKeyCount	Returns the number of subkeys that are this key's direct children.
ToString	Returns the key's name.
ValueCount	Returns the number of values stored in this key.

The following example opens the HKEY_CURRENT_USER\Software\VB and VBA Program Settings\RegistrySettings\Config key. It reads the CurrentDirectory value from that key using the default value C:\ and saves the result in the variable current_directory. It closes the key and then uses the DeleteSubKey method to delete the RegistrySettings application's Config section.

```
' Open the application's Config subkey.
Dim config_section As Microsoft.Win32.RegistryKey =
    My.Computer.Registry.CurrentUser.OpenSubKey(
        "Software\VB and VBA Program Settings\RegistrySettings\Config\")

' Get the CurrentDirectory value.
Dim current_directory As String =
    CType(config_section.GetValue("CurrentDirectory", "C:\"), String)

' Close the subkey.
config_section.Close()

' Delete the application's whole Config section.
My.Computer.Registry.CurrentUser.DeleteSubKey(
    "Software\VB and VBA Program Settings\RegistrySettings\Config")
```

The following code shows the equivalent operations using the native registry methods of Visual Basic:

```
' Get the CurrentDirectory value.
Dim current_directory As String =
GetSetting("RegistrySettings", "Config", "CurrentDirectory", "C:\")

' Delete the application's whole Config section.
DeleteSetting("RegistrySettings", "Config")
```

It is generally easier to use the native registry methods of Visual Basic. Those methods work only with values in the HKEY_CURRENT_USER\Software\VB and VBA Program Settings Registry subtree, however. If you need to access keys and values outside of this subtree, you must use the My.Computer.Registry objects.

Example program MyComputerRegistry demonstrates many useful My.Computer.Registry operations. It does the same things as program RegistrySettings mentioned in the previous section except it uses My.Computer.Registry instead of Visual Basic's native registry methods.

CONFIGURATION FILES

Configuration files let you store information for a program to use at run time in a standardized external file. You can change the values in the configuration file, and the program will use the new value the next time it starts. That enables you to change some of the application's behavior without needing to recompile the executable program.

One way to use configuration files is through dynamic properties. Dynamic properties are automatically loaded from the configuration file at run time by Visual Basic.

Start by defining the settings you will bind to the dynamic properties. In Solution Explorer, double-click My Project and select the Settings tab to see the property page shown in Figure 28-1. Use this page to define the settings that you will load at run time.

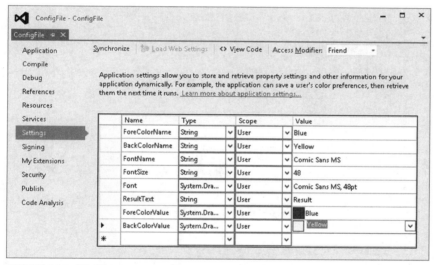

FIGURE 28-1: Use this page to define application settings.

A setting's scope can be Application or User. A setting with Application scope is shared by all of the program's users. Settings with User scope are stored separately for each user so different users can use and modify their own values.

Next, add a control to a form and select it. In the Properties window, open the ApplicationSettings entry, click the PropertyBinding sub-item, and click the ellipsis to the right to display a list of the control's properties.

Select the property that you want to load dynamically and click the drop-down arrow on the right to see a list of defined settings that you might assign to the property. Figure 28-2 shows the Application

FIGURE 28-2: Use the drop-down list to assign a setting to the dynamic property.

Setting dialog box with this drop-down list displayed for a control's Text property. From the list, select the setting that you want to assign to the property.

Visual Studio adds the setting to the program's configuration file. If you open Solution Explorer and double-click the app.config entry, you'll see the new dynamic property.

The following text shows the configuration setting sections of an `App.config` file. The userSettings section defines the settings shown in Figure 28-1.

```xml
<?xml version="1.0" encoding="utf-8" ?>
<configuration>
    ...
    <userSettings>
        <ConfigFile.My.MySettings>
            <setting name="ForeColorName" serializeAs="String">
                <value>Blue</value>
            </setting>
            <setting name="BackColorName" serializeAs="String">
                <value>Yellow</value>
            </setting>
            <setting name="FontName" serializeAs="String">
                <value>Comic Sans MS</value>
            </setting>
            <setting name="FontSize" serializeAs="String">
                <value>48</value>
            </setting>
            <setting name="Font" serializeAs="String">
                <value>Comic Sans MS, 48pt</value>
            </setting>
            <setting name="ResultText" serializeAs="String">
                <value>Result</value>
            </setting>
            <setting name="ForeColorValue" serializeAs="String">
                <value>Blue</value>
            </setting>
            <setting name="BackColorValue" serializeAs="String">
                <value>Yellow</value>
            </setting>
        </ConfigFile.My.MySettings>
    </userSettings>
</configuration>
```

When the application starts, Visual Basic loads the `App.config` file, reads the settings, and assigns their values to any properties bound to them.

So far, this is just a very roundabout way to set the control's property values. The real benefit of this method comes later when you want to change a setting. If you look in the compiled application's directory (normally the bin\Debug directory when you're developing the program), you'll find a file with the same name as the application but with a `.config` extension. If the application is called `ConfigFile.exe`, then this file is called `ConfigFile.exe.config`.

If you open this file with any text editor and change the value of a setting, the program uses the new value the next time it runs. For example, if you change the value of BackColorValue from Yellow to

Orange, then the next time the program runs, any controls that use that color for their backgrounds will now be orange. Instead of recompiling the whole application, you only need to change this text file. If you have distributed the application to a large number of users, you only need to give them the revised configuration file and not a whole new executable.

When you make a new setting, Visual Basic automatically generates code that adds the setting to the My.Settings namespace, so the program can easily get the setting's value. For example, the following code displays the values of the txtFontSize and txtFontName settings:

```
MessageBox.Show(My.Settings.FontSize & "pt " & My.Settings.FontName)
```

The My.Settings namespace provides several other properties and methods that make working with settings easy. The following table summarizes the most useful My.Settings properties and methods:

PROPERTY OR METHOD	PURPOSE
Item	A name-indexed collection of the values for the settings.
Properties	A name-indexed collection of SettingsProperty objects that contain information about the settings, including their names and default values.
Reload	Reloads the settings from the configuration file.
Save	Saves any modified settings into the configuration file. The program can modify settings with user scope. Settings with application scope are read-only.

Example program ShowSettings uses the following code to display the settings listed in the My.Settings.Properties collection:

```
Imports System.Configuration

Public Class Form1
    Private Sub Form1_Load() Handles MyBase.Load
        For Each settings_property As SettingsProperty In My.Settings.Properties
            Dim new_item As New ListViewItem(settings_property.Name)
            new_item.SubItems.Add(settings_property.DefaultValue.ToString)
            lvSettings.Items.Add(new_item)
        Next settings_property

        lvSettings.Columns(0).Width = -2
        lvSettings.Columns(1).Width = -2
    End Sub
End Class
```

When a program closes, it automatically saves any changes to User scope settings. However, if the program crashes, it does not have a chance to save any changes. If you want to be sure changes are saved, call My.Settings.Save after the user changes settings.

Example program SaveSettings uses two settings: a User scope color named FormColor that determines the form's background color and an Application scope color named ButtonColor that determines the background colors of the program's two buttons. The program provides Form Color and Button Color buttons to let you change the two color settings. If you change the colors, close the program, and restart it, you'll see that the User scope form color is saved, but the Application scope button color is not.

RESOURCE FILES

Resource files contain text, images, and other data for the application to load at run time. The intent of resource files is to let you easily replace one set of resources with another.

One of the most common reasons for using resource files is to provide different resources for different languages. To create installation packages for different languages, you simply ship the executable and a resource file that uses the right language. Alternatively, you can ship resource files for all of the languages you support and then let the application pick the appropriate file at run time based on the user's computer settings.

Resource files are not intended to store application configuration information and settings. They are intended to hold values that you might want to change, but only infrequently. You should store frequently changing data in configuration files or the system registry rather than in resource files.

The distinction is small and frankly somewhat artificial. Both configuration files and resource files store data that you can swap without recompiling the application. Rebuilding resource files can be a little more complex, however, so perhaps the distinction that configuration and setting data changes more frequently makes some sense.

Resource files can also be embedded within a compiled application. In that case, you cannot swap the resource file without recompiling the application. Although this makes embedded resource files less useful for storing frequently changing information, they still give you a convenient place to group resource data within the application. This is particularly useful if several parts of the application must use the same pieces of data. For example, if every form should display the same background image, it makes sense to store the image in a common resource file that they can all use.

The following sections describe the three most common types of resources: application, embedded, and localization.

Application Resources

To create application resources in Visual Basic, open Solution Explorer, double-click the My Project entry, and select the Resources tab. Use the drop-down on the left to select one of the resource categories: Strings, Images, Icons, Audio, Files, or Other. Figure 28-3 shows the application's Resources tab displaying the application's images.

If you double-click an item, Visual Studio opens an appropriate editor. For example, if you double-click a bitmap resource, Visual Studio opens the image in an integrated bitmap editor.

Click the Add Resource drop-down list and select Add Existing File to add a file to the program's resources. Use the drop-down's Add New String, Add New Icon, or Add New Text File commands

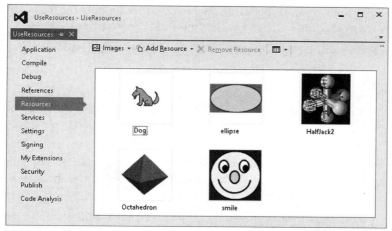

FIGURE 28-3: The Resources tab contains images and other resources used by the application.

to add new items to the resource file. The drop-down's New Image item opens a cascading submenu that lets you create new PNG, bitmap, GIF, JPEG, and TIFF images.

Using Application Resources

When you create application resources, Visual Studio automatically generates code that adds strongly typed resource properties to the My.Resources namespace. If you open Solution Explorer and click the Show All Files button, you can see the `Resources.Designer.vb` file that contains this code. The Solution Explorer path to this file is My Project/Resources.resx/Resources .Designer.vb.

The following code shows the property that `Resources.Designer.vb` contains to retrieve the Octahedron image resource:

```
Friend ReadOnly Property Octahedron() As System.Drawing.Bitmap
    Get
        Dim obj As Object =
            ResourceManager.GetObject("Octahedron", resourceCulture)
        Return CType(obj,System.Drawing.Bitmap)
    End Get
End Property
```

The following code shows how a program can use these My.Resources properties. It sets the lblGreeting control's Text property to the string returned by the My.Resources.Greeting property. Then it sets the form's BackgroundImage property to the image resource named Dog.

```
Private Sub Form1_Load() Handles MyBase.Load
    lblGreeting.Text = My.Resources.Greeting
    Me.BackgroundImage = My.Resources.Dog
End Sub
```

Because these property procedures are strongly typed, IntelliSense can offer support for them. If you type My.Resources, IntelliSense lists the values defined in the application's resource file.

Example program UseResources uses similar code to set a label's text and to display an image.

Embedded Resources

In addition to storing resources in the application's resource file Resources.resx, you can add other resource files to the application. Open the Project menu and select the Add New Item command. Pick the Resources File template, give the file a meaningful name, and click OK.

After you add a resource file to the project, you can double-click it in Solution Explorer to open it in the resource editor. Then you can add resources to the file exactly as you do for the application's resource file.

Just as it generates strongly typed properties for application resources, Visual Studio generates similar code for other embedded resource files. You can access these properties by adding the resource file's name after My.Settings and before the resource name. For example, to get the image resource named Dog from the Images resource file, the program would use My.Settings.Images.Dog.

Example program EmbeddedResources uses the following code to set a Label's text to the resource named Greeting in the file Strings.resx and to set the form's background image to the resource named Dog in the file Images.resx:

```
Public Sub Form1_Load() Handles MyBase.Load
    lblGreeting.Text = My.Resources.Strings.Greeting
    Me.BackgroundImage = My.Resources.Images.Dog
End Sub
```

Localization Resources

One of the most important reasons for inventing resource files was to allow localization: supporting different text, images, and other items for different languages and cultures. Resources make localization in Visual Studio .NET easy.

First, create a form using whatever language you typically use from day to day. For me, that's English as spoken in the United States. Open the form in the form designer and give it whatever controls you need. Set the form's and controls' properties as usual.

Next, set the form's Localizable property to True. Then set the form's Language property to the first language you want to support other than the default language that you have been working with so far. Modify the controls' properties for the new language.

As you modify a form, Visual Studio saves the changes you make to a new resource file attached to the form. If you open Solution Explorer and click the Show All Files button, you can see these resource files below the form's file.

Example program Localized uses default settings for United States English. It also includes localizations for generic German (as opposed to German as spoken in Switzerland, Germany, Liechtenstein, or some other country). If you expand the form's entry in Solution Explorer, you'll find the files `Form1.resx` holding the default settings and `Form1.de.resx` holding the German settings.

At run time, the application automatically checks the user's computer and selects the best resource file based on the system's regional settings.

Normally, you should let the application pick the appropriate resource file automatically, but you can explicitly select a resource file for testing purposes. To do that, open the Solution Explorer and click the Show All Files button. Find the form's design file (for example, `Form1.Designer.vb`) and open it.

At the top of the file, import the System.Threading and System.Globalization namespaces.

Next, create a parameterless constructor for the form. Add a call to MyBase.New and then set the current thread's CurrentCulture and CurrentUICulture properties to a CultureInfo object that represents the culture that you want to use.

The LocalizedUseGerman example program uses the following code to select the German localization when it starts:

```
Imports System.Threading
Imports System.Globalization

<Global.Microsoft.VisualBasic.CompilerServices.DesignerGenerated()> _
Partial Class Form1
    Inherits System.Windows.Forms.Form

    Public Sub New()
        MyBase.New()

        ' Set the culture and UI culture to German.
        Thread.CurrentThread.CurrentCulture = New CultureInfo("de-DE")
        Thread.CurrentThread.CurrentUICulture = New CultureInfo("de-DE")

        ' This call is required by the designer.
        InitializeComponent()

        ' Add any initialization after the InitializeComponent() call.

    End Sub
    ...
End Class
```

CULTURE COMES FIRST

The program must set the culture and user interface culture before it calls InitializeComponent because InitializeComponent is where the program sets the form and control properties.

The rest is automatic. When the form's InitializeComponent method executes, it loads the resources it needs for the culture you selected.

Example program LocalizedUseGerman, which is available for download on the book's website, uses this code to open the form localized for German even if your system would not normally select that version.

For a list of culture codes, see `http://msdn.microsoft.com/library/ee825488.aspx`.

APPLICATION

The Application object represents the running application at a very high level. It provides properties and methods for starting an event loop to process Windows messages, possibly for a form. It also provides methods for controlling and stopping the event loop.

Don't confuse the Application object with the My.Application namespace. The two have somewhat similar purposes but very different features.

The following sections describe the Application object's most useful properties, methods, and events.

Application Properties

The following table describes the Application object's most useful properties.

PROPERTY	PURPOSE
CommonAppDataPath	Returns the path where the program should store application data shared by all users. By default, this path has the form base_path\company_name\product_name\product_version. The base_path is typically `C:\Documents and Settings\All Users\Application Data`.
CommonAppDataRegistry	Returns the registry key where the program should store application data shared by all users. By default, this path has the form HKEY_LOCAL_MACHINE\Software\company_name\product_name\product_version.
CompanyName	Returns the application's company name.
CurrentCulture	Gets or sets the CultureInfo object for this thread.
CurrentInputLanguage	Gets or sets the InputLanguage for this thread.
ExecutablePath	Returns the fully qualified path to the file that started the execution, including the filename.
LocalUserAppDataPath	Returns the path where the program should store data for this local, non-roaming user. By default, this path has the form base_path\company_name\product_name\product_version. The base_path is typically `C:\Documents and Settings\user_name\Local Settings\Application Data`.

PROPERTY	PURPOSE
MessageLoop	Returns True if the thread has a message loop. If the program begins with a startup form, this loop is created automatically. If it starts with a custom Sub Main, the loop doesn't initially exist and the program must start it by calling Application.Run.
OpenForms	Returns a collection holding references to all of the application's open forms.
ProductName	Returns the application's product name.
ProductVersion	Gets the product version associated with this application.
StartupPath	Returns the fully qualified path to the directory where the program starts.
UserAppDataPath	Returns the path where the program should store data for this user. By default, this path has the form base_path\company_name\product_name\product_version. The base_path is typically `C:\Documents and Settings\user_name\Application Data`.
UserAppDataRegistry	Returns the registry key where the program should store application data for this user. By default, this path has the form HKEY_CURRENT_USER\Software\company_name\product_name\product_version.
UseWaitCursor	Determines whether this thread's forms display a wait cursor. Set this to True before performing a long operation, and set it to False when the operation is finished.

To set the CompanyName, ProductName, and ProductVersion, open Solution Explorer, double-click the My Project entry, and select the Application tab. Then click the Assembly Information button and enter the values on the Assembly Information dialog box.

Application Methods

The following table describes the Application object's most useful methods.

METHOD	PURPOSE
AddMessageFilter	Adds a message filter to monitor the event loop's Windows messages.
DoEvents	Processes Windows messages that are currently in the message queue. If the thread is performing a long calculation, it would normally prevent the rest of the thread from taking action such as processing these messages. Calling DoEvents lets the user interface catch up with the user's actions. Note that you can often avoid the need for DoEvents if you perform the long task on a separate thread.

continues

(continued)

METHOD	PURPOSE
Exit	Ends the whole application. This is a rather abrupt halt, and any forms that are loaded do not execute their FormClosing or FormClosed event handlers.
ExitThread	Ends the current thread. This is a rather abrupt halt, and any forms running on the thread do not execute their FormClosing or FormClosed event handlers.
OnThreadException	Raises the Application object's ThreadException event, passing it an exception. If your application throws an uncaught exception in the IDE, the IDE halts. That makes it hard to test Application .ThreadException event handlers. You can call OnThreadException to invoke the event handler.
RemoveMessageFilter	Removes a message filter.
Run	Runs a message loop for the current thread. If you pass this method a form object, it displays the form and processes its messages until the form closes.
SetSuspendState	Makes the system suspend operation or hibernate. When the system hibernates, it writes its memory contents to disk. When you restart the system, it resumes with its previous desktop and applications running. When the system suspends operation, it enters low-power mode. It can resume more quickly than a hibernated system, but memory contents are not saved, so they will be lost if the computer loses power.

Application Events

The Application object provides a few events that give you information about the application's state. The following table describes these events:

EVENT	PURPOSE
ApplicationExit	Occurs when the application is about to shut down.
Idle	Occurs when the application finishes executing some code and is about to enter an idle state to wait for events.
ThreadException	Occurs when the application throws an unhandled exception.
ThreadExit	Occurs when a thread is about to exit.

When you end an application by unloading its form, the program receives the events FormClosing, FormClosed, ThreadExit, and ApplicationExit, in that order.

If you end the application by calling the Application object's Exit method, the program only receives the ThreadExit and ApplicationExit events. If more than one thread is running, they each receive ThreadExit events, and then they each receive ApplicationExit events.

SUMMARY

Visual Studio provides many ways to store and use application configuration and resource information. Some of the most useful of these methods include environment variables, the registry, configuration files, and resource files. The My namespace and the Application object make working with some of these easier.

Store configuration information that changes relatively often in configuration files. Store less changeable resources that determine the application's appearance in resource files. If you will distribute the application in multiple languages, use localized resource files to manage the different languages. If necessary, you can change the data stored in configuration and resource files and redistribute them to your users without rebuilding the entire application.

You can store small pieces of information between program runs in the system registry. Use databases, XML files, and other files to store larger amounts of data.

Using all of these techniques, you can make your application easily configurable. You can satisfy the needs of different kinds of users and customize the application without recompiling it.

This chapter explained ways that a program can save configuration and resource information using tools such as the registry, environment variables, and resource files. Generally, these kinds of data are of relatively limited size. If an application needs to store larger amounts of data, it generally uses a database or file.

Chapter 29, "Streams," explains classes that a Visual Basic application can use to work with stream data in general and files in particular. Using streams attached to files, a program can read and write large amounts of data without cluttering up the registry, environment variables, or resource files.

29

Streams

WROX.COM CODE DOWNLOADS FOR THIS CHAPTER

The wrox.com downloads for this chapter are found at http://www.wrox.com/remtitle .cgi?isbn=9781118314074 on the Download Code tab. The code for this chapter is divided into the following major examples:

➤ FileStreamWrite

➤ MemoryStreamWrite

➤ StringWriterReader

➤ ReadLines

➤ OpenCreateAppendText

STREAM CONCEPTS

At some very primitive level, all pieces of data are just piles of bytes. The computer doesn't really store invoices, employee records, and recipes. At its most basic level, the computer stores bytes of data (or even bits, but the computer naturally groups them in bytes). It is only when a program interprets those bytes that they acquire a higher-level meaning that is valuable to the user.

Although you generally don't want to treat high-level data as undifferentiated bytes, there are times when thinking of the data as bytes lets you handle it in more uniform ways.

One type of byte-like data is the *stream*, an ordered series of bytes. Files, data flowing across a network, messages moving through a queue, and even the memory in an array all fit this description.

Defining the abstract idea of a stream lets applications handle these different types of objects uniformly. If an encryption or serialization routine manipulates a generic stream of bytes, it doesn't need to know whether the stream represents a file, a chunk of memory, plaintext, encrypted text, or data flowing across a network.

Visual Studio provides several classes for manipulating different kinds of streams. It also provides higher-level classes for working with this kind of data at a more abstract level. For example, it provides classes for working with streams that happen to represent files and directories.

This chapter describes some of the classes you can use to manipulate streams. It explains lower-level classes that you may use only rarely and higher-level classes that let you read and write strings and files relatively easily.

The following table summarizes the most useful stream classes:

CLASS	USE
FileStream	Read and write bytes in a file.
MemoryStream	Read and write bytes in memory.
BinaryReader, BinaryWriter	Read and write specific data types in a stream.
StringReader, StringWriter	Read and write text with or without new lines in a string.
StreamReader, StreamWriter	Read and write text with or without new lines in a stream (usually a file stream).

STREAM

The Stream class defines properties and methods that derived stream classes must provide. These let the program perform relatively generic tasks with streams such as determining whether the stream allows writing.

The following table describes the Stream class's most useful properties:

PROPERTY	PURPOSE
CanRead	Returns True if the stream supports reading.
CanSeek	Returns True if the stream supports seeking to a particular position in the stream.
CanTimeout	Returns True if the stream supports timing out of read and write operations.
CanWrite	Returns True if the stream supports writing.
Length	Returns the number of bytes in the stream.

PROPERTY	PURPOSE
Position	Returns the stream's current position in its bytes. For a stream that supports seeking, the program can set this value to move to a particular position.
ReadTimeout	Determines the number of milliseconds that a read operation will wait before timing out.
WriteTimeout	Determines the number of milliseconds that a write operation will wait before timing out.

The following table describes the Stream class's most useful methods:

METHOD	PURPOSE
BeginRead	Begins an asynchronous read.
BeginWrite	Begins an asynchronous write.
Close	Closes the stream and releases any resources it uses (such as file handles).
EndRead	Waits for an asynchronous read to finish.
EndWrite	Ends an asynchronous write.
Flush	Flushes data from the stream's buffers into the underlying storage medium (device, file, memory, and so forth).
Read	Reads bytes from the stream and advances its position by that number of bytes.
ReadByte	Reads a byte from the stream and advances its position by one byte.
Seek	If the stream supports seeking, sets the stream's position.
SetLength	Sets the stream's length. If the stream is currently longer than the new length, it is truncated. If the stream is shorter than the new length, it is enlarged. The stream must support both writing and seeking for this method to work.
Write	Writes bytes into the stream and advances the current position by this number of bytes.
WriteByte	Writes one byte into the stream and advances the current position by one byte.

You can learn about the other members of the Stream class at http://msdn.microsoft.com/ system.io.stream.aspx.

FILESTREAM

The FileStream class provides a stream representation of a file.

The FileStream class's parent class Stream defines most of its properties and methods. See the preceding section "Stream" for descriptions of those properties and methods.

FileStream adds two useful new properties to those it inherits from Stream. First, IsAsync returns True if the FileStream was opened asynchronously. Second, the Name property returns the filename passed into the object's constructor.

The class also adds two new useful methods to those it inherits from Stream. The Lock method locks the file, so other processes can read it but not modify it. Unlock removes a previous lock.

Overloaded versions of the FileStream class's constructor let you specify the following:

➤ Filename or handle

➤ File mode (Append, Create, CreateNew, Open, OpenOrCreate, or Truncate)

➤ Access mode (Read, Write, or ReadWrite)

➤ File sharing (Inheritable, which allows child processes to inherit the file handle, None, Read, Write, or ReadWrite)

➤ Buffer size

➤ File options (Asynchronous, DeleteOnClose, Encrypted, None, RandomAccess, SequentialScan, or WriteThrough)

Example program FileStreamWrite uses the following code to create a file. It creates a file and uses a Universal Transformation Format (UTF) UTF8Encoding object to convert a string into an array of bytes. It writes the bytes into the file and then closes the FileStream.

```
Dim file_name As String = Application.StartupPath & "\test.txt"
Using file_stream As New FileStream(file_name, FileMode.Create)
    Dim bytes As Byte() = New UTF8Encoding().GetBytes("Hello world!")

    file_stream.Write(bytes, 0, bytes.Length)
    file_stream.Close()
End Using
```

> **NOTE** *The 8-bit UTF encoding is the most popular type on the web, although there are other encoding formats such as UTF-7 and UTF-16. For additional information, see* http://unicode.org/faq/utf_bom.html *and* http://en.wikipedia.org/wiki/Unicode.

As this example demonstrates, the FileStream class provides only low-level methods for reading and writing files. These methods let you read and write bytes, but not integers, strings, or the other types of data that you are more likely to want to use.

The BinaryReader and BinaryWriter classes let you read and write binary data more easily than the FileStream class does. The StringReader and StringWriter classes let you read and write string data more easily than the other classes. See the section "StringReader and StringWriter" describing these classes later in this chapter for more information.

MEMORYSTREAM

Like FileStream, the MemoryStream class inherits from the Stream class. This class represents a stream with data stored in memory. Like the FileStream, it provides only relatively primitive methods for reading and writing data. Usually, you will want to attach a higher-level object to the MemoryStream to make using it easier.

Example program MemoryStreamWrite uses the following code to write and read from a MemoryStream object:

```
Dim memory_stream As New MemoryStream()
Dim binary_writer As New BinaryWriter(memory_stream)
binary_writer.Write("Peter Piper picked a peck of pickled peppers.")

Dim binary_reader As New BinaryReader(memory_stream)
memory_stream.Seek(0, SeekOrigin.Begin)
MessageBox.Show(binary_reader.ReadString())
binary_reader.Close()
```

This program first creates the MemoryStream. It then creates a BinaryWriter attached to the MemoryStream and uses it to write some text into the stream. Next, the program makes a BinaryReader object attached to the same MemoryStream. It uses the stream's Seek method to rewind the stream to its beginning, and then uses the BinaryReader's ReadString method to read the string out of the MemoryStream.

The following example does the same things as the previous example, except it uses the StreamWriter and StreamReader classes instead of BinaryWriter and BinaryReader. Note that this version must call the StreamWriter class's Flush method to ensure that all of the text is written into the MemoryStream before it can read the memory using the StreamReader.

```
Using memory_stream As New MemoryStream()
    Dim stream_writer As New StreamWriter(memory_stream)
    stream_writer.Write("Peter Piper picked a peck of pickled peppers.")
    stream_writer.Flush()

    Dim stream_reader As New StreamReader(memory_stream)
    memory_stream.Seek(0, SeekOrigin.Begin)
    MessageBox.Show(stream_reader.ReadToEnd())
    stream_reader.Close()
End Using
```

BINARYREADER AND BINARYWRITER

The BinaryReader and BinaryWriter classes are not stream classes. Instead, they are helper classes that work with stream classes. They let you read and write data in files using a specific encoding. For example, the BinaryReader object's ReadInt32 method reads a 4-byte (32-bit) signed integer from the stream. Similarly, the ReadUInt16 method reads a 2-byte (16-bit) unsigned integer.

These classes still work at a relatively low level, and you should generally use higher-level classes to read and write data if possible. For example, you shouldn't tie yourself to a particular representation of an integer (32- or 16-bit) unless you really must.

BinaryReader and BinaryWriter objects are attached to stream objects that provide access to the underlying bytes. Both of these classes have a BaseStream property that returns a reference to the underlying stream. Note also that the Close method provided by each of these classes automatically closes the underlying stream.

The following table describes the BinaryReader class's most useful methods.

METHOD	PURPOSE
Close	Closes the BinaryReader and its underlying stream.
PeekChar	Reads the stream's next character but does not advance the reader's position, so other methods can still read the character later.
Read	Reads characters from the stream and advances the reader's position.
ReadBoolean	Reads a Boolean from the stream and advances the reader's position by 1 byte.
ReadByte	Reads a byte from the stream and advances the reader's position by 1 byte.
ReadBytes	Reads a number of bytes from the stream into a byte array and advances the reader's position by that number of bytes.
ReadChar	Reads a character from the stream and advances the reader's position appropriately for the stream's encoding.
ReadChars	Reads a number of characters from the stream, returns the results in a character array, and advances the reader's position appropriately for the stream's encoding.
ReadDecimal	Reads a decimal value from the stream and advances the reader's position by 16 bytes.
ReadDouble	Reads an 8-byte floating-point value from the stream and advances the reader's position by 8 bytes.

METHOD	PURPOSE
ReadInt16	Reads a 2-byte signed integer from the stream and advances the reader's position by 2 bytes.
ReadInt32	Reads a 4-byte signed integer from the stream and advances the reader's position by 4 bytes.
ReadInt64	Reads an 8-byte signed integer from the stream and advances the reader's position by 8 bytes.
ReadSByte	Reads a signed byte from the stream and advances the reader's position by 1 byte.
ReadSingle	Reads a 4-byte floating-point value from the stream and advances the reader's position by 4 bytes.
ReadString	Reads a string from the current stream and advances the reader's position past it. The string begins with its length.
ReadUInt16	Reads a 2-byte unsigned integer from the stream and advances the reader's position by 2 bytes.
ReadUInt32	Reads a 4-byte unsigned integer from the stream and advances the reader's position by 4 bytes.
ReadUInt64	Reads an 8-byte unsigned integer from the stream and advances the reader's position by 8 bytes.

The following table describes the BinaryWriter class's most useful methods.

METHOD	PURPOSE
Close	Closes the BinaryWriter and its underlying stream.
Flush	Writes any buffered data into the underlying stream.
Seek	Sets the position within the stream.
Write	Writes a value into the stream. This method has many overloaded versions that write characters, arrays of characters, integers, strings, unsigned 64-bit integers, and so forth.

You can learn about the other members of the BinaryWriter and BinaryReader classes at http://msdn.microsoft.com/system.io.binarywriter.aspx and http://msdn.microsoft.com/system.io.binaryreader.aspx, respectively.

TEXTREADER AND TEXTWRITER

Like the BinaryReader and BinaryWriter classes, the TextReader and TextWriter classes are not stream classes, but they provide properties and methods for working with text, which is stream-related. TextReader and TextWriter are abstract (MustInherit) classes that define behaviors for derived classes that read or write text characters. For example, the StringWriter and Stream Writer classes derived from TextWriter let a program write characters into a string or stream, respectively. Normally, you would use these derived classes to read and write text, but you might want to use the TextReader or TextWriter classes to manipulate the underlying classes more generically. You may also encounter a method that requires a TextReader or TextWriter object as a parameter. In that case, you could pass the method either a StringReader/String Writer or a StreamReader/StreamWriter. For more information on these classes, see the sections "StringReader and StringWriter" and "StreamReader and StreamWriter" later in this chapter.

The following table describes the TextReader object's most useful methods.

METHOD	PURPOSE
Close	Closes the reader and releases any resources that it is using.
Peek	Reads the next character from the input without changing the reader's state, so other methods can read the character later.
Read	Reads data from the input. Overloaded versions of this method read a single character or an array of characters up to a specified length.
ReadBlock	Reads data from the input into an array of characters.
ReadLine	Reads a line of characters from the input and returns the data in a string.
ReadToEnd	Reads any remaining characters in the input and returns them in a string.

The TextWriter class has three useful properties. Encoding specifies the text's encoding (ASCII, UTF-8, Unicode, and so forth). The FormatProvider property returns an object that controls formatting. For example, you can build a FormatProvider object that knows how to display numbers in different bases (such as hexadecimal or octal). The NewLine property gets or sets the string used by the writer to end lines. Usually, this value is something similar to a carriage return or a carriage return plus a line feed.

The following table describes the TextWriter object's most useful methods.

METHOD	PURPOSE
Close	Closes the writer and releases any resources it uses.
Flush	Writes any buffered data into the underlying output.
Write	Writes a value into the output. This method has many overloaded versions that write characters, arrays of characters, integers, strings, unsigned 64-bit integers, and so forth.
WriteLine	Writes data into the output followed by the new line sequence.

You can learn about the other members of the TextWriter and TextReader classes at `http://msdn .microsoft.com/system.io.textwriter.aspx` and `http://msdn.microsoft.com/system .io.textreader.aspx`, respectively.

STRINGREADER AND STRINGWRITER

The StringReader and StringWriter classes let a program read and write text in a string.

These classes are derived from TextReader and TextWriter and inherit the definitions of most of their properties and methods from those classes. See the preceding section "TextReader and TextWriter" for details.

The StringReader provides methods for reading lines, characters, or blocks of characters from a string. Its ReadToEnd method returns any of the string that has not already been read. The StringReader class's constructor takes as a parameter the string that it should process.

The StringWriter class lets an application build a string. It provides methods to write text into the string with or without a new-line sequence. Its ToString method returns the StringWriter class's string.

The StringWriter stores its string in an underlying StringBuilder class. StringBuilder is designed to make incrementally building a string more efficient than building a string by concatenating a series of values onto a String variable. For example, if an application needs to build a very large string by concatenating a series of long substrings, it may be more efficient to use a StringBuilder rather than add the strings to a normal String variable. StringWriter provides a simple interface to the StringBuilder class.

The most useful method provided by StringWriter that is not defined by the TextWriter parent class is GetStringBuilder. This method returns a reference to the underlying StringBuilder object that holds the class's data.

Example program StringWriterReader uses the following code to demonstrate the StringWriter and StringReader classes:

```
' Use a StringWriter to write into a string.
Using string_writer As New StringWriter()
    string_writer.WriteLine("The quick brown fox")
```

```
        string_writer.WriteLine("jumps over the lazy dog.")
        MessageBox.Show(string_writer.ToString)

        ' Use a StringReader to read from the string.
        Using string_reader As New StringReader(string_writer.ToString)
            string_writer.Close()
            MessageBox.Show(string_reader.ReadLine())
            MessageBox.Show(string_reader.ReadToEnd())
            string_reader.Close()
        End Using
    End Using
End Using
```

This code creates a StringWriter object and uses its WriteLine method to add two lines to the string. It then displays the result of the writer's ToString method, which returns the writer's current contents.

Next, the program creates a StringReader, passing its constructor the string from which it will read. It closes the StringWriter because it is no longer needed.

The code displays the result of the StringReader class's ReadLine method. Because the StringWriter created the string as two separate lines, this displays only the first line, "The quick brown fox." Next, the code uses the StringReader class's ReadToEnd method to read and display the rest of the text, "jumps over the lazy dog." The code finishes by closing the StringReader.

STREAMREADER AND STREAMWRITER

The StreamReader and StreamWriter classes let a program read and write data in a stream. The underlying stream is usually a FileStream. You can pass a FileStream into these classes' constructors, or you can pass a filename and the object will create a FileStream automatically.

The StreamReader provides methods for reading lines, characters, or blocks of characters from the stream. Its ReadToEnd method returns any of the stream that has not already been read. The EndOfStream method returns True when the StreamReader has reached the end of the stream.

Example program ReadLines uses the following code fragment to read the lines from a file and add them to a ListBox control:

```
' Open the file.
Dim stream_reader As New StreamReader("Animals.txt")

' Read until we reach the end of the file.
Do Until stream_reader.EndOfStream()
    lstValues.Items.Add(stream_reader.ReadLine())
Loop

' Close the file.
stream_reader.Close()
```

The StreamWriter class provides methods to write text into the stream with or without a new-line character.

StreamReader and StreamWriter are derived from the TextReader and TextWriter classes and inherit the definitions of most of their properties and methods from those classes. See the section "TextReader and TextWriter" earlier in this chapter for a description of these properties and methods.

The StreamWriter class adds a new AutoFlush property that determines whether the writer flushes its buffer after every write.

Example program StreamWriterReader uses the following code to demonstrate the StreamReader and StreamWriter classes:

```
Dim file_name As String = Application.StartupPath & "\test.txt"
Using stream_writer As New StreamWriter(file_name)
    stream_writer.Write("The quick brown fox")
    stream_writer.WriteLine(" jumps over the lazy dog.")
    stream_writer.Close()
End Using

Using stream_reader As New StreamReader(file_name)
    MessageBox.Show(stream_reader.ReadToEnd())
    stream_reader.Close()
End Using
```

This code generates a filename and passes it into a StreamWriter class's constructor. It uses the StreamWriter class's Write and WriteLine methods to place two pieces of text in the file and then closes the file. If you were to open the file at this point with a text editor, you would see the text.

The program then creates a new StreamReader, passing its constructor the same filename. It uses the reader's ReadToEnd method to grab the file's contents and displays the results.

This example would have been much more awkward using a FileStream object's lower-level Write and Read methods to manipulate byte arrays. Compare this code to the example in the "FileStream" section earlier in this chapter.

OPENTEXT, CREATETEXT, AND APPENDTEXT

The File class in the System.IO namespace provides four shared methods that are particularly useful for working with StreamReader and StreamWriter objects associated with text files. The following table summarizes these four methods.

METHOD	PURPOSE
Exists	Returns True if a file with a given path exists.
OpenText	Returns a StreamReader that lets you read from an existing text file.
CreateText	Creates a new text file, overwriting any existing file at the given path, and returns a StreamWriter that lets you write into the new file.
AppendText	If the indicated file does not exist, creates the file. Whether the file is new or previously existing, returns a StreamWriter that lets you append text at the end of the file.

The OpenCreateAppendText example program lets you open an existing file, create a new file, or append text at the end of an existing file. It uses the following code to demonstrate the Exists and OpenText methods:

```
Dim file_name As String = Application.StartupPath & "\test.txt"
If Not Exists(file_name) Then
    txtData.Text = " < File not found > "
Else
    Using sr As StreamReader = OpenText(file_name)
        txtData.Text = sr.ReadToEnd()
        sr.Close()
    End Using
End If
```

This code uses Exists to see if the file exists. If the file does exist, the code uses OpenText to open the file and get a StreamReader associated with it. It uses the StreamReader class's ReadToEnd method to display the file's text in the text box txtData.

The OpenCreateAppendText program uses the following code to create a new text file:

```
Dim file_name As String = Application.StartupPath & "\test.txt"
Using sw As StreamWriter = CreateText(file_name)
    sw.Write(txtData.Text)
    sw.Close()
End Using
```

The code uses CreateText to create a new text file named `test.txt`. If `test.txt` already exists, CreateText overwrites it without warning. The program uses the StreamWriter returned by CreateText to write the contents of the txtData text box into the file and closes the file.

The OpenCreateAppendText program uses the following code to demonstrate the AppendText method:

```
Dim file_name As String = Application.StartupPath & "\test.txt"
Using sw As StreamWriter = AppendText(file_name)
    sw.Write(txtData.Text)
    sw.Close()
End Using
```

This code uses AppendText to create the file if it doesn't already exist or open it for appending if it does exist. The program uses the StreamWriter returned by AppendText to write into the file and then closes the file.

CUSTOM STREAM CLASSES

Visual Studio provides a few other stream classes with more specialized uses.

The CryptoStream class applies a cryptographic transformation to data that passes through it. For example, if you attach a CryptoStream to a file using a particular cryptographic transformation and then use it to write data, the CryptoStream automatically transforms the data and produces an encrypted file. Similarly, you can use a CryptoStream to read an encrypted file and recover the original text. For more information about the CryptoStream class, see `http://msdn.microsoft` `.com/library/system.security.cryptography.cryptostream.aspx`.

The NetworkStream class represents a socket-based stream over a network connection. You can use this class to make different applications communicate over a network. For more information about this class, see `http://msdn.microsoft.com/library/system.net.sockets.network` `stream.aspx`.

Three other special uses of streams are standard input, standard output, and standard error. Console applications define these streams for reading and writing information to and from the console. An application can interact directly with these streams by accessing the Console.In, Console.Out, and Console.Error properties. It can change these streams to new stream objects such as StreamReaders and StreamWriters by calling the Console.SetIn, Console.SetOut, and Console.SetError methods. For more information on these streams, see `http://msdn.microsoft.com/library/system.console` `.aspx`.

SUMMARY

Streams let a program consider a wide variety of data sources in a uniform way. If a subroutine takes a stream as a parameter, it doesn't need to worry about whether the stream is attached to a string, file, block of memory, or network connection.

Many applications use the StringReader and StringWriter classes to read and write text in strings, and the StreamReader and StreamWriter classes to read and write text in streams (usually files). The Exists, OpenText, CreateText, and AppendText methods are particularly useful for working with StreamReader and StreamWriter objects associated with text files.

The other stream classes are often used at lower levels or as more abstract classes to allow a routine to process different kinds of streams in a uniform way. If you focus on the four classes (StringReader, StringWriter, StreamReader, and StreamWriter), you will quickly learn how to perform the most common stream operations.

Programs often use the StreamReader and StreamWriter classes to read and write files. Chapter 30, "Filesystem Objects," describes classes that let a Visual Basic application interact with the filesystem in other ways. These classes let a program examine, rename, move, and delete files and directories.

30

Filesystem Objects

WROX.COM CODE DOWNLOADS FOR THIS CHAPTER

The wrox.com downloads for this chapter are found at `http://www.wrox.com/remtitle.cgi?isbn=9781118314074` on the Download Code tab. The code for this chapter is divided into the following major examples:

- ➤ RandomAccessEmployees
- ➤ UseFileSystemWatcher
- ➤ GetDriveInfo
- ➤ ShowSpecialDirectories
- ➤ UseFindInFiles

PROGRAMMING APPROACHES

Visual Basic includes a bewildering assortment of objects that you can use to manipulate drives, directories, and files. The stream classes described in Chapter 29 enable you to read and write files, but they don't really capture any of the special structure of the filesystem.

A Visual Basic application has two main choices for working with the filesystem: Visual Basic methods and .NET Framework classes. This chapter describes these two approaches and the classes that they use. It finishes by describing some of the My namespace properties and methods that you can use to access filesystem tools more easily. For more information on the My namespace, see the section "My" in Chapter 28, "Configuration and Resources," and Appendix S, "The My Namespace."

PERMISSIONS

An application cannot perform a task if the user running it doesn't have the appropriate permissions. Although this is true of any operation a program must perform, permission issues are particularly common when working with files, and recent versions of the Windows operating system are particularly strict about enforcing permission requirements.

A common mistake is for developers to build and test an application while logged in as a user who has a lot of privileges. Sometimes, developers even have system administrator privileges, so their programs can do pretty much anything on the computer. To ensure that users will have the permissions needed by an application, develop or at least test the code using an account with the privileges that typical users will have.

VISUAL BASIC METHODS

Visual Basic provides a number of commands for manipulating the filesystem. These commands are relatively flexible and easy to understand. Most of them have been around since the early days of Visual Basic, so many long-time Visual Basic developers prefer to use them rather than the newer .NET Framework methods.

One disadvantage to these methods is that they do not natively allow you to read and write nonstandard data types. They can handle string, date, integer, long, single, double, and decimal data. They can also handle structures and arrays of those types. They cannot, however, handle classes themselves. You can use XML serialization to convert a class object into a string and then use these methods to read and write the result, but that requires an extra step with some added complexity.

The section "File System Methods" later in this chapter describes the native filesystem methods of Visual Basic. The sections "Sequential-File Access," "Random-File Access," and "Binary-File Access" later in this chapter describe specific issues for working with sequential, random, and binary files.

File Methods

The following table describes the methods Visual Basic provides for working with files:

METHOD	PURPOSE
EOF	Returns True if a file open for reading is at the end of file. (EOF stands for End Of File.)
FileClose	Closes an open file.
FileGet	Reads data from a file opened in Random or Binary mode into a variable.
FileGetObject	Reads data as an object from a file opened in Random or Binary mode into a variable.
FileOpen	Opens a file for reading or writing. Parameters indicate the mode (Append, Binary, Input, Output, or Random), access type (Read, Write, or ReadWrite), and sharing (Shared, LockRead, LockWrite, or LockReadWrite).
FilePut	Writes data from a variable into a file opened for Random or Binary access.
FilePutObject	Writes an object from a variable into a file opened for Random or Binary access.
FreeFile	Returns a file number that is not currently associated with any file in this application. You should use FreeFile to get file numbers rather than use arbitrary numbers such as 1.
Input	Reads data written into a file by the Write method back into a variable.
InputString	Reads a specific number of characters from the file.
LineInput	Returns the next line of text from the file.
Loc	Returns the current position within the file.
LOF	Returns the file's length in bytes. (LOF stands for Length Of File.)
Print	Prints values into the file. Multiple values separated by commas are aligned at tab boundaries.
PrintLine	Prints values followed by a new line into the file. Multiple values separated by commas are aligned at tab boundaries.
Seek	Moves to the indicated position within the file.
Write	Writes values into the file, delimited appropriately so that they can later be read by the Input method.
WriteLine	Writes values followed by a new line into the file, delimited appropriately so that they can later be read by the Input method.

Many of the Visual Basic file methods use a file number to represent an open file. The file number is just a number used to identify the file. There's nothing magic about it. You just need to be sure not to use the same file number for more than one file at the same time. The FreeFile method returns a number that is not in use so that you know it is safe to use as a file number.

The following example uses FreeFile to get an available file number. It uses FileOpen to open a file for reading. Then, while the EOF method indicates that the code hasn't reached the end of the file, the program uses LineInput to read a line from the file and it displays the line. When it finishes reading the file, the program uses FileClose to close it.

```
' Get an available file number.
Dim file_num As Integer = FreeFile()

' Open the file.
FileOpen(file_num, "C:\Temp\test.txt",
    OpenMode.Input, OpenAccess.Read, OpenShare.Shared)

' Read the file's lines.
Do While Not EOF(file_num)
    ' Read a line.
    Dim txt As String = LineInput(file_num)
    Debug.WriteLine(txt)
Loop

' Close the file.
FileClose(file_num)
```

File System Methods

Visual Basic also provides several methods for working with the filesystem. The following table describes methods that manipulate directories and files:

METHOD	PURPOSE
ChDir	Changes the application's current working directory.
ChDrive	Changes the application's current working drive.
CurDir	Returns the application's current working directory.
Dir	Returns a file matching a directory path specification that may include wildcards, and matching certain file properties such as ReadOnly, Hidden, or Directory. The first call to Dir should include a path. Subsequent calls can omit the path to fetch the next matching file for the same initial path. Dir returns filenames without the path and returns Nothing when no more files match.
FileCopy	Copies a file to a new location.
FileDateTime	Returns the date and time when the file was created or last modified.

METHOD	PURPOSE
FileLen	Returns the length of a file in bytes.
GetAttr	Returns a value indicating the file's attributes. The value is a combination of the values vbNormal, vbReadOnly, vbHidden, vbSystem, vbDirectory, vbArchive, and vbAlias.
Kill	Permanently deletes a file.
MkDir	Creates a new directory.
Rename	Renames a directory or file.
RmDir	Deletes an empty directory.
SetAttr	Sets the file's attributes. The attribute value is a combination of the values vbNormal, vbReadOnly, vbHidden, vbSystem, vbDirectory, vbArchive, and vbAlias.

Sequential-File Access

With sequential-file access, a program reads or writes the contents of a file byte by byte from start to finish with no jumping around. In contrast, in a random-access file, the program can jump freely to any position in the file and write data wherever it likes.

A text file is a typical sequential file. The program can read the text in order, and read it one line at a time, but it cannot easily jump around within the file.

The Input, InputString, LineInput, Print, PrintLine, Write, and WriteLine methods provide sequential access to files.

The Print and PrintLine methods provide mostly unformatted results. If you pass these methods multiple parameters separated by commas, they align the results on tab boundaries. Write and WriteLine, on the other hand, delimit their output so that it can be easily read by the Input method.

A program cannot directly modify only part of a sequential file. For example, it cannot modify, add, or remove a sentence in the middle of a paragraph. If you must modify the file, you should read it into a string, make the changes you want, and then rewrite the file.

If you must frequently modify text in the middle of a file, you should consider using random or binary access, or storing the data in a database.

Random-File Access

A random-access file contains a series of fixed-length records. For example, you could create an employee file that contains a series of values defining an employee. Each record would have fixed-length fields to hold an employee's ID, first name, last name, street address, and so forth, as shown in the following structure definition:

```
Structure Employee
    Public Id As Long
    <VBFixedString(20)> Public FirstName As String
    <VBFixedString(20)> Public LastName As String
    <VBFixedString(40)> Public Street As String
    ...
End Structure
```

When you open a file for random access, you can jump to any record in the file. That makes certain kinds of file manipulation easier. For example, if the file is sorted, you can use a binary search to locate records in it.

You can overwrite the values in a record within the file, but you cannot add or remove records in the middle of the file. If you must make those sorts of changes, you must load the file into memory and then rewrite it from scratch.

The FileGet, FileGetObject, FilePut, and FilePutObject methods read and write records in random-access files. Example program RandomAccessEmployees uses the following code to demonstrate the FilePut and FileGet methods:

```
Public Class Form1
    Public Structure Employee
        Public ID As Integer
        <VBFixedString(15) > Public FirstName As String
        <VBFixedString(15) > Public LastName As String

        Public Sub New(new_id As Integer, first_name As String,
         last_name As String)
            ID = new_id
            FirstName = first_name
            LastName = last_name
        End Sub

        Public Overrides Function ToString() As String
            Return ID & ": " & FirstName & " " & LastName
        End Function
    End Structure

    Private Sub btnMakeRecords_Click() Handles btnMakeRecords.Click
        ' Declare a record variable.
        Dim emp As New Employee

        ' Get an available file number.
        Dim file_num As Integer = FreeFile()

        ' Open the file.
        FileOpen(file_num, "MYFILE.DAT", OpenMode.Random,
            OpenAccess.ReadWrite, OpenShare.Shared, Len(emp))

        ' Make some records.
```

```
        FilePut(file_num, New Employee(1, "Alice", "Altanta"))
        FilePut(file_num, New Employee(2, "Bob", "Bakersfield"))
        FilePut(file_num, New Employee(3, "Cindy", "Chicago"))
        FilePut(file_num, New Employee(4, "Dan", "Denver"))
        FilePut(file_num, New Employee(5, "Erma", "Eagle"))
        FilePut(file_num, New Employee(6, "Fred", "Frisco"))

        ' Fetch and display the records.
        Dim obj As ValueType = DirectCast(emp, ValueType)
        For Each i As Integer In New Integer() {3, 1, 5, 2, 6}
            FileGet(file_num, obj, i)
            emp = DirectCast(obj, Employee)
            Debug.WriteLine("[" & emp.ToString() & "]")
        Next i

        ' Close the file.
        FileClose(file_num)
    End Sub
End Class
```

First, the code defines a structure named Employee to hold the data in a record. Notice how the code uses the VBFixedString attribute to flag the strings as fixed length. The structure must have a fixed length if you want to jump randomly through the file because Visual Basic calculates a record's position by multiplying a record's size by its index in the file. If records contained strings of unknown length, the calculation wouldn't work.

When the user clicks the Make Records button, the btnMakeRecords_Click event handler executes. This code declares a variable of the record type, Employee. It uses the FreeFile method to get an available file number and uses FileOpen to open the file for random access. The final parameter to FileOpen is the length of the file's records. To calculate this length, the program uses the Len function, passing it the Employee instance emp.

Next, the program uses the FilePut method to write six records into the file. It passes FilePut the file number and a new Employee structure. The structure's constructor makes initializing the new records easy.

The program then uses FileGet to retrieve the six records using their indexes as keys, fetching them out of numeric order to demonstrate random access. It then displays each record's data in the Output window surrounded by brackets so you can see where the data starts and ends.

There are two key points to notice here. First, the file numbers records starting with 1 not 0, so the first record in the file has index 1.

Second, the FileGet method does not have an overloaded version that takes an Employee structure as a parameter. Because this example has Option Strict set to On, the code must pass FileGet a ValueType variable and then convert it into an Employee.

If you set Option Strict to Off, you can pass an Employee variable directly into FileGet.

After it has read and displayed the records, the program uses FileClose to close the file.

The following text shows the result. Notice that the first and last names are padded with spaces to 15 characters, the length of the Employee structure's fixed-length strings. The last names are also padded to 15 characters.

```
[3: Cindy          Chicago         ]
[1: Alice          Altanta         ]
[5: Erma           Eagle           ]
[2: Bob            Bakersfield     ]
[6: Fred           Frisco          ]
```

Binary-File Access

Binary access is similar to random access, except that it does not require its data to fit into neat records. You get control over pretty much every byte in the file, and you can jump to an arbitrary byte number in the file. If the items in the file are not fixed-length records, however, you cannot jump to a particular record because you cannot calculate where that record would begin.

.NET FRAMEWORK CLASSES

The System.IO namespace provides several classes for working with the filesystem. The Directory and File classes provide shared methods that you can use to manipulate the filesystem without creating instances of helper objects.

The DirectoryInfo and FileInfo classes let you work with specific relevant filesystem objects. For example, a FileInfo object represents a particular file and provides methods to create, rename, delete, and get information about that file.

The following sections describe these and the other classes that the Framework provides to help you work with the filesystem.

Directory

The Directory class provides shared methods for working with directories. These methods let you create, rename, move, and delete directories. They let you enumerate the files and subdirectories within a directory, and get and set directory information such as the directory's creation and last access time.

The following table describes the Directory class's shared methods:

METHOD	PURPOSE
CreateDirectory	Creates a directory and any missing ancestors (parent, grandparent, and so on).
Delete	Deletes a directory and its contents. It can delete all subdirectories, their subdirectories, and so forth to remove the entire directory tree.
Exists	Returns True if a path points to an existing directory.

METHOD	PURPOSE
GetCreationTime	Returns a directory's creation date and time.
GetCreationTimeUtc	Returns a directory's creation date and time in Coordinated Universal Time (UTC).
GetCurrentDirectory	Returns the application's current working directory.
GetDirectories	Returns an array of strings holding the fully qualified names of a directory's subdirectories.
GetDirectoryRoot	Returns the directory root for a path (the path need not exist). For example, `C:\`.
GetFiles	Returns an array of strings holding the fully qualified names of a directory's files.
GetFileSystemEntries	Returns an array of strings holding the fully qualified names of a directory's files and subdirectories.
GetLastAccessTime	Returns a directory's last access date and time.
GetLastAccessTimeUtc	Returns a directory's last access date and time in UTC.
GetLastWriteTime	Returns the date and time when a directory was last modified.
GetLastWriteTimeUtc	Returns the date and time in UTC when a directory was last modified.
GetLogicalDrives	Returns an array of strings listing the system's logical drives as in `A:\`. The list only includes drives that are attached. For example, it lists an empty floppy drive and a connected flash disk but doesn't list a flash disk after you disconnect it.
GetParent	Returns a DirectoryInfo object representing a directory's parent.
Move	Moves a directory and its contents to a new location on the same disk volume.
SetCreationTime	Sets a directory's creation date and time.
SetCreationTimeUtc	Sets a directory's creation date and time in UTC.
SetCurrentDirectory	Sets the application's current working directory.
SetLastAccessTime	Sets a directory's last access date and time.
SetLastAccessTimeUtc	Sets a directory's last access date and time in UTC.
SetLastWriteTime	Sets a directory's last write date and time.
SetLastWriteTimeUtc	Sets a directory's last write date and time in UTC.

File

The File class provides shared methods for working with files. These methods let you create, rename, move, and delete files. They also make working with file streams a bit easier.

The following table describes the File class's most useful shared methods:

METHOD	PURPOSE
AppendAll	Adds text to the end of a file, creating it if it doesn't exist, and then closes the file.
AppendText	Opens a file for appending UTF-8 encoded text and returns a StreamWriter class attached to it.
Copy	Copies a file.
Create	Creates a new file and returns a FileStream attached to it.
CreateText	Creates or opens a file for writing UTF-8 encoded text and returns a StreamWriter class attached to it.
Delete	Permanently deletes a file.
Exists	Returns True if the specified file exists.
GetAttributes	Gets a file's attributes. This is a combination of flags defined by the FileAttributes enumeration: Archive, Compressed, Device, Directory, Encrypted, Hidden, Normal, NotContextIndexed, Offline, ReadOnly, ReparsePoint, SparseFile, System, and Temporary.
GetCreationTime	Returns a file's creation date and time.
GetCreationTimeUtc	Returns a file's creation date and time in UTC.
GetLastAccessTime	Returns a file's last access date and time.
GetLastAccessTimeUtc	Returns a file's last access date and time in UTC.
GetLastWriteTime	Returns a file's last write date and time.
GetLastWriteTimeUtc	Returns a file's last write date and time in UTC.
Move	Moves a file to a new location.
Open	Opens a file and returns a FileStream attached to it. Parameters let you specify the mode (Append, Create, CreateNew, Open, OpenOrCreate, or Truncate), access (Read, Write, or ReadWrite), and sharing (Read, Write, ReadWrite, or None) settings.
OpenRead	Opens a file for reading and returns a FileStream attached to it.

METHOD	PURPOSE
OpenText	Opens a UTF-8-encoded text file for reading and returns a StreamReader attached to it.
OpenWrite	Opens a file for writing and returns a FileStream attached to it.
ReadAllBytes	Returns a file's contents in an array of bytes.
ReadAllLines	Returns a file's lines in an array of strings.
ReadAllText	Returns a file's contents in a string.
Replace	Takes three file paths as parameters, representing a source file, a destination file, and a backup file. If the backup file exists, this method permanently deletes it. It then moves the destination file to the backup file, and moves the source file to the destination file.
SetAttributes	Sets a file's attributes. This is a combination of flags defined by the FileAttributes enumeration: Archive, Compressed, Device, Directory, Encrypted, Hidden, Normal, NotContextIndexed, Offline, ReadOnly, ReparsePoint, SparseFile, System, and Temporary.
SetCreationTime	Sets a file's creation date and time.
SetCreationTimeUtc	Sets a file's creation date and time in UTC.
SetLastAccessTime	Sets a file's last access date and time.
SetLastAccessTimeUtc	Sets a file's last access date and time in UTC.
SetLastWriteTime	Sets a file's last write date and time.
SetLastWriteTimeUtc	Sets a file's last write date and time in UTC.
WriteAllBytes	Creates or replaces a file, writes an array of bytes into it, and closes the file.
WriteAllLines	Creates or replaces a file, writes an array of strings into it, and closes the file.
WriteAllText	Creates or replaces a file, writes a string into it, and closes the file.

DriveInfo

A DriveInfo object represents one of the computer's drives. The following table describes the properties provided by this class. Note that some of these properties are available only when the drive is ready, as indicated in the Must Be Ready column. If you try to access them when the drive is not ready, Visual Basic throws an exception. The program should check the IsReady property to determine whether the drive is ready before trying to use the AvailableFreeSpace, DriveFormat, TotalFreeSpace, or VolumeLabel properties.

DRIVEINFO PROPERTY	PURPOSE	MUST BE READY
AvailableFreeSpace	Returns the amount of free space available on the drive in bytes.	True
DriveFormat	Returns the name of the filesystem type such as NTFS (NT File System) or FAT32 (32-bit File Allocation Table). (For a comparison of these, see `http://www.ntfs.com/ntfs_vs_fat.htm`.)	True
DriveType	Returns a DriveType enumeration value indicating the drive type. This value can be CDRom, Fixed, Network, NoRootDirectory, Ram, Removable, or Unknown.	False
IsReady	Returns True if the drive is ready. Many DriveInfo properties are unavailable and raise exceptions if you try to access them while the drive is not ready.	False
Name	Return's the drive's name. This is the drive's root name (as in `A:\` or `C:\`).	False
RootDirectory	Returns a DirectoryInfo object representing the drive's root directory. See the following section "DirectoryInfo" for more information on this class.	False
TotalFreeSpace	Returns the total amount of free space on the drive in bytes.	True
VolumeLabel	Gets or sets the drive's volume label.	True

The DriveInfo class also has a public shared method GetDrives that returns an array of DriveInfo objects describing the system's drives.

DirectoryInfo

A DirectoryInfo object represents a directory. You can use its properties and methods to create and delete directories and to move through a directory hierarchy.

The following table describes the most useful public properties and methods provided by the DirectoryInfo class:

PROPERTY OR METHOD	PURPOSE
Attributes	Gets or sets flags for the directory from the FileAttributes enumeration: Archive, Compressed, Device, Directory, Encrypted, Hidden, Normal, NotContentIndexed, Offline, ReadOnly, ReparsePoint, SparseFile, System, and Temporary.
Create	Creates the directory. You can create a DirectoryInfo object, passing its constructor the fully qualified name of a directory that doesn't exist, and then call the object's Create method to create the directory.
CreateSubdirectory	Creates a subdirectory within the directory and returns a DirectoryInfo object representing it. The subdirectory's path must be relative to the DirectoryInfo object's directory, but can contain intermediate subdirectories. For example, the following code creates the Tools subdirectory and the Bin directory inside that: `dir_info.CreateSubdirectory("Tools\Bin")`.
CreationTime	Gets or sets the directory's creation time.
CreationTimeUtc	Gets or sets the directory's creation time in UTC.
Delete	Deletes the directory if it is empty. A parameter lets you tell the object to delete its contents, too, if it isn't empty.
Exists	Returns True if the directory exists.
Extension	Returns the extension part of the directory's name. Normally, this is an empty string for directories.
FullName	Returns the directory's fully qualified path.
GetDirectories	Returns an array of DirectoryInfo objects representing the directory's subdirectories. An optional parameter gives a pattern to match. This method does not recursively search the subdirectories.
GetFiles	Returns an array of FileInfo objects representing files inside the directory. An optional parameter gives a pattern to match. This method does not recursively search subdirectories.
GetFileSystemInfos	Returns a strongly typed array of FileSystemInfo objects, representing subdirectories and files inside the directory. The items in the array are DirectoryInfo and FileInfo objects, both of which inherit from FileSystemInfo. An optional parameter gives a pattern to match. This method does not recursively search subdirectories.
LastAccessTime	Gets or sets the directory's last access time.
LastAccessTimeUtc	Gets or sets the directory's last access time in UTC.
LastWriteTime	Gets or sets the directory's last write time.

continues

(continued)

PROPERTY OR METHOD	PURPOSE
LastWriteTimeUtc	Gets or sets directory's last write time in UTC.
MoveTo	Moves the directory and its contents to a new path.
Name	The directory's name without the path information.
Parent	Returns a DirectoryInfo object, representing the directory's parent. If the directory is its filesystem's root (for example, C:\), this returns Nothing.
Refresh	Refreshes the DirectoryInfo object's data. For example, if the directory has been accessed since the object was created, you must call Refresh to load the new LastAccessTime value.
Root	Returns a DirectoryInfo object representing the root of the directory's filesystem.
ToString	Returns the directory's fully qualified path and name.

FileInfo

A FileInfo object represents a file. You can use its properties and methods to create and delete files.

The following table describes the most useful public properties and methods provided by the FileInfo class:

PROPERTY OR METHOD	PURPOSE
AppendText	Returns a StreamWriter that appends text to the file.
Attributes	Gets or sets flags for the file from the FileAttributes enumeration: Archive, Compressed, Device, Directory, Encrypted, Hidden, Normal, NotContentIndexed, Offline, ReadOnly, ReparsePoint, SparseFile, System, and Temporary.
CopyTo	Copies the file and returns a FileInfo object, representing the new file. A parameter lets you indicate whether the copy should overwrite an existing file. If the destination path is relative, it is relative to the application's current directory, not to the FileInfo object's directory.
Create	Creates the file and returns a FileStream object attached to it. For example, you can create a FileInfo object, passing its constructor the name of a file that doesn't exist, and then call the Create method to create the file.

PROPERTY OR METHOD	PURPOSE
CreateText	Creates the file and returns a StreamWriter attached to it. For example, you can create a FileInfo object passing its constructor the name of a file that doesn't exist, and then call the CreateText method to create the file.
CreationTime	Gets or sets the file's creation time.
CreationTimeUtc	Gets or sets the file's creation time in UTC.
Delete	Deletes the file.
Directory	Returns a DirectoryInfo object representing the file's directory.
DirectoryName	Returns the name of the file's directory.
Exists	Returns True if the file exists.
Extension	Returns the extension part of the file's name, including the period. For example, the extension for game.txt is .txt.
FullName	Returns the file's fully qualified path and name.
IsReadOnly	Returns True if the file is marked read-only.
LastAccessTime	Gets or sets the file's last access time.
LastAccessTimeUtc	Gets or sets the file's last access time in UTC.
LastWriteTime	Gets or sets the file's last write time.
LastWriteTimeUtc	Gets or sets the file's last write time in UTC.
Length	Returns the number of bytes in the file.
MoveTo	Moves the file to a new location. If the destination uses a relative path, it is relative to the application's current directory, not to the FileInfo object's directory. When this method finishes, the FileInfo object is updated to refer to the file's new location.
Name	The file's name without the path information.
Open	Opens the file with various mode (Append, Create, CreateNew, Open, OpenOrCreate, or Truncate), access (Read, Write, or ReadWrite), and sharing (Read, Write, ReadWrite, or None) settings. This method returns a FileStream object attached to the file.
OpenRead	Returns a read-only FileStream attached to the file.
OpenText	Returns a StreamReader with UTF-8 encoding attached to the file for reading.
OpenWrite	Returns a write-only FileStream attached to the file.

continues

(continued)

PROPERTY OR METHOD	PURPOSE
Refresh	Refreshes the FileInfo object's data. For example, if the file has been accessed since the object was created, you must call Refresh to load the new LastAccessTime value.
Replace	Replaces a target file with this one, renaming the old target as a backup copy. If the backup file already exists, it is deleted and replaced with the target.
ToString	Returns the file's fully qualified name.

FileSystemWatcher

The FileSystemWatcher class keeps an eye on part of the filesystem and raises events to let your program know if something changes. For example, you could make a FileSystemWatcher monitor a work directory. When a new file with a .job extension arrives, the watcher could raise an event and your application could process the file.

The FileSystemWatcher class's constructor takes parameters that tell it which directory to watch and that give it a filter for selecting files to watch. For example, the filter might be "*.txt" to watch for changes to text files. The default filter is "*.*", which catches changes to all files that have an extension. Set the filter to the empty string "" to catch changes to all files including those without extensions.

The following table describes the FileSystemWatcher class's most useful properties:

PROPERTY	PURPOSE
EnableRaisingEvents	Determines whether the component is enabled. Note that this property is False by default, so the watcher will not raise any events until you set it to True.
Filter	Determines the files for which the watcher reports events. You cannot watch for multiple file types as in *.txt and *.dat. Instead use multiple FileSystemWatcher objects. If you like, you can use AddHandler to make all of the FileSystemWatcher classes use the same event handlers.
IncludeSubdirectories	Determines whether the object watches subdirectories within the main path.
InternalBufferSize	Determines the size of the internal buffer. If the watcher is monitoring a very active directory, a small buffer may overflow.
NotifyFilter	Determines the types of changes that the watcher reports. This is a combination of values defined by the NotifyFilters enumeration and can include the values Attributes, CreationTime, DirectoryName, FileName, LastAccess, LastWrite, Security, and Size.
Path	Determines the path to watch.

The FileSystemWatcher class provides only two really useful methods. The first method, Dispose, releases resources used by the component. When you are finished using a watcher, call its Dispose method to allow garbage collection to reclaim its resources more efficiently.

The second method, WaitForChanged, waits for a change synchronously (with an optional timeout). When a change occurs, the method returns a WaitForChangedResult object, giving information about the change that occurred.

When the FileSystemWatcher detects a change asynchronously, it raises an event to let the program know what has happened. The following table describes the class's events:

NAME	DESCRIPTION
Changed	A file or subdirectory has changed.
Created	A file or subdirectory was created.
Deleted	A file or subdirectory was deleted.
Error	The watcher's internal buffer overflowed.
Renamed	A file or subdirectory was renamed.

The following simple example shows how to use a FileSystemWatcher to look for new files in a directory:

```
Private WithEvents JobFileWatcher As FileSystemWatcher

Private Sub Form1_Load() Handles MyBase.Load
    Dim watch_path As String =
        FileSystem.GetParentPath(Application.StartupPath)
    JobFileWatcher = New FileSystemWatcher(watch_path, "*.job")
    JobFileWatcher.NotifyFilter = NotifyFilters.FileName
    JobFileWatcher.EnableRaisingEvents = True
End Sub

Private Sub JobFileWatcher_Created(sender As Object,
 e As FileSystemEventArgs) Handles JobFileWatcher.Created
    ' Process the new file.
    MessageBox.Show("Process new job: " & e.FullPath)

    File.Delete(e.FullPath)
End Sub
```

The program uses the WithEvents keyword to declare a FileSystemWatcher object. When the program's main form loads, the Form1_Load event handler allocates this object. Its constructor sets the object's path to the program's startup directory's parent. It sets the object's filter to "*.job" so that the object will watch for changes to files that end with a .job extension.

The event handler sets the watcher's NotifyFilter to FileName, so it will raise its Created event if a new filename appears in the target directory. Unfortunately, the NotifyFilter values (Attributes, CreationTime, DirectoryName, FileName, LastAccess, LastWrite, Security, and Size) do not match up well with the events provided by the FileSystemWatcher, so you need to figure out which NotifyFilter values to set to raise different kinds of events.

The Form1_Load event handler finishes by setting the watcher's EnableRaisingEvents property to True so the object starts watching.

When a `.job` file is created in the watcher's target directory, the program's fswJobFiles_Created executes. The program processes and then deletes the file. In this example, the program processes the file by displaying a message giving its fully qualified name. A more realistic example might read the file; parse fields, indicating the type of job this is; assign it to an employee for handling; and then e-mail it to that employee.

The UseFileSystemWatcher example program, which is available for download on the book's website, uses similar code without the filter to look for any new file in the program's startup directory.

Path

The Path class provides shared properties and methods that you can use to manipulate paths. Its methods return the path's filename, extension, directory name, and so forth. Other methods provide values that relate to system-generated paths. For example, they can give you the system's temporary directory path, or the name of a temporary file.

The following table describes the Path class's most useful public properties.

PROPERTY	PURPOSE
AltDirectorySeparatorChar	Returns the alternate character used to separate directory levels in a hierarchical path. Typically this is /.
DirectorySeparatorChar	Returns the character used to separate directory levels in a hierarchical path. Typically this is \ (as in `C:\Tests\Billing\2008q2.dat`).
InvalidPathChars	Returns a character array that holds characters that are not allowed in a path string. Typically, this array includes characters such as ", <, >, and |, as well as nonprintable characters such as those with ASCII values between 0 and 31.
PathSeparator	Returns the character used to separate path strings in environment variables. Typically this is a semicolon (;).
VolumeSeparatorChar	Returns the character placed between a volume letter and the rest of the path. Typically this is a colon (:).

The following table describes the Path class's most useful methods.

METHOD	PURPOSE
ChangeExtension	Changes a path's extension.
Combine	Returns two path strings concatenated.
GetDirectoryName	Returns a path's directory.
GetExtension	Returns a path's extension.
GetFileName	Returns a path's filename and extension.
GetFileNameWithoutExtension	Returns a path's filename without the extension.

GetFullPath	Returns a path's fully qualified value. This can be particularly useful for converting a partially relative path into an absolute path. For example, this statement:
	
	`Path.GetFullPath("C:\Tests\OldTests\`
	`Software\..\..\New\Code")`
	
	returns this result:
	
	`"C:\Tests\New\Code"`

GetInvalidFileNameChars	Returns an array listing characters that are invalid in filenames.
GetInvalidPathChars	Returns an array listing characters that are invalid in file paths.
GetPathRoot	Returns a path's root directory string.
GetRandomFileName	Returns a random filename.
GetTempFileName	Creates a uniquely named, empty temporary file and returns its fully qualified path. Your program can open that file for scratch space, do whatever it needs to do, close the file, and then delete it. A typical filename might be `C:\Documents and Settings\Rod\Local Settings\Temp\tmp19D.tmp`.
GetTempPath	Returns the path to the system's temporary folder. This is the path part of the filenames returned by GetTempFileName.
HasExtension	Returns True if a path includes an extension.
IsPathRooted	Returns True if a path is an absolute path. This includes `\Temp\Wherever` and `C:\Clients\Litigation`, but not `Temp\Wherever` or `.\Uncle`.

MY.COMPUTER.FILESYSTEM

The My.Computer.FileSystem object provides tools for working with drives, directories, and files. The following table summarizes this object's properties.

PROPERTY	DESCRIPTION
CurrentDirectory	Gets or sets the fully qualified path to the application's current directory.
Drives	Returns a read-only collection of DriveInfo objects describing the system's drives.
SpecialDirectories	Returns a SpecialDirectoriesProxy object that has properties giving the locations of various special directories (such as the system's temporary directory and the user's MyDocuments directory). See the following section "My.Computer.FileSystem.SpecialDirectories" for more information.

The following list describes the My.Computer.FileSystem object's methods:

METHOD	PURPOSE
CombinePath	Combines a base path with a relative path reference and returns a properly formatted fully qualified path. For example, the following code displays the name of the directory that is the parent of the application's current directory: `MessageBox.Show(My.Computer.FileSystem.CombinePath (My.Computer.FileSystem.CurrentDirectory(), "..")`.
CopyDirectory	Copies a directory. Parameters indicate whether to overwrite existing files, whether to display a progress indicator, and what to do if the user presses Cancel during the operation.
CopyFile	Copies a file. Parameters indicate whether to overwrite existing files, whether to display a progress indicator, and what to do if the user presses Cancel during the operation.
CreateDirectory	Creates a directory. This method will create ancestor directories if necessary.
DeleteDirectory	Deletes a directory. Parameters indicate whether to recursively delete subdirectories, prompt the user for confirmation, or move the directory into the Recycle Bin.
DeleteFile	Deletes a file. Parameters indicate whether to prompt the user for confirmation or move the file into the Recycle Bin, and what to do if the user presses Cancel while the deletion is in progress.
DirectoryExists	Returns True if a specified directory exists.

METHOD	PURPOSE
FileExists	Returns True if a specified file exists.
FindInFiles	Returns a read-only collection of strings listing files that contain a target string.
GetDirectories	Returns a string collection listing subdirectories of a given directory. Parameters tell whether to recursively search the subdirectories, and the wildcards to match.
GetDirectoryInfo	Returns a DirectoryInfo object for a directory.
GetDriveInfo	Returns a DriveInfo object for a drive.
GetFileInfo	Returns a FileInfo object for a file.
GetFiles	Returns a string collection holding the names of files within a directory. Parameters indicate whether the search should recursively search subdirectories, and give wildcards to match.
GetParentPath	Returns the fully qualified path of a path's parent. For example, this returns a file's or directory's parent directory.
MoveDirectory	Moves a directory. Parameters indicate whether to overwrite files that have the same name in the destination directory and whether to prompt the user when such a collision occurs.
MoveFile	Moves a file. Parameters indicate whether to overwrite a file that has the same name as the file's destination and whether to prompt the user when such a collision occurs.
OpenTextFieldParser	Opens a TextFieldParser object attached to a delimited or fixed-field file such as a log file. You can use the object to parse the file.
OpenTextFileReader	Opens a StreamReader object attached to a file. You can use the object to read the file.
OpenTextFileWriter	Opens a StreamWriter object attached to a file. You can use the object to write into the file.
ReadAllBytes	Reads all of the bytes from a binary file into an array.
ReadAllText	Reads all of the text from a text file into a string.
RenameDirectory	Renames a directory within its parent directory.
RenameFile	Renames a file within its directory.
WriteAllBytes	Writes an array of bytes into a binary file. A parameter tells whether to append the data or rewrite the file.
WriteAllText	Writes a string into a text file. A parameter tells whether to append the string or rewrite the file.

MY.COMPUTER.FILESYSTEM.SPECIALDIRECTORIES

The My.Computer.FileSystem.SpecialDirectories property returns an object that has properties giving the locations of various special directories such as the system's temporary directory and the user's MyDocuments directory.

The following table describes these special directory properties.

PROPERTY	PURPOSE
AllUsersApplicationData	Application settings for all users
CurrentUserApplicationData	Application settings for the current user
Desktop	The current user's desktop directory
MyDocuments	The current user's MyDocuments directory
MyMusic	The current user's MyMusic directory
MyPictures	The current user's MyPictures directory
Programs	The current user's Programs directory
ProgramFiles	The current user's Program Files directory
Temp	The current user's temporary directory

DIRECTORY DEFICIENCIES

Note that these directories may not all exist on a particular system. For example, a system may not define the MyMusic or MyPictures directories. Trying to access the value of a missing directory causes a DirectoryNotFoundException. You can use a Try Catch block to protect the program from the exception.

SUMMARY

Visual Basic provides a native set of methods for reading and writing files, including FreeFile, FileOpen, Input, LineInput, Print, Write, and FileClose. It also provides methods for working with the filesystem (such as ChDir, MkDir, Kill, and RmDir). If you have a lot of previous experience with Visual Basic, you may prefer these familiar methods.

The System.IO namespace offers many objects that provide even more powerful capabilities than the native Visual Basic methods. Classes such as Directory, DirectoryInfo, File, and FileInfo make it easy to create, examine, move, rename, and delete directories and files. The File class's methods make it particularly easy to read or write an entire file and to create streams attached to files for reading or writing.

The FileSystemWatcher class lets an application keep an eye on a file or directory and take action when it is changed. For example, a program can watch a spooling directory and take action when a new file appears in it.

The Path class provides miscellaneous support for working with paths. For example, it provides methods for examining a path's filename or extension, and for combining paths.

The My.Computer.FileSystem namespace provides shortcuts to some of the more useful of the methods offered by the other filesystem classes. Its methods let you create, examine, and delete files and directories. The SpecialDirectories object also provides information about the locations of system directories.

There is considerable overlap among all of these tools, so you don't need to feel that you have to use them all. Take a good look so you know what's there, and then pick the tools that you find the most comfortable.

The chapters in this book cover a wide variety of Visual Basic programming topics. In the first part of the book, Chapters 1 through 6 described the Visual Studio integrated development environment and many of the tools that you use to build Visual Basic programs. In the second part of the book, Chapters 7 through 21 explained basic topics of Visual Basic programming (such as the language itself, using standard controls, and drag and drop). In the third part of the book, Chapters 22 through 26 described object-oriented concepts (such as class and structure declaration, namespaces, and generics). In the fourth part of the book, Chapters 27 through 30 explained the ways a program can interact with its environment by printing and using techniques such as configuration files, the registry, streams, and filesystem objects.

The rest of this book contains appendices that provide a categorized reference for Visual Basic .NET. You can use them to quickly review the syntax of a particular command, select from among several overloaded versions of a routine, or refresh your memory about what a particular class can do.

PART V
Appendices

A

Useful Control Properties, Methods, and Events

A control interacts with a program or user through properties, methods, and events. Although each type of control provides different features, they are all derived from the Control class. This class provides many useful properties, methods, and events that other controls inherit if those other controls don't take special action to override them. The following sections describe some of the most useful of these inherited features.

CLASSY CONTROLS

You can learn more about the Control class at `http://msdn.microsoft.com/system.windows.forms.control.aspx`.

PROPERTIES

The following table lists properties implemented by the Control class. All controls that inherit from this class inherit these properties unless those other controls override the Control class's behavior.

PROPERTY	PURPOSE
BackColor	The control's background color.
BackgroundImage	The control's background image.
BackgroundImageLayout	Determines how the control's background image is used to fill the control. This can be Center, None, Stretch, Tile, or Zoom.

continues

(continued)

PROPERTY	PURPOSE
Bottom	The distance between the top edge of the control's container and the bottom edge of the control in pixels. This is read-only. Modify the Top and Height properties to change this value.
Bounds	Determines the control's size and location, including nonclient areas.
Capture	Determines whether the control has captured the mouse.
CausesValidation	Determines whether the control makes other controls validate when it receives the focus.
ClientRectangle	Represents the control's client area.
ClientSize	Holds the control's height and width.
ContainsFocus	Indicates whether the control or one of its child controls has the input focus. This is read-only.
ContextMenuStrip	The context menu strip associated with the control.
Controls	Collection containing references to the controls contained within this control.
Cursor	The cursor that the control displays when the mouse is over it.
DataBindings	The control's DataBindings, used to bind the control to a data source.
DisplayRectangle	A Rectangle giving the control's display area. Figure A-1 shows two GroupBoxes with the same size. The GroupBox on the right contains two labels that cover its ClientRectangle and DisplayRectangle.
Dock	Determines the edge of the control's parent to which the control is docked. This can be Left, Right, Top, Bottom, Fill, or None.
Enabled	Determines whether the control will interact with the user.
Focused	Indicates whether the control has the input focus. This is read-only.
Font	The control's font.
ForeColor	The control's foreground color.
Handle	The control's window handle. This is read-only.
HasChildren	Indicates whether the control holds any child controls. This is read-only. Also see the Controls property.
Height	The control's height in pixels.

PROPERTY	PURPOSE
InvokeRequired	Returns True if the calling code is running on a thread different from the control's thread and therefore must use an invoke method to interact with the control. See also the Invoke method.
Left	The X coordinate of the control's left edge in pixels.
Location	The position of the control's upper-left corner.
Margin	Determines the spacing between this control and another control's margin within an arranging container.
MaximumSize	The control's largest allowed size.
MinimumSize	The control's smallest allowed size.
ModifierKeys	Indicates which modifier keys (Shift, Ctrl, and Alt) are pressed. This is read-only.
MouseButtons	Indicates which mouse buttons (Left, Right, Middle, None) are pressed. This is read-only.
MousePosition	The mouse's current position in screen coordinates (where the point (0, 0) is in the screen's upper-left corner). This is read-only.
Name	The control's name.
Padding	The spacing of the control's contents.
Parent	The parent containing the control.
PreferredSize	A size that is big enough to hold the control's contents.
Region	Determines the control's window region. This is the area in which the control may draw.
Right	The distance between the left edge of the control's container and the right edge of the control in pixels. This is read-only. Modify the Left and Width properties to change this value.
Size	The control's size including client and nonclient areas.
TabIndex	The control's position in its container's tab order. If more than one control has the same TabIndex, they are traversed front to back using the stacking order.
TabStop	Determines whether the user can tab to the control.
Tag	This property can hold any object that you want to associate with the control.

continues

(continued)

PROPERTY	PURPOSE
Text	The control's text.
Top	The Y coordinate of the control's top edge in pixels.
TopLevelControl	The control's top-level ancestor. Usually that is the outermost Form containing the control. This is read-only.
Visible	Determines whether the control is visible.
Width	The control's width in pixels.

METHODS

The following table lists useful methods implemented by the Control class. All controls that inherit from this class inherit these methods unless they override the Control class's behavior.

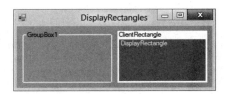

FIGURE A-1: The DisplayRectangle property gives the area in which you should normally place items within a control.

METHOD	PURPOSE
Sub BringToFront()	Brings the control to the front of the stacking order.
Function Contains(ByVal target As Control) As Boolean	Returns True if target is contained by this control.
Function CreateGraphics() As Graphic	Creates a Graphics object that you can use to draw on the control's surface.
Sub DrawToBitmap(ByVal bm As Bitmap, ByVal rect As Rectangle)	Draws an image of the control including contained controls onto the Bitmap in the indicated Rectangle.
Function Focus() As Boolean	Gives the control the input focus.

METHOD	PURPOSE
Function GetChildAtPoint (ByVal pt As Point) As Control	Returns the control's child that contains the indicated point. If more than one control contains the point, the method returns the control that is higher in the stacking order.
Function GetPreferredSize (ByVal proposed_size) As Size	Returns a size that is big enough to hold the control's contents.
Function GetType() As Type	Returns a Type object representing the control's class. You can use this object to get information about the class.
Sub Invalidate()	Invalidates some or all of the control and sends it a Paint event so that it redraws itself.
Sub Invoke(ByVal delegate As Delegate)	Invokes a delegate on the thread that owns the control.
Function PointToClient (ByVal screen_point Point) As Point	Converts a Point in screen coordinates into the control's coordinate system.
Function PointToScreen (ByVal control_point As Point) As Point	Converts a Point in control coordinates into the screen coordinate system.
Function RectangleToClient (ByVal screen_rect As Rectangle) As Rectangle	Converts a Rectangle in screen coordinates into the control's coordinate system.
Function RectangleToScreen (ByVal control_rect As Rectangle) As Rectangle	Converts a Rectangle in control coordinates into the screen coordinate system.
Sub Refresh()	Invalidates the control's client area, so the control redraws itself and its child controls.
Sub Scale(ByVal scale_factor As Single)	Scales the control and any contained controls by multiplying the Left, Top, Width, and Height properties by scale_factor.
Sub Select()	Moves the input focus to the control. Some controls have overloaded versions.

continues

(continued)

METHOD	PURPOSE
Function SelectNextControl (ByVal ctl As Control, ByVal forward As Boolean, ByVal tab_stop_only As Boolean, ByVal include_nested As Boolean, ByVal wrap As Boolean) As Boolean	Moves the input focus to the next control contained within this one.
Sub SendToBack()	Sends the control to the back of the stacking order.
Sub SetBounds(ByVal x As Integer, ByVal y As Integer, ByVal width As Integer, ByVal height As Integer)	Sets the control's position and size.
Sub Show()	Displays the control by setting its Visible property to True.
Function ToString() As String	Returns a textual representation of the control. This is generally the type of the control followed by its most commonly used property.
Sub Update()	Makes the control redraw any invalidated areas.

EVENTS

The following table lists useful events implemented by the Control class. All controls that inherit from this class inherit these events unless they override the Control class's behavior.

EVENT	PURPOSE
Click	Occurs when the user clicks the control. This event is at a higher logical level than the MouseClick event, and it can be triggered by actions other than a mouse click (such as pressing the Enter key or a shortcut key).
ControlAdded	Occurs when a new control is added to the control's contained child controls.
ControlRemoved	Occurs when a control is removed from the control's contained child controls.

EVENT	PURPOSE
DoubleClick	Occurs when the user double-clicks the control.
Enter	Occurs when the control is entered. This event fires before the GotFocus event.
GotFocus	Occurs when the control receives the input focus. This event fires after the Enter event. Generally, the Enter event is preferred.
HelpRequested	Occurs when the user requests help for the control. For example, if the user moves the focus to a TextBox and presses F1, the TextBox raises this event.
Invalidated	Occurs when part of the control is invalidated.
KeyDown	Occurs when the user presses a key while the control has the input focus.
KeyPress	Occurs when the user presses and releases a key while the control has the input focus.
KeyUp	Occurs when the user releases a key while the control has the input focus.
Leave	Occurs when the input focus leaves the control. This event fires before the LostFocus event.
LostFocus	Occurs when the input focus leaves the control. This event fires after the Leave event. Generally, the Leave event is preferred.
MouseClick	Occurs when the user clicks the mouse on the control.
MouseDoubleClick	Occurs when the user double-clicks the mouse on the control.
MouseDown	Occurs when the user presses a mouse button down over the control.
MouseEnter	Occurs when the mouse enters the control.
MouseHover	Occurs when the mouse hovers over the control.
MouseLeave	Occurs when the mouse leaves the control.
MouseMove	Occurs when the mouse moves over the control.
MouseUp	Occurs when the user releases a mouse button over the control.
MouseWheel	Occurs when the user moves the mouse wheel while the control has the input focus.
Move	Occurs when the control is moved. This event fires before the LocationChanged event fires.

continues

(continued)

EVENT	PURPOSE
Paint	Occurs when the control must redraw itself. Normally the program draws on the control during this event (if it draws on the control at all).
Resize	Occurs while the control is resizing. This event occurs after the Layout event but before the SizeChanged event.
SizeChanged	Occurs while the control is resizing. This event occurs after the Layout and Move events.
TextChanged	Occurs when the control's Text property changes.
Validated	Occurs when the control has successfully finished validating its data.
Validating	Occurs when the control should validate its data.

Variable Declarations and Data Types

This appendix provides information about variable declarations and data types.

VARIABLE DECLARATIONS

The following code shows a standard variable declaration:

```
[attribute_list] [accessibility] [Shared] [Shadows] [ReadOnly] _
Dim [WithEvents] name[?] [(bounds_list)] [As [New] type[?]] _
[= initialization_expression]
```

The following list describes the pieces of this declaration:

➤ attribute_list — Comma-separated list of attributes specific to a particular task. For example, <XmlAttributeAttribute(AttributeName:="Cost")>.

➤ accessibility — Public, Protected, Friend, Protected Friend, Private, or Static.

➤ Shared — Means that all instances of the class or structure containing the variable share the same variable.

➤ Shadows — Indicates that the variable hides a variable with the same name in a base class.

➤ ReadOnly — Indicates that the program can read, but not modify, the variable's value. You can set the value in an initialization statement or in an object constructor.

➤ Dim — Officially tells Visual Basic that you want to create a variable. You can omit the Dim keyword if you specify Public, Protected, Friend, Protected Friend, Private, Static, or ReadOnly.

➤ `WithEvents` — Tells Visual Basic that the variable is of a specific object type that can raise events that you may want to catch.

➤ `name` — Gives the name of the variable.

➤ `?` — Indicates this should be a nullable variable. For more information, see the section "Nullable Types" in Chapter 14, "Data Types, Variables, and Constants."

➤ `bounds_list` — Bounds for an array.

➤ `New` — Use New to make a new instance of an object variable. Include parameters for the class's constructor if appropriate.

➤ `type` — Variable's data type.

➤ `initialization_expression` — Expression that sets the initial value for the variable.

Visual Basic enables you to declare and initialize more than one variable in a single declaration statement, but this can make the code more difficult to read. To avoid possible later confusion, declare only variables of one type in a single statement.

INITIALIZATION EXPRESSIONS

Initialization expressions assign a value to a new variable. Simple expressions assign a literal value to a simple data type. The following example sets the value of a new string variable:

```
Dim txt As String = "Test"
```

The assignment expression can also initialize a variable to the result of a function or constructor, as in the following example:

```
Dim a_person As Person = New Person("Rod", "Stephens") ' Constructor.
Dim num_tools As Integer = CountTools()                ' Function.
```

An initialization expression for an object can use the With keyword to specify values for the object's public properties as in the following example, which sets the object's FirstName and LastName properties:

```
Dim emp As New Employee With {.FirstName = "Rod", .LastName = "Stephens"}
```

To initialize a one-dimensional array, put the array's values inside braces separated by commas as in the following code:

```
Dim fibonacci() As Integer = {1, 1, 2, 3, 5, 8, 13, 21, 34, 55, 89}
```

To initialize higher-dimensional arrays, place lower-dimensional array values inside braces and separate them with commas as in the following example, which initializes a two-dimensional array:

```
Dim int_values(,) As Integer =
{
    {1, 2, 3},
    {4, 5, 6}
}
```

Visual Basic's type inference system can guess the data type of an array from its initialization if Option Strict is Off. For example, in the following code, Visual Basic concludes that the array values hold Integers:

```
Dim values() = {1, 2, 3} ' Integer
```

If an array initializer holds values of more than one compatible data type, Visual Basic assumes the array holds the more general type. For example, the following array holds Doubles:

```
Dim values() = {1, 2, 3.4} ' Double
```

If an array holds values of multiple incompatible data types, Visual Basic makes the array hold Objects, as in the following example:

```
Dim values() = {1, 2.3, "three"} ' Object
```

WITH

When you create a new object variable, you can include a With clause to initialize the object's properties. The following code uses the Person class's parameterless constructor to make a new Person object. The With statement then sets values for the object's FirstName and LastName values.

```
Dim author As New Person() With {.FirstName = "Rod", .LastName = "Stephens"}
```

FROM

When you declare a collection, you can use the From keyword to initialize the collection. For example, the following code creates a collection of strings:

```
Dim fruits As New Collection() From {"Apple", "Banana", "Cherry"}
```

This works for any collection class that has an Add method.

If the collection's Add method takes more than one parameter, group parameters in brackets, as in the following example:

```
Dim fruits As New Dictionary(Of Integer, String)() From
    {{1, "Apple"}, {2, "Banana"}, {2, "Cherry"}}
```

If a class does not provide an Add method, you can create one with extension methods. For example, the following code creates Add methods for the Stack and Queue classes:

```
Module CollectionExtensions
    ' Add method for the Stack class.
    <Extension()>
    Public Sub Add(the_stack As Stack, value As Object)
        the_stack.Push(value)
    End Sub

    ' Add method for the Queue class.
    <Extension()>
    Public Sub Add(the_queue As Queue, value As Object)
        the_queue.Enqueue(value)
    End Sub
End Module
```

USING

To make it easy to call an object's Dispose method, you can declare a variable in a Using statement. When the code reaches the corresponding End Using statement, Visual Basic automatically calls the object's Dispose method.

You can only place Using statements inside code blocks, not at the module level, so the syntax is somewhat simpler than the syntax for declaring a variable in general. The following code shows the syntax for declaring a variable in a Using statement:

```
Using name [(bounds_list)] [As [New] type] [= initialization_expression]
    ...
End Using
```

The parts of this statement are described in the section "Variable Declarations" earlier in this appendix.

If it declares the variable, the Using statement must also initialize it either with the As New syntax or with an initialization expression.

ENUMERATED TYPE DECLARATIONS

The syntax for declaring an enumerated type is as follows:

```
[attribute_list] [accessibility] [Shadows] Enum name [As type]
    [attribute_list] value_name [= initialization_expression]
    [attribute_list] value_name [= initialization_expression]
    ...
End Enum
```

Most of these terms (including *attribute_list* and *accessibility*) are similar to those used by variable declarations. See the section "Variable Declarations" earlier in this appendix for more information.

XML VARIABLES

To initialize XML data, declare an XElement variable and set it equal to properly formatted XML code. For example, the following code declares a variable named *book_node* that contains XML data representing a book:

```
Dim book_node As XElement =
    <Book>
        <Title>The Bug That Was</Title>
        <Year>2012</Year>
        <Pages>376</Year>
    </Book>
```

OPTION EXPLICIT AND OPTION STRICT

When Option Explicit is on, you must explicitly declare all variables before using them. When Option Explicit is off, Visual Basic creates a variable the first time it is encountered if it has not yet been declared. To make your code easier to understand, and to avoid problems (such as Visual Basic creating a new variable because of a typographical error), you should always turn Option Explicit on.

When Option Strict is on, Visual Basic will not implicitly perform narrowing type conversions. For example, if you set an Integer variable equal to a String value, Visual Basic will raise an error because the String might not contain an Integer value. When Option Strict is off, Visual Basic will silently attempt narrowing conversions. It tries to convert the String value into an Integer and raises an error if the String doesn't contain an integral value. To avoid confusion and potentially slow conversions, always turn Option Strict on.

OPTION INFER

When Option Infer is on, Visual Basic can infer the data type of a variable from its initialization expression. For example, Visual Basic would infer that the variable *txt* in the following code has data type String:

```
Dim message = "Hello!"
```

Because inferred data types do not explicitly give the variable's data type, they can make the code harder to understand. To avoid confusion, leave Option Infer off unless you really need it.

For example, LINQ (Language Integrated Query) lets a program generate results that have an anonymous type. LINQ creates a data type to hold results but the type is not given a name for the program to use. Instead type inference allows the program to manipulate the results without ever referring to the type by name. In this case, Option Infer must be on. For more information on LINQ, see Chapter 20, "LINQ."

DATA TYPES

The following table summarizes the Visual Basic data types.

TYPE	SIZE	VALUES
Boolean	2 bytes	True or False
Byte	1 byte	0 to 255 (unsigned byte)
SByte	1 byte	−128 to 127 (signed byte)
Char	2 bytes	0 to 65,535 (unsigned character)
Short	2 bytes	−32,768 to 32,767
UShort	2 bytes	0 through 65,535 (unsigned short)
Integer	4 bytes	−2,147,483,648 to 2,147,483,647
UInteger	4 bytes	0 through 4,294,967,295 (unsigned integer)
Long	8 bytes	−9,223,372,036,854,775,808 to 9,223,372,036,854,775,807
ULong	8 bytes	0 through 18,446,744,073,709,551,615 (unsigned long)
Decimal	16 bytes	0 to +/−79,228,162,514,264,337,593,543,950,335 with no decimal point 0 to +/−7.9228162514264337593543950335 with 28 places
Single	4 bytes	−3.4028235E+38 to −1.401298E-45 (negative values) 1.401298E−45 to 3.4028235E+38 (positive values)
Double	8 bytes	−1.79769313486231570E+308 to −4.94065645841246544E−324 (negative values) 4.94065645841246544E−324 through 1.79769313486231570E+308 (positive values)
String	variable	Depending on the platform, approximately 0 to 2 billion Unicode characters
Date	8 bytes	January 1, 0001 0:0:00 to December 31, 9999 11:59:59 pm
Object	4 bytes	Points to any type of data
Structure	variable	Structure members have their own ranges

DATA TYPE CHARACTERS

The following table lists the Visual Basic data type characters.

CHARACTER	DATA TYPE
%	Integer
&	Long
@	Decimal
!	Single
#	Double
$	String

Using data type characters alone to determine a variable's data type can be confusing, so I recommend that you use an As clause instead. For example, the following code defines two integer variables and then uses them in nested loops. The declaration of *j* is more explicit and easier to understand.

```
Dim i%
Dim j As Integer

For i = 1 To 10
    For j = 1 To 10
        Debug.WriteLine(i * 100 + j)
    Next j
Next i
```

LITERAL TYPE CHARACTERS

The following table lists the Visual Basic literal type characters.

CHARACTER	DATA TYPE
S	Short
US	UShort
I	Integer
UI	UInteger

continues

(continued)

CHARACTER	DATA TYPE
L	Long
UL	ULong
D	Decimal
F	Single (F for "floating point")
R	Double (R for "real")
c	Char (note that this is a lowercase "c")

DATA TYPE CONVERSION FUNCTIONS

The following table lists the Visual Basic data type conversion functions.

FUNCTION	CONVERTS TO
CBool	Boolean
CByte	Byte
CChar	Char
CDate	Date
CDbl	Double
CDec	Decimal
CInt	Integer
CLng	Long
CObj	Object
CSByte	SByte
CShort	Short
CSng	Single
CStr	String

FUNCTION	CONVERTS TO
CUInt	UInteger
CULng	ULong
CUShort	UShort

Remember that data types have their own parsing methods in addition to these data type conversion functions. For example, the following code converts the String variable *a_string* into an Integer value:

```
an_integer = Integer.Parse(a_string)
```

These methods are faster than the corresponding data type conversion functions (in this case, CInt).

The Convert class also provides methods for converting from one data type to another. The following table lists the most useful Convert class functions.

FUNCTION

ToBoolean	ToInt64
ToByte	ToSByte
ToChar	ToSingle
ToDateTime	ToString
ToDecimal	ToUInt16
ToDouble	ToUInt32
ToInt16	ToUInt64
ToInt32	

All of the Convert class functions provide many overloaded versions to convert different kinds of values. For example, ToInt32 has different versions that take parameters that are Boolean, Byte, String, and other data types.

The integer functions ToInt16, ToInt32, ToInt64, ToUInt16, ToUInt32, and ToUInt64 also provide overloaded versions that take as parameters a string value and a base, which can be 2, 8, 10, or 16 to indicate whether the string is in binary, octal, decimal, or hexadecimal, respectively. For example, the following statement converts the binary value 00100100 into the integer value 36:

```
Dim value As Integer = Convert.ToInt32("00100100", 2)
```

CTYPE, DIRECTCAST, AND TRYCAST

The CType and DirectCast statements also perform type conversion. CType converts data from one type to another type if the types are compatible. For example, the following code converts the string 1234 into an integer:

```
Dim value As Integer = CType("1234", Integer)
```

DirectCast converts an object reference to a desired type provided the object's true type inherits from or has an implementation relationship with the desired type. For example, suppose the Employee class inherits from the Person class, and consider the following code:

```
Dim emp1 As New Employee

' Works because emp1 is an Employee and a Person.
Dim per1 As Person = DirectCast(emp1, Person)

' Works because per1 happens to point to an Employee object.
Dim emp2 As Employee = DirectCast(per1, Employee)

Dim per2 As New Person

' Fails because per2 is a Person but not an Employee.
Dim emp3 As Employee = DirectCast(per2, Employee)
```

This code creates an Employee object. It then uses DirectCast to convert the Employee into a Person and then to convert the new Person back into an Employee. This works because this object is both an Employee and a Person.

Next, the code creates a Person object and tries to use DirectCast to convert it into an Employee. This fails because this Person is not an Employee.

The CType and DirectCast statements throw exceptions if an object cannot be converted into the desired type. The TryCast statement performs a conversion much as DirectCast does except it returns Nothing if the conversion fails.

For example, the final line in the previous example throws an exception when it tries to convert a Person object into an Employee object because a Person is not an Employee. If you replace the DirectCast statement with TryCast, the statement would return Nothing and the code would set the value of the variable *emp3* to Nothing instead of throwing an exception.

Operators

The Visual Basic operators fall into five main categories: arithmetic, concatenation, comparison, logical, and bitwise. The following sections explain these categories and the operators they contain. The end of this appendix describes special Date and TimeSpan operators, as well as operator overloading.

ARITHMETIC OPERATORS

The following table lists the arithmetic operators provided by Visual Basic.

OPERATOR	PURPOSE	EXAMPLE	RESULT
^	Exponentiation	2 ^ 3	(2 to the power 3) = 2 * 2 * 2 = 8
–	Negation	–2	–2
*	Multiplication	2 * 3	6
/	Division	3 / 2	1.5
\	Integer division	17 \ 5	3
Mod	Modulus	17 Mod 5	2
+	Addition	2 + 3	5
–	Subtraction	3 – 2	1
<<	Bit left shift	&H57 << 1	&HAE
>>	Bit right shift	&H57 >> 1	&H2B

The bit shift operators deserve a little extra discussion. These operators shift the binary representation of a number by a given number of bits either left or right. Unfortunately, Visual Basic doesn't understand binary so you must manually translate between binary and decimal, octal, or hexadecimal.

For example, the hexadecimal value &H57 is 01010111 in binary. If you shift this one bit to the left, you get 10101110, which is &HAE in hexadecimal. If you shift the original value one bit to the right, you get 00101011, which is &H2B in hexadecimal.

When working with binary values, many developers prefer to work in hexadecimal because each hexadecimal digit corresponds to four binary bits so you can work with each group of four bits separately.

CONCATENATION OPERATORS

Visual Basic provides two concatenation operators: & and +. Both join two strings together. Because the + symbol also represents an arithmetic operator, your code will be easier to read if you use the & symbol for concatenation.

COMPARISON OPERATORS

The following table lists the comparison operators provided by Visual Basic.

OPERATOR	PURPOSE	EXAMPLE	RESULT
=	Equals	A = B	True if A equals B
<>	Not equals	A <> B	True if A does not equal B
<	Less than	A < B	True if A is less than B
<=	Less than or equal to	A <= B	True if A is less than or equal to B
>	Greater than	A > B	True if A is greater than B
>=	Greater than or equal to	A >= B	True if A is greater than or equal to B
Is	Equality of two objects	emp Is mgr	True if emp and mgr refer to the same object
IsNot	Inequality of two objects	emp IsNot mgr	True if emp and mgr refer to different objects
TypeOf ... Is ...	Object is of a certain type	TypeOf obj Is Manager	True if obj points to a Manager object
Like	Matches a text pattern	value Like "###-####"	True if value contains three digits, a dash, and four digits

The following table lists characters that have special meanings to the Like operator.

CHARACTER(S)	MEANING
?	Matches any single character
*	Matches any zero or more characters
#	Matches any single digit
[characters]	Matches any of the characters between the brackets
[!characters]	Matches any character not between the brackets
A–Z	When inside brackets, matches any character in the range A to Z

The following table lists some useful Like patterns.

PATTERN	MEANING
[2–9]##–####	Seven-digit U.S. phone number
[2–9]##–[2–9]##–####	Ten-digit U.S. phone number including area code
1–[2–9]##-[2–9]##–####	Eleven-digit U.S. phone number beginning with 1 and area code
#####	Five-digit U.S. ZIP code
#####–####	Nine-digit U.S. ZIP+4 code
?*@?*.?*	E-mail address
[A–Z][0–9][A–Z] [0–9][A–Z][0–9]	Canadian postal code

LOGICAL OPERATORS

The following table summarizes the Visual Basic logical operators.

OPERATOR	PURPOSE	EXAMPLE	RESULT
Not	Logical negation	Not A	True if A is false
And	Logical And	A And B	True if A and B are both true
Or	Logical Or	A Or B	True if A or B or both are true

continues

(continued)

OPERATOR	PURPOSE	EXAMPLE	RESULT
Xor	Logical exclusive Or	A Xor B	True if A or B (but not both) is true
AndAlso	Logical And with short-circuit evaluation	A AndAlso B	True if A and B are both true
OrElse	Logical Or with short-circuit evaluation	A OrElse B	True if A or B or both are true

BITWISE OPERATORS

Bitwise operators work much as logical operators do, except that they compare values one bit at a time. Visual Basic provides bitwise versions of Not, And, Or, and Xor but not bitwise versions of AndAlso or OrElse.

OPERATOR PRECEDENCE

The following table lists the operators in order of precedence. When evaluating an expression, the program evaluates an operator before it evaluates those lower than it in the list. When operators are on the same line in the table, the program evaluates them from left to right as they appear in the expression.

OPERATOR	DESCRIPTION
^	Exponentiation
–	Negation
*, /	Multiplication and division
\	Integer division
Mod	Modulus
+, –, +	Addition, subtraction, and concatenation
&	Concatenation
<<, >>	Bit shift
=, <>, <, <=, >, >=, Like, Is, IsNot, TypeOf ... Is ...	All comparisons

OPERATOR	DESCRIPTION
Not	Logical and bitwise negation
And, AndAlso	Logical and bitwise And with and without short-circuit evaluation
Xor, Or, OrElse	Logical and bitwise Xor, and Or with and without short-circuit evaluation

Use parentheses to change the order of evaluation and to make expressions easier to read.

ASSIGNMENT OPERATORS

The following table summarizes the Visual Basic assignment operators.

OPERATOR	EXAMPLE	LONG SYNTAX EQUIVALENT
=	A = B	A = B
^=	A ^= B	A = A ^ B
*=	A *= B	A = A * B
/=	A /= B	A = A / B
\=	A \= B	A = A \ B
+=	A += B	A = A + B
-=	A -= B	A = A - B
&=	A &= B	A = A & B
<<=	A <<= B	A = A << B
>>=	A >>= B	A = A >> B

There are no assignment operators corresponding to Mod or the Boolean operators.

CHOOSE, IF, AND IIF

The Choose, If, and IIf statements return values that you can assign to a variable. These statements are not really assignment operators (you need to use = to assign their results to a variable) and they perform decisions so they are described in Appendix E, "Control Statements."

DATE AND TIMESPAN OPERATORS

The Date and TimeSpan data types are related through their operators. The following list shows the relationships between these two data types:

➤ Date – Date = TimeSpan

➤ Date + TimeSpan = Date

➤ TimeSpan + TimeSpan = TimeSpan

➤ TimeSpan – TimeSpan = TimeSpan

The following table lists examples demonstrating convenient methods provided by the Date data type.

SYNTAX	MEANING
result_date = date1 .Add(timespan1)	Returns *date1* plus *timespan1*
result_date = date1 .AddYears(num_years)	Returns the date plus the indicated number of years
result_date = date1 .AddMonths(num_months)	Returns the date plus the indicated number of months
result_date = date1 .AddDays(num_days)	Returns the date plus the indicated number of days
result_date = date1 .AddHours(num_hours)	Returns the date plus the indicated number of hours
result_date = date1 .AddMinutes(num_minutes)	Returns the date plus the indicated number of minutes
result_date = date1 .AddSeconds(num_seconds)	Returns the date plus the indicated number of seconds
result_date = date1 .AddMilliseconds(num_milliseconds)	Returns the date plus the indicated number of milliseconds
result_date = date1 .AddTicks(num_ticks)	Returns the date plus the indicated number of ticks (100 nanosecond units)
result_timespan = date1 .Subtract(date2)	Returns the time span between *date2* and *date1*
result_integer = date1 .CompareTo(date2)	Returns a value indicating whether *date1* is greater than, less than, or equal to *date2*
result_boolean = date1 .Equals(date2)	Returns True if *date1* equals *date2*

OPERATOR OVERLOADING

The syntax for defining an operator for a class is as follows:

```
[ <attributes> ] Public [ Overloads ] Shared [ Shadows ] _
[ Widening | Narrowing ] Operator symbol ( operands ) As type
    ...
End Operator
```

The operator's symbol can be:

OPERATOR SYMBOLS

+	>>	Not
–	=	And
*	<>	Or
/	<	Xor
\	>	Like
^	<=	IsTrue
&	>=	IsFalse
<<	Mod	CType

For example, the following code defines the + operator for the ComplexNumber class. This class has two public properties, Re and Im, that give the number's real and imaginary parts.

```
Public Shared Operator +(c1 As ComplexNumber, c2 As ComplexNumber) _
  As ComplexNumber
    Return New ComplexNumber With
    {
        .Re = c1.Re + c2.Re,
        .Im = c1.Im + c2.Im
    }
End Operator
```

Some operands come in pairs, and if you define one, you must define the other. The pairs are = and <>, < and >, <= and >=, and IsTrue and IsFalse.

If you define And and IsFalse, Visual Basic uses them to define the AndAlso operator. Similarly, if you define Or and IsTrue, Visual Basic automatically provides the OrElse operator.

Subroutine and Function Declarations

This appendix provides information about subroutine, function, and generic declarations. A property procedure includes a subroutine and function pair, so they are also described here.

SUBROUTINES

The syntax for writing a subroutine is as follows:

```
[attribute_list] [inheritance_mode] [accessibility]
Sub subroutine_name [(parameters)] [ Implements interface.procedure ]
    [ statements ]
End Sub
```

The *inheritance_mode* can be one of the following values: Overloads, Overrides, Overridable, NotOverridable, MustOverride, Shadows, or Shared. These values determine how a subroutine declared within a class inherits from the parent class or how it allows inheritance in derived classes.

The *accessibility* clause can take one of the following values: Public, Protected, Friend, Protected Friend, or Private. These values determine which pieces of code can invoke the subroutine.

FUNCTIONS

The syntax for writing a function is as follows:

```
[attribute_list] [inheritance_mode] [accessibility] _
Function function_name([parameters]) [As return_type]
[ Implements interface.function ]
    [ statements ]
End Function
```

This is the same as the syntax used for declaring a subroutine, except that a function includes a return type and ends with End Function.

The *inheritance_mode* can be one of the values Overloads, Overrides, Overridable, NotOverridable, MustOverride, Shadows, or Shared. These values determine how a subroutine declared within a class inherits from the parent class or how it allows inheritance in derived classes.

The *accessibility* clause can take one of the following values: Public, Protected, Friend, Protected Friend, or Private. These values determine which pieces of code can invoke the subroutine.

A function assigns its return value by using the Return statement.

PROPERTY PROCEDURES

The syntax for read/write property procedures is as follows:

```
Property property_name() As data_type
    Get
        ...
    End Get
    Set(Value As data_type)
        ...
    End Set
End Property
```

The syntax for a read-only property procedure is as follows:

```
Public ReadOnly Property property_name() As data_type
    Get
        ...
    End Get
End Property
```

The syntax for a write-only property procedure is as follows:

```
Public WriteOnly Property property_name() As data_type
    Set(Value As data_type)
        ...
    End Set
End Property
```

In all three of these cases, you don't need to remember all the declaration details. If you type the first line (including the ReadOnly or WriteOnly keywords if you want them) and the last line, then Visual Basic displays an error indicator telling you that you didn't include the Get and Set procedures. If you hover the mouse over the error indicator, the error correction options provide a link you can click to generate empty procedures automatically.

Auto-implemented properties let you create simple read/write properties without providing Get and Set. The following code shows the syntax:

```
Property property_name() As data_type [= initial_value]
```

Visual Basic automatically makes a backing variable to hold the property's value, and Get and Set routines to access the value.

Note that Visual Basic cannot provide auto-implemented ReadOnly or WriteOnly properties.

LAMBDA FUNCTIONS AND EXPRESSIONS

A *lambda function* (also called an *inline function*) is a function declared within another routine. You can use lambda functions to initialize a delegate or to pass the function to a method that takes a delegate as a parameter.

For example, the following code creates an inline delegate named F. It then displays the value of F(12).

```
Dim F = Function(x As Integer) Sin(x / 2) + 2 * Cos(x / 3)
Debug.WriteLine(F(12))
```

The following code calls subroutine ApplyFunction. This function takes as parameters an array of values and a function that it should apply to each of the values. The code passes an inline delegate that doubles a number into ApplyFunction to double each of the values.

```
ApplyFunction(values, Function(x As Single) 2 * x)
```

A *lambda subroutine* is similar to a lambda function except it doesn't return a value. The syntax is similar to the syntax for lambda functions except you use the type Action instead of Function. The following code creates and invokes a lambda subroutine:

```
Dim echo As Action(Of Integer) = Sub(x As Integer) Debug.WriteLine(x)
echo(123)
```

The following code creates a lambda subroutine inline as a parameter to a call to the Array.ForEach method:

```
Dim states() As String = {"CO", "UT", "KS", "WY"}
Array.ForEach(Of String)(states,
    Sub(str As String) MessageBox.Show(str))
```

You can make multiline lambda functions or subroutines. Start a new line after the Sub or Function statement, include the lines of code that you need, and finish with End Sub or End Function.

The following code shows a call to Array.ForEach that uses a multiline lambda subroutine:

```
Array.ForEach(Of String)(states,
    Sub(str As String)
        Debug.WriteLine(str)
        MessageBox.Show(str)
    End Sub
)
```

EXTENSION METHODS

An extension method adds a new method to an existing class, even if you don't have access to the class's code. For example, you could add a ToFileSize extension method to the Long class to convert a Long value into a formatted file size string as in 1.23 KB or 4.5 GB. Then if `size` is a Long variable, the program could invoke the method as in the following code:

```
MessageBox.Show("The file size is " & size.ToFileSize())
```

To make an extension method, place a method in a code module and decorate it with the Extension attribute. (The Extension attribute is defined in the System.Runtime.CompilerServices namespace. You may want to import that namespace to make your code easier to read.)

The first parameter to the method determines the class that the method extends. For example, the following code gives the String class a MatchesRegexp method that returns True if the String matches a regular expression:

```
Module StringExtensions
    <Extension()>
    Public Function MatchesRegexp(the_string As String,
     regular_expression As String) As Boolean
        Dim reg_exp As New Regex(regular_expression)
        Return reg_exp.IsMatch(the_string)
    End Function
End Module
```

Control Statements

Control statements tell an application which other statements to execute under a particular set of circumstances.

The two main categories of control statements are decision statements and looping statements. The following sections describe the decision and looping statements provided by Visual Basic .NET.

DECISION STATEMENTS

A decision statement represents a branch in the program. It marks a place where the program can execute one set of statements or another or possibly no statements at all. These include If, Choose, and Select Case statements.

Single-Line If Then

A single-line If Then statement tests a condition and, if the condition is true, executes a piece of code. The code may include more than one simple statement separated by a colon.

Optional Else If clauses let the program evaluate other conditions and execute corresponding pieces of code. A final optional Else clause lets the program execute a piece of code if none of the previous conditions is true.

The syntax for different variations are as follows:

```
If condition Then statement
If condition Then statement1 Else statement2
If condition1 Then statement1 Else If condition2 Then statement2 _
    Else statement3
If condition Then statement1: statement2
If condition Then statement1: statement2 Else statement3: statement4
```

Complicated single-line If Then statements can be confusing and difficult to read, so I recommend using the multiline versions if the statement includes an Else clause or executes more than one statement.

Multiline If Then

A multiline If Then statement is similar to the single-line version, except the pieces of code executed by each part of the statement can include multiple lines. Each piece of code ends before the following ElseIf, Else, or End If keywords. In complex code, this format is often easier to read than a complicated single-line If Then statement.

The syntax is as follows:

```
If condition1 Then
    statements1...
ElseIf condition2
    statements2...
Else
    statements3...
End If
```

The multiline If statement can contain any number of ElseIf sections.

Select Case

A Select Case statement lets a program execute one of several pieces of code based on a test value. Select Case is equivalent to a long If Then Else statement.

The syntax is as follows:

```
Select Case test_value
    Case comparison_expression1
        statements1
    Case comparison_expression2
        statements2
    Case comparison_expression3
        statements3
        ...
    Case Else
        else_statements
End Select
```

A comparison expression can contain multiple expressions separated by commas, can use the To keyword to specify a range of values, and can use the Is keyword to evaluate a logical expression using the test value. The following example's first case looks for a string in the range "A" to "Z" or "a" to "z." Its second and third cases look for values less than "A" and greater than "Z," respectively.

```
Select Case key_pressed
    Case "A" To "Z", "a" To "z"
        ...
```

```
        Case Is < "A"
            ...
        Case Is > "Z"
            ...
    End Select
```

Many developers always include a Case Else section to catch unexpected situations. If every possible situation should be covered by other cases, some developers throw an exception inside the Case Else section to make it easier to find errors.

If and IIf

IIf takes a Boolean value as its first parameter. It returns its second parameter if the value is True, and it returns its third parameter if the value is False.

The syntax is as follows:

```
    variable = IIf(condition, value_if_true, value_if_false)
```

Note that IIf always evaluates all of its arguments. For example, if the condition is True, IIf only returns the second argument, but it evaluates both the second and third arguments.

The If function does the same thing as IIf except it uses short-circuit evaluation, so it only evaluates the second and third arguments if necessary. If the condition is True in the following code, If evaluates the second argument but not the third:

```
    variable = If(condition, value_if_true, value_if_false)
```

A second form if the If function takes two parameters: an object reference or a nullable type and a return value. The If function returns the first parameter if it is not Nothing and the second argument if it is Nothing. The following code shows the syntax:

```
    variable = If(nullable_value, default_if_nothing)
```

IIf and If are often confusing and IIf is slower than an If Then Else statement, so you may want to use If Then Else instead.

Choose

Choose takes an index value as its first parameter and returns the corresponding one of its other parameters.

The syntax is as follows:

```
    variable = Choose(index, value1, value2, value3, value4, ...)
```

Choose is rarely used, so it can be confusing. To avoid unnecessary confusion, you may want to use a Select Case statement instead.

LOOPING STATEMENTS

A looping statement makes the program execute a series of statements repeatedly. The loop can run for a fixed number of repetitions, run while some condition holds True, run until some condition holds True, or run indefinitely.

For Next

A For Next loop executes a piece of code while a loop control variable ranges from one value to another.

The syntax is as follows:

```
For variable [As data_type] = start_value To stop_value [Step increment]
    statements
    [Exit For]
    statements
Next [variable]
```

For Each

A For Each loop executes a piece of code while a loop control variable ranges over all of the items contained in a group such as a collection or array.

The syntax is as follows:

```
For Each variable [As object_type] In group
    statements
    [Exit For]
    statements
Next [variable]
```

The *group* in this code can also be a LINQ (Language Integrated Query) query. The following code creates a LINQ query to select information from the book_data array and then uses a For Each loop to display the results:

```
Dim book_query = From book_info In book_data
    Select book_info
    Where book_info.Year > = 2000
    Order By book_info.Year
For Each bi In book_query
    Debug.WriteLine(bi.Title)
Next bi
```

For more information about LINQ, see Chapter 20, "LINQ."

Do Loop

Do Loop statements come in three forms. First, if the statement has no While or Until clause, the loop repeats infinitely or until the code uses an Exit Do, Exit Sub, or some other statement to break out of the loop.

The syntax is as follows:

```
Do
    statements
    [Exit Do]
    statements
Loop
```

The other two forms of Do Loop statements execute as long as a condition is True (Do While condition) or until a condition is True (Do Until condition).

The second form of Do Loop statement tests its condition before it executes, so the code it contains is not executed even once if the condition is initially False.

The syntax is as follows:

```
Do {While | Until} condition
    statements
    [Exit Do]
    statements
Loop
```

The third form of Do Loop statement tests its condition after it executes, so the code it contains is executed at least once even if the condition is initially False.

The syntax is as follows:

```
Do
    statements
    [Exit Do]
    statements
Loop {While | Until} condition
```

While End

The While End loop executes a series of statements as long as a condition is True. It tests its condition before it executes, so the code it contains is not executed even once if the condition is initially False.

The syntax is as follows:

```
While condition
    statements
    [Exit While]
    statements
End While
```

This statement is equivalent to the Do Loop:

```
Do While condition
    statements
    [Exit Do]
    statements
Loop
```

Error Handling

This appendix provides information on structured error handling that uses the Try Catch statement.

A Try block attempts to execute some code and reacts if errors occur. The syntax is as follows:

```
Try
    try_statements...
[Catch ex As exception_type_1
    exception_statements_1...]
[Catch ex As exception_type_2
    exception_statements_2...]
...
[Catch
    final_exception_statements...]
[Finally
    finally_statements...]
End Try
```

When an error occurs, the program examines the Catch statements in order until it finds one that matches the current exception. The program executes the *finally_statements* after the *try_statements* succeed or after any Catch block is done executing.

THROWING EXCEPTIONS

Use the Throw statement to throw an exception, as in the following code:

```
Throw New ArgumentException("Width must be greater than zero")
```

Exception classes provide several overloaded constructors so you can indicate such things as the basic error message, the name of the variable that caused the exception, and an inner exception.

For information on useful exception classes and custom exception classes, see Appendix O, "Useful Exception Classes."

Windows Forms Controls and Components

This appendix summarizes the standard controls and components provided by Visual Basic .NET for use by Windows Forms applications. Some of these are quite complicated, providing dozens or even hundreds of properties, methods, and events, so it would be impractical to describe them all completely here. However, it's still worthwhile having a concise guide to the most important controls so you know which to pick for a particular task.

MORE INFORMATION

You can find information about most of these controls under the "System.Windows .Forms Namespace" topic in the MSDN help at http://msdn.microsoft.com /system.windows.forms.aspx.

Note that components inherit from the Component class and controls inherit from the Control class. Except where overridden, the components and controls inherit the properties, methods, and events defined by the Component and Control classes. Chapter 8, "Using Windows Forms Controls," discusses some of the more useful properties, methods, and events provided by the Control class, and many of those apply to these controls as well. Appendix A, "Useful Control Properties, Methods, and Events," summarizes the Control class's most useful properties.

Figure G-1 shows the Visual Basic Toolbox displaying the standard Windows Forms controls.

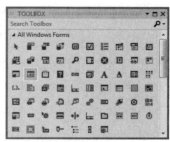

FIGURE G-1: Visual Basic provides a large number of standard components and controls for Windows Forms.

TUNING THE TOOLBOX

You can add and remove controls from the Toolbox. You can add controls built by Microsoft, other companies, yourself, or other Visual Basic programmers. Some extra controls even come installed with Visual Basic but are not displayed by default in the Toolbox. Right-click the Toolbox and select Choose Items to add or remove items.

The following table lists the components shown in Figure G-1 in the same order in which they appear in the figure. Read the table by rows. For example, the first several entries (Pointer, BackgroundWorker, BindingNavigator, BindingSource, Button, and so on) correspond to the first controls in the first row in Figure G-1.

Pointer	BackgroundWorker	BindingNavigator	BindingSource
Button	CheckBox	CheckedListBox	ColorDialog
ComboBox	ContextMenuStrip	DataGridView	DataSet
DateTimePicker	DirectoryEntry	DirectorySearcher	DomainUpDown
ErrorProvider	EventLog	FileSystemWatcher	FlowLayoutPanel
FolderBrowserDialog	FontDialog	GroupBox	HelpProvider
HScrollBar	ImageList	Label	LinkLabel
ListBox	ListView	MaskedTextBox	MenuStrip
MessageQueue	MonthCalendar	NotifyIcon	NumericUpDown
OpenFileDialog	PageSetupDialog	Panel	PerformanceCounter
PictureBox	PrintDialog	PrintDocument	PrintPreviewControl
PrintPreviewDialog	Process	ProgressBar	PropertyGrid
RadioButton	RichTextBox	SaveFileDialog	SerialPort
ServiceController	SplitContainer	Splitter	StatusStrip
TabControl	TableLayoutPanel	TextBox	Timer
ToolStrip	ToolStripContainer	ToolTip	TrackBar
TreeView	VScrollBar	WebBrowser	

CONTROL PURPOSES

The following table summarizes the controls' purposes.

CONTROL	PURPOSE
Pointer	This isn't a control, it's a tool that lets you select controls in the Windows Form Designer.
BackgroundWorker	A component that simplifies multithreading. It lets you run code on a separate thread and receive events to indicate the code's progress.
BindingNavigator	A control that provides a user interface so the user can control a data source. It initially appears as a toolbar docked to the top of the form, although you can move it if you like.
BindingSource	Provides control of bound data on a form. It provides programmatic methods for navigating through the data, adding items, deleting items, and otherwise managing the data at the code level.
Button	A simple push button. You can use it to let the user tell the program to do something.
CheckBox	Displays a box that enables the user to select or clear an option.
CheckedListBox	Displays a series of items with check boxes in a list format. This enables the user to pick and choose similar items from a list of choices.
ColorDialog	Displays a dialog box that enables the user to select a color from a standard palette or from a custom color palette.
ComboBox	Contains a text box where the user can enter a value. It also provides a list box or drop-down list where the user can select a value.
ContextMenuStrip	Represents a context menu that you can attach to other controls' ContextMenuStrip properties.
DataGridView	Displays a table-like grid showing data from an underlying data source such as a DataSet or BindingSource. The program can also add rows and columns directly to the DataGridView.
DataSet	Holds data in a relational format. A DataSet provides all the features you need to build, load, store, manipulate, and save data similar to that stored in a relational database. For example, it can hold multiple tables related with complex parent/child relationships and uniqueness constraints.
DateTimePicker	Allows the user to select a date and time. The control can display one of several styles including a series of up/down controls that let the user scroll through date values (month, day, year), and a drop-down calendar display.

continues

(continued)

CONTROL	PURPOSE
DirectoryEntry	Represents a node or object in an Active Directory hierarchy. (Active Directory is a service that provides a common, hierarchical view of distributed resources and services on a network.)
DirectorySearcher	Performs searches on an Active Directory hierarchy. See the online help for more information on Active Directory (`http://msdn.microsoft.com/aa286486.aspx`) and the DirectorySearcher component (`http://msdn.microsoft.com/system.directoryservices.directorysearcher.aspx`).
DomainUpDown	Displays a list of items that the user can select by using the arrow keys or by clicking the up and down arrow buttons beside the control. For example, the control might let the user select one of the values High, Medium, and Low.
ErrorProvider	Displays an error indicator next to controls.
EventLog	Lets an application manipulate event logs. Provides methods to create logs, write and read log messages, and clear logs. For more information, see the MSDN topic "Logging Application, Server, and Security Events" (`http://msdn.microsoft.com/e6t4tk09.aspx`).
FileSystemWatcher	Monitors part of the filesystem and raises events to let your program know if something changes. For example, it can notify your program if a file is created in a particular directory. For more information, see Chapter 30, "Filesystem Objects," and Appendix U, "Filesystem Classes."
FlowLayoutPanel	Displays the controls that it contains in rows or columns.
FolderBrowserDialog	Displays a dialog box that lets the user select a folder (directory) in the filesystem. The program can set the component's root folder to indicate where the search should begin.
FontDialog	Displays a dialog box that lets the user select a font's name, size, style (bold, italic), color, and other characteristics.
GroupBox	Displays a caption and border.
HelpProvider	When associated with a control, if the user sets focus to the control and presses the F1 key, the HelpProvider displays help for the control. The HelpProvider either displays a small tooltip-like pop-up displaying a help string or opens a help file.
HScrollBar	A horizontal scroll bar.
ImageList	Stores a series of images for use by other controls or by the program's code.

CONTROL	PURPOSE
Label	Displays a piece of read-only text.
LinkLabel	Displays a label that is associated with a hyperlink.
ListBox	Displays a list of items that the user can select.
ListView	Displays a list of items in one of five possible views: Details (item and sub-item text on a row), LargeIcon (large icons above the item's text, List (small icons to the left of the item's text with each item on its own row), SmallIcon (small icons to the left of the item's text with multiple items per row), and Tile (large icons to the left of the item's text).
MaskedTextBox	A text box that provides a mask to help guide the user in entering a value in a particular format. The mask determines which characters are allowed at different positions in the text.
MenuStrip	Represents a form's menus, submenus, and menu items.
MessageQueue	Provides access to a queue on a message-queuing server. An application can use a message queue to communicate with other applications. For more information, see `http://msdn.microsoft.com/system .messaging.messagequeue.aspx`.
MonthCalendar	Displays a calendar that allows the user to select a range of dates. (This calendar is similar to the one that the DateTimePicker control can display.)
NotifyIcon	Displays an icon in the system tray that can indicate the program's state. The icon can also display a context menu.
NumericUpDown	Displays a number with up and down arrows that you can use to change the number. If you click an arrow and hold it down, the number changes repeatedly.
OpenFileDialog	Displays a standard dialog box that lets the user select a file to open.
PageSetupDialog	Displays a dialog box that lets the user specify properties for printed pages. For example, the user can specify the printer's paper tray, page size, margins, and orientation (portrait or landscape).
Panel	A container for other controls. By setting the Anchor and Dock properties of the contained controls, you can make those controls arrange themselves when the Panel is resized. The control also forms a grouping for any RadioButtons that it contains and provides a very useful auto-scroll capability.
PerformanceCounter	Represents a Windows NT–style performance counter. You can use the component's methods to read, increment, and decrement the counters. For more information, see `http://msdn.microsoft.com/system .diagnostics.performancecounter.aspx`.

continues

(continued)

CONTROL	PURPOSE
PictureBox	Displays images. A program can also draw on it in a Paint event handler.
PrintDialog	Displays a dialog box that lets the user prepare to print. The dialog box lets the user select a printer, modify printer properties, select the pages to print, and determine the number of copies to print.
PrintDocument	Represents an object that will be printed. The program generates a printout by responding to this object's events, notably the PrintPage event.
PrintPreviewControl	Displays a print preview within one of the program's forms. Usually it's easier to use a PrintPreviewDialog instead.
PrintPreviewDialog	Displays a dialog box that shows what a print document will look like when it is printed.
Process	Provides access to the processes running on the computer. You can use this object to start, stop, and monitor processes.
ProgressBar	Lets a program display a visible indication of its progress during a long task.
PropertyGrid	Displays and lets the user edit information about an object in a format similar to the one used by the Properties window at design time.
RadioButton	Represents one of an exclusive set of options.
RichTextBox	A text box that supports rich text extensions such as text that is bold, underlined, italicized, indented, and in different fonts and has other special visual properties.
SaveFileDialog	Displays a dialog box that lets the user select a file for saving.
SerialPort	Represents one of the computer's physical serial ports. It provides properties and methods for reading and configuring the port's baud rate, break signal, Data Set Ready (DSR) state, port name, parity, and stop bits.
ServiceController	Represents a Windows service process. It provides methods that let you connect to a running or stopped service to control it or get information about it.
SplitContainer	Represents an area divided into two regions either vertically or horizontally. The control contains a bar (called the splitter) that the user can drag to adjust the amount of space given to each region.
Splitter	Provides the thin strip that users can grab to resize the two panes of a SplitContainer. A program can also use a Splitter directly to separate any two other controls.

CONTROL	PURPOSE
StatusStrip	Provides an area where the application can display brief status information, usually at the bottom of the form.
TabControl	Displays a series of tabs attached to separate pages. Each page is a control container, holding whatever controls you want for that tab. When you click a tab at design time or the user clicks one at run time, the control displays the corresponding page.
TableLayoutPanel	Displays the controls that it contains in rows and columns. This makes it easy to build grids of regularly spaced controls.
TextBox	A typical everyday text box. The user can enter and modify text, click and drag to select text, press Ctrl+C to copy the selected text to the clipboard, and so forth. Note that a TextBox can use only one foreground color, background color, and font. For text that uses multiple colors or fonts, use a RichTextBox.
Timer	Periodically raises a Tick event so the program can take action at specific intervals.
ToolStrip	Displays a series of buttons, drop-downs, and other tools that the user can access quickly without navigating through a series of menus.
ToolStripContainer	Contains a ToolStripPanel along each of its edges where ToolStrip controls can dock. The control's center is filled with another ToolStripPanel that can contain other controls that are not part of the tool strips.
ToolTip	Associates controls with tooltips that should be displayed if the mouse hovers over the controls.
TrackBar	Allows the user to drag a pointer along a bar to select a numeric value. This control is very similar to a horizontal scroll bar, but with a different appearance.
TreeView	Displays a hierarchical data set graphically. The user can click indicators beside nodes to collapse or expand their subtrees.
VScrollBar	Similar to the HScrollBar control, except that it is oriented vertically instead of horizontally.
WebBrowser	Displays the contents of web pages, XML documents, text files, and other documents understood by the browser. The control can automatically follow links that the user clicks in the document and provides a standard web browser context menu, containing commands such as Back, Forward, Save Background As, and Print.

H

WPF Controls

This appendix lists the most useful Windows Presentation Foundation (WPF) controls and briefly describes their purposes. This list does not include all of the hundreds of classes that WPF defines; it lists only the tools most likely to appear in the window designer's Toolbox.

These controls are part of the System.Windows.Controls namespace. In contrast, the controls used in Windows Forms are contained in the System.Windows.Forms namespace. Many of the controls in the two namespaces serve very similar purposes, although they have different capabilities. For example, both namespaces have buttons, labels, combo boxes, and check boxes but only the System.Windows.Controls classes provide foreground and background brushes, render transformations, complex content, and XAML-defined triggers.

For much more information about WPF controls and WPF in general, see my book *WPF Programmer's Reference* (Stephens, Wrox 2010). You can learn more about the book at http://www.vb-helper.com/wpf.htm.

Note that not all of the controls described here are available by default when you create a new WPF application. You need to add some of these controls to the Toolbox before you can use them. To add a control that is missing, right-click a Toolbox section and select Choose Items. On the Choose Toolbox Items dialog box, select the WPF Components tab to display the dialog box shown in Figure H-1. Check the boxes next to the controls that you want, and click OK.

Controls in the following table are marked with superscripts [0], [1], or [2] to indicate whether they can hold 0, 1, or 2 children, respectively. Controls with no superscripts can hold any number of children.

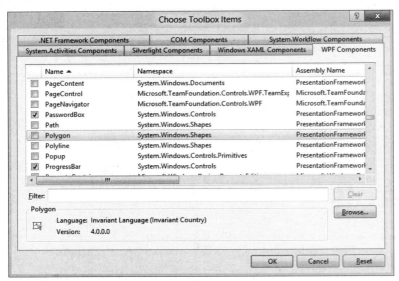

FIGURE H-1: Use this dialog box to add new WPF controls to the Toolbox.

CONTROL	PURPOSE
Border[1]	Provides a visible border around or background behind its contents.
BulletDecorator[2]	Contains two children. The first is used as a bullet and the second is aligned with the first. For example, you can use this to align bullet images next to labels.
Button[1]	Displays a button that the user can click. Raises a Click event that the program can catch to perform an action.
Canvas	Creates an area in which you can explicitly position children by specifying their Width, Height, Canvas.Left, and Canvas.Top properties.
CheckBox[1]	Allows the user to select or deselect an item. Each CheckBox choice is independent of all others.
ComboBox	Allows the user to select an item from a drop-down list. The list can contain all sorts of objects, but typically holds a series of ComboBoxItems.
ComboBoxItem[1]	Represents an item in a ComboBox control's list.
ContentControl[1]	Represents a control that contains a single piece of content. Note, however, that the content may, in turn, contain other objects.

CONTROL	PURPOSE
ContextMenu	Builds a pop-up menu for a control. This element should be inside the control's ContextMenu property (for example, inside a <Button .ContextMenu> element). Normally the ContextMenu contains MenuItem controls.
DockPanel	Docks its children to its left, right, top, or bottom much as the Dock property does in a Windows Forms application. If the control's LastChildFill property is True, the control makes its last child control fill the remaining space.
DocumentViewer[1]	Displays a FixedDocument. See the section "Fixed Documents" in Chapter 11, "Using WPF Controls."
Ellipse[0]	Displays an ellipse.
Expander[1]	Displays a header and lets the user expand and contract a single detail item. The <Expander.Header> sub-element contains the content displayed in the header.
FlowDocumentPageViewer[1]	Displays a FlowDocument one page at a time. If the control is wide enough, it may display multiple columns although it still only displays one page at a time. See the section "Flow Documents" in Chapter 11.
FlowDocumentReader[1]	Displays a FlowDocument in one of three modes. When in *single page* mode, it acts as a FlowDocumentPageViewer. When in *scrolling* mode, it acts as a FlowDocumentScrollViewer. In *book reading mode*, it displays two pages side by side much as a real book does. See the section "Flow Documents" in Chapter 11.
FlowDocumentScrollViewer[1]	Displays a FlowDocument as a single, long, vertically scrolling page. See the section "Flow Documents" in Chapter 11.
Frame[0]	Supports navigation and content display. The control can navigate to a .NET Framework object or to HTML content.
Grid	Displays children in rows and columns. This is similar to the Windows Forms TableLayoutPanel control.
GridSplitter[0]	Acts as a splitter that allows the user to resize rows or columns in a Grid.
GridView	Displays data in columns within a ListView control.
GridViewColumnHeader[1]	Represents a column header for a GridViewColumn.
GroupBox[1]	Displays a visible border with a header. The Header property determines the content displayed in the header. The control also forms a grouping for any RadioButtons that it contains.

continues

(continued)

CONTROL	PURPOSE
GroupItem[1]	Used to group items in other controls such as a TreeView.
HeaderedContentControl[2]	This is the base class for controls that have a single content element and a header. Although you can create one directly, usually it's better to use a subclass such as GroupBox.
HeaderedItemsControl	Displays a header and multiple content elements.
Image[0]	Displays an image. Can optionally stretch the image with or without distortion.
InkCanvas	Displays or captures ink strokes.
InkPresenter[0]	Displays ink strokes.
ItemsControl	Displays a collection of content items.
Label[1]	Displays non-editable text.
Line[0]	Draws a line segment.
ListBox	Lets the user select items from a list. ListBoxItem objects hold the items. The control automatically displays scroll bars when needed.
ListBoxItem[1]	Holds content for display by a ListBox object.
ListView	Displays a group of items in various display modes.
ListViewItem[1]	Contains the content for an item displayed in a ListView.
MediaElement[0]	Presents audio and video. To let you control the media, it provides Play, Pause, and Stop methods, and Volume and SpeedRatio properties.
Menu	Builds a menu that is visible, in contrast to a ContextMenu, which is hidden until displayed. Normally, the Menu contains MenuItem controls representing the top-level menus. Those items contain other MenuItem controls representing commands.
MenuItem	Defines a top-level menu, submenu, or menu item for a ContextMenu or Menu.
NavigationWindow[0]	Navigates to content and displays it, keeping a navigation history. Similar to Frame.
Panel	Panel is the parent class for Canvas, DockPanel, Grid, TabPanel, ToolbarOverflowPanel, UniformGrid, StackPanel, VirtualizingPanel, and WrapPanel. Usually, you should use one of those classes instead of Panel, but you can use Panel to implement your own custom panel controls.

CONTROL	PURPOSE
PasswordBox[0]	A text box where the user can enter sensitive information such as passwords. The control's PasswordChar property determines the character displayed for each character the user types. By default, this is a solid black circle.
Path[0]	Contains a series of drawing instructions that make line segments, arcs, curves, ellipses, and so forth. For more information, see the section "Drawing Objects" in Chapter 11.
Polygon[0]	Draws a closed polygon.
Polyline[0]	Draws a series of connected line segments.
Popup[1]	Displays content in a window above another control. Usually, you can use the Tooltip and ContextMenu controls instead of a Popup.
PrintDialog[0]	Displays a standard Windows print dialog box. You shouldn't place a PrintDialog on a window. Instead use code to build and display the PrintDialog.
ProgressBar[0]	Indicates the fraction of a long task that has been completed. Usually, the task is performed synchronously, so the user is left staring at the form while it completes. The ProgressBar lets the user know that the operation is not stuck.
RadioButton[1]	Lets the user pick from among a set of options. If the user checks one RadioButton, all others with the same parent become unchecked.
Rectangle[0]	Draws a rectangle, optionally with rounded corners.
RepeatButton[1]	Acts as a Button that raises its Click event repeatedly when it is pressed and held down.
ResizeGrip[0]	Displays a resize grip similar to the one used on the lower-right corner of a window.
RichTextBox[1]	Similar to a TextBox but contains text in the form of a document object. See the section "Managing Documents" in Chapter 10 for more information on documents.
ScrollBar[0]	Allows the user to drag a "thumb" to select a numeric value. Usually scroll bars are used internally by other controls such as the ScrollViewer, and your applications should use a Slider instead.
ScrollViewer[1]	Provides vertical and horizontal scroll bars for a single content element. Makes a scrollable area that can contain other controls.

continues

(continued)

CONTROL	PURPOSE
Separator[0]	Draws a vertical or horizontal separator in controls that contain other controls, such as StatusBar, Menu, ListBox, or ToolBar.
Slider[0]	Enables the user to select a value from a range by sliding a Thumb along a Track. Similar to the Windows Forms TrackBar control.
StackPanel	Arranges children in a single row or column. If there are too many controls, those that don't fit are clipped.
StatusBar	Displays a container at the bottom of the form where you can place controls holding status information. Although you can place anything inside a StatusBar, this control is intended to hold summary status information, not tools. Generally, menus, combo boxes, buttons, toolbars, and other controls that let the user manipulate the application do not belong in a StatusBar.
StatusBarItem[1]	Contains an item in a StatusBar.
TabControl	Arranges children in tabs. TabItem controls contain the items that should be displayed in the tabs.
TabItem[1]	Represents an item in a TabControl. The Header property determines the content displayed on the tab, and the Content property determines what's displayed on the tab's body.
TextBlock	Displays more complex non-editable text. This control's contents can include inline tags to indicate special formatting. Tags can include AnchoredBlock, Bold, Hyperlink, InlineUIContainer, Italic, LineBreak, Run, Span, and Underline.
TextBox[0]	Allows the user to enter simple text. Optionally can allow carriage returns and tabs, and can wrap text.
Thumb[0]	Represents an area that the user can grab and drag as in a ScrollBar or Slider.
ToggleButton[1]	This is the base class for controls that toggle between two states such as a CheckBox or RadioButton. You can make one directly, but it's easier to use CheckBox or RadioButton.
ToolBar	Contains a series of tools, typically Button controls, ComboBox controls, and other small controls. The Header property gives the ToolBar a header.
ToolBarTray	Contains ToolBars and allows the user to drag them into new positions.

CONTROL	PURPOSE
ToolTip[1]	Displays a tooltip. To give a control a simple textual tooltip, set its Tooltip property. Use the Tooltip control to build more complex tooltips. For example, a Tooltip control might contain a StackPanel that holds other controls.
TreeView	Displays hierarchical data with a series of nested collapsible nodes. TreeViewItems contain the items displayed in the hierarchy.
TreeViewItem	Represents an item within a TreeView. The Header attribute or sub-element determines the content displayed for the item.
UserControl[1]	A container that you can use to create a simple compound control. Note, however, that classes derived from UserControl do not support templates.
Viewbox[1]	Stretches its single child to fill the Viewbox. The Stretch property determines whether the control stretches its child uniformly (without changing the width-to-height ratio).
VirtualizingStackPanel	Generates child items to hold items that can fit in the available area. For example, when working with a ListBox bound to a data source, the VirtualizingStackPanel generates only the items that will fit within the ListBox. If the control is not bound to a data source, this control behaves like a StackPanel.
Window[1]	Represents a window, the WPF equivalent of a form. The window includes two areas: the client area where you normally put controls and the non-client area where the window displays borders, title bar, caption, system menus, and so on. Normally, you add a window to an application by using the Project menu's Add New Item command.
WrapPanel	Arranges children in rows or columns depending on its Orientation property. When a row or column is full, the next child moves to a new row or column. This is similar to the Windows Forms FlowLayoutPanel control.

For more detailed descriptions plus examples using these and other controls, see the Microsoft online help. You can find a reference for System.Windows.Controls classes at `http://msdn .microsoft.com/system.windows.controls.aspx`. You can find a reference for the System .Windows.Controls.Primitives classes, which include base classes used by other controls, at `http://msdn.microsoft.com/system.windows.controls.primitives.aspx`.

For much more information about WPF controls and WPF in general, see my book *WPF Programmer's Reference*. You can learn more about the book at `http://www.vb-helper.com/ wpf.htm`.

Visual Basic Power Packs

When Visual Basic .NET first appeared, it was missing many features that developers had found extremely useful in Visual Basic 6. Power Packs were invented to provide objects and tools to fill the need for these missing features and to make programming easier and more productive in general.

This appendix describes Visual Basic Power Tools provided by Microsoft and other compatibility tools that you may find useful.

MICROSOFT POWER PACKS

Originally Microsoft provided its Power Packs as a download but now they are included in Visual Basic. Near the bottom of the Toolbox, you should be able to find a section of tools named Visual Basic Power Packs that you can add to your forms. The following sections describe the Power Pack tools. You can learn more about the Power Packs at `http://msdn .microsoft.com/en-us/library/microsoft.visualbasic.powerpacks.aspx`.

DataRepeater

The DataRepeater control allows you to define a template of controls to display a piece of data. The repeater then repeats your template for each row in a data source and displays the result in a scrollable container.

Line and Shape Controls

The LineShape, OvalShape, and RectangleShape controls let you easily place lines, ovals, and rectangles on a form without using pens, brushes, and Graphics objects.

Properties let you set the controls' pens and brushes at design time. The controls support events such as Click and DoubleClick, and many of the graphical methods provided in the

System.Drawing namespace. The OvalShape and RectangleShape controls even support linear gradient brushes that let you add interesting graphical effects at design time.

PrintForm Component

In Visual Basic 6 and earlier versions, the Form control had a PrintForm method that sent an image of the form to the printer. The result was a bitmap image that usually looked grainy on the printout. It did not take full advantage of the printer's high resolution, and it didn't add extra data that might not fit on the monitor but that could fit on a printout.

Despite these drawbacks, PrintForm was extremely easy to use. The program simply called the form's PrintForm method. This is much simpler than generating a high-resolution printout, so developers often used it to give early versions of an application a printing capability. For many applications, PrintForm was good enough, and it gave users a WYSIWYG (what you see is what you get) printing tool, so that's all many programs needed.

Similarly the PrintForm component enables a Visual Basic .NET application to print a form's image quickly and easily.

CAPTURE OR PRINT

You can also use the Form object's DrawToBitmap method to capture an image of the form in a bitmap. You can then print the image, display a print preview, save it into a file, or do anything else that you can do with a bitmap. For an example, see `http://www.vb-helper.com/howto_2005_drawtobitmap.html`. That example was written in Visual Basic 2005 but works in later versions, too.

GOTDOTNET POWER PACK

The GotDotNet Visual Basic Power Pack includes seven useful controls. Although they were written in Visual Basic 2003, they can still be useful. The Power Pack comes with source code so you can upgrade them to Visual Basic 2012 or use their code as a starting point for building your own controls.

The following list summarizes the seven controls:

- ➤ **BlendPanel** — Provides a background with linear gradient shading. Note that the WPF LinearGradientBrush class provides a similar, but more flexible, effect. Other WPF classes such as RadialGradientBrush provide even more shading features.

- ➤ **UtilityToolbar** — A toolbar that has a look and feel similar to the Microsoft Internet Explorer toolbar.

- ➤ **ImageButton** — A button with a transparent background. You can use it, for example, to display a round button over a gradient shaded, or complex, background, without messing up the background.

- ➤ **NotificationWindow** — Displays text and graphics in a pop-up notification window.
- ➤ **TaskPane** — A container that provides collapsible panes similar to the WPF Expander control.
- ➤ **FolderViewer** — Displays a hierarchical view of a directory tree.
- ➤ **FileViewer** — Displays a list of the files in a directory.

Unfortunately, Microsoft closed the GotDotNet website in 2007. Before the site disappeared, however, I saved a copy of the Power Pack. You can get more information and download it at `http://www.vb-helper.com/tip_gotdotnet_powerpack.html`.

Form Objects

This appendix describes the most useful properties, methods, and events provided by the Windows Form class.

The Form class inherits indirectly from the Control class (Control is the Form class's "great-grandparent"), so in many ways, a form is just another type of control. Except where overridden, Form inherits the properties, methods, and events defined by the Control class. Chapter 8, "Using Windows Forms Controls," discusses some of the more useful properties, methods, and events provided by the Control class, and most of those apply to the Form class as well. Appendix A, "Useful Control Properties, Methods, and Events," summarizes the Control class's most useful properties.

PROPERTIES

The following table describes some of the most useful Form properties.

PROPERTY	DESCRIPTION
AutoScroll	Determines whether the form automatically provides scroll bars when it is too small to display all of the controls it contains.
AutoScrollMargin	If AutoScroll is True, the control will provide scroll bars if necessary to display its controls plus this much margin.
AutoScrollPosition	Adjusts the AutoScroll scroll bars so this point on the form is placed at the upper-left corner of the visible area (if possible). For example, if a button has location (100, 20), the statement AutoScrollPosition = New Point(100, 20) scrolls the form so the button is in the upper-left corner of the visible area.

continues

(continued)

PROPERTY	DESCRIPTION
BackColor	Determines the form's background color.
BackgroundImage	Determines the image displayed in the form's background.
BackgroundImageLayout	Determines how the BackgroundImage is displayed. This can be None (the image is displayed at up to normal scale, or compressed, if necessary, to make it fit vertically or horizontally), Tile (the image is tiled to fill the form), Center (the image is centered on the form at up to normal scale, or compressed, if necessary, to make it fit vertically or horizontally), Stretch (the image is resized to fill the form exactly), or Zoom (the image is resized to fill the form as much as possible without distorting it).
Bottom	Returns the distance between the form's bottom edge and the top edge of its container.
Bounds	Determines the form's size and location within its container. These bounds include the form's client and non-client areas (such as the borders and caption area).
CancelButton	Determines the button that clicks when the user presses the Escape key. This button basically gives the form a cancel action. If the form is being displayed modally, clicking this button either manually or by pressing Escape automatically closes the form.
Capture	Determines whether the form has captured mouse events. While this is True, all mouse events go to the form's event handlers. For example, pressing the mouse button sends the form a MouseDown event even if the mouse is over a control on the form or if it is off of the form completely.
ClientRectangle	Returns a Rectangle object representing the form's client area.
ClientSize	Gets or sets a Size object representing the client area's size. If you set this value, the form automatically adjusts to make the client area this size while allowing room for its non-client areas (such as borders and title bar).
ContainsFocus	Returns True if the form or one of its controls has the input focus.
ContextMenuStrip	Gets or sets the form's context menu. If the user right-clicks the form, Visual Basic automatically displays this menu. Note that controls on the form share this menu unless they have context menus of their own. Also note that some controls have their own context menus by default. For example, a TextBox displays a Copy, Cut, Paste menu, unless you explicitly set its ContextMenu property.

PROPERTY	DESCRIPTION
ControlBox	Determines whether the form displays a control box (the Minimize, Maximize, Restore, and Close buttons) on the right side of its caption area.
Controls	Returns a collection containing references to all of the controls on the form. This includes only the controls contained directly within the form, and not controls contained within other controls.
Cursor	Determines the cursor displayed by the mouse when it is over the form.
DesktopBounds	Determines the form's location and size on the desktop as a Rectangle.
DesktopLocation	Determines the form's location on the desktop as a Point.
DialogResult	Gets or sets the form's dialog box result. If code displays the form modally using its ShowDialog method, the method returns the DialogResult value the form has when it closes. Setting the form's DialogResult value automatically closes the dialog box. Triggering the form's CancelButton automatically sets DialogResult to Cancel and closes the dialog box.
DisplayRectangle	Gets a Rectangle representing the form's display area. This is the area where you should display things on the form. In theory, this might not include all of the client area and could exclude form decorations, although in practice it seems to be the same as ClientRectangle.
Enabled	Determines whether the form will respond to user events. If the form is disabled, all of its controls are disabled and drawn grayed out. The user can still resize the form, and its controls' Anchor and Dock properties still rearrange the controls accordingly. The user can also click the form's Minimize, Maximize, Restore, and Close buttons. Note that you cannot display a form modally using ShowDialog if it is disabled.
Font	Determines the form's font.
ForeColor	Determines the foreground color defined for the form.
FormBorderStyle	Determines the form's border style. This can be None, FixedSingle, Fixed3D, FixedDialog, Sizeable, FixedToolWindow, or SizeableToolWindow.
Handle	Returns the form's integer window handle (hWnd). You can pass this value to API functions that work with window handles.
HasChildren	Returns True if the form contains child controls.

continues

(continued)

PROPERTY	DESCRIPTION
Height	Determines the form's height.
HelpButton	Determines whether the form displays a Help button with a question mark in the caption area to the left of the close button. The button is only visible if the MaximizeBox and MinimizeBox properties are both False. If the user clicks the Help button, the mouse pointer turns into a question mark arrow. When the user clicks the form, Visual Basic raises the form's HelpRequested event. The form can provide help based on the location of the click and, if it provides help, it should set the event handler's hlpevent.Handled parameter to True.
Icon	Determines the form's icon displayed in the left of the form's caption area, in the taskbar, and by the Task Manager. Typically, this icon should contain images at the sizes 16 x 16 pixels and 32 x 32 pixels, so different displays can use an image with the correct size without resizing.
KeyPreview	Determines whether the form receives key events before they are passed to the control with the input focus. If KeyPreview is True, the form's key event handlers can see the key, take action, and hide the key from the control that would normally receive it, if necessary.
Left	Determines the distance between the form's left edge and the left edge of its container.
Location	Determines the coordinates of the form's upper-left corner.
MainMenuStrip	Gets or sets the form's main menu.
MaximizeBox	Determines whether the form displays a Maximize button on the right of its caption area.
MaximumSize	This Size object determines the maximum size the form can take.
MinimizeBox	Determines whether the form displays a Minimize button on the right of its caption area.
MinimumSize	This Size object determines the minimum size the form can take.
Modal	Returns True if the form is displayed modally.
Name	Gets or sets the form's name. Initially, this is the form's class name, but your code can change it to anything, possibly even duplicating another form's name.
Opacity	Determines the form's opacity level between 0.0 (transparent) and 1.0 (opaque). At design time this is displayed as a percentage 0% (transparent) to 100% (opaque).

PROPERTY	DESCRIPTION
OwnedForms	Returns an array listing this form's owned forms. To make this form own another form, call this form's AddOwnedForm method, passing it the other form. Owned forms are minimized and restored with the owner and can never lie behind the owner. Typically, they are used for things like toolboxes and search forms that should remain above the owner form.
Region	Gets or sets the region that defines the area that the form can occupy. Pieces of the form that lie outside of the region are clipped.
Right	Returns the distance between the form's right edge and the left edge of its container.
ShowIcon	Determines whether the form displays an icon in its title bar. If this is False, the system displays a default icon in the taskbar and Task Manager if ShowInTaskbar is True.
ShowInTaskbar	Determines whether the form is displayed in the taskbar and Task Manager.
Size	Gets or sets a Size object representing the form's size, including client and non-client areas.
SizeGripStyle	Determines how the resize grip is shown in the form's lower-right corner. This can be Show, Hide, or Auto.
StartPosition	Determines the form's position when it is first displayed at run time. This can be Manual (use the size and position specified by the form's properties), CenterScreen (center the form on the screen taking the taskbar into account), WindowsDefaultLocation (use a default position defined by Windows and use the form's specified size), and WindowsDefaultBounds (use a default position and size defined by Windows).
Tag	Gets or sets an object associated with the form. You can use this for whatever purpose you see fit.
Text	Determines the text displayed in the form's caption.
Top	Determines the distance between the form's top edge and the top edge of its container.
TopMost	Determines whether the form is a topmost form. A topmost form always sits above all other non-topmost forms, even when the other forms have the input focus.

continues

(continued)

PROPERTY	DESCRIPTION
TransparencyKey	Gets or sets a color that determines the areas of the form that are shown as transparent. This applies to the form itself and any controls it contains. For example, if you set TransparencyKey to the color Colors.Control, the whole form and the bodies of many of its controls are invisible, so you will see text and borders floating above whatever forms lie behind.
UseWaitCursor	Determines whether the form is currently displaying the wait cursor.
Visible	Determines whether the form is visible. If the form is not visible, the user cannot interact with it. If you set Visible = False, the form's icon is also removed from the taskbar and Task Manager.
Width	Determines the form's width.
WindowState	Gets or sets the form's state. This can be Normal, Minimized, or Maximized.

METHODS

The following table describes some of the most useful Form methods.

METHOD	DESCRIPTION
Activate	Activates the form and gives it the focus. Normally, this pops the form to the top. Note that forcing a form to the top takes control of the desktop away from the user, so you should use this method sparingly. For example, if the user dismisses one form, you might activate the next form in a logical sequence. You should not activate a form to get the user's attention every few minutes.
AddOwnedForm	Adds an owned form to this form. Owned forms are minimized and restored with the owner and can never lie behind the owner. Typically, they are used for things like toolboxes and search forms that should remain above the owner form.
BringToFront	Brings the form to the top of the Z-order. This applies only to other forms in the application. This form will pop to the top of other forms in this program, but not forms in other applications.
Close	Closes the form. The program can still prevent the form from closing by catching the FormClosing event and setting e.Cancel to True.

METHOD	DESCRIPTION
Contains	Returns True if a specified control is contained in the form. This includes controls inside GroupBox controls, Panel controls, and other containers, which are not listed in the form's Controls collection.
CreateGraphics	Creates a Graphics object that the program can use to draw on the form's surface. Note that the Paint event handler provides a Graphics object in its e.Graphics parameter when the form needs to be redrawn. You should use that object rather than a new one returned by CreateGraphics while inside a Paint event handler. Otherwise, the Paint event handler's version will draw over anything that you draw using the object returned by CreateGraphics.
GetChildAtPoint	Returns a reference to the child control at a specific point. Note that the control is the outermost control at that point. For example, if a GroupBox contains a Button and you call GetChildAtPoint for a point above the Button, GetChildAtPoint returns the GroupBox. To find the Button, you would need to use the GroupBox control's GetChildAtPoint method. Note also that the position of the Button within the GroupBox is relative to the GroupBox control's origin, so you would need to subtract the GroupBox control's position from the X and Y coordinates of the point relative to the form's origin.
GetNextControl	Returns the next control in the tab order. Parameters indicate the control to start from and whether the search should move forward or backward through the tab order.
Hide	Hides the form. This sets the form's Visible property to False.
Invalidate	Invalidates some or all of the form's area and generates a Paint event.
PointToClient	Converts a point from screen coordinates into the form's coordinate system.
PointToScreen	Converts a point from the form's coordinate system into screen coordinates.
RectangleToClient	Converts a rectangle from screen coordinates into the form's coordinate system.
RectangleToScreen	Converts a rectangle from the form's coordinate system into screen coordinates.
Refresh	Invalidates the form's client area and forces it to redraw itself and its controls.
RemoveOwnedForm	Removes an owned form from this form's OwnedForms collection.

continues

(continued)

METHOD	DESCRIPTION
Scale	Resizes the form and the controls it contains by a scale factor. A second overloaded version scales by different amounts in the X and Y directions. Note that this doesn't change the controls' font sizes, just their dimensions.
ScrollControlIntoView	If the form has AutoScroll set to True, this scrolls to make the indicated control visible.
SelectNextControl	Activates the next control in the tab order. Parameters indicate the control to start at, whether the search should move forward or backward through the tab order, whether the search should include only controls with TabStop set to True or all controls, whether to include controls nested inside other controls, and whether to wrap around to the first/last control if the search passes the last/first control.
SendToBack	Sends the form to the back of the Z-order. This puts the form behind all other forms in all applications, although it *does not remove the focus from this form*.
SetAutoScrollMargin	If AutoScroll is True, this method sets the AutoScroll margin. The control will provide scroll bars if necessary to display its controls plus this much margin.
SetBounds	Sets some or all of the form's bounds: X, Y, Width, and Height.
SetDesktopBounds	Sets the form's position and size in desktop coordinates. See SetDesktopLocation for more information.
SetDesktopLocation	Sets the form's position in desktop coordinates. Desktop coordinates include only the screen's working area and do not include the area occupied by the taskbar. For example, if the taskbar is attached to the left edge of the screen, the point (0, 0) in *screen coordinates* is *beneath the taskbar*. However, the point (0, 0) in *desktop coordinates* is just *to the right of the taskbar*. If you set the form's location to (0, 0), part of the form is hidden by the taskbar. If you set the form's desktop location to (0, 0), the form is visible just to the right of the taskbar.
Show	Displays the form. This has the same effect as setting the form's Visible property to True.
ShowDialog	Displays the form as a modal dialog box. The user cannot interact with other parts of the application before this form closes. Note that some other processes may still be running within the application. For example, a Timer control on another form still raises Tick events and the program can still respond to them.

EVENTS

The following table describes some of the most useful Form events.

EVENT	DESCRIPTION
Activated	Occurs when the form activates.
Click	Occurs when the user clicks the form. Normally, if the user clicks a control, the control rather than the form receives the Click event. If the form's Capture property is set to True, however, the event goes to the form.
Deactivate	Occurs when the form deactivates.
DoubleClick	Occurs when the user double-clicks the form. Normally, if the user double-clicks a control, the control rather than the form receives the DoubleClick event. If the form's Capture property is set to True, however, the first click goes to the form and the second goes to the control.
FormClosed	Occurs when the form is closed. The program can still access the form's properties, methods, and controls, but it is definitely going away. See also the FormClosing event. Note that if the program calls Application.Exit, the form's FormClosed and FormClosing events do not occur. If you want the program to free resources before the form disappears, it should do so before calling Application.Exit.
FormClosing	Occurs when the form is about to close. The program can cancel the close (for example, if some data has not been saved) by setting the event handler's e.Cancel parameter to True.
GotFocus	Occurs when focus moves into the form.
HelpRequested	Occurs when the user requests help from the form, usually by pressing F1 or by pressing a context-sensitive Help button (see the HelpButton property) and then clicking a control on the form. Help requests move up through control containers until a HelpRequested event sets its hlpevent.Handled parameter to True. For example, suppose that the user sets focus to a TextBox contained in the form and presses F1. The TextBox control's HelpRequested event handler executes. If that routine doesn't set hlpevent.Handled to True, the event bubbles up to the TextBox control's container, the form, and its HelpRequested event handler executes.
KeyDown	Occurs when the user presses a keyboard key down.
KeyPress	Occurs when the user presses and releases a keyboard key.

continues

(continued)

EVENT	DESCRIPTION
KeyUp	Occurs when the user releases a keyboard key.
Layout	Occurs when the form should reposition its child controls. If your code needs to perform custom repositioning, this is the event where it should do so.
Load	Occurs after the form is loaded but before it is displayed. You can perform one-time initialization tasks here.
LostFocus	Occurs when the focus moves out of the form.
MouseClick	Occurs when the user clicks the form. You should consider the Click event to be on a logically higher level than MouseClick. For example, the Click event may be triggered by actions other than an actual mouse click (such as the user pressing the Enter key).
MouseDoubleClick	Occurs when the user double-clicks the form. You should consider the DoubleClick event to be on a logically higher level than MouseDoubleClick.
MouseDown	Occurs when the user presses the mouse down over the form. Also see the Capture property.
MouseEnter	Occurs when the mouse first moves so it is over the form. If the mouse moves over one of the form's controls, that counts as leaving the form, so when it moves back over an unoccupied part of the form, it raises a MouseEnter event.
MouseHover	Occurs when the mouse remains stationary over the form for a while. This event is raised once when the mouse first hovers and then is not raised again until the mouse leaves the form and returns. Note that the mouse moving over one of the form's controls counts as leaving.
MouseLeave	Occurs when the mouse leaves the form. Note that the mouse moving over one of the form's controls counts as leaving.
MouseMove	Occurs when the mouse moves while over the form.
MouseUp	Occurs when the user releases a mouse button. When the user presses a mouse button down, the form captures subsequent mouse events until the user releases the button. While the capture is in place, the form receives MouseMove events, even if the mouse is moved off of the form. It will receive a MouseHover event, even if the mouse is off of the form, if no such event has been raised since the last time the mouse moved over the form. When the user finally releases the button, the form receives a MouseUp event and then, if the mouse is no longer over the form, a MouseLeave event.

EVENT	DESCRIPTION
MouseWheel	Occurs when the user moves the mouse wheel. The event's e.X and e.Y parameters give the mouse's current position. The e.Delta parameter gives the signed distance by which the wheel has been rotated. Currently, this is defined as 120 *detents* per notch of the wheel. (A detent is a unit of the wheel's rotation. A notch is the amount by which the wheel rotates with a discrete click. So every time you turn the wheel 1 notch, e.Delta changes by 120 detents.) Standards dictate that you should scroll data when the accumulated delta reaches plus or minus 120 detents, and that you should then scroll the data by the number of lines given by SystemInformation.MouseWheelScrollLines (currently this is 3). If higher-resolution mouse wheels are added some day, a notch might send a value smaller than 120, and you could update the data more often, but you should keep the same ratio: SystemInformation.MouseWheelScrollLines lines per 120 detents.
Move	Occurs when the form is moved.
Paint	Occurs when part of the form must be redrawn. You can use the e.ClipRectangle parameter to see what area needs to be drawn. For very complicated drawings, you may be able to draw more quickly if you only draw the area indicated by e.ClipRectangle. Note also that Visual Basic clips drawings outside of this rectangle and may clip some areas inside this rectangle that do not need to be redrawn. That makes drawing faster in some cases. The idea here is that part of the form has been covered and exposed so only that part must be redrawn. If you need to adjust the drawing when the form is resized, you should invalidate the form in the Resize event handler to force a redraw of the whole form.
Resize	Occurs when the form is resized.
ResizeBegin	Occurs when the user starts resizing the form.
ResizeEnd	Occurs when the user has finished resizing the form.
SizeChanged	Occurs when the form is resized.

When focus moves into and out of a form, the sequence of events is: Activated, GotFocus, Deactivate, Validating, Validated, LostFocus.

Typically, when the user clicks the form, the sequence of events is: MouseDown, Click, MouseClick, MouseUp.

Typically, when the user double-clicks the form, the sequence of events is: MouseDown, Click, MouseClick, MouseUp, MouseDown, DoubleClick, MouseDoubleClick, MouseUp.

When code resizes the form, the sequence of events is: Resize, SizeChanged.

When the user resizes the form, the sequence of events is: ResizeBegin, Resize, SizeChanged, Resize, SizeChanged, . . ., ResizeEnd.

PROPERTY-CHANGED EVENTS

The Form class provides several events that fire when certain form properties change. The name of each of these events has the form *PropertyName*Changed where *PropertyName* is the name of the corresponding property. For example, the BackColorChanged event fires when the form's BackColor property changes.

The following is a list of these events.

BackColorChanged	MaximumSizeChanged
BackgroundImageChanged	MinimumSizeChanged
ContextMenuChanged	ParentChanged
CursorChanged	SizeChanged
DockChanged	StyleChanged
EnabledChanged	SystemColorsChanged
FontChanged	TextChanged
ForeColorChanged	VisibleChanged
LocationChanged	

The names of most of these events are self-explanatory, so they are not described here. The exception is the SystemColorsChanged event. This occurs when the system's colors are changed either by the user or programmatically.

For example, suppose that you want the form to draw using its ForeColor property and you want that property to match the active title bar text color. Then, you could use the following code to update ForeColor when the user changed the system colors:

```
Private Sub Form2_SystemColorsChanged() Handles MyBase.SystemColorsChanged
    Me.ForeColor = SystemColors.ActiveCaptionText
End Sub
```

Note that Visual Basic invalidates the form after raising the SystemColorsChanged event, so the form immediately repaints itself using the new settings.

Classes and Structures

This appendix provides information about class and structure declarations.

CLASSES

The syntax for declaring a class is:

```
[attribute_list] [Partial] [accessibility] [Shadows] [inheritance] _
Class name [(Of type_list)]
    [Inherits parent_class]
    [Implements interface]
    statements
End Class
```

The attribute_list can include any number of attribute specifiers separated by commas.

The accessibility clause can take one of the following values: Public, Protected, Friend, Protected Friend, and Private.

The Partial keyword indicates that this is only part of the class declaration and that the program may include other partial declarations for this class.

The Shadows keyword indicates that the class hides the definition of some other entity in the enclosing class's base class.

The inheritance clause can take the value MustInherit or NotInheritable.

The type_list clause defines type parameters for a generic class. For information on generics, see Chapter 26, "Generics."

The Inherits statement tells the class from which this class inherits. A class can include at most one Inherits statement and, if present, this must be the first non-comment statement after the Class statement.

The Implements statement specifies an interface that the class implements. A class can implement any number of interfaces. You can specify interfaces in separate Interface statements or in a single statement separated by commas.

The following example declares a simple Person class and an Employee class that inherits from it:

```
Public Class Person

End Class

Public Class Employee
    Inherits Person

End Class
```

STRUCTURES

The syntax for writing a structure is as follows:

```
[attribute_list] [Partial] [accessibility] [Shadows] _
Structure name [(Of type_list)]
    [Implements interface]
    statements
End Structure
```

The structure's attribute_list, Partial, accessibility, Shadows, type_list, and Implements statements are the same as those for classes. See the previous section for details.

The major differences between a structure and a class are:

➤ Structures cannot use the MustInherit or NotInheritable keyword (because you cannot inherit from a structure).

➤ Structures cannot use the Inherits clause.

➤ Structures are *value types*, whereas classes are *reference types*. See Chapter 23, "Classes and Structures," for information on the consequences of this difference.

CONSTRUCTORS

A *constructor* is a special subroutine named New.

Class constructors can take any number of parameters. If you provide no constructors, Visual Basic allows a default empty constructor that takes no parameters. If you provide *any* constructor, Visual Basic does not provide a default empty constructor. If you want to allow the program to use an empty constructor in that case, you must either provide one or provide a constructor with all optional parameters.

Structure constructors are very similar to class constructors with two major exceptions. First, you cannot make a structure constructor that takes no parameters. Second, Visual Basic always provides a default empty constructor, even if you give the structure other constructors.

EVENTS

An *event* lets an object notify the application that something potentially interesting has occurred.

The syntax for declaring an event is:

```
[accessibility] [Shadows] Event event_name(parameters)
```

The accessibility clause can take one of the following values: Public, Protected, Friend, Protected Friend, or Private.

Use the Shadows keyword to indicate that the event shadows an item with the same name in the parent class. Any type of item can shadow any other type of item. For example, an event can shadow a subroutine, function, or variable. This would be rather bizarre and confusing, but it is possible.

The parameters clause specifies the parameters that you will pass when raising the event. An event handler catching the event will receive those parameters. Use ByRef parameters to allow the event handler to provide feedback to the code that raises the event.

The syntax for raising an event is as follows:

```
RaiseEvent event_name(arguments)
```

The arguments that you pass to the event handler must match the parameters declared in the Event statement.

The following code shows pieces of a SeatAssignment class that raises a NameChanged event when its Name property changes:

```
Public Class SeatAssignment
    Public Event NameChanged()
    ...
    Private m_Name As String
    Public Property Name() As String
        Get
            Return m_Name
        End Get
        Set(ByVal value As String)
            m_Name = Ðvalue
            RaiseEvent NameChanged()
        End Set
    End Property
    ...
End Class
```

LINQ

This appendix provides syntax summaries for the most useful LINQ methods. For more detailed information, see Chapter 20, "LINQ."

BASIC LINQ QUERY SYNTAX

The following text shows the typical syntax for a LINQ query:

```
From ... Where ... Order By ... Select ...
```

The following sections describe these four basic clauses. The sections after those describe some of the other most useful LINQ clauses.

From

The From clause tells where the data comes from and defines the name by which it is known within the LINQ query.

```
From var1 In data_source1, var2 In data_source2, ...
```

Examples:

```
Dim query1 = From cust As Customer In all_customers
Dim query2 = From stu In students, score In TestScores
```

Usually, if you select data from multiple sources, you will want to use a Where clause to join the results from the sources.

Where

The Where clause applies filters to the records selected by the From clause. The syntax is:

```
Where conditions
```

Use comparison operators (>, <, =), logical operators (Not, Or, AndAlso), object methods (ToString, Length), and functions to build complex conditions.

For example, the following query selects student and test score data, matching students to their test scores:

```
Dim query = From stu In students, score In TestScores
    Where stu.StudentId = score.StudentId
```

The following example selects only students with last names starting with S:

```
Dim query = From stu In students, score In TestScores
    Where stu.StudentId = score.StudentId AndAlso
        stu.LastName.ToUpper.StartsWith("S")
```

Order By

The Order By clause makes a query sort the selected objects. For example, the following query selects students and their scores and orders the results by student last name followed by first name:

```
Dim query = From stu In students, score In TestScores
    Where stu.StudentId = score.StudentId
    Order By stu.LastName, stu.FirstName
```

Add the Descending keyword to sort a field in descending order. The following example orders the results by descending TestAverage value:

```
Dim query = From stu In students, score In TestScores
    Where stu.StudentId = score.StudentId
    Order By stu.TestAverage Descending
```

Select

The Select clause lists the fields that the query should select into its result. If this is omitted, the query selects all of the data in the data sources. You can add an alias to the result.

The following query selects customers' FirstName and LastName values concatenated and gives the result the alias Name. It also selects the customers' AccountBalance value and gives it the alias Balance.

```
Dim query = From cust In all_customers
    Select Name = cust.FirstName & " " & cust.LastName,
        Balance = Cust.AccountBalance
```

You can pass values from the data sources into functions or constructors. For example, suppose the Person class has a constructor that takes first and last names as parameters. Then the following query returns a group of Person objects created from the selected customer data:

```
Dim query = From cust In all_customers
    Select New Person(cust.FirstName, cust.LastName)
```

Distinct

The Distinct keyword makes a query return only one copy of each result. The following example selects the distinct CustId values from the all_orders list:

```
Dim query = From ord In all_orders
    Select ord.CustId
    Distinct
```

Join

The Join keyword selects data from multiple data sources matching up corresponding fields. The following pseudo-code shows the Join command's syntax:

```
From variable1 In datasource1
Join variable2 In datasource2
On variable1.field1 Equals variable2.field2
```

For example, the following query selects corresponding objects from the all_customers and all_orders lists:

```
Dim query = From cust As Customer In all_customers
    Join ord In all_orders
    On cust.CustId Equals ord.CustId
```

Note that you can get a similar result by using a Where clause. The following query selects a similar set of objects without using the Join keyword:

```
Dim query = From cust As Customer In all_customers, ord In all_orders
    Where cust.CustId = ord.CustId
```

Group By

The Group By clause lets a program select data from a flat, relational style format and build a hierarchical arrangement of objects. The following code shows the basic Group By syntax:

```
Group items By value Into groupname = Group
```

Here, *items* is a list of items whose properties you want selected into the group, *value* tells LINQ on what field to group objects, and *groupname* gives a name for the group.

The following query selects objects from the all_orders list. The Group By statement makes the query group orders that have the same CustId value.

```
Dim query1 = From ord In all_orders
    Order By ord.CustId, ord.OrderId
    Group ord By ord.CustId Into CustOrders = Group
```

The result is an IEnumerable that contains objects with two fields. The first field is the CustId value used to define a group (the value part in the syntax shown earlier). The second field is an IEnumerable named CustOrders that contains the group of order objects for each CustId value.

The following code shows how a program might display the results in a TreeView control:

```
Dim root1 As TreeNode = trvResults.Nodes.Add("Orders grouped by CustId")
For Each obj In query1
    ' Display the customer id.
    Dim cust_node As TreeNode = root1.Nodes.Add("Cust Id: " & obj.CustId)

    ' List this customer's orders.
    For Each ord In obj.CustOrders
        cust_node.Nodes.Add("OrderId: " & ord.OrderId &
            ", Date: " & ord.OrderDate)
    Next ord
Next obj
```

Another common type of query uses the Group By clause to apply some aggregate function to the items selected in a group. The following query selects order and order item objects, grouping each order's items and displaying each order's total price:

```
Dim query1 = From ord In all_orders, ord_item In all_order_items
    Order By ord.CustId, ord.OrderId
    Where ord.OrderId = ord_item.OrderId
    Group ord_item By ord Into
        TotalPrice = Sum(ord_item.Quantity * ord_item.UnitPrice),
        OrderItems = Group
```

The following code shows how a program might display the results in a TreeView control named trvResults:

```
Dim root1 As TreeNode = trvResults.Nodes.Add("Orders")
For Each obj In query1
    ' Display the customer id.
    Dim cust_node As TreeNode =
        root1.Nodes.Add("Order Id: " & obj.ord.OrderId &
            ", Total Price: " & FormatCurrency(obj.TotalPrice))

    ' List this customer's orders.
    For Each ord_item In obj.OrderItems
        cust_node.Nodes.Add(ord_item.Description & ": " &
            ord_item.Quantity & " @ " &
            FormatCurrency(ord_item.UnitPrice))
    Next ord_item
Next obj
```

Limiting Results

LINQ includes several keywords for limiting the results returned by a query.

The Take statement makes the query keep a specified number of results and discard the rest.

The Take While statement makes the query keep selected results as long as some condition holds and then discard the rest.

The Skip statement makes the query discard a specified number of results and keep the rest.

The Skip While statement makes the query discard selected results as long as some condition holds and then keep the rest.

The following code demonstrates each of these commands:

```
Dim q1 = From cust In all_customers Take 5
Dim q2 = From cust In all_customers Take While cust.FirstName.Contains("n")
Dim q3 = From cust In all_customers Skip 3
Dim q4 = From cust In all_customers Skip While cust.FirstName.Contains("n")
```

USING QUERY RESULTS

A LINQ query expression returns an IEnumerable containing the query's results. A program can iterate through this result and process the items that it contains.

If the selected data has a well-understood data type, such as strings or objects from a known class, you can iterate through the result by using an explicitly typed looping variable. The following example selects customer names and then displays them. The looping variable is explicitly typed as a string.

```
Dim query = From cust In all_customers
    Select Name = cust.FirstName & " " & cust.LastName
For Each cust_name As String In query
    Debug.WriteLine(cust_name)
Next cust_name
```

If the returned data type is less well understood, you can use a looping variable with an inferred data type. The following code selects customers and their orders. It then loops through the results displaying order dates and numbers, together with the names of the customers who placed the orders. The looping variable *obj* has an inferred type.

```
Dim query = From cust In all_customers, ord In all_orders
    Where cust.CustId = ord.CustId
    Order By ord.OrderDate

For Each obj In query
    Debug.WriteLine(obj.ord.OrderDate & vbTab & obj.ord.OrderId &
        vbTab & obj.cust.Name)
Next obj
```

LINQ FUNCTIONS

The following table summarizes LINQ extension methods that are not available from Visual Basic LINQ query syntax.

FUNCTION	PURPOSE
Aggregate	Uses a function specified by the code to calculate a custom aggregate.
Concat	Concatenates two sequences into a new sequence.
Contains	Returns True if the result contains a specific value.
DefaultIfEmpty	Returns the query's result or a default value if the query returns an empty result.
ElementAt	Returns an element at a specific position in the query's result.
ElementAtOrDefault	Returns an element at a specific position in the query's result or a default value if there is no such position.
Empty	Creates an empty IEnumerable.
Except	Returns the items in one IEnumerable that are not in a second IEnumerable.
First	Returns the first item in the query's result.
FirstOrDefault	Returns the first item in the query's result or a default value if the query contains no results.
Intersection	Returns the intersection of two IEnumerable objects.
Last	Returns the last item in the query's result.
LastOrDefault	Returns the last item in the query's result or a default value if the query contains no results.
Range	Creates an IEnumerable containing a range of integer values.
Repeat	Creates an IEnumerable containing a value repeated a specific number of times.
SequenceEqual	Returns True if two sequences are identical.
Single	Returns the single item selected by the query.
SingleOrDefault	Returns the single item selected by the query or a default value if the query contains no results.
Union	Returns the union of two IEnumerable objects.

The following table summarizes LINQ data type conversion functions.

FUNCTION	PURPOSE
AsEnumerable	Converts the result to IEnumerable(Of T).
AsQueryable	Converts an IEnumerable to IQueryable.
OfType	Removes items that cannot be cast into a specific type.
ToArray	Places the results in an array.
ToDictionary	Places the results in a Dictionary.
ToList	Converts the result to List(Of T).
ToLookup	Places the results in a Lookup (one-to-many dictionary).

LINQ TO XML

LINQ provides methods to move data in and out of XML.

LINQ into XML

To select data into XML objects, use the special characters <%= and %> to indicate a "hole" within the XML literal. Inside the hole, place a LINQ query.

For example, the following code builds an XElement object that contains Customer XML elements for objects in the all_customers list:

```
Dim x_all As XElement =
    <AllCustomers>
        <%= From cust In all_customers
            Select New XElement("Customer",
            New XAttribute("FirstName", cust.FirstName),
            New XAttribute("LastName", cust.LastName),
            New XText(cust.Balance.ToString("0.00")))
        %>
    </AllCustomers>
```

LINQ out of XML

XML classes such as XElement provide LINQ functions that allow you to use LINQ queries on them just as you can select data from IEnumerable objects.

The following code extracts the descendants of the x_all XElement object that have negative balances. It selects each XML element's FirstName and LastName attributes, and balance (saved in the element's value).

```
Dim select_all = From cust In x_all.Descendants("Customer")
    Where CDec(cust.Value) < 0
    Select FName = cust.Attribute("FirstName").Value,
           LName = cust.Attribute("LastName").Value,
           Balance = cust.Value
```

The following table summarizes LINQ methods supported by XElement.

FUNCTION	RETURNS
Ancestors	IEnumerable containing all ancestors of the element.
AncestorsAndSelf	IEnumerable containing this element followed by all ancestors of the element.
Attribute	The element's attribute with a specific name.
Attributes	IEnumerable containing the element's attributes.
Descendants	IEnumerable containing all descendants of the element.
DescendantsAndSelf	IEnumerable containing this element followed by all descendants of the element.
DescendantNodes	IEnumerable containing all descendant nodes of the element. These include all nodes such as XElement and XText.
DescendantNodesAndSelf	IEnumerable containing this element followed by all descendant nodes of the element. These include all nodes such as XElement and XText.
Element	The first child element with a specific name.
Elements	IEnumerable containing the immediate children of the element.
ElementsAfterSelf	IEnumerable containing the siblings of the element that come after this element.
ElementsBeforeSelf	IEnumerable containing the siblings of the element that come before this element.
Nodes	IEnumerable containing the nodes that are immediate children of the element. These include all nodes such as XElement and XText.
NodesAfterSelf	IEnumerable containing the sibling nodes of the element that come after this element.
NodesBeforeSelf	IEnumerable containing the sibling nodes of the element that come before this element.

The following table gives examples of shorthand expressions for node axes and their functional equivalents.

SHORTHAND	MEANING	EQUIVALENT
x...<Customer>	Descendants named Customer.	x.Descendants("Customer")
x.<Child>	An element named Child that is a child of this node.	x.Attributes("Child")
x.@<FirstName> Or: x.@FirstName	The value of the FirstName attribute.	x.Attributes("FirstName").Value

LINQ TO DATASET

LINQ to DataSet refers to methods provided by database objects that support LINQ queries.

The DataSet class itself doesn't provide many LINQ features, but the DataTable objects that it holds do. The DataTable has an AsEnumerable method that converts the DataTable into an IEnumerable, which supports LINQ.

The following list summarizes the key differences between a DataTable query and a normal LINQ to Objects query:

➤ The code must use the DataTable object's AsEnumerable method to make the object queryable.

➤ The code can access the fields in a DataRow as in stu!LastName or as in stu.Field(Of String) ("LastName").

➤ If you want to display the results in a DataGrid control, use the query's ToList method.

The following example shows a query that selects student data from the dtStudents DataTable where the LastName comes before D. It selects the students' FirstName and LastName fields, and displays the result in a DataGrid control.

```
Dim before_d =
    From stu In dtStudents.AsEnumerable()
    Where stu!LastName < "D"
    Order By stu.Field(Of String)("LastName")
    Select First = stu!FirstName, Last = stu!LastName

dgStudentsBeforeD.DataSource = before_d.ToList
```

Method-Based Queries

LINQ query keywords including Where, Order By, and Select actually correspond to methods that take parameters giving the functions they should use to perform their tasks. For example, the Where method takes as a parameter the address of a function that returns True if an item should be selected in the query result.

In addition to using standard LINQ query syntax, you can use method-based queries to select data. The following example selects data from all_customers where the OwesMoney function returns True. The OrderByAmount function returns values that can be used to order the results and SelectFields returns an object that contains selected fields for a selected item.

```
Dim q2 = all_customers.
    Where(AddressOf OwesMoney).
    OrderBy(AddressOf OrderByAmount).
    Select(AddressOf SelectFields)
```

Instead of passing the address of a function to these methods, you can pass lambda functions. The following code returns a result similar to the preceding query but using lambda functions instead of addresses of functions:

```
Dim q3 = all_customers.
    Where(Function(c As Customer) c.AccountBalance < 0).
    OrderBy(Of Decimal)(Function(c As Customer) c.AccountBalance).
    Select(Of CustInfo)(
        Function(c As Customer, index As Integer)
            Return New CustInfo() With
                {.CustName = c.Name, .Balance = c.AccountBalance}
    )
```

PLINQ

Adding parallelism to LINQ is remarkably simple. First, add a reference to the System.Threading library to your program. Then add a call to the AsParallel to the enumerable object that you're searching. For example, the following code uses AsParallel to select the even numbers from the array numbers:

```
Dim evens =
    From num In numbers.AsParallel()
    Where num Mod 2 = 0
```

Generics

This appendix summarizes generic classes, extensions, and methods. The final section in this appendix describes items that you cannot make generic.

GENERIC CLASSES

The syntax for declaring a generic class is as follows:

```
[attribute_list] [Partial] [accessibility] [Shadows] [inheritance] _
Class name [(Of type_list)]
    [Inherits parent_class]
    [Implements interface]
    statements
End Class
```

All of these parts of the declaration are the same as those used by a normal (non-generic) class. See Chapter 25, "Classes and Structures," and Appendix K for information about non-generic classes.

The key to a generic class is the (Of type_list) clause. Here, type_list is a list of data types separated by commas that form the generic's parameter types. Each type can be optionally followed by the keyword As and a list of constraints that the corresponding type must satisfy. The constraint list can contain any number of interfaces and, at most, one class. It can also contain the New keyword to indicate that the corresponding type must provide a parameterless constructor. If a constraint list contains more than one item, the list must be surrounded by braces.

The following code defines the generic MyGeneric class. It takes three type parameters. The first is named Type1 within the generic's code and has no constraints. The second type, named Type2, must satisfy the IComparable interface. The third parameter, named Type3, must provide a parameterless constructor, must satisfy the IDisposable interface, and must inherit directly or indirectly from the Person class.

```
Public Class MyGeneric(Of _
  Type1,
  Type2 As IComparable,
  Type3 As {New, IDisposable, Person})
```

GENERIC EXTENSIONS

Because of their somewhat idiosyncratic nature, extension methods add an extra level of complexity to generics.

Normally, a generic class declaration includes the types on which it depends and the code within the class can use those types. For example, consider the Schedule class shown in the following code, which represents a schedule of tasks:

```
' Represents a schedule of Tasks.
Public Class Schedule(Of Task)
    Public Sub AddTask(ByVal new_task As Task)
        ...
    End Sub
    ...
End Class
```

The type list for the Schedule class includes a type named Task and the class's code can use the type Task. In this example, the AddTask subroutine takes a parameter of this type.

Now suppose you want to add an extension method named Prioritize to the generic Schedule class. The first parameter in the extension method's declaration indicates the class that the method extends. In this case, that should be Schedule(Of Task), but the extension method itself must also be generic, so it must use a type list just as any other generic method does.

The result is the following declaration.

```
Imports System.Runtime.CompilerServices

Public Module ScheduleExtensions
    ' Prioritizes the schedule.
    <Extension()>
    Sub Prioritize(Of T)(sched As Schedule(Of T))
        Debug.WriteLine("Prioritizing Schedule of " & GetType(T).Name)
        ...
    End Sub
End Module
```

The Prioritize method first includes a type list indicating that it generically depends on a type named T within this method. It then includes the extension method parameter list. The first parameter (the only parameter in this example) gives the class that the method extends: Schedule(Of T).

The following code fragment shows how a program could create a Schedule of Job objects and then call the Prioritize extension:

```
Dim sched As New Schedule(Of Job)
...
sched.Prioritize()
```

Generic extension methods can become extremely complicated. For more detailed information about extension methods in general, see Chapter 16, "Subroutines and Functions," and the Microsoft Visual Basic Team blog post at `http://blogs.msdn.com/vbteam/pages/articles-about-extension-methods.aspx`, paying special attention to Part 5, "Generics and Extension Methods."

GENERIC METHODS

In addition to generic classes and extension methods, you can create generic methods. This is simply a method that takes generic parameters. The following code shows a Switcher class that has a shared generic Switch method:

```
Public Class Switcher
    Public Shared Sub Switch(Of T)(ByRef thing1 As T, ByRef thing2 As T)
        Dim temp As T = thing1
        thing1 = thing2
        thing2 = temp
    End Sub
End Class
```

The Switcher class is not generic, but it contains a generic method. Both generic and non-generic classes can define both generic and non-generic methods. For example, the following code shows a code module that contains a generic Switch method:

```
Module SwitchStuff
    ' Switch two variables' values.
    Public Sub Switch(Of T)(ByRef thing1 As T, ByRef thing2 As T)
        Dim temp As T = thing1
        thing1 = thing2
        thing2 = temp
    End Sub
End Module
```

The only difference between this code and the previous version is that the previous version includes the Shared keyword so the program can use the class's method without instantiating the class.

PROHIBITED GENERICS

Unfortunately (or perhaps fortunately because this could be extremely complicated and confusing), you cannot make generic lambda functions. The following code shows a lambda function that is allowed and a generic lambda function that is not allowed:

```
' Allowed.
Dim max_index1 = Function(lst As List(Of Integer)) lst.Count - 1

' Prohibited.
Dim max_index2 = Function(Of T)(lst As List(Of T)) lst.Count - 1
```

You also cannot make generic properties, operators, events, or constructors.

Graphics

This appendix provides information about graphics classes used by Windows Forms applications.

GRAPHICS NAMESPACES

This section describes the most important graphics namespaces and their most useful classes, structures, and enumerated values.

System.Drawing

This namespace defines the most important graphics objects such as Graphics, Pen, Brush, Font, FontFamily, Bitmap, Icon, and Image. The following table describes the namespace's most useful classes and structures.

CLASSES AND STRUCTURES	PURPOSE
Bitmap	Represents a bitmap image defined by pixel data.
Brush	Represents area fill characteristics.
Color	Defines a color's red, green, blue, and alpha components as values between 0 and 255. Alpha = 0 means the object is transparent, and alpha = 255 means it is opaque.
Font	Represents a particular font (name, size, and style, such as italic or bold).
FontFamily	Represents a group of typefaces with similar characteristics.
Graphics	Represents a drawing surface. Provides methods to draw on the surface.

continues

(continued)

CLASSES AND STRUCTURES	PURPOSE
Icon	Represents a Windows icon.
Image	Abstract base class from which Bitmap, Icon, and Metafile inherit.
Metafile	Represents a graphic metafile that contains drawing commands (in contrast to rasterized bitmap data).
Pen	Represents line drawing characteristics such as color, thickness, and dash style.
Pens	Provides a large number of predefined pens with different colors and thickness 1.
Point	Defines a point's X and Y coordinates.
PointF	Defines a point's X and Y coordinates with floating-point values.
Rectangle	Defines a rectangle using a Point and a Size.
RectangleF	Defines a rectangle using a PointF and a SizeF (with floating-point values).
Region	Defines a shape created from rectangles and paths for use in filling, hit testing, or clipping.
Size	Defines a width and height.
SizeF	Defines a width and height with floating-point values.
SolidBrush	Represents a solid brush.

System.Drawing.Drawing2D

This namespace contains classes for more advanced two-dimensional drawing. Some of these classes refine more basic drawing classes. For example, the HatchBrush class represents a specialized type of Brush that fills with a hatch pattern. Other classes define values for use by other graphics classes. For example, the Blend class defines color-blending parameters for a LinearGradientBrush.

The following table describes this namespace's most useful classes and enumerations.

CLASSES AND ENUMERATIONS	PURPOSE
Blend	Defines blend characteristics for a LinearGradientBrush.
ColorBlend	Defines blend characteristics for a PathGradientBrush.
DashCap	Enumeration that determines how the ends of each dash in a dashed line are drawn.

CLASSES AND ENUMERATIONS	PURPOSE
DashStyle	Enumeration that determines how a dashed line is drawn.
GraphicsPath	Represents a series of connected lines and curves for drawing, filling, or clipping.
HatchBrush	Defines a Brush that fills an area with a hatch pattern.
HatchStyle	Enumeration that determines the hatch style used by a HatchBrush object.
LinearGradientBrush	Defines a Brush that fills an area with a linear color gradient.
LineCap	Enumeration that determines how the ends of a line are drawn.
LineJoin	Enumeration that determines how lines are joined by a method that draws connected lines such as Graphics.DrawLines or Graphics.DrawPolygon.
Matrix	Represents a transformation matrix.
PathGradientBrush	Defines a Brush that fills an area with a color gradient that follows a path.

System.Drawing.Imaging

This namespace contains objects that deal with more advanced bitmap graphics. It includes classes that define image file formats such as GIF and JPG, classes that manage color palettes, and classes that define metafiles. The following table describes this namespace's most useful classes.

CLASS	PURPOSE
ColorMap	Defines a mapping from old color values to new ones.
ColorPalette	Represents a palette of color values.
ImageFormat	Specifies an image's format (`.bmp`, `.emf`, `.gif`, `.jpg`, and so on).
Metafile	Represents a graphic metafile that contains drawing instructions.
MetafileHeader	Defines the attributes of a Metafile object.
MetaHeader	Contains information about a Windows metafile (WMF).
WmfPlaceableFileHeader	Specifies how a metafile should be mapped to an output device.

System.Drawing.Printing

This namespace contains objects for printing and managing the printer's characteristics. The following table describes the most useful of these classes.

CLASS	PURPOSE
Margins	Defines the margins for the printed page.
PageSettings	Defines the page settings either for an entire PrintDocument or for a particular page. This object has properties that are Margins, PaperSize, PaperSource, PrinterResolution, and PrinterSettings objects.
PaperSize	Defines the paper's size.
PaperSource	Defines the printer's paper source.
PrinterResolution	Defines the printer's resolution.
PrinterSettings	Defines the printer's settings.

System.Drawing.Text

This namespace contains only three classes, all of which are for working with installed fonts. The following table describes these classes.

CLASS	PURPOSE
FontCollection	Base class for the derived InstalledFontCollection and PrivateFontCollection classes.
InstalledFontCollection	Provides a list of the system's installed fonts.
PrivateFontCollection	Provides a list of the application's privately installed fonts.

DRAWING CLASSES

The basic steps for drawing in Visual Basic are to obtain a Graphics object and use its methods to draw shapes. Brush classes determine how shapes are filled, and Pen classes determine how lines are drawn.

The following sections describe the most useful properties and methods provided by key drawing classes, including the Graphics, Pen, and Brush classes.

Graphics

The Graphics object represents a drawing surface. It provides many methods for drawing shapes, filling areas, and determining the appearance of drawing results.

All of the drawing methods (as opposed to the filling methods) except DrawString take a Pen object as a parameter to determine the lines' color, thickness, dash style, and other properties. DrawString takes a Brush object instead of a Pen object as a parameter.

The following table lists the Graphics object's drawing methods.

DRAWING METHOD	PURPOSE
DrawArc	Draws an arc of an ellipse.
DrawBezier	Draws a Bézier curve.
DrawBeziers	Draws a series of connected Bézier curves.
DrawClosedCurve	Draws a smooth closed curve that connects a series of points, joining the final point to the first point.
DrawCurve	Draws a smooth curve that connects a series of points.
DrawEllipse	Draws an ellipse.
DrawIcon	Draws an Icon onto the Graphics object's drawing surface.
DrawIconUnstretched	Draws an Icon object onto the Graphics object's drawing surface without scaling.
DrawImage	Draws an Image object onto the Graphics object's drawing surface.
DrawImageUnscaled	Draws an Image object onto the drawing surface without scaling.
DrawLine	Draws a line.
DrawLines	Draws a series of connected lines.
DrawPath	Draws a GraphicsPath object.
DrawPie	Draws a pie slice taken from an ellipse.
DrawPolygon	Draws a polygon.
DrawRectangle	Draws a rectangle.
DrawRectangles	Draws a series of rectangles.
DrawString	Draws text.

The following table lists the Graphics object's area filling methods. These methods take Brush objects as parameters to determine the filled shape's color, hatch pattern, gradient colors, and other fill characteristics.

FILLING METHOD	PURPOSE
FillClosedCurve	Fills a smooth curve that connects a series of points.
FillEllipse	Fills an ellipse.
FillPath	Fills a GraphicsPath object.
FillPie	Fills a pie slice taken from an ellipse.
FillPolygon	Fills a polygon.
FillRectangle	Fills a rectangle.
FillRectangles	Fills a series of rectangles.
FillRegion	Fills a Region object.

The following table lists other useful Graphics object properties and methods.

PROPERTIES AND METHODS	PURPOSE
AddMetafileComment	Adds a comment to a metafile.
Clear	Clears the Graphics object and fills it with a specific color.
Clip	Determines the Region object used to clip any drawing the program does on the Graphics surface.
Dispose	Releases the resources held by the Graphics object.
DpiX	Returns the horizontal number of dots per inch (DPI) for this object's surface.
DpiY	Returns the vertical number of dots per inch (DPI) for this object's surface.
EnumerateMetafile	Invokes a callback method for each record defined in a metafile.
ExcludeClip	Updates the Graphics object's clipping region to exclude the area defined by a Region or Rectangle.
FromHdc	Creates a new Graphics object from a device context handle (hDC).
FromHwnd	Creates a new Graphics object from a window handle (hWnd).
FromImage	Creates a new Graphics object to draw on an Image object.
InterpolationMode	Controls anti-aliasing when drawing scaled images to determine how smooth the result is.

PROPERTIES AND METHODS	PURPOSE
IntersectClip	Updates the Graphics object's clipping region to be the intersection of the current clipping region and the area defined by a Region or Rectangle.
IsVisible	Returns True if a specified point is within the Graphics object's visible clipping region.
MeasureCharacterRanges	Returns an array of Region objects that show where each character in a string will be drawn.
MeasureString	Returns a SizeF structure that gives the size of a string drawn on the Graphics object with a particular font.
MultiplyTransform	Multiplies the Graphics object's current transformation matrix by another transformation matrix.
PageScale	Determines the amount by which drawing commands are scaled.
PageUnit	Determines the units of measurement: Display (depends on the device, typically pixel for monitors and 1/100 inch for printers), Document (1/300 inch), Inch, Millimeter, Pixel, or Point (1/72 inch).
RenderingOrigin	Determines the point used as a reference when hatching.
ResetClip	Resets the object's clipping region so that the drawing is not clipped.
ResetTransformation	Resets the object's transformation matrix to the identity matrix.
Restore	Restores the Graphics object to a state saved by the Save method.
RotateTransform	Adds a rotation to the object's current transformation.
Save	Saves the object's current state.
ScaleTransform	Adds a scaling transformation to the Graphics object's current transformation.
SetClip	Sets or merges the Graphics object's clipping area to another Graphics object, a GraphicsPath object, or a Rectangle.
SmoothingMode	Controls anti-aliasing when drawing lines, curves, or filled areas.
TextRenderingHint	Controls anti-aliasing and hinting when drawing text.
Transform	Gets or sets the Graphics object's transformation matrix.
TransformPoints	Applies the object's current transformation to an array of points.
TranslateTransform	Adds a translation transformation to the Graphics object's current transformation.

Pen

The Pen object determines the appearance of drawn lines. It determines such properties as a line's width, color, and dash style. The following table lists the Pen object's most useful properties and methods.

PROPERTIES AND METHODS	PURPOSE
Alignment	Determines whether the line is drawn inside or centered on the theoretical perfectly thin line specified by the drawing routine.
Brush	Determines the Brush used to fill the line.
Color	Determines the line's color.
CompoundArray	Lets you draw a line that is striped lengthwise.
CustomEndCap	Determines the line's end cap.
CustomStartCap	Determines the line's start cap.
DashCap	Determines the cap drawn at the ends of dashes.
DashOffset	Determines the distance from the start of the line to the start of the first dash.
DashPattern	An array of Singles that specifies a custom dash pattern.
DashStyle	Determines the line's dash style.
EndCap	Determines the cap used at the end of the line.
LineJoin	Determines how lines are joined by a method that draws connected lines such as DrawPolygon.
MultiplyTransform	Multiplies the Pen object's current transformation by another transformation matrix.
ResetTransform	Resets the Pen object's transformation to the identity transformation.
RotateTransform	Adds a rotation transformation to the Pen object's current transformation.
ScaleTransform	Adds a scaling transformation to the Pen object's current transformation.
SetLineCap	This method takes parameters that let you specify the Pen object's StartCap, EndCap, and LineJoin properties at the same time.
StartCap	Determines the cap used at the start of the line.
Transform	Determines the transformation applied to the initially circular "pen tip" used to draw lines.
Width	The width of the pen.

Brushes

The Brush class is an abstract class, so you cannot make instances of it. Instead, you must make instances of one of its derived classes: SolidBrush, TextureBrush, HatchBrush, LinearGradient Brush, or PathGradientBrush. The following table briefly describes these classes.

CLASS	PURPOSE
SolidBrush	Fills areas with a single solid color.
TextureBrush	Fills areas with a repeating image.
HatchBrush	Fills areas with a repeating hatch pattern.
LinearGradientBrush	Fills areas with a linear gradient of two or more colors.
PathGradientBrush	Fills areas with a color gradient that follows a path.

GraphicsPath

The GraphicsPath object represents a path defined by lines, curves, text, and other drawing commands. You can use Graphics object methods to fill and draw a GraphicsPath, and you can use a GraphicsPath to define a clipping region. The following table lists the GraphicsPath object's most useful properties and methods.

PROPERTIES AND METHODS	PURPOSE
CloseAllFigures	Closes all open figures by connecting their last points with their first points and then starts a new figure.
CloseFigure	Closes the current figure by connecting its last point with its first point and then starts a new figure.
FillMode	Determines how the path handles overlaps when you fill it. This property can take the values Alternate and Winding.
Flatten	Converts any curves in the path into a sequence of lines.
GetBounds	Returns a RectangleF structure representing the path's bounding box.
GetLastPoint	Returns the last PointF structure in the PathPoints array.
IsOutlineVisible	Returns True if the indicated point lies beneath the path's outline.
IsVisible	Returns True if the indicated point lies in the path's interior.
PathData	Returns a PathData object that encapsulates the path's graphical data.
PathPoints	Returns an array of PointF structures giving the points in the path.

continues

(continued)

PROPERTIES AND METHODS	PURPOSE
PathTypes	Returns an array of Bytes representing the types of the points in the path.
PointCount	Returns the number of points in the path.
Reset	Clears the path data and resets FillMode to Alternate.
Reverse	Reverses the order of the path's data.
StartFigure	Starts a new figure, so future data is added to the new figure.
Transform	Applies a transformation matrix to the path.
Warp	Applies a warping transformation defined by mapping a parallelogram onto a rectangle to the path.
Widen	Enlarges the curves in the path to enclose a line drawn by a specific pen.

StringFormat

The StringFormat object determines how text is formatted. It enables you to draw text that is centered vertically or horizontally, aligned on the left or right, and wrapped or truncated. The following table lists the StringFormat object's most useful properties and methods.

PROPERTIES AND METHODS	PURPOSE
Alignment	Determines the text's horizontal alignment. This can be Near (left), Center (middle), or Far (right).
FormatFlags	Gets or sets flags that modify the StringFormat object's behavior.
GetTabStops	Returns an array of Singles giving the positions of tab stops.
HotkeyPrefix	Determines how the hotkey prefix character is displayed. This can be Show, Hide, or None.
LineAlignment	Determines the text's vertical alignment. This can be Near (top), Center (middle), or Far (bottom).
SetMeasureableCharacter Ranges	Sets an array of CharacterRange structures representing ranges of characters that will later be measured by the Graphics object's MeasureCharacterRanges method.
SetTabStops	Sets an array of Singles giving the positions of tab stops.
Trimming	Determines how the text is trimmed if it cannot fit within a layout rectangle.

Image

The Image class represents the underlying physical drawing surface hidden below the logical layer created by the Graphics class. Image is an abstract class, so you cannot directly create instances of it. Instead, you must create instances of its child classes Bitmap and Metafile.

The following table describes the Image class's most useful properties and methods, which are inherited by the Bitmap and Metafile classes.

PROPERTIES AND METHODS	PURPOSE
Dispose	Frees the resources associated with this image.
Flags	Returns attribute flags for the image.
FromFile	Loads an image from a file.
FromHbitmap	Loads a Bitmap image from a Windows bitmap handle.
FromStream	Loads an image from a data stream.
GetBounds	Returns a RectangleF structure representing the rectangle's bounds.
GetPixelFormatSize	Returns the color resolution (bits per pixel) for a specified PixelFormat.
GetThumbnailImage	Returns a thumbnail representation of the image.
Height	Returns the image's height.
HorizontalResolution	Returns the horizontal resolution of the image in pixels per inch.
IsAlphaPixelFormat	Returns True if the specified PixelFormat contains alpha information.
Palette	Determines the ColorPalette object used by the image.
PhysicalDimension	Returns a SizeF structure giving the image's dimensions in pixels for Bitmaps and 0.01 millimeters for Metafiles.
PixelFormat	Returns the image's pixel format.
RawFormat	Returns an ImageFormat object representing the image's raw format.
RotateFlip	Rotates, flips, or rotates and flips the image.
Save	Saves the image in a file or stream with a given data format.
Size	Returns a Size structure containing the image's width and height in pixels.
VerticalResolution	Returns the vertical resolution of the image in pixels per inch.
Width	Returns the image's width.

Bitmap

The Bitmap class represents an image defined by pixel data. It inherits the Image class's properties and methods described in the previous section. The following table describes some of the most useful new methods added by the Bitmap class.

METHOD	PURPOSE
FromHicon	Loads a Bitmap image from a Windows icon handle.
FromResource	Loads a Bitmap image from a Windows resource.
GetPixel	Returns a Color representing a specified pixel.
LockBits	Locks the Bitmap image's data in memory, so it cannot move until the program calls UnlockBits.
MakeTransparent	Makes all pixels with a specified color transparent by setting the alpha component of those pixels to 0.
SetPixel	Sets a specified pixel's Color value.
SetResolution	Sets the Bitmap image's horizontal and vertical resolution in dots per inch (DPI).
UnlockBits	Unlocks the Bitmap image's data in memory so that the system can relocate it, if necessary.

Metafile

The Metafile class represents an image defined by metafile records. Those records define drawing commands so the image can be smoothly scaled. In contrast, a Bitmap contains pixel data that cannot be resized without some jagged or fuzzy appearance.

The Metafile class inherits the Image class's properties and methods described in the section "Image" earlier in this appendix. The following table describes some of the most useful new methods added by the Metafile class.

METHOD	PURPOSE
GetMetafileHeader	Returns the MetafileHeader object associated with this Metafile.
PlayRecord	Plays a metafile record. Use the Graphics class's EnumerateMetafile method to get the data needed to play metafile records.

Useful Exception Classes

When your program throws an exception, it's easy enough to use a TryCatch block to catch the exception and examine it to determine its class. When you want to throw your own exception, however, you must know what exception classes are available so that you can pick the right one.

For more information on error handling, see Chapter 18, "Error Handling," and Appendix F.

STANDARD EXCEPTION CLASSES

The following table lists some of the most useful exception classes in Visual Basic .NET. You can use one of these when you need to throw an error.

CLASS	PURPOSE
AmbiguousMatchException	The program could not figure out which overloaded object method to use.
ApplicationException	This is the ancestor class for all nonfatal application errors. When you build custom exception classes, you should inherit from this class, or from one of its descendants.
ArgumentException	An argument is invalid.
ArgumentNullException	An argument that cannot be Nothing has the value Nothing.
ArgumentOutOfRangeException	An argument is out of its allowed range.

continues

(continued)

CLASS	PURPOSE
ArithmeticException	An arithmetic, casting, or conversion operation has occurred.
ArrayTypeMismatchException	The program tried to store the wrong type of item in an array.
ConfigurationException	A configuration setting is invalid.
ConstraintException	A data operation violates a database constraint.
DataException	The ancestor class for ADO.NET exception classes.
DirectoryNotFoundException	A needed directory is missing.
DivideByZeroException	The program tried to divide by zero.
DuplicateNameException	An ADO.NET operation encountered a duplicate name (for example, it tried to create two tables with the same name).
EvaluateException	Occurs when a DataColumn's Expression property cannot be evaluated.
FieldAccessException	The program tried to access a class property improperly.
FormatException	An argument's format doesn't match its required format.
IndexOutOfRangeException	The program tried to access an item outside of the bounds of an array or other container.
InvalidCastException	The program tried to make an invalid conversion. For example, Integer.Parse("ten").
InvalidOperationException	The operation is not currently allowed.
IOException	The ancestor class for input/output (I/O) exception classes. A generic I/O error occurred.
EndOfStreamException	A stream reached its end.
FileLoadException	Error loading a file.
FileNotFoundException	Error finding a file.
InternalBufferOverflowException	An internal buffer overflowed.
MemberAccessException	The program tried to access a class member improperly.
MethodAccessException	The program tried to access a class method improperly.
MissingFieldException	The program tried to access a class field that doesn't exist.
MissingMemberException	The program tried to access a class member that doesn't exist.

CLASS	PURPOSE
MissingMethodException	The program tried to access a class method that doesn't exist.
NotFiniteNumberException	A floating-point number is PositiveInfinity, NegativeInfinity, or NaN (Not a Number). You can get these values from the floating-point classes (as in Single.Nan or Double.PositiveInfinity).
NotImplementedException	The requested operation is not implemented.
NotSupportedException	The requested operation is not supported. For example, the program might be asking a routine to modify data that was opened as read-only.
NullReferenceException	The program tried to use an object reference that is Nothing.
OutOfMemoryException	There isn't enough memory. Note that sometimes a program cannot recover from an OutOfMemoryException because it doesn't have enough memory to do anything useful. This exception is most useful if you can predict beforehand that you will run out of memory before you actually use up all of the memory and crash the program. For example, if the user wants to generate a really huge data cache, you may be able to predict how much memory the program will need, see if it is available, and throw this error without actually allocating the data cache.
OverflowException	An arithmetic, casting, or conversion operation created an overflow. For example, the program tried to assign a large Integer value to a Byte variable.
PolicyException	Policy prevents the code from running.
RankException	A routine is trying to use an array with the wrong number of dimensions.
ReadOnlyException	The program tried to modify read-only data.
SecurityException	A security violation occurred.
SyntaxErrorException	A DataColumn's Expression property contains invalid syntax.
Unauthorized Access Exception	The system is denying access because of an I/O or security error.

Use the Throw statement to raise an exception. The following code throws a DivideByZeroException:

```
Throw New DivideByZeroException("No employees are defined.")
```

This code passes the exception class's constructor a message describing the exception. In this case, the divide by zero exception occurred because the application did not have any employees defined.

Notice that the message explains the reason for the exception, not the mere fact that a division by zero occurred.

CUSTOM EXCEPTION CLASSES

To define a custom exception class, make a class that inherits from an exception class. To give developers who use the class the most flexibility, provide four constructors that delegate their work to the parent class's corresponding constructors.

The following code shows the InvalidWorkAssignmentException class. The parameterless constructor passes the Exception class's constructor a default error message. The other constructors simply pass their arguments to the Exception class's other constructors.

```
Public Class InvalidWorkAssignmentException
    Inherits ApplicationException

    Public Sub New()
        MyBase.New("This work assignment is invalid")
    End Sub

    Public Sub New(msg As String)
        MyBase.New(msg)
    End Sub

    Public Sub New(msg As String, inner_exception As Exception)
        MyBase.New(msg, inner_exception)
    End Sub

    Public Sub New(info As SerializationInfo, context As StreamingContext)
        MyBase.New(info, context)
    End Sub
End Class
```

For more information on custom exception classes, see Chapter 18 and the online documentation for topics such as "Designing Custom Exceptions" (http://msdn.microsoft.com/ms229064 .aspx) and "Design Guidelines for Exceptions" (http://msdn.microsoft.com/ms229014.aspx), or search the web for articles such as "Custom Exceptions in VB 2005" by Josh Fitzgerald (http://www.developer.com/net/vb/article.php/3590931).

P

Date and Time Format Specifiers

A program uses date and time format specifiers to determine how dates and times are represented as strings. For example, the Date object's ToString method returns a string representing a date and time. An optional parameter to this method tells the object whether to format itself as in 8/20/2012, 08.20.12 A.D., or Monday, August 20, 2012 2:37:18 pm.

Visual Basic provides two kinds of specifiers that you can use to determine a date and time value's format: standard format specifiers and custom format specifiers.

STANDARD FORMAT SPECIFIERS

A standard format specifier is a single character that you use alone to indicate a standardized format. For example, the format string d indicates a short date format (as in 8/20/2012).

The following table lists standard format specifiers that you can use to format date and time strings. The results depend on the regional settings on the computer. The examples shown in this table are for a typical computer in the United States.

SPECIFIER	MEANING	EXAMPLE
d	Short date.	8/20/2012
D	Long date.	Monday, August 20, 2012
t	Short time.	2:37 PM
T	Long time.	2:37:18 PM
f	Full date/time with short time.	Monday, August 20, 2012 2:37 PM
F	Full date/time with long time.	Monday, August 20, 2012 2:37:18 PM

continues

(continued)

SPECIFIER	MEANING	EXAMPLE
g	General date/time with short time.	8/20/2012 2:37 PM
G	General date/time with long time.	8/20/2012 2:37:18 PM
m or M	Month and date.	August 20
r or R	RFC1123 pattern. Formatting does not convert the time to Greenwich Mean Time (GMT), so you should convert local times to GMT before formatting.	Mon, 20 Aug 2012 14:37:18 GMT
S	Sortable ISO 8601 date/time.	2012-08-20T14:37:18
u	Universal sortable date/time. Formatting does not convert the time to universal time, so you should convert local times to universal time before formatting.	2012-08-20 14:37:18Z
U	Universal full date/time. This is the full universal time, not the local time.	Monday, August 20, 2012 9:37:18 PM
y or Y	Year and month.	August 2012

You can learn more about RFC1123 at `http://www.faqs.org/rfcs/rfc1123.html`. You can learn more about ISO 8601 at `http://www.iso.org/iso/support/faqs/faqs_widely_used_standards/widely_used_standards_other/date_and_time_format.htm`.

CUSTOM FORMAT SPECIFIERS

Custom format specifiers describe pieces of a date or time that you can use to build your own customized formats. For example, the specifier ddd indicates the abbreviated day of the week, as in Wed.

The following table lists characters that you can use to build custom formats for date and time strings.

SPECIFIER	MEANING	EXAMPLE
d	Date of the month.	3
dd	Date of the month with two digits.	03
ddd	Abbreviated day of the week.	Wed
dddd	Full day of the week.	Wednesday
f	Fractions of seconds, one digit. Add additional f's for up to seven digits (fffffff).	8

SPECIFIER	MEANING	EXAMPLE
g	Era.	A.D.
h	Hour, 12-hour clock with one digit, if possible.	1
hh	Hour, 12-hour clock with two digits.	01
H	Hour, 24-hour clock with one digit, if possible.	13
HH	Hour, 24-hour clock with two digits.	07
m	Minutes with one digit, if possible.	9
mm	Minutes with two digits.	09
M	Month number (1–12) with one digit, if possible.	2
MM	Month number (1–12) with two digits.	02
MMM	Month abbreviation.	Feb
MMMM	Full month name.	February
s	Seconds with one digit, if possible.	3
ss	Seconds with two digits.	03
t	AM/PM designator with one character.	A
tt	AM/PM designator with two characters.	AM
y	Year with up to two digits, not zero-padded.	12
yy	Year with two digits.	12
yyyy	Year with four digits.	2012
z	Time zone offset (hours from GMT in the range −12 to +13).	−7
zz	Time zone offset with two digits.	−07
zzz	Time zone offset with two digits of hours and minutes.	−07:00
:	Time separator.	
/	Date separator.	
"..."	Quoted string. Displays the enclosed characters without trying to interpret them.	
'...'	Quoted string. Displays the enclosed characters without trying to interpret them.	
%	Displays the following character as a custom specifier. (See the following discussion.)	
\	Displays the next character without trying to interpret it.	

Some of the custom specifier characters in this table are the same as characters used by standard specifiers. For example, if you use the character d alone, Visual Basic interprets it as the standard specifier for a short date. If you use the character d in a custom specifier, Visual Basic interprets it as the date of the month.

If you want to use a custom specifier alone, precede it with the % character. The following shows two queries and their results executed in the Immediate window:

```
?Now.ToString("d")
"8/20/2012"
?Now.ToString("%d")
"20"
```

Custom specifiers are somewhat sensitive to the computer's regional settings. For example, they at least know the local names and abbreviations of the months and days of the week.

The standard specifiers have even more information about the local culture, however. For example, the date specifiers know whether the local culture places months before or after days. The d specifier gives the result 8/20/2012 for the en-US culture (English, United States), and it returns 20/08/2012 for the culture en-NZ (English, New Zealand).

To avoid cultural problems on different computers, you should use the standard specifiers whenever they will satisfy your needs rather than build your own custom format specifiers. For example, use d instead of M/d/yyyy.

Other Format Specifiers

A program uses format specifiers to determine how objects are represented as strings. For example, by using different format specifiers, you can make an integer's ToString method return a value as –12345, –12,345, (12,345), or 012,345–.

Visual Basic provides standard format specifiers in addition to custom specifiers. The standard specifiers make it easy to display values in often-used formats (such as currency or scientific notation). Custom specifiers provide more control over how results are composed.

STANDARD NUMERIC FORMAT SPECIFIERS

Standard numeric format specifiers enable you to easily display commonly used numeric formats. The following table lists the standard numeric specifiers.

SPECIFIER	MEANING
C or c	Currency. The exact format depends on the computer's internationalization settings. If a precision specifier follows the C, it indicates the number of digits that should follow the decimal point. On a standard system in the United States, the value –1234.5678 with the specifier C produces ($1,234.57).
D or d	Decimal. This specifier works only with integer types. It simply displays the number's digits. If a precision specifier follows the D, it indicates the number of digits the result should have, padding on the left with zeros, if necessary. If the value is negative, the result has a minus sign on the left. The value –1234 with the specifier D6 produces –001234.

continues

(continued)

SPECIFIER	MEANING
E or e	Scientific notation. The result always has exactly one digit to the left of the decimal point, followed by more digits, an E or e, a plus or minus sign, and at least three digits of exponent (padded on the left with zeros, if necessary). If a precision specifier follows the E, it indicates the number of digits the result should have after the decimal point. The value –1234.5678 with the specifier e2 produces –1.23e+003.
F or f	Fixed point. The result contains a minus sign if the value is negative, digits, a decimal point, and then more digits. If a precision specifier follows the F, it indicates the number of digits the result should have after the decimal point. The value –1234.5678 with the specifier f3 produces –1234.568.
G or g	General. Either scientific or fixed-point notation depending on which is more compact.
N or n	Number. The result has a minus sign if the value is negative, digits with thousands separators, a decimal point, and more digits. If a precision specifier follows the N, it indicates the number of digits the result should have after the decimal point. The value –1234.5678 with the specifier N3 produces –1,234.568.
P or p	Percentage. The value is multiplied by 100 and then formatted according to the computer's settings. If a precision specifier follows the P, it indicates the number of digits that should follow the decimal point. On a typical computer, the value 1.2345678 with the specifier P produces 123.46%.
R or r	Round trip. The value is formatted in such a way that the result can be converted back into its original value. Depending on the data type and value, this may require 17 digits of precision. The value 1/7 with the specifier R produces 0.14285714285714285.
X or x	Hexadecimal. This works for integer types only. The value is converted into hexadecimal. The case of the X or x determines whether hexadecimal digits above 9 are written in uppercase or lowercase. If a precision specifier follows the X, it indicates the number of digits the result should have, padding on the left with zeros, if necessary. The value 183 with the specifier x4 produces 00b7.

CUSTOM NUMERIC FORMAT SPECIFIERS

Custom numeric format specifiers describe how a number should be formatted. The following table lists characters that you can use to build custom numeric formats.

SPECIFIER	MEANING
0	A digit or zero. If the number doesn't have a digit in this position, the specifier adds a 0. The value 12 with the specifier 000.00 produces 012.00.
#	A digit. If the number doesn't have a digit in this position, nothing is printed.

SPECIFIER	MEANING
,	If used between two digits (either 0 or #), adds thousands separators to the result. Note that it will add many comma separators if necessary. The value 1234567 with the specifier #,# produces 1,234,567.
,	If used immediately to the left of the decimal point, the number is divided by 1000 for each comma. The value 1234567 with the specifier #,#,. produces 1,235.
%	Multiplies the number by 100 and inserts the % symbol where it appears in the specifier. The value 0.123 with the specifier .00% produces 12.30%.
E0 or e0	Displays the number in scientific notation inserting an E or e between the number and its exponent. Use # and 0 to format the number before the exponent. The number of 0s after the E determines the number of digits in the exponent. If you place a + sign between the E and 0, the result's exponent includes a + or − sign. If you omit the + sign, the exponent only includes a sign if it is negative. The value 1234.5678 with the specifier 00.000E+000 produces 12.346E+002.
\	Displays the following character literally without interpreting it. Use \\ to display the \ character. The value 12 with the specifier #\% produces 12%, and the same value with the specifier #% produces 1200%.
'ABC' or "ABC"	Displays the characters in the quotes literally. The value 12 with the specifier #'%' (single quotes around the % symbol) produces 12%.

NUMERIC FORMATTING SECTIONS

A numeric format specifier may contain one, two, or three sections separated by semicolons. If the specifier contains one section, the specifier is used for all numeric values.

If the specifier contains two sections, the first is used to format values that are positive or zero, and the second is used to format negative values.

If the specifier contains three sections, the first is used to format positive values, the second is used to format negative values, and the third is used to format values that are zero.

The following text shows output from the Immediate window for three values using the format specifier #,#.00;<#,#.00>;ZERO:

```
?(1234.5678).ToString("#,#.00; <#,#.00>;ZERO")
1,234.57
?(-1234.5678).ToString("#,#.00; <#,#.00>;ZERO")
<1,234.57>
?(0).ToString("#,#.00; <#,#.00>;ZERO")
ZERO
```

COMPOSITE FORMATTING

The String.Format, Console.WriteLine, and TextWriter.WriteLine methods provide a different method for formatting strings. These routines can take a composite formatting string parameter that contains literal characters plus placeholders for values. Other parameters to the methods give the values.

The value placeholders have the following format:

```
{index[,alignment][:format_specifier]}
```

The *index* value gives the index numbered from 0 of the parameter that should be inserted in this placeholder's position.

The optional alignment value tells the minimum number of spaces the item should use and the result is padded with spaces, if necessary. If this value is negative, the result is left-justified. If the value is positive, the result is right-justified.

The format_specifier indicates how the item should be formatted.

For example, consider the following code:

```
Dim emp As String = "Crazy Bob":
Dim sales As Single = -12345.67
MessageBox.Show(String.Format("{0} {1:earned;lost} {1:c} this year", emp, sales))
```

The first placeholder refers to parameter number 0, which has the value "Crazy Bob." The second placeholder refers to parameter number 1 and includes a two-part format specifier that displays "earned" if the value is positive or zero, and "lost" of the value is negative. The third placeholder refers to parameter number 1 again, this time formatted as currency.

The following code shows the result:

```
Crazy Bob lost ($12,345.67) this year
```

ENUMERATED TYPE FORMATTING

Visual Basic provides special formatting capabilities that can display the values of enumerated variables. For example, consider the following code:

```
Private Enum Dessert
    Cake = 1
    Pie = 2
    Cookie = 3
    IceCream = 4
End Enum
...
Dim dessert_choice As Dessert = Dessert.Cake
MessageBox.Show(dessert_choice.ToString)
```

This code displays the string "Cake."

For variables of an enumerated type such as dessert_choice, the ToString method can take a specifier that determines how the value is formatted.

The specifier G or g formats the value as a string if possible. If the value is not a valid entry in the Enum's definition, the result is the variable's numeric value. For example, the previous code does not define a Dessert enumeration for the value 7 so, if you set dessert_choice to 7, then dessert_choice .ToString("G") returns the value 7.

If you define an enumerated type with the Flags attribute, variables of that type can be a combination of the Enum's values, as shown in the following code:

```
<Flags()>
Private Enum Dessert
    Cake = 1
    Pie = 2
    Cookie = 4
    IceCream = 8
End Enum
...
Dim dessert_choice As Dessert = Dessert.IceCream Or Dessert.Cake
MessageBox.Show(dessert_choice.ToString("G"))
```

In this case, the G format specifier returns a string that contains all of the flag values separated by commas. In this example, the result is "Cake, IceCream." Note that the values are returned in the order in which they are defined by the enumeration, not the order in which they are assigned to the variable.

If you do not use the Flags attribute when defining an enumerated type, the G format specifier always returns the variable's numeric value if it is a combination of values rather than a single value from the list. In contrast the F specifier returns a list of comma-separated values if it makes sense. If you omit the Flags attribute from the previous code, dessert_choice.ToString("G") returns 9, but dessert_choice.ToString("F") returns "Cake, IceCream."

The D or d specifier always formats the variable as a number.

The specifier X or x formats the value as a hexadecimal number.

The Application Class

The Application class provides static properties and methods for controlling the application. This appendix contains a summary of the Application class's most useful properties, methods, and events. Chapter 28, "Configuration and Resources," has a bit more to say about the Application class and provides some example code.

PROPERTIES

The following table describes the Application class's most useful properties.

PROPERTY	PURPOSE
CommonAppDataPath	Returns the path where the program should store application data that is shared by all users. By default, this path has the form base_path\company_name\product_name\product_version. The base_path is typically C:\Documents and Settings\All Users\ Application Data.
CommonAppDataRegistry	Returns the registry key where the program should store application data that is shared by all users. By default, this path has the form HKEY_LOCAL_MACHINE\Software\ company_name\product_name\product_version.
CompanyName	Returns the application's company name.
CurrentCulture	Gets or sets the CultureInfo object for this thread. The CultureInfo object specifies information about a specific culture (such as its name, writing system, and calendar, and its formats for dates, times, and numbers).

continues

(continued)

PROPERTY	PURPOSE
CurrentInputLanguage	Gets or sets the InputLanguage for this thread. The InputLanguage object defines the layout of the keyboard for the culture. It determines how the keyboard keys are mapped to the characters in the culture's language.
ExecutablePath	Returns the fully qualified path to the file that started the execution, including the file's name.
LocalUserAppDataPath	Returns the path where the program should store data for this local, non-roaming user. By default, this path has the form base_path\company_name\product_name\product_version. The base_path is typically C:\Documents and Settings\user_name\Local Settings\Application Data.
MessageLoop	Returns True if the thread has a message loop. If the program begins with a startup form, this loop is created automatically. If it starts with a custom Sub Main, then the loop doesn't initially exist, and the program must start it (if it needs a message loop) by calling Application.Run.
OpenForms	Returns a collection holding references to all of the application's open forms.
ProductName	Returns the application's product name.
ProductVersion	Gets the product version associated with this application.
StartupPath	Returns the fully qualified path to the file that started the execution, including the file's name.
UserAppDataPath	Returns the path where the program should store data for this user. By default, this path has the form base_path\company_name\product_name\product_version. The base_path is typically C:\Documents and Settings\user_name\Application Data.
UserAppDataRegistry	Returns the registry key where the program should store application data for this user. By default, this path has the form HKEY_CURRENT_USER\Software\company_name\product_name\product_version.
UseWaitCursor	Determines whether this thread's forms display a wait cursor. Set this to True before performing a long operation, and set it to False when the operation is finished.

METHODS

The following table describes the Application class's most useful methods.

METHOD	PURPOSE
AddMessageFilter	Adds a message filter to monitor the event loop's Windows messages.
DoEvents	Processes Windows messages that are currently in the message queue. If the thread is performing a long calculation, it would normally prevent the rest of the thread from taking action (such as processing these messages). Calling DoEvents lets the user interface catch up with the user's actions. Note that you can often avoid the need for DoEvents if you perform the long task on a separate thread.
Exit	Ends the whole application. This is a rather abrupt halt, and any loaded forms do not execute their FormClosing or FormClosed event handlers, so be sure the application has executed any necessary clean-up code before calling Application.Exit.
ExitThread	Ends the current thread. This is a rather abrupt halt, and any forms on the thread do not execute their FormClosing or FormClosed event handlers.
OnThreadException	Raises the Application object's ThreadException event, passing it an exception. (If your application throws an uncaught exception in the IDE, the IDE halts. That makes it hard to test Application .ThreadException event handlers. You can call OnThreadException to invoke the event handler.)
RemoveMessageFilter	Removes a message filter.
Run	Runs a message loop for the current thread. If you pass this method a form object, it displays the form and processes its messages until the form closes.
SetSuspendState	Makes the system suspend operation or hibernate. When the system *hibernates*, it writes its memory contents to disk. When you restart the system, it resumes with its previous desktop and applications running. When the system *suspends* operation, it enters low-power mode. It can resume more quickly than a hibernated system, but memory contents are not saved, so they will be lost if the computer loses power.

EVENTS

The following table describes the Application object's events.

EVENT	PURPOSE
ApplicationExit	Occurs when the application is about to shut down.
Idle	Occurs when the application finishes executing some code and is about to enter an idle state to wait for events.
ThreadException	Occurs when the application throws an unhandled exception.
ThreadExit	Occurs when a thread is about to exit.

The My Namespace

The My namespace provides shortcuts to make performing common tasks easier. The following sections describe the major items within the My namespace and describe the tools that they make available.

MY.APPLICATION

My.Application provides information about the current application. It includes properties that tell you the program's current directory, culture, Log object, and splash screen. It also includes information about the application's assembly, including the program's version numbering.

The following table describes the most useful My.Application properties, methods, and events.

ITEM	PURPOSE
ApplicationContext	Returns an ApplicationContext object for the currently executing thread. It provides a reference to the thread's form. Its ExitThread method terminates the thread, and its ThreadExit event fires when the thread is exiting.
ChangeCurrentCulture	Changes the thread's culture used for string manipulation and formatting.
ChangeCurrentUICulture	Changes the thread's culture used for retrieving resources.
CommandLineArgs	Returns a collection containing the command-line arguments used when the application was started. The first entry (with index 0) is the fully qualified name of the executable application.

continues

(continued)

ITEM	PURPOSE
CurrentCulture	Returns a CultureInfo object that represents the settings used for culture-specific string manipulation and formatting. This includes calendar information, date and time specifications, the culture's name, keyboard layout, number formats for general numbers (for example, the thousands separator character and decimal character), currency, and percentages.
CurrentUICulture	Returns a CultureInfo object that represents the culture-specific settings used by the thread to retrieve resources. It determines the culture used by the Resource Manager and My.Resources.
Deployment	Returns the application's current ApplicationDeployment object used for ClickOnce deployment. Normally, you don't need to manage deployment yourself, but this object lets you check for updates, start an update synchronously or asynchronously, download files, and restart the updated application.
DoEvents	Makes the application process all of the Windows messages currently waiting in the message queue. Doing this allows controls to process messages and update their appearances while the program is performing a long calculation. Often, you can avoid using DoEvents by performing long calculations on a separate thread, so the user interface can continue running normally.

GetEnvironmentVariable	Returns the value of the specified environment variable. For example, the following code displays the value of the PATH environment variable:
	
	`MessageBox.Show(`
	`    My.Application.GetEnvironmentVariable("PATH"))`
	
	This method raises an exception if the named environment variable doesn't exist. The method Environment.GetEnvironmentVariable performs the same function, except that it returns Nothing if the variable doesn't exist.

Info	Returns an AssemblyInfo object that provides information about the assembly such as assembly name, company name, copyright, trademark, and version.
IsNetworkDeployed	Returns True if the application was deployed over the network. You should check this property and only try to use the My.Application.Deployment object if it returns True.
Log	An object of the class MyLog. You can use this object's WriteEntry and WriteException methods to log messages and exceptions.

ITEM	PURPOSE
MainForm	Gets or sets the application's main form.
NetworkAvailability Changed	The application raises this event when the network's availability changes.
OpenForms	Returns a collection containing references to all of the application's open forms.
Shutdown	The application raises this event when it is shutting down. This event occurs after all forms' FormClosing and FormClosed event handlers have finished. Note that it fires only if the program shuts down normally. If it exits, these events don't fire.
SplashScreen	Gets or sets the application's splash screen.
Startup	The application raises this event when it is starting up before it creates any forms.
StartupNextInstance	The application raises this event when the user tries to start a second instance of a single-instance application.
UICulture	Gets the thread's culture used for retrieving resources.
UnhandledException	The application raises this event if it encounters an unhandled exception.

The following table lists the Info object's properties. Note that these properties have default blank values unless you set them by opening the project's property pages, selecting the Application tab, and clicking the Assembly Information button.

PROPERTY	PURPOSE
AssemblyName	Gets the assembly's name.
CompanyName	Gets the assembly's company name.
Copyright	Gets the assembly's copyright information.
Description	Gets the assembly's description.
DirectoryPath	Gets the directory where the assembly is stored.
LoadedAssemblies	Returns a collection of Assembly objects for the application's currently loaded assemblies.
ProductName	Gets the assembly's product name.

continues

(continued)

PROPERTY	PURPOSE
StackTrace	Gets a stack trace.
Title	Gets the assembly's title.
Trademark	Gets the assembly's trademark information.
Version	Gets the assembly's version number.
WorkingSet	Gets the number of bytes mapped to the process context.

The project's Application property page gives you access to most of the Info values at design time. To open the Application property page, open Solution Explorer, double-click the My Project entry, and select the Application tab.

To set Info values at design time, open the Application property page and click the Assembly Information button, and then enter the assembly information in the dialog box shown in Figure S-1 and click OK.

To place code in the My.Application object's NetworkAvailabilityChanged, Shutdown, Startup, StartupNextInstance, or UnhandledException event handlers, open the Application property page and click the View Application Events button.

To make the application a single-instance application, open the Application property page and check the "Make single instance application" box.

FIGURE S-1: Enter assembly information such as the application title and version number on the Assembly Information dialog box.

MY.COMPUTER

My.Computer provides methods for understanding and controlling the computer's hardware and the system software. It lets you work with the audio system, clock, keyboard, clipboard, mouse, network, printers, registry, and filesystem.

The following sections describe the properties, methods, and events available through My.Computer in detail.

Audio

This object provides access to the computer's audio system. Its methods let you play a `.wav` file synchronously or asynchronously, stop a file playing asynchronously, or play a system sound. For example, the following code plays the system's exclamation sound:

```
My.Computer.Audio.PlaySystemSound(SystemSounds.Exclamation)
```

The following table describes the Audio object's methods.

METHOD	PURPOSE
Play	Plays `.wav` data from a file, byte array, or stream. The second parameter can be Background (play asynchronously in the background), BackgroundLoop (play asynchronously in the background and repeat when it ends), or WaitToComplete (play synchronously).
PlaySystemSound	Plays a system sound. The parameter should be a member of the SystemSounds enumeration and can have the value Asterisk, Beep, Exclamation, Hand, or Question.
Stop	Stops the sound currently playing asynchronously.

Clipboard

The Clipboard object enables you to move data in and out of the system's clipboard. The My.Computer.Clipboard object provides extra tools that simplify some clipboard operations. The following table briefly summarizes the My.Computer.Clipboard object's methods.

METHOD	PURPOSE
Clear	Removes all data from the clipboard.
ContainsAudio	Returns True if the clipboard contains audio data.
ContainsData	Returns True if the clipboard contains data in a specific custom format.
ContainsFileDropList	Returns True if the clipboard contains a file drop list.
ContainsImage	Returns True if the clipboard contains image data.
ContainsText	Returns True if the clipboard contains textual data.
GetAudioStream	Gets audio data from the clipboard.
GetData	Gets data in a specific custom format from the clipboard.
GetDataObject	Gets a DataObject from the clipboard.
GetFileDropList	Gets a StringCollection holding the names of the files selected for drop from the clipboard.
GetImage	Gets image data from the clipboard.

continues

(continued)

METHOD	PURPOSE
GetText	Gets textual data from the clipboard.
SetAudio	Saves audio data to the clipboard.
SetData	Saves data in a specific custom format to the clipboard.
SetDataObject	Saves a DataObject to the clipboard.
SetFileDropList	Saves a StringCollection containing a series of fully qualified filenames to the clipboard.
SetImage	Saves an image to the clipboard.
SetText	Saves textual data to the clipboard.

Clock

This property returns an object of type Clock that you can use to learn about the current time. The following table describes this object's properties.

PROPERTY	PURPOSE
GmtTime	Returns a Date object that gives the current local date and time converted into Coordinated Universal Time (UTC) or Greenwich Mean Time (GMT).
LocalTime	Returns a Date object that gives the current local date and time.
TickCount	Returns the number of milliseconds since the computer started.

For example, suppose that you live in Colorado, which uses Mountain Standard Time (MST), seven hours behind Greenwich Mean Time. If My.Computer.Clock.LocalTime returns 2:03 PM, then My.Computer.Clock.GmtTime returns 9:03 PM.

If you must store a date and time for later use (for example, in a database), you should generally store it in UTC. Then you can meaningfully compare that value with other times stored on other computers in different time zones such as those across the Internet.

FileSystem

The FileSystem object provides tools for working with drives, directories, and files. The following table summarizes this object's properties and methods.

ITEM	DESCRIPTION
CombinePath	Returns a properly formatted combined path as a string.
CopyDirectory	Copies a directory.
CopyFile	Copies a file.
CreateDirectory	Creates a directory.
CurrentDirectory	Determines the fully qualified path to the application's current directory.
DeleteDirectory	Deletes a directory.
DeleteFile	Deletes a file.
DirectoryExists	Returns True if a directory exists.
Drives	Returns a read-only collection of DriveInfo objects describing the system's drives. See Chapter 30, "Filesystem Objects," for information about the DriveInfo class.
FileExists	Returns True if a file exists.
FindInFiles	Returns a collection holding names of files that contain a search string.
GetDirectories	Returns a String collection representing the pathnames of subdirectories within a directory.
GetDirectoryInfo	Returns a DirectoryInfo object for the specified path.
GetDriveInfo	Returns a DriveInfo object for the specified path.
GetFileInfo	Returns a FileInfo object for the specified path.
GetFiles	Returns a read-only String collection representing the names of files within a directory.
GetParentPath	Returns a string representing the absolute path of the parent of the provided path.
MoveDirectory	Moves a directory.
MoveFile	Moves a file.
OpenTextFieldParser	Opens a TextFieldParser object attached to a delimited or fixed-field file (such as a log file). You can use the object to parse the file.
OpenTextFileReader	Opens a TextReader object attached to a file. You can use the object to read the file.

continues

(continued)

ITEM	DESCRIPTION
OpenTextFileWriter	Opens a TextWriter object attached to a file. You can use the object to write into the file.
ReadAllBytes	Reads all data from a binary file.
ReadAllText	Reads all text from a text file.
RenameDirectory	Renames a directory within its parent directory.
RenameFile	Renames a file within its directory.
SpecialDirectories	Returns a SpecialDirectoriesProxy object that has properties giving the locations of various special directories such as the system's temporary directory and the user's MyDocuments directory. See the section "My.Computer.FileSystem.SpecialDirectories" in Chapter 30 for more information.
WriteAllBytes	Creates a file and writes byte data into it.
WriteAllText	Creates a text file and writes text into it.

Info

The My.Computer.Info object provides information about the computer's memory and operating system. The following list describes this object's properties:

PROPERTY	PURPOSE
AvailablePhysicalMemory	Returns the computer's total amount of free physical memory in bytes.
AvailableVirtualMemory	Returns the computer's total amount of free virtual address space in bytes.
InstalledUICulture	Returns the current user-interface culture.
LoadedAssemblies	Returns a collection of the assemblies loaded by the application.
OSFullName	Returns the computer's full operating-system name as in Microsoft Windows XP Home Edition.
OSPlatform	Returns the platform identifier for the operating system of the computer. This can be Unix, Win32NT (Windows NT or later), Win32S (runs on 16-bit Windows to provide access to 32-bit applications), Win32Windows (Windows 95 or later), or WinCE.

PROPERTY	PURPOSE
OSVersion	Returns the operating system's version in a string with the format major.minor.build.revision.
StackTrace	Returns a string containing the application's current stack trace.
TotalPhysicalMemory	Returns the computer's total amount of physical memory in bytes.
TotalVirtualMemory	Returns the computer's total amount of virtual address space in bytes.
WorkingSet	Returns the amount of physical memory mapped to the process context in bytes.

Keyboard

This object returns information about the current keyboard state. The following table describes this object's properties.

PROPERTY	PURPOSE
AltKeyDown	Returns True if the Alt key is down.
CapsLock	Returns True if Caps Lock is on.
CtrlKeyDown	Returns True if the Ctrl key is down.
NumLock	Returns True if Num Lock is on.
ScrollLock	Returns True if Scroll Lock is on.
ShiftKeyDown	Returns True if the Shift key is down.

The My.Computer.Keyboard object also provides one method named SendKeys. This method sends keystrokes to the currently active window just as if the user had typed them. You can use this method to provide some automated control over applications.

Mouse

The My.Computer.Mouse object provides information about the computer's mouse. The following table describes this object's properties.

PROPERTY	DESCRIPTION
ButtonsSwapped	Returns True if the functions of the mouse's left and right buttons have been switched. This can make using the mouse easier for left-handed users.
WheelExists	Returns True if the mouse has a scroll wheel.
WheelScrollLines	Returns a number indicating how much to scroll when the mouse wheel rotates one notch.

Name

The My.Computer.Name property simply returns the computer's name.

Network

The My.Computer.Network object provides a few simple properties and methods for working with the network. Its single property, IsAvailable, returns True if the network is available.

The following table describes the object's methods.

METHOD	DESCRIPTION
DownloadFile	Downloads a file from a remote computer. Parameters give such values as the filename, username, password, and connection timeout.
IsAvailable	Returns True if the network is available.
Ping	Pings a remote computer to see if it is connected to the network.
UploadFile	Uploads a file to a remote computer. Parameters give such values as the filename, username, password, and connection timeout.

This object also provides one event, NetworkAvailabilityChanged, that you can catch to learn when the network becomes available or unavailable.

Ports

This object provides one property and a single method. Its SerialPortNames property returns an array of strings listing the names of the computer's serial ports.

The OpenSerialPort method opens the serial port with a particular name (optional parameters give the baud rate, parity, and other port configuration information) and returns a reference to a SerialPort object.

The SerialPort class is much more complex than the My.Computer.Ports object. The following table describes the SerialPort class's most useful properties.

PROPERTY	PURPOSE
BaseStream	Returns the underlying Stream object.
BaudRate	Gets or sets the port's baud rate.
BreakState	Gets or sets the break signal state.
BytesToRead	Returns the number of bytes of data in the receive buffer.
BytesToWrite	Returns the number of bytes of data in the send buffer.
CDHolding	Returns the state of the port's Carrier Detect (CD) line.
CtsHolding	Returns the state of the port's Clear-to-Send (CTS) line.
DataBits	Gets or sets the standard length of data bits per byte.
DiscardNull	Determines whether null characters are ignored.
DsrHolding	Returns the state of the Data Set Ready (DSR) signal.
DtrEnable	Determines enabling of the Data Terminal Ready (DTR) signal.
Encoding	Determines the character encoding for text conversion.
Handshake	Determines the handshaking protocol.
IsOpen	Returns True if the port is open.
NewLine	Determines the end-of-line sequence for the ReadLine and WriteLine methods. This is a linefeed by default.
Parity	Determines the parity-checking protocol.
ParityReplace	Determines the character used to replace invalid characters when a parity error occurs.
PortName	Gets or selects the port.
ReadBufferSize	Determines the port's read buffer size.
ReadTimeout	Determines the read timeout in milliseconds.
ReceivedBytesThreshold	Determines the number of bytes in the input buffer before a ReceivedEvent is raised.
RtsEnable	Determines whether the Request to Transmit (RTS) signal is enabled.
StopBits	Determines the standard number of stop bits per byte.
WriteBufferSize	Determines the port's write buffer size.
WriteTimeout	Determines the write timeout in milliseconds.

The following table describes the SerialPort object's most useful methods.

METHOD	PURPOSE
Close	Closes the port.
DiscardInBuffer	Discards any data that is currently in the read buffer.
DiscardOutBuffer	Discards any data that is currently in the write buffer.
GetPortNames	Returns an array of strings holding the serial ports' names.
Open	Opens the port's connection.
Read	Reads data from the read buffer.
ReadByte	Synchronously reads one byte from the read buffer.
ReadChar	Synchronously reads one character from the read buffer.
ReadExisting	Reads all immediately available characters in both the stream and the read buffer.
ReadLine	Reads up to the next NewLine value in the read buffer.
ReadTo	Reads a string up to the specified value in the read buffer.
Write	Writes data into the port's write buffer.
WriteLine	Writes a string and a NewLine into the write buffer.

The SerialPort object also has a few events that you can use to learn about changes in the port's status. The following table describes the object's most useful events.

EVENT	PURPOSE
DataReceived	Occurs when the port receives data. The e.EventType parameter indicates the type of data and can be SerialData.Eof (end of file received) or SerialData.Chars (characters were received).
ErrorEvent	Occurs when the port encounters an error. The e.EventType parameter indicates the type of error and can be Frame (framing error), Overrun (character buffer overrun), RxOver (input buffer overrun), RxParity (hardware detected parity error), or TxFull (output buffer full).
PinChangedEvent	Occurs when the port's serial pin changes. The e.EventType parameter indicates the type of change and can be Break (break in the input), CDChanged (Receive Line Signal Detect, or RLSD, signal changed state), CtsChanged (CTS signal changed state), DsrChanged (DSR signal changed state), and Ring (detected a ring indicator).

Registry

My.Computer.Registry provides objects that manipulate the registry. My.Computer.Registry has seven properties that refer to objects of type RegistryKey that represent the registry's main subtrees or "hives."

The following table lists these objects and the corresponding registry hives.

MY.COMPUTER.REGISTRY PROPERTY	REGISTRY SUBTREE
ClassesRoot	HKEY_CLASSES_ROOT
CurrentConfig	HKEY_CURRENT_CONFIG
CurrentUser	HKEY_CURRENT_USER
DynData	HKEY_DYNAMIC_DATA
LocalMachine	HKEY_LOCAL_MACHINE
PerformanceData	HKEY_PERFORMANCE_DATA
Users	HKEY_USERS

My.Computer.Registry also provides two methods, GetValue and SetValue, that get and set registry values, respectively.

The program can use the RegistryKey objects to work with the corresponding registry subtrees. The following table describes the most useful properties and methods provided by the RegistryKey class.

PROPERTY OR METHOD	PURPOSE
Close	Closes the key and writes it to disk if it has been modified.
CreateSubKey	Creates a new subkey or opens an existing subkey within this key.
DeleteSubKey	Deletes the specified subkey.
DeleteSubKeyTree	Recursively deletes a subkey and any child subkeys it contains.
DeleteValue	Deletes a value from the key.
Flush	Writes any changes to the key into the registry.
GetSubKeyNames	Returns an array of strings giving subkey names.
GetValue	Returns the value of a specified value within this key.

continues

(continued)

PROPERTY OR METHOD	PURPOSE
GetValueKind	Returns the type of a specified value within this key. This can be Binary, DWord, ExpandString, MultiString, QWord, String, or Unknown. (Unknown is particularly important because the registry can contain just about any custom data type.)
GetValueNames	Returns an array of strings giving the names of all of the values contained within the key.
Name	Returns the key's registry path.
OpenSubKey	Returns a RegistryKey object representing a descendant key. A parameter indicates whether you need write access to the key.
SetValue	Sets a value within the key.
SubKeyCount	Returns the number of subkeys that are this key's direct children.
ToString	Returns the key's name.
ValueCount	Returns the number of values stored in this key.

Visual Basic's native registry methods SaveSetting and GetSetting are generally easier to use than My.Computer.Registry, although they provide access to only part of the registry.

Screen

The My.Computer.Screen property returns a Screen object representing the computer's main display. The following table describes the Screen object's most useful properties.

PROPERTY	PURPOSE
AllScreens	Returns an array of Screen objects representing all of the system's screens.
BitsPerPixel	Returns the screen's color depth in bits per pixel.
Bounds	Returns a Rectangle giving the screen's bounds in pixels.
DeviceName	Returns the screen's device name as in \\.\DISPLAY1.
Primary	Returns True if the screen is the computer's primary screen.

PROPERTY	PURPOSE
PrimaryScreen	Returns a reference to a Screen object representing the system's primary display. For a single display system, the primary display is the only display.
WorkingArea	Returns a Rectangle giving the screen's working area bounds in pixels. This is the desktop area excluding taskbars, docked windows, and docked toolbars.

The following table describes the Screen class's most useful methods.

METHOD	PURPOSE
FromControl	Returns a Screen object representing the display that contains the largest piece of a specific control.
FromHandle	Returns a Screen object representing the display that contains the largest piece of the object with a given handle.
FromPoint	Returns a Screen object representing the display that contains a given point.
FromRectangle	Returns a Screen object representing the display that contains the largest piece of a given Rectangle.
GetBounds	Returns a Rectangle giving the bounds of the screen that contains the largest piece of a control, rectangle, or point.
GetWorkingArea	Returns a Rectangle giving the working area of the screen that contains the largest piece of a control, rectangle, or point.

The AllScreens and PrimaryScreen properties, and all of these methods, are shared members of the Windows.Forms.Screen class.

The WorkingArea property does not update after you access the Screen object. If the user moves the system taskbar, the WorkingArea property does not show the new values.

However, the GetWorkingArea method retrieves the screen's current working area. If you must be certain that the user has not moved the taskbar or a docked object, use the GetWorkingArea method.

MY.FORMS

My.Forms provides properties that give references to an instance of each of the types of forms defined by the application. If the program begins with a startup form, the corresponding My.Forms entry refers to that form. For example, suppose the program begins by displaying Form1. Then, My.Forms.Form1 refers to the startup instance of the Form1 class.

You can also refer to these forms directly. For example, the following two statements set the text and display the predefined instance of the Form2 class:

```
My.Forms.Form2.Text = "Hello!"
Form2.Show()
```

Other forms that you create using the New keyword are separate instances from those provided by My.Forms.

If you know you will only want one instance of a particular form, for example, if the form is a dialog box, you can use the instance defined in the My.Forms collection instead of creating new instances of the class. If you will need to use more than one instance of the form at the same time, you must use New to create them.

You can set these properties to Nothing to dispose of the forms, but you can never set them to anything else. In particular, you cannot set them to new instances of their form classes later. When you destroy one of these instances, it is gone forever. If you will need to reuse the form later, set its Visible property to False rather than set it equal to Nothing. Alternatively, you can just create new instances of the class when you need them and ignore the forms in My.Forms.

MY.RESOURCES

My.Resources provides access to the application's resources. Its ResourceManager property returns a reference to a ResourceManager object attached to the project's resources. You can use this object to retrieve the application's resources.

My.Resources also provides strongly typed properties that return the application's resources. For example, if you create a string resource named Greeting, the following code sets the form's caption to that string's value:

```
Me.Text = My.Resources.Greeting
```

See Chapter 28, "Configuration and Resources," for more information on using My.Resources to access the application's resources.

MY.USER

My.User returns information about the current user. The following table describes the My.User object's most useful properties.

PROPERTY OR METHOD	PURPOSE
CurrentPrincipal	Gets or sets an IPrincipal object used for role-based security.
InitializeWithWindowsUser	Sets the thread's principal to the Windows user who started it.
IsAuthenticated	Returns True if the user's identity has been authenticated.
IsInRole	Returns True if the user belongs to a certain role.
Name	Returns the current user's name in the format domain\user_name.

Streams

Visual Studio provides several classes that treat data as a stream — an ordered series of bytes. These classes are not difficult to use, but they are similar enough to be confusing. This appendix summarizes the stream classes and describes their properties and their methods. See Chapter 29, "Streams," for more information on streams.

STREAM CLASS SUMMARY

The following table lists the Visual Studio stream classes. It can provide you with some guidance for selecting a stream class.

CLASS	PURPOSE
BinaryReader, BinaryWriter	Read and write data from an underlying stream using routines that manage specific data types (such as ReadDouble and ReadUInt16).
BufferedStream	Adds buffering to another stream type. This sometimes improves performance on relatively slow underlying devices.
CryptoStream	Applies a cryptographic transformation to its data.
FileStream	Represents a file as a stream. Usually, you can use a helper class such as BinaryReader or TextWriter to make working with a FileStream easier.
MemoryStream	Lets you read and write stream data in memory. This is useful when you need a stream but don't want to read or write a file.
NetworkStream	Sends and receives data across a network connection.

continues

(continued)

CLASS	PURPOSE
Stream	A generic stream class. This is a virtual (MustInherit) class, so you cannot create one directly. Instead, you must instantiate one of its subclasses.
StreamReader, StreamWriter	These classes inherit from TextReader and TextWriter. They provide methods for reading and writing text into an underlying stream, usually a FileStream.
StringReader, StringWriter	These classes inherit from TextReader and TextWriter. They provide methods for reading and writing text into an underlying string.
TextReader, TextWriter	These virtual (MustInherit) classes define methods that make working with text on an underlying stream easier.

STREAM

The following table describes the Stream class's most useful properties.

PROPERTY	PURPOSE
CanRead	Returns True if the stream supports reading.
CanSeek	Returns True if the stream supports seeking to a particular position in the stream.
CanTimeout	Returns True if the stream supports timeouts.
CanWrite	Returns True if the stream supports writing.
Length	Returns the number of bytes in the stream.
Position	Returns the stream's current position in its bytes. For a stream that supports seeking, the program can set this value to move to a particular position.
ReadTimeout	Determines the stream's read timeout in milliseconds.
WriteTimeout	Determines the stream's write timeout in milliseconds.

The following table describes the Stream class's most useful methods.

METHOD	PURPOSE
BeginRead	Begins an asynchronous read.
BeginWrite	Begins an asynchronous write.
Close	Closes the stream and releases any resources it uses (such as file handles).
EndRead	Waits for an asynchronous read to finish.
EndWrite	Ends an asynchronous write.
Flush	Flushes data from the stream's buffers into the underlying storage medium (device, file, and so on).
Read	Reads bytes from the stream and advances its position by that number of bytes.
ReadByte	Reads a byte from the stream and advances its position by 1 byte.
Seek	If the stream supports seeking, sets the stream's position.
SetLength	Sets the stream's length. If the stream is currently longer than the new length, it is truncated. If the stream is shorter than the new length, it is enlarged. The stream must support both writing and seeking for this method to work.
Write	Writes bytes into the stream and advances the current position by this number of bytes.
WriteByte	Writes 1 byte into the stream and advances the current position by 1 byte.

The FileStream and MemoryStream classes add only a few methods to those defined by the Stream class. The most important of those are new constructors specific to the type of stream. For example, the FileStream class provides constructors for opening files in various modes (append, new, and so forth).

BINARYREADER AND BINARYWRITER

These are stream helper classes that make it easier to read and write data in specific formats onto an underlying stream. The following table describes the BinaryReader class's most useful methods.

METHOD	PURPOSE
Close	Closes the BinaryReader and its underlying stream.
PeekChar	Reads the reader's next character, but does not advance the reader's position, so other methods can still read the character later.
Read	Reads characters from the stream and advances the reader's position.
ReadBoolean	Reads a Boolean from the stream and advances the reader's position by 1 byte.
ReadByte	Reads a byte from the stream and advances the reader's position by 1 byte.
ReadBytes	Reads a number of bytes from the stream into a byte array and advances the reader's position by that number of bytes.
ReadChar	Reads a character from the stream and advances the reader's position according to the stream's encoding and the character.
ReadChars	Reads a number of characters from the stream, returns the results in a character array, and advances the reader's position according to the stream's encoding and the number of characters.
ReadDecimal	Reads a decimal value from the stream and advances the reader's position by 16 bytes.
ReadDouble	Reads an 8-byte floating-point value from the stream and advances the reader's position by 8 bytes.
ReadInt16	Reads a 2-byte signed integer from the stream and advances the reader's position by 2 bytes.
ReadInt32	Reads a 4-byte signed integer from the stream and advances the reader's position by 4 bytes.
ReadInt64	Reads an 8-byte signed integer from the stream and advances the reader's position by 8 bytes.
ReadSByte	Reads a signed byte from the stream and advances the reader's position by 1 byte.
ReadSingle	Reads a 4-byte floating-point value from the stream and advances the reader's position by 4 bytes.
ReadString	Reads a string from the current stream and advances the reader's position past it. The string begins with its length.
ReadUInt16	Reads a 2-byte unsigned integer from the stream and advances the reader's position by 2 bytes.

METHOD	PURPOSE
ReadUInt32	Reads a 4-byte unsigned integer from the stream and advances the reader's position by 4 bytes.
ReadUInt64	Reads an 8-byte unsigned integer from the stream and advances the reader's position by 8 bytes.

The following table describes the BinaryWriter class's most useful methods.

METHOD	DESCRIPTION
Close	Closes the BinaryWriter and its underlying stream.
Flush	Writes any buffered data into the underlying stream.
Seek	Sets the position within the stream.
Write	Writes a value into the stream. This method has many overloaded versions that write characters, arrays of characters, integers, strings, unsigned 64-bit integers, and so on.

TEXTREADER AND TEXTWRITER

These are stream helper classes that make it easier to read and write text data onto an underlying stream. The following table describes the TextReader class's most useful methods.

METHOD	PURPOSE
Close	Closes the reader and releases any resources that it is using.
Peek	Reads the next character from the text without changing the reader's state so other methods can read the character later.
Read	Reads data from the input. Overloaded versions of this method read a single character, or an array of characters up to a specified length.
ReadBlock	Reads data from the input into an array of characters.
ReadLine	Reads a line of characters from the input and returns the data in a string.
ReadToEnd	Reads any remaining characters in the input and returns them in a string.

The following table describes the TextWriter class's most useful properties.

PROPERTY	PURPOSE
Encoding	Specifies the data's encoding (ASCII, UTF-8, Unicode, and so forth).
FormatProvider	Returns an object that controls formatting.
NewLine	Gets or sets the stream's new-line sequence.

The following table describes the TextWriter class's most useful methods.

METHOD	PURPOSE
Close	Closes the writer and releases any resources it is using.
Flush	Writes any buffered data into the underlying output.
Write	Writes a value into the output. This method has many overloaded versions that write characters, arrays of characters, integers, strings, unsigned 64-bit integers, and so forth.
WriteLine	Writes data into the output followed by the new-line sequence.

STRINGREADER AND STRINGWRITER

The StringReader and StringWriter classes let a program read and write text in a string. They implement the features defined by their parent classes TextReader and TextWriter. See the section "TextReader and TextWriter" earlier in this appendix for a list of those features.

STREAMREADER AND STREAMWRITER

The StreamReader and StreamWriter classes let a program read and write data in an underlying stream, often a FileStream. They implement the features defined by their parent classes TextReader and TextWriter. See the section "TextReader and TextWriter" earlier in this appendix for a list of the features.

TEXT FILE STREAM METHODS

The System.IO.File class provides several handy methods for working with text files. The following table summarizes these methods.

METHOD	PURPOSE
AppendText	Creates a text file or opens it for appending if it already exists. Returns a StreamWriter for writing into the file.
CreateText	Creates a text file, overwriting it if it already exists. Returns a StreamWriter for writing into the file.
Exists	Returns True if a file exists. It is better practice (and much faster) to only try to open the file if Exists returns True, rather than just try to open the file and catch errors with a Try Catch block.
OpenText	Opens an existing text file and returns a StreamReader to read from it. This method throws a FileNotFoundException if the file doesn't exist.

U

Filesystem Classes

A Visual Basic application can take three basic approaches to filesystem manipulation: Visual Basic methods, System.IO Framework classes, and the My.Computer.FileSystem namespace. This appendix summarizes the properties, methods, and events provided by these approaches. For more information on filesystem objects, see Chapter 30, "Filesystem Objects."

VISUAL BASIC METHODS

The following table summarizes the Visual Basic methods for working with files. They let a program create, open, read, write, and learn about files.

METHOD	PURPOSE
EOF	Returns True if the file is at the end of file.
FileClose	Closes an open file.
FileGet	Reads data from a file opened in Random and Binary mode into a variable.
FileGetObject	Reads data as an object from a file opened in Random and Binary mode into a variable.
FileOpen	Opens a file for reading or writing. Parameters indicate the mode (Append, Binary, Input, Output, or Random), access type (Read, Write, or ReadWrite), and sharing (Shared, LockRead, LockWrite, or LockReadWrite).
FilePut	Writes data from a variable into a file opened for Random or Binary access.

continues

(continued)

METHOD	PURPOSE
FilePutObject	Writes an object from a variable into a file opened for Random or Binary access.
FreeFile	Returns a file number that is not currently associated with any file in this application. You should use FreeFile to get file numbers rather than use arbitrary numbers such as 1.
Input	Reads data written into a file by the Write method back into a variable.
InputString	Reads a specific number of characters from the file.
LineInput	Returns the next line of text from the file.
Loc	Returns the current position within the file.
LOF	Returns the file's length in bytes.
Print	Prints values into the file. Multiple values separated by commas are aligned at tab boundaries.
PrintLine	Prints values followed by a new line into the file. Multiple values separated by commas are aligned at tab boundaries.
Seek	Moves to the indicated position within the file.
Write	Writes values into the file, delimited appropriately so that they can later be read by the Input method.
WriteLine	Writes values followed by a new line into the file, delimited appropriately so that they can later be read by the Input method.

The following table describes Visual Basic methods that manipulate directories and files. They let an application list, rename, move, copy, and delete files and directories.

METHOD	PURPOSE
ChDir	Changes the application's current working directory.
ChDrive	Changes the application's current working drive.
CurDir	Returns the application's current working directory.

METHOD	PURPOSE
Dir	Returns a file matching a directory path specification that may include wildcards, and matching certain file properties such as ReadOnly, Hidden, or Directory. The first call to Dir should include a path. Subsequent calls can omit the path to fetch the next matching file for the initial path. Dir returns filenames without the path and returns Nothing when no more files match.
FileCopy	Copies a file to a new location.
FileDateTime	Returns the date and time when the file was created or last modified.
FileLen	Returns the length of a file in bytes.
GetAttr	Returns a value indicating the file's attributes. The value is a combination of the values vbNormal, vbReadOnly, vbHidden, vbSystem, vbDirectory, vbArchive, and vbAlias.
Kill	Permanently deletes a file.
MkDir	Creates a new directory.
Rename	Renames a directory or file.
RmDir	Deletes an empty directory.
SetAttr	Sets the file's attributes. The value is a combination of the values vbNormal, vbReadOnly, vbHidden, vbSystem, vbDirectory, vbArchive, and vbAlias.

FRAMEWORK CLASSES

The System.IO namespace provides several classes for working with the filesystem. The following sections describe the properties, methods, and events provided by these classes.

Directory

The Directory class provides shared methods for working with directories. The following table summarizes its shared methods.

METHOD	PURPOSE
CreateDirectory	Creates all of the directories along a path.
Delete	Deletes a directory and its contents. It can recursively delete all subdirectories.
Exists	Returns True if the path points to an existing directory.

continues

(continued)

METHOD	PURPOSE
GetCreationTime	Returns a directory's creation date and time.
GetCreationTimeUtc	Returns a directory's creation date and time in Coordinated Universal Time (UTC).
GetCurrentDirectory	Returns the application's current working directory.
GetDirectories	Returns an array of strings holding the fully qualified names of a directory's subdirectories.
GetDirectoryRoot	Returns the directory root for a path, which need not exist (for example, C:\).
GetFiles	Returns an array of strings holding the fully qualified names of a directory's files.
GetFileSystemEntries	Returns an array of strings holding the fully qualified names of a directory's files and subdirectories.
GetLastAccessTime	Returns a directory's last access date and time.
GetLastAccessTimeUtc	Returns a directory's last access date and time in UTC.
GetLastWriteTime	Returns the date and time when a directory was last modified.
GetLastWriteTimeUtc	Returns the date and time when a directory was last modified in UTC.
GetLogicalDrives	Returns an array of strings listing the system's logical drives as in A:\. The list includes drives that are attached. For example, it lists an empty floppy drive and a connected flash disk but doesn't list a flash disk after you disconnect it.
GetParent	Returns a DirectoryInfo object representing a directory's parent directory.
Move	Moves a directory and its contents to a new location on the same disk volume.
SetCreationTime	Sets a directory's creation date and time.
SetCreationTimeUtc	Sets a directory's creation date and time in UTC.
SetCurrentDirectory	Sets the application's current working directory.
SetLastAccessTime	Sets a directory's last access date and time.
SetLastAccessTimeUtc	Sets a directory's last access date and time in UTC.
SetLastWriteTime	Sets a directory's last write date and time.
SetLastWriteTimeUtc	Sets a directory's last write date and time in UTC.

File

The File class provides shared methods for working with files. The following table summarizes its most useful shared methods.

METHOD	PURPOSE
AppendAllText	Adds text to the end of a file, creating it if it doesn't exist, and then closes the file.
AppendText	Opens a file for appending UTF-8 encoded text and returns a StreamWriter attached to it. (For more information on UTF-8, see http://en.wikipedia.org/wiki/UTF-8.)
Copy	Copies a file.
Create	Creates a new file and returns a FileStream attached to it.
CreateText	Creates or opens a file for writing UTF-8 encoded text and returns a StreamWriter attached to it.
Delete	Permanently deletes a file.
Exists	Returns True if the specified file exists.
GetAttributes	Gets a file's attributes. This is a combination of flags defined by the FileAttributes enumeration, which defines the values Archive, Compressed, Device, Directory, Encrypted, Hidden, Normal, NotContextIndexed, Offline, ReadOnly, ReparsePoint, SparseFile, System, and Temporary.
GetCreationTime	Returns a file's creation date and time.
GetCreationTimeUtc	Returns a file's creation date and time in UTC.
GetLastAccessTime	Returns a file's last access date and time.
GetLastAccessTimeUtc	Returns a file's last access date and time in UTC.
GetLastWriteTime	Returns a file's last write date and time.
GetLastWriteTimeUtc	Returns a file's last write date and time in UTC.
Move	Moves a file to a new location.
Open	Opens a file and returns a FileStream attached to it. Parameters let you specify the mode (Append, Create, CreateNew, Open, OpenOrCreate, or Truncate), access (Read, Write, or ReadWrite), and sharing (Read, Write, ReadWrite, or None) settings.
OpenRead	Opens a file for reading and returns a FileStream attached to it.

continues

(continued)

METHOD	PURPOSE
OpenText	Opens a UTF-8 encoded text file for reading and returns a StreamReader attached to it.
OpenWrite	Opens a file for writing and returns a FileStream attached to it.
ReadAllBytes	Returns a file's contents into an array of bytes.
ReadAllLines	Returns a file's lines into an array of strings.
ReadAllText	Returns a file's contents into a string.
Replace	This method takes three file paths as parameters representing a source file, a destination file, and a backup file. If the backup file exists, the method permanently deletes it. It then moves the destination file to the backup file, and moves the source file to the destination file. This method throws an exception if either the source file or the destination file doesn't exist.
SetAttributes	Sets a file's attributes. This is a combination of flags defined by the FileAttributes enumeration, which defines the values Archive, Compressed, Device, Directory, Encrypted, Hidden, Normal, NotContextIndexed, Offline, ReadOnly, ReparsePoint, SparseFile, System, and Temporary.
SetCreationTime	Sets a file's creation date and time.
SetCreationTimeUtc	Sets a file's creation date and time in UTC.
SetLastAccessTime	Sets a file's last access date and time.
SetLastAccessTimeUtc	Sets a file's last access date and time in UTC.
SetLastWriteTime	Sets a file's last write date and time.
SetLastWriteTimeUtc	Sets a file's last write date and time in UTC.
WriteAllBytes	Creates or overwrites a file, writes an array of bytes into it, and closes the file.
WriteAllLines	Creates or overwrites a file, writes an array of strings into it, and closes the file.
WriteAllText	Creates or overwrites a file, writes a string into it, and closes the file.

DriveInfo

A DriveInfo object represents one of the computer's drives. The following table describes the properties provided by this class. The final column in the table indicates whether a drive must be ready for the property to work without throwing an exception. Use the IsReady property to see whether the drive is ready before using those properties.

PROPERTY	PURPOSE	MUST BE READY?
AvailableFreeSpace	Returns the amount of free space available on the drive in bytes. This value takes quotas into account, so it may not match TotalFreeSpace.	True
DriveFormat	Returns the name of the filesystem type such as NTFS or FAT32. (For more information on NTFS and FAT filesystems, search the web. For example, the page http:// www.ntfs.com/ ntfs_vs_fat.htm compares the FAT, FAT32, and NTFS filesystems.)	True
DriveType	Returns a DriveType enumeration value indicating the drive type. This value can be CDRom, Fixed, Network, NoRootDirectory, Ram, Removable, or Unknown.	False
IsReady	Returns True if the drive is ready. Many DriveInfo properties are unavailable and raise exceptions if you try to access them while the drive is not ready.	False
Name	Return's the drive's name. This is the drive's root name as in A:\ or C:\.	False
RootDirectory	Returns a DirectoryInfo object representing the drive's root directory. See the section "DirectoryInfo" later in this appendix for more information.	False
TotalFreeSpace	Returns the total amount of free space on the drive in bytes.	True
TotalSize	Returns the total amount of space on the drive in bytes.	True
VolumeLabel	Gets or sets the drive's volume label.	True

DirectoryInfo

A DirectoryInfo object represents a directory. The following table summarizes its most useful properties and methods.

PROPERTY OR METHOD	PURPOSE
Attributes	Gets or sets flags from the FileAttributes enumeration for the directory. These flags can include Archive, Compressed, Device, Directory, Encrypted, Hidden, Normal, NotContentIndexed, Offline, ReadOnly, ReparsePoint, SparseFile, System, and Temporary.
Create	Creates the directory. You can create a DirectoryInfo object, passing its constructor the fully qualified name of a directory that doesn't exist. You can then call the object's Create method to create the directory.
CreateSubdirectory	Creates a subdirectory within the directory and returns a DirectoryInfo object representing it. The subdirectory's path must be relative to the DirectoryInfo object's directory but can contain intermediate subdirectories. For example, the statement dir_info. CreateSubdirectory("Tools\Bin") creates the Tools subdirectory and the Bin directory inside that.
CreationTime	Gets or sets the directory's creation time.
CreationTimeUtc	Gets or sets the directory's creation time in UTC.
Delete	Deletes the directory if it is empty. A parameter lets you tell the object to delete its contents, too, if it isn't empty.
Exists	Returns True if the directory exists.
Extension	Returns the extension part of the directory's name. Normally, this is an empty string for directories.
FullName	Returns the directory's fully qualified path.
GetDirectories	Returns an array of DirectoryInfo objects representing the directory's subdirectories. An optional parameter gives a pattern to match. This method does not recursively search the subdirectories.
GetFiles	Returns an array of FileInfo objects representing files inside the directory. An optional parameter gives a pattern to match. This method does not recursively search subdirectories.
GetFileSystemInfos	Returns a strongly typed array of FileSystemInfo objects representing subdirectories and files inside the directory. The items in the array are DirectoryInfo and FileInfo objects, both of which inherit from FileSystemInfo. An optional parameter gives a pattern to match. This method does not recursively search subdirectories.

PROPERTY OR METHOD	PURPOSE
LastAccessTime	Gets or sets the directory's last access time.
LastAccessTimeUtc	Gets or sets the directory's last access time in UTC.
LastWriteTime	Gets or sets the directory's last write time.
LastWriteTimeUtc	Gets or sets the directory's last write time in UTC.
MoveTo	Moves the directory and its contents to a new path.
Name	Returns the directory's name without the path information.
Parent	Returns a DirectoryInfo object representing the directory's parent. If the directory is its filesystem's root (for example, C:\), this returns Nothing.
Refresh	Refreshes the DirectoryInfo object's data. For example, if the directory has been accessed since the object was created, you must call Refresh to load the new LastAccessTime value.
Root	Returns a DirectoryInfo object representing the root of the directory's filesystem.
ToString	Returns the directory's fully qualified path and name.

FileInfo

A FileInfo object represents a file. The following table summarizes its most useful properties and methods.

PROPERTY OR METHOD	PURPOSE
AppendText	Returns a StreamWriter that appends text to the file.
Attributes	Gets or sets flags from the FileAttributes enumeration for the file. These flags can include Archive, Compressed, Device, Directory, Encrypted, Hidden, Normal, NotContentIndexed, Offline, ReadOnly, ReparsePoint, SparseFile, System, and Temporary.
CopyTo	Copies the file and returns a FileInfo object representing the new file. A parameter lets you indicate whether the copy should overwrite the destination file if it already exists. If the destination path is relative, it is relative to the application's current directory, not to the FileInfo object's directory.

continues

(continued)

PROPERTY OR METHOD	PURPOSE
Create	Creates the file and returns a FileStream object attached to it. For example, you can create a FileInfo object passing its constructor the name of a file that doesn't exist. Then you can call the Create method to create the file.
CreateText	Creates the file and returns a StreamWriter attached to it. For example, you can create a FileInfo object passing its constructor the name of a file that doesn't exist. Then you can call the CreateText method to create the file.
CreationTime	Gets or sets the file's creation time.
CreationTimeUtc	Gets or sets the file's creation time in UTC.
Delete	Deletes the file.
Directory	Returns a DirectoryInfo object representing the file's directory.
DirectoryName	Returns the name of the file's directory.
Exists	Returns True if the file exists.
Extension	Returns the extension part of the file's name including the period. For example, the extension for game.txt is .txt.
FullName	Returns the file's fully qualified path and name.
IsReadOnly	Returns True if the file is marked read-only.
LastAccessTime	Gets or sets the file's last access time.
LastAccessTimeUtc	Gets or sets the file's last access time in UTC.
LastWriteTime	Gets or sets the file's last write time.
LastWriteTimeUtc	Gets or sets the file's last write time in UTC.
Length	Returns the number of bytes in the file.
MoveTo	Moves the file to a new location. If the destination uses a relative path, it is relative to the application's current directory, not to the FileInfo object's directory. When this method finishes, the FileInfo object is updated to refer to the file's new location.
Name	The file's name without the path information.
Open	Opens the file with different mode (Append, Create, CreateNew, Open, OpenOrCreate, or Truncate), access (Read, Write, or ReadWrite), and sharing (Read, Write, ReadWrite, or None) settings. This method returns a FileStream object attached to the file.

PROPERTY OR METHOD	PURPOSE
OpenRead	Returns a read-only FileStream attached to the file.
OpenText	Returns a StreamReader with UTF-8 encoding attached to the file for reading.
OpenWrite	Returns a write-only FileStream attached to the file.
Refresh	Refreshes the FileInfo object's data. For example, if the file has been accessed since the object was created, you must call Refresh to load the new LastAccessTime value.
Replace	Replaces a target file with this one, renaming the old target as a backup copy. If the backup file already exists, it is deleted and replaced with the target.
ToString	Returns the file's fully qualified name.

FileSystemWatcher

The FileSystemWatcher class lets an application watch for changes to a file or directory. The following table summarizes its most useful properties.

PROPERTY	PURPOSE
EnableRaisingEvents	Determines whether the component is enabled. Note that this property is False by default, so the watcher will not raise any events until you set it to True.
Filter	Determines the files for which the watcher reports events. You cannot watch for multiple file types as in `*.txt` and `*.dat`. Instead, use multiple FileSystemWatchers. If you like, you can use AddHandler to make all of the FileSystemWatchers use the same event handlers.
IncludeSubdirectories	Determines whether the object watches subdirectories within the main path.
InternalBufferSize	Determines the size of the internal buffer. If the watcher is monitoring a very active directory, a small buffer may overflow.
NotifyFilter	Determines the types of changes that the watcher reports. This is a combination of values defined by the NotifyFilters enumeration and can include the values Attributes, CreationTime, DirectoryName, FileName, LastAccess, LastWrite, Security, and Size.
Path	Determines the path to watch.

The following table summarizes the FileSystemWatcher class's two most useful methods.

METHOD	PURPOSE
Dispose	Releases resources used by the object.
WaitForChanged	Synchronously waits for a change to the target file or directory.

The following table summarizes the class's events.

NAME	DESCRIPTION
Changed	A file or subdirectory has changed.
Created	A file or subdirectory was created.
Deleted	A file or subdirectory was deleted.
Error	The watcher's internal buffer overflowed.
Renamed	A file or subdirectory was renamed.

Path

The Path class provides shared properties and methods that you can use to manipulate paths. The following table summarizes its most useful public properties.

PROPERTY	PURPOSE
AltDirectorySeparatorChar	Returns the alternate character used to separate directory levels in a hierarchical path (typically /).
DirectorySeparatorChar	Returns the character used to separate directory levels in a hierarchical path (typically \, as in C:\Tests\Billing\2010q2.dat).
InvalidPathChars	Returns a character array that holds characters that are not allowed in a path string. Typically, this array will include characters such as ", <, >, and |, as well as nonprintable characters such as those with ASCII values between 0 and 31.
PathSeparator	Returns the character used to separate path strings in environment variables (typically ;).
VolumeSeparatorChar	Returns the character placed between a volume letter and the rest of the path (typically :, as in C:\Tests\Billing\2010q2.dat).

The following table summarizes the Path class's most useful methods.

METHOD	PURPOSE
ChangeExtension	Changes a path's extension.
Combine	Returns two path strings concatenated. This does not simplify the result as the My.Computer.FileSystem.CombinePath method does.
GetDirectoryName	Returns a path's directory.
GetExtension	Returns a path's extension.
GetFileName	Returns a path's filename and extension.
GetFileNameWithout Extension	Returns a path's filename without the extension.
GetFullPath	Returns a path's fully qualified value. This can be particularly useful for converting a partially relative path into an absolute path. For example, the statement Path.GetFullPath("C:\Tests\OldTests\Software\..\..\New\ Code") returns C:\Tests\New\Code.
GetInvalidFileNameChars	Returns a character array that holds characters that are not allowed in filenames.
GetPathRoot	Returns a path's root directory string. For example, the statement Path.GetPathRoot("C:\Invoices\Unpaid\Deadbeats") returns C:\.
GetRandomFileName	Returns a random filename.
GetTempFileName	Creates a uniquely named, empty temporary file, and returns its fully qualified path. Your program can open that file for scratch space, do whatever it needs to do, close the file, and then delete it. A typical filename might be `C:\Documents and Settings\Rod\Local Settings\Temp\tmp19D.tmp`.
GetTempPath	Returns the path to the system's temporary folder. This is the path part of the filename returned by GetTempFileName.
HasExtension	Returns True if a path includes an extension.
IsPathRooted	Returns True if a path is an absolute path. This includes \Temp\ Wherever and C:\Clients\Litigation, but not Temp\Wherever or ..\Uncle.

MY.COMPUTER.FILESYSTEM

The My.Computer.FileSystem object provides tools for working with drives, directories, and files. The following table summarizes this object's properties.

PROPERTY	DESCRIPTION
CurrentDirectory	Gets or sets the fully qualified path to the application's current directory.
Drives	Returns a read-only collection of DriveInfo objects describing the system's drives. See Chapter 30, "Filesystem Objects," for information about the DriveInfo class.
SpecialDirectories	Returns a SpecialDirectoriesProxy object that has properties giving the locations of various special directories such as the system's temporary directory and the user's My Documents directory. See the section "My.Computer.FileSystem.SpecialDirectories" later in this appendix for more information.

The following list summarizes the My.Computer.FileSystem object's methods:

METHOD	PURPOSE
CombinePath	Combines a base path with a relative path reference and returns a properly formatted fully qualified path.
CopyDirectory	Copies a directory. Parameters indicate whether to overwrite existing files, whether to display a progress indicator, and what to do if the user presses Cancel during the operation.
CopyFile	Copies a file. Parameters indicate whether to overwrite existing files, whether to display a progress indicator, and what to do if the user presses Cancel during the operation.
CreateDirectory	Creates all of the directories along a path.
DeleteDirectory	Deletes a directory. Parameters indicate whether to recursively delete subdirectories, prompt the user for confirmation, or move the directory into the Recycle Bin.
DeleteFile	Deletes a file. Parameters indicate whether to prompt the user for confirmation, or move the file into the Recycle Bin, and what to do if the user presses Cancel while the deletion is in progress.
DirectoryExists	Returns True if a specified directory exists.
FileExists	Returns True if a specified file exists.
FindInFiles	Returns a collection holding names of files that contain a search string.

METHOD	PURPOSE
GetDirectories	Returns a string collection listing subdirectories of a given directory. Parameters tell whether to recursively search the subdirectories and wildcards to match.
GetDirectoryInfo	Returns a DirectoryInfo object for a directory. See the section "DirectoryInfo" earlier in this appendix for more information.
GetDriveInfo	Returns a DriveInfo object for a drive. See the section "DriveInfo" earlier in this appendix for more information.
GetFileInfo	Returns a FileInfo object for a file. See the section "FileInfo" earlier in this appendix for more information.
GetFiles	Returns a string collection holding the names of files within a directory. Parameters indicate whether the search should recursively search subdirectories and give wildcards to match.
GetParentPath	Returns the fully qualified path of a path's parent.
MoveDirectory	Moves a directory. Parameters indicate whether to overwrite files that have the same name in the destination directory and whether to prompt the user when such a collision occurs.
MoveFile	Moves a file. Parameters indicate whether to overwrite a file that has the same name as the file's destination and whether to prompt the user when such a collision occurs.
OpenTextFieldParser	Opens a TextFieldParser object attached to a delimited or fixed-field file (such as a log file). You can use the object to parse the file.
OpenTextFileReader	Opens a StreamReader object attached to a file. You can use the object to read the file.
OpenTextFileWriter	Opens a StreamReader object attached to a file. You can use the object to write into the file.
ReadAllBytes	Reads all the bytes from a binary file into an array.
ReadAllText	Reads all the text from a text file into a string.
RenameDirectory	Renames a directory within its parent directory.
RenameFile	Renames a file within its directory.
WriteAllBytes	Writes an array of bytes into a binary file. A parameter tells whether to append the data or rewrite the file.
WriteAllText	Writes a string into a text file. A parameter tells whether to append the string or rewrite the file.

MY.COMPUTER.FILESYSTEM.SPECIALDIRECTORIES

The My.Computer.FileSystem.SpecialDirectories property returns a SpecialDirectoriesProxy object that has properties giving the locations of various special directories (such as the system's temporary directory and the user's My Documents directory). The following table summarizes these special directory properties.

PROPERTY	PURPOSE
AllUsersApplicationData	The directory where applications should store settings for all users (typically, something like C:\ProgramData\WindowsApplication1\WindowsApplication1\1.0.0.0).
CurrentUserApplicationData	The directory where applications should store settings for the current user (typically, something like C:\Users\CrazyBob\AppData\Roaming\WindowsApplication1\WindowsApplication1\1.0.0.0).
Desktop	The current user's desktop directory (typically, C:\Users\CrazyBob\Desktop).
MyDocuments	The current user's My Documents directory (typically, C:\Users\CrazyBob\Documents).
MyMusic	The current user's My Music directory (typically, C:\Users\CrazyBob\Music).
MyPictures	The current user's My Pictures directory (typically, C:\Users\CrazyBob\Pictures).
ProgramFiles	The Program Files directory (typically, C:\Program Files).
Programs	The current user's Programs directory (typically, C:\Users\CrazyBob\AppData\Roaming\Microsoft\Windows\Start Menu\Programs).
Temp	The current user's temporary directory (typically, C:\Users\CrazyBob\AppData\Local\Temp).

Visual Studio Versions

Most of the code in this book was written with a prerelease "release candidate" (RC) version of Visual Studio Ultimate 2012. The code does not require any of the special tools that are included in the Ultimate edition so they should run in Professional and Premium editions, too.

However, the free product Visual Studio 2012 Express for Windows 8 is another matter. With the Visual Studio 2012 release, Microsoft introduced Metro-style applications. To strongly encourage developers to move away from Windows desktop-style applications and toward Metro-style development, Visual Studio 2012 Express for Windows 8 does not include templates for building Windows desktop-style applications.

Because Windows desktop programming is a relatively stable and straightforward technology, I used Windows desktop applications for most of the examples in this book. That means you may have trouble running or reproducing those examples if you are using Visual Studio 2012 Express for Windows 8.

Fortunately all is not lost! After much impassioned feedback by early testers including Microsoft MVPs (Most Valuable Professionals), Microsoft decided to create a new edition: Visual Studio Express 2012 for Windows Desktop. That version, which will let you create Windows desktop applications, was not available when this was written but should be available in the fall of 2012.

For more information on the Visual Studio 2012 Ultimate, Premium, and Professional editions, see `http://www.microsoft.com/visualstudio/11/en-us/products/compare`.

To download Visual Studio Express RC for Windows 8, see `http://msdn.microsoft.com/windows/apps/hh852659.aspx`. (The location of this information may move when Microsoft posts the final release. You should be able to find it easily by searching online for "Visual Studio Express RC for Windows 8.")

INDEX

B

M

N